INSIGHT GUIDES

SCANDINAVIA

APA PUBLICATIONS

Part of the Langenscheidt Publishing Group

INSIGHT GUIDE

SCANDINAVIA

Editorial

Project Editor
Jane Hutchings
Managing Editor
Tom Le Bas
Series Manager
Rachel Fox

Distribution

North America
Langenscheidt Publishers, Inc.
36–36 33rd Street 4th Floor
Long Island City, NY 11106
orders@langenscheidt.com

UK & Ireland
GeoCenter International Ltd
Meridian House, Churchill Way West
Basingstoke, Hampshire RG21 6YR
sales@geocenter.co.uk

Australia
Universal Publishers
1 Waterloo Road
Macquarie Park, NSW 2113
sales@universalpublishers.com.au

New Zealand
Hema Maps New Zealand Ltd (HNZ)
Unit 2, 10 Cryers Road
East Tamaki, Auckland 2013
sales.hema@clear.net.nz

Worldwide
**Apa Publications GmbH & Co.
Verlag KG (Singapore branch)**
7030 Ang Mo Kio Avenue 5
08-65 Northstar @ AMK
Singapore 569880
apasin@singnet.com.sg

Printing

CTPS - China

©2008 Apa Publications GmbH & Co.
Verlag KG (Singapore branch)
All Rights Reserved
First Edition 2001
Updated 2008
Reprinted 2010

CONTACTING THE EDITORS
We would appreciate it if readers
would alert us to errors or out-
dated information by writing to:
**Insight Guides, P.O. Box 7910,
London SE1 1WE, England.**
insight@apaguide.co.uk

ABOUT THIS BOOK

The first Insight Guide pioneered the use of creative full-colour photography in travel guides in 1970. Since then, we have expanded our range to cater for our readers' need not only for reliable information about their chosen destination but also for a genuine understanding of the culture and workings of that destination.

Now, when the internet can supply inexhaustible (but not always reliable) facts, our books marry text and pictures to provide those much more elusive qualities: knowledge and discernment. To achieve this, they rely heavily on the authority of locally based writers and photographers.

How to use this book

This first edition of *Insight Guide: Scandinavia* is carefully structured to convey an understanding of the countries of Denmark, Norway, Sweden and Finland and their cultures as well as to guide readers through their sights and activities:

◆ The **Features** section, indicated by a yellow bar at the top of each page, covers the history and culture of the countries in a series of informative essays.

◆ The main **Places** section, indicated by a blue bar, is a complete guide to all the sights and areas worth visiting. Places of special interest are coordinated by number with the maps.

◆ The **Travel Tips** section, with an orange bar,

provides a handy point of reference for information on travel, hotels, shops, restaurants and more.

The contributors

Insight Guide: Scandinavia was edited by **Jane Hutchings**, under the guidance of managing editor **Tom Le Bas**. The book builds on the solid foundations laid by the late **Doreen Taylor-Wilkie**, editor of the original Insight Guides to each of the four countries.

The history of Scandinavia was the work of **Rowlinson Carter**. Art historian **Kathryn Boyer** wrote about Scandinavia's culture and from her base in Trollhättan covered Sweden's West Coast and Great Lakes. Stockholm-based journalist **Amy Brown** contributed the feature on the Great Outdoors, and the chapters on Stockholm, Southern Sweden and Dalarna. The writer **Debra Williamson** provided her comments on The Swedes and the Insight on the Vikings. From Arjeplog in Lapland **Illona Fjellström** covered Northern Sweden. **Joanie Rafidi Oxhammar** compiled the Insight on the Stockholm Archipelago.

From Århus, Denmark, journalist **Jack Jackson** wrote about the Scandinavian passion for food and drink and contributed chapters on The Danes, Copenhagen and Jutland, and the Insight on Danish Design.

The chapters on Norway were compiled by the journalist and author **Michael Brady** with the assistance of **Samtext** in Oslo. Brady, a long-time resident of Norway, has written extensively about the country. Other contributors included **Lance Price** and Olso columnist **Yngve Kvistad**.

Joan Gannij, an Amsterdam-based American journalist and "Finnatic", contributed the chapters on Finland and The Finns. She also compiled the Insight on the Hurtigruten in Norway. Writers whose text has been adapted from individual *Insight Guides* to the countries include: Denmark, **Fradley Garner**, **Bryan Wilder**; Norway, **Anita Peltonen**, **Robert Spark**, **John Harley**; Sweden, **Philip Ray**; Finland, **Anne Roston**, **Sylvie Nickels**, **Robert Spark**.

The Travel Tips section was compiled by **Anna Lia Bright** in Copenhagen, **Liv Bente T. Dybfest** in Oslo, **Elisabet Lim** in Stockholm and for Finland, **Joan Gannij**. The section was edited by **Sue Platt**.

This edition was updated by **Fran Parnell**. After studying Scandinavian history at Cambridge University, she became a freelance writer specialising in the region.

Paula Soper edited the book. Thanks go to **Stewart Wild** for proofreading.

Map Legend

▬ ▪▪	International Boundary
▬ ▬ ▬	Province/County Boundary
⊖	Border Crossing
▬•▬	National Park/Reserve
▬ ▬ ▬	Ferry Route
Ⓜ Ⓣ	Metro
Ⓢ	S-Tog (S-Train)
Ⓣ	Tunnelbanan
✈ ✈	Airport: International/Regional
🚌	Bus Station
🅿	Parking
❶	Tourist Information
✉	Post Office
✝ ✝ ✝	Church/Ruins
✝	Monastery
☾	Mosque
✡	Synagogue
🏰 🏚	Castle/Ruins
∴	Archaeological Site
∩	Cave
⌶	Statue/Monument
★	Place of Interest

The main places of interest in the Places section are coordinated by number with a full-colour map (e.g. ❶), and a symbol at the top of every right-hand page tells you where to find the map.

CONTENTS

Maps

Scandinavia **78**
DENMARK **92**
Copenhagen **94**
Zealand **114**
Bornholm **118**
Funen **124**
Jutland **130**
Greenland **138**
Faroe Islands **142**
NORWAY **156**
Oslo **158**
Oslo Fjord **168**
South & Cent. Norway **174**
Bergen **186**
Norway's Northwest
Coast **206**
Norway's Far North **212**
SWEDEN **228**
Stockholm **230**
Around Stockholm **242**
Southern Sweden **250**
Sweden's West Coast **256**
Göteborg **258**
Sweden's Great Lakes **262**
Dalarna **268**
Central Sweden **272**
Northern Sweden **278**
FINLAND **296**
Helsinki **298**
Lakes & South Finland **316**
Turku **324**
Tampere **332**
Finland's West Coast **338**
Karelia & Kuusamo **342**
Lapland **346**

Introduction

Best of Scandinavia **6**
Northerly Neighbours **15**

History

Decisive Dates **18**
Beginnings **21**
War and Peace **31**
The Modern Age **39**

Features

Art and Culture **51**
Food and Drink **61**
Great Outdoors **65**

People

The Danes **89**
The Norwegians **153**
The Swedes **225**
The Finns **293**

Insight on ...

The Vikings 28
Danish Design 110
Hurtigruten 202
The Stockholm Archipelago   246
Finnish Saunas 312

Information panels

Royal Families 42
Cool Looks............................. 54
Life in Lapland 70
Christiania 106
Andersen and Nielsen.......... 127
Heroes of Telemark 180
Stiklestad 209
Drottningholm Palace 245
Gotland 253
Sweden by Canal 265
On the Trail of Jugendstil...... 306
Åland Islands 321
Canoeing 335

Travel Tips

Denmark 356
Norway 372
Sweden 394
Finland 416

◆ **Full Travel Tips index
is on page 355**

MAIN PICTURE: Vibrant
colours in springtime,
southern Sweden.

Places

DENMARK
Introduction 87
Copenhagen 97
Zealand 113
Bornholm 118
Funen 123
Jutland 129
Greenland 137
The Faroe Islands 141
NORWAY
Introduction 151
Oslo and its Fjord 161
Southern Norway 173
Bergen 185
The Heart of Norway 191
The Northwest Coast 205
Norway's Far North.............. 211

SWEDEN
Introduction 223
Stockholm 233
Southern Sweden 249
Sweden's West Coast 255
Sweden's Great Lakes 261
Dalarna 267
Central Sweden 271
Northern Sweden 277
FINLAND
Introduction 291
Helsinki 301
Southern Finland 315
Turku 323
Finland's Lakeland 327
Finland's West Coast 337
Karelia and Kuusamo 340
Finnish Lapland 345

THE BEST OF SCANDINAVIA

Stunning scenic journeys, the best museums, festivals, family fun and unique attractions... here, at a glance, are our recommendations for a memorable visit to Scandinavia, plus some money-saving tips

BEST JOURNEYS

Here's your chance to experience the sheer beauty of Scandinavia.

- **Hurtigruten** (Norway) The world-famous postal boat sails up Norway's fjord-lined coast, stopping in at 34 picturesque ports along its 12-day route. *See page 202.*
- **Göta Kanal** (Sweden) Cross the entire country in the most leisurely manner possible, along Sweden's 19th-century engineering masterpiece, the Göta Kanal. *See page 265.*
- **Flåmsbana** (Norway) The mountain railway journey from Myrdal to Flåm packs the most dramatic scenery – ravines, rivers and toppling waterfalls – into its 20-km (12-mile) route. *See page 197.*
- **Karelian Circle Trek** (Finland) Pull on your walking boots and launch yourself into the wilderness on this 1,000-km (620-mile) trail, which takes in four national parks. *See page 68.*
- **Hærvejen** (Denmark) Cycle through Denmark's peaceful countryside on this bicycle path, which stretches from Germany all the way to Viborg in central Jutland. *See page 69.*

FRESH AIR FUN

- **Dog- and reindeer-sledding** (Finland) Explore Lapland's icy wastes in traditional fashion, driven along by a team of huskies or reindeer.
- **Cycling** (Denmark) Flat countryside and fabulous bike paths make Danish cycling a dream. Try the island of Bornholm for a taste of two-wheeled freedom.
- **Cross-country Skiing** (Oslo, Norway) The Marka area around Oslo has an incredible 2,500km (1,500 miles) of cross-country skiing trails.
- **Snowmobiling** (Kusamo, Finland) Roar across endless snow-fields on a snow-mobile in northern Finland.
- **Hiking** (Jotunheimen, Norway) Scandinavia offers exceptional hiking, but there's something magical about the Jotunheimen National Park.
- **Sailing** (Stockholm, Sweden) With Viking blood flowing through their veins, Scandinavians thrive in boats. Experience the joy of sailing for yourself around the Stockholm Archipelago.

LEFT: the railway from Flåm to Myrdal winds through magnificent mountain scenery.
ABOVE: sleighing through Lapland's snow-laden terrain.

BEST MUSEUMS

● **Vasa Museum** (Stockholm, Sweden) Carvings of cherubs and mermaids festoon the Vasa, a spectacular 17th-century warship. *See page 239.*

● **Skansen** (Stockholm, Sweden) Over 150 traditional Swedish buildings are at the world's oldest open-air museum. *See page 238.*

● **Louisiana** (Humlebæk, Denmark) This huge modern-art gallery contains an impressive permanent collection, including works by Giacometti and Andy Warhol. *See page 115.*

● **Alvar Aalto Museum** (Jyväskylä, Finland) See into the creative soul of Finland's best-loved furniture designer and architect. *See page 331.*

● **Nasjonalgalleriet** (Oslo, Norway) Amongst the paintings in Norway's National Gallery is Edvard Munch's *Skrik (The Scream). See page 163.*

FINEST FOOD TRADITIONS

Scandinavia is a gastronomic treat, with fresh seafood in abundance.

● **Crayfish parties** In July and August, crayfish parties are the seasonal speciality in Finland and Sweden.

● **Artistic sandwiches** *Smørrebrød* in Denmark, *smörgåsbord* in Sweden, and *voileipäpöytä* in Finland – all wonderfully dainty hot-and-cold buffet dishes.

● **Pickled herring** An acquired taste, but one that will always bring back fond memories of Scandinavia.

● **Cloudberries** Picked and devoured in Scandinavian forests in late summer and early autumn.

ONLY IN SCANDINAVIA

Some of the unique attractions that make Scandinavia special.

● **Northern lights** Nothing can prepare you for the eerie flickering of the aurora borealis.

● **Lumilinna** (Kemi, Finland) Each year, the marvellous Snow Castle is constructed from blocks of snow. *See page 339.*

● **Saunas** The genuine sauna experience requires clouds of steam, freshly cut birch leaves, and snow to roll around in. *See page 312.*

● **Christiania** (Copenhagen, Denmark) A fascinating social experiment, the "Free City" is open to curious visitors. *See page 106.*

● **Father Christmas** (Finland) Several places in Scandinavia lay claim to Santa Claus. Joulupukin Pajakylä, near Rovaniemi, allegedly has the real Man in Red.

LEFT: experience the Swedish way of life, preserved at Skansen in Stockholm.
BELOW: the aerial light display of aurora borealis is best seen between September and February.

SCANDINAVIA FOR FAMILIES

Some of the best family fun that will keep the children amused.

● **Legoland** (Billund, Denmark) Win eternal admiration by taking your children to Legoland, with waterpark, rides and the marvellous Miniland, created from 20 million bricks. *See page 131.*

● **Tivoli** (Copenhagen, Denmark) Utterly delightful theme park and gardens, right in the heart of the capital city. Fountains and fairground rides as well as jugglers and acrobats make this a fun family day out for everyone. *See page 99.*

● **Moominworld** (Naantali, Finland) A theme park for smaller children based on the Moomin books by Tove Jansson. The blue-coloured Moomin House is the main attraction. *See page 325.*

● **Glassriket** (Småland, Sweden) For something a little different, let your children paint, engrave and even blow their own glass at a traditional glassworks. *See page 252.*

● **Egeskov Slot** (Funen, Denmark) One of Denmark's most famous historic sights. This well-preserved fairytale castle has a gardenful of endearing attractions, including one of the world's biggest permanent mazes. *See page 125.*

● **The International Museum of Children's Art** (Oslo, Norway) A museum devoted entirely to children's art from 150 countries, where young visitors are encouraged to paint, dance and draw. *See page 164.*

ABOVE: celebrating Midsummer with a bonfire on the beach, in West Jutland, Denmark.
BELOW LEFT: all aboard the train bound for Legoland, in Billund, East Jutland, Denmark.

BEST FESTIVALS

● **Midsummer** Celebrated with bonfires and great gusto across Scandinavia on the nearest weekend to 23rd June.

● **Savolinna Opera Festival** (Finland) International artists perform at Olavinlinna castle, on Lake Pihlajavesi, during July at Finland's most famous cultural festival.

● **Holmenkollen Ski Festival** (Norway) Oslo's Holmenkollen ski jump is the focus of this traditional sports event, held annually in March.

● **Horsens Middle Ages Festival** (Denmark) Medieval history is brought to life in late August at this lively festival, with music, dancing, and theatrical performances.

● **Dalhalla Summer Music** (Sweden) There's something to appeal to everyone at this cavernous open-air arena, set in the depths of an abandoned limestone quarry near Rättvik. Their summer-long music programme encompasses opera, jazz, pop and rock.

● **Roskilde** (Denmark) Northern Europe's largest annual music festival, held over four days in early July, features world-famous rock and pop bands.

● **Tromsø International Film Festival** (Norway) Norway's biggest festival attracts over 30,000 visitors.

BEST IN SCANDINAVIAN DESIGN

- **Oslo Opera House** (Oslo, Norway) A stage with perfect acoustics; a sleek design that engages with its surroundings and its visitors; a construction that came in ahead of schedule and under budget. Oslo's brand-new opera house shows why Scandinavians still design. *See page 163.*

- **Carl Larsson's House** (Sundborn, Denmark) The artist's beautiful riverside cottage is a humbling example of love, family life and Swedish design working in

perfect harmony. *See page 269.*
- **Finnish Jugendstil** (Finland) The National Romantics used art and architecture to express independence from Russian rule: admire their Art Nouveau buildings in Helsinki's Katajanokka area. *See page 306.*
- **Danish Museum of Art and Design** (Copenhagen, Denmark) Ceramics, furniture, textiles, prints and posters – the best in Danish design is here. *See page 110.*
- **Central Train Station** (Helsinki, Finland) Designed by Eliel Saarinen, it links two of Helsinki's most prevalent styles: National Romanticism and functionalism. The entrance to the station is guarded by two granite giants holding translucent lanterns. *See page 302.*

BELOW LEFT: the fabulous granite and marble Oslo Opera House.
ABOVE: Päijänne Lakes; the popular view of Finland, endless lakes and forests.

NATURAL WONDERS

Phenomenal natural wonders abound from fabulous fjords to gigantic glaciers.

- **Icebergs** (Greenland) Qeqertarsuaq makes a good viewing place to watch vast blue-white towers of ice drifting by. *See page 137.*
- **Preikestolen** (Norway) Featured in every tourist brochure on Norway, majestic Pulpit Rock has unbeatable fjord views. *See page 177.*
- **Jostedalsbreen Glacier** (Sognefjorden, Norway)

Europe's largest glacier. *See page 197.*
- **Päijänne Lakes** (Finland) 33,000 islands are yours to explore in Finland's watery Lakeland. *See page 327.*
- **Cliffs of Møn** (Denmark) Hunt for fossils along the edges of Denmark's most famous landscape, the shining white chalk cliffs of Møn. *See page 116.*

MONEY-SAVING TIPS

Tourist Cards Larger cities such as Stockholm, Oslo and Göteborg offer 24- and 48-hour tourist cards, which are well worth the money as the price includes admission to many museums, galleries and tourist attractions, and usually free access to public transport or car-parking.

Hostels Youth hostels in Scandinavia are well worth considering: they tend to be good value, family-orientated and have excellent facilities. Bring your own sheets and towels to save on rental costs. *See pages 365, 387 and 407.*

City Bikes Getting around Scandinavian cities by bicycle is generally a liberating experience. Borrow bicycles for free in Norway (Bergen, Oslo and Trondheim) and Denmark (Copenhagen) and explore further afield.

Food Self-service buffet breakfasts in hostels and hotels are a great boon to the thrifty traveller. Fill up in the morning; at lunchtime snack on sandwiches or look for the daily special on restaurant menus; and many places do "early bird" evening

deals, usually between 5.30pm and 7pm.

Nature Wild, empty space is Scandinavia's greatest treasure. Get back to nature with a tent and immerse yourself in solitude.

Free Festivals Check what's on and when. Many Scandinavian festivals have free as well as ticketed events: for example, at the Copenhagen Jazz Festival in July, the city streets become a venue.

NORTHERLY NEIGHBOURS

At the top of the map, but no longer aloof, the
Scandinavian countries are Europe's best-kept secret

To fly over Scandinavia is to discover a vast, sparsely inhabited, natural landscape of sparkling fjords and rocky mountains, glassy lakes and rushing rivers, dense forests and frozen tundra, extending from temperate Denmark far north to the land of the Sami and including Greenland and the Faroe Islands.

Norway, Denmark, Sweden and Finland are among Europe's most ancient civilisations. Theirs is an eventful shared history of prowess and intrigue. Early Norse traders ventured deep into Asia leaving graphic runic inscriptions on stones which provide clues as to their exploits. Later, the infamous Vikings who pillaged their way round the coasts of Ireland, Britain and France laid the foundations for kingdoms and Christianity across Scandinavia. They were followed by kings, queens and tsars who schemed and battled. Borders shifted, unions came and went, and by the start of the 20th century four distinct nations emerged which have grown into the modern, highly individualistic countries we know today.

The Danes are probably the most garrulous of the Scandinavians, though all will ensure the visitor receives a warm welcome. The Nordic reputation for cool reservedness has had its day, but not for cool design. Everything from beer bottle openers to the latest building has the stamp of chic understatement.

The Scandinavian capitals of Copenhagen, Oslo, Stockholm and Helsinki are vibrant cities housing some of the most inspirational museums and finest art collections in Europe, with concerts and festivals bringing music and life to the streets. In fact, at the slightest excuse Scandinavians will take to the outdoors, whether on a bicycle along the winding lanes of Denmark, skiing on floodlit trails around Oslo, escaping to little red-painted waterside cottages in Sweden, or plunging from sauna to ice pool in Finland. An inherent love of nature is deeply rooted within the national psyches. Perhaps this has to do with the long dark days of winter and the need to soak up the summer light. Arrive in any of the Scandinavian countries in mid- to late June and you'll find the locals dancing and feasting around Midsummer maypoles and bonfires.

Transport and communications are excellent: roads join southerly Denmark with the North Cape, railways penetrate Lapland, ferries ply the fjords and link remote islands and lakeside villages, and planes cut the journey times. And with the opening of the Øresund bridge in 2000 from Denmark to Sweden, Scandinavia is just a short step from its European neighbours. ❑

PRECEDING PAGES: the forested north of Sweden; a Sami family in their colourful traditional costumes.
LEFT: market day at the harbour, Helsinki.

Decisive Dates

EARLY HISTORY: 10,000 BC–AD 800

From 10,000 BC Hunter-gatherer tribes follow the melting ice northwards, establishing settlements and farming communities in southern Scandinavia. Tribes from Eastern Europe settle the Arctic coast.

1500 BC Trade routes are forged through the rivers of Eastern Europe to the Danube.

c.500 BC–AD 800 Iron Age "Grauballe Man" and "Tollund Man" are buried in peat bogs in Denmark to be unearthed in the 1950s in remarkable condition.

c.AD 100 The historian Tacitus mentions the Fenni

(the Sami of Finland) in his *Germania* and describes the Sveas who inhabit what is now central Sweden.

c.AD 400 Suomalaiset (Baltic Finns) cross the Baltic and settle in Finland. Sweden's influence over its "eastern province" begins. In Norway farmers push inland; forts have been found on Lake Mjøsa.

THE VIKING AGE

800–1060 The Scandinavian Vikings earn a reputation as sea warriors. In 862, at the invitation of the Slavs, Prince Rurik leads the Swedish Vikings (Varangians) east to bring order to the principality of Novgorod. They soon control the trade routes to Byzantium.

830 A Benedictine monk, Ansgar (801–865), lands on Björkö in Sweden and founds a church.

861 Vikings sack Paris.

866 After repeated raids along the English and French coasts and the plundering of monasteries, the Vikings control most of England and Normandy.

940–95 Harald Bluetooth brings Christianity to Denmark; Olav Tryggvason uses force in his attempts to convert the Norwegian Vikings.

1001 The sagas relate that it was Leifur Eiríksson who discovered Vinland (America).

1030 Battle of Stiklestad in Norway and the death of King Olav Haraldsson who later becomes St Olav.

1050 Harald Hardrada of Norway founds Oslo.

1066 Defeat in England at the Battle of Stamford Bridge brings the Viking Age to an end.

MIDDLE AGES c.1100–1500

1100 The first bishoprics appear, among them the see of Nidaros (Trondheim) in Norway.

1155 King Erik of Sweden launches a crusade into Finland; further Swedish invasions take place in 1239 and 1293 subjugating large areas of the country.

1319–43 Inter-Scandinavian royal marriages produce a joint Norwegian–Swedish monarchy.

1362 Finland becomes a province of Sweden.

1397 A union is forged by Queen Margarethe and signed at Kalmar which unites the kingdoms of Norway, Denmark and Sweden.

1417 Eric VII of Denmark makes Copenhagen his capital and builds a palace at Helsingør.

1460 Kristian I secures the duchies of Schleswig and Holstein for Denmark.

WARS AND REFORMATION

1520 Kristian II of Denmark invades Sweden and massacres the nobility in the "Stockholm Bloodbath". Gustav Vasa drives him out and the Kalmar Union is disbanded. Norway remains under Danish rule.

1523 In Sweden, Gustav Vasa (1523–60) ascends the throne, marking the start of the Vasa dynasty (1523–1720), which also holds power in Finland. Under Gustav II Adolf (1611–32) Sweden becomes a great European power, only to decline during the reign of Karl XII (1697– 1718), the "warrior king". Fine arts flourish under Gustav III (1771–92).

1530 The Reformation passes through the Scandinavian countries and the Lutheran faith is introduced. In Finland Mikael Agricola's translation of the Bible forms the basis of Finnish literary language.

1536 Norway ceases to be an independent kingdom as the Danes take control.

1588–1648 Denmark flourishes under the long rule of Kristian IV (1577–1648). Attempts to regain territory lost to Sweden end in failure.

1625–57 The Thirty Years War launched by the Danish king, Kristian IV, to check Swedish expansion ends in defeat for Denmark.

1714–41 "Great Wrath" and "Lesser Wrath": Russia and Sweden battle over Finland. Under the Treaty of Turku (1743) Russia moves its border westwards.

NINETEENTH-CENTURY MANOEUVRES

1801–14 During the Napoleonic Wars English fleets twice bombard Copenhagen. Denmark sides with Napoleon and suffers further defeat. In 1814 the victorious powers dissolve the Denmark–Norway union and Norway is ceded to Sweden (1814–1905). A new Norwegian constitution is adopted at Eidsvoll.

1807–1905 Tsar Alexander I occupies Finland in 1807. The Treaty of Hamina cedes Finland to Russia. A programme of "Russification" is introduced in Finland; in 1899 the composer Jean Sibelius writes his patriotic *Finlandia* as part of a protest against Russian suppression. Finnish resistance grows. In 1905 events in Russia lead to a degree of autonomy for Finland.

1812 Tsar Alexander makes Helsinki Finland's capital.

1815–1907 In Sweden, Jean-Baptiste Bernadotte, French marshal of Napoleon, succeeds to the throne as Karl XIV Johan (1818–44). The great exodus to the United States takes place.

1864 Denmark and Prussia at war. Denmark loses Schleswig-Holstein.

MODERN TIMES

1905 Referendum in Norway leads to the end of the union with Sweden. The Danish prince Håkon VII is invited to be King of Norway.

1906 Finnish women become the first in Europe to be given the vote.

1917–19 Finland declares its independence from the new Soviet Union, but is plunged into civil war in 1918 over attempts by radicals to introduce a Russian-style revolution. The White Guard (government troops), under General Mannerheim, defeats the Red Guard.

1919 The Republic of Finland comes into being under its first president, K.J. Ståhlberg.

1919 Denmark recovers Schleswig, but not Holstein.

1930s Sweden and Denmark establish welfare states.

1939–48 Soviet territorial demands spark off the Winter War between Finland and the Soviet Union. The Continuation War follows. Finland is forced to cede land to the USSR. War reparations are severe. In 1948 Finland and the Soviet Union sign the Treaty of Friendship, Co-operation and Mutual Assistance. Sweden remains neutral in World Wars I and II. Norway proclaims neutrality in World War II, but is attacked by the Germans, who also occupy Denmark. Norwegian resistance force numbers 50,000.

1949 Denmark becomes a founding member of NATO.

1951–86 In Sweden, Social Democrats hold office for several years at a time; the monarch's constitutional powers are removed. In 1986 Olof Palme, Swedish prime minister and international peacemaker, is killed.

1955 Finland is admitted to the United Nations. Helsinki becomes a centre for international peace and arms limitation talks in the late 20th century.

1960s Norway begins oil exploration in the North Sea.

1973 Denmark joins the EEC (now European Union).

1995 Finland and Sweden join the European Union. Norway votes against membership (1972 and 1994).

2000 Øresund bridge opens between Denmark and Sweden, establishing new links across Scandinavia.

2005 Norway celebrates 100 years of independence from Sweden.

2006 Finland's first female president, Tarja Halonen, narrowly wins re-election. Cartoons of the Prophet Muhammad printed in a Danish newspaper spark protest and outrage throughout the world.

2008 World financial crisis catches up with Scandinavia as central banks of Denmark, Sweden and Norway bail out Iceland. King Harald V of Norway opens the Oslo Opera House in Bjørvika, ahead of schedule and under budget. ❏

PRECEDING PAGES: Sweden loses Finland at the battle of Poltava, 1709. **LEFT:** King Gustav Vasa of Sweden. **RIGHT:** Tarja Halonen, Finland's first female president.

BEGINNINGS

As the ice floes retreated, so the hunter-gatherers moved north,
colonising the Nordic lands and giving rise to the Viking Age

For 1.6 million years, Scandinavia languished under an ice-sheet that oozed out of the Jostedalsbreen in Norway, stretched as far as the British Isles and Moscow, and was 3,000 metres (9,800 ft) thick. When eventually it melted, nomadic hunters and gatherers went after the plants and animals that surfaced in its wake. Some 12,000 years ago, the peninsula celebrated its final liberation from the crushing weight of the ice by rising like bread in an oven. Unleavened Denmark, however, remained barely above sea level, the land bridge with Norway and Sweden broken.

The first inhabitants

Some of the earliest arrivals in this re-sculptured land brought with them tame dogs, knew how to make leather boats, and kept a well-stocked armoury of bows, arrows, harpoons and spears. Not much else is known about them, so a case has been made for recognising the nomadic Lapps, also known as Sami, as Scandinavia's quasi-aboriginals. Other schools of thought put them down as comparatively recent arrivals from Siberia. In any case, Lapp women and children these days generally live in houses while their men in shrinking numbers drive reindeer herds over a territory which encompasses parts of Norway, Sweden, Finland and the Russian Kola Peninsula.

As for the Finns, the second group of somewhat exceptional Scandinavians, a 19th-century scholar, M.A. Castren, suggested that they and anyone else speaking a Finno-Ugric language, which includes Hungarians, Estonians and indeed Lapps, hailed from Outer Mongolia and could therefore claim kinship with the likes of Genghis Khan. After searching self-examination, an increasing number of Finns see themselves as indigenous Baltic folk who drifted into their present location between the

LEFT: Viking raiding party sets out across the North Sea, 9th century.
RIGHT: latter-day Viking in traditional garb at one of Denmark's popular re-enactments.

Bronze Age and the start of the great European migration in the 5th century AD.

The real majority of Scandinavians are legendary types, like the 11th-century Norman crusader Bohemund who stopped in Constantinople on his way to the Holy Land. "Like no other man ever seen in the Byzantine Empire

whether barbarian or Greek," gushed the emperor's daughter, Anna Comnenus, "so tall in body that he exceeded even the tallest man by almost 50 centimetres… so narrow in the belly and flanks… so broad in the chest and shoulders… so strong in the arms. His whole stature could be described as neither constricted nor over-endowed with flesh, but blended as perfectly as possible."

Nevertheless, there were always significant numbers of shorter, darker people with more rounded skulls in the region, although more so in Denmark than in the northern forests and fjords. Lapps and Finns aside, they all spoke the same Primitive Nordic language, one of the

Germanic group, and had common notions of religion, law and culture. Bronze Age rock-carvings reveal a well-appointed world of horse-drawn carts, ships with curious beaks at either end, weapons and a religion devoted to the worship of the sun and fertility.

Travellers' tales

In 500 BC, however, a drastic turn in the weather killed off livestock which had previously spent the whole year outdoors, wrecked agriculture and forced men into trousers instead of belted cloaks. In the meantime, sun-drenched Athenians were building the Parthenon and,

Suiones (Uppland Swedes) had developed a healthy respect for wealth, recognised a king "with an unchallengeable right to obedience", and built powerful ships "unusual in that there is a prow at each end". Augustus and Nero sent expeditions to find out more, and it was possibly through contact with Rome that the Scandinavians were inspired to produce their own runic alphabet.

Jordanes, the 6th-century historian of the Goths, was the first to identify "Dani" among the local tribes, all of whom were said to be taller than Germans and ferocious fighters. Procopius, the Byzantine historian, singled out

like most Europeans, had no idea whatsoever of Scandinavia until the voyager Pytheas of Marseilles returned a little before 300 BC with tales of a land north of Britain where it was either dark for six months at a time or light enough, even at midnight, to pick lice out of a shirt. The local population were barbarians who lived on millet, herbs, roots and fruit because, he noticed, they had hardly any domestic animals, and threshing generally had to be done indoors. Nevertheless, grain fermented with honey produced a giddying drink they enjoyed.

Four centuries later, the Roman historian Tacitus reported significant improvements. The

the Lapps as people who had neither crops nor wine and wore animal skins held together with sinews. Lapp babies, he said, did not touch milk. Put into skin cradles and left dangling from trees while their mothers worked, they tucked into bone marrow. He also described hunters on skis and an excessive enthusiasm for human sacrifice.

Raiding parties

In 789, however, the Scandinavians spoke up for themselves. Three ships of an unfamiliar design appeared off the coast of Dorset in southwest England and the local magistrate ambled down to welcome them. Heavily armed warriors leapt ashore and subjected the hapless man to a fate known as "kissing the thin lips of the axe". As his head rolled, they stormed off to fill their ships with whatever caught their fancy, including a number of attractive natives, and were gone. The bemused *Anglo-Saxon Chronicle* could only say that they were apparently "Northmen from Hordaland" (Norwegians from the Bergen area). They returned four years later. As committed pagans, the raiders were unaffected by the sanctity of Chris-

navigable grid between the Gulf of Finland and the Caspian and Black seas. At the far end lay Constantinople, the richest city on earth and an inexhaustible market for northern products like amber, furs, weapons and above all fresh-faced European slaves. The Arab traveller and diplomat Ibn Fadlan was impressed by the physical attributes of the Swedes – "perfect physical specimens, tall as date palms, blond and ruddy" – but had reservations about their insistence on exercising seigneurial rights

RUNIC WRITING

To facilitate carving in wood or stone, the runic alphabet consisted of permutations of straight lines. It was used initially only for names and invocations against evil spirits.

tian monasteries stuffed with valuables. Beginning with Lindisfarne in Northumbria, they murdered monks and ransacked coastal monasteries all around the British Isles, and repeated the performance every summer. Prayers went up everywhere for delivery from so-called Northmen. They, however, called themselves Vikings, whose meaning is disputed.

At more or less the same time, Swedish counterparts were capitalising on the fact that lakes and rivers formed an almost uninterrupted

LEFT: Bronze Age Sun Chariot, National Museum of Denmark, Copenhagen.
ABOVE: rock carvings at Hjemmeluft, Sweden.

over the merchandise in public and en masse. "A man will have sexual intercourse with slave girls while his companions look on," he said.

On a third contemporary front, Charlemagne's crusade against the heathen Saxons of northwest Germany brought him into contact with their Danish neighbours on the other side of the Eider, whose look he liked even less. As the Danes felt exactly the same way about him and his Franks, they built the Danevirke wall across the Jutland peninsula to keep them at bay and to secure the border town of Hedeby, the trade bridge between the North Sea and the Baltic. Thus were sown the seeds of the Schleswig-Holstein imbroglio, a territorial dispute of such complexity that any-one dragged into it even 1,000 years later, according to a 19th-century British prime minister himself involved, was in danger of going mad or dying.

Al-Tartushi, another Arab traveller, went to see Hedeby, "a large town at the farthest end of the world ocean." The carcasses of sacrificed animals swung from poles, but the main food was fish "as there is so much of it".

Both men and women used eye make-up, he said (not that anyone else ever noticed),

> ### NO LOVE LOST
>
> In Arthurian romances the Vikings were described as being "wild and savage and had not in them the love of God nor their neighbours".

and women could unilaterally divorce their husbands whenever they felt like it.

Taken together, these developments across three fronts signalled the start of the "Viking Age" in which they went abroad to conquer most of the British Isles, carve a Norman province out of France, invade Germany, Spain and Italy, settle Iceland and Greenland, discover America, terrorise the Mediterranean, dominate the Baltic region, Poland, Russia and Ukraine, fight for and against Byzantium, attack the Muslim Caliphate in

Baghdad, and contribute to the liberation of Jerusalem. Meanwhile, the pack of warring chieftainships and petty kingdoms at home was being shuffled and cut down to form the separate states as exist today.

Trade with Byzantium

Various factors combined to produce this explosive energy. The disruption of traditional trade by the 9th-century Muslim conquests in Europe, for one, encouraged the Swedes to open up the alternative routes through Russia. They put it about that the Slavs begged them to take over the running of the territory. "Our land is large and fruitful but it lacks order," the message

> ### VIKING SHIP DESIGN
>
> A Viking's ticket to foreign parts was the latest evolution of the ship design first shown in Bronze Age rock carvings. The prows at either end were the extremities of a keel made out of a single oak. It could twist like a tree in the wind, hence its immense strength. A fighting ship of the type found at Gokstad in Norway was 25 metres (82 ft) long, 6 metres (19 ft) wide, and carried a crew of 70. Clinker-built, caulked with tarred animal hair or wool, it had a hinged steering oar that swung out of the way so the ships could be aimed at a beach at full speed. An important innovation was the use of sail. Viking ships could cross the North Sea to England in 72 hours.

allegedly read. "Come over and rule us." By 900, Swedish influence radiated throughout Eastern Europe from their strongholds at Novgorod and Kiev. The Swedes were soon assimilated under the weight of Slavic numbers, but they left an indelible mark in the name by which they were locally known, Rus.

Polygamy and primogeniture were also forces behind the Viking Age. Big as Scandinavia was, only a tiny proportion of the land was actually habitable, and the useful land in remote valleys or fjords could only be subdivided so many times. As the whole of a patrimony generally went to the eldest son, or

foray in 844 opened with a rebuff at La Coruña on Spain's Atlantic coast, improved with the sacking of Lisbon, Cádiz and Seville, and ended with the loss of two ships crammed with gold, silver and prisoners to the Moors.

Terrorising the Mediterranean

Back again in 859 with a fleet of 62 red-sailed ships, Hasting negotiated the Straits of Gibraltar, sacked Algeciras, spent a week in Morocco rounding up "blue men" for subsequent sale in Ireland and then wintered on La Camargue in the Rhône Delta, "causing great annoyance and detriment to the inhabitants." Come spring, he

rather the eldest surviving son, Swedish kings with 40 women in their harem, or Norwegian earls with a dozen sons by various wives and concubines, were sure recipes for orgiastic fratricide. Harald Fairhair's ascendancy, *c*.890, went a long way towards defining Norway, but it necessarily involved stripping and disbanding numerous lesser dynasties, whose scions had no real choice but to try their luck abroad.

To begin with, Viking enterprise abroad was a matter of independent initiative, as epitomised by a certain Hasting. Born in Denmark, his first

LEFT: Viking burial ground, Jutland, Denmark.
ABOVE: runic script, National Museum, Copenhagen.

was ready for Italy. After looting Pisa, he turned south and came across a city of such marbled magnificence that it could only be Rome.

Hasting dispatched messengers with the story that their leader, a Christian of unparalleled piety, was dying, and his last wish was to be given a Christian burial in such hallowed ground as now lay before them. Permission granted, the gates admitted a coffin followed by a long procession of mournful Vikings. As the local bishop was praying over the coffin it flew open and out leapt Hasting himself. The startled bishop was on his back, run through with Hasting's sword, as the mourners went off to reduce the city to ashes. Only then did Hasting learn that he had destroyed Luna, not Rome, and felt so cheated that he ordered the massacre of all male prisoners. His next port of call was Alexandria in Egypt. The campaign closed in 862 with an overland march to sack Pamplona.

England under attack

Three years later, in 865, Hasting appeared at the mouth of the Thames with a new fleet of 80 ships just as "a big heathen horde", according to the *Anglo-Saxon Chronicle*, arrived elsewhere in England under Ivar the Boneless. Their immediate mission was to avenge a private grievance, the cruel death of their father

Ragnar in a pit full of snakes, but with Hasting's fleet and other Danish private armies dotted around the country, the show took on the appearance of a concerted Danish conquest. The outcome was a Danish kingdom in England and the imposition of a stiff tax, Danegeld.

Ironically, Harald Bluetooth of Denmark (*c*.910–985) was in turn obliged to prostrate himself. His *bête noire* was the crusading Holy Roman Emperor Otto I, a German, who could be appeased only by Harald's submission to Christian baptism. Most of Europe had been Christian for five centuries or more, but Scandinavia was not inclined to abandon paganism. Harald's son and successor, Swein Forkbeard,

brushed aside his father's baptism as an aberration. The Norwegian king Olav Tryggvason (*c*.965–1000), a hell-raising pirate from the age of 12, was supposedly convinced by a wise hermit in the Scillies in England, but the methods he then employed to convert his subjects were pure Viking. Sweden remained true to paganism by turning Christian missionaries into martyrs. Sacrifices in the golden temple at Uppsala continued into the late 11th century.

Norman conquest

In France, Vikings who sailed up the Seine and attacked Paris were given 3,000 kg (3 tons) of silver by Charles the Bald of France to go away, while his successor Charles the Simple was ready to cede an entire province as protection money to Rolf (or "Rollo") the Ganger, a Viking too big to ride any horse. The province became the Duchy of Normandy, and within two centuries it was the springboard for the 1066 Norman conquest of Anglo-Danish England. But if the conquest was a great triumph for Norman arms, it also accelerated the end of the Viking Age.

Harald Hardrada of Norway (1015–66), the "Thunderbolt of the North", had tried to pre-empt William's seizure of England with an invasion of his own, and it was not long before Danish and Norwegian forces attempted to unseat William. But England under the Normans was a tough nut to crack; Normandy itself was no longer open to disgruntled Scandinavians, and Iceland was full. Greenland was the next possibility, and it was from here that Leifur Eiríksson set sail to see if he could find something better in the unknown world to the west.

As it was Leifur's own father who had coined the deceptive tease "Greenland", sceptics might have wondered about the son's tales of Vinland, a land of warm sunshine, trees, grass and, as the name implied, grapes. But his brother Thorvaldur believed him, followed his directions, and on landing in Vinland walked straight into an Indian arrow. The next assessment of the land's potential was by a fearsome woman, Freydís, who murdered most of her party en route. She was not over-impressed. The future America, she thought, was not more than "all right". ❑

LEFT: Lejre Iron Age village, Roskilde, Denmark.
RIGHT: Odin, the mythological Norse god of wisdom, war, culture and the dead.

MEDIEVAL THUGS OR MERCHANT TRADERS?

The Vikings plundered their way into the annals of Scandinavian history. But archaeology reveals there's more to these raiders than meets the eye

At first glance the Viking legacy appears to be little more than an impressive catalogue of violence and piracy. Archaeological finds have, however, shed light not only on the way the Vikings lived (everything from the food they ate to the clothing they wore) but also on their burial traditions.

Today, the Vikings are recognised for their skills as craftsmen, traders and of course as sailors.

The Viking longship, essential for both raiding and trading, was also used to bury kings and chieftains. Superb examples can be seen at the Viking ship museums in Roskilde, Denmark, and in Oslo, Norway, where textiles, household utensils and other artefacts excavated from the burial mounds around the Oslo Fjord are also on display. In Denmark, Funen's Ladby Ship Museum houses a magnificent burial ship with a dragon's head and tail.

Sites and open-air museums such as those at Birka outside Stockholm (*see right*), and Denmark's Fyrkat and Trelleborg, offer a unique look into the daily lives of the Vikings. Other places of interest include the burial ground at Lindholm Høje, Jutland and Jelling in Zealand, with its runes and burial mounds, often referred to as Denmark's "birth certificate". With a host of activities and re-enactments, these sites offer visitors a chance to relive the Viking experience first-hand.

▷ **CARVED IN STONE**
The Vikings would commemorate an event or a death on runestones like this one on Öland.

▷ **BURIAL SHIP**
The Oseberg ship in Oslo's Vikingskipshuset is thought to be the tomb of a queen buried in 834 with her maidservant and most valued possessions.

△ **ANCIENT LIFESTYLE**
Reliving life the Viking way in Fyrkat, Denmark. Viking re-enactments are popular attractions in Jutland.

▽ **GRAVE OBJECTS**
Tools found in the graves at Birka, Sweden, are testimony to the society of skilled craftsmen who lived in the town.

△ DWELLING PLACE
The reconstructed longhouse at Fyrkat, in Denmark, where four earth fortifications enclosed 16 large houses.

▽ SAILING ONWARD
Unlike other burial sites, graves at Lindholm Høje, Denmark, were marked by stones. This one is in the shape of a ship.

THE VIKING SILK ROUTE

This bishop's crosier from Ireland, pictured above, was found at the site of Sweden's first Viking town, Birka. Situated 30 km (19 miles) west of Stockholm, Birka was founded towards the end of the 8th century.

Archaeological excavations have revealed trade networks stretching east to Byzantium and as far as China. The finds, which include silks from the Far East, Arabic coins and glass beads from the Arabic Caliphate, have challenged the belief that the Viking age was all murder and mayhem. They point instead to a burgeoning, prosperous society made up of merchants, traders and farmers.

Birka was the first town in Sweden to come into contact with Christianity. But the town was never evangelised and in some graves Thor's hammer was found alongside a crucifix.

The museum at Birka is open between May and mid-September. Boats leave from outside Stockholm City Hall, at Stadshusbron.

△ MONEY MATTERS
Danish, Frankish and Arabic coins were found at Birka. This one depicts a trading vessel.

◁ HAIR CARE
Combs were popular items. Many fine examples were found in the graves excavated at Birka.

△ SHIPSHAPE
Manoeuvrability and speed were the key features of Viking ship design. A number of replicas have been built in Norway, like this one in Oslo harbour.

WAR AND PEACE

From the end of the Viking Age to the dawn of the 20th century, kings battled for supremacy, land changed hands and unions were made and broken

As the Viking Age drew to a close in the 11th century, the kings of Norway, Sweden and Denmark – "all handsome and big men, of noble looks and well-spoken" – met at Konghelle on the Göta River in 1098 to acknowledge one another's legitimacy and to adopt a common policy on robbery and theft, ever the crimes of greatest concern. To seal the pact, King Magnus of Norway – known as "Barelegs" since returning from Scotland sporting a kilt – married Inge of Sweden's daughter Margaret, hence "The Peace Maiden".

Five years later, however, Magnus fulfilled one of his own favourite sayings – "a king stands for his country's honour and glory, not for a long life" – by being killed in action in Ireland. Norway was then carved up among his three young sons, thereby undoing not only the single Norwegian kingdom hammered together by Harald Fairhair but also any real prospect of smooth Scandinavian co-existence.

Converting the heathens

Denmark's particular difficulty was not fragmentation but a succession of kings so ineffectual (e.g. "Harald the Hen") that several were simply taken out to sea and drowned. In Sweden, the throne bobbed between two dynasties who routinely murdered the opposing encumbent. Next to these goings-on, the princes of the new power in the land, the Church, looked purposeful. As comfortable in the saddle as the pulpit, Bishop Absalon of Roskilde (1128–1201) personally sorted out "the heathen Wend", a tribe of defiant Baltic pagans whose headquarters were on Rügen island. Smashing the four-headed god Svantevit, he offered everyone the choice of embracing Christ or dying immediately. The island then became part of his booming diocese. With bishops like Absalon around, ambitious kings were obliged to demonstrate their religious credentials by "taking the

Cross" and joining a crusade. Sigurd of Norway, one of Barelegs' sons ("not good-looking but well-grown and manly; his few words were most often not friendly") went to the Holy Land. Valdemar I (1131–82), a more dashing king than Denmark had seen for some time, fought 28 battles against heathens of one sort or

another. His successor Valdemar II concentrated on Estonians, and in spite of a fleet of 1,000 ships was only rescued from one certain defeat by the miraculous apparition of a red-and-white banner in the heavens. It became Denmark's national flag.

Sweden annexes Finland

Erik I of Sweden did his crusader service among the Finns during the 12th century, marking the start of Sweden's 700-year annexation of Finland and Erik's climb to the status of his country's patron saint. But aggrandisement was all too easily reversed, as occurred in Denmark on Valdemar II's exit. "The crown

---

LEFT: Gustav Vasa (1523–60), first king of the Vasa dynasty, laid the foundations of the Swedish state.
RIGHT: Kristian II of Denmark (1513–23).

fell off the head of the Danes," a chronicle wailed, "and they became the laughing stock for all their neighbours through civil wars and mutual destruction."

In Sweden, the saintly Erik I was murdered by the son of the king he had removed, Sverker, leaving Erik's son in no doubt about what was expected of him. He did not disappoint.

Like the Church, German and Dutch Hansa traders recognised the chaotic absence of government as an excellent opportunity for themselves. The obvious fact

THE DANISH FLAG

The oldest national flag in the world is a source of pride among Danes. It must never touch the ground and only a pennant version may be flown at night.

Fishing vessels raced from all over Europe until some 40,000 were crammed into the Sound, temporarily loosening the Hansa's grip on the market. The 14th-century king, Valdemar IV of Denmark, launched a snap invasion of the Hansa's base at Visby in Gotland and, flushed with success, assumed the title of "King of the Goths". The Hansa were neither impressed nor amused. Throwing the resources of their 77 towns and cities into a military alliance with Sweden, they bounced Valdemar off his Danish throne and

of Scandinavian economic life was an abundance of fish versus a shortage of grain. By tying up the markets in both commodities, and the shipping in between, the Hansa had a goose of pure gold, and it gave them a network of strategic ports and market towns across the continent. But if Scandinavia was sapped by an extortionate exchange rate between fish and grain, it was then poleaxed by the Black Death in 1349. With the population of Norway, for example, cut by more than half, economics reverted to the Stone Age.

One interlude in the slow reconstruction process was the arrival of shoals of herring so dense that fish could be caught with bare hands.

invited applications. Margarethe, the young wife of King Håkon VI of Norway, proposed their son Oluf. He was five years old.

A scheming queen

Margarethe, who had married in 1363 at the age of 10 and given birth to Oluf at 17, knew what she was doing. With Denmark under Oluf's little belt and the Norwegian crown bound to follow in due course, she encouraged him to think of himself as "the true heir to Sweden" as well, a presumption that infuriated Albrecht, the reigning king of Sweden.

Nevertheless, Margarethe (described as "of dark complexion and somewhat masculine in appearance") had to think again when Oluf died at 17. While personally keeping the Danish throne warm, she persuaded the Norwegian nobility to recognise her grandnephew Erik of Pomerania as Oluf's successor. Erik, too, was five at this turning point in his career. Margarethe went behind Albrecht's back to offer the Swedish nobles perpetual rights to their property and privileges in exchange for their support against him. Albrecht could take no more. Raising an army of German mercenaries, he demanded satisfaction at Falköping. A chronicler was surprised by the outcome: "God gave an unexpected victory into the hands of a woman."

of a war with Holstein when she collapsed. The Danish nobility were inclined to ask aloud whether their interests might be better served by Erik's nephew, Christopher of Bavaria, and the talk in Sweden was of a separate constitution and a fresh crowned head. Meanwhile, Erik retired to Visborg Castle in Gotland and applied himself, privately and very profitably, to the business of piracy.

Stockholm Bloodbath

After more than one trial separation Denmark and Sweden were together again under the Danish king, Kristian II (1481–1559). Anti-

Margarethe's grand scheme was at last realised at Kalmar in 1397 when Eric, now 14, donned the three crowns of Norway, Denmark and Sweden. "Rash, violent and obstinate," he faced the tall order of running an empire from the Arctic Circle (including Swedish Finland) to the Eider, and west to Greenland, with no money or support from the wary nobility. Margarethe had her hands full nursing the damage caused by Erik's railings against these constraints, and she was addressing the aftermath

LEFT: the Swedish army is defeated by Peter the Great of Russia at the battle of Poltava, 1709.
ABOVE: a depiction of medieval life at Turku Castle.

Danish feeling was growing apace in Sweden when the Swedish assembly voted to burn the fortress of the Archbishop of Sweden, a pro-Dane, Gustav Trolle. In the event Trolle was merely imprisoned, but in 1520 the Papal Court excommunicated the Swedish regent, Sten Sture the Younger, for this act. Kristian II had the justification he sought for invading Sweden. He invited Sweden's leading nobles to a feast in Stockholm at which he chopped off the heads of 82 of Sweden's finest. This "Stockholm Bloodbath" provoked a rebellion.

Kristian was driven out of Sweden and Gustav Vasa, a nobleman whose family had been victims in the massacre, seized power.

Thus began a Swedish dynasty of exceptional distinction and durability.

Hounded out of Denmark, Kristian II sought refuge in the Netherlands. Norway's clergy, staunchly loyal to Rome, made him an offer of the Norwegian throne, which provoked violent intervention by Danish and Hanseatic forces with far-reaching consequences. Kristian spent the rest of his life in Sonderborg Castle, while the Norwegian church was purged of Roman Catholics to make it Lutheran, and the Norwegian monarchy was abolished. Norway was thereafter a mere province of Denmark. The tripartite Kalmar Union was dead.

squadrons crossed the ice and a resounding victory cost Denmark all its territory on the Swedish side of the Sound.

The warrior king

In Karl XII (1682–1718), Sweden seemed to acquire a reincarnation of the Vikings who fought and caroused their way across Russia. Taking over the mantle of the traditional Germanic *Drang nach Osten* (drive to the east), he collided with Peter the Great of Russia.

The Russians eventually got the better of a titanic struggle, putting Karl in the impossible position of trying to rule Sweden from his bolt-

Battle on ice

A larger-than-life character, Kristian IV (1577–1648) was on the Danish throne for 52 years, building palaces and towns, trebling the size of the navy, and sending explorers to investigate the possibility of a northwest passage to Asia. He took an avuncular interest in Norway, renaming Oslo after himself ("Kristiania"), but never managed to achieve friendly relations with Sweden and the two countries inevitably entered the Thirty Years War on opposite sides. The battling continued, but it was the Swedish King Karl X Gustav who seized an opportunity when the Sound (Øresund) froze over during the winter of 1657. Two cavalry

hole in Turkey. Finally, he rode home with two companions, a journey of 1,300 miles, only to find that in his absence Sweden had been stripped of all his recent gains. His plan to put matters right began and ended with a siege of Frederiksten in southern Norway. The bullet through his head may have been fired by a genuine enemy sniper or a contracted assassin, but in any case Sweden decided to give absolutism a rest and explore constitutional government.

Denmark's first taste of quasi-constitutional government was deferred until the 1770s and even so only materialised in strange circumstances. Kristian VII's increasingly erratic behaviour clearly needed medical attention, a task entrusted to a German doctor, Johann Friederich Struensee. The patient was off his head, Struensee decided, so the best he could do was to run the country himself. And so he did.

In little more than a year, Struensee drew up 1,069 bills introducing freedom of speech and the press, a national budget, the decriminalisation of fornication and adultery, and the abolition of capital punishment for all but the most unspeakable crimes.

He could not have envisaged, as he extended his stately role to touch on the void in Queen Caroline Matilde's conjugal life, that he would be dragged out of bed at dawn and charged with

Britain bombarded Copenhagen, Tsar Alexander I occupied Finland, bringing the ages-old Swedish rule initiated by St Erik to a close.

Russia wins Finland

Russia later changed sides and was sitting with the victors when reparations were decided after the Battle of Waterloo (1815). Russia was allowed to keep Finland; Norway was detached from Denmark and handed to Sweden, albeit not as a colony but as a supposed equal in a union under a common crown.

The king in question was a curious choice: Jean-Baptiste Bernadotte was French and not

just such a crime, one that still carried the supreme penalty. Locked up in Kronborg Castle at Helsingør, his partner in crime was rescued from her fate by an English warship sent by George III, himself showing signs of instability but her brother nonetheless.

The same navy was again under the guns of Kronborg Castle at the outbreak of the Napoleonic War in the early 19th century, in this instance because Denmark had sided with Russia, at that stage Napoleon's ally. While

LEFT: the Swedish royal palace of Drottningholm, designed in the 17th century by Tessin the Elder.
ABOVE: *Conversation at Drottningholm, 1779.*

THE GREAT EXODUS

The 19th century witnessed a mass exodus of Scandinavians in search of a better life in the New World. "Potatoes, peace and vaccination" were blamed for a population explosion at home which contributed to an outflow of 750,000 Norwegian and one million Swedish emigrants – a quarter of the Swedish population.

The new settlers sent back glowing accounts of their lives in America, and money to support those left behind. These signs of prosperity and other factors such as The United States Homestead Act of 1862, which promised land almost free to settlers who dared to travel west, encouraged others to follow.

only a former general of the French Revolution but a key member of Napoleon's staff. If taking the name Karl Johan was meant to help him to blend into his new surroundings, this was offset by his refusal to speak anything but French.

Thus reorganised, the Scandinavian states stepped into the frenzy of romantic nationalism that swept across Europe and inspired phenomenal scientific progress and a flowering of the arts. In these respects Scandinavia did its bit and more. Sweden was especially strong in the sciences;

> **TROUBLED UNION**
>
> Sweden typically bribed North African pirates not to attack their ships, but to plunder those of the Norwegians who insisted on sailing under their own colours.

consider, for one, Linnaeus, the naturalist *(see box, below)*. Denmark's most notable contributions were the writer Hans Christian Andersen *(see page 127)* and the philosopher, Søren Kierkegaard. Norway offered Edvard Grieg (composer), Henrik Ibsen (dramatist) and Edvard Munch (painter), and Finland (pre-Sibelius) contributed the *Kalevala*, an epic which Elias Lönnrot compiled from old ballads and songs to reinvent his country's hitherto elusive past.

Language became a vexing issue in Finland and Norway. Mikael Agricola, the Bishop of Turku, had produced a Finnish translation of the Bible as early as 1642, and although Finnish had always been spoken by the majority of the population, it had no official status. The Russians even banned books written in Finnish.

In Norway, Old Norse had gone to Iceland with the Viking settlers, while the language in Norway itself had been affected by Danish connections. Pure Danish was used for official business, in literature and by the educated classes. In the 19th century Norwegian nationalists wanted to revert to untainted Norwegian. They concocted a cocktail from Norway's surviving rural dialects called "New Norwegian".

Friends and foes

One 19th-century development was that Swedish, Danish and Norwegian (but not yet Finnish) historians could at last get together for a chat without coming to blows, and in this spirit Swedish and Danish university students took advantage of the atrocious winter of 1838, when the Sound again froze over, to walk across the ice, meet in the middle, and improvise odes to Scandinavian solidarity.

If this was reminiscent of Magnus Barelegs and company at Konghelle, the dream was again upset by events in Norway, where the union with Sweden was in trouble. Norway strengthened its border fortifications, and Sweden had its army on alert before a compromise was worked out. The union dissolved in 1905 and, as Norway went shopping for a new king, Scandinavia braced itself for the 20th century.   ❑

LINNAEUS, THE PLANTSMAN

Carl Linnaeus (also known as von Linné), the Swedish naturalist who devised the modern classification system for plants and animals, was one of the great scientists of 18th-century Scandinavia. Born in 1707, he studied medicine at the University of Lund and botany at Uppsala. He travelled widely and was a leading figure in the founding of the Swedish Academy of Science. As chair of botany, dietetics and *materia medica* at Uppsala, he pursued his research into nomenclature. His publications included *Systema Naturae* (1735), *Philosophia Botanica* (1750), and *Species Plantarum* (1753). Linnaeus died in 1778. His house and botanical garden can be visited at Uppsala.

LEFT: Alfred Nobel (1833–96), Swedish chemist, inventor of dynamite and founder of the Nobel Prizes.
RIGHT: Sami girls in traditional costume, 1898.

THE MODERN AGE

Two world wars took their toll on the Nordic countries, but by the end of the
20th century they had emerged as sophisticated economic powers

The 20th century dawned with not only the union of Sweden and Norway on the rocks but also the special relationship between Finland and Russia. A new tsar, the ill-fated Nicholas II, did not share his predecessors' fond view of Finland as a separate grand duchy and liked even less the privileges that went with it. So while breakaway Norway recruited Håkon VII, né Prince Carl of Denmark, as its first independent king for 600 years, Finland was delivered into the hands of Nikolai Ivanovich Bobrikov, a hard-boiled martinet whose previous assignment had been to knock some sense into Russia's wayward Baltic provinces.

King Håkon accepted the job only after a plebiscite indicated that three-quarters of the Norwegian population wanted him. Bobrikov did not bother with such trifles. Having abolished the Finns' exemption from service in the Russian imperial forces, he was systematically shredding the freedom of speech and other rights when he was met on the staircase to the Senate by Eugen Schauman, a civil servant. Schauman put three bullets into the brute before turning the revolver on himself.

The onset of World War I

Fortunately for Finland, the tsar was too involved in war with Japan and later in the St Petersburg uprising to avenge Bobrikov's murder. Every one of 40 previous wars with Russia had gone badly for the Finns, but they were always ready to try again. The first whiff of World War I saw volunteers flocking to Germany to join a special "Jagar battalion" which duly entered the field against Russia alongside Kaiser Wilhelm's forces.

For their part, the three kings of Scandinavia met at Malmö in Sweden in December 1914 and declared their neutrality. However, putting the proclamation into practice was not so easy. After centuries of anguish over Schleswig-

Holstein, Denmark was not Germany's greatest admirer, but it was in no position to defy the kaiser's orders to mine Danish sea-lanes against the British navy. Conversely, Norway received a warning from Britain that selling fish, iron pyrites or copper to Germany would not be tolerated, and Sweden was in fact blockaded,

eventually to suffer acute food shortages, for trading too eagerly with Wilhelm. The worst blow, though, was Germany's declaration of unrestricted submarine warfare in 1916. Hundreds of Scandinavian ships and crews "on charter" to Britain had in fact been commandeered, but they went to the bottom all the same and with heavy losses.

On Russia's withdrawal from the war after the Bolshevik revolution in 1917, Lenin made a direct appeal to sympathisers in Scandinavia and Finland in particular. "Rise, rise instantly," he cried, "take over the government in the hands of organised labour." The Finnish Red Guard, about 30,000 strong, accordingly seized

LEFT: flag-waving during the annual National Day celebrations in Norway on 17 May.
RIGHT: evacuated Finnish family, 1939.

government offices in Helsinki and proclaimed a Socialist Workers' Republic. The government's response was to raise a White Guard, including the Jagar battalion, Swedish volunteers and 12,000 German troops, under the command of General Baron Gustaf Mannerheim, a former White Russian cavalry officer. The revolution lasted less than four months, but there were 24,000 casualties and a comparable number of Red sympathisers were subsequently executed or left to die in internment camps.

Consideration was then given to turning Finland into a kingdom with one of Kaiser Wilhelm's sons on the throne, but Germany's

MED WAFFEN-⚡⚡ OG
DEN NORSKE LEGION
MOT DEN FELLES FIENDE . . . .

UNDERCOVER OPERATIONS

The Resistance movement in Denmark and Norway was crucial in undermining the German campaign during World War II. Anders Lassen epitomised the 20,000-strong Danish Resistance. By the time he died aged 24, he had fought in France, Greece, the Balkans and Italy. His commanding officer said, "Anders caused more discomfort to the enemy over five years of war than any other man of his rank and age". Other heroes included the Norwegians who knocked out the heavy water plant at Rjukan *(Heroes of Telemark, see page 180)*. Two museums, Frihedsmuseet, Copenhagen, and Norges Hjemmefront-museum, Oslo, document the movement's history.

defeat in the war turned opinion in favour of a republic under the presidency of Kaarlo Juho Ståhlberg, a local professor of law. The Soviet Union raised no objection to Finland's independence and signed the Treaty of Tartu to that effect, but Finland's fanatical Christian fundamentalists, the Lapua pietists, were determined to clear the nest of vipers. Suspected communists were kidnapped, beaten and dumped at the Soviet border. The pietists forced the government to ban communism completely and were arming themselves for a full-scale coup d'état when the army decided they had been around too long for any good they were doing.

Sweden sailed through the post-war years on a wave of international demand for Swedish steel and ball bearings, Ericsson telephones and Electrolux vacuum cleaners. While also doing well, Norway and Denmark clashed over Greenland and the Arctic islands of Svalbard (Spitzbergen) and Jan Mayen, which raised issues rooted in Viking times. Asked to arbitrate, the international court at The Hague gave Greenland to Denmark, the islands to Norway.

Scandinavia emerged from the second crisis of the interwar years, the Great Depression, with improved political systems. The severity of the situation forced small parties with narrow interests – farmers' parties being a prime example – to remove their blinkers and join broader coalitions, the front runners generally calling themselves "Social Democrats".

World War II

With the Depression out of the way it was not long until the storm clouds of World War II gathered. Hitler's rise was especially worrying to Denmark because Germany had never formally agreed to the Schleswig-Holstein border as defined by plebiscite after World War I. Accepting his surprising offer of a non-aggression pact, Denmark nevertheless joined Sweden and Norway in another declaration of neutrality.

Finland was again a special case. When Hitler invaded Poland, Stalin assumed Russia would be next and seized a strip of Finnish territory to strengthen the defences around Leningrad. The 1939 Nazi-Soviet pact removed this threat, but at the same time it allowed Stalin

---

LEFT: World War II poster published during the German occupation of Norway, 1941.
RIGHT: German aircraft on Finland's tundra, 1941.

a free hand in Finland, and he ordered an invasion. Marshal Mannerheim, now in his seventies, came out of retirement to lead Finland in what came to be known as the Winter War.

Almost invisible in the white uniforms against driving snow, Finnish troops went into action on skis against Russian tanks. As Swedish volunteers arrived to help, Hitler had to restrain Mussolini ("that great man across the Alps") from sending in the Italian air force to give Stalin one in the eye. What really mattered, though, was the collapse of the Nazi-Soviet pact and Germany's invasion of Russia. The Finns went in at the same time to recover their recent losses (the "War of Continuation") and were therefore stigmatised as Hitler's allies.

German aggression

The German invasion of Denmark and Norway began on 9 April 1940. Some troops crossed the Jutland border into Denmark, others emerged from hiding in German merchant ships in Copenhagen harbour, and paratroops landed at key points around the country. The Danish army was in barracks, the navy was too surprised to fire a single shot, and the air force was destroyed on the ground. If nothing else, the Royal Life Guards at Amalienborg Palace in

THE DEMON DRINK

Stringent laws on the purchase of alcohol in Norway and Sweden have been somewhat at odds with the figure these countries have wanted to cut in the modern world. The time-honoured yearning for drink can be blamed on long winter nights, but ancient Scandinavians also drank like fish because their food was preserved with lashings of salt. King Sverre of Norway experimented with prohibition as early as the 12th century. In 1775, however, King Gustav III of Sweden turned the distillation and sale of spirits into a royal monopoly and encouraged his subjects to drink because he needed the money. Against this backdrop, 20th-century prohibitionists had problems. The conundrum in Norway was that France, Spain and Portugal, major consumers of Norwegian fish, had always bartered with wine or brandy. The issue of prohibition led to the downfall of three successive governments in the early 20th century.

Sweden, however, put its faith in the "Bratt Liquor Control System", a certain Dr Ivan Bratt having worked out exactly how much alcohol an individual could consume according to age, physique and other considerations, with the result that it was almost impossible for a married woman to qualify for a single drink in any circumstances. Today, as in Gustav III's time, the sale of wines and spirits in both countries, as well as in Finland, is a state monopoly.

The Royal Line

I t used to be said, not so long ago, that there would soon be just five kings left in the world: of England, clubs, hearts, spades and diamonds. However, at the present time, there are still seven monarchies alive in Europe, three of them in Scandinavia. Moreover, the royal families of Denmark, Sweden and Norway are probably as secure and popular as ever they have been.

Monarchy could hardly be more entrenched than in Denmark. Queen Margrethe II is the 53rd in an unbroken line of sovereigns spanning more than

1,000 years. Sweden, too, has had more than 60 kings since 980. The present King Carl Gustaf may be "XVI" but his direct line begins with Jean-Baptiste Bernadotte, the French marshal who became heir apparent in 1810 and Sweden's king in 1818. Norway's royal line ceased when Norway became a Danish province and the monarchy was only restored, after a referendum, following the dissolution in 1905 of the subsequent union with Sweden. The present king, Harald V, is the third of the modern line, the "V" notwithstanding. Finland also considered a monarchy on breaking away from Russia, but chose to become a republic instead.

Nevertheless, not a little craft has gone into keeping the Scandinavian monarchies in robust health. When Carl XVI Gustaf ascended the Swedish throne in 1973, the Constitution began with: "The King alone shall govern the realm..." Lest he got the wrong impression, this was hastily changed to: "All public power in Sweden emanates from the people..." The king decided his own official motto ought to be: "For Sweden – in Keeping with the Times". This was the cue for changing the rules of succession so that they no longer discriminated against daughters. Consequently, next in line is Crown Princess Victoria rather than her younger brother. Their mother, Queen Silvia, is the daughter of a German businessman.

Carl Gustaf is not averse to tearing around in a Ferrari and was reported to the police in Denmark for doing an alleged 250 kph (155 mph) on the Copenhagen expressway. Nonsense, the king retorted. He admitted having a lot to do on his way to Queen Margrethe's 60th birthday but had not exceeded 150. In contrast, King Harald loves boats, representing Norway at the Olympic Games, and winning the European Championship in 2005 – right after a heart bypass. Unlike his Swedish counterpart, Harald would not be seen dead in a Ferrari. He uses public transport. Queen Sonja is the daughter of an Oslo shopkeeper and their children went to state schools. Fittingly, the Crown Prince found himself a bachelor flat in an unfashionable part of Oslo but let the side down, as it were, by sharing it with a waitress, and her three-year-old son by a man who was in prison for drug offences; they are now married.

If conscientious exercises in non-charisma go down well in Norway, Queen Margrethe could not hope to do the same in Denmark. She has been showered with genuine academic honours from the likes of Cambridge, Oxford and the London School of Economics. While trying unsuccessfully to hide her distinguished output as a painter, writer and designer behind a string of aliases, she has at least persuaded her friends to call her Daisy. Crown Prince Frederik, her heir, is not much better at disguise. Dressing down for a night on the town, he turned out so scruffy that the bar refused to let him in. The situation was saved by an extremely attractive stranger, one Bettina Odum, stepping forward to say that he was with her. As a trained soldier, no mean dancer and the leader of a husky-drawn expedition across Greenland, Frederik's status as dashing bachelor ended in marriage to Australian Mary Donaldson, with whom he now has two children. ❑

LEFT: Queen Sonja of Norway in relaxed mood at Holmenkollen Ski Festival.

Copenhagen prevented the Germans from capturing King Kristian X just long enough for him to order a surrender. Denmark remained in theory a sovereign state under German protection, but when the king ignored Hitler's effusive greetings on his birthday in 1942, the pretence was dropped. A new government was expected to jump at Hitler's whim, but it refused to sanction death sentences on members of the increasingly active Resistance movement and made arrangements to smuggle Denmark's endangered Jews to safety in Sweden.

Norway is overrun

In Norway's case, gunners in an old fortress on Oslo fjord had the satisfaction of sinking the German cruiser *Blücher* on the first day of the invasion, killing around 830 of those on board. While Hitler's local stooge, Vidkun Quisling, the leader of the fascist National Unity Party, proclaimed himself prime minister, King Håkon and most members of the government escaped to Tromsø in northern Norway and remained there while a combined force of British, French, Polish and Norwegian units recaptured the iron-ore port of Narvik. The sudden collapse of France, however, created a greater demand for the expeditionary force elsewhere, so as the Allies withdrew the king and his entourage were evacuated to England.

Neutral throughout the war, Sweden took in 300,000 refugees. The Swedish Red Cross, led by Count Folke Bernadotte, a nephew of the king, secured the release of 30,000 prisoners of various nationalities from German concentration camps, and the diplomat Raoul Wallenberg played "Schindler" to Jews in Hungary. But it was also the case that German troops and materials were given permission to cross Sweden on their way to Norway in 1940 and thereafter when they went on leave. Moreover, Sweden supplied iron ore critical to the German war machine. These are matters which Norwegians to this day cannot easily forget.

Peacetime recovery

The last stage of the war, with German forces scorching the earth in their retreat from the advancing Soviets, hurt northern Norway but was utterly devastating in Finland. The latter,

then, could hardly have been in a worse position to meet Soviet demands for US$600 million in reparations. These were to be paid within 10 years in goods other than what remained of the Finnish economy, namely trees. Barred by Moscow from accepting Marshall aid, Finland nevertheless beat the deadline by creating a diversified industrial economy from scratch.

Reparations out of the way, the bottomless Soviet market kept these new industries – shipbuilding, oil refineries, textiles – working flat out, with the extra bonus that the USSR paid for goods in dirt-cheap oil. So the eventual collapse of the Soviet Union was politically a pleasure but

at the same time a threat to the Finnish economy – until, among numerous aspects of the country's second economic miracle, Nokia recognised the potential of the mobile phone and Porsche decided to build its new Boxster model in Finland. By the turn of the millennium, Finland was a member of the European Union.

A new way of life

Recovery from the war in Denmark and Norway was set in motion by the Marshall Plan, and within a decade or so they were able to join Sweden in presenting a seemingly united Scandinavian front to the outside world. In certain quarters, the image was a paradox, a combina-

RIGHT: the great long-distance runner Paavo Nurmi lights the Olympic flame at the 1952 Helsinki Games.

tion of beautiful and talented people, an enviable standard of living, robust health, exceptional generosity to the Third World – and at the same time rather too much promiscuity, self-righteousness and suicide.

At the heart of all this lay the desire to find a compromise between capitalism and socialism, in Sweden's case "the Middle Way". While Denmark and Norway joined NATO after the war, Sweden remained nonaligned and spent a huge proportion of the national budget on its arms industry in the belief, or at least hope, that its products would therefore never be required.

To begin with, Scandinavians were willing to live with the punitive taxation needed to cover the cost of their vaunted "cradle-to-grave" social security if only because memories of bitterly hard times without it were still fresh. But if new generations were less susceptible to these fears and consequently concerned about the enormous cost of maintaining the safety, in Norway and Denmark it suddenly didn't matter. They struck oil.

The new oil-rich nations

Denmark's agriculture was always on its toes. Characteristically quick to breed a pig that produced the streaky bacon popular on British breakfast tables, and with companies like Lego, Bang & Olufsen and Carlsberg, which proved adept at exploiting particular market niches, it was the first time the country had enjoyed the luxury of natural resources since the herring shoals in the 14th century. Ironically, Denmark's North Sea windfall arrived in the middle of concerted efforts to start "wind farms", fields full of power-generating turbines.

Measured against population, the prize in Norway was much bigger and triggered lavish expenditure on items such as road tunnels through solid rock which served no indispensable purpose that anyone could think of. At one point it looked as if Norway might have blown more oil revenue than existed under the North Sea, but new discoveries, especially of gas, put such fears to rest.

Deprived of any share of the North Sea bonanza, Sweden's Middle Way showed signs of turning into a cul-de-sac. Industry had long been pampered with low taxes on profits while individual taxpayers were bled white. Companies like Volvo had a proud international profile but even they complained loudly of burdens like the costs attached to each employee in the form of national insurance, shorter working weeks, longer holidays and so on. Nevertheless, most Swedes were astonished and dismayed when Saab was swallowed by General Motors, Volvo by Ford, and a regiment of other prestigious companies decamped abroad.

Bridge to the future

While more than one proposed business merger along pan-Scandinavian lines tripped up on mutual misgivings as ancient as the Kalmar Union, the new millennium found a cure for the oldest schism of all. The Øresund road and rail bridge rejoined Denmark and Sweden in 2000, a connection broken by the cataclysmic convulsion at the end of the Ice Age. Although the bridge has strengthened pan-Scandinavian links, it has conversely fuelled the traditional suspicion of the European Union, symbolised by the Euro. To this point, only Finland has adopted the single currency and Norway has not even joined the EU, signifying the Nordic countries' independence. ❑

LEFT: Olof Palme, prime minister of Sweden and international peace campaigner, assassinated in 1986.
RIGHT: Øresund bridge linking Denmark and Sweden.

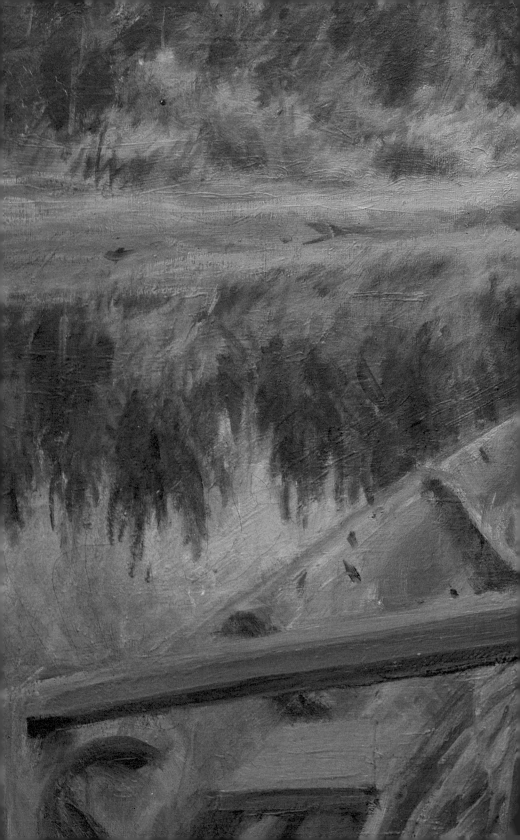

ART AND CULTURE

Rich in art, music and literature, and pioneers of modern design,
Scandinavians are justifiably proud of their cultural heritage

The history of Denmark, Norway, Sweden, and Finland has been so intertwined through the centuries that, while each country possesses a unique culture, there are strong similarities, perhaps best seen in design and an overall "feel" for visual expression. A bias towards simplicity pervades with clean lines, natural materials and a lack of pretence.

Although much of what is considered Scandinavian style is a product of the 20th century *(see page 54)* there is an underlying cultural heritage that complements the modern look. Exceptions exist, such as work commissioned by royalty with French design in mind, but the tastes of the people over the past 200 years make the strongest impression on the visitor.

DENMARK

The rich cultural history of Denmark finds expression in centuries-worth of art and artefacts, including Viking treasures, numerous castles and manor houses, churches (many from the Middle Ages), fortresses, stimulating museums, and some of the finest contemporary design in the world.

Denmark's strongest art tradition is literary, reaching back to sagas and medieval folk songs, to the most popular Danish playwright, Ludvig Holberg (1684–1754) in the Age of Enlightenment, the Romantic poet Adam Oehlenschläger (1779–1850) and, in the 19th century, to Hans Christian Andersen (1805–75) and Søren Kierkegaard (1813–55).

Thanks to stories such as *The Little Mermaid*, Andersen is probably still the most widely read Danish writer today. His children's tales – including *The Ugly Duckling*, *The Emperor's New Clothes* and *The Princess and the Pea* – gained him worldwide fame, and their popularity has not waned as a source for plays, ballets, films, visual arts and bedtime reading. In

the 20th century, Karen Blixen (1885–1962), working under the pseudonym Isak Dinesen, gained international recognition for her 1937 memoir of her years in Kenya, *Out of Africa*, which became a Hollywood movie in 1985.

The Danish philosopher Søren Kierkegaard, known as the father of existentialism, wrote in

the first half of the 19th century, but his work had the most impact in the mid-20th century, when in translation it became an important source for existentialists.

Masters of dance

More than a third of the state funds allocated for the theatre in Denmark finance the Det Kongelige Teater (Royal Theatre) in Copenhagen, founded in 1748. This building also houses the Royal Danish Opera, the Royal Danish Orchestra and the Royal Danish Ballet. The ballet company, formed 150 years ago, is one of the most influential worldwide. It has attracted great masters such as August Bournonville

---

PRECEDING PAGES: Norwegian composer Edvard Grieg; *Midnight* by Sweden's Anders Zorn, 1891.
LEFT: *The Girl in the Kitchen*, Anna Ancher, 1883–6.
RIGHT: Karen Blixen, Denmark, author of *Out of Africa*.

(1805–79), creator of today's "classical ballet" and choreographer of more than 50 productions, including the popular *La Sylphide*.

The big screen

Denmark's Nordisk Film Kompagni, founded in 1906, is the oldest film company still in operation. Carl Theodor Dreyer (1889–1968), a master of psychological realism who started his career here, produced classics such as *The Passion of Joan of Arc* (1928) and *The Word* (1955). Today the government-supported Danish Film Institute is the heart of a vibrant Danish film industry. *Babette's Feast* (1986), based on a story by Karen Blixen, directed by Gabriel Axel, and *Pelle the Conqueror* (1987), directed by Bille August, both won Academy Awards for Best Foreign Film. In the last 10 years, Lars von Trier's *Dancer in the Dark*, Thomas Vinterberg's *The Celebration* and Susanne Bier's *After the Wedding* have attracted international acclaim. These directors are signatories (along with Kristian Levring) of the Dogma 95 Manifesto. This set of "chastity" rules, which holds that films should be made on location without artificial lighting or sound, using hand-held cameras, was intended as a personal challenge to help reinvigorate the art of film-making.

LOUISIANA MUSEUM OF MODERN ART

Small museum treasures may be found throughout Denmark, but the most complete and satisfying of them all is the Louisiana Museum of Modern Art, situated in a sublime spot in Humlebæk, 35 km (22 miles) north of Copenhagen. Louisiana houses a splendid collection of 20th-century art, including pieces by Pablo Picasso, Andy Warhol, Alberto Giacometti and Asger Jorn. It lies on the water's edge, and the extensive sculpture garden, featuring work by Henry Moore and Alexander Calder, that surrounds the unassuming building (much of its space is underground) is backdropped by exquisite coastal scenery and landscaping (www.louisiana.dk).

The Skagen painters

In the visual arts, Denmark's most notable contributions were produced in the 19th and 20th centuries. C.W. Eckersberg (1783–1853), the father of Danish painting, and those who studied under him absorbed the artistic lessons offered from France, particularly a sense of classical nature. At the end of the 19th century, a group of artists – including P.S. Krøyer (1851–1909) and Michael and Anna Ancher (1859–1935) – based themselves in Skagen at the northernmost tip of Jutland. Known as the "Skagen painters", they turned away from Impressionism, the favoured French style of the day, while still being highly indebted to it. Their works captured the special northern light within images of the maritime landscape.

In the middle of the 20th century, Asger Jorn (1914–73), a member of the CoBrA art movement (including artists from Copenhagen, Brussels and Amsterdam), created large, bold, brightly coloured paintings. His expressionistic and experimental works on canvas and ceramics played a key role in the development and promotion of modern Danish art.

SWEDEN

Along with being the conqueror rather than the conquered throughout history, Sweden

King Gustav III (1771–92), the "Theatre King", took many of his cues from the royal court of France and was a great patron of drama and the arts. In 1773, he built the Kungliga Teatern (Royal Theatre, known today as the Royal Opera), and Kungliga Dramatiska Teatern (Royal Dramatic Theatre or *Dramaten*) in 1788. In addition, he hired Swedish actors and singers, forming the basis for a tradition of opera and drama performed in Swedish instead of in the original French or Italian.

The most notable of Swedish dramatic venues is Drottningholms Slottsteater (Drottningholm Court Theatre), in the grounds of

developed strong cultural traditions, particularly in theatre, music and dance.

Diplomatic as well as commercial ties with European cultural centres provided conduits for importing styles that left their mark on architecture and the performing arts. The prosperity of the Swedish monarchy resulted in the patronage of cultural venues, theatre troupes and court painters. Their private collections became the basis for national art museums.

LEFT: Drottningholms Slottsteater, near Stockholm, built by "Theatre King" Gustav III in the 18th century.
ABOVE: interior at Sundborn, Sweden, by Carl Larsson.

Drottningholm Palace outside Stockholm. Built in 1766 and rediscovered and restored in the mid-20th century, every summer this intimate stage draws spectators from all over the world eager to see Baroque and rococo operas in an intact 18th-century theatre, complete with original backdrops and stage machinery.

Award-winning writers

One of the best-known (at least among Swedes) and still popular writers of the past is Carl Bellman (1740–95), a troubadour, whose lyrics and poems immortalised 18th-century daily life.

Works such as *The Red Room* by August Strindberg (1849–1912) and *Gösta Berlings Saga*

Cool looks

Say "Scandinavian design"and most people visualise furniture, glass and domestic ware with pure forms and simple, clean lines. The aesthetic is immediately recognisable, especially since the Swedish home-furnishing giant IKEA invaded the world.

Elegant, light, sparse – these are all descriptive of the Scandinavian look – along with a respect for natural materials and superb craftsmanship. The key is not only good looks, but also utility. This picture of Scandinavian design, while having roots in

traditional crafts, is very much a product of the 20th century and the age of Functionalism.

Taking off in the 1920s, led by architects and artists such as Le Corbusier in France and Walter Gropius in Germany, Functionalism applies to various movements such as the International Style and Bauhaus. In Scandinavia it has been a source of inspiration since the 1930s.

The move away from ornamentation in favour of clean shapes and lines, allowing for the pure expression of the essence of structures, was more than a mere change in taste. Adherents to this style, which manifested itself in new materials (tubular metal, steel and glass), also embraced a vision for a new world, one where architecture and design could contribute to the levelling out of injustices in modern society. In Scandinavia, not only were the aesthetics of the modern, international style eagerly adopted, the social agenda behind the style was also very popular.

Earlier in the 1900s, Carl and Karin Larsson, taking their cue from the English Arts and Crafts movement, revived an interest in traditional Swedish crafts and craftsmanship. Their home at Sundborn, now a museum of Swedish country style *(see page 269)*, features textiles with simple checked and striped patterns, against a background of sparse wall designs, wooden floors, striped rag runners and furniture brightened with uncomplicated embellishments.

The influences of Art Nouveau were an important inspiration, but in the hands of Danish designers in the mid-20th century, the fluid lines that had served as mere decoration in southern countries became the impulse behind the quest for a satisfying form that fitted a function, as seen in the chairs of Hans Wegner and Arne Jacobsen from the 1940s and 1950s *(see page 110)*. Designers also began to heed ergonomic research at industrial companies like the car-makers Saab and Volvo. Today, the adage "form follows function" is taken to a high science in Scandinavia. Aesthetics are fused with efficiency for everything from utensils to welding equipment, as seen in the products of Ergonomi Design Gruppen (Sweden). Numerous pieces from the early 20th century remain as popular as ever, for example, stools by the Finnish architect and designer, Alvar Aalto.

The success of Nordic design has made it a standard far beyond the boundaries of Northern Europe – from time-tested pieces, such as the Stokke Tripp Trapp chairs by the Norwegian, Peter Opsvik, to the works of the multitalented Stefan Lindfors, whose output includes designs for Finnish companies Arabia (porcelain) and Marimekko (textiles); from glass and crystal designed for Kosta and Orrefors (Sweden) by Ulrika Hydman-Vallien to Nokia telephones (Finland) by Frank Nuovo.

In a part of the world forsaken by the sun for half the year, Scandinavians exploit interiors to maximise light. Even national characteristics may be seen as a source of style. Just as their design is characterised as rather stark, cool, unadorned, the Scandinavian character is often reserved, sombre – hardly excessively embellished. ❏

LEFT: contemporary furniture design at the Kunstmuseet Trapholt, Kolding, Denmark.

by Selma Lagerlöf (1858–1940), two of the country's finest writers, set the foundation for modern Swedish literature. Strindberg, whose personal life was marked by a series of failed marriages, alcoholism and instability, produced books, stories and screenplays that often featured social criticism, satire and emotional angst.

> **THE SOUND OF JOIK**
>
> Joik is a form of singing traditional among the Sami. Composed in response to an event or emotion, it sounds like a yodelling chant.

The creative output of Lagerlöf, the first woman to win a Nobel prize for Literature (1909), is sharply distinct from Strindberg, depending more on legend, history and tradition, and childhood memories (*Jerusalem*, 1901–02, *The Wonderful Adventures of Nils*, 1906).

Other Swedes have been honoured with Nobel Literature prizes (Verner von Heidenstam, 1916; Erik Axel Karlfeldt, 1931; Pär Lagerkvist, 1951; Eyvind Johnson and Harry Martinson, 1974), and many other novelists have had their work translated for publication abroad, such as Vilhelm Moberg, whose four-volume novel, beginning with *The Emigrants*, is the inspiration for the hit musical *Kristina from Duvemåla*.

Undoubtedly the most widely read Swedish writer is Astrid Lindgren, the indefatigable creative mind behind *Pippi Longstocking*, *Emil in Lönneberga*, and many other free-spirited child heroines and antiheroines.

Swedish design

The "Swedish look", as it is understood today, is greatly indebted to the graphic work and paintings of Carl Larsson (1853–1919) as well as to the design of his home at Sundborn (*see box, page 269*). Larsson's images are marked by strong outline, subdued colours, and a gentle curvilinear quality.

Today, however, Swedish visual arts are extraordinarily multifaceted and bear little resemblance to preconceived notions of the Swedish look. Artists such as Ann-Sofi Sidén, Elin Wikström and Carl Michael von Hausswolff work in a variety of media, addressing complex contemporary issues. These trends can be seen at Moderna Museet in Stockholm, which reopened in 1998 in a new building by Rafael Moneo. The museum has a fine collection of modern Swedish and international art.

NORWAY

After being a world power during the Viking Age, Norway went through various unions with and occupations by Denmark and Sweden until independence in 1905. Over the centuries the country's culture was suppressed rather than enhanced by those of Denmark and Sweden. Culture with a capital "C" was something the overlords brought with them from foreign capitals. And it was something they took away with them when they left. Under Danish rule Norwegian "dialects" were forbidden for

> **INGMAR BERGMAN**
>
> Although Sweden was a cinematic powerhouse in the age of silent films, since the advent of sound it has been a relatively small player, with the exception of exports such as Greta Garbo and Ingrid Bergman, and one of the giants of film and theatre, Ingmar Bergman (1918–2007).
>
> Bergman made his breakthrough with *Smiles of a Summer Night* in 1955. Among his most acclaimed films are *The Seventh Seal* (1956), *Wild Strawberries* (1957) and *Cries and Whispers* (1973). *Fanny and Alexander* (1982) was his final film, although he remained active in the theatre until his death. His work offers a very personal perspective on what is Swedish, yet universal.

RIGHT: Ingmar Bergman, internationally acclaimed Swedish playwright and film producer.

official documents and communications. As a result, the heritage of Norwegian culture is identified in the arts and crafts of rural populations.

The recreation of a national identity began in earnest in the 19th century. Not surprisingly, inspiration came from the sublime nature, ancient verbal traditions, and heroic sagas of a mighty Norway and Viking lords of long ago.

Henrik Ibsen (1828–1906) wrote many plays inspired by folklore. His best-known works include *Peer Gynt* (1867), to which Edvard Grieg composed the incidental music, *A Doll's House* (1879) and *Hedda Gabler* (1890). Ibsen delved into the individual struggle for freedom

EDVARD MUNCH

Edvard Munch (1863–1944), perhaps Norway's most reproduced artist, is honoured with a museum in Oslo dedicated to his work, as well as an entire floor of the National Gallery. A forerunner of Expressionism, his introspective, symbolist and angst-ridden paintings and prints, such as *The Scream* (1893), *The Kiss* and *The Vampire* (both 1895), verge on the dark side and are a product of Scandinavian themes, artistic developments in France and Germany where he studied, as well as personal idiosyncrasies and obsessions (Munchmuseet, Oslo, tel: 23 49 35 00, www.munch.museum.no; Nasjonalgalleriet, Oslo, tel: 21 98 20 00, www.nationalmuseum.no).

and self-knowing. He commented on Norway's relationship with Denmark and Sweden as well as on the individual's relationship with a society which would have him conform.

Sigrid Undset (1882–1949) won the Nobel Prize for Literature for *Kristin Lavransdatter*, her epic trilogy about medieval Norway.

Rustic arts

The country's ancient stave churches represent some of the most distinctive examples of Norwegian artistic production. The rich ornamental carvings on door frames, around windows and on capitals in the interior owe more, stylistically, to the design motifs of the Viking period – dragons, tendrils, leaf patterns – than to Christian iconography found elsewhere in Europe. The most famous stave churches still standing can be seen in Borgund, Heddal and Urnes.

Another very "Norwegian" visual expression is found in the *rosemaling* or "rose painting" (more aptly called "rustic painting") of which there are as many styles as villages, since each isolated community developed its own interpretation. This decorative painting, used to adorn household utensils as well as interiors, features organic patterns and flowers, figurative representations and even geometric design. Most "genuine" *rosemaling* dates from the early 18th century to the late 19th century, but today many artisans continue the traditions of this very native art.

Golden age of music

Norwegian music flowered in the early 19th century, mainly as a result of the union with Sweden and the influence of the Royal Swedish Court. The violin virtuoso Ole Bull (1810–80), "The Nordic Paganini", proved a model for musicians and writers alike.

The late 1800s became known as the Golden Age of Norwegian music with such prominent composers as Halfdan Kjerulf (1815–68), Edvard Grieg (1843–1907) and Johan Svendsen (1840–1911). Generally, they incorporated elements of folk music in their work, including Grieg, who fused folk music with Romanticism.

Bergen hosts an International Music Festival each May, and Oslo's incredible submerged opera house, opened in 2008, is a must-see.

LEFT: *The Scream* by Edvard Munch, 1893.
RIGHT: the Alvar Aalto Museum, Jyväskylä, celebrates the work of Finland's renowned architect-designer.

FINLAND

What may properly be called "Finnish culture" has existed for only a little over a century. Until the late 19th century, the arts in Finland fell under the influence of the invading powers of Sweden and Russia. Prior to Finnish independence (from Russia) in 1917, talented artists and composers normally studied and worked in Stockholm or St Petersburg.

Today, Finnish architecture and design are the nation's most influential cultural exports

> **TURNING POINT**
>
> The 19th-century artist Akseli Gallén-Kallela was a seminal figure in Finnish culture whose contribution laid the foundations for contemporary Finnish design.

(see box, below). Purely modern and very Scandinavian, they combine a love of natural materials and purity of form and functionalism with an exquisite aesthetic.

As is true for all the Nordic countries, the innovations that emanated from France and Germany preoccupied Finland's artists, with Finnish nature and themes lending the art a special character. Albert Edelfelt (1854–1905) was one of the nation's greatest artists of the 19th century. Later the national style created by Akseli Gallén-Kallela

FINNISH ARCHITECTURE AND DESIGN

One of the more prominent architects of Helsinki is Carl Ludwig Engel (1778–1840) from Germany, who designed much of the capital, including Senate Square and the cathedral. But despite the neoclassical imprint of this import, his creations are not representative of what is considered Finnish architecture, which, by many definitions, is no more than a century old.

The National Romanticism of Armas Lindgren (1874–1929), Herman Gesellius (1874–1916) and Eliel Saarinen (1873–1950) defined Finnish architecture of the late 19th and early 20th century, gradually turning from a Gothic look to embrace Art Nouveau.

Alvar Aalto (1898–1976), Finland's most celebrated architect, designed the Finnish Pavilion at the New York World's Fair in 1939, gaining international recognition for himself and the unadorned Functionalist style. He designed many buildings around the world. In Finland he left his mark on housing, schools, governmental and industrial buildings, theatres and churches. His finest building, Helsinki's Finlandia Hall, was built in 1971 during his "white" period.

Possibly Aalto's most indelible imprint on the world is from his classic chairs and stools and instantly recognisable curving glass vase (Alvar Aalto Museo, Alvar Aallon katu 7, Jyväskylä; tel: 014 624 809; www.alvaraalto.fi).

(1865–1931) became so popular that Finnish painters in the early 20th century tended to ignore foreign influences. The peasant and the landscape were considered to be representative of true Finnish qualities.

Musical notes

Although Jean Sibelius (1865–1957) still ranks as the most notable Finnish name in music, the contemporary scene is teeming with internationally acclaimed composers, conductors, opera singers and classical

musicians. Sibelius exemplified 19th-century Romanticism in his compositions, which drew inspiration from Finnish nature, folk music and poetry. His career began while Finland was still under Russian rule, and works such as *Finlandia* (1899; revised 1900) provoked such patriotic and nationalistic feelings that they were banned by the Russian authorities. His early symphonies, such as *Kullervo*, used material and motifs from Elias Lönnrot's classic poem *Kalevala*.

A generous policy of funding for musicians, musical institutes (of which there are nearly 130), conservatories and the celebrated Sibelius Academy has spawned a remarkable pool of

---

OPERA FESTIVAL

Even the most recalcitrant sopranos come home for the annual Savonlinna Opera Festival. Held in a 500-year-old castle, it is one of the most delightful summer opera festivals in the world.

---

modern talent. Supporting this talent are numerous professional and semi-professional or chamber orchestras and ensembles. Finnish artists such as the principal conductor Esa-Pekka Salonen, the opera singer Karita Mattila, and cellists Arto Noras and Erkki Rautio appear the world over. At home, musical festivals abound, of which the Savonlinna Opera Festival (www.operafestival.fi) and the Pori Jazz Festival (www.porijazz.fi), both in July, are international attractions.

Literary heritage

Precious little writing in the Finnish language exists from prior to the early 19th century. Until Sweden ceded Finland to Russia in 1809, the Swedish language dominated Finnish culture.

In 1835, after many years of studying and collecting folk poetry and ballads, Elias Lönnrot (1802–84) published his remarkable poem, *Kalevala*. The work is a heroic epic on the scale of *The Odyssey* or *The Iliad* as well as a ragbag of narratives and light interludes, existing to preserve old customs and songs. The context – sea, farm, forest – is entirely Finnish.

The *Kalevala* has had an enormous impact on Finnish literature, art and music, not only in the 19th century where it inspired a nationalistic surge in writing in Finnish, but even today it continues to be a source of inspiration.

At the same time that Lönnrot was working, Aleksis Kivi (1834–72) wrote the first proper Finnish novel set in Finland, *Seven Brothers*, which celebrated rural life and contributed to a burgeoning national consciousness. The stage performance of Kivi's *Leah* in the late 19th century marked the beginning of Finnish drama. The Finns love theatre and even amateur groups perform to capacity audiences.

F.E. Sillanpää (1888–1964) took home the country's sole literary Nobel prize, in 1939.

Today, international audiences are probably most familiar with the Moomintroll books by Tove Jansson. However, contemporary literature is vibrant and more introspective and critical than the roots of Finnish literature. ❑

LEFT: the composer Jean Sibelius (1865–1957) set the scene for modern music in Finland.
RIGHT: Ingrid Bergman (1915–82), Swedish actress.

FOOD AND DRINK

Brace yourself for a gastronomic treat: fresh seafood, wild berries and succulent mountain meat washed down by fiery aquavit is the order of the day

Scandinavian food gets down to the basics of nature, finding deep flavour in simple and healthy ways. Meats and fish might be smoked, then served with little else than steaming new potatoes, fresh dill, rich butter and tart redcurrants. The general rule says "less is more", and Scandinavian cooks – from the fanciest restaurant to the basic home kitchen – make good use of native fruits and vegetables, grains, fish, meat and game.

Fruits of the sea

Denmark, Sweden, Norway and Finland each have their own food cultures, but they share some gastronomic ground. Seafood is king, and this king spreads its rule into society. In Denmark, for example, model ships hang in every church, as if to remind parishioners to give thanks for the fruits of the sea. The North and Baltic seas have provided a solid economic base for strong fishing industries – and the societies that have revolved around them.

Herring might be the fish most associated with the region, and each country prepares it in variations on the same themes: marinated in sugar and vinegar with onions and herbs, or spiced with sandalwood (like *matjes*, which the Swedes frequently eat with boiled potatoes and sour cream); fried and then marinated; seasoned with mustard, curry, or sherry; smoked; salted; or baked. Usually, the dishes are eaten cold, and washed down with aquavit.

A Swedish summertime favourite is the smelly *surströmming*, fermented Baltic herring, eaten with raw onion, cheese and potatoes. Norwegians have a similar dish, *rakfisk*, a pungent, aged salt-cured trout. The uninitiated to these dishes run for cover in the opposite direction.

Other fish have their place on the dinner table or in the finest local restaurants, including plaice, cod, haddock, mackerel and eel. *Klippfisk*, a salty splitcod, is hung and dried in the open air in Norway's coastal villages. Salmon is king in Finland, where it is commonly made into a simple, tasty soup. *Fraavi lohi*, salmon marinated for a day in salt and herbs, is sometimes called the Finnish version of *sushi*. Danes, Swedes and Norwegians eat sweet, cured gravlax as a lunch-time delicacy.

Feasting on open sandwiches

Fish is the focus of a Danish or Swedish lunch-time feast. In Denmark the *smørrebrød* (open sandwiches) start with rye bread. Extremely dense and packed with all kinds of seeds and grains, this bread could be used to build walls if one ran out of bricks. Sliced and spread with goose lard or butter, the Danish rye is topped with arty combinations of foods and eaten with knife and fork.

Some restaurants, most notably Slotskælderen in Copenhagen, feature *smørrebrød* menus on scrolls several feet long. But certain unwritten rules apply to the feast, even at home: "You must have two or three kinds of herring,"

LEFT: tempting Danish cakes and pastries on display.
RIGHT: *Klippfisk* (dried, salted split cod) is a major Norwegian export.

explains Hanne Christensen from Funen. Her husband, Carl, adds that fiery shots of cold aquavit must "go down like hailstones".

"Then you need a little warm dish, like fried fish with lemon and remoulade," Hanne says.

"Sliced meats," adds Carl. "Small tenderloin steaks. Danish meatballs with red cabbage."

"And then cheese and fruit salad at the end," says Hanne.

The Swedish *smörgåsbord* and Finnish *voileipäpöytä* are equally artistic and elegant, with cold and hot dishes – similar to those eaten at a Danish lunch – laid out buffet-style on a table, to which guests visit five times. Special to these countries are dishes such as roasted reindeer, Swedish meatballs and a baked anchovy-potato-cream casserole called "Jansson's Temptation". The Finnish dishes tend to be less sweet than those in Sweden, and Finns serve a greater variety of bread.

In Norway, a large selection of breads and toppings comes at breakfast, *frokost*, with copious amounts of cold meats, crispbreads, cheeses, caviar from a tube and black coffee. *Geitost* is a food of national pride, a type of brown, sweet, goat's milk cheese, which tastes like caramel. At home and at celebrations Norwegians also enjoy *rømmegrøt*, a thick and extremely rich porridge

SKÅL! TO THE SPIRIT OF LIFE

No herring dish in Scandinavia is complete without aquavit, literally "water of life". Distilled from potatoes or grain and flavoured with a variety of herbs and seasonings – such as caraway seed, cumin, fennel, dill or St John's wort – ice-cold aquavit warms the body (and mood). One of the best versions is Norway's Løiten Linie, which is matured partly by a sea voyage in oak casks across the equator and back (each bottle carries details of its "voyage" on the label). The Finns tend to pour bigger glasses of the drink, but they are also masters at distilling and drinking vodka.

To gain instant friends in Scandinavia, lift your drink and say the word for cheers: *"skål"* (pronounced *"skoal"*). The correct way to *skål* is to look at the person, say the word, lift the glass slightly, drink and look at the person again. There are some rules about when to *skål* at formal occasions. Never drink until the host has given a welcome toast. A gentleman must ensure that the woman on his right has something on her plate and in her glass. She must be the first he *skåls*, followed by the woman on his left. The host will *skål* each guest. The hostess may also *skål* her guests. It is not good form to *skål* a person who is older or of higher rank. Let them take the initiative and return the gesture within three minutes. A gentleman should *skål* the man sitting on the left of his partner, as well as her.

made from cream, butter and milk. At Easter, the Finns eat *mämmi*, a whipped rye and malt porridge that takes up to a day to make.

Sausage fare

Sausage is common in all four countries, and its flavour and consistency depends upon the region where it is made. In Tampere in southwest Finland, *mustamakkara* (black sausage) is flavoured with spices, barley and blood. The Danes also make a blood sausage, *blødpølse*, which is seen commonly around Christmas; the south Jutland

CRAYFISH SEASON

Crayfish is eaten widely in Finland and Sweden in July and August, when it is boiled and peeled and served at outdoor parties.

Fruits of the forest

Along the same lines, nearly all Scandinavians do a hunting of a different sort in the summer and autumn – that is for mushrooms or berries (from raspberries to cloudberries and blueberries). Some restaurants have gained fame for their use of foraged foods sold by enthusiasts, fresh back from the woods.

Sweet treats

It almost goes without saying that the traditional Danish pastry *(wienerbrød)* became

ølpølse (beer sausage) is a tasty snack found at the local butcher. Swedes eat little pork links *(prinskorv)* at a *smörgåsbord*.

Besides elk and venison, the Norwegians, Swedes and Finns eat reindeer, which can be found on the menus of fine restaurants – as well as stocked up in freezers across the area.

After a bracing trek in the Finnish wilderness, try the hearty *poronkäristys* (reindeer casserole). Karelian stew, made of meats, liver and kidney and slow cooked for hours, is another speciality.

FAR LEFT: Norway's celebrated Løiten Linie aquavit.
LEFT: Danish open sandwiches *(smørrebrød)*.
ABOVE: the fish market in Bergen, Norway.

famous for a reason. When in Denmark, visit a bakery and try a rich, chewy "chocolate snail" pastry in the morning, or a layered cream cake in the afternoon. Danish waffle cones filled with ice cream, marshmallow topping and marmalade are also not to be missed.

The Finns eat *pulla* (wheat buns) with their coffee and indulge in cream cakes topped with strawberries. In Skåne in southern Sweden, *spettkaka* is a local speciality, a tower-shaped confectionery of sugar, eggs and potato flour baked over an open fire. Norwegians enjoy fresh waffles and a variety of cakes, such as *bløtkake* – a rich sponge cake topped with strawberries. ❑

THE GREAT OUTDOORS

Scandinavians are passionate about nature and the outdoor life.
Unfazed by the weather, they hike, ski, skate, sail, fish and climb

The people of the Nordic countries are so at home in their natural surroundings that they seldom pause to consider how intertwined their daily lives are with the climate, the seasons, and the amazing and diverse beauty of the northern landscape. In winter, they take to their skis to traverse fields and forests, and pull on skates to blaze paths across icy lakes. They'll fish through the ice and even climb a frozen waterfall. Winter poses no obstacle to the hardy Scandinavian. In spring and summer, the mountains will beckon backpackers to scale their heights while the Swedish archipelago will be dotted with thousands of sailing boats, and the forests of the Nordic countries will be full of berry-pickers, picnickers, and hikers.

Danes will head for their magnificent beaches while Swedes, Norwegians, and Finns will celebrate the cool refreshing plunge of the thousands of lakes that dot the landscape. Come autumn, the people of the Nordic lands are combing the forests for mushrooms and admiring the gold- and red-hued foliage of the forest.

For Scandinavians, the great outdoors is a reflection of their national identity, an expression of their individuality and sporting spirit, and a valuable national asset that they will go to great lengths to protect. Some of the world's strongest green movements are to be found in Denmark, Sweden, Norway and Finland.

Country retreats

In a region where winter days are short and nasty weather can crop up any time of the year, comfort translates to secure shelter, often your own. A quarter of Norway's households own a holiday home, or *hytte*, a cottage or cabin.

In Sweden, many families save for years in order to buy a *stuga* (cottage) in the country or on the coast. Others are lucky enough to have inherited their little spot in a meadow. Most

Swedes are only a generation or two away from rural life and many have relatives who still live in their original home districts.

At the water's edge

Denmark and Sweden offer varied coastlines and a beach-life that is unique to each country's

topography. There are 8,000 km (5,000 miles) of coastline in Sweden, offering clean, if often chilly, water to swim in, and rocks to sun on (but few sandy beaches). The most spectacular seascape is the Stockholm archipelago, with its 24,000 islands, but nearly as thrilling are the waves crashing on the rocks of Bohuslän's archipelago.

The Danes, on the other hand, are blessed with sandy beaches. With more than 7,400 km (4,600 miles) of coastline, the waters surrounding Denmark are a playground for outdoor activities. No point in the country is more than a 45-minute drive from the sea and many inland waterways or fjords are even

LEFT: Norway, Sweden and Finland offer exciting opportunities for winter sports enthusiasts.
RIGHT: jet-boarding off Bornholm, Denmark.

closer. Kayaks, canoes, rowing boats, smaller sailing or motor craft may be hired at resorts along the coasts or on the larger lakes. The air is hardly still in Denmark, and the wind-surfing is excellent. Seasoned surfers may prefer the exhilaration of the North Sea, while beginners can try their hand in the lee of a fjord, bay or on a lake.

Norway has its fjords, which can be explored by steamers in summertime. In winter, when the fjords freeze over, families take Sunday "walks" on skates among the rocks and islets. Increased tourism along Finland's lake system is bringing the steamers back into business.

There are now regular passenger routes on several of the lake systems, but the oldest and probably the most romantic are those across Saimaa's vast expanse.

Hitting the trails

The Nordic region is known for its great open landscapes and is a mecca for hikers and backpackers. The greatest proportion of Sweden is virgin country. You can stroll for miles along tracks without seeing another human being, or drive a car on serpentine gravel roads and never have to pass another vehicle, or cycle through untouched land on special bicycle trails.

Norwegians are quite at home in their wild, unspoilt country, and have a great feeling for its mountains. Finland also offers pristine wilderness, quaint historical attractions, peace and quiet and free access to practically anywhere – all forests are potentially yours for trekking, berry- and mushroom-picking or short-term camping.

The Danish countryside is an appealing patchwork of dense forests, coastal dunes, marshes, moors and meticulously manicured farmland. In every type of landscape walkers will find paths or trails that stretch for miles, and a labyrinth of winding country roads.

Throughout Sweden, there's an excellent network of waymarked footpaths. Close to

Stockholm is the 850-km (530-mile) Sörmlandsleden (Sörmland trail), starting at Björkhagen underground station. Carefully laid out, the trail offers hikers constantly changing vistas of deep forest, historic sites, lookout points and lakes. It passes several camps where you can eat, rest and buy supplies, with shelters at regular intervals. Sörmlandsleden is an easy hike, but it offers plenty of excitement. You rarely meet another soul, particularly in spring, autumn and winter, but you will spot deer, elk, capercaillie, hawks and grouse. The area is full of mushrooms and berries to pick. For the most exotic views, however, head for the Kungsleden trail which runs for 450 km (280 miles) between Abisko and Hemavan.

Waymarked footpaths are found in the more scenically outstanding areas like the national parks. These areas are often well away from towns and villages, and as a result many of them have a chain of mountain stations set a day's walk from one another along the footpaths, providing shelter for walkers. Most of the mountain stations are equipped with cooking facilities, a shop and comfortable beds. Some even have a self-service restaurant and a sauna. They are not hotels, but simple accommodation designed to provide a haven at the end of the day for tired walkers.

In Norway, the bulk of the trails and lodges are conveniently in the middle of the triangle bounded by the cities of Oslo, Bergen and Trondheim. A central entry point is Finse, situated above the timber line at 1,200 metres (4,000 ft). Finse's main street is the station platform; there are no cars because there are no roads. When a train has gone and the last passengers have left, Finse returns to normal, a speck in a seemingly infinite expanse of rock, ice and snow.

Accessible mountaineering

To the north of Finse lie the Jotunheimen mountains, the range that took its name from Norse mythology, literally "Home of the Giants". The name is appropriate: peaks jut a

---

FOLLOW THE SIGNS

In Sweden and Norway, the extensive networks of walking and hiking trails are marked by a red "T". Lodges and cabins offer accommodation along the way.

---

kilometre and more skywards from lake-studded, moraine-strewn flats, all above the timber line. Nonetheless, even the loftiest of the Jotunheimen peaks, Galdhøpiggen and Glittertind, which are the highest in Northern Europe with summits rising more than 2,400 metres (7,900 ft), rank low on the international scale of noteworthy mountains where sheer altitude, not challenge, is the main criterion. Though this fact has led to relative anonymity – few Norwegian peaks appear in the classic

mountaineering literature – it does mean that you can ascend the equivalent of the Matterhorn or Mont Blanc without having to cope with the problems associated with high altitude. Most Jotunheimen trails meander from around 900–1,200 metres (3,000–4,000 ft) above sea level and there are no acclimatisation difficulties at that height.

Some of the glaciers that hewed the Norwegian landscape left offspring. One, Jostedalsbreen (Jostedal Glacier), is the largest on the mainland of Europe. Jostedalsbreen and its siblings throughout the country are the places to see crampon-shod parties wielding ice axes from spring until autumn.

LEFT: the "Sjaelland Rundt" yacht race circumnavigates the Danish island of Zealand.
RIGHT: climbing in the mountains of Norway.

Contact with the ice that shaped their land is currently the Norwegians' fastest-growing wilderness recreation and many centres now organise specialist courses.

Wilderness experience

In Finland, you can enjoy some of the region's best hiking along the Karelian Circle Trek, Finland's longest trekking route with approximately 1,000 km (620 miles) of marked trails. The Karelian Circle Trek offers genuine wilderness routes, variety in four different national parks, and the possibility to combine walking with mountain biking, canoeing, fishing or

hunting. Bears are rare but walkers are advised to tie a small bell to their backpack to warn them of their presence. Bed-and-breakfast accommodation is available, as are free wilderness huts (or ones that have to be reserved in advance). Pitching a tent is legal (and free) almost everywhere along this route.

On two wheels

Visitors to Denmark will notice within minutes of their arrival two signs of the country's greenness: windmills and bicycles. Windmills dot the landscape – including the area around Copenhagen's airport – churning out clean energy.

NATIONAL PARKS

The Nordic region has many national parks, each with its own claim to unique native flora and fauna. Hiking trails are marked and it's often possible to engage a guide. Large areas of Norway have been designated as national parks to protect special habitats and support biodiversity.

In Sweden, strict laws protect the rarer mammals such as the bear, wolf, wolverine, lynx, musk-ox, Arctic fox and otter. Among the more common animals, roe deer live in the forest and only in Scandinavia will you see the traffic sign "Danger, Elk". National parks cover highland and lowland regions. To see herbaceous flora and listen to birdsong in Sweden, Dalby Söderskog near Lund in Skåne

is at its best in the spring, while Store Mosse in Småland is worth a detour for birdwatchers interested in whooper swans, marsh harriers and cranes.

Denmark's first national park, established in 2007, is Thy National Park, a 12-km (7-mile) wide stretch of dunes, heathland and lakes on the West Jutland coast.

Finland's park network is mostly administered by the Forest and Park Service, which controls 30 or so national parks, including the rugged rift valley of Hiidenporrttin Kansallis-puisto in Karelia and the Ramsholmen Nature Reserve on the Åland Islands. The organisation rents interesting accommodation in isolated wilderness cottages.

The bicycle, meanwhile, is an important mode of transport for Danes and visitors alike. Bikes outnumber cars in some city areas, where the streets have bicycle lanes and traffic lights.

Denmark has thousands of miles of foot and cycle paths and bikes may be taken on most trains and ferries. Tourist offices can provide detailed maps of routes. Hærvejen is a bicycle and walking trail that stretches from the German border to Viborg in north-central Jutland. Traders and travellers beat this path a few thousand years ago, and much of it still looks as it did during Viking times. All along the route there are inns, hotels or hostels, as well as shops for provisions.

there is the Sverigeleden (Sweden Bicycle Route), from Stockholm to Göteborg – a distance of 2,600 km (1,600 miles).

Cast your line

Anglers are beginning to appreciate the wealth of excellent fishing that Scandinavia provides.

One of the most remarkable and most accessible places to fish is right in the centre of Stockholm, in the fast-moving Strömmen channel which links the freshwater of Lake Mälaren with the Baltic Sea. A clean-up programme has brought salmon and sea trout back to the very heart of the capital. What is more, the fishing

Cycling and, in recent years, mountain biking, are also popular outdoor sports for Swedes, and there are many well-designed and well-lit cycle routes all over the country. You could spend a week touring the island of Gotland on a bike. Keen cyclists also head for Östergötland, particularly along the banks of the Göta Kanal where the towpaths make ideal cycling tracks. Bikes can be hired at several places, and the most popular route for cyclists is between Berg and Borensberg. For the truly ambitious,

LEFT: the wide open spaces of northern Sweden and Finland offer superb wilderness trekking.
ABOVE: the Danes and Swedes are keen cyclists.

here is completely free of charge. Big salmon and sea trout can also be caught almost anywhere in Sweden – in world-famous waters like the Mörrum River in southern Sweden and, above all, in the large and wild rivers of northern Sweden, as well as along the coast when the fish are on their migration.

The salmon season varies between rivers, but it usually starts during the summer and continues well into the autumn. The sea trout tend to arrive a little later. Both spinning and fly-fishing can produce good salmon catches, but sturdy tackle is advised.

To Norwegians, fish is the standby staple. Even in modest markets, the variety of fish and

Life in Lapland

They call themselves "the people of the eight seasons". They are the Sami who live in Sweden, Norway, and Finland's most northerly provinces: vast wildernesses where nature and reindeer set the course of the year. Traces of their presence stretch back more than 8,000 years. They have their own language, religious traditions, and customs. While the life of the Sami has changed in modern times, the annual cycle of the reindeer – rutting, herding, separating, slaughtering, calving, marking – continues to shape the Lap-

land calendar. The winter round-ups are among Europe's most colourful events, resembling scenes from a Wild West film transposed to an Arctic setting. Visitors can enjoy this ancient culture at festivals and ceremonial occasions held throughout the year, where one can sample reindeer delicacies and marvel at Sami handicrafts.

A vivid way to experience the Sami lifestyle and landscape is to get outdoors. In spring and summer the mountains blossom with Sami heather, globe flowers, cloudberries and countless other species, inviting the visitor to take to the trails and woods of the many national parks in the Sami regions of Scandinavia. One not to miss is Padjelanta, the biggest national park in Sweden. The name comes from a Sami word that means "the higher mountain", and it is one of Sweden's most beautiful areas, with rolling plains, gently rounded mountain massifs, and huge lakes, such as Vastenjaure and Virihaure. Almost the entire park is above the tree line. There are many small streams, which the Lapps call *jokk*, and it has always been an important pasture for their reindeer herds.

For golf enthusiasts, nothing can quite top the thrill of golfing under the Midnight Sun in the glorious days of summer, where (depending on latitude and cloud cover) the sun is visible for up to 70 summer days. Anglers will find a true paradise in the primeval wilderness of the north, laced by swift rivers and streams and punctuated by lakes and pools. Big salmon and sea trout can be caught almost anywhere in northern Scandinavia.

To enjoy the wintry wilderness in an entirely different way, try dog-sledging, which is offered by many firms in northern Scandinavia. Drive the dog-sledge yourself or sit back in the vast silence of the mountains and be driven by a team of huskies. Your guide will tell you how to take care of a sledge dog and share bits of trivia, like the fact that in the Inuit language there are 18 different words for snow. Dog-sledging, common in Greenland, is now well established in Sweden and is growing in popularity in Finland's northern wilderness around Muonio.

The Sami winter vistas can also be enjoyed on reindeer sleigh rides and snowshoe treks. Ice climbing is popular, too. Fishing through the ice is common on most lakes and rivers.

To really soak up the hard life of the Sami, the visitor can stay in the world's largest igloo, the Jukkasjärvi Ice Hotel in Sweden. Each autumn, as the Arctic temperature plummets, Laplanders rebuild this celebrated igloo from thousands of tons of snow and ice. Inside it houses a church, hotel, gallery, golf room, cinema and bar named appropriately Absolut Ice. Guests sleep in warm sleeping bags on mattresses of spruce bough and reindeer skins. Temperatures average –4°C (25°F). The hearty fare served from the kitchen and the activities waiting outdoors don't leave guests much time to feel cold. Next morning, the hotel will issue a certificate of survival. It's not quite the same as herding reindeer, but it brings you one step closer to understanding how climate, custom, and sheer human persistence have made the Sami what they are today. ❑

LEFT: a young Sami boy from northern Sweden dressed for winter in a traditional pom-pom hat.

fish products is amazing, and Norwegians look on a proper fresh fish shop as an asset to a community. It is not surprising, then, that Norway is a country of fishermen of all kinds, both commercial fishermen and anglers.

The long coastline is a mecca for saltwater angling, yet freshwater angling is the more popular pastime, and there are a quarter of a million fishable inland lakes and ponds. The most common of around 40 freshwater species are trout and char; in the northernmost parts, and in lakes and ponds at higher elevations, they are the only fish. Grayling and pike are more common in larger lakes and rivers in eastern and central areas.

Ice fishing is a prime winter-time hobby. It's a straightforward form of angling, which requires only a baited hand line or short pole and line, warm clothing, and lots of patience.

Sporting nations

Norway, Denmark and Finland consider sport both a pleasure and an athletic pursuit. Sweden is one of the world's most sporting nations, with nearly half the population engaged in some form of sport or outdoor recreation. One in four Norwegians competes in a sport.

From the broad base of people for whom sport is a major leisure activity come the élite, competitors who enter the many national championships and represent their countries in international sports meetings. In Sweden, great sportsmen like Björn Borg have made Swedish tennis prowess legendary.

The runner, Paavo Nurmi (1897–1973), put Finland on the map, breaking multiple world records and winning four gold medals, Nurmi first competed in the 1920 Olympics. Variously known as the Flying Finn, the Phantom Finn and the Phenomenal Finn, he is still remembered for his extraordinary running style, speed, and tough character.

These days the Finns are better known for being world-class rally drivers. Mika Häkkinen, Tommi Mäkinen, Ari Vatanen and Hannu Mikkola may be known only to lovers of motor

> **TEEING OFF**
>
> Golf is the fastest-growing sport in Scandinavia, and its popularity has exploded in Denmark in recent years. In Scandinavia's far north enthusiasts like to play golf under the Midnight Sun.

sports, but probably more non-Finns could name one of these sportsmen than could identify Finland's current prime minister.

Traditionally, Norwegian prowess has been in winter sports and in sailing, but they have also won international medals in a wide range of events, including weight lifting, women's football, cycling, boxing, wrestling, shooting, handball, karate, canoeing, rowing and marathon running – Grete Waitz won the New York marathon a record nine times.

All the Nordic countries share the European passion for football. Clubs are supported through funds from the football pools and from the sale of players to major European leagues, in particular the English and Scottish Premier Leagues.

Winter sports

Not surprisingly, given the long winters and the beckoning snow-topped mountains, Swedes, Norwegians and Finns all excel at winter sports.

Downhill skiing in Sweden attracts a growing number of visitors thanks to artificially produced snowfall, the reduced risk of avalanches compared to Alpine resorts, and

RIGHT: the Scandinavian countries are an angler's dream with numerous lakes, rivers and a varied coastline all offering a good catch.

the variety of slopes. While slalom champion Ingemar Stenmark put Sweden on the international skiing map, it is Anja Pärson, the World and Olympic champion skier, who is keeping the country in the spotlight. As a result, Swedish downhill resorts such as Åre attract skiers from all over Europe. Sälen is the largest ski resort in Sweden with various Alpine and cross-country skiing facilities. World Cup Ski Championships are held in Åre, so there are hundreds of top-class, superbly groomed pistes served by high-speed lifts and cabins. Half-pipes and snow parks are available for snowboarding fanatics.

Norway has witnessed a reawakening of interest in the style of skiing called Telemark, which evolved in Morgedal, in the southern county of Telemark. In the mid-1800s, Sondre Norheim, a young farmer, devised bindings (devices that hold ski boots to skis) that were firm and were the first to give the feet control over the skis. He also gave the skis what is known as "sidecut", the slight hourglass profile of a ski seen from above. Sidecut is what enables skis to run true and turn easily, even to this day.

Norheim and his fellow Morgedal skiers used the new designs to perfect new skiing manoeuvres, including landing from airborne flights off snow-covered rooftops and natural outcrops.

Soon, they were ready to show off their new skills and this led to the first ski-jumping contest in 1879. The bent-knee stance with one ski trailing soon became known as the "Telemark".

In modern Telemark skiing, the heel is free to lift up from the ski and turns are steered, with one ski trailing and at an angle to the other. Competitive Telemark ski races are now held on packed slopes, as are Alpine ski races, but true Telemark skiing has spawned the revival of skiathlons, in which competitors must ski jump, ski through a slalom course, and run a cross-country ski race, all on the same pair of skis.

The Vasaloppet

Another world-famous ski competition takes place in Mora, in the Dalarna region of Sweden. The Vasaloppet, a 90-km (56-mile) cross-country skiing race, is the most popular sporting event in the country. It is held every March to commemorate King Gustav Vasa's flight from his enemies in the 16th century. Each year the race includes more than 15,000 competitors, who in the past have included the present king, Carl XVI Gustaf. The first Vasaloppet was run on 19 March 1922. A victory in Vasaloppet is regarded by most of the world's best skiers as highly as a podium place in the Olympic games or the World Championships.

Skiing is also one of the top sports in Finland, and the sport most readily associated with this snow-covered nation. Along with its Scandinavian neighbours, Finland has produced champion cross-country and downhill skiers, who benefit from an extended winter season in which to perfect their sport.

Skiing is not the only winter sport in which the nation excels. Ice hockey is one of the most important team sports in Finland. Almost all males participate at school, and the élite are filtered through and chosen for the best teams. Ice hockey is highly commercialised: one of the leading teams, Jokerit (the Jokers, referring to a deck of cards rather than humour) is run like a large company. Teams in Helsinki, Tampere and Turku are usually the best and spectators can number up to 10,000 for a game. Many Finns play in the North American NHL and many foreigners play in Finnish teams. ❏

LEFT: skiing, both downhill and cross-country, is a national sport in Norway, Sweden and Finland.
RIGHT: hikers enjoy the solitude of the far north.

PLACES

*A detailed guide to the Scandinavian countries, with
principal sites cross-referenced by number to the maps*

Whether you're in a car or coach, on a bicycle, boat or train, on
foot or on skis, the Scandinavian countries of Denmark,
Norway, Sweden and Finland have an enormous variety of
sights and scenery to beguile the visitor.

Denmark is neatly beautiful rather than grand, with its white sand
beaches, well-groomed farmland and gentle hills. Nurtured by the
mild climate, the countryside in spring glows with fruit blossom and
sharp yellow rape seed, and in late summer with the golden tinge of
harvest fields. Brightly painted half-timbered buildings echo nature's
colours and Renaissance castles dot the landscape. Copenhagen is
one of Europe's most enjoyable cities, a relaxed place with pedestrianised streets, pavement cafés, superb shops and entertainment.
This is the cultural as well as the political capital, but every Danish
town has its museum and art gallery, every castle its collection.

Far out to sea, remote from the rest of Scandinavia but part of the
Danish realm, lie the Faroe Islands – a paradise for bird-watchers –
and Greenland, a fascinating destination for the adventurous.

As if to compensate for the flatter terrain of its neighbours, Norway is made up of mountains, not craggy like the Alps, but curved
and etched with beautiful fjords and dramatic valleys. From the
beaches and pastures of the south, the coastline stretches far north to
the Arctic Circle and beyond, dotted with islands, fishing villages and
historic towns such as Bergen. Inland, the rugged landscape beckons
walkers and skiers. The capital, Oslo, offers all the attractions of a
European city, but with a very Norwegian imprint.

A short journey from Copenhagen across the Øresund bridge brings
you to southern Sweden, the rolling landscape of Skåne and the sunny
islands of Öland and Gotland. At the heart of Sweden lie two vast
lakes, Vänern and Vättern linked by the Göta Kanal, a pleasure-
boaters' mecca. Further north the folklore province of Dalarna gives
way to lakes and forests, winter-sports centres and the rugged landscape of Lapland. Stockholm lies majestically on an archipelago of
Baltic islands, the most sophisticated of the Scandinavian capitals.

For many centuries Finland came under Sweden's wing; later the
Russians took control. Remnants of both cultures can be found, but
with independence Finland's own identity has emerged. The south
coast is a summer playground of islands and beaches, fortresses and
painted towns. The capital, Helsinki, with its wealth of architecture,
new and old, is known as the "Daughter of the Baltic". Lakes and
forests cover central Finland, while easterly Karelia is a hiker's
delight. Lapland, land of the Midnight Sun, attracts anglers, white-
water enthusiasts and those in search of true peace and solitude. ❑

PRECEDING PAGES: modern reproductions of typical Norwegian boats
at the Sunnmøre Boat Museum, Ålesund.
LEFT: the spectacular Dalsnibba panorama at Geirangerfjord, Norway.

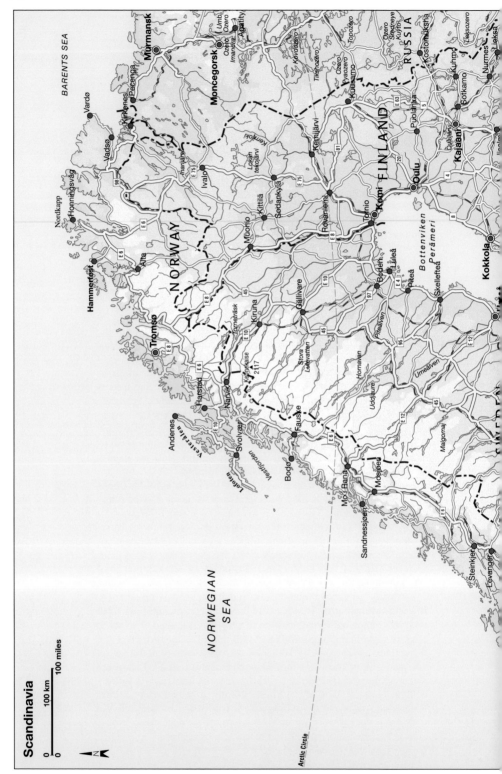

Scandinavia

0 — 100 km
0 — 100 miles

N

BARENTS SEA

NORWEGIAN SEA

Murmansk
Moncegorsk
RUSSIA
FINLAND
NORWAY
Kokkola
Kajaani
Oulu
Kemi
Tornio
Rovaniemi
Kemijärvi
Kittilä
Sodankylä
Muonio
Ivalo
Inarijärvi
Kenujoki
Kirkenes
Pecenga
Vardø
Vadsø
Honningsvåg
Nordkapp
Hammerfest
Alta
Tromsø
Harstad
Narvik
Andenes
Svolvær
Bodø
Fauske
Mo-i-Rana
Mosjøen
Sandnessjøen
Steinkjer
Levanger
Kiruna
Gällivare
Boden
Luleå
Piteå
Skellefteå
Gruvträsk
Kvikkjokk
Uddjaure
Storavan
Stora Lulevatten
Umeälven
Piteälven
Pecenga
Apatity
Kuusamo
Puolanka
Sotkamo
Kuhmo
Nurmes
Lieksa
Ozero Imandra
Umbi Ozero
Bottenviken
Perämeri

Arctic Circle

Vesterålen
Lofoten
Vestfjorden

E 6
E 8
E 10
E 75
E 12
E 45
45

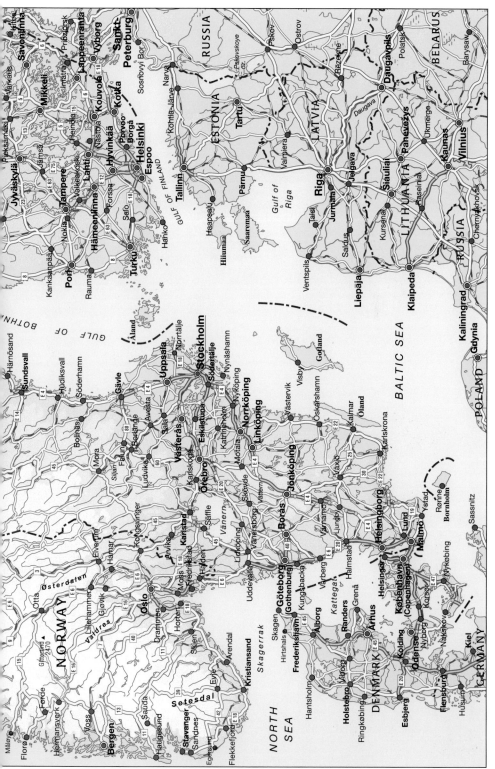

DENMARK

Small, but perfectly formed, Denmark is a country of fun-loving, environmentally conscious people

Hamlet was wrong – there is nothing rotten in the State of Denmark. Yes, the winters can be dreary, but they're not biting cold and there is little snow – the Danes go to Sweden and Norway to ski – and summers can be sunny, with long hours of daylight. Yes, the tax rate is among the world's highest. But taxes are reinvested to help make this a country "where few have too much and fewer too little".

The world's oldest kingdom may be no empire as of yore, but the sons of those Vikings continue to pack plenty of clout. These days they're spreading their seed far and wide in canisters of frozen nitrogen: Denmark is the biggest supplier of meticulously screened and frozen human sperm on the planet – and a major purveyor of computer elements and electronic devices, windmills, agricultural products, arts and crafts and skilled professionals.

Denmark is also a nation of cyclists and recyclers – more than half the country's rubbish is turned into either steam heat for homes or other new things. Energy supplies are also as green as possible. Natural gas and windmills are the preferred energy sources of this windy country.

Nowhere is very far away, especially now that a network of motorways, railway lines and spectacular bridges link west to east from Germany, through Denmark to Copenhagen and across the Øresund to Sweden. Ferries still play their part, linking islands and crossing "fjords" as the Danes call their larger lakes, for this is a nation with a strong seafaring past.

Zealand, in the east, holds the capital, Copenhagen, Scandinavia's liveliest city, and Hamlet's castle, Kronborg at Helsingør (Elsinore). Jutland, in the west, is Denmark's link with mainland Europe. The North Jutland seascapes have captivated artists over the centuries; west-coast sands stretching as far as the eye can see draw summer holiday-makers. East Jutland has an intricate lake system, well-used for canoeing and water sports, and also Århus, Denmark's second city, with an international arts festival in the autumn. Funen, sandwiched between Jutland and Zealand, is the "garden of Denmark", with Odense, the birthplace of Denmark's most famous writer, Hans Christian Andersen. Out in the Baltic is the island of Bornholm, home to craftspeople and a popular holiday destination.

Far to the west and north lie the outposts of the Danish kingdom; the windswept Faroe Islands ("Sheep Islands"), a favourite haunt for birdwatchers; and Greenland, a true adventure travel destination offering stunning scenery and a pristine natural environment. ❏

PRECEDING PAGES: mustard field, Djursland; Den Gamle By, the historic old town of Århus, Jutland; Valdemars Slot (castle) on the island of Tåsinge, Funen Archipelago.
LEFT: Amagertorv and the Stork Fountain in Copenhagen's main shopping area.

THE DANES

They're generally warm, witty and welcoming. But they can also be cool and reserved. It depends where you meet them

Danes have two reputations in the world; one at home and another abroad. Outside their homeland, Danes are known as warm, curious, friendly, funny, charming. In their modest way, Danish travellers bring on laughs and a sense of pure enjoyment for life. They try not to act too offended when, outside Europe, people ask: "Is Denmark the capital of Sweden?" or "What language do you speak – Dutch?" A short, firm geography lesson is given on the spot, but modesty usually prevents the Dane from pointing out that Denmark is the oldest monarchy in the world, dating from AD 935.

At home, Danes are seen by foreign visitors as distant, sombre, even cold. They keep to themselves. Danes blame this image on the wet, cool climate. "Not much of our social life happens on the pavements or out in front of the home," says Frans Kjær Nielsen, a teacher. "We spend much of our time indoors with our families and friends."

Cosiness prevails

Inside this thin barrier of social contact, Denmark is one of the warmest countries in the world. People are genuine. They speak their minds. They thrive on making life cosy, relaxing and enjoyable – from festive occasions to mundane coffee breaks. This is what Danish *hygge* is all about. *Hygge* (pronounced **whoo-guh**) stands for any and every sense of cosiness, and it is found everywhere in Denmark. A good meal has *hygge*, a house can have *hygge*, a story, a walk in the woods, a meeting at a café, even a person can have *hygge*.

Parties for weddings, birthdays, anniversaries and the like have *hygge* at their core. Tables are decorated with flowers and candles and creatively folded napkins. A three-course meal is usually interspersed with songs and speeches, which end in a collective "Hurrah!" Wine flows freely. As the Danish poet and troubadour

Benny Andersen wrote in a song well known among Danes: "One must keep the mood wet. I'm drunk and I'm feeling great".

Six hours into such a celebration and filled with spirits, a party-goer has a chance to get up from the table, dance a bit, then fetch some coffee and cookies and sit down again. Later, the

DENMARK: THE ESSENTIALS

Population 5.5 million.
Capital Copenhagen (pop. 1.7 million).
Notable towns Århus, Odense.
Climate Average maximum temperature in July: 22°C (71°F). In February: 5.5°C (42°F).
Top museums Nationalmuseet, Louisiana Museum of Modern Art, Vikingeskibshallen.
Famous home Hans Christian Andersen Hus, Odense.
Historic sights Christiansborg, Copenhagen; Kronborg, Helsingør; Roskilde Cathedral; Vikingeborgen, Trelleborg.
Natural wonders Råbjerg Mile sand dune; cliffs of Møn.
Tourist information www.visitdenmark.com

LEFT: jazz on a summers day at the Riverboat Jazz Festival, Silkeborg, Jutland.
RIGHT: the modern face of Danish industry.

hosts serve the final course, called "get out food", and guests gradually take the hint.

Hygge was born, no doubt, indoors during the grey winter months. From November to February, Danes go to work in darkness and return home in darkness. Warm candlelight fills flats, homes and offices in natural defence. During *Jul* (Christmas), live candles decorate Christmas trees indoors, around which families join hands and sing carols. Local ferries light up the black water with strings of white lights. On New Year's Eve, the Queen gives her annual talk to the nation on television, and fireworks spark and pop, lighting up the midnight sky.

A whiff of spring

By February, winter seems to drag on forever. In his essay, *Oh! To be Danish*, the author Klaus Rifbjerg writes of this time: "Sure, it can be grim, and now and then we might want to turn our collar up and jump in the river. But then the light suddenly changes and there's a melody in the air, a whiff of spring to come, the smell of the sea and a blackbird singing on a rooftop."

Fields of fluorescent yellow winter rape blossom in May, and the days turn longer. In spring and summer, urban Danes cycle out to their garden houses on the edge of town, and rural Danes collect dead branches and greenery into

huge piles on the beaches and in the countryside. On the evening of 23 June, Midsummer's Eve, those piles of wood are topped with an effigy of a witch and set on fire to drive bad spirits from the land as Danes gather around the bonfires and sing. In July, nearly the whole country goes on holiday for three weeks. Barbecues are lit and bathing-suits donned.

By late summer, farmers' tractors haul grain and hay, holding up traffic. Towns hold harvest festivals, children start school and families hunt for mushrooms and berries in the forests. People complain about the diminishing light and increasing rain, and soon the frost hits and temperatures can drop so low the sea freezes solid. So, the

Danes light a candle, make some *hygge* with hot cocoa and buns, and look forward to *Jul* again.

A sense of togetherness and looking out for each other can be felt not only in family *hygge*, but in society as well, starting with the generous welfare system. Workers unions are strong, and the cooperative spirit prevails. Only four out of 100 Danes do not belong to an association.

"We have a joke that if two Danes sit together for five minutes, they will start an association," says Frans Kjær Nielsen.

> **MANY VOICES**
>
> More than 100 dialects are spoken in Denmark. Some vary greatly. People in South Jutland are hardly understood by the residents of Copenhagen.

newcomers and Danes alike. Denmark found itself unprepared in how to deal with cultural misunderstandings, how to teach Danish effectively to thousands of immigrants, and how to help integrate them into the job market and society.

In 1985, the only option for recent immigrants were local night schools, which also offered classes like painting and gardening. Fortunately, things have improved. The country passed immigrant education laws and also improved teacher-training. Yet unem-

The new Danes

In the 1960s and 1970s, Denmark experienced the first recent wave of immigrants – Turkish "guest workers". It was not until the early 1980s, however, that the effects of immigration on the Danish culture were felt, when refugees from the Far East, Middle East, the Balkans, Somalia, and elsewhere came to the country. The Danish social democracy, traditions, norms and welfare system were suddenly thrown into question by

ployment remains high among immigrants.

Immigration remains an emotive issue and typical Danish tolerance seems to be eroding. The right-wing, anti-immigration Danish People's Party has consistently increased its share of the vote since its formation in 1995. When Denmark came under intense criticism across the Islamic world in 2005, after the newspaper *Jyllands-Posten* sparked protests, boycotts and death threats by publishing cartoons depicting the prophet Mohammed, the party's popularity increased. In elections held in November 2007, they won 13.9 percent of the vote, making them the third largest political party in Denmark. ❏

LEFT: arts and music festivals are regular fixtures on the Danish cultural calendar.
ABOVE: drinks on the waterfront.

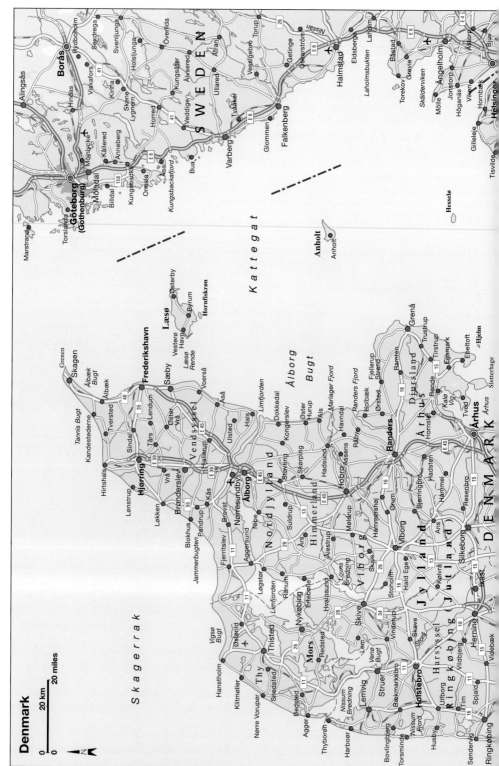

Denmark

0 20 km
0 20 miles

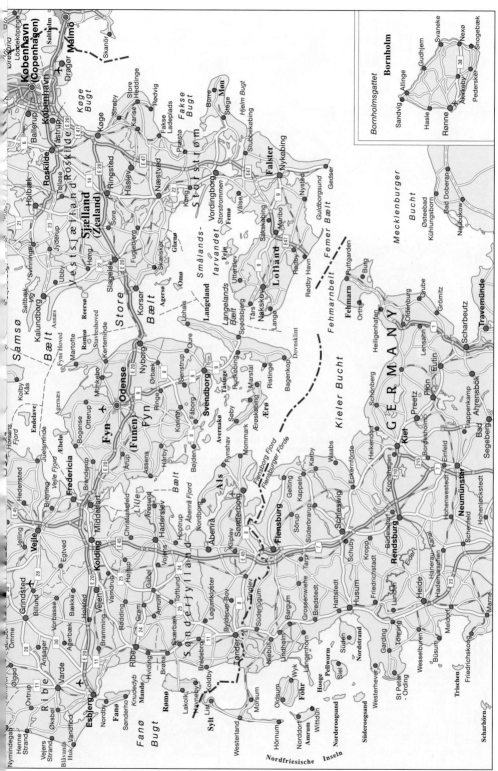

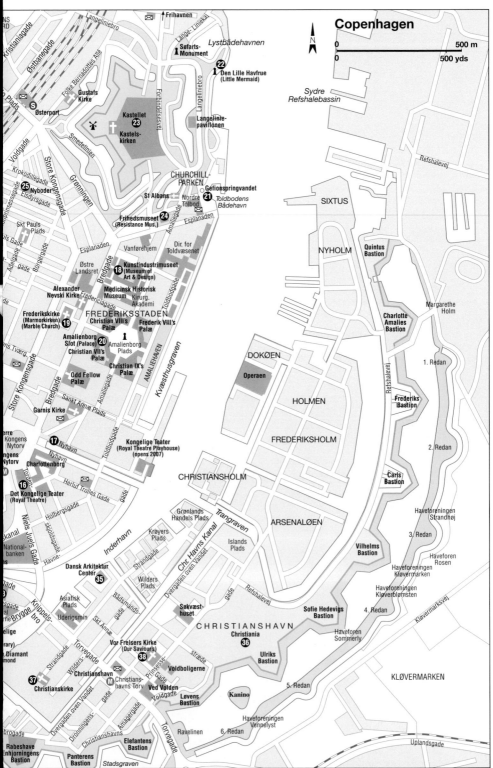

Copenhagen

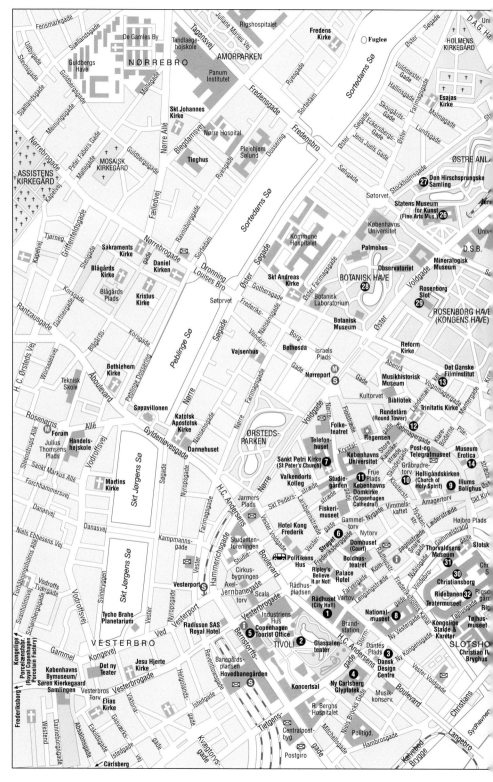

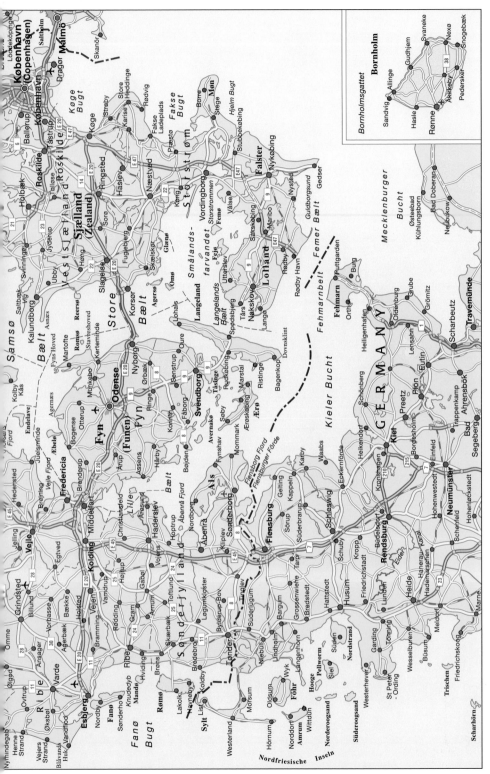

COPENHAGEN

*Denmark's capital city is the most exuberant in Scandinavia.
Pedestrians and cyclists rule, shopping is a pleasure,
cultural sights abound, and by night the city buzzes*

Map
on pages
94–95

Copenhagen (København) is the "city of green spires". Copper plates, etched green by salt air, clad the spires of castles and churches in the old city, and tower over the medieval street network and newer houses. The Old Town you visit today would have looked different but for two devastating fires and a terrible bombardment. Blazes in 1728 and 1795 licked and leaped along the straw-roofed houses and turned most of the half-timbered medieval town to ashes. Only a few solidly built structures survived – among them, the Round Tower (**Rundetårn**). When Admiral Lord Nelson and the British fleet bombarded Copenhagen in 1801 the toll was also heavy. Six years later, Wellington besieged the city, destroying 300 houses and capturing the Danish fleet.

Copenhagen is the liveliest – and many claim the most fetching – of the Scandinavian capitals, with things to see and do all the time. With Europe's longest pedestrian mall, this was the first capital to offer the pleasures of ambling through a network of streets free of motor vehicles and exhaust fumes.

A good way to get a first feel of Copenhagen is from the water. Take one of the 50-minute canal boat trips from Gammel Strand (mid-Mar–mid-Dec; every 30 minutes from 10am; tel: 33 13 31 05). If you're the adventuresome type you could explore the waterways in a kayak for two hours, starting at the

LEFT: the bright lights of Tivoli.
BELOW: meeting for drinks.

FACT FILE

Situation Copenhagen is located on the east coast of Zealand facing the sound between Denmark and Sweden.
Population 1.7 million in the Copenhagen area.
Climate Afternoon temperatures in February average 5.5°C (42°F); in July they are around 21 or 22°C (70–72°F).
Transport Metro, bus and S-train network; bike hire.
Discount card Buy a Copenhagen Card for free entrance to museums, galleries, and free transport.
Best sightseeing tour Guided Walking Tour *(see panel, page 103)*; canal boat trip from Gammel Strand.
Best shopping Strøget, Europe's longest pedestrian mall.
Top attraction Tivoli Gardens (open summer, Hallowe'en and Christmas).
Finest building Rosenborg Slot (Castle).
Best museums Nationalmuseet, Ny Carlsberg Glyptotek, Statens Museum for Kunst (National Museum for Fine Arts), the ruins of Absalon's castle beneath Christiansborg.
Best views of the city Rådhuset tower; Rundetårn (Round Tower); Vor Frelsers Kirke, Christianshavn.
Best *smørrebrød* Slotskælderen, Fortunstræde 4, tel: 33 11 15 37.
Tourist information office Vesterbrogade 4A (just across from the Tivoli), tel: 70 22 24 42; www.visitcopenhagen.com

TIP

One of the best ways to enjoy Denmark is by bicycle. The City of Copenhagen provides 2,000 free bicycles. All you have to do is deposit a DKK 20 coin (about $4) in one of the 110 City Bike Parking places dotted about the city centre, and ride off. The DKK 20 is refunded when the cycle is returned (1 May to end November only).

BELOW: the palace of Christiansborg, Denmark's seat of government.

same place. A guide paddles ahead of you (Copenhagen Adventure Tours; tel: 40 50 40 06; www.kajakole.dk).

Rådhuspladsen (City hall Square) is the nexus of Copenhagen, grandly lit up at night with its coloured signs, digital news headlines and blinking neon, with the enormous **Rådhuset ❶** (City Hall; Mon–Fri 8.30am–4.30pm, Sat 10am–1pm, free; tours in English for a fee, 3pm; tel: 33 66 25 82) at its heart. Constructed in the National Romantic style, its inspiration was drawn from medieval Danish and Norwegian architecture with a touch of the Palazzo style of northern Italy. The facade and interior are trimmed with historic details from Nordic mythology. Looking for a bird's-eye view of the city's spires and towers? The 106-metre (347-ft) tower (daily; entrance charge) is for you.

Inside the Rådhuset's foyer, look for the entrance to **Jens Olsen's World Clock** (Mon–Fri 8.30am–4.30pm, Sat 10am–1pm; entrance charge). Its star dial mechanism shows the path of the pole star in resettable periods, making it one of the most accurate and complicated clocks in the world. Unsurprisingly, this masterpiece of time-telling took 27 years to build.

Bordering the square to the east on Vester Voldgade are two of Copenhagen's fine traditional hotels. Closest to City Hall is the **Palace Hotel**, one of the few buildings in the Jugendstil (Art Nouveau style), and further north, past the square, **Hotel Kong Frederik** with the smart and pricey Queen's Pub restaurant.

Between the two hotels is the beginning of Strøget, Europe's longest pedestrianised shopping street, and the kingdom of wonder that is **Ripley's Believe It or Not! Museum** (mid-June–Aug daily 10am–10pm, Sept–mid-June Sun–Thur 10am–6pm, Fri–Sat 10am–8pm; entrance charge; tel: 33 32 31 31; www.topattractions.dk). Forget educational value, and take the family to marvel

HISTORIC TRADING POST

Before 1167, Copenhagen was just a trading post called Havn (Harbour), which gave easy access to Skåne (Scania) across the Sound. Skåne is now part of Sweden, but in those days southern Sweden was part of Denmark, and the village of Havn enjoyed a position in the middle of the kingdom. As wars and unrest changed the geography of Denmark, København (Merchants' Harbour) gradually moved to its point on the eastern shore of Zealand.

In 1167, King Valdemar I commanded the local bishop, Absalon of Roskilde, to fortify Havn in order to protect it against Wendic pirates. Absalon built a fortress on the spot where the Parliament building now looms across the canal from Højbro Plads (Square). Copenhagen was on the way to becoming Denmark's biggest and most important town. The fortress became Christiansborg, *borg* meaning castle. Centuries later, it remains the seat of Danish politics, housing the Folketing (Parliament).

During the long reign of Kristian IV (1588–1648), Copenhagen solidified its role as the country's seat of power. This visionary town planner built Børsen, said to be the oldest stock exchange in Europe, a Renaissance structure with a spire of four entwined dragons, steep copper roofs, tiny windows and gables galore.

at shrunken heads, optical illusions, and a picture of Queen Margrethe carefully constructed from pocket fluff.

On the western side of Rådhuspladsen is one of Denmark's purest delights, the charming, timeless **Tivoli Gardens** ❷ (late-Apr–late-Sept Sun–Thur 11am–11pm, Fri 11am–12.30am, Sat 11am–midnight; also open at Hallowe'en and Christmas; entrance charge; tel: 33 15 10 01; www.tivoli.dk). Tivoli is a Scandinavian rainbow of gardens, open-air amusements, restaurants, cafés, theatres, an open-air stage and a major concert hall, home of Sjællands Symphony Orchestra. Tivoli is also the place to enjoy a good meal, coffee and cake, or a drink. The park has more than 20 restaurants. For children, the greatest thrills come from the rides, roller-coasters and merry-go-rounds. In recent years the lake has been machine-frozen for winter ice-skating, and the pleasure mecca's portals are thrown open for an old-fashioned market at Christmas time.

Danish design

A two-minute walk south of the City Hall on H.C. Andersens Boulevard is the **Dansk Design Centre** ❸ (Mon–Fri 10am–5pm, Sat–Sun 11am–4pm; entrance charge; tel: 33 69 33 69), with ongoing Danish and international exhibitions *(see Insight on Danish Design, page 110).*

Across the road is **Ny Carlsberg Glyptotek** ❹ (Tues–Sun 10am–4pm; entrance charge; tel: 33 41 81 41). This exquisite museum offers a grand art collection begun by the brewer Carl Jacobsen and maintained by the New Carlsberg Foundation. There are collections of ancient Egyptian, Greek, Roman and Etruscan sculptures, as well as some French masterpieces from Cézanne, Gauguin and Rodin. The lush, palm-lined indoor Winter Garden has a wonderful café.

Map on pages 94–95

The tall tubes in front of the Moorish-style palace restaurant in Tivoli contain bubbling water. This unusual sculpture was designed by the Danish nuclear physicist Niels Bohr.

BELOW: City Hall dominates the bustling central square of Rådhuspladsen.

On Bernstorffsgade, across from Tivoli's west entrance, is the **Hovedbanegården** (Central Railway Station). Beyond it to the west lies **Vesterbro**, one of Copenhagen's oldest residential districts, today a multicultural community, vibrant with bizarre shops, exotic restaurants and its red-light boulevard, **Istedgade**.

The **Copenhagen Tourist Office ❺** lies across the street from Central Station on Bernstorffsgade, near the corner of Vesterbrogade. This travellers' ganglion has it all: information on sights, cultural activities, transport, eating places and events. A prime source of information is the free magazine *Copenhagen This Week* (www.ctw.dk).

The medieval city

If Rådhuspladsen is the heart of Copenhagen, then **Strøget ❻**, the 1.8-km (1-mile) pedestrian shopping street, is the spine. It has endless shops, street vendors, buskers and cellar galleries. Strøget (*"stroy-yet"*) is where Copenhageners and visitors alike go to shop or just to promenade. The mainstream shops and eateries are on Strøget proper, while the more quirky boutiques, cafés and restaurants are situated on the quieter side streets.

Starting at Rådhuspladsen, Strøget meanders through five streets and four squares before it runs into Kongens Nytorv, the largest square in the old town. Good landmarks and meeting places are the squares at **Gammeltorv** (Old Square) and at Strøget's major crossroads, the crane fountain at **Amagertorv**. Here, another main pedestrian artery, **Købmagergade**, branches off to the north.

Near Gammeltorv, the area behind **Vestergade** is one of the few remaining residential areas in the inner city. Living in the picturesque neoclassical houses

is a mixture of old-time Copenhageners, artists and students, and here you find some of the more exotic clothes shops and galleries – try Skt Pedersstræde for starters. **Sankt Petri Kirke ❼** (St Peter's Church), on the corner of Nørregade and Skt Pedersstræde, is the oldest church in Copenhagen, its chancellery built in 1450. Hans Christian Andersen lived in No. 19 Vestergade when, as a young man, he first arrived in Copenhagen from Odense. Another famous Dane, the 19th-century philosopher Søren Kierkegaard, lived in the house on the corner of Nytorv and Frederiksberggade at Gammeltorv.

One block south and running parallel to Strøget, is **Kompagnistræde**, with shops specialising in antiques, china and pewter.

Two blocks south, across from the canal on Ny Vestergade, is Denmark's **Nationalmuseet ❽** (National Museum; Tues–Sun 10am–5pm; tel: 33 13 44 11), the country's most-visited museum. It's highly recommended for its newly revamped collections of ancient "bog" finds from the Stone, Bronze and Iron Ages including unique treasures such as the golden Chariot of the Sun, the enigmatic Gundestrup Cauldron and Egtved Girl. A fascinating and well-structured museum that takes days to cover, it also has an interesting section on Danish cultural history.

From Nytorv, continue along Strøget towards Amagertorv. For a close encounter of the rich and sweet, stop at one of Copenhagen's premier confectioners, **Konditori La Glace**, a few stops from Strøget at Skoubogade. Here, cream layer-cakes reign supreme. The opposite side of Amagertorv is occupied by the shops most often visited by tourists: **Illums Bolighus** ❾, showcase for superb Danish and international design; and the flagship stores of **Royal Copenhagen Porcelain** and **Georg Jensen** silver.

Latin Quarter

The streets to the north of Amagertorv form the old **Latin Quarter**, featuring the cosy **Gråbrødretorv** ❿ (Greyfriars Square). The cobblestone square is a popular place to enjoy lunch at one of several outdoorsy restaurants or dinner (Peder Oxe is a local favourite).

The streets just to the north hold **Københavns Domkirke** ⓫ (Copenhagen's Cathedral) and the main building of the **University of Copenhagen**. The seat of the University Board, beside Nørregade, dates from 1420 and is the oldest building in Copenhagen. A fun stop for children is the sweet factory on Nørregade 36, **Sømod's Bolcher**, where confectioners make old-fashioned boiled sweets by hand (demonstrations Mon–Fri 9.15am–3pm; tel: 33 12 60 46). **Fiolstræde** is known for its antiquarian bookshops, and **Krystalgade** is the site of Copenhagen's synagogue. Try a sandwich from the busy, bowler-hatted organic butchers, **Slagteren ved Kultorvet** (Coal Square), on the open plaza near the Nørreport subway station, at the top of traffic-free Købmagergade.

On Købmagergade itself is one of Copenhagen's most fascinating buildings. The **Rundetårn** ⓬ (Round Tower; mid-Sept–May 10am–5pm; June– mid-Sept

BELOW: Gråbrødretorv.

10am–8pm; entrance charge; tel: 33 73 03 73) was built in 1642 as an observatory possibly inspired by the work of Denmark's world-renowned astronomer, Tycho Brahe. The viewing platform on the top offers a breathtaking panorama on clear days and nights. The tower stands 36 metres (118 ft) high, and to reach the roof one walks up a 209-metre (685-ft) spiral ramp. In 1716 Tsar Peter the Great rode a horse to the top while his wife followed in a carriage.

Around the corner off Landemærket is **Det Danske Filminstitut** ⑬, home of Cinemateket, which celebrates Denmark's trailblazing successes in cinematography, and shows a programme of international and Danish films (performances Tues–Fri 9.30am–10pm, Sat–Sun noon–10pm; tel: 33 74 34 00; www.dfi.dk).

A few blocks south on Købmagergade is **Museum Erotica** ⑭ (May–Sept 10am–11pm; Oct–Apr 11am–8pm; entrance charge; tel: 33 12 03 11; www.museumerotica.dk), one of the best examples in town of the liberal-minded Danes. Here sex and sensuality are not an issue – they *are* the issue.

Haunts of the rich and famous

The last section of Strøget, from the Crane Fountain to Kongens Nytorv, is the home of the exclusive and expensive: fashion shops, furriers and jewellers.

At the end of Strøget, facing **Kongens Nytorv** (King's New Square), stands the grand old hotel of the city, **Hotel D'Angleterre** ⑮. The majestic buildings dominating Kongens Nytorv are **Det Kongelige Teater** ⑯ (Royal Theatre) – the national stage for ballet, opera and drama. The present building was designed in the 1870s, taking the Paris Opera Garnier as its ideal. Next door is **Charlottenborg**, since 1754 the home of the **Royal Academy of Fine Arts**, where painters, sculptors and architects receive their formal training.

TIP

For a taste of brewing, visit the famous Carlsberg Brewery and stables, Gammel Valby Langgade 1, Valby, and sample a glass of the best (Tues–Sun 10am–4pm; entrance charge; tel: 33 27 13 14).

BELOW: the colourful quayside at Nyhavn.

Nyhavn quayside

At the narrow waterway of **Nyhavn** ⑰, a famous landmark from 1673, colourful old wooden schooners line the quay, and the north side is a charming combination of sailors' bars and new restaurants. The south side was always "the nice side" but the north side used to be "the naughty side" where sailors on shore leave would spend their liberty drinking, whoring, and getting tattooed. Times have changed, and Nyhavn is now one of the most popular spots in town for a different type of visitor.

From Nyhavn, Bredgade and its parallel twin, Store Kongensgade, are the main shopping streets of the residential **Frederiksstaden** to the north. The area was planned and built in the 18th century for the well-to-do who wanted stately homes close to the centre.

At Bredgade 68 is **Kunstindustrimuseet** ⑱ (The Danish Museum of Decorative Art; Tues–Sun 11am–5pm; entrance charge; tel: 33 18 56 56) which features not only European and Oriental works, but classic Danish design as well. The building dates from 1757 and was originally a hospital. Opposite the museum, three domes tower over **Alexander Nevski Russian Orthodox Church**, which was built in 1881 by the Russian government and contains a number of fine icons.

Close by, there is almost no way one can miss the grand copper dome of **Frederikskirke** ⑲, popularly known as the **Marble Church**. The church was meant to be a majestic rococo monument, but the king, Frederik V, ran out of money and the project was cancelled in 1770. The church was not completed until 1894. When the project was resumed it was built not in marble but in limestone. From the dome, which is accessible to visitors (mid-June–Aug daily

Map on pages 94–95

Nyhavn still retains some of the character of bygone days, when it was a haunt for sailors on leave.

BELOW: exhibits at the Danish Museum of Art and Design.

THE WALK OF THE TOWN

On your feet is the best way to discover this old town of narrow streets and cobbled courtyards. The "Guided Walking Tour of Copenhagen" starts outside the Tourist Information Office on Bernstorffsgade, across from Central Station (all year Sat–Sun 11am, also June–Aug: Thur and Fri 11am; tel: 70 22 24 42).

The first stop is Rådhuspladsen, where the western wall came down in the 1850s to let the city expand, "it was dirty and terribly crowded inside". The guide sets off along streets following the curve of the canal which once extended to Strøget – now Europe's longest pedestrian mall – pausing at the City Court House, profiled like a Greek temple. By the canal a buxom woman serves fishcakes. Over Amagertorv looms a Dutch Renaissance building from 1616, the mayor's residence taken over in 1911 by Royal Copenhagen Porcelain. Today, side by side, are Royal Copenhagen, Georg Jensen silver, Holmegaard glass and Illums Bolighus with Danish gifts and furnishings. Then there's the Royal Theatre and the elegant Hotel D'Angleterre, where Victor Borge used to stay. And Nyhavn, where you can take a canal tour. What's this – Amalienborg Palace? Just in time for the noon-time changing of the guard.

1 and 3pm; Sept–mid-June Sat–Sun only; entrance charge), there is a splendid view across the Sound to Sweden. The statues outside the church represent important Danish churchmen and theologians.

Royal residence

Amalienborg Slot ⓴ (Amalienborg Palace), directly across Bredgade towards the harbour, is the winter residence of the Royal Family, one of Europe's less assuming royal domiciles, built in the 18th century. One wing of the palace houses the **Amalienborg Museum** (May–Oct daily 10am–4pm, Nov–mid-Dec and Jan–Apr Tues–Sun 11am–4pm; entrance charge; tel: 33 12 21 86), whose reconstructed rooms contain exhibitions on the monarchy from 1863 to 1972.

The Royal Guard are always on duty, and the changing of the guard at noon every day attracts both children and adults. If the flag is flying, then the Queen is in residence and the full ceremony will take place. The exquisite equestrian statue in the square represents Frederik V and was made by the French sculptor Jacques Saly.

Along the promenade

BELOW: royal guards on duty at Amalienborg Palace.
RIGHT: rococo splendour at the Marble Church.

The other end of the east–west axis through the plaza ends in **Amaliehaven**, a modern park donated to the city by the A.P. Møller shipping company in 1983. Following the promenade to the north, you will find the dazzling fountain, **Gefionspringvandet ㉑**, dedicated to the Nordic goddess Gefion.

At the start of Langelinie is *the* symbol of Copenhagen, **Den Lille Havfrue ㉒** (The Little Mermaid). This bronze statue of the character from the Hans Christian Andersen fairy tale was created by Edvard Eriksen in 1913.

The quay of Langelinie follows, and Europe's busiest cruise ship pier is to the north of this at **Frihavnen** (Free Harbour). Renovations have been taking place to rejuvenate the area. The most architecturally interesting of the new buildings is **Paustians Hus**, designed by Jørn Utzon, who also designed the Sydney Opera House. Paustian is one of Copenhagen's finest furniture stores and the building also houses a good restaurant.

Map on pages 94–95

War resistance

Return to the city centre via **Kastellet ㉓** (The Citadel), a fortification that has kept its old ramparts intact. Part of the area is still military property.

Churchillparken, a tiny park just south of Kastellet, provides a home for the **Frihedsmuseet ㉔** (Danish Resistance Museum; Tues–Sun, May–Sept 10am–5pm, Oct–Apr 10am–3pm; free; tel: 33 47 39 21), which commemorates the Danish underground fighters of World War II.

Continue past Store Kongensgade to visit Denmark's oldest housing development, **Nyboder ㉕**. The long rows of ochre-coloured houses were built in 1638 by Kristian IV as quarters for the Danish Royal Navy, and the 616 apartments are still used for staff and retired officers.

The Little Mermaid (Lille Havfrue), by Edvard Eriksen, was modelled on his wife.

Nearby, where Øster Voldgade and Sølvgade meet, is the superb **Statens Museum for Kunst ㉖** (National Museum for Fine Arts; Thur–Sun and Tues 10am–5pm, Wed 10am–8pm; permanent collection free, entrance charge for exhibitions; tel: 33 74 84 94). A new extension houses four storeys of modern art within stunning glass and whitewashed walls. Other Danish and European works are displayed permanently, along with changing international exhibitions. Behind the museum and across the park is the **Den Hirschsprungske Samling ㉗**

BELOW: the ochre-coloured houses of the Nyboder district.

CHRISTIANIA – THE ALTERNATIVE CITY

In a beautiful position on Copenhagen's waterfront, Christiania offers a way of life far removed from the bustle of a city

In 1971, a group of alternative thinkers founded Christiania, a 34-hectare (84-acre) "Free City" with woods, dirt roads, workshops, restaurants and funky houses.

The hippie playground in the heart of the city – only 1 km (½ mile) from the Parliament buildings – occupies what was previously an abandoned 19th-century military barracks in Christianshavn. The Christianites, about 1,000 people of all ages, cultures and income levels, have converted barrack blocks, workshops and powder magazines into a place where they can live and work. There are only four rules: no hard drugs, no cars, no gang insignia, no weapons or violence.

From the entrance on, Christiania is a sensory overload. Buildings are painted with rainbows, spiritual figures and politically defiant graffiti. There are barefoot cyclists, their baskets full of vegetables; earthy-smelling organic markets; recycling warehouses; workshops and stables. Resident children play in an "organic kindergarten", where modern equipment is replaced with nature. Houses along the leafy path have names such as "The Blue Banana" or "The Pyramid".

Christiania has some of the best restaurants in the city, including SpiseLoppen (The Eating Flea), in the warehouse by the front entrance. In the same building is Loppen, a music club. Månefiskeren (The Moon Fisher), a café in the heart of the collective, serves excellent coffee in a "far-out" atmosphere.

For years, Christiania's unusual social experiment was tolerated, but since 2004 the Danish government has stepped up measures to "normalise" the area. A police crackdown on "Pusher Street", where marijuana was once sold openly, drove the drugs trade underground. In 2006 the government proposed that all buildings should be privately owned, a suggestion fiercely rejected by the Christiania collective. When government workers entered Christiania in 2007 with a police guard and began to demolish a derelict building, tension quickly turned to violent protest, with 59 arrests.

Christiania's future looks uncertain, as government and big business press to turn a spirit-of-Woodstock piece of prime real estate into an affluent suburb. Visit while it still exists.

An inexpensive walking tour leaves at 3pm from the front entrance (July–Aug daily, rest of year weekends) – this is the best way to see the Free City and get a broader perspective. Christiania's tourist guide (10 DKK) provides a detailed history and self-guided walks. ❑

TOP LEFT: murals decorate many of Christiania's buildings. **LEFT:** relaxed lifestyle. **TOP:** child of the New Age. **ABOVE:** the streets are car-free.

(Hirschsprungske Collection; Wed–Mon 11am–4pm; entrance charge; tel: 35 42 03 36), a commendable private collection of 19th-century Danish art – including many of the originals from the Skagen painters.

Map on pages 94–95

Gardens and jewels

The **Botanisk Have** ❷ (Botanical Gardens) are just across the street, with the main entrance on Gothersgade (summer daily 8.30am–6pm; winter Tues–Sun 8.30am–4pm; free; tel: 35 32 22 22). Visit the rosarium, the perennials and a huge conservatory with tropical and subtropical plants.

One of Copenhagen's most attractive sights is **Rosenborg Slot** ❷ (opening times vary; entrance charge; tel: 33 15 32 86), the fairy-tale castle across from the Botanical Gardens. King Kristian IV's exquisite palace in Dutch Renaissance style is now a museum, and contains three centuries-worth of royal treasures, as well as the crown jewels. The garden surrounding it, **Kongens Have**, has been a favourite with Copenhageners for centuries.

For treasure and trash visit the city's antique and flea markets. Try Israels Plads on Saturday, 8am–3pm, and Gammel Strand, Friday 7am–6pm and Saturday 8am–4pm, both late April to September.

Centre of government

To the southeast of Strøget and the main shopping area lies **Slotsholmen** (Castle Island). Surrounded by canals, the island is the seat of the Danish Parliament and government ministries. The imposing **Christiansborg** ❸, built on the same spot as the original old castle of Copenhagen, contains Parliament, the Prime Minister's office, the Supreme Court and the Royal Reception Chambers. The public may join conducted tours of the **Folketinget** (House of Parliament), and the **Royal Reception Chambers** (in English Oct–Apr Tues–Sun at 3pm and May–Sept at 11am, 1 and 3pm; entrance charge; tel: 33 92 64 92).

Bishop Absalon built a fortress on this little islet in 1167, and from 1416 it was the home of the Danish king. Absalon's fortress was replaced by a new castle in 1367 and in the 1730s King Kristian VI ordered a new palace. This one, a magnificent baroque building, burned in 1794 and was replaced yet again with a new palace which, ill-fated as it was, burned down in 1884. The present version of Christiansborg is around 100 years old, built between 1907 and 1928. The granite facade was made from stones gathered in every parish in the country. The equestrian statue, erected on the Palace Square, depicts King Frederik VII (1843–63).

The **Ruins of Absalon's Old Fortress** (May–Sept daily 10am–4pm; Oct–Apr Tues–Sun 10am–4pm; entrance charge) and the medieval castle are now accessible to visitors and make an interesting "underground" visit.

The **Palace Chapel**, inaugurated in 1826, is located to the north of Christiansborg. Behind the chapel is **Thorvaldsens Museum** ❸, which contains the works of Denmark's great sculptor, Bertel Thorvaldsen (1770–1844), who lived and worked in Rome for 40 years (Tues–Sun 10am–5pm; entrance charge; tel: 33 32 15 32).

In front of Christiansborg is the **Ridebanen** ❸, the royal riding grounds from the 1740s bordered by the only surviving buildings from the first Christiansborg. The royal horses are still exercised here and their

BELOW: exploring Copenhagen's waterways by boat.

Map
on pages
94–95

stables can be visited on the southeast side of the square – the **Kongelige Stalde og Kareter** (Museum of Royal Stables and Coaches; May–Sept Fri–Sun 2–4pm; Oct–Apr Sat–Sun 2–4pm; entrance charge; tel: 33 40 26 76). Adjacent to the stables, the **Teatermuseet** is one of the oldest court theatres in the world, designed in 1766 by the French architect Nicolas-Henri Jardin (Tues–Thur 11am– 3pm, Sat–Sun 1–4pm; entrance charge; tel: 33 11 51 76). The equestrian statue on the riding grounds depicts King Kristian IX, who died in 1906.

East of Christiansborg is another of Copenhagen's best-known buildings, the **Børsen** ❸ (Stock Exchange), built in 1619 in Dutch Renaissance style by Kristian IV. Its prominent spire is formed by the entwined tails of four dragons said to protect the building from fire. On the southeast side of the island is the **Det Kongelige Bibliotek** ❸ (Royal Library) and its "Black Diamond" – an architectural wonder of old and new. Det Kongelige Bibliotek dates back to 1482 and is the largest library in Scandinavia, with more than 2½ million volumes. The Black Diamond, completed in 1999, is a modern extension in black polished granite perched on the water's edge.

The 17th-century Vor Frelsers Kirke on Christianshavn.

BELOW: the city's Botanical Gardens. **RIGHT:** Carlsberg Brewery drayman.

Colourful Christianshavn

Cross the harbour via the Knippelsbro bridge to reach **Christianshavn**, one of Copenhagen's oldest and most colourful residential areas. Christianshavn was built on an island in 1617 by Kristian IV and is surrounded by the original star-shaped ramparts. Along the harbour wall, one of the meticulously restored warehouses is well worth a visit, the **Dansk Arkitektur Center** ❸ (Danish Architecture Centre; daily 10am–5pm, until 9pm on Wed; entrance charge; tel: 32 57 19 30), which features various exhibitions, a bookshop and café.

Until recently a run-down, working-class area and Denmark's largest shipyard, Christianshavn has changed enormously and now features a mixture of smartly renovated 18th-century city houses, big apartment blocks, old and new industry, a good deal of the state's administration and Copenhagen's new **Operaen** (Opera House).

Take a stroll down the streets of Christianshavn and glance into the courtyards of some of the old houses on **Strandgade**. Amagergade 11, at the other end of Christianshavn, is said to have the finest courtyard in town, and is surrounded by old galleries.

Christianshavn is also the home of **Christiania** ❸, the hippie-style "free city" *(see Christiania, page 106).* The main entrance is on Prinsessegade.

Two of Copenhagen's more notable churches are on Christianshavn. **Christianskirke** ❸ in Strandgade is a rococo building from 1754. It was built as a theatre with boxes, including one for the royal family. **Vor Frelsers Kirke** ❸ (Church of Our Saviour; tel: 32 54 68 83) in Prinsessegade attracts the most attention. Built in red brick in 1694, its tall copper-clad tower with a spiralling, external stairway can be seen from all over the city. The tower is generally open in summer to visitors who are brave enough to climb through a maze of roof timbers and up the 150 gilded steps. However, it was closed for renovations at the time of writing. ❏

A FLAIR FOR DESIGN: FUNCTION WITH FORM

When a nation of craftsmen mixed with a late move towards industrialisation in the 1900s, an influential new school of design was born

A chair may be something to sit in, and a lamp may help to light up a room, but Danish designers have made these ordinary objects extraordinary over the past 50 years. Whether in museums or in conference rooms and homes, Danish design has brought a sense of elegance to everyday life.

"It always starts with a task," says designer Hans J. Wegner. "I never say to myself I'm going to make a piece of art. I tell myself I want to make a good chair" (Wegner's Round Chair, above). Danish designers "subtract and subtract" unnecessary elements from products and tools to find true function and form, says Jens Bernsen of the Danish Design Centre. "Sometimes these designs even turn out to be beautiful."

In Copenhagen, you should visit the Danish Museum of Art and Design, Bredgade 68 (open Tues–Sun 11am–5pm, closed Mon; entrance charge; tel: 33 18 56 56), and the Danish Design Centre, H.C. Andersens Boulevard 27 (Mon–Fri 10am–5pm, Wed until 9pm, Sat–Sun 11am–4pm; entrance charge; tel: 33 69 33 69). A good place to buy furniture is Illums Bolighus.

△ **URSULA**
Ursula Munch-Petersen designed this well-loved table service for Royal Copenhagen.

▽ **PH LAMP**
Poul Henningsen saw a light fixture as more than just light, but something to create a sense of space.

▽ **CYLINDA LINE**
The architect Arne Jacobsen designed this stainless steel line of household objects for the company Stelton, and it is now one of the most recognised in Denmark.

DESIGN IN THE HOME

For all its elegance, Danish design is not something limited to galleries and museums. In Denmark, it is found everywhere – hotels, restaurants, cafés, offices, and most importantly, homes. Nearly every Dane, it seems, has some sort of sleek designer lamp hanging over the dinner or coffee table.

For special occasions, such as weddings, birthdays and office receptions, Danes give presents such as arty salad sets, candle holders, salt and pepper grinders, pot holders – even mixing bowls *(pictured above)*.

"The kitchen drawer is good design's enemy number one," says Erik Bagger, whose wine-serving tools are well known in Denmark. Danish-designed products are meant to be used, however, meaning that Denmark probably has the most stylish contents of kitchen drawers anywhere in the world.

The visually striking sound systems designed by Bang & Olufsen are praised worldwide, and are found in many a Danish home. Even such prosaic items as cupboard handles and other household fittings are given due attention by Danish designers.

◁ **EGG CHAIR**
Many of Arne Jacobsen's designs were intended for specific buildings or, in this case, hotel lobbies.

▽ **IC3 TRAIN**
Gone are the days of lumpish locomotives. Even Danish trains have a high quality of design.

ZEALAND

Map on page 114

*Venture north from Copenhagen to Hamlet's castle at Helsingør,
or south to the white cliffs of Møn, and discover Zealand,
a colourful land rich in culture and tradition*

The island of Zealand is Denmark's largest, yet it is still compact and most of its many attractions make ideal day-trips from the capital. The area north of Copenhagen makes a classic tour for visitors, with its undulating countryside, beech forests, lakes and good beaches, as well as castles, manor houses, royal hunting lodges, art galleries and museums. The southern and western areas of Zealand have traditionally been the port of entry for new people and ideas coming from the Continent. This side of the island is an enchanting expanse of rolling hills, woodland and some wonderful seaside scenery.

Historically, Zealand played an important political role in the development of Denmark. The Viking influence was strong and the town of Roskilde, a trading post in Viking times, became the seat of kings and an important religious centre.

The Danish Riviera

The coast road from **Copenhagen ❶** to Helsingør is officially called Strandvejen, but is also known as the "Danish Riviera" for its stylish houses and fine views across the Øresund to Sweden. Small protected harbours shelter working fishing boats and millionaires' yachts alike, and converted marine buildings now house fresh fish restaurants.

While it's true that the essence of North Zealand can be glimpsed in a day, it really warrants more time, either by an overnight stop at a charming Danish *kro* (inn) or by taking several day tours from Copenhagen.

From Copenhagen, drive north through fashionable Charlottenlund to **Klampenborg ❷**. In just 15 minutes you'll come to an ancient deer park, **Klampenborg Dyrhaven** (daily), first mentioned in official documents in 1231. Leave your car and take a horse and carriage through the woods and parkland. Forest walks are indicated by yellow spots painted on trees.

Within the deer park lies the world's oldest fun fair, **Bakken** (mid-Mar–Aug Mon–Fri noon–10pm, Sat 11am–midnight, Sun 11am–10pm; tel: 39 96 20 96). **Peter Lieps'** rustic forest restaurant is where locals go to drink hot chocolate after winter walks. Art lovers will enjoy the quiet elegance of nearby **Ordrupgaard** (Vilvordevej 110; Tues, Thur, Fri 1–5pm, Wed 10am–6pm, Sat–Sun 11am–5pm; entrance charge; tel: 39 64 11 83). Its permanent collection of Danish and French paintings includes works by Matisse and Gauguin. The museum has newly incorporated the home of Finn Juhl, architect and furniture-designer extraordinaire.

Out of Africa

A further 12 km (7 miles) brings you to **Rungsted ❸**, site of **Rungstedlund** (May–Sept Tues–Sun 10am–5pm; Oct–Apr Wed–Fri 1–4pm, Sat–Sun 11am–4pm;

LEFT: the chalk face of Møns Klint.
BELOW: the chapel at Frederiksborg.

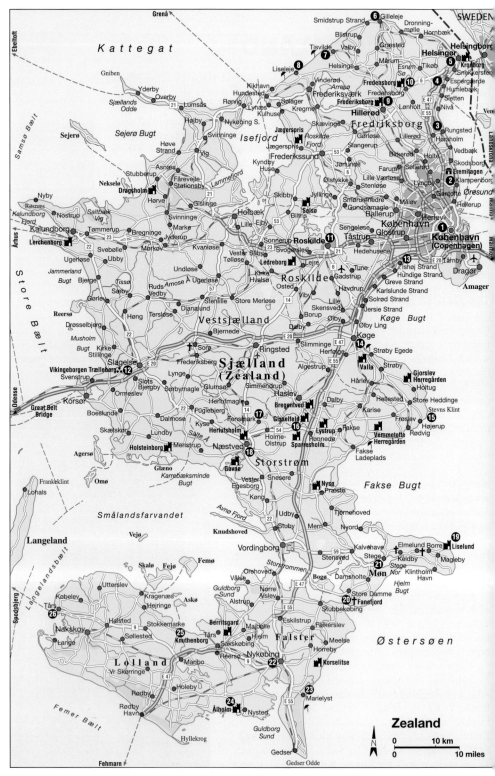

Zealand

0   10 km

0   10 miles

entrance charge; tel: 45 57 10 57), the family home of Karen Blixen, the Danish writer known as Isak Dinesen whose best-selling book, *Out of Africa*, became a film starring Meryl Streep and Robert Redford.

At **Humlebæk ❹**, art lovers could easily spend an entire day at the **Louisiana Museum for Moderne Kunst** (Louisiana Museum for Modern Art, Gl. Strandvej 13; Tues–Fri 11am–10pm, Sat–Sun 11am–6pm; entrance charge; tel: 49 19 07 19). A rich permanent collection is supplemented by frequent international exhibitions held in a breathtaking setting overlooking the Øresund to Sweden. Sculptures adorn the gardens and there is a children's wing *(see box, page 52)*.

Hamlet's Helsingør

Helsingør ❺ is best known for its massive Renaissance-style **Kronborg**, Hamlet's "Castle of Elsinore" (May–Sept daily 10.30am–5pm; Oct and Apr Tues–Sun 11am–4pm, Nov–March Tues–Sun 11am–3pm; entrance charge; tel: 49 21 30 78). Originally built by King Eric of Pomerania when he introduced the "Sound Dues" (fees paid to the Danish crown by all ships passing through to the Baltic), Kronborg has been rebuilt several times. It has provided a backdrop for many productions of Shakespeare's *Hamlet*. Inside, the richly decorated King's and Queen's chambers and the 62-metre (203-ft) long Great Hall are worth seeing.

Taking on the elements: a Zealand skipper.

Helsingør is one of Denmark's most historic towns, with entire streets of colour-washed buildings. The 15th-century **Skt Mariæ Kirke** and the **Carmelite Kloster** (Convent) are among the best-preserved Gothic buildings in the world. Hans Christian Andersen described it as "one of the most beautiful spots in Denmark, close to the Sound, which is a mile wide and looks like a blue stream swelling between Denmark and Sweden".

BELOW: author Karen Blixen lived at Rungsted.

The coast road leads on to **Gilleleje ❻**, the most northerly town of Zealand, a small working fishing port. **Adamsen's Fisk**, an unpretentious harbourside takeaway, is a great spot for a fish lunch.

If the weather is good, you could stop at the sun-worshippers' beaches of **Tisvilde ❼** or **Liseleje ❽**.

As one turns back towards Copenhagen, Denmark's National History Museum is at the spectacular Renaissance palace **Frederiksborg ❾** (mid-Mar–Oct daily 10am–5pm; Nov–mid-Mar daily 11am–3pm; entrance charge; tel: 48 26 04 39), built between 1605 and 1621 in **Hillerød**. The most notable rooms are the Council Hall, Knights' Hall and the chapel with its original Compenius organ (1610). Outside is one of the best baroque gardens in Northern Europe.

Just 9 km (5 miles) from Hillerød is the royal palace of **Fredensborg ❿**. The palace was built in Italian style in 1722, and is now used as a residence for the Danish Royal Family in spring and autumn (guided tours, July daily 1–4.30pm; tel: 33 40 31 87).

Viking town

A major highlight of Zealand is the town of **Roskilde ⓫**, the island's second-largest town, 20 minutes by train west of Copenhagen. The wonderful **Domkirke** (Cathedral; Apr–Sept Mon–Sat 9am–5pm; Sun 12.30–4pm; Oct–Mar Tues–Sat 10am–4pm, Sun 12.30–4pm; entrance charge), built in 1170, is the

Kronborg, Hamlet's "Castle of Elsinore" at Helsingør.

burial place of generations of Danish monarchs. The **Vikingeskibsmuseet** (Viking Ship Museum; daily 10am–5pm; entrance charge; tel: 46 300 200; www.vikingeskibsmuseet.dk) is one of the great delights of Denmark. Its five ships were found in 1962 at the mouth of Roskildefjord, sunk by the 11th-century defenders of Roskilde to block the fjord against enemy attack. The restored ships are awe-inspiring and include a dreaded Viking man o' war. Costumed re-enactors demonstrate Viking crafts and the restaurant has *mjød* (mead) to quaff.

Still on the Viking theme, **Vikingeborgen Trelleborg** ⑫ (June–Aug Sat–Thur 10am–5pm, Sept–May Sat–Thur 10am–4pm; entrance charge; tel: 58 54 95 06), near Slagelse in western Zealand, is an abandoned Viking fortress some 1,000 years old. It was once a huge fortified camp that housed 1,000 Vikings and one of the houses has been reconstructed.

Southern Zealand

The first stop for modern art enthusiasts south of Copenhagen is the sleek white **Arken Museet for Moderne Kunst** (Thur–Sun and Tues 10am–5pm, Wed until 9pm; entrance charge; tel: 43 54 02 22; www.arken.dk) at **Ishøj** ⑬. **Køge** ⑭ is popular for its beaches, crowded with sun-loving Danes. Inhabitants claim that Køge has more half-timbered houses than any other town in Denmark. The oldest, dated 1527, stands at 20 Kirkestræde. **Skt Nikolai Kirke** has one of Denmark's most beautiful town church interiors. Not far from the market is **Hugo's Vinkælder**, a historic inn serving old-fashioned draught porter.

The cliffs of **Stevns Klint** ⑮ on the south headland of Køge Bay may not be quite as dramatic as those on the island of Møn, but they are impressive when the sun illuminates them in brilliant hues of white.

Inland, 5 km (3 miles) south of the ancient town of **Haslev**, Hans Christian Andersen found inspiration for what is perhaps his most famous story, *The Ugly Duckling*, in **Gisselfeld Slot** ⑯ (grounds and stables daily), a castle built in 1554. To the west of Gisselfeld at **Fensmark** ⑰ is the **Holmegård Danish Glassværk** (Glassworks; tours Jan Mon–Fri 10am–4pm, Feb–Dec daily 10am–4pm, until 6pm July–mid-Aug; entrance charge; tel: 55 54 50 00). Here, visitors can watch fine pieces being formed. The **Glass Museum** has a notable collection, and at the museum shop, seconds often make superb bargains.

Næstved ⑱, 5 km (3 miles) southwest of Fensmark, has been an important trading town for most of its history and has an attractive city centre. About 6 km (4 miles) to the southwest is **Gavnø Slot** (Apr–Sept 10am–5pm; entrance charge; tel: 55 70 02 00), situated among magnificent gardens on a tiny island linked by road. In the 13th century it was used as a pirates' castle; today it houses Scandinavia's largest privately owned picture collection.

Cliffs of Møn

The island of **Møn** ("The Maid") to the east is linked to Zealand by road bridges. According to legend, its spectacular stretches of luminous white chalk cliffs, topped with beech woods and studded with fossils, became a refuge for the most powerful of Nordic gods,

BELOW: Arken, the modern art museum at Ishøj.

Map on page 114

Odin, when Christianity left him homeless. The brand-new **Geocenter Møns Klint** (May–Oct 10am–5pm; entrance charge; tel: 55 86 36 00; www.moensklint.dk) explains the area's geology brilliantly.

Liselund Slot ⑲ (May–Sept Wed–Sun 10.30am–3.30pm, by guided tour only; entrance charge; tel: 55 81 21 78) is a thatched mini-château, built in 1796. Andersen wrote *The Tinder Box* and *The Little Match Girl* in a summer house on the estate. Møn's churches are noted for their frescoes, particularly those at **Keldby**, **Elmelund** and **Fanefjord ⑳**, the last standing on an isolated hill overlooking the narrows of Grønsund. Beside the church is the longest barrow grave in Denmark, **Grønjægers Høj**. The main town of **Stege ㉑** has medieval ramparts.

Falster and Lolland

The Farø bridges connect Zealand to **Falster**, and the ferry routes to Germany. The main town on the island is **Nykøbing ㉒**, noted for the **Czarens Hus** (Tsar's House), where Peter the Great stayed in 1716 and which now houses the local **Gulborgsund Museum** (Mon–Sat 10am–4pm; entrance charge; tel: 54 85 26 71). The area around **Marielyst ㉓**, to the southeast, has miles of white sand dunes where families take beach holidays. There is a choice of bridges from Falster to **Lolland**, to reach **Ålholm Slot ㉔** near Nysted. The 12th-century castle is closed to visitors, but you can visit the rare cars at the Automobile Museum (May–Oct; tel: 54 87 19 11) in its grounds. From Aalholm, the road north runs past lakes to **Knuthenborg ㉕** (May–Oct 11am–5pm; entrance charge; tel: 54 78 80 89), a safari park. In the far west, the **Tårs ㉖** to **Spodsbjerg** crossing connects the island with Langeland and Funen. ❑

TIP

On Midsummer's Eve along the coast north of Copenhagen, beach bonfires and fireworks light the skies and a procession of ships passes through the Øresund, blasting their horns to celebrate the peak of the short Danish summer.

BELOW: farmland landscape, North Zealand.

The beautiful **Kastellet** (citadel) is on the east side of town; today it is a military museum, **Forsvarsmuseet** (June–Aug Tues–Sat 11am–5pm, May and Sept Tues–Sat 1–5pm; entrance charge; tel: 56 95 65 83).

Bornholm has inspired many Danish painters, as well as having produced a few of its own: Oluf Høst is the best known. **Bornholms Museum** (Skt Mortensgade 29; Jan–mid-May and late-Oct–Dec Mon–Sat 1–4pm, mid-May–June and Sept–late-Oct Mon–Sat 10am–5pm, July–Aug daily 10am–5pm; entrance charge; tel: 56 95 07 35) and its collection of paintings and exhibits from pre-history onwards relating to the island's past, is worth visiting. It also includes a charming model of the Bornholm railway.

Åkirkeby ⑤ (pop. 1,400) is the main town in the southern part of Bornholm, and the only one of the larger towns situated inland. It was an ecclesiastical centre and its church, **Åkirke**, was built around 1150 as a chapter house in the Archbishopric of Lund. The large tower was extended around 1200, and at the same time it was fortified with walls even heavier than those of Hammershus. It is notable for its sandstone baptismal font depicting the life of Christ in 11 relief carvings; the figures are explained in runic script, and end with the signature of the stonecutter, "Sighraf, master".

The easternmost town in Denmark, **Svaneke ⑥**, prospered with the success of its shipping captains. The largest buildings were originally merchants' houses. North of the town is an old Dutch mill, and nearby an untraditional water tower, built by the architect Jørn Utzon in 1951.

Cycling downhill is forbidden in **Gudhjem ⑦** ("good home"), a very pretty place, built on steep slopes down to the water. Windmills around the town once provided electricity. There is an open-air agricultural museum, **Landbrugsmuseet Melstedgård** (July–Aug daily 10am–5pm, mid-May–June and Sept–late Oct Sun–Fri 10am–5pm; entrance charge; tel: 56 48 55 98), just southeast of Gudhjem at **Melsted**, complete with horses, pigs and poultry.

Bornholm celebrates classical music with a festival from mid-July to September, which attracts music lovers from around the world.

BELOW:
a great breakfast.

Fortress in the sea

From Gudhjem Harbour one can sail to the group of islands collectively known as **Ertholmene**. The largest of these are **Christiansø ⑧** and **Frederiksø**. A naval base was constructed here in about 1864, but today only fishermen and their families live on this "fortress in the sea". It makes an interesting place to visit. The islands are quite rocky, with castle towers, batteries and cannon all serving as reminders of the past.

Round churches

Østerlars Kirke ⑨ (consecrated to St Laurentius), just over 4 km (2½ miles) southwest from Gudhjem, is the largest of the four medieval "round churches" of Bornholm, which include **Nylars**, **Nyker** and **Olsker**. When the Slavic Wends ravaged the island they were occasionally used as places of refuge and in the 14th–16th century Hanseatic merchants from northern Germany would move in during the herring season. At Østerlars the enormous support pillars create the impression of a fortress, which was

Map on page 118

the second purpose of the structure. Inside the church (built around 1150), the vault is painted with fine frescoes of biblical scenes. On the north wall of the oval-shaped choir, stone steps lead to the second storey, where the hollow central pillar has two entrances. The outer wall has a watchman's gallery. The double altarpiece was painted by the local artist Poul Høm.

Edible delicacies

During the summer months, freshly landed herrings are delivered to the island's smokehouses. Here they are turned from their original silver colour into the "golden Bornholmers" dearly loved by Danes, which can often be seen drying on stands outside. Elderwood gives them their special taste. You can eat them warm from the oven or put them on black bread, sprinkle them with salt, and add chopped chives, radishes and an egg yolk on top.

Pickled herrings are a lunchtime speciality. The best spiced herrings are produced on Christiansø. Baltic salmon, said to be the finest edible fish in the world, is normally available, too.

A cheerful sign attracts diners. Try a delicious "golden Bornholmer", the island's smoked herring speciality.

Bornholm by bike

The best way to travel around Bornholm is by bicycle. An extensive network of cycle paths has been established and it's easy to find houses, hotels and campsites en route. The island's residents often rent rooms or houses to visitors, but remember to book accommodation in advance during the summer months, especially in the southeast part of the island where the wonderful beaches of **Dueodde** ❿ and **Balka** in particular attract crowds of holiday-makers in high season. ❑

BELOW:
Gudhjem village, on the north coast.

FUNEN

Map on page 124

Bridging the water between Zealand and Jutland is the island of Funen, the "Garden of Denmark", with the buzzing cultural centre of Odense at its heart

Denmark's central island of **Funen** (*Fyn* in Danish) is known for its natural beauty, flowered gardens, castles and manor houses. Danes call it "the Garden of Denmark". Cycling tours take you along hundreds of kilometres of marked routes. Here, too, lies historic Odense, the birthplace of author Hans Christian Andersen *(see page 127)*. South Funen and the island archipelago are a paradise for anglers and yachtsmen.

The Funen circle

When coming from Copenhagen, the usual way to reach Funen is by train or car across the mighty Store Bælt bridge to Nyborg on Funen's east coast. The Lille Bælt bridge links it to east central Jutland on the opposite side. Your choice then is circling the islands from Nyborg or Middelfart, and basing yourself either in Odense or Svendborg to make excursions. Driving is easy, but the most satisfying way to see Funen is on a bicycle. You can lean your bike beside one of the little whitewashed churches to take a look inside, and inhale the scent of the wild flowers that lie beneath roadside rose hedges.

LEFT: young visitor at Hans Christian Andersen's house in Odense.
BELOW: decorative doorway in Ærøskøbing.

Before heading north out of **Nyborg ❶** for Kerteminde and the Hindsholm Peninsula, take a look at **Nyborg Slot** (Mar–May and Sept–Oct Tues–Sun 10am–3pm; June and Aug until 4pm; entrance charge; tel: 65 31 02 07), which dates from 1170. It was built to defend the country from the Wends of North Germany and, during the Middle Ages, was the meeting place for the three ruling powers of monarchy, nobility and clergy. However, in 1722, much of Nyborg Slot was demolished to provide building materials for Odense Castle. Part of the original ramparts and moat remain, and the castle has a fine interior of great echoing, empty rooms.

About 15 km (9 miles) north from Nyborg, near Kerteminde, are the underground remains of a Viking chieftain's burial ship at the **Vikingemuseet** (June–Aug daily 10am–5pm; Mar–May and Sept–Oct Tues–Sun 10am– 4pm; Nov–Feb Wed–Sun 11am–3pm; entrance charge) at **Ladby ❷**. With him in his 22-metre (72-ft) Viking ship, the chief took what he prized most: his weapons, hunting dogs and 11 horses.

Kerteminde ❸ is Funen's foremost fishing village, with old half-timbered houses. Most towns in Funen have craftspeople of many different skills, and Kerteminde offers stoneware and pottery at local shops.

Odense

In the centre of Funen lies the quaint but lively capital of Funen, **Odense ❹**, Denmark's third-largest city (pop. 187,000). Its name stems from Old Norse and means "the sanctuary of Odin", the wise and mighty

The Kerteminde landscape has attracted some of Denmark's most renowned artists. Their work can be seen at the village's Johannes Larsen Museum at Møllebakken (tel: 65 32 11 77).

chief god. So the place was important enough to be worthy of Odin's protection before the Christian conversion of Denmark. The Gothic cathedral, **Skt Knuds Domkirke**, is one of the most beautiful landmarks of Odense. It was named after King Knud (Canute) II, who was murdered in the town in 1086 by his rebellious subjects and later canonised by the Pope. It's adorned with a gilded altarpiece made by Claus Berg in Germany in 1521. In the crypt lie the remains of Skt Knud.

Munkemøllestræde, west of the cathedral, is the cobblestone street where the storyteller Hans Christian Andersen grew up in the early 1800s (July–Aug daily 10am–4pm; Sept–June Tues–Sun 11am–3pm; entrance charge). Northeast of the cathedral is the outstanding **Hans Christian Andersen Museum** (Bangs Boder 29; Sept–June Tues–Sun 10am–4pm; July–Aug daily 9am–6pm; entrance charge; tel: 65 51 46 01). The museum's collection is devoted to the writer's life, with manuscripts, and other personal belongings.

Denmark's foremost composer, Carl Nielsen *(see page 127)*, spent his early years in the city and the **Carl Nielsen Museet** (Claus Bergs Gade 11; June–Aug

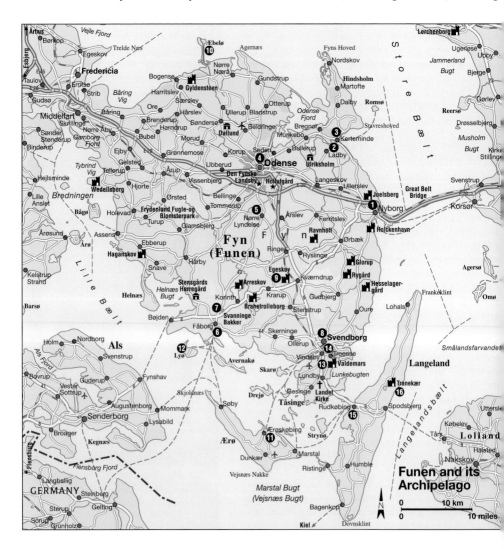

Fri–Sun noon–4pm; Sept–May Mon–Wed 2–5pm; free; tel: 65 51 46 01) is devoted both to his life and work and to that of his wife, Anne Marie Nielsen, a sculptor. His childhood home can be visited at **Nørre Lyndelse ❺** (May–Sept Tues–Sun 11am–3pm; entrance charge; tel: 65 51 46 01), 15 km (9 miles) south of Odense.

Few other cities have a river that is clean enough to offer amateur fishermen both sea trout and eel. This is an accomplishment for what was once a polluted industrial centre. Today, the quarter around the old factory buildings at Kongensgade and Vestergade has been revitalised and is a popular magnet for young people. The former textile mill, **Brandts Klædefabrik**, off Vestergade, is now a multipurpose cultural centre, complete with **Museet for Fotokunst** (Museum of Photographic Art); **Kunsthallen** art gallery, featuring a varied programme of exhibitions; **Danmarks Mediemuseum** (Danish Media Museum); and **Tidens Samling** (Time Collection) which follows daily life and fashion since 1900 (all Tues–Wed, Fri–Sun 10am–5pm, Thur noon–9pm; entrance charge), plus cafés, bars and concert halls.

Just south of Odense is a delightful spot, **Den Fynske Landsby** (Funen Village, Sejerskovvej 20; Apr–June and mid-Aug–mid-Oct Tues–Sun 10am–5pm, July–mid-Aug daily 10am–7pm, mid-Oct–March Sun and holidays only 11–3pm; entrance charge; tel: 65 51 46 01). It contains old farm buildings from different areas, with a vicarage, workshops, a windmill and water mill.

Tuneful Fåborg

Fåborg ❻ on south Funen is a peaceful little town where **Klokketårnet**, Europe's largest carillon, chimes out a hymn four times a day (mid-June–mid-Sept daily 11am–3pm). Other low-key attractions include **Fåborg Museum for Fynsk Kunst** (Grønnegade 75; Apr–Oct daily 10am–4pm; Nov–Mar Tues–Sun 11am–3pm; entrance charge; tel: 62 61 06 45), an art gallery featuring the "Funen artists" (1880–1920), including Peter Hansen, Fritz Syberg and Johannes Larsen, with sculptures by Kai Nielsen.

The heather-covered **Svanninge Bakker ❼**, about 10 km (6 miles) north of Fåborg, is a national park. Heading eastwards, **Svendborg ❽** is a beautiful market town and makes a good centre for touring. Along with Fåborg, it is the gateway to the southern islands.

The unmissable **Egeskov Slot ❾** (May–Sept daily 10am–5pm, closes later in summer; entrance charge; tel: 62 27 10 16), 14 km (9 miles) north of Svendborg, is one of Denmark's most famous historic sights, a moated castle set in magnificent baroque and Renaissance gardens. Egeskov means oak forest – legend says that an entire forest of the trees was felled around 1540 to form the piles the castle stands on.

The castle and grounds are filled with wonders, including a mysterious Wooden Man sculpture, the awesomely detailed doll's house **Titania's Palace**, three large, leafy **mazes**, a tree-top walk and six museums, including a **Veteranmuseum** (Veteran Motor Museum), containing a fine collection of vintage cars, aircraft and motor cycles.

Map on page 124

BELOW: book sale on Funen.

Map on page 124

TIP

Whether driving, cycling or walking, follow the "Daisy Routes" marked by a flower sign. These guide you past some of the most beautiful scenery in Funen.

BELOW: Egeskov Slot, built in the 16th century.

Along the west coast

From Fåborg, turn northwest to explore Funen's west coast. Around 15 km (9 miles) north from Assens on the road to **Middelfart**, a broad west-facing bay at **Tybrind Vig** is a site for underwater archaeology. North of Middelfart dramatic steep cliffs line the shore.

About 3 km (2 miles) east of **Bogense** is the castle of **Gyldensteen**, a late-Renaissance building with an impressive gatehouse (closed to the public). Here, Karen Blixen (pen name Isak Dinesen), author of *Out of Africa*, wrote some of her books during the German Occupation of Denmark in World War II. From Bogense, you can complete the Funen circle by touring along the sparsely populated north coast to the Hindsholm Peninsula and Kerteminde. At low tide you can walk to the island of **Æbelø** ⑩, an unspoilt landscape rich in wildlife.

To the islands

You could spend a lifetime trying to visit all the islands of the Funen Archipelago and still miss a few. Only 19 are inhabited permanently, and even the largest hold no more than a few thousand people. You can take day trips aboard wooden sailing ships or longer cruises through the archipelago. This is also an angler's paradise.

From Fåborg, it is just a short trip to the most beautiful island of all, **Ærø**. Hire a bike for the short cycle run from Søby to **Ærøskøbing** ⑪, the main town, and on to the old naval port of **Marstal**. Cycling is easy and the roads wind past fertile fields and thatched farmhouses, medieval churches and windmills. The American author, Temple Fielding, said that Ærøskøbing was one of the five places in the world one should see. Certainly, the cobbled streets with their brightly coloured houses almost seem like a film set.

From Fåborg, ferries also run to the smaller islands of **Avernakø** and **Lyø** ⑫; both have good inns.

Svendborg is the ferry port for the southern islands. The first island, reached by a narrow bridge, is **Tåsinge**, with some 5,000 inhabitants. **Valdemars Slot** ⑬ is one of Denmark's oldest privately owned castles, with a wonderful view over Svendborgsund (May–Aug daily 10am–5pm, until 6pm in July; Sept Tues–Sun 10am–5pm; entrance charge; tel: 62 22 61 06). It was built in 1640 by King Kristian IV for one of his sons, Prince Valdemar Kristian. Most interesting is the castle church, with an excellent restaurant beneath. Beyond the Tea Pavilion, mirrored in its own lake, is a tiny swimming beach beside Lunkebugten Bay. The loveliest village on Tåsinge is **Troense** ⑭. Watching the slim masts of the sailing boats gather in the harbour against a darkening sea is one of the pleasures of a Funen summer.

Langeland, literally "long land", is connected to Tåsinge by a bridge. H.C. Ørsted, the discoverer of electromagnetism, was born in the main town of **Rudkøbing** ⑮.

North at **Tranekær** ⑯ lies TICKON, a peaceful wooded sculpture park. To the south is fascinating **Langelandsfort** (May–Sept Mon–Fri 10am–5pm, Sat–Sun 11am–5pm; Mar–Apr until 4pm), a Cold-War listening station with cannons, bunkers, planes and a U-boat. To the south, **Ristinge** and **Bagenkop** both have excellent bathing beaches. ❑

ANDERSEN AND NIELSEN: FUNEN'S FAMOUS SONS

In the 19th century, two Funen boys, the storyteller Hans Christian Andersen and the the composer Carl Nielsen, set off to make their fortunes in the world

Two of Denmark's most noted literary and musical figures, Hans Christian Andersen and Carl Nielsen respectively, were born on the island of Funen.

At the height of his fame, the composer Carl Nielsen (1865–1931) told an audience that his mother had always said to him: "Don't forget that Hans Christian Andersen was a poor boy like you." There may have been something in the Funen air that inspired poor boys to rise to fame, but it is more likely that Nielsen was inspired by Andersen, 60 years his senior. Both came from humble homes, both left Odense to seek their fortune in Copenhagen.

Andersen (1805–75) was born in Odense and spent his childhood in a small half-timbered house in Munkemøllestræde, now a museum. Quite apart from his skill as a writer, Andersen had a good singing voice and gifts as an artist. At the age of 14 he set off to Copenhagen to attend the Royal Theatre School. The Theatre Board recognised his skills and he was found a place at a grammar school in Helsingør.

After school, Andersen travelled widely; *Shadow Picture of a Journey to the Harz Mountains and Saxony* (1831) was the result of his early adventures. Throughout his life he continued to write poems, novels and plays. His autobiographical novel, *The Improvisatore*, described the rise to fortune of a poor Italian boy. His early fairy tales, including *The Tinder Box* and *The Princess and the Pea* (1835), brought him immortality. In 1840 he met and fell in love with the singer Jenny Lind, "The Swedish Nightingale", though she always called him "brother". His fairy tale, *The Nightingale*, was inspired by her.

When he was made an honorary citizen of Odense in 1867, Andersen said it was "an honour greater than I had ever dreamt of".

Carl Nielsen was born in Nørre Lyndelse, where his childhood home is now a museum. His father was a folk musician and Carl played the violin. His earliest compositions, at the age of eight, were two dance tunes. Like Andersen, Nielsen wrote an autobiography, *My Childhood in Funen.*

At the Royal Theatre Orchestra in Copenhagen, where Nielsen became second violinist, the Norwegian conductor, Johan Svendsen, encouraged him to compose. At 25, Nielsen won a fellowship which allowed him to travel, and went to Dresden to steep himself in Wagner's ideas. Nielsen composed two operas: the dark drama, *Saul og David*, and a comic opera, *Maskarade*, along with symphonies and choral works, such as *Hymnus Amoris*. ❑

TOP LEFT AND RIGHT: composer Carl Nielsen.
ABOVE LEFT: Hans Christian Andersen.
RIGHT: actor Ejnar Hans Jensen plays Andersen.

JUTLAND

The dune-fringed shores of Jutland have captured the imagination of both painters and holiday-makers, while music lovers head for Århus, "the world's smallest big city"

Map on page 130

Jutland *(Jylland)* is the Danish peninsula that juts up above Germany, the "mainland" in this nation of islands. When Copenhageners talk about the provinces, they usually mean Jutland. With its rolling hills crisscrossed with rivers and creeks, patched with forests, crusted by sand dunes and scattered with palaces, Viking monuments and remains, Jutland is a land of contrasts.

Jutland's capital city is **Århus ❶**, a lively college town known for its music, theatre, ballet, art and cafés, as well as its fun Festival Week every autumn. Denmark's second-largest city – with a population of 300,000, only a fraction of Copenhagen's size – this harbour town is noted for its nearby forests, beaches and castles. The pointed spire of the **Domkirken** (Cathedral of St Clement; May–Sept Mon–Sat 9.30am–4pm; rest of year 10am–3pm; entrance charge to tower), is 93 metres (316 ft) high and offers a superb view from its belfry. Nearby are the winding, cobblestone streets of the Latin Quarter, with quirky boutiques and trendy cafés and restaurants. The AROS **Århus Kunstmuseum** (Museum of Art; Tues, Thur–Sun 10am–5pm, Wed until 10pm; entrance charge; tel: 87 30 66 00) gives an overview of Danish art from the 18th century to the present. The **City Hall** (Rådhus) was built in 1941 and designed by Arne Jacobsen, one of Denmark's most notable architects and designers.

Den Gamle By (The Old Town; open all year; times vary; entrance charge; tel: 86 12 31 88) is an open-air, national museum of culture and history, with reconstructions of 75 Danish town buildings. From the entrance on, the museum is a sensory overload in an environment that feels genuinely historic – with merchant and artisan houses and workshops, gardens, shops, stalls, streets and alleys.

One of the best museum exhibits in Denmark is the 2,000-year-old Grauballe Man at the **Moesgård Museum** (Museum of Prehistory; Apr–Sept daily 10am–5pm, Oct–Mar Tues–Sun 10am–4pm; entrance charge; tel: 89 42 11 00) at **Moesgård ❷**, 8 km (5 miles) south of Århus. To stand centimetres from the twisted body of this Iron-Age man, found perfectly preserved in a peat bog in 1952, is a chilling experience.

The ruins of the **Kalø Slot ❸**, built in 1313, are situated on a small island north of Århus bay, linked to the mainland by a causeway. The nearby hills of **Mols Bjerge ❹**, where Viking relics abound in beautiful nature, are well worth a visit. Several artists have set up shop on the pretty Djursland peninsula.

Island haven

West of Mols Bjerge is the immaculate town of **Ebeltoft ❺**, with its small, unaltered town hall from 1789. The island of **Samsø** can be seen from here, but it must be reached by ferry from **Hou ❻**, 25 km

LEFT: dappled forest of East Jutland.
BELOW: beach life, West Jutland.

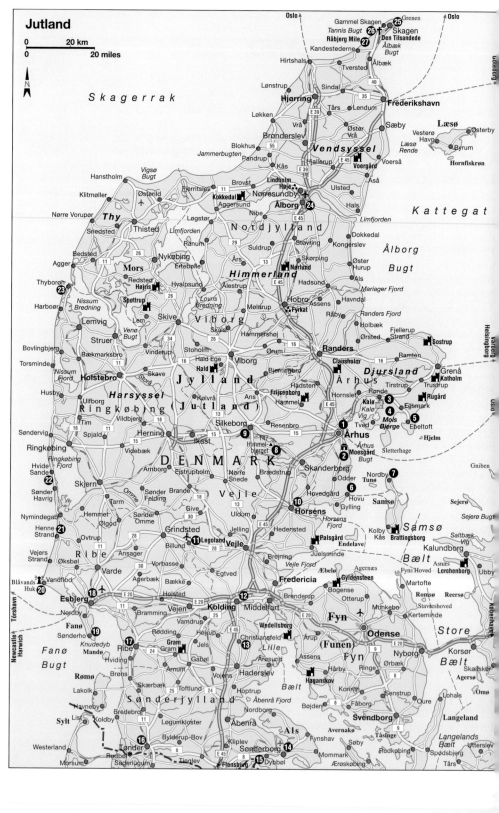

(15 miles) south of Århus. A haven for artists, farmers and nature lovers alike, Samsø is renowned for its new potatoes and cheese. **Nordby ❼**, on the northern tip, contains a wealth of colourful, crossbeam houses, as well as small art galleries. Also worth a visit in Nordby is **Samsø Labyrinten**, the world's largest permanent maze (Easter and mid-July–Aug daily 11am–5pm; Sat only Apr–June and Sept–early Oct; entrance charge; tel: 86 59 66 59 for times). Its 5 km (3 miles) of passages wind through a dense fir forest covering 6 hectares (15 acres). In the south of the island, **Brundby Rock Hotel**, owned by a group of Danish rock musicians, is a festive place to have dinner and hear live music.

Lake district

A series of lakes snake through forested hills west of Århus, and a fun way to see them is from the paddle steamer *MS Hjejlen* (May–Sept daily 9am–5pm; Oct–Apr Mon–Fri 9am–5pm; tel: 86 82 07 66; www.hjejlen.com), which has carried passengers from Ry to Silkeborg since 1861. For a bird's-eye view, climb **Himmelbjerget ❽** (Sky Mountain), at 147 metres (482 ft) one of Denmark's highest "mountains". The nearby town of **Silkeborg ❾** features the **Silkeborg Kunstmuseum** (Silkeborg Museum of Art; Apr–Oct Tues–Sun 10am–5pm; Nov–Mar Tues–Fri noon– 4pm, Sat–Sun 10am–5pm; entrance charge; tel: 86 82 53 88), built around the glorious, playful work of the painter Asger Jorn and others from the 20th-century CoBrA group. **Silkeborg Museum** (May–Oct 10am–5pm, Nov–Apr Sat–Sun noon–4pm; entrance charge; tel: 86 82 14 99) houses one of Denmark's best-known bog bodies, Tollund Man.

Further south, historical **Horsens ❿** hosts an annual Middle Ages Festival in the autumn, which is highly recommended (www.middelalderfestival.dk). At **Billund**, 50 km (31 miles) southwest of Horsens, 1.5 million people a year visit **Legoland ⓫** (May–June weekdays 10am–6pm, weekends until 8pm; July–mid-Aug 10am–9pm; Mar, Apr, Sept and Oct hours vary; entrance charge; tel: 75 33 13 33), coming to marvel at the miniature world created from more than 45 million of the studded plastic bricks.

A good salami

South Jutland has some of the most patriotic Danes in the country, particularly the generations who remember the area when it was officially part of Germany's Schleswig duchy from 1864 to 1920. **Kolding ⓬** was a border town on the Danish side at the time, and historical sights abound. Particularly of interest are the remains of **Koldinghus Slot** (daily 10am–5pm; entrance charge; tel: 76 33 81 00), a castle built in 1268, and the **Kunstmuseet Trapholt** (Trapolt Museum of Art; Tues–Sun 10am–5pm, until 8pm on Wed; entrance charge; tel: 76 30 05 30) with a fine collection of modern art.

Driving south 15 km (9 miles), the Danish Moravian town of **Christiansfeld ⓭** is famous for its scrumptious honey cakes. Further south, close to the German border, **Sønderborg ⓮** is a striking town on **Als Island**, with a colourful harbour and the mighty **Sønderborg Slot** (May–Sept daily 10am–5pm; Oct–Mar Tues–Sun 1–4pm; Apr Tues–Sun 10am–4pm; tel: 74 42 25 39), a

Map on page 130

Miniature world: Lego was developed by Ole Kirk Christiansen and his family in Billund in 1949.

BELOW: timber-framed cottages, Ebeltoft.

TIP

A good place to try South Jutland's local speciality of "marsh sausage" is the Rudbøl Grænsekro, an inn in the village of Rudbøl (southwest of Tønder) that has been serving this delicacy since 1791.

fortress built around 1100. Provincial Sønderborg happens to have one of the best cafés in Denmark, **Café Druen**, not far from the castle. South Jutland is known for its meats – particularly salamis. Stop at a local butcher to try a beer sausage.

Just to the west, **Dybbøl** ⑮ was a key battlefield in the 1864 war with Germany: the Danish army suffered a huge defeat. **Dybbøl Mill**, restored and painted white, is now a national historic park and its museum dedicated to the battle is open to the public (mid-Apr–mid-Oct daily 10am–5pm; entrance charge; tel: 74 48 69 91).

On the western side of South Jutland is **Tønder** ⑯, a lace-making centre in the 17th century, documented in **Tønder Museum** (June–Aug daily 10am–5pm; Sept–May closed Mon; entrance charge; tel: 74 72 89 89). Tønder has attractive 17th- and 18th-century houses, many with distinctive painted doorways. At **Møgeltønder**, 3 km (2 miles) to the west, the village street is lined with lime trees. **Schackenborg Slot** is home to Prince Joachim (fourth in succession) and his second wife Princess Marie, who were married in May 2008.

Night watchmen

Ribe ⑰, built around its 12th-century cathedral, ranks high on the list of historic centres in Scandinavia. Its brick and half-timbered houses, courtyards and *kroer* (inns) are much as they were hundreds of years ago.

Ribe Domkirke (Cathedral; Nov–Mar daily 11am–3pm, Sun noon–3pm; Apr and Oct daily 11am–4pm; May–Sept daily 10am–5pm, Sun noon–4pm; free; tel: 75 42 06 19) stands on the site of one of Denmark's earliest wooden churches, built around AD 860. The "Cat Head Door" was said to be the entrance for the Devil. The choir has been stunningly decorated by CoBrA artist Carl-Henning Petersen. There are splendid views from the tower (July–mid-Aug; entrance charge).

BELOW: the Jelling Stones, *circa* 983.

HARALD BLUETOOTH WAS HERE

Viking sights abound in Jutland. **Lindholm Høje** (Easter–Oct daily 10am–5pm; Nov–Easter Tues and Sun 11am–4pm; entrance charge; tel: 99 31 74 40), just north of Ålborg, is a necropolis with 700 graves, a reconstructed village from the early Iron Age and Viking times, and a museum. Many of the graves are in the shape of Viking ships.

Elsewhere, near Hobro, is the Viking fort of **Fyrkat**. Four earth fortifications once enclosed 16 large houses on the site, and one of these longhouses has been reconstructed. Finds from Fyrkat are on display in **Hobro Museum** (May–Sept 11am–4pm; entrance charge; tel: 98 51 05 55). On the Mols peninsula near Århus is the **Poskjær Stenhus** barrow, which lies along the road from Agri to Grønfeld.

A memorial referred to as Denmark's "birth certificate" can be found in Jelling. The **Jelling Stones** (Jellingstenene) are covered with runic script that King Harald Bluetooth had carved over 1,000 years ago to proclaim his conversion to Christianity, and to honour his parents, King Gorm the Old and Queen Thyra Danebrod, who were buried in the mounds beside Jelling town church. For a flavour of life in Viking times, re-enactments, including battles and blood oaths, can be experienced at Moesgård, and in Jels in July.

Ribe continues the Middle Ages tradition of night watchmen. On summer evenings at 8pm and 10pm, the watchman walks around singing the traditional songs that once told the people that they could sleep soundly, all was well.

Map on page 130

Western shores

West Jutland has a sense of space and time different from the rest of the region. In winter, the weather can be rugged, with storms blowing in off a turbulent North Sea. In summer this part of Denmark, with its sandy beaches, is popular with holiday-makers.

Esbjerg ⑱ is the biggest port town on the coast, the main gateway for ferries from Britain. A 20-minute ferry ride away is the island of **Fanø**, a major ship-building centre in the 18th and 19th centuries. **Sønderho** ⑲ village in the south of the island has colourful thatch-roofed cottages, an inn and Seamen's Church (1782). The island is characteristic for West Jutland: a superb stretch of white sandy beach, dunes, heath and forest.

Back on the Jutland coast, 30 km (19 miles) northwest, is **Blåvands Huk** ⑳ lighthouse, a popular holiday spot with a nature reserve nearby. At the beach during low tide if you see people standing in water up to their ankles staring down, don't be alarmed. They are hunting for nuggets of amber, a golden-coloured petrified tree resin that frequently washes ashore here.

The night watchman of Ribe who recounts the town's history in song on his rounds.

Some 25 km (16 miles) to the north, at **Henne** ㉑, Denmark's television chef Hans Beck Thomsen runs the **Henne Kirkeby Kro** (tel: 75 25 54 00) in summer.

A narrow strip of land runs north from Nymindegab to Søndervig, separating the sea from **Ringkøbing Fjord**, a broad, shallow, saltwater "lake". Driving north towards the fishing village of **Hvide Sande** ㉒, the crashing waves from the North

BELOW: re-enacting the Middle Ages.

Map on page 130

Shell-covered house at Thyborøn.

BELOW: church in the sands. **RIGHT:** Hennes Strand.

Sea can be heard but are hidden from view by tall sand dunes. No matter how many times one walks to the top of these dunes, the experience is breathtaking.

From here to the northern tip at Skagen, the scenery is similar, broken by several attractive fishing villages and bathing resorts. At **Thyborøn** ㉓, a native has decorated a house with shells, covering all surfaces, inside and out. Take the 10-minute ferry from here across the Limfjorden to Vendsyssel, north Jutland.

At its advantageous location for trade on the Limfjorden, **Ålborg** ㉔ – Denmark's fourth-largest city with a population of 195,000 – is full of historical buildings, castles and Viking monuments. The best-known building in town is the opulent six-storey **Stenhus** (Stone House) on Østerågade, built in 1624 by a merchant, Jens Bang, to show off his wealth. Bang was annoyed that he had never become a town councillor; on the south facade of Stenhus is a carving of him sticking his tongue out at the town hall across the street. Also across the street lies the tourist information centre (tel: 99 31 75 00). The town's main entertainment artery is **Jomfru Ane Gade**, lined with restaurants and bars in courtyards and half-timbered buildings. This is the place to try Ålborg's most famous product: *aquavit*, the strong aperitif flavoured with caraway seeds that accompanies the traditional Danish *smørrebrød* (open-faced sandwiches).

Nordic light

Situated on a narrow piece of land with the North Sea on one side and the Baltic on the other, **Skagen** ㉕ has a magical quality to it. The air shimmers with a certain light that must be experienced in person to believe it. This was an irresistible lure to the Skagen painters, who made it their home in the second half of the 19th century, with Brøndums Hotel as their rallying ground. Works by artists from this period, such as Anna and Michael Ancher, P.S. Krøyer, and Viggo Johansen can be seen in **Skagens Museum** (May–Aug daily 10am–5pm, until 9pm Wed; Sept–Apr Tues–Sun 10am–5pm; entrance charge; tel: 98 44 64 44), and **Ancher's Hus** (Anchers House; Apr and Oct Sat–Thur 11am–3pm; May–Sept daily 10am–5pm; Nov and Feb–Mar Sat 11am–3pm; entrance charge; tel: 98 44 30 09), bought by the Anchers in 1884. The artists' colony still lives on in Skagen. A few kilometres southwest is **Gammel Skagen** (Old Skagen), a cosmopolitan resort known for its sun-yellow homes with red-tiled roofs and its gourmet fish restaurants.

Just west of Gammel Skagen, Den Tilsandede Kirke ㉖ (the Sand Covered Church; June–Aug daily 11am–5pm; entrance charge; tel: 98 44 43 71) peeps out of the dunes with only its steeple visible. (Another church is on the way to a more dramatic end at **Lønstrup** on the west coast. Here, the powerful waves are eating away at the cliffs under Mårup Kirke, starting with its cemetery.) To see migrating dunes up close, you need go no further than **Råbjerg Mile** ㉗, 10 km (6 miles) south of Skagen. Pushed by the wind and sea, the dunes travel as much as 20 metres (65 ft) every year.

For a thrilling experience of nature, go to **Grenen**, 5 km (3 miles) north of Skagen, Denmark's northernmost point. At the tip, you can actually see the North and Baltic seas crash into each other. ☐

GREENLAND

Map on page 138

In spring and summer when the ice retreats and the temperature rises, Greenland's spectacular landscape becomes accessible for some of the most adventurous travellers

The world's largest island is a place of stunning natural beauty, dramatic weather and fascinating culture. Greenland (www.greenland.com), like the Faroe Islands, is a former Danish colony that has become a member of the kingdom, but with its own home-rule government.

Greenland is like no other place. Its vast Arctic solitude is profound and its silence almost consumes you. Here, where the North Atlantic meets the Arctic Ocean, is the cleanest environment in the world, and measurably the oldest. Where else can you sip a drink cooled by a 1,000-year-old ice cube?

Greenland is called Kalaallit Nunaat (the land of the people) by its own people. They number only about 50,000 (plus an additional 7,000 Danes) in an area of 2,175,600 sq km (840,000 sq miles). The distance north to south is 2,670 km (1,655 miles), and the widest part east to west is 1,000 km (620 miles). Its closest neighbour is Canada. The capital is **Nuuk** ❶ (Godthåb) on the west coast.

Greenlanders are Inuit and live in small towns around the coasts, mainly on the milder western side. Most of these people still earn their livelihoods by fishing and hunting. But thanks to its long association with Denmark, Greenland has a modern infrastructure and burgeoning tourist industry.

More than four-fifths of the country lies under 3 km (2 miles) of pack ice, which rate of melting has increased recently; but the southern coastal regions, especially to the west, are green and mild during late spring and summer. Daytime temperatures here can climb to a balmy 21°C (70°F) or more, but northerly winds in winter can make the mercury plunge to a bone-cracking -32°C (-25°F). Conditions in spring and summer make for excellent hiking and camping, not to mention some of the best fishing anywhere.

LEFT: Greenland coastal settlement. **BELOW:** fisherman's hideaway.

Adventure tours

The classic way of touring Greenland is by dog sled. You can hire a team and driver for a short sightseeing tour or for a longer journey. The season is usually from late February to May. In western Greenland it is possible to arrange trips from **Sisimiut** ❷, **Qeqertarsuaq** ❸ (Disko Island) and points further north. On the barely populated east coast, you can dog sled from **Tasiilaq** ❹ and **Ittoqqortoormiit** ❺.

A classic, though physically demanding, dog sled tour is the eight-day trip between Sisimiut and **Kangerlussuaq** ❻ at Søndre Strømfjord on the west coast, which is best done in March, April or early May. The route takes you through the vast and beautiful landscapes of mid-Greenland, across frozen lakes and over hilly terrain. You sleep in hunting huts or tents.

Boat tours also offer breathtaking scenery and wildlife. Summer cruises to towns along the east and west coasts take you through sparkling seas alive with

Arctic foxes are common along Greenland's coastal areas; other species found in the harsh environment include polar bear, musk ox and caribou.

seals and other marine life, even whales. You can disembark at harbours and settlements for hiking trips, or dog sled tours in season. Between ports, you sail past icebergs and glaciers. On land you might see reindeer and musk oxen, and polar bears have been spotted. Bird life is not abundant in Greenland, but you can encounter Arctic terns, ravens, peregrine falcons and eagles.

Helicopters are an important, often essential, means of transport here. Chopper tours are a breathtakingly beautiful way to travel around Greenland.

A novel way of exploring Greenland's nature is aboard a traditional Inuit vessel – the kayak. Although full-on sea-kayaking here is only for experts, beginners can explore sheltered fjord waters from many towns.

This vast, half-frozen island draws an increasing number of anglers each year. They come to fish for trout and Arctic char in the lowland lakes, rivers and streams. Off the coast and sometimes through ice, they reel in Greenland halibut, Norway haddock, catfish and cod. Fishing licences are required.

Among the spectacular natural phenomena in Greenland are the Northern Lights and the Midnight Sun. The *aurora borealis* occurs all year long but is only visible in a clear night sky in autumn and winter. These ethereal lights can appear as colourful curtains, veins of silk ribbon, or as ghostly souls flying to heaven. In summer, the midnight sun keeps the night sky blue.

Ruled by the weather

Some cruise ships include Nuuk on their itineraries; otherwise the only way to travel to Greeland is by air, from Copenhagen; Keflavik, Iceland; Baltimore, US; or Ottawa, Canada. Once in Greenland, sailing is an option year-round, but schedules are highly dependent on the weather. The same applies to air services.

BELOW: dressed in traditional costume.

In a climate which changes from hot sun and clear skies to a deluge of rain in a moment, the weather decides whether it's possible to keep to a plan made the day before. Many a visitor has been forced to "overnight" at **Narsarsuaq ⑦** in the south because aircraft couldn't land.

Most towns in Greenland have modern hotels in various categories of comfort. These and the local tourist offices are the best places to book excursions. The more footloose visitor may prefer a hostel, seaman's home, or a cabin. Camping sites are appearing and tent-roughing is permitted virtually everywhere, so long as campers observe the rules of nature and common politeness.

Fruits of the sea

Heart disease is a rarity for Greenlanders, thanks to a diet based heavily on the sea. Greenlandic specialities also include fowl, game and berries. The national dish is *svaassat*, seal meat cooked with rice and onions. A particular delicacy is *mattak*, pieces of whale skin with a thin layer of blubber. Slow chewing brings out its nutty flavour. If your taste buds are more "Western", try musk ox steak or Greenlandic lamb cutlets, considered to be some of the best in the world. The reindeer venison and honey-roasted eider duck breast aren't bad, either. Then, of course, there is any kind of fresh Greenlandic seafood. This includes trout, salmon, Atlantic halibut, redfish, whale, bay scallops and the world-renowned large Greenlandic prawns. Smoked fish is a traditional lunch.

In summer, families take to the highlands to cook in traditional Greenlandic style. This involves building a raised, flat stone base, gathering heather and branches for a fire and placing a pot or a piece of meat directly on the stone. Soon comes the delicious aroma of heather smoke and cooking fish or seal meat. ❏

Map on page 138

TIP

If you travel to Greenland in summer, it's wise to take shorts, gloves, and everything in between, plus waterproof clothing. Light waterproof hiking boots are the most appropriate footwear.

BELOW: Greenland's icy waters.

THE FAROE ISLANDS

Map on page 142

The fruits of the sea have brought prosperity to the far-flung Faroe Islands. Visitors are attracted by the natural beauty and remarkable bird life

The remote Faroe Islands lie far to the north of mainland Europe, halfway between Iceland and the Shetland Islands. The sailing distance between this self-governing Danish outpost and Copenhagen is around 1,500 km (900 miles). The sea is serious business here, and nothing shows that more clearly than **Tórshavn's** ❶ harbour. It is stuffed with boats of all kinds – visiting ships, inter-island ferries, sailing boats and other pleasure craft and, most numerous of all, the fishing boats which disgorge their cargoes at one of the big fish processors scattered around the islands' coasts.

The fishing fleet is one of the most modern in Europe. Fish products make up 94 percent of the country's export earnings and the not-to-be missed tang of fish permeating the harbour is also the smell of money.

Although the Faroe islanders are prosperous with a high standard of living – for example, they claim to have more televisions per head than anyone else in the world – everything is relative. Only 48,668 live on the 17 inhabited islands – a dozen more are home only to the huge colonies of birds. Much of the surface area is virtually bare rock, and only a few areas are habitable. As though to contrast with the muted blues, greens and greys of rocks, sea and hills, modern Faroese favour brightly painted houses. Traditional, living, green turf roofs are becoming popular once more.

Warm and wet

Far north as the islands are and feel, the Gulf Stream keeps the climate mild and moist. In the coldest month the average temperature is around 3°C (37°F), although wind chill makes it feel much colder. In the warmest, it reaches only 11°C (52°F). The weather is very changeable; one minute the sun is warm against the back, the next there is driving rain and mist.

No self-respecting tree could grow to a reasonable height against the islands' constant wind – though, as a joke, the Faroese call the small copse in the shelter of the park in the capital, Tórshavn, the islands' "forest".

The islands' name in Faroese, Føroyar, means "sheep islands" – even today, there are around 20,000 more sheep than people, and lamb is a basic staple. Arable land is extremely limited. Small kitchen gardens have robust plants, leeks, cabbages, carrots. Outside, people hang fish and lamb to dry in the wind.

On the trail

The inland trails cover a wonderland of stunning terrain. Footpaths crisscross all the islands and were originally the main routes between settlements. Most of the paths are marked by cairns, but some of them are not regularly maintained, and it's imperative to carry a map and compass. Campers may pitch tents

LEFT: the turf-roofed church at Saksun set against the green Faroese landscape.
BELOW: fishing boats at anchor in Tórshavn harbour.

The puffin is a Faroese delicacy, caught during the open season in July. The meat has a distinctively tangy flavour.

virtually anywhere, but many a tent has been swept into the North Atlantic by powerful gusts, so remember to find a sheltered spot and weight the tent down.

Bird cliffs

Although the Faroe Islands have few mammals, the bird life is outstanding. The towering faces of the stacks and cliffs are home to thousands of sea birds and in the sheltered pools live phalaropes and red-throated divers. The stiff-winged flight of the fulmars follows the boats without ever tiring and clown-faced puffins gaze solemnly from cliff burrows. The Faroese national bird, the black and white oystercatcher, calls worriedly from every hillock.

For the seafaring adventurer, boat operators sail from **Vestmanna** on an excursion of the islands to view the **Vestmannabjørgini ❷**, or **Enniberg** bird cliffs. The restored sloop, *Urðardrangur*, takes visitors on a tour of the islands, sailing into fjords and grottoes; and the island of **Mykines ❸** attracts bird-watchers from many lands.

Anglers may find great challenges in the brooks and lochs which hold trout and salmon. The season extends from 1 May to 31 August. Contact the tourist office in Tórshavn for permits and details (tel: 30 24 25; www.visit-faroes.com).

Early settlers

The islands' first substantial settlers came from Norway in the 9th century. Even before that time, an early township, **Kirkjubøur ❹**, had been the centre of life for a group of Irish friars who colonised the islands around the 8th century. In 1380, as Norway came under Danish rule, the islands, too, became part of Denmark and, when the union dissolved in 1814, the Faroes continued as a

BELOW: fish hanging up to dry – a common sight on the Faroe Islands.

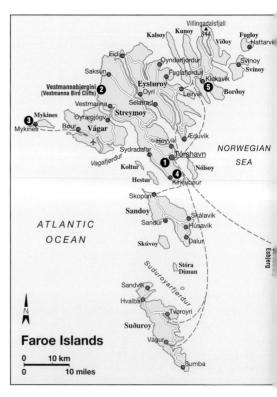

Faroe Islands

0   10 km
0   10 miles

Danish county. The present system of Home Rule dates from 1948 and the Faroe Islands also send two representatives to the Danish Parliament.

The islands' long seafaring history is traced in the **Fornminnissavn** (National Museum; mid-May–mid-Sept Mon–Fri 10am–5pm, Sat–Sun 2–5pm; entrance charge) at Hoyvik, 2 km (1 mile) north of Tórshavn, and also in the **Norđoya Fornminnissavn** (North Islands Museum; mid-May–mid-Sept daily 1–4pm) at **Klaksvík ❺**, on **Borđoy** island.

Map
on page
142

Dancing with the Faroese

The Faroese are proud of the rich culture and traditions of their islands, where the language, costumes and customs are kept very much alive. On festive occasions everyone joins in the Faroese chain dance, a slow, hypnotic dance accompanied by chanting. An older tradition that is still practised is the "door schnapps". Visitors are greeted at the door with a horn full of schnapps *(akvavit)* and everybody takes a sip before entering.

When visiting the **Roykstovan** (Smoke Room; June–Aug Mon–Sat 10am–5.30pm, Sun 2–5pm) in Kirkjubøur, the first order of the day is a nip from the horn. The building is allegedly the oldest wooden structure in the world, built from logs that were towed from Norway.

In the summer months a series of events encompassing literature, music, theatre and, of course, chain dancing – known as the **Faroese Cultural Evening** – is held on the island of **Eysturoy** and at Tórshavn. In late June and July the **Summartónar Music Festival** is staged at venues around the islands. The **Tórshavnar Jazz, Folk and Blues Festival** is a four-day event held from the end of July to early August, and the **Folk Music Festival** takes place in mid-July in Tórshavn. ❑

 TIP

For the thirsty, Faroe is not the easiest place to find a drink. Alcoholic beverages are sold only at state-run monopoly stores *(Rúsdrekkasøla Landsins)*. Hotels generally have fully stocked bars, as do restaurants.

BELOW: stacking hay Faroese-style.

NORWAY

*Breathtaking scenery, historic sights and modern cities
are the big attractions for the traveller to Norway*

Norway is a land of contrasts: its landscape is both beautiful and brutal, hospitable and hostile; barren rock submits to soft fertile plains; majestic mountains tower above mysterious fjords; harsh winters are relieved by glorious summers; and long polar nights give way to the radiant Midnight Sun. It is one of Europe's oldest civilisations but only became an independent nation in 1905. The Norwegians themselves have adapted rather quickly – the lusty Vikings have turned into global peacemakers. Norway has both urban excitement and rural tranquillity: shopping malls and Mercedes rub shoulders with compass and rucksack; hi-technology parallels steadfast tradition.

A thriving offshore oil industry has brought prosperity, and as a consequence, social habits are changing rapidly, though, in a society where the divorce rate is high and cohabitation the norm, the home and family still remain important. Murray's *Handbook for Travellers in Norway* described the Norwegians in 1874 thus: "Great patriotism and hospitality are two of the leading characteristics of the Norwegians; they are often cold and reserved, and combine great simplicity of manner with firmness and kindness. 'Deeds, not words' is their motto." Today, little has changed.

Norway is a long narrow strip of a country, stretching north from mainland Europe far into the Arctic. The ancient capital of Trondheim is 500 km (350 miles) from the modern capital of Oslo, yet only a quarter of the way up the country's jagged coast. The southern coast is as far from Monaco as it is from the Nordkapp (North Cape), and Norway's northernmost outpost, the islands of Svalbard (Spitsbergen), are hundreds of kilometres further still. With a population of less than 5 million, Norway has, above all else, space.

Yet travel is not difficult. From early times, the Norwegians were magnificent sailors, and this old way of travel continues today through the Hurtigruten coastal steamers and other ferries that link coastal communities. The Gulf Stream warms the western coastline so that the seas are ice-free all the year round. On land, the Norwegians have achieved the seemingly impossible, connecting even the most isolated settlements by building railways, roads and bridges across their fjords and by tunnelling deep into mountains and under the sea. Oslo, Stavanger, Bergen, Trondheim and Tromsø are small manageable cities that make good use of the surrounding countryside.

Norwegians are an outdoor people, and Norway a country where inhabitants and visitors alike can make the most of limitless space for walking, skiing, touring and just breathing in the clear air. ❑

PRECEDING PAGES: rocky outline of the Lofoten Islands; the reindeer reigns supreme in the far north; Art Nouveau architecture in the fishing town of Ålesund. **LEFT:** intrepid settlers built their homes in the most secluded spots.

THE NORWEGIANS

Forget the stereotypical image of a cool Scandinavian, visitors to Norway can be assured of a warm and friendly welcome

Even to their nearest neighbours in Scandinavia, the Norwegians are a bit of a conundrum. To visitors from further afield they offer so many, often conflicting, faces that many leave Norway feeling they haven't even come close to understanding the people.

They can be cool almost to the point of rudeness when you first meet them, but once they've got to know you a little their warmth and hospitality are unmistakable. They are slow to offer opinions but when they do their views are forthright. They pride themselves on their internationalism and yet can be incredibly inward looking. They have strong cultural and economic links with the rest of Europe but stubbornly insist on staying outside the European Union. Where many people have national pride, for the Norwegians it's a passion. Their way is the best in just about everything and if the rest of the world hasn't noticed, well too bad.

One Hans Christian Andersen character proclaims: "I'm a Norwegian. And when I say I'm Norwegian, I think I've said enough. I'm as firm in my foundations as the ancient mountains of old Norway… It thrills me to the marrow to think what I am, and let my thoughts ring out in words of granite."

Andersen was a Dane, and he was teasing the Norwegians, as their Scandinavian neighbours are still apt to do.

Many people put this self-reliance down to history and to resentment over centuries of foreign rule and neighbourly condescension. Others use one word to explain it: oil. The Norwegians can afford to go it alone and say a polite *"nei takk"* ("no thanks") to the advice of outsiders.

Proud self-reliance

Historically, Norway is one the oldest nations in Europe, if not the oldest. Its people can trace an unbroken line of descent from those who inhabited the area in prehistoric times.

During the era of the Vikings (*circa* 800–1050), Norway controlled an enormous territory from Russia to the British Isles, and the common European tongue was Old Norse. Yet today's Norway was reconstituted as late as 1905 when the union with Sweden was finally dissolved. The dominance of Old Norse may

NORWAY: THE ESSENTIALS

Population 4.7 million, including 20,000 Sami.
Capital Oslo (pop. just over 560,000).
Notable towns Bergen, Stavanger, Trondheim, Tromsø.
Climate Afternoon temperatures in January are around −2°C (28°F), but lower in the north; July, 20°C (68°F).
Top museums Vikingskipshuset, Nasjonalgalleriet, Oslo.
Historic sights Gamle Bergen; Trondheim Cathedral; Røros; stave churches including Borgund and Heddal.
Natural wonders Fjord coastline; Preikestolen (Pulpit Rock); Lofoten Islands; North Cape; Jostedalsbreen glacier.
Outdoor activities Water sports, hiking, skiing, fishing.
Tourist information www.visitnorway.com

LEFT: a warm welcome awaits visitors to Norway.
RIGHT: a Sami woman in traditional dress, decorated with colourful ribbons and exquisite pendants.

have gone but today's Norwegians have regained their pride.

World War II, and the Nazi occupation, was a massive shock to the Norwegian psyche. Still today there's a deep-felt anger against the supposedly neutral Swedes for permitting the transit of German troops into Norway. After the war, the Norwegians realised with some reluctance that strategically they had no choice but to seek the protection of others. So they signed up to NATO, not least as protection against Russia, another unreliable neighbour in the north. But they turned their backs on the European Union. The importance of fishing and farming

and the security of the oil revenues meant that economically they preferred to go it alone.

At times it seems that the enthusiasm of so many Norwegians to participate in commercial whaling has less to do with its value as an industry and more to do with a hatred of being told what to do by the international community.

It's too easy, however, to equate this self-reliance with xenophobia. Norwegians don't fear or dislike foreigners. Their foreign aid budget is usually the highest per capita of developed nations and they play a role on the world stage, particularly in the field of conflict resolution, that is impressive for a country of less than five million people.

Home comforts

Hospitality is second nature to a Norwegian, whether he or she lives in Oslo or in the remotest corner of Finnmark. If you're planning to visit people at home be prepared – there's a lot of coffee to be drunk and usually cakes to be eaten.

Traditionally the host would light a candle as the guest arrived. It still happens, though not so religiously these days, and probably harks back to the days when, compounded by the long hours of winter darkness, houses shuttered against the cold were rather gloomy. The food will be plentiful and wholesome; your host will expect nothing in return except some appreciative comments about the welcome and maybe the décor.

Thanks to all that oil, and a very generous social security system, there is relatively little poverty in Norway. But nor are they at all ostentatious about their wealth and, especially in rural areas, life can still be very simple.

The more enigmatic aspects of the Norwegian character – including the Nordic gloom which can descend after a drink too many – have been famously scrutinised by native Norwegian, Henrik Ibsen. He was brought up in small communities and, during a long exile, turned his critical eye on the experience. One of the themes running through Ibsen's work is the double-edged nature of life in such a community: mutual support in adversity weighed against a suffocating lack of privacy at other times.

The lesser-known, Danish/Norwegian Aksel Sandemose wrote Ten Commandments for Village Life in a fictional novel about a town called Jante, the essence being humility bordering on self-abasement. They included: "You must not think that you are worth anything; you must not think that you are better than anyone else; you must not think yourself capable of anything worthwhile; and you must not think that you are in any way exceptional." Scandinavians today are still guided by this fictional Jante law (janteloven).

Land of many dialects

The essentially rural nature of so much of Norway has compounded one of their thorniest problems, language. The issue has split the country for over a century. Throwing off the Danish dominated bokmål (book language) was crucial to the independence activists of the 19th century. Unfortunately there was no Norwegian alternative on offer, just a variety of often very divergent dialects. Various attempts were made to bring these together into a truly national language known as *nynorsk* (new Norwegian) but these were never more than a partial success and even now there are huge regional variations in the spoken tongue.

Most Norwegians speak English extremely well and are more than happy to do so. Long before the French, for example, they realised it was taking national pride too far to deny the pre-eminence of English. Indeed many an urbanite will claim to find it much eas-

THE DOOMSDAY VAULT

In February 2008, the remote Spitsbergen Global Seed Bank officially opened. Built to be war and disaster proof, it acts as a living library of all known varieties of the world's crops.

which were easier to cross in winter on skis than in summer on foot, they effectively lived in worlds apart. Families managed on their own, a resourcefulness which still runs in the blood. It is not unknown for young couples living in Oslo today to solicit the help of a few friends to build their first home with their own hands.

Whether it's the outdoor life or all the fish in the diet, Norwegians enjoy amazing longevity. They manage to look remarkably healthy all their lives, and the octo-

ier to understand a foreigner speaking English than one of their own compatriots speaking in their regional dialect.

Worlds apart

Norway's geography and its sparse population have entrenched cultural and economic fragmentation too. Rural lives depended on agriculture, and the land was too poor to support more than a family or two in a single valley. Separated from their neighbours by mountains,

genarian grandmother whizzing by on skis is not entirely a myth. Yet one more reason why they feel rather pleased with themselves.

The Swedish king who reluctantly oversaw Norway's independence predicted that bureaucratic incompetence would soon have Norwegians begging to be returned to the fold. That, of course, never happened and modern Norway is a strong, successful socialist state. But they've never forgiven the patronising attitude of their eastern neighbours.

So, if even now they're reluctant to admit that they're capable of making a mistake, it may just be that they're still trying to prove that Swedish king wrong. ❏

LEFT: conscripts undergoing winter training in the far north of Norway.
ABOVE: rural life.

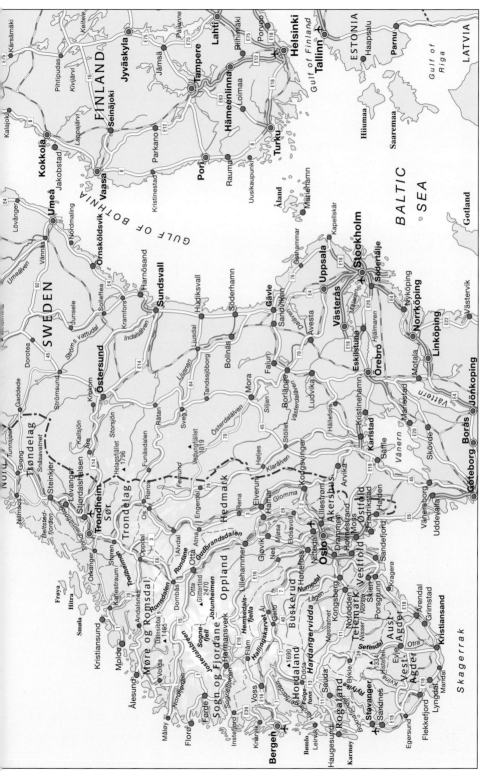

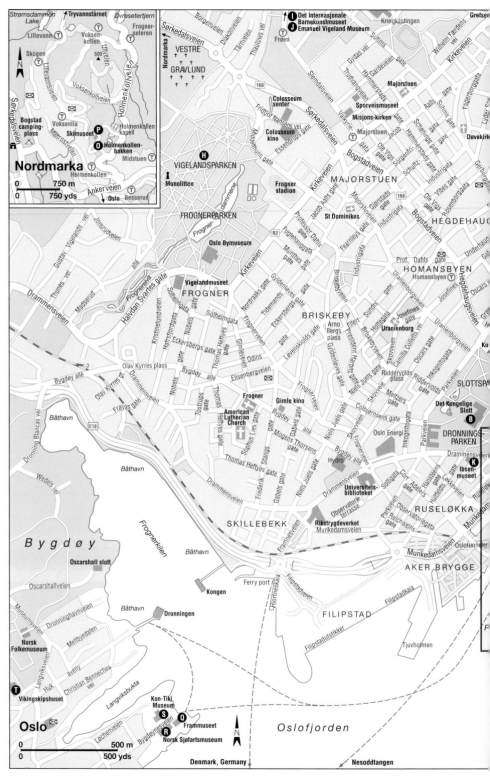

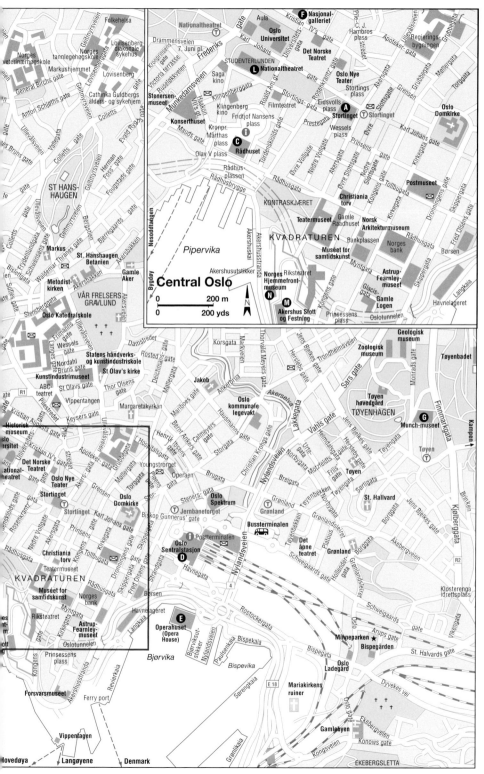

Central Oslo

OSLO AND ITS FJORD

Norway's capital offers a lively mix of galleries, museums, shops, restaurants and nightlife, with magnificent forests, ski trails and the beautiful Oslo Fjord close at hand

Maps:
City 158
Area 168

O slo: the name has an English connection. According to the *Snorre Saga*, the city was founded by Harald III (1015–66), the half-brother of Olaf II (later St Olaf). Crowned in 1045, Harald ruled so harshly as to earn the nickname Hardrade (Harsh Ruler). In 1066, he invaded England to claim its throne following the death of Edward the Confessor. The attempt failed; he was killed at Stamford Bridge on 25 September, barely three weeks before the Battle of Hastings that so changed English history.

Back home, Harald's subjects kept the name Oslo for six centuries, until 1624, when King Christian IV of Denmark and Norway immodestly renamed it Christiania. In 1877, at the height of the national romantic period following the dissolution of the union with Denmark in 1814, the government officially Norwegianised the spelling to Kristiania, and the city followed suit in 1897. State and municipal bureaucrats were obliged to use the new spelling, but the citizenry were divided and arguments raged. In 1924, the Storting (Parliament) settled the argument by reinstating the name Oslo. But the pronunciation has yet to settle down. The British say "Ozlo". The natives say "Osslo" or "Oschlo", depending on whether they are East Siders or West Siders. Linguistic purists do it straight: "Os-lo", with two distinct syllables. Ask two Osloites to pronounce

LEFT: sculpture by Gustav Vigeland in Vigelandsparken.
BELOW: cafés spill out onto the street in summer.

FACT FILE

Situation Oslo lies in southeast Norway at 59°55'N.
Size 454 sq km (175 sq miles).
Population just over 560,000.
Climate Average afternoon temperature in winter: –2°C (28°F); in summer: 16°C (61°F). Annual precipitation: 763 mm (30 inches).
Transport Train, T-bane (underground), tram, bus, boat and commuter rail services. Trafikanten information, tel: 177.
Airports Gardermoen, 51 km (32 miles) north; Torp at Sandefjord, 117 km (73 miles) south; Moss at Rugge, 66 km (41 miles) southeast.
Biggest attraction Vigeland Park, featuring 212 works by the sculptor Gustav Vigeland.
Newest attraction National Opera House.
Finest building Akershus Slott og Festning (Castle), 1300.
Best view of the city Tryvannstårnet (Tryvann Tower).
Best museums Vikingskiphuset, Norsk Folkemuseum, Skimuseet, Barnekunstmuseet (Children's Art Museum).
Annual events Jazz Festival (Aug).
Best ski resort Tryvann Winter Park – 14 slopes and seven ski lifts just above Holmenkollen. Open Dec–Apr.
Tourist information Fridtjof Nansens plass 5 and Oslo S Railway Station, tel: 815 30 555; www.visitoslo.com

The classical facade of Oslo's Det Kongelige Slott (Royal Palace).

the city name and you trigger debate. Today the dialects of the city are declining, under the influence of television and an ever more mobile population.

The industrial complex that lined the banks of Akerselva (Aker River) from the 1840s is no more. The city's remnant heavy industry, the Aker Shipyards, where 550 ships were built, closed in 1982. In its place is Aker Brygge (Aker Docks), a gentrified complex of trendy boutiques, international eateries and luxury apartments overlooking the fjord.

Likewise, civil servants and service-sector professionals have displaced industrial workers as the stalwarts of the city. The myth of the blond, blue-eyed Viking weakens, as an influx of foreigners enriches the city. Oslo has the country's greatest percentage of immigrants with Poles making up the greatest number, followed by Swedes then Germans. On the East Side, in the city districts of Torshov, Grünerløkka, Dælen, Tøyen, Grønland and Gamlebyen, daily life and business are conducted as much in Turkish, Vietnamese and Urdu as they are in Norwegian. Here are most of the city's ethnic eateries and shops, as well as mosques and Islamic organisations to serve the burgeoning Muslim population.

The 19th century today

In many ways **Oslo ❶** retains the features of the ideal city of the 19th century. Within easy walking distance, nestled around the northern tip of the fjord, are all the accoutrements of a capital: **Stortinget Ⓐ** (Parliament; tours in English July and Aug 10am, 11.30am and 1pm; free; tel: 23 31 35 96), **Det Kongelige Slott Ⓑ** (Royal Palace; mid-June–mid-Aug, 3 English guided tours daily, tickets on sale from Mar, tel: 81 53 31 33; park open all year; free; changing of the guard daily 1.30pm), **Rådhuset Ⓒ** (City Hall; May–Aug daily 9am–5pm;

BELOW: the stunning Oslo Opera House.

Sept–Apr until 4pm; entrance charge; tel: 23 46 16 00), **Oslo Sentralstasjon** (Oslo Central Station), Oslo's spanking new **Operahuset** ❺ (Opera House), **Nasjonalgalleriet** ❻ (National Gallery; Tues, Wed and Fri 10am–6pm, Thur until 7pm, Sat–Sun 11am–5pm; free; tel: 21 98 00 00) where you can view a version of *Skrik* (The Scream) by Munch *(see below)*, embassies, larger hotels and shops. On Rådhusplassen is **Nobels Fredssenter** (The Nobel Peace Center; daily 10am–6pm; entrance charge; www.nobelpeacecenter.no), an institution unique to Oslo, celebrating the Nobel Peace Prize. **Museet for Samtidskunst** (Museum of Contemporary Art; Tues Wed Fri 11am–5pm, Thur until 7pm, Sat–Sun noon–5pm; free; www.nationalmuseum.no) on Bankplassen, has works of post-WWII Scandinavian and international art. The attractions not in this compact grid of streets are just a few stops away on the T-Bane (underground).

The **Munch-museet** ❼ (Munch Museum; June–Aug daily 10am–6pm; Sept–May Tues–Fri 10am–4pm, Sat–Sun 11am–5pm; summer entrance charge; tel: 23 49 35 00), near the Tøyen underground station to the east of the city centre, is dedicated to the works of Edvard Munch (1863–1944), the painter and graphic artist who fathered German expressionism. His *Skrik* (The Scream), stolen by armed robbers and recovered in 2004, is probably Scandinavia's most famed work of art *(see box, page 56)*.

The works of one of Munch's contemporaries, sculptor Gustav Vigeland (1869–1943), dominate **Vigelandsparken** ❽ (Vigelands Park; open year-round; free) at Frogner Park to the west of the city centre, an extensive display of human life and emotion cast in stone and bronze. No matter that English novelist Evelyn Waugh called it a "subhuman zoo"; it remains one of Scandinavia's most visited attractions, drawing more than a million visitors each year.

Maps:
City 158
Area 168

TIP

Buy an Oslo Pass for free admission to the city's museums, free public transport and parking, discounts at shops, restaurants and on car hire. Obtainable from tourist offices and hotels.

BELOW: sculptures at Vigeland Park.

OSLO OPERA HOUSE

Rising like an iceberg from the waves, Norway's dramatic harbourside opera house opened on 12 April 2008 to international acclaim. The design is a truly Nordic concoction, built to resemble snow fields and floating ice and with fabulous acoustics.

Constructed using 4.4 billion kroners of public money, the opera house was deliberately planned so that even non-opera goers could find something to enjoy. Two sweeping slopes of Italian Carrara marble flank the main bulk of the building, allowing the public to stroll onto the roof, sunbathe, picnic – in short, to claim the building as their own. The harbourside location and radical design have lent the opera house two unusual features. Much of the building is actually below sea level – orchestra members in the main auditorium actually sit 15m "underwater". It's also the only opera house in the world to have its own underwater sea defences, a barrier to protect it should the Oslo-Copenhagen car ferry ever drift off course. The dramatic exterior is matched by equal artistry on the inside, including the actual stages and their carefully planned acoustics so that audiences can hear anything from opera to rock played to perfection. For programme details, see www.operaen.no.

At Frøen, a short stroll north, is the unique **Det Internasjonale Barnekunst-museet ❶** (International Museum of Children's Art; Lille Frøens vei 4; July–Aug Tues–Thur, Sun 11am–4pm; Sept–mid-Dec and mid-Jan–June Tues–Thur 9.30am–2pm, Sun 11am–4pm; entrance charge; www.barnekunst.no). The museum exhibits children's art from 150 countries. A few blocks uphill near Slemdal T-Bane station is the **Emanuel Vigeland Museum ❷** (Grimelunds-veien 8; Sun noon–4pm; entrance charge; tel: 22 14 57 88). Emanuel Vigeland (1875–1948), Gustav Vigeland's brother, made his living painting the great personages of his time. But he was fascinated by themes of life and death, and used them in the alfresco decoration of a crypt, entitled *Vita* ("life"), the museum's major attraction.

Back to the city centre, on the south side of Drammensveien from Dronningsparken, **Ibsen-museet ❸** (Ibsen Museum; mid-May–mid-Sept Tues–Sun 11am–6pm; until 4pm mid-Sept–mid-May; tours hourly; entrance charge; tel: 22 12 35 50) is located partly in the flat once occupied by Henrik Ibsen (1828–1906), Norway's most noted playwright and one of the world's outstanding pioneers of social drama. A statue of Ibsen stands in front of the rococo **Nationaltheatret ❹** (National Theatre; Johanne Dybwads plass 1), built in 1899, the venue of the annual international Ibsen Festival in August.

History and the outdoors

The river that divides the city shares the root of its name with **Akershus Slott og Festning ❺** (Akershus Castle and Fortress; castle May–Aug Mon–Sat 10am–4pm, Sun 12.30–4pm; entrance by tour; bastions and ramparts open 6am–9pm; free entrance to grounds), a major complex begun in 1300, finished

Children will enjoy the old-fashioned candy store and horse and carriage rides at the Norsk Folkemuseum on Bygdøy peninsula (Museumsveien 10; open daily; tel: 22 12 37 00), where more than 150 historic timber houses and a stave church are on display (see picture page 166).

BELOW: off duty at the Royal Palace.

in 1308 and extended through the 15th century. It was built principally to defend the city against attack from Sweden. The fort remains an imposing symbol of past military importance. **Norges Hjemmefrontmuseum**  (Norway's Resistance Museum; June–Aug Mon–Sat 10am–5pm, Sun 11am–4pm; closes 4pm rest of year; entrance charge; tel: 23 09 31 38) is located here, near the place where members of the Resistance were executed during World War II. It illustrates the intense story of occupied Norway.

Map
on pages
158–159

Capital sports

High on the hills overlooking the city is **Holmenkollen Ski Jump**  (open all year; free except during ski meets), Norway's top visitor attraction and venue of the annual Holmenkollen Ski Festival. Adjoining the ski jump is **Skimuseet**  (Holmenkollen Ski Museum; May and Sept daily 10am–5pm; June–Aug 9am–8pm; Oct–Apr 10am–4pm; entrance charge; tel: 22 92 32 00), featuring 4,000 years of skiing history. Outside is a statue of King Olav V (1903–91) in a cross-country skiing pose, because here skiing is the sport of commoner and king alike. One Olympic Winter Games (1952) and three World Nordic Ski Championships (1930, 1966 and 1982) have been held in Oslo, and the latter will be held here again in 2011.

Akershus Slott, built to defend against attacks from Sweden.

Oslo's sporty profile is due in part to the closeness of outdoor recreation. On one side there's the fjord, a broad, sheltered expanse of water ideal for windsurfing and boating. On the other side is a huge woodland recreation area known as **Oslomarka** (Oslo's fields), covering some 1,700 sq km (656 sq miles). Here there are 2,600 km (1,600 miles) of ski trails marked with red-painted slashes on trees and rings round sign-poles at trail intersections. The total length of the

BELOW LEFT: Aker Brygge complex.
BELOW RIGHT: Holmenkollen.

summer-time walking trails is even longer; they are marked in blue, the difference being that red-marked trails can cross lakes and marshes frozen in the winter, while blue-marked trails cannot. Some 110 km (68 miles) of these trails are illuminated until 10pm for night skiing with their trailheads at car parks or underground stations, for ease of after-dark access. All the illuminated trails, as well as some 500 km (300 miles) of other trails, are regularly maintained with tracks set by machine. Trail use is free, as cross-country skiing is regarded as part of public recreation. Along the trails, there are some 44 staffed lodges with lounges, cafeterias and toilets; most are open at weekends and during school holidays, and in the winter, some are open in the evening. There are also 16 Alpine ski lift hills and 48 ski jumps.

Although Norway gave the word "ski" (meaning "piece of split wood") to the world, the language has no verb equivalent to the act of skiing.

For details, contact Skiforeningen (tel: 22 92 32 00), or Skogvesen (Oslo Municipal Forestry Service; tel: 22 08 22 00), which maintains trails, and operates the illuminated trails and 11 of the trailside lodges. For snow conditions in the Oslo area, phone Tryvann Winter Park (tel: 40 46 27 00).

Great explorers

The pines and waters of Oslo were the training ground for Fridtjof Nansen (1861–1930) and Roald Amundsen (1872–1928), two of the greats of the heroic age of polar exploration. Their ships, *Fram* and *Gjøa*, are preserved in two museums on the **Bygdøy** peninsula, **Frammuseet Q** (Fram Museum; June–Aug daily 9am–6pm; May and Sept 10am–5pm; Mar–Apr and Oct 10am–4pm; Nov–Feb 10am–3pm; entrance charge; tel: 23 28 29 50) and **Norsk Sjøfartsmuseum R** (Norwegian Maritime Museum; mid-May–Aug daily 10am–6pm; Sept–mid-May 10.30am–4pm; entrance charge; tel: 24 11 41 50). Nearby, the **Kon-Tiki Museum S** (Apr, May and Sept daily 10am–5pm; June–Aug 9.30am–5.30pm; Oct–Mar 10.30am–3.30pm; entrance charge; tel: 23 08 67 67) has a fine collection of Easter Island artefacts as well as detailed displays of the preserved *Kon-Tiki* and *Ra II* craft used by ethnographic explorer Thor Heyerdahl (1914–2002), and **Vikingskipshuset T** (Viking Ship Museum; May–Sept daily 9am–6pm; Oct–Apr 11am–4pm; entrance charge; tel: 22 13 52 80) features the world's best-preserved collection of the elegant long-ships of the Viking Age.

BELOW: old-style country store at the Norsk Folkemuseum on the Bygdøy peninsula.

Historic coat of arms

An event during the era of the city's founding is depicted in its coat of arms. One day, Hallvard Husaby (*d.*1053) came upon a young, pregnant girl being pursued by three men. He took her in his boat in an attempt to escape on the fjord. But the villains caught and slew them both, tied a millstone around his neck, and tossed the bodies into the fjord. A few days later, Hallvard's body was found floating on the fjord, millstone still securely tied to his neck. A saint was born. City coats of arms and seals depicting St Hallvard have been in use since the 14th century. The current version, designed in 1924, shows Hallvard on a lion throne, the three lethal arrows in his left hand, the millstone in his right, and the girl at his feet. Around the periphery is the Latin motto: *Unanimiter et Constanter* (Unanimous and Eternal). Can an increasingly multicultural city be unanimous about anything? Perhaps. In the late 1980s, the public transport authorities decreed that trams were to be repainted red to promote visibility in traffic. The citizens were not pleased. Adamant that trams in Oslo are blue, preferably the cobalt blue of the city flag, they obliged the authorities to surrender. Cobalt blue now is the standard tram colour.

Maps:
City 158
Area 168

And the eternal? It also survives, subliminal in the soul of the city. Novelist Knut Hamsun (1859–1952), awarded the Nobel Prize for Literature in 1920, observed in his novel *Sult* (*Hunger*, 1888) that Oslo is "a strange city that nobody leaves without being marked by it". Translated to today's idiom, Oslo might be said to be memorable because it is a different sort of city.

Outward and southward

If you stand at a vantage point in Oslo and look south down the fjord, almost everything in view is in Akershus county. Further south, the fjord is flanked on the east by Østfold county and on the west by Vestfold county. Aside from being home to one in three residents of the country, the city and these counties play a key role in contemporary events and history.

The excellent Kon-Tiki Museum displays Thor Heyerdahl's Kon-Tiki and Ra II craft as well as artefacts from Easter Island.

In Akershus county, some 67 km (42 miles) north of Oslo, lies **Eidsvoll** ❷, a town that grew around the iron works built in 1624. The works closed in 1825; Eidsvoll might be just another post-industrial town, save for the happenings of the spring of 1814. Following the dissolution of the union with Denmark, 112 representatives convened at the headquarters of the iron works, then the only convenient large building, to draw up the Norwegian Constitution. The **Eidsvollbygningen** (Memorial Building; May–Aug daily 10am–5pm; Sept and Apr Tues–Fri 10am–3pm, Sat–Sun noon–5pm; Oct–Mar Wed–Fri 10am–3pm,

BELOW: outdoor café, Aker Brygge.

Traditional architecture in Drøbak, south of the capital.

Sat–Sun noon–5pm; entrance charge; tel: 63 92 22 10) is now a museum to the constitution and includes the room where the document was signed on 17 May 1814. The country's first railway, built in 1845, connected Oslo and Eidsvoll, and it's now on the E6 highway, the major north-south artery.

Historic provincial cities and towns are scattered throughout Østfold and Vestfold counties. The best way to explore the counties, whether you travel by bus, car or boat, is via **Drøbak ❸**. By road, you will pass Vinterbro, at the junction of the E6 and E18 highways, the location of **TusenFryd ❹**, the country's major amusement park (mid-June–mid-Aug daily 10.30am–7pm; early June to 4pm; May, late Aug and Sept weekends only; entrance charge; tel: 64 97 66 99).

Picturesque Drøbak grew out of a fishermen's settlement, and fishing vessels still dock to sell fresh catch on the quayside. Places of interest include **Follo Museum** (Heritage Museum; late May–mid-Sept Tues–Fri 11am–4pm, Sun 11am–4pm; entrance charge; tel: 64 93 99 90) and **Oscarsborg Festning** (Fort) out in the fjord, whose cannons sunk the German heavy cruiser *Blücher* on the day the country was invaded in 1940 (guided boat trips from the harbour). Another point of pride is the cross-timbered **Drøbak Kirke** (Church; built 1776; open all year; free), with an elaborately carved model of a ship inside, a common church decoration in seafaring towns.

Further south, **Fredrikstad ❺** is a gem among Østfold towns, and Scandinavia's only completely preserved fortress town, dating from 1567. History and prehistory figure largely hereabouts. The **Oldtidsveien** (Highway of the Ancients), the 18-km (11-mile) stretch of National Highway 110 between Fredrikstad and Skjeberg, has three **Helleristningsfelt** (literally "rock wall carving areas"; open all year; free access to grounds) with Bronze Age pictographs.

Halden **❻**, south of Skjeberg and close by the Swedish border, is dominated by **Fredriksten Fort** (Festning), a largely intact ruin with many of its buildings serving as small theme museums. The streets below were laid out along the cannons' blast lines to give the fortress's defenders freedom to fire. In summer, passenger launches travel the **Haldenkanal** (canal) that runs east and then north, through several sets of massive locks. The **Kanalmuseum** (Kanalmuseum; mid–June–mid-Aug Tues–Sun noon–6pm; Sept–Apr times vary; entrance charge; tel: 69 81 10 21) at the locks at **Ørje ❼** displays the implements of canal operations. It also arranges charter tours on the *Engebret Soot*, named after the designer of the canal and now the world's oldest propeller-driven steamship in service.

Throughout Østfold, *Olsok* (St Olav's day, 29 July) is celebrated with a great show of folk costume, music and dance. One of the best displays is at the **Borgarsyssel Museum** (mid-May–Aug Tues–Fri 10am–4pm, Sat–Sun noon–4pm; entrance charge; tel: 69 11 56 50) in **Sarpsborg ❽**, north of Skjeberg.

Viking Vestfold

The Moss-Horten car ferry connects Østfold and Vestfold in just under an hour. The **Marinemuseet** (Naval Museum; May–Sept daily noon–4pm, Oct–Apr Sun only; free; tel: 33 03 33 97) at **Horten ❾**, home port of Sjøforsvaret (the Royal Norwegian Navy), bulges with maritime history. There are also museums of photography and veteran cars in Horten (both open all year; entrance fee).

To the south lies the heart of eastern Viking country, and **Borre Nasjonalpark ❿** (open all year; free access to grounds), en route to Tønsberg, contains large turf-covered mounds concealing the graves of Viking kings. Keeping to the coastline along Road 311, **Munch's Lille Hus** (Munch's Little House; June–

Map on page 168

TIP

A pleasant way to travel to fjord towns is by boat. Contact any travel agent or Trafikanten at Oslo S station for information on ferry and launch services (tel: 177).

BELOW:
Drøbak, a fishing port on Oslo Fjord.

Map on page 168

TIP

Oslo has a wide variety of restaurants, both Norwegian and international. Cafés and *konditoris* offer coffee and pastries. For low-budget meals, look for a *kafeteria*.

BELOW: stave church at the Norsk Folkemuseum, Bygdøy peninsula. **RIGHT:** a typical fjord retreat.

Aug, times vary; entrance charge; tel: 33 08 21 31) at **Åsgårdstrand** ⓫ is where the artist lived when in Norway. It was a setting for many of his paintings.

Between Åsgårdstrand and Tønsberg is a burial mound, **Oseberghaugen** ⓬, the most important Viking site yet discovered (open all year; grounds free). Oslo's Vikingskipshuset *(see page 166)* contains the finds, including the 20-metre (65-ft) arch-ended wooden ship. Only the mound itself, near Slagen church, remains, but as a symbol Oseberghaugen has a subtle, magnetic power.

Just south is historic **Tønsberg** ⓭, established in the 9th century. On the 65-metre (200-ft) high **Slottsfjellet** are the fortress remains and tower. The main street, **Storgata**, is flanked by Viking graves. These were excavated and incorporated, under glass, into the ground floor of the new library.

The most renowned king to hold court in Tønsberg was Håkon Håkonson IV (1204–63). The ruins of his court can be seen on **Nordbyen**, a street with old houses hunched along it. A more recent native son is Roald Amundsen, the polar explorer. Less known outside Norway is Svend Foyn, the Tønsberg whaling captain who invented the explosive-powered harpoon.

The steamship *Kysten I* (built 1909), moored on Byfjorden near the old customs house, operates a three-hour islands tour.

Summer playground

To the south of Tønsberg, along the eastern side of the fjord, the islands of **Nøtterøy** and **Tjøme**, and the skerries, are fantastic summer hangouts. **Verdens Ende** ⓮ (World's End) is at the end – but for a few boulders – of the chain. The old lighthouse here is a beautifully simple structure made of stone.

On the other side of Tønsbergfjorden lies **Sandefjord** ⓯, a whaling town and home to Oslo's second airport. The sea still dominates life here. One of the main industries is marine paint production. The town centre is compact, and near **Badeparken** are the former spa and the old town. **Preståsen** is the hilly park above it.

Just outside Sandefjord is another burial site, **Gokstadhaugen** ⓰ (open all year; May–Sept guided tours; entrance charge to grounds), in which the *Gokstad* ship, now in Oslo's Vikingskipshuset, was discovered in 1880. The **Vesterøy** peninsula is a supremely peaceful place, ideal for walking, cycling and boating.

Larvik ⓱ was home to two legendary boat lovers, ethnographic explorer Thor Heyerdahl and master boatbuilder Colin Archer (1832–1921), designer of the polar ship *Fram*. Archer's first house was at Tollerodden, on the fjord. At Larvik's back is Farris lake and **Farriskilde** (Farris Spring), the country's only natural mineral-water spring.

People who live around Oslofjorden have a strange modesty-pride complex. They are the first to point out that the fjords of the west are more beautiful, the central mountain ranges far higher. But once these are out of the way, the superlatives begin to flow. The birthplaces of the most intrepid explorers are here, as are the best sailing races, the warmest summers, the finest archaeological discoveries, the best drinking water and summer resorts; for when it comes to this part of Norway neither modesty nor pride is false. ❑

SOUTHERN NORWAY

Norway's southern beaches and picturesque seaside towns are a magnet for summer visitors. The west coast is blessed with glorious fjords and the oil-rich city of Stavanger

Map on pages 174–175

D raw an upward arc on the map from Oslo in the east to Bergen in the west, and south of it you see the part of Norway where the bulk of the natives take their home country holidays. Here is where much of the history of the country happened and where the myriad roots of the contemporary Norwegian character remain intact. In clockwise order starting at Oslo, Southern Norway can be divided into the principal regions of **Sørlandet** (Southern country) comprising Telemark, Aust-Agder and Vest-Agder counties and their coasts around to about 7 o'clock; **Rogaland** county centred at the city of Stavanger on the west coast; and **Hordaland** county around Bergen.

Sørlandet

Kristiansand ❶ is the unofficial capital of the southern coast, and rightfully so. In 1639, King Christian IV of Denmark and Norway selected the site of the city for a fort to control the approaches to the North Sea and the Baltic. Much survives of the first of many forts built here, such as **Christiansholm Festning** (fortress; May–Sept daily 9am–9pm; free; tel: 38 07 51 50). Present-day Kristiansand, a pleasant city laid out in a rectangular pattern by Christian IV's directive, invites strolling. The nearby **Kristiansand Dyrepark** (mid-June–mid-Aug daily 10am–7pm, times vary rest of year; entrance charge; tel: 38 04 97 00) is a combined zoo, water park and amusement park, and is the most-visited attraction in Norway.

West of Kristiansand, the **Lindesnes Fyr ❷** (lighthouse; open all year; entrance charge) marks the southernmost point of Norway. The last town before Vest Agder rises to meet Rogaland is the port of **Flekkefjord** and the idyllic island of **Hidra**. The terrain is mountainous, with many splendid waterfalls, especially around **Kvinesdal ❸**.

Coastal journey

The principal centres along the coast east from Kristiansand are, in order, Lillesand, Grimstad and Arendal. **Lillesand ❹** is a popular holiday town with a fine selection of cafés and restaurants around the harbour. **Grimstad ❺** is indelibly associated with Ibsen. It was here that he served his apprenticeship to a chemist. Ibsen and his works are commemorated in the **Ibsen Museum** (Ibsen-museet i Grimstad; mid-May–mid-Sept daily 11am–5pm; entrance charge; tel: 37 04 04 90). **Arendal ❻** was struck by fire in 1863, and lost the houses on stilts that had earned it the nickname "Little Venice". Now overflowing onto a number of small islands, it retains its lovely setting.

The **Arendal Bymuseum** (Town Museum; Tues–Fri 10am–3pm, Sat 10am–2pm; entrance charge; tel:

LEFT: Preikestolen (the Pulpit Rock), one of Rogaland's best-known landmarks.
BELOW: cascading waters of the southwest.

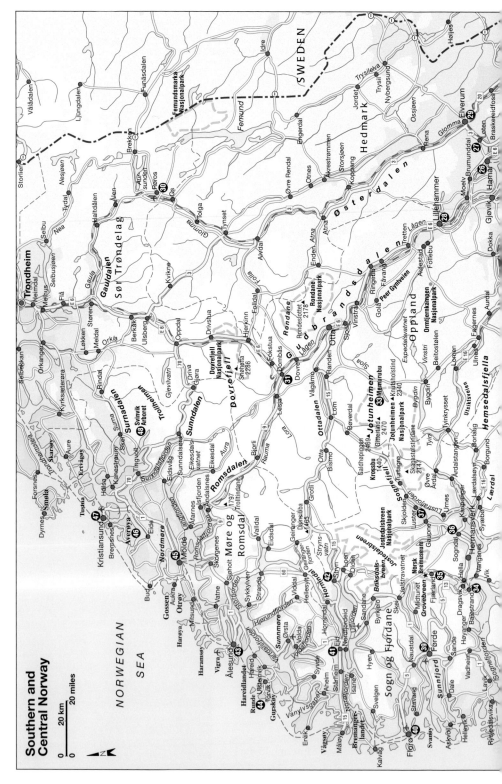

Southern and Central Norway

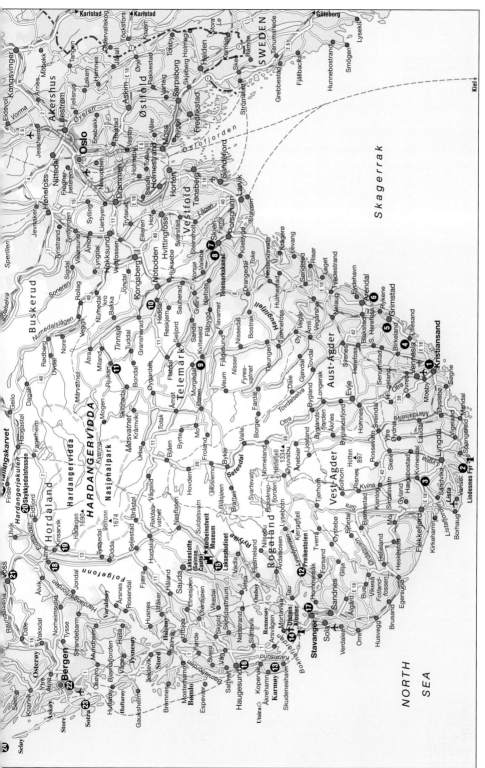

TIP

Express trains speed
between Oslo and
Kristiansand in 4 hours
and 45 minutes, and
between Kristiansand
and Stavanger in 3
hours and 15 minutes.

37 02 59 25) has extensive displays delineating local history, and the **Rådhus** (Town Hall), previously the home of a merchant, is said to be one of the largest wooden buildings ever constructed in Norway.

Telemark

Travelling northeast, the capital of Telemark is **Skien** ❼, which originally came into existence on the back of an industry producing stone projectiles for military slingshots. Norway's great playwright, Henrik Ibsen (1828–1906) spent his childhood here and his home, Venstøp, forms part of the **Telemark Museum** (Brekke Park; mid-May–Aug Mon–Fri noon–6pm, Sat and Sun 11am–6pm; entrance charge; tel: 35 52 57 49). Tulips bloom en masse in the gardens in summer.

Northwest of Skien lies **Ulefoss**, a village that until the end of the 19th century was a major exporter of ice, which was transported along waterways that became **Telemarkskanalen** ❽, which is still trafficked by passenger launches, such as the *MV Victoria* and *MV Henrik Ibsen* (late May–early Sept; tel: 35 90 00 20).

Although a finger of Telemark reaches the sea at **Kragerø**, not far from the mouth of Oslofjorden, the county is most associated with its inland terrain. Indeed, whenever a modern skier performs a Telemark turn, homage is done to the village of **Morgedal** ❾. It was here that Sondre Norheim (1825–97), the son of a sharecropper, first improved utilitarian skis and ski bindings for greater control in turns and consequently became regarded as the father of modern downhill skiing.

One of the major attractions west of **Notodden**, along Road 11, is at **Heddal** ❿, where the **Heddal Stavkirke** (stave church) is the country's largest (late May, early June and early Sept Mon–Sat 10am–5pm; mid-June–mid-Aug 9am–7pm; entrance charge; tel: 35 01 39 90). Its ornate carvings are rivalled only by the beau-

BELOW: southerly Mandal's popular bathing beach.

tiful period rose paintings in the Ramberg room of the nearby **Heddal Bygdetun** (rural museum; mid-June–mid-Aug 10am–5pm, until 7pm July; entrance charge).

Map on pages 174–175

About 10 km (6 miles) further on, Road 37 branches north past Tinnsjø lake towards **Rjukan** ⓫. The principal attraction of Rjukan is the hydroelectric plant where heavy water once was produced; see "Heroes of Telemark" *(page 180)* for an account of the daring sabotage that took place here in 1943. Today, the plant is the **Norsk Industriarbeidermuseum** (Norwegian Industrial Workers Museum; May–Sept daily 10am–4pm; Oct–Apr Tues–Fri noon–3pm, Sat–Sun 11am–4pm; entrance charge; tel: 35 09 90 00). Rjukan lies in the shade of the surrounding mountains, and from **Gvepseborg** (860 metres/2,800 ft) it is said that one can see about one-sixth of Norway.

Rogaland

Though Bergen is known as the capital of fjord country, Rogaland county, centred on the west-coast port of Stavanger, has some of the country's more spectacular fjord and mountain sights. It also has the country's highest average temperature, and in winter there is little snow and the fertile fields are green for most of the year. The Ryfylke area northeast of Stavanger is true fjord country. It starts with Lysefjorden and stretches north past long narrow lakes that once were open fjords, until it reaches Vindafjorden, Saudafjorden and Suldalsvatn. Every visitor should try to walk out through the heather moor to stand on the top of **Preikestolen** ⓬ (The Pulpit), a rock outcropping 597 metres (1,958 ft) above Lysefjorden, and the country's most famous vantage point.

The sheltered bay north of Stavanger, and outer islands such as **Karmøy** ⓭, protect Ryfylke's inshore islands from the North Sea. Christianity flourished early

The ornate altar at the Heddal Stavkirke, Norway's largest stave church.

BELOW: sheltered marinas dot the south coast.

COUNTRY AFLOAT

To the world, Norway and seafaring are synonymous. From the age of sail until after World War II, the Norwegian merchant fleet was one of the world's largest, and Norwegian could be heard in ports worldwide.

Norwegians seem happiest when they are in, on or around the sea. Each year, more than a third of the population spend their summer holidays partly or completely in craft that range from small dinghies to motor launches and ocean-going yachts. In all, there are more than 400,000 boats over 4.5 metres (15 ft) in length, and an untold number of smaller boats in the country. Most are motor boats, though sailing is popular on the fjords and as a competitive sport.

Geography and topography are the deciding factors. There are thousands of islands, and the fjords and coastal archipelagos are a paradise for competitive and recre - ational sailors, king and commoner alike. King Olav V (1903–91), the father of present King Harald V, won a Gold Medal in sailing in the 1928 Olympic Games, which made him the world's only Olympic medallist monarch.

Norway's first sailing club was founded in 1868 in Tønsberg, since when the nation has been a major force in championship sailing and regattas worldwide.

here under the protection of the bishops of Stavanger and the islands have many churches. The 12th-century **Utstein Kloster** ⓮ on **Mosterøy** makes a beautiful setting for concerts (mid-May–mid-Sept Tues–Sat 10am–4pm, Sun noon–5pm; mid-Sept–Nov and Mar–mid-May Sun only; entrance charge; tel: 51 72 47 05).

Following chemical analysis, it has been confirmed that the copper used to cover New York's Statue of Liberty came from one of the old Visnes mines on the island of Karmøy.

The many lighthouses are not only landmarks for islanders and seafarers but make excellent bird-watching sites. The waters around these peaceful islands are a sea kingdom for sailors, with enough coastline to give every boat a bay to itself and many yacht harbours. Most of the island grocers also provide boat services, and it is easy to hire rowing boats and small craft with outboard engines.

In the northeast highlands of Rogaland, the fjords, lakes and rivers are rich in fish and fine for sailing and canoeing. All these inland, eastern areas of Rogaland have good cross-country skiing tracks in winter and excellent Alpine slopes.

Among the best holiday areas is the Suldal district, stretching from Sand on the Sandsfjorden, along the Suldalslågen River – where the rushing waters have produced large salmon. At the Sand end of Suldalslågen is **Laksestudioet** ⓯ (mid-June–mid-Aug daily 10am–6pm; mid-Aug–mid-Sept noon–4pm; entrance charge; tel: 52 79 05 60), an observation studio built under a waterfall where visitors look through a large window at the salmon resting before their next leap up the fish ladder. Where river meets lake is **Kolbeinstveit Museum** (Rural Museum; mid-June–mid-Aug Tues–Sun 11am–5pm; entrance charge; tel: 52 79 93 04), a "living" museum on an old farm, part of which dates to the 13th century.

Back to the coast

BELOW: Utstein Kloster (cloister) on Mosterøy.

The sea route to **Bergen** is a popular way to see the coast. By taking an express boat (a cross between a catamaran and a hydrofoil) you can drop off at any of

the harbour stops and stay a night or a week according to your whim (tel: 177; www.kolumbus.no). Karmøy, the island at the south of the outer islands chain, is big enough to merit its own boat service, which goes to Skudeneshavn in the south, an idyllic old port with white, wooden houses along narrow streets. The north of the island is linked to the mainland just south of **Haugesund** , the first sizeable coastal town north of Stavanger. Haugesund has long been a centre for fishing, shipping and farming. Today its harbour is filled with pleasure boats; the town also hosts Sildajazz, the International Jazz Festival (tel: 52 74 33 70; www.sildajazz.no) and the Norwegian Film Festival (both in Aug; Tourist Office tel: 52 01 08 30).

Stavanger

The sea has blessed **Stavanger** ⓱, Norway's fourth-largest city. As its once-lucrative fishing industry declined, the city discovered North Sea oilfields and has been booming ever since. The sea has also taken Stavanger's citizens around the world, returning with new people, products and ideas. Today, nearly one in ten of its 120,000 inhabitants was born abroad. The city's cosmopolitan nature was acknowledged when it became a European Capital of Culture in 2008.

The Anglo-Norman cathedral at Stavanger dates from the 12th century.

In the 19th and early 20th centuries, Stavanger was the principal port of embarkation for the great waves of Norwegian emigration to the United States: the first 52 emigrants left in 1825, bound for New York on the sloop *Restauration*. Those wishing to trace their roots can contact the **Det Norske Utvandrersenteret** (Emigration Centre; Mon–Fri 9am–3pm; tel: 51 53 88 60; www.utvandrersentret.no) for assistance.

BELOW: the harbour at Stavanger.

The Heroes of Telemark

The most celebrated act of resistance in Norway during World War II was the sabotage of the Vemork heavy water plant at Rjukan, in Telemark, in February 1943. No visitor to Rjukan, dwarfed and darkened by mountains all round, could fail to be awed by the audacity of the saboteurs. More importantly, successful production of heavy water in the plant could conceivably have aided German development of an atomic bomb.

The operation was originally planned for a joint force of Norwegian volunteers and British commandos in two towed gliders. It ended disastrously when both gliders and one of the aircraft towing them crashed in bad weather, and the survivors were tortured and executed by the Gestapo.

The next attempt was an all-Norwegian affair. "Gunnerside" was the code name for six men who had been trained in England.

They parachuted onto a frozen lake where they joined up with "Swallow", an advance party who had been on the ground since the first failed operation, subsisting for almost four winter months on moss, lichen and a single reindeer.

The men skied to the ridge above Rjukan for the perilous descent, up to their waists in snow. Just after midnight, the covering party took up positions while the six-man demolition team cut a chain on the gates and crept forward to the basement of the concrete building where the most vital equipment and the heavy water storage tanks were located. All agreed that anyone captured would take his own life.

The best way in appeared to be a funnel carrying cables and piping. Two went through it. The solitary Norwegian guard was astonished but agreed to lead them to vital components. "I had placed half the charges in position when there was a crash of broken glass behind me," one of the pair wrote later. The other members of the team, not realising that their leaders had managed to get in, had decided to smash in through a window. With the rest of the charges laid, the six began a rapid withdrawal. The party had only gone a few yards when there was what members later variously described as "a cataclysmic explosion" and "a tiny, insignificant pop".

Of the 10 saboteurs, six reached Sweden after a 400-km (250-mile) journey on skis in indescribably difficult conditions; the other four remained in Norway. Of the Swallow party, Claus Helberg had the liveliest time. He was chased through the mountains by German soldiers, but escaped. Then he fell over a cliff and broke an arm. The next day he walked into a German patrol but had a good enough story to be taken to a hotel to await treatment. Most of the hotel guests (but not the injured Norwegian) were turned out of their rooms to make way for Reichskommissar Joseph Terboven (the Nazi who ruled Norway). Later, and through no fault of his own, he was bundled along with the remaining guests "into a bus and sent off to the Grini concentration camp". Helberg jumped from the bus. Later, he turned up in Britain, reporting for further duties. ❑

LEFT: Kirk Douglas played a saboteur in the 1965 film *The Heroes of Telemark*.

Map on pages 174–175

The Stavanger *siddis* (colloquialism for a person from Stavanger, a contraction of "citizen" in English) claim to be the oldest true Norwegians, tracing their lines to the Battle of Hafrsfjord. This decisive battle that first united the country under King Harald I Hårfagre, *c.*880, took place at a bay just southwest of the city. On the shore there is a monument to the event, **Sverd i fjell**, three larger-than-life Viking swords seemingly thrust into bedrock.

The heart of modern Stavanger is the area around **Breiavatnet**, the small lake in the middle of the city, near the **Domkirken** (cathedral). Work began on the cathedral in 1125 in the Anglo-Norman style. Massive interior pillars give it a feeling of austere strength and contrast with the elegant arches of the chancel. One of the finest pieces is the ornate 16th-century pulpit by Andrew Smith.

Northwest of the cathedral are the winding cobbled streets and old timber houses of **Gamle Stavanger** (Old Stavanger), one of the most coveted places to live in the town. Around 1870, as fishing and shipping were in decline, the fishermen turned their attention to *brisling* (small herring), which were cured and canned in the town and sent as Norwegian "sardines" all over the world. Stavanger thrived on sardines until the 1950s. Today, the **Hermetikkmuseet** (Canning Museum; mid-June–Aug daily 11am–4pm; Sept–mid-June Tues–Sun; entrance charge; tel: 51 84 27 00) is a reminder of the former smell of money.

Violas growing wild by the roadside in southern Norway.

In 1966, the city became the base for oil exploration in the North Sea. The black gold has brought prosperity to Stavanger – the city is third only to Russia and Saudi Arabia in oil exports. Visit the interactive **Norsk Oljemuseum** (Norwegian Petroleum Museum; June–Aug daily 10am–7pm; Sept–May daily 10am–4pm, until 6pm on Sun; entrance charge; tel: 51 93 93 00) for an insight into this source of energy. Sadly, not all advances come without their disasters: in the suburb of **Kvernevik** the **Alexander Kielland Minnesmerke** (monument) commemorates the loss of 123 lives when the *Alexander Kielland* offshore oil platform capsized in 1980.

BELOW: sardines, once the lifeblood of Stavanger.

Hordaland

Hordaland county includes two of the country's prime natural attractions: **Hardangervidda**, the central mountain plateau at 1,300 metres (4,500 ft) above sea level and **Hardangerfjorden**, which gave its name to Norway's national musical instrument, the eight-stringed Hardanger fiddle, and provided inspiration for the composer Edvard Grieg (1843–1907), and the violinist Ole Bull (1810–80). Among these mountains and fjords, Grieg and Bull travelled on foot and horse, absorbing the old melodies of the land. Like today's visitors, they came to Hardanger for its waterfalls, for the beauty of smaller fjords that lead almost to the plateau above, and for glaciers and mountains that rarely lose their snow-caps, contrasted with orchards lining the fjordside.

In days gone by, the fjords provided West Norway's main transport arteries, and **Utne** ⑱ was an important junction between east and west. Two establishments here that sum up Hardanger life over the past centuries are the **Hardanger Folkemuseum** (May–Sept daily 10am–4pm; Oct–Apr Mon–Fri 10am–3pm; entrance charge), and the **Utne Hotel**, founded in 1722, the oldest hotel in Norway still in operation.

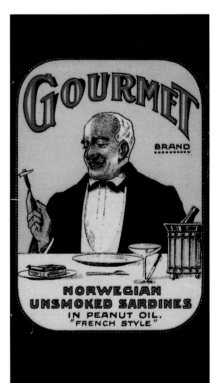

Map
on pages
174-175

A ferry service connects Utne with **Kinsarvik** ⑲ on the east side of Sørfjorden, an arm of the Hardangerfjord. Heading northeast on National Highway 13, you'll find a beautiful stretch of water, Eidfjorden. It cuts far into the dramatic landscape that includes the beautiful **Skykkjedalsfossen** ⑳ waterfall.

Hang-gliding to skiing

Edvard Grieg used to visit a small "hytte" poised on the edge of Hardangerfjorden, near the village of Ullensvang, where with piano and writing desk at hand, he would compose surrounded by the beauty of the Norwegian fjords.

If you loop back northwest, crossing Eidfjord by ferry and continuing on Highway 13, you come to **Voss** ㉑, which lies next to lake Vangsvatnet in the middle of rich farmland. The Voss district *(kommune)* makes full use of its surroundings to attract visitors. In summer they come for touring, fjord excursions, mountain walking, parachuting, hang-gliding and paragliding from Hangurfjell, and fishing and watersports on Vangsvatnet. In winter, everything changes and Voss becomes one of the best centres for Alpine and cross-country skiing.

The top station of the cable car up Hangurfjell at 610 metres (2,000 ft) gives one of the best prospects of Voss in its bowl-shaped valley. The town has long been a centre for artists and musicians, and their monuments are scattered around. It is one of the best places to hear the Hardanger fiddle and see the old dances performed in beautiful costumes. On the main street is a shop where you can buy the ornate silver belts and jewellery that go with the traditional Norwegian costume.

BELOW: Heddal
Stave Church.
RIGHT: dramatic
Hordaland fjord.

Around Bergen and north

From Voss the E16 highway or the train take you to **Bergen** ㉒ *(see page 185).* Bergen's islands are linked so closely together that sometimes it is hard to realise that you have crossed water, but those such as **Askøy** and **Osterøy** to the north of the city have their own character, and the area round the Bjørnafjorden (Bear Fjord) to the south is particularly mild and green.

The long narrow island of **Sotra** ㉓ shelters Bergen from the North Sea. It is a good base for sea-canoeing in and out of the small offshore islands and rocks and, in good weather, as far as the open sea to combine canoeing with ocean fishing. In any case, shelter is never far away.

North of Bergen is **Nordhordland**, a district of islands that stretches as far north as Sognefjorden. Today, fish farming is the prime livelihood and the region exports salmon and trout all round the world. Fish farmers are now attempting to rear cod, halibut and other species. Some fish farms are open to the public. There is good sea fishing for cod and coalfish, and rosy-coloured trout inhabit many of the lakes. Diving and sub-aqua fishing, as well as treasure hunting, are easy in these transparent waters. Oil is a modern, though not conflicting, industry in this area with the Mongstad refinery illuminated at night.

To the north and most remote of all is the island of **Fedje** ㉔, an important navigation point for many centuries with two 19th-century lighthouses still in use today. Norwegian maritime rules insist that all ships must carry a Norwegian pilot, which here is vital, as tankers serving the Mongstad refinery navigate through the ever-changing waters. ◼

BERGEN

Gateway to the fjords, mountains and islands, Norway's western seaport has a relaxed atmosphere, stunning setting and vibrant cultural life

Map on page 186

Should you tell a Bergenser that your spouse or a good friend hails from the city, the spontaneous response may be "how fortunate". Mirth is the currency of life in Bergen, humour among its better-known exports. A Bergenser wants you to laugh at a local joke, but seldom forewarns you that in laughing you might find yourself caught in a mental mousetrap.

During the city's official 900th anniversary celebrations in 1970, King Olav V visited an archaeological excavation and asked Councilman Knut Tjonneland "How old is the city, really?" "That depends, your majesty," replied Tjonneland, "on the amounts appropriated for further excavation."

Although Bergen is said to have been founded in AD 1070 by the Viking king, Olav Kyrre, the city is probably older. Recent archaeological finds have dated the earliest settlements to 50 BC or earlier. The name Bergen derives from the old Norse *Bjørgvin*, still the name of the diocese.

International connections

Surrounded by seven mountains, Bergen is now a major port with 10 km (6 miles) of dockside. Until the railway eastwards over the high mountain plateau to Oslo was opened in November 1909, Bergen was isolated from the rest of Norway. Scotland by ship was closer than Oslo, England less distant than Copenhagen. As the western-most city in Scandinavia, Bergen soon became a crossroads of the north and, in the 13th century, the capital of a united Norway. Its favourable location with respect to the other ports of Europe drew Hanseatic tradesmen, who established a commercial community at the harbour.

Fullriggers plied the port, with peak traffic in 1644, when more than 400 ships docked from Scotland alone. Many current everyday objects first came to Norway on ships docking here – not least wallpaper, which first appeared in the late 17th century in the homes of ships' captains who plied the Oriental trade routes. With nine centuries of maritime tradition, it is hardly surprising that most "real" Bergensers have their roots elsewhere. Composer Edvard Grieg's family of diplomats, writers and musicians, for example, is an offspring of the Scottish McGregor clan.

Street and place names ring the register of central European origins. Even the crisp Bergen dialect bears the indelible stamp of international influence. To most Norwegians, an Englishman is an *engelskmann*, but to the Bergenser, an *englender*, from the German *Engländer*. A parade in Bergen is a *prosesjon*, from the English "procession"; the rest of Norway says *tog*.

Individuality prevails. Edvard Grieg was a Bergen-ser, a self-professed misfit at the 130-year-old Tanks

LEFT: beautiful Bergen.
BELOW: selling fish in Bergen's famous fish market.

TIP

Buy a Bergenskortet
(Bergen Card) from
the Tourist Information
Office in Vågsall-
menningen. Benefits
include free admission
or discounts for
museums and free
public transport.

School, where he was known as Pupil No. 139. Yet, today, annual summer concerts attract music lovers from all over the world to his home, **Troldhaugen**, 8 km (5 miles) south of the city (May–Sept daily 9am–6pm; Oct–Apr times vary; entrance charge; tel: 55 92 29 92), and the **Grieghallen** ❹ music hall is renowned in Europe as the home of one of the world's oldest orchestras, Harmonien, founded in 1765, as well as of the annual Bergen Music Festival.

Most of the time, the city's backdrop is the glacial quiet of the mountains, but music, one is frequently reminded, is very much a part of its heritage. "Rat-a-tat-tat, rat-a-tat-tat." The sound pierces the mind. It's the **Buekorps**, an organisation for 10–20-year-old boys – and girls, since the 1990s. They're easily recognised by their natty tunics and tasselled tam-o'-shanter caps dating from the 1850s, when the organisation was founded in emulation of the home guards, then the backbone of the country's defence. From mid-April until 17 May, when the brigades march in formation in the annual Constitution Day parade, they practise before going to school, which makes early morning sleep a rarity.

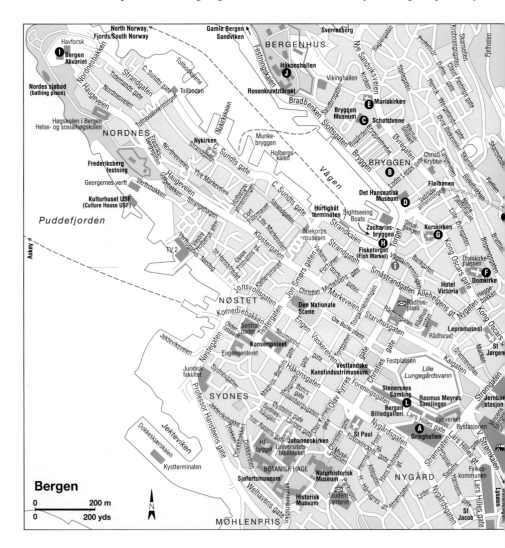

Bergen

0   200 m
0   200 yds

Map
on page
186

Water, water...

The Gulf Stream blesses Bergen with a benign climate and a harbour that is ice-free year round. But it also brings rain, some 2,250 mm (89 inches), making Bergen the country's wettest city. A local saying holds that "*I Bergen by, går alle med paraply*" ("In Bergen town, everyone carries an umbrella"). Bergen also has the world's only umbrella-repair shop. In other parts of the world, in other parts of Norway, teenagers refuse to carry umbrellas no matter how wet the weather. In Bergen, they are customary confirmation gifts.

Reminders of the city's seafaring tradition abound. The magnificently preserved full-rigged *Statsraad Lehmkuhl*, named after Christopher Lehmkuhl, a Bergenser and a man of the sea who ultimately became a cabinet minister, has her home port in the city. Today, Bergen is a port of call for cruise ships heading to and from the fjords. As the American movie producer Woody Allen said, "There is enough scenery for a dozen films." Quite rightly, the city calls itself the capital of fjord country.

Moreover, many of the Hanseatic **Bryggen** ⓑ buildings remain – a film set in themselves, meticulously preserved and listed as a UNESCO World Heritage Site. A walk through Bryggen is a step back in time, to before the Reformation. Here are galleries, craft shops, fashion boutiques and eating places, interspersed with sailmakers, a freight company and a scrap metal dealer.

The earliest archaeological remains are in **Bryggen Museum** ⓒ (May–Aug daily 10am–5pm; Sept–Apr Mon–Fri 11am–3pm, Sat noon–3pm, Sun noon–4pm; entrance charge; tel: 55 58 80 10). Guides from the museum conduct tours through the row of Hansa houses and warehouses that line Bryggen. These were built after the great fire of 1702, which destroyed many buildings. A key to understanding the Hansa merchants' way of life is to visit the **Hanseatisk Museum** ⓓ (June–Aug daily 9am–5pm; Sept–May hours vary; entrance charge; tel: 55 54 46 90).

Nearby is the oldest building still in use in the city, **Mariakirken** ⓔ (St Mary's Church), built in the early 12th century and justly proud of its rich Baroque pulpit. The other medieval churches to survive the periodic fires are the present **Domkirke** ⓕ (cathedral) and **Korskirken** ⓖ, both of which merit a visit.

Fish for sale

To buy fish year-round in the open-air **Fisketorget** ⓗ (Fish Market) on the nearby harbour is to walk in and out of a continuous conversation. Fishmongers from as far afield as Asia ward their solid masonry tanks teeming with live cod or crawling with crustaceans. To the Bergenser, a fresh fish is one with the tail still flipping.

Bergen's shopping centre is situated south of the Fish Market around **Torgalmenningen**, a broad, traffic-free street where many of the best shops are to be found. Crowded in summer, these thoroughfares, known as *almenning*, were deliberately built wide to prevent flames from spreading to the opposite side of the street.

The view from the Nordnes peninsula over the town to the mountain of Fløyen is characterised by the contrast between the green woodland, blue sea and the mainly white-painted wooden houses. At the point of the peninsula is **Bergen Akvariet** ⓘ (Aquarium;

King Harald Hårfagre sculpture at Bryggens Museum.

BELOW: statue of the violinist Ole Bull.

The summer home of Edvard Grieg (1843–1907) at Troldhaugen.

May–Aug daily 9am–7pm; Sept–Apr 10am–6pm; entrance charge; tel: 55 55 71 71), one of the most extensive collections of sea life in Europe.

Historic highs

Håkonshallen ❶ (mid-May–Aug daily 10am–4pm; Sept–mid-May daily noon–3pm, Thur until 6pm; entrance charge; tel: 55 31 60 67), northwest of Bryggen, is an imposing Gothic festival hall built in 1261, one of Scandinavia's best examples of middle-age profane architecture. In it resides the fierce pride of the Bergenser. During World War II, Håkonshallen was nearly destroyed when the *Voorbode*, a Dutch ship carrying German munitions, blew up in the harbour. The explosion flung parts of the ship 25 km (16 miles) from town and killed or injured its crew, dozens of Russian prisoner dock workers and more than 5,000 townspeople. One of the *Voorbode's* anchors still lies where it hit the ground, on **Fløyen mountain** ❷, some 300 metres (1,000 ft) higher than where the ship had been docked. A small park has been built around the anchor. Stand there, and you can tell the true Bergenser who pass by: they're the ones who doff their hats.

A funicular, **Fløibanen** (daily 7.30am–11pm, Sat from 8am, Sun from 9am; May–Aug closes at midnight) connects the city centre to Fløyen mountain, with its panoramic views of Bergen, restaurant, eight walking routes and summer concerts. For a longer ride, the **Ulriksbanen** cable car, opening in 2009, will take you to the top of Ulriken mountain.

Lakeside galleries

Bergen has several strong art collections, mostly centred on Lille Lungegårdsvann, an octagonal-shaped lake near Grieghallen. Here are the **Bergen Billedgalleri** ❸

BELOW: Fløibanen on its way up Fløyen, one of Bergen's seven hills.

(Municipal Art Gallery) with a large collection of Norwegian painting; the **Rasmus Meyer Samlinger** (Rasmus Meyers Collection), which also specialises in Norwegian art, including Edvard Munch; and the **Stenersens Samling**, with work by Munch, Picasso and Klee among others (all open daily 11am–5pm; mid-Sept–mid-May closed Mon; entrance charge; tel: 55 56 80 00).

The outgoing nature, taste for trade and concern for others typical of Bergensers are best reflected in Thoralf Rafto (1922–86). Before the fall of Communism, Rafto dedicated his energies to awakening the West to the human rights abuses in the East, particularly of Soviet Jews. An annual Rafto Prize for Human Rights commemorates his work; fittingly it is administered at **Raftohuset – Menneskerettighetenes Hus** (Rafto Human Rights House; Menneskerettighetenes Plass 1; Mon–Fri 9am–5pm; tel: 55 21 09 50).

Excursions from Bergen

Not to be missed is the **Fantoft Stave Church**, 8 km (5 miles) south of the city in Paradis (mid-May–mid-Sept daily 10.30am–2pm, 2.30–6pm; entrance charge; tel: 55 28 07 10). It was built around 1150 and is one of the oldest wooden buildings in Europe. In 1992, it burned down, but has since been completely restored.

A short ferry ride across Lysefjorden brings you to the beautiful island of **Lysøen** (Island of Light) and the onion-domed summer residence of the violin virtuoso Ole Bull (1810–80). Bull called the villa, built in 1873, his "Little Alhambra" and often invited fellow musicians and artists. In summer, the old music room resounds to the music Bull played here with violin recitals and small ensembles (mid-May–Aug Mon–Sat noon–4pm, Sun 11am–5pm; ferry from Buena quay; entrance charge; tel: 56 30 90 77). ❑

Map on page 186

TIP

The Hotel Terminus, across Kaaes Gate from Bergen's railway station, is known for putting on one of the country's most sumptuous breakfast tables.

BELOW: National Day celebrations.

THE HEART OF NORWAY

Map on pages 174–175

Central Norway encompasses a remarkable landscape from the shimmering fjords of the west across the peaks, plateaux and valleys that have inspired great writers and composers

The heartland of Norway is the upper part of the southern bulge of the country, extending from above Oslo and Bergen to below Trondheim. The area encompasses the highest mountains in Scandinavia, and freshwater lakes and watercourses abound. To the east there are two long valleys, **Østerdalen** (literally "Easterly Valley") and **Gudbrandsdalen**, orientated roughly parallel to the border with Sweden and knifing through the high interior cordillera to provide the major north–south land transport arteries. In the middle there are the lofty peaks and high plateau of the Rondane and Jotunheimen ranges, and to the west lies the coast with its fjords and archipelago in waters plied by boats since the land was first settled. Indeed, this part of the country embodies the *fjord og fjell* (fjord and mountain) landscape so deeply etched in the Norwegian ethos.

Lake Mjøsa, a slender jewel

The glaciers that gouged the fjords also worked the inland and left **Mjøsa** ㉕, a jewel of a lake. Its southern end is at Minnesund just north of Eidsvoll, and its northern tip is at Lillehammer, 101 km (63 miles) to the northwest. It's slender – only 15 km (9 miles) at its broadest – and like a fjord, deep – up to 449 metres (1,472 ft). Around Mjøsa lies some of the most arable land in the country, and its shores greet undulating countryside with large farms backed by densely forested hills. One of the best ways to enjoy the lake and its surroundings is a trip on the *Skibladner*, the world's oldest paddle-wheel steamship still in service, named after a sailing ship of Nordic mythology. In summer, the *Skibladner* carries up to 230 passengers on excursions six days a week; contact any tourist information office in the region or her home port at **Hamar** ㉖ for schedules (tel: 61 14 40 80).

Hamar was a medieval centre of Roman Catholicism in Norway and the seat of a bishop. It is still a bishopric, but only ruins remain of its imposing cathedral, now protected under a spectacular glass structure at **Hedemarks-museet og Domkirkeodden** (Hedemark Museum and Cathedral Point; mid-May–mid-Sept Tues–Sun 10am–4pm, July daily until 5pm; entrance charge). In the 19th century Hamar became a railway junction with a locomotive works. The works are gone, but there's a reminder: **Jernbanemuseet** (National Museum of Railway Transport; daily 11am–3pm, July–mid-Aug until 5pm; entrance charge), with stations, railway buildings and vintage rolling stock. There are regular excursions on a narrow-gauge steam train.

Fertile local lands long ago led to cities and towns producing comestibles. Most stimulating, perhaps, is that seven of the country's eight distilleries are located hereabouts. One of them, **Løten Brænderi** (guided tours; entrance charge; tel: 62 59 49 10), at **Løten** ㉗,

LEFT: Ålesund abounds with Art Nouveau buildings. **BELOW:** legendary Norwegian troll.

Lillehammer's coat of arms reflects a national pastime.

13 km (8 miles) east of Hamar, is open to the public. A fascinating one-man show (mid-June–Aug Fri, Sat and Sun 6pm, entrance charge) recounts the history of the distillery and the production of *akevitt*, the Norwegian liquor made from potato and caraway seeds. Also worth visiting on the same site is **Løiten Lys** (Mon–Fri 10am–8pm; Sat 10am–6pm, Sun noon–6pm), a candle factory with a display of candles in every conceivable shape and size.

Two weeks of fame

Lillehammer ㉘ is best known in the world of winter sports as the venue of the 1994 Olympic Winter Games. Many of the Olympic facilities still stand, such as the ice event rinks at Hamar and Gjøvik, and luge and bobsleigh tracks. There's also an Alpine ski area at nearby **Hafjell**, and 500 km (300 miles) of cross-country skiing tracks. The cross-country arena now is the finish for the annual trans-mountain Birkebeiner race, one of the world's oldest citizens' races.

For summer visitors, the biggest attraction is the open-air museum, **Maihaugen** (mid-May–Sept daily 10am–5pm, Oct–mid-May Tues–Sun 11am–4pm; entrance charge), with some 185 vintage buildings brought into the 40-hectare (100-acre) site from all over Gudbrandsdalen, including a stave church and two farms. The museum was the life's work of Anders Sandvig. He came to Lillehammer in 1885 suffering from tuberculosis and with a life expectancy of just two years. Whether or not it was his interest in the museum he founded in 1887 which kept him alive, he lived another 65 years. The **Norsk Vegmuseum** (Road Transport Museum) at **Fåberg**, to the north of Lillehammer on the E6 highway, has everything from horse-drawn sleighs to modern cars (mid-May–Aug daily 10am–6pm; Sept–mid- May Tues–Sun 10am–3pm; free).

BELOW: the historic copper-mining town of Røros.

RØROS

Røros, a UNESCO World Heritage site on the E30 north of Alvdal, was until recently the archetypal company town, with life and society revolving around the mining business. Isolated, exposed, nearly 600 metres (2,000 ft) above sea level and surrounded by mountains, it owed its existence to copper, which was mined here from 1644 to 1972. Now the inhabitants make their living from sawmills, furniture making, wool processing and reindeer meat, as well as tourism. It is a harsh spot; the lowest temperatures in the whole of Norway are often recorded here.

By some miracle Røros escaped the fires that so often laid waste to the wooden buildings in Norwegian towns, and it has retained much of its mining town atmosphere. The wealthy folk lived to the east of the river in Bergmannsgate, while the miners had to make do with the area beneath the slagheaps and the smelter. Picturesque log houses remain, while the crooked houses in Slaggveien are particularly interesting. The most noticeable feature is the stone church, "the pride of the mining town", which was dedicated in 1784. Paintings of clergymen and mining officials decorate the interior. The smelter was the focal point of the town and has been restored as a museum.

Østerdalen

To the east of Mjøsa lake lies **Østerdalen**, carved through the mountains by the Glomma – the country's longest river – stretching 617 km (383 miles). The valley carries one of the north–south railway lines as well as National Highway 3. It starts at **Elverum** ㉙ in the south and continues northward for 250 km (150 miles) becoming broader and more open further north. Just south of **Aursunden**, one of the source lakes for the Glomma River, lies the old copper-mining town of **Røros** ㉚ *(see box, page 192)*, a UNESCO World Heritage site.

Gudbrandsdalen

To the west of Østerdalen lies **Gudbrandsdalen**, the country's second-longest valley, cut by the River Lågen flowing south to Lillehammer. Perhaps because mountains surround it, the valley has a long tradition of folk dancing and folk music and is known for its wood carving and rose painting, sold by handicraft shops in the villages.

For Norwegians everywhere, as well as for curious visitors, Gudbrandsdalen is best remembered as the place where the indigenous Norwegian *geitost* (whey cheese made from goat's milk) was first made in the mid-19th century. The real variety, *ekte geitost*, made entirely of goat's milk, is still produced in the valley and elsewhere in the country. Tribute to the original cheese is paid in the name of *Gudbrandsdalost* (Gudbrandsdalen cheese), made from 10 percent goat's milk and 90 percent cow's milk, the cheese most likely to adorn all breakfast tables, from humble bed and breakfasts to the best of hotels.

About midway along the valley lies **Dombås** ㉛, a principal rail and road junction just southwest of the **Dovrefjell** (Dovre Mountains). The Dovre

Map on pages 174–175

The unsung hero of the Gudbrandsdalen valley is Anne Haav, the "budeia" (farm maiden) who first made the uniquely Norwegian "geitost" (goat's cheese) in the 19th century.

BELOW: canoeing is a popular pastime in summer.

A local hazard for drivers: elk on the road.

BELOW: carved ravens offer protection over this household in Stordalselva.

summits are lofty, but even the highest, **Snøhetta**, at 2,286 metres (7,498 ft), is lower than the peaks of the Jotunheimen. Yet the Dovre Mountains have a place in the national psyche like no other, embodied in the saying about the strength of the country, *"Enig og tro til Dovre Faller"* ("United and faithful till Dovre falls"). Fittingly, the name Dombås derives from *Domba*, the name of a river, and *ås*, meaning "mountain ridge".

Home of the giants

South of Dombås is an extensive area of peak and plateau. The Norwegian mountains are made for walking. As explorer Paul Belloni Du Chaillu observed in *Land of the Midnight Sun* (1881): "The difference between the mountains of Switzerland and Norway is this: those of the former are much higher, more bold and pointed, and sharp in the outlines of their thousand forms. On the other hand, the Norwegian mountains have a grave and sombre character, appearing like a gigantic stony wave, with a peak here and there, impressing more by their vastness than their height and ruggedness."

This "gigantic stony wave" has many hiking trails marked by red letter Ts painted on rocks and cairns. They meander between *hytta* (lodges), mostly above the timberline, between 950 and 1,600 metres (3,100–5,250 ft) above sea level, and the highest summits are around 2,400 metres (7,900 ft). Hence the lack of mention in mountaineering anthologies, where sheer elevation is the criterion. Therein lies part of the secret: you can enjoy the high-altitude experience without needing high-altitude lungs.

Moreover, in summer you can travel to the heart of the range in only a few steps, by boarding one of the passenger launches that ply the waters of lakes

cut right through the mountain to the renowned **Geirangerfjorden** to the north. **Stryn ꊨ** is known for summer skiing on the northeast of Strynsvatn, where the ground rises to Tystigbreen. Until you watch, it is hard to imagine skiers in swimsuits or shorts and T-shirts with deep tans, but there they enjoy every moment.

Map on pages 174–175

Møre og Romsdal

Coastal vessels have long called at Ålesund, Molde and Kristiansund on their way to Trondheim and the north. Looking at the coastline, islands and fjord mouths on a map, it is difficult to distinguish where sea and islands end and fjords and mainland begin. Yet move inland and half the area lies above 600 metres (1,800 ft).

Ålesund **ꊩ** is Norway's largest fishing town. Yet it is best known for its Art Nouveau architecture, built in 1904 after fire destroyed its centre. First to the rescue came Kaiser Wilhelm II of Germany, who sent architecture students and four ships laden with supplies and building materials. With help and donations from all over Europe, the people of Ålesund completed the rebuilding of their town.

Until the 1950s, fishing supported Ålesund, and *klippfisk* (traditional Norwegian split dried cod) was its principal export, mainly to the Mediterranean. But as fishing changed so did Ålesund, which added fish processing and aquaculture. Many former warehouses are now offices and restaurants, where you can try one of the more unlikely local specialities such as *bacalao* (Spanish for cod), made from boned *klippfisk*.

TIP

Explore the colourful Art Nouveau town of Ålesund: guided walks depart Saturdays at noon from the Tourist Information Office (Rådhuset; June–Aug; tel: 70 15 76 00).

Bird island

To the southwest of Ålesund is **Runde ꊪ**, the island that draws naturalists from around the world, as more than 200 bird species have been recorded here. One

BELOW: the magnificent setting of Geirangerfjorden.

Map
on pages
174–175

of the best ways of seeing the island is by taking a four-hour tour on one of the boats departing from **Ulsteinvik** daily from June to August. As a bonus, the waters round the island close over myriad wrecks; in 1972, divers found a hoard of gold and silver coins on board the *Akerendam*, a Dutch vessel that sank in 1725; it was one of the largest finds of sunken treasure ever.

Detail from the marble church on the island of Giske, near Ålesund.

Roses, jazz and ocean driving

Molde ⓭, halfway along the coast from Ålesund north to Kristiansund, is part of an archipelago sheltered from the Norwegian Sea; its mild climate, lush vegetation and rose gardens earn it the title "Town of Roses". It is known at home for the might of its football team and for the annual Molde International Jazz Festival (mid-July; many free concerts; tel: 71 20 31 50).

From **Bud** on the coast west of Molde, a road leads to the **Atlanterhavsveien** (Atlantic Road) to Kristiansund, over **Averøya** ⓯, the biggest island in the area. It heads north across the rim of the ocean, so driving seems like a voyage. Averøya deserves more than the view from a car window. Archaeologists believe that this was one of the first places to be settled after the last Ice Age, and their finds include remnants of the early Fosna Culture that existed around 7000 BC.

The *klippfisk* capital

BELOW: Molde is the "Town of Roses". **RIGHT:** at the foot of the Jostedalsbreen Glacier.

Unlike Ålesund and Molde, **Kristiansund** ⓮ has little protection from the worst the North Atlantic can do. It is right on the coast, with weather-beaten rocks pounded by the sea, yet not far inland are grassy areas and small woods. This is the *klippfisk* town, for long the biggest exporter of Norwegian dried cod. A recent census counted only 22,000 inhabitants but, because of the centuries-old links with other countries through its sailors and fishermen, and the foreign merchants who settled here, the atmosphere is cosmopolitan. Like most Norwegian towns with "Kristian" in their title, Kristiansund was named after King Christian VI. A good introduction is by *sundbåtene*, the harbour boats that for more than 100 years have linked four of the town's five islands.

Mellemverftet, once one of four shipyards in Vågen, is working again as a centre for preserving the craft of shipbuilding, carefully restoring the beautiful lines of traditional Norwegian boats.

Land of the trolls

Inland, the northern part of Møre og Romsdal ends in a crisscross of fjords eating into the islands and peninsulas which lead to **Trollheimen**, the "Home of the Trolls", where the mountains reach nearly 1,600 metres (5,000 ft). This haunt of climbers and skiers is bounded by two important valleys, Surnadalen and Sunndalen, with between them the tiny Todalfjorden. Beside the latter is the surprise of the **Svinvik Arboretum** ⓰ (arboretum), beautiful gardens with thousands of rhododendrons, conifers and other plants (mid-May–Aug Mon–Fri 10am–4pm, Sat–Sun 11am–5pm; entrance charge; tel: 71 66 35 80). Despite the northern latitude, plants from all over the world grow at Svinvik, run by Trondheim University. ❑

NORWAY'S MOST BEAUTIFUL VOYAGE

The splendid coastal voyage from Bergen to the North Cape and beyond has long been regarded as one of the great sea journeys of the world

To travel on board the Hurtigruten (literally "swift route") steamships is to partake in what has been described as one of the world's most beautiful voyages. What began in 1891 as an idea to provide an express shipping service along the rugged Norwegian coast between Trondheim and Hammerfest has evolved into a lucrative form of tourism. Yet part of the charm is watching a working ship going about its business. Out of season, it reverts to its traditional role of carrying west-coast Norwegians, who treat it as a bus, for business and pleasure.

PORTS OF CALL

In spring and autumn, the 12-day round trip from Bergen across the Arctic Circle to the Nordkapp (North Cape) and Kirkenes lets you feast on the dramatic seasonal changes. In May, the fjord valleys are brilliantly in bloom, and the hills and the mountains of the north are still covered with snow. Returning south one meets the swift Norwegian summer marching north.

The Hurtigruten makes 34 ports of call along this ever-changing coast, some at places no bigger than a handful of houses round a harbour, others at cities such as Trondheim and Tromsø with time ashore to explore.

▷ **OUTWARD BOUND**
In the summer months the Hurtigruten take on the trimmings of cruise ships with dancing, film shows and day trips. Guides are on hand for hikes and vigorous climbs.

▽ **TEMPTING TREATS**
No matter what season, the meals on board offer a feast of Norwegian specialities, with abundant buffets, assorted cheeses and a mouthwatering selection of desserts.

▷ **FULL STEAM AHEAD**
Captain Ernstsen, *M/S Nordlys*, and his crew, along with those of the other ships in the fleet, ensure generally smooth sailings in and out of the islands along the coast.

◁ **STUNNING SCENERY**
Tranquil Trollfjorden: from fjords to open sea, fertile land to barren rock, fishing hamlets to cities, the voyage is a mix of the workaday and the spectacular.

△ **ARCHITECTURAL SIGHT**
Ishavskatedralen, the Arctic Ocean Cathedral at Tromsø, is a symbol of the north. Built in 1964, the cathedral features one of Europe's largest works of stained glass.

△ **VIEW FROM THE DECK**
With thousands of islands and skerries, mountains and glaciers, the landscape is constantly changing and no two days are alike.

◁ **NIGHT SKY**
The Northern Lights (Aurora Borealis) is a fascinating spectacle, whether a sparkling multicoloured vision or dancing white streaks.

COMMUNICATIONS REVOLUTION

Over the past century more than 70 ships have served in the Hurtigruten fleet.

These diverse vessels led a communications revolution, enabling the population and industries along the rugged Norwegian coast to keep in touch in a new way. Previously, it took three weeks in summer or five months in winter to send a letter from Trondheim to Hammerfest; the Coastal Express reduced this time to a few days.

Places such as the Lofoten Islands, Trollfjorden and the North Cape *(symbol pictured above)* became accessible to travellers who wanted to see the Midnight Sun, and so the tourist business began to grow. Nature lovers and birdwatchers are attracted by the scenery and the many bird colonies, which include puffins, kittiwakes and guillemots.

As time went by, ships were built specifically with cold storage and freezer rooms, vehicle roll on/roll off capacity and conference facilities, as well as comfortable cabins.

Two companies now run 11 ships, ranging from the grand old *M/S Lofoten* to the *M/S Midnatsol*, built in 2003.

THE NORTHWEST COAST

North of Trondheim, Norway's religious and cultural capital, lies a beautiful, but often harsh landscape that crosses the Arctic Circle into the land of the Midnight Sun

Map on page 206

The northwest coast is where Norway gets thinner, from Trondheim – a large city for its latitude and the gateway to the north – up to Bodø, which lies beyond the Arctic Circle. The land along this narrow conduit is mostly forested, with the benign influence of the Gulf Stream ensuring temperate conditions persist far to the north.

Trondheim ❶ is a name rooted in Nordic mythology: *Trond* comes from the Old Norse "*throendr*", the name of the people of the region and meaning "strong and virile", and *heim* comes from the word for habitation. It is a pleasant city, with clean air, wide streets, low buildings and a compact centre. Its relatively modest population of 165,000 swells by nearly a sixth in term-time, as this is a university town, as well as the country's leading hi-tech research centre. It is, as American sociologists have proclaimed, a most ideal city to live in.

As with all Norwegian cities, the outdoors is close at hand. Trondheim's back garden is Bymarka to the west, where **Gråkallen** (Old Man) at 520 metres (1,700 ft) high is a favourite walking and cross-country skiing area. Indeed, outdoor sports are a leading local pastime, and the city has acted as host to the World Nordic Ski Championships. The River Nidelva is known for the size of its salmon, and the fjord itself is ideal for sea fishing from boat or shore.

LEFT: overview of the city of Trondheim.
BELOW: Nidaros Cathedral, venue for Norwegian coronations.

NIDAROS CATHEDRAL

In 997 the settlers of Nidaros could not have known, but the sheltered site they picked at the mouth of the Nid River was to become a pivotal city in Europe.

In the late 11th century, work started on a major church at Nidaros, erected over the grave of St Olav, the king who brought Christianity to the Vikings *(see page 209)*. Apparently the Pope found that fact auspicious, as he appointed an archbishop there and made the bishops of Greenland, Iceland, the Isle of Man, Orkney and the Faroe Islands, and the bishops in Norway responsible to him.

The church became a cathedral, one of the holy sites of Europe and the goal for many pilgrimages. It has become the national shrine and according to the 1814 Constitution the venue for the coronation of Norwegian kings.

The name Nidaros endured; the cathedral is Nidaros - domen (Nidaros Cathedral). The city that grew up around it became Trondhjem, a name rooted in Nordic mythology. In January 1930, when the city celebrated its 900th anniversary, the origin of the cathedral was honoured by changing the city name to Nidaros. The renaming triggered a debate that ended in March 1931 when the name reverted to Trondheim, with the spelling "*hjem*" amended to "*heim*" to please linguistic purists.

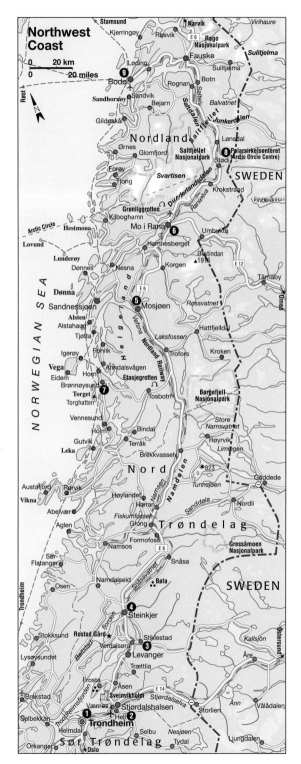

Viking city

The well-preserved buildings of the old harbour, the imposing **Nidarosdomen** (cathedral; *see box, page 205*; daily: hours vary; entrance charge includes admission to adjacent Archbishop's Palace) and the statue of a Viking king, Olav Tryggvason, on a high pedestal in the centre of the city, belie the heritage of more than a millennium. Tryggvason founded the city in 997, and his successor, Olav Haraldsson, brought Christianity to the country *(see page 209)*. It was Haraldson's martyrdom that triggered the building of the cathedral, where Norwegian kings are crowned, most recently King Harald V in 1991. The **Norwegian Crown Jewels** (May–Aug Mon–Fri 9am–6pm, Sat 9am–2pm, Sun 1–4pm; Sept–Apr times vary; entrance charge) are kept in the cathedral, and the regalia for king, queen and crown prince are on display in the Archbishop's Palace.

Throughout history, the cathedral also had influence on secular life. In pre-Reformation Europe, kings would often extend the powers of the clerics to civil and mercantile matters, including the issuing of coins. At Nidaros, that happened in 1222, when young King Håkon Håkonsson issued an edict empowering Archbishop Guttorm of Nidaros to mint and circulate coins. The archbishop and his successors exercised that right until 1537, when the Reformation ousted the last archbishop. Examples of the coins struck at the archbishop's mint were found in the following centuries, then in the early 1990s archaeologists discovered the mint beneath the ruins of a building that had burned down in 1640. The mint, the oldest found in Europe, forms part of the exhibits at the **Archbishop's Palace** (Erkebispegården) next to the cathedral.

Giving cyclists a lift

Trondheim has done much to relieve traffic congestion, including implementing a toll ring round the city. Cycling is encouraged on a network of dedicated cycle paths. Yet topography challenges cycling: the flat centre is surrounded by steep hills. So in 1995, the resourceful city built

Trampe, the world's first bicycle lift, 130 metres (426 ft) up Brubakken hill. The lift operates like a ski tow, and cyclists pay using keycards at the bottom of the hill. Not surprisingly, the annual **Styrkeprøven** (Trial of Strength) trans-mountain bicycle race (June) starts in Trondheim. It finishes 540 km (336 miles) south, in Oslo.

Map on page 206

And you can go to...

Some Norwegian words tempt *double entendre* in English, most notably the name of the village closest to Trondheim's Værnes airport. It's **Hell ❷**. Notwithstanding the derivation of the name from the Old Norse word for cavern, postcards of the railway station at Hell sell astonishingly well. So when in Trondheim, you can indeed go to Hell; it's only 33 minutes east by commuter train. The station here must be one of the most photographed in the country. In September Hell hosts an annual blues festival which attracts international stars and fans to this otherwise quiet settlement.

St Olav's battleground

Many European countries claim histories highlighted by a decisive medieval battle. For Norway, it's the **Battle of Stiklestad** on 29 July 1030, some 36 years before England's momentous Battle of Hastings. Unlike Hastings, which enabled the winning Normans to conquer the country, at **Stiklestad ❸** it was the loser who ultimately won. The forces of King Canute of Denmark and England were victorious and King Olav Haraldson of Norway was slain. Olav was later to become a saint *(see page 209)*. Stiklestad, located east of the E6 highway about 100 km (60 miles) north of Trondheim, is the venue for the annual St Olav's Play *(Spelet om Heilag Olav)* performed every July in an open-air amphitheatre dur-

Northern road signs appear in Norwegian and Finnish.

BELOW: Bodø, port of call for the coastal steamers.

Map on page 206

The Arctic Circle at 66°N is defined not by temperature, but by light. It is the latitude at which the sun is above the horizon at noon on 21 June. At Bødo, the "Mørketid" (Arctic Night) lasts from 15 to 29 December.

BELOW: the bus runs whatever the weather.

ing the 11-day St Olav Festival. A 12th-century church marks the spot where King Olav died, and a museum (St Olav's Kulturhus) chronicles the events.

Trade essential

Despite their reputation as marauders, the Vikings were principally farmers and traders who settled and worked the land wherever they went. **Steinkjer ④**, the first sizeable town north of Trondheim, reflects this. Its name comes from the Old Norse word for a river dam built to trap fish, and indeed in Viking times it was a trading centre. In 1857 it became an export port for timber and agricultural produce, a status that underscores the comparatively mild climate of the region, as here at 64°N the land is fertile and forests abound.

North of Steinkjer, the railway and the E6 highway follow the sheltered Namdalen valley to **Mosjøen ⑤** at the head of the Vefsnfjorden and then to **Mo i Rana ⑥** at the head of Ranafjorden. The word *Mo*, which means sand or gravel flats, is a common place name in Norway. Consequently, Mo at the head of Ranafjorden is called Mo i Rana to distinguish it from other towns named Mo. As for Steinkjer, trade triggered the first settlement of Mosjøen and Mo i Rana. Today the towns support heavy industries, starting in the mid-1950s with the **Norsk Jernverk** iron works at Mo i Rana and **Mosjøen Aluminumverk** aluminium plant at Mosjøen. From a business viewpoint, the locations of these industries in small, northern towns may be questioned. They are there as part of the government's efforts to provide jobs that keep people in the region. A similar effort is the more recent centralisation of the nine principal government registers at **Brønnøysund ⑦**, on the coast south of Mosjøen. If, say, you take out a loan to buy a car anywhere in Norway, the relevant details will be registered at Brønnøysund.

Crossing the Arctic Circle

Most people experience an inexplicable thrill as they cross the **Polarsirkel** (Arctic Circle). Perhaps the reason is celestial: unlike the equator, set by geometry, or the International Date Line, drawn by timekeepers, the Arctic Circle marks the southern boundary of a different sort of world, the Land of The Midnight Sun.

The only building in this landscape is **Polarsirkelsenteret ⑧** (Arctic Circle Centre; June and Aug daily 9am–8pm; July 8am–10pm; May and 1–15 Sep 10am–6pm; free). Situated on the Circle, alongside the railway and the E6 highway, it has a cafeteria, gift shop and exhibitions, including Europe's largest stuffed polar bear. Outside stands a memorial to the thousands of Russian and Yugoslav World War II prisoners of war who built the railway and perished in the bitter winter conditions.

Further north, **Bodø ⑨** was founded as a trading centre, to compete with Bergen. It competed unsuccessfully, but today the Hurtigruten coastal steamers (*see Insight on Hurtigruten, page 202*) call on their way from Bergen. Bodø also features the world's strongest maelstrom – Saltstraumen – with whirlpools up to 10 metres (30 ft) in diameter. Bodø is the northern end of the rail network and a staging post for summer visitors. As the crow flies, it is as far from Kristiansand, the southernmost station, as Kristiansand is from Paris. ❑

STIKLESTAD: THE MAKING OF A SAINT

The site of the Battle of Stiklestad near Trondheim in 1030 marks a pivotal point in the history of the Norwegian nation and the adoption of Christianity

Stiklestad, north of Trondheim, is a name which is revered by Norwegians. This ancient battlefield is the place that saw the foundation of Norwegian unity and the adoption of the Christian faith.

In the 11th century Norway was a country constantly disrupted by disputes between rival chieftains. The ambition of the reigning king, Olav Haraldson, was a united Norway. He also wanted to create a Christian country with Christian laws and churches and clergy.

He was not the first to attempt this. In the previous century Olav Tryggvason had been converted to Christianity in England. He returned to Norway in 995 with the express purpose of crushing the chieftains and imposing his new-found faith. But Olav Tryggvason's conversion had not swept away all his Viking instincts and in his zeal he used great cruelty to convert the populace. His chieftains became disenchanted and Olav was killed in the Battle of Svolder in the year 1000.

Olav Haraldson ascended the throne in 1015, but like Olav Tryggvason he foolishly made too great a use of the sword to establish Christianity. King Canute of Denmark and England, with his eye on the Norwegian throne, gave support to discontented factions within the country and in 1028 invaded Norway, forcing King Olav to flee to Russia.

Undaunted, Olav returned with a few followers, but his support had dwindled. He met his end on 29 July 1030 at the Battle of Stiklestad. Olav's corpse was taken to the then capital, Nidaros, and buried on the banks of the Nidelva river. When the body was disinterred a year later, it showed no signs of corruption: his face was unchanged and his nails and hair had grown. This was taken as a sign of sanctity.

Following this revelation, Olav was proclaimed a saint and his body placed in a silver shrine in Nidaros Cathedral. Faith in the holiness of King Olav – St Olav – spread and his shrine became a centre of pilgrimage.

Canute's victory at the Battle of Stiklestad was brief. He ceded power to his son, Svejn, but as rumours of Olav's sanctity grew, popular support for Canute evaporated and Svejn was exiled to Denmark in 1035. Meanwhile, St Olav's son, Magnus, had been in exile in Russia. Norway now invited him to return and accept the crown.

From that time Stiklestad has been a place of pilgrimage. It now has a beautiful open-air theatre, and on the anniversary of the battle a cast of 300 actors, choristers, dancers and musicians re-enact the events of July 1030. ❏

TOP LEFT: statue of St Olav. **ABOVE LEFT:** a rune stone marks the place where King Olav died. **TOP RIGHT AND RIGHT:** the annual St Olav's Play.

NORWAY'S FAR NORTH

Map on pages 212–213

Far removed from the rest of Europe, Norway's spectacular North extends through Arctic latitudes from the rugged Lofoten Islands to the Russian border. Beyond is the remote archipelago of Spitsbergen

The far north of Norway, comprising Troms and Finnmark counties and the Lofoten Islands, is unique in the Arctic, thanks to the warming currents of the Gulf Stream. Here lies more than a third of the land of Norway, which one resident in 20 calls home.

Imposing wall, tricky waters

Viewed from the mainland across Vestfjorden north of Bodø, the **Lofoten Islands** present an imposing wall of rugged peaks rising from the sea. On the west, these mountains form a mighty shield against the onslaught of Norwegian Sea weather, so most of their habitation is along their east coasts, facing the mainland. **Svolvær ❶**, the main town, has been a trading and fishing centre since the 17th century. Fishing has long been the traditional calling of the islanders, and today *Lofot torsk* (Lofoten cod) remains choice throughout the country. Between February and April, **Kabelvåg**, to the south, is the undisputed fishing capital of northern Norway. Up to 10,000 vessels make for Vestfjord during these months for the colourful *Lofotfiske*, the annual cod-fishing event.

LEFT: sunset by a frozen waterfall on the Lofoten Islands.
BELOW: a tribute to the explorer Roald Amundsen.

The southernmost of the larger Lofoten Islands, **Moskenesøya** is the most photographed, perhaps because of the picturesque fishing village of **Reine ❷**. Between Lofotodden, its southern cape, and the islet of Mosken lies **Moskenstraumen ❸**, a 4-km (2½-mile) wide, shallow channel. Here tidal currents reach speeds of up to 6 knots in their alternating flow between the Norwegian Sea and Vestfjorden, and water always swirls around a submerged rock in the middle of the channel. Sailing here is risky, as Dutch navigators first noted on maps published in 1595 in *Mercator's Atlas*, where the current was called "*Maelstrom*". Internationally, it has since been known by that name, and writers, including Jules Verne and Edgar Allan Poe, have amplified it to a huge whirlpool that engulfs ships and men. Maelstrom now is a synonym for a whirlpool treacherous to navigation and, by extension, turbulent confusion.

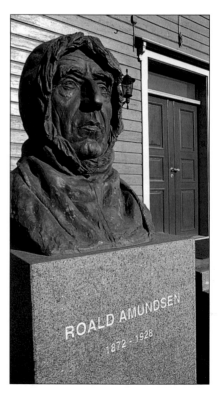

Paris of the North

Tromsø ❹ has long been a leading city in northern Norway and now is regarded as the region's unofficial capital. International trade and influence came early, and by the 1860s the women of the town were so stylishly dressed as to cause a visiting tourist to remark that the city seemed to be "The Paris of the North". That nickname persists, and now may apply as well to Tromsø's abundant and varied nightlife, with an average of one seat in an eatery or place of entertainment for every three residents. The city is built mostly on an island between the mainland and the larger coastal

ROALD AMUNDSEN 1872 - 1928

For panoramic views of Tromsø, take the Fjellheisen cable car 420 metres (1,378 ft) above sea level. It even operates until 1am when the Midnight Sun is shining.

island of **Kvaløya**. The sheltered location made it an ideal port for commercial operations in Arctic waters as well as the last port of call for polar expeditions. Intrepid polar explorers are the centre of attention at the **Polarmuseet** (Polar Museum; mid-June–mid-Aug daily 10am–7pm; Mar–mid-June and mid-Aug–Sept 11am–5pm; Oct–Feb 11am–3pm) in the historic harbour area.

The city is the cultural centre of the North. The **Nordnorsk Kunstmuseum** (Art Museum of Northern Norway; mid-June–Aug daily noon–6pm; Sept–mid-June Tues–Fri 10am–5pm, Sat–Sun noon–5pm; free) has been going from strength to strength since moving in 2001 to its first permanent home facing Roald Amundsens Square. Sami and Northern Norwegian art is well represented in the permanent collection. The museum has some excellent visiting exhibitions throughout the year as well. The **Tromsø Museum** (June–Aug daily 9am–8pm; Sept–May Mon–Fri 9am–3.30pm, Sat noon–3pm, Sun 11am–4pm; entrance charge; tel: 77 64 50 00) has a splendid collection of Sami art and contains a reconstructed Viking longhouse.

Just over the bridge, on the mainland, is the striking **Ishavskatedral** (Arctic Ocean Cathedral; June–mid-Aug Mon–Sat 9am–7pm, Sun from 1pm; mid-Aug–May daily 4–6pm; entrance charge), an impressive modern work by the architect Jan Inge Hovig. Its entire east wall, 23 metres (75 ft) high, consists of a *dalle* (French for "flagstone") technique stained-glass window by Victor Sparre.

Tromsø is also home to Europe's northernmost brewery, **Mack** (tel: 77 62 45 00), established in 1845. Here you can sample its famous Arctic Ale, *Mackøl*.

Though it is in the Arctic, the city enjoys a benign climate. The average midday temperature in January is the same as in Oslo and summer temperatures are about the same as in Trondheim.

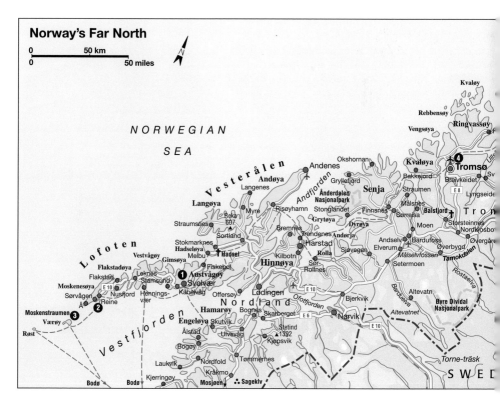

Norway's Far North

Heritage of the centuries

Alta ❺, the largest town in Finnmark, is known among fishermen for having one of the world's best salmon rivers. It is also home to the **Alta Museum** at **Hjemmeluft** (late May and mid-Aug–Sept daily 9am–6pm; June–mid-Aug 8am–9pm; Oct–late May Mon–Fri 9am–3pm, Sat–Sun 11am–4pm; entrance charge) on the southern outskirts, a collection of rock carvings dating from 4200 to 500 BC. These remarkable "stories in pictures" of people, animals (particularly reindeer), boats and weapons, are now a UNESCO World Heritage site.

South of Alta on the E93 lies **Kautokeino** ❻, a centre for the Sami, the indigenous people of northern Scandinavia and the Kola Peninsula of Russia. They are sometimes called Lapps, but prefer their own name Sami, which designates the land where they have lived for thousands of years. The size of the Sami population is not known, but is conservatively estimated at 70,000, of whom about half live in Norway. Their native languages are related to Finnish, Hungarian and Estonian and have little in common with Norwegian. Traditionally, the Sami have been hunters, fishermen and reindeer herders. Some still follow these callings, while others practise more modern trades. One of the more famous among them is film director Nils Gaup, whose *Pathfinder* (1987), the first feature-length Sami film, was nominated for an Academy Award. Like indigenous minorities elsewhere, the Sami were long suppressed, but now have their own flag and own parliament, *Sámediggi*, at **Karasjok** ❼.

After two months of winter darkness, Vardø, Norway's easternmost town, celebrates the return of the sun around 20 January with a gun salute on the first day that the entire disk is visible above the horizon.

Northernmost point

Nordkapp ❽ (The North Cape) at 71°10' 21"N is considered by many to be the most northerly point of mainland Europe. But in fact the tip of **Knivskjelodden**,

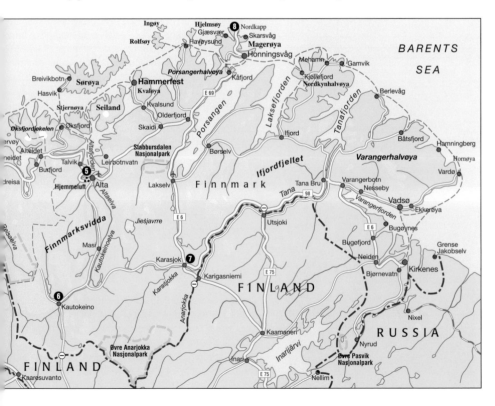

Map on pages 212–213

Part of the Children of the World Monument at the North Cape.

BELOW: polar bear on Svalbard.
RIGHT: Sami woman rounds up reindeer.

a low, slim peninsula to the west of Nordkapp, lies 47 seconds of latitude farther north. No matter; the North Cape, a name first used in 1553 by English sailor Richard Chancellor, is the imposing headland that draws visitors from around the world. Residents further south know the annual signs: in early summer, a stream of cars with southern European number plates heads north, many of them with "To the North Cape" written on their boots. Later, the stream reverses, and the cars come south, reindeer horns strapped to their roof racks. They have attained their goal. Tablets attest that even royalty have been here, King Oscar II of Sweden in 1873, King Chulalangkorn of Thailand in 1907.

Nordkapphallen (North Cape Hall; Apr–early Oct times vary; mid-June–early Aug daily 9am–1am; entrance charge) has a café, restaurant and other facilities for visitors. The **Nordkappmuséet** (North Cape Museum; June–mid-Aug Mon–Sat 10am–7pm, Sun from noon; mid-Aug–May Mon–Fri noon–4pm; entrance charge; tel: 78 47 72 00), near the Hurtigruten quay in **Honningsvag** has a variety of displays about the cape and its history.

North to Svalbard

The **Svalbard** (Spitsbergen) archipelago lies 640 km (400 miles) north of the mainland. It was first mentioned in 1194 by Icelandic sailors. In 1596, the Dutch navigator Willem Barents, searching for the Northeast Passage, sighted the largest of its four main islands, which he called Spitsbergen (Pointed Peaks). Indeed, the terrain resembles that of the Alps, and Spitsbergen covers an area almost as large as Switzerland. In 1920, an international treaty gave Norway sovereignty over Svalbard and granted 35 signatory countries the right to exploit its resources. Only three countries have exercised their right on a commercial scale. In 1906, John Longyear, an American industrialist, founded the Arctic Coal Company on Spitsbergen. Today, the principal village, **Longyearbyen** (pop. 2,000) is named after him, but only Norway and Russia remain as mine operators.

The climate is relatively mild for the Arctic: midday temperatures at Longyearbyen average –7°C (19°F) in February and 7°C (45°F) in July. But permafrost prevails year-round. In 1998 it made the international news, when Canadian pathologists exhumed the well-preserved corpses of six Svalbard coal miners who had died in the 1918 influenza pandemic, to search for clues that might reveal its origin.

Today, hi-tech is supplanting mining as a leading livelihood. The **Svalbard Satellite Station** near Longyearbyen is positioned to download images from all earth observation satellites in polar orbits, and the **Rocket Range** at **Ny Ålesund** is now instrumental in weather research.

With daily flights between Tromsø and Longyearbyen, tourism is growing. In summer, the stark mountains around the village are offset by a valley which has meadows spangled with flowers. Here you will find cassiope and purple saxifrage, and, perhaps, a patch of boreal Jacob's ladder, *Polemonium boreale*, an Arctic rarity. The polar winter is another matter. The sun does not rise above the horizon and everything is locked in darkness, lit only by the moon and the multicoloured rays of the **Aurora Borealis**, the Northern Lights. ❑

SWEDEN

From sophisticated Stockholm to mountain wilderness,
Sweden offers the traveller immense variety

A subtle change in Swedish attitudes has been emerging in recent years. Not so long ago the country was an introverted Fortress Sweden perched uneasily on the edge of Western Europe. Indeed, many Swedes still talked about travelling "to Europe" as if it was on a different continent. All that changed with the country's admission to the European Union in the 1990s and the opening in 2000 of the Öresund bridge across the straits separating Sweden from Denmark. The Swedes have finally become "good Europeans".

As such, Sweden is attracting many more visitors, not just to the bustling big cities and cultural centres of Stockholm, Göteborg and Malmö, but also to the rural regions and the vast wilderness areas of Lapland and the Bothnian coast. Where else can you stay in an hotel made entirely from ice, play golf under the Midnight Sun or dance with abandon around a maypole at Midsummer?

It is an ideal country for those who like the great outdoors and activities such as angling, golf, riding, fell-walking, skiing, sailing or canoeing. Even Greater Stockholm, which covers a much wider area than you might expect for its 2 million population, is a region of sea, lake and open spaces, and never far from the thousands of islands that form its archipelago, reaching out into the waters of the Baltic.

The southern provinces, including Skåne, were for centuries part of Denmark and a faintly Danish accent persists. Much of south-central Sweden is dominated by the great lakes of Vänern and Vättern, the heart of a network of waterways that make it possible to cross this widest part of Sweden by boat along the Göta Kanal, which links Stockholm to Göteborg.

Further north, the geographical centre of Sweden holds Dalarna, the folklore province where old customs linger. At the end of the long road or rail route north are the mountains. This is home to Scandinavia's second race, the Sami, whose wanderings with their reindeer herds take little account of national boundaries.

Culturally, well-preserved sites like the remains of the Viking capital of Birka, state-of-the-art museums, and the homes of artists such as Carl Larsson, who inspired the clean lines of contemporary Swedish design, are all open to the visitor. On the musical front, Göteborg's Symphony Orchestra is in the top rank of world orchestras. Sweden has even become a centre of gastronomic excellence.

This northern land is also a popular year-round destination. The winter climate is less harsh than many people imagine and the period around Christmas, with its traditional markets, brightly decorated streets and St Lucia processions, is a magical time of year. ❑

PRECEDING PAGES: the smooth rocks of the Bohuslän coast; enjoying a dip outside; Stockholm, city of islands.
LEFT: decorative ironwork at Stockholm's Royal Palace.

THE SWEDES

Beneath the cool, sophisticated exterior, the surprisingly mirthful Swede
harbours a deep commitment to nature, tradition and schnapps

Contrary to popular opinion, Swedes do have a sense of humour. Armies of dissenters will no doubt beg to differ and sceptics will balk at the very idea. But the Swedish sense of humour is a peculiar thing: as elusive as Garbo and as fleeting as a Swedish summer. Blink and you'll miss it. Their reputation for being dry, sombre and painfully serious is itself the cause of much mirth for these Scandinavian jokers. And when the uninitiated confuse Sweden with Switzerland, it always raises an eyebrow and just the smallest trace of a knowing smile.

But don't let the cool exterior of this Scandinavian fool you. They may certainly seem calm and collected on the outside, but they're every bit as prone to hysterical fits as the next person. Even if they do recover much faster and the smile that flashed across those solemn features vanishes as quickly as it came.

Blond and beautiful

When it comes to Sweden, popular misconceptions are rife. It is commonly held that most people in Sweden are blond, at least 6ft 3in tall and drive Volvos. In fact, only half the population are natural blonds, the average male is 5ft 10in and the BMW is the preferred mode of transport for upwardly mobile Swedes today. Though the more stereotypical images of Sweden – leggy blonde beauties, pickled herring, meatballs and seemingly unflappable tennis players – certainly run true to form, Sweden today is a country of growing cultural and social diversity. A country in which the traditional mingles with the ultramodern and in which society and the political arena have been shaped by a strong democratic tradition.

First encounters with Swedes can be somewhat confusing. They are a baffling blend of the cosmopolitan and the provincial. For this sophisticated urbanite is every bit at home in the concrete jungle, sipping cappuccinos at a pavement café, as going barefoot at their place in the country. It's no exaggeration to say that Swedes are potty about nature. It's somehow a part of the Swedish soul. They are quick to wax lyrical about the grassy plains of Skåne, expound the virtues of lakeside Dalarna and

SWEDEN: THE ESSENTIALS

Population 9.2 million.
Capital Stockholm (pop. 795,000).
Notable towns Göteborg, Malmö.
Climate Average afternoon temperatures in Stockholm in July are 22°C (71°F); in January, –1°C (30°F).
Top museums Vasamuséet, Nordiska Muséet, Skansen, Stockholm; Universeum, Göteborg; Silvermuséet, Arjeplog.
Historic sights Drottningholm Palace, Gripsholms Slott, Uppsala Cathedral, Gammelstad, Luleå.
Best midsummer festivity Dalarna.
Outdoor activities watersports, hiking, fishing, skiing.
Tourist information www.visitsweden.com.

LEFT: the Swedes are a blend of the cosmopolitan and the provincial.
RIGHT: growing up in modern Sweden.

remind you that theirs is the only true wilderness left in all Europe. Ask any Swede to recount tales of their childhood and they'll dreamily recall summers spent in the country with a noticeable softening of facial expression, a voice tinged with more than just a hint of nostalgia and a faraway look in their eye.

National pride

Next to nature, there's nothing Swedes like to talk about more than Sweden itself. Get them started on this subject at your peril. This is not to say that Swedes are braggarts, far from it. A more humble, self-deprecating tribe you'd be

hard pushed to find. But their modesty is a thin veil in the face of such obvious national pride. For all young Swedes are well versed in the achievements of their countrymen, be it Alfred Nobel or August Strindberg; even the exploits of their marauding ancestors are today taught in schools with pride.

At first glance a Swede may appear a very cool customer. But underneath that composed exterior and self-satisfaction with all things Swedish, you'll find a warm, friendly individual, who having decided to let their guard down and befriend you, will be a friend for life.

The image of the bloodthirsty Viking,

WINING AND DINING

Oddly enough, this "vodka-belt" nation has a rather uneasy relationship with alcohol. The liberalism that once made Sweden the envy of more conservative societies makes the prevailing attitude towards drinking, with its moral pontificating, all the more perplexing.

Despite EU membership and its initial effects, alcohol remains a contentious issue. Exorbitant prices and an unyielding state monopoly have conspired to create a sense of deprivation and prohibition. A Friday evening ritual is played out at state off-licences up and down the country, in which Swedes queue with stoical aplomb to buy a bottle of wine and a six-pack. It's not so strange then that when

the chance to indulge presents itself, Swedes have few qualms about throwing themselves into the fray.

Whatever your take on the Swedes' drinking habits, when it comes to dining their manners are impeccable. Be it state banquets or family get-togethers, Swedes are sticklers for etiquette. From arriving punctually to observing the niceties of fine dining, the formalities are upheld to the last drop of schnapps. At birthdays and anniversaries, coffee and cake are served with the precision of a military exercise. Yet Swedes will happily tuck into a crayfish feast, ripping off claws with their hands and clashing beer glasses in a fashion reminiscent of their Viking forebears.

plundering all in his path, is one the Swedes have taken centuries to live down. Nowadays the little red cottage is Sweden's most enduring image and there's nothing Swedes like better than to take off to the country for a spell. An affinity for the land runs deep within the Swedish soul and they are never happier than when they can kick off their shoes, swim naked and bond with nature.

Life in Sweden is intrinsically linked to the natural rhythms of the changing seasons.

SKÅL!

Friendships are often sealed over schnapps. Delicately flavoured with fruits or spices, schnapps is a perennial favourite and every Swede can name his or her tipple.

soaking up the first warming rays of spring. Summers are woefully short, often hot and always much longed for.

Swedes today come in a variety of creeds and colours. Immigration continues to influence the country's social, cultural and political landscape. During the turbulent 1990s Sweden was forced to re-evaluate its global position in the face of new economic challenges and growing questions of social inequality. The high standard of living once enjoyed by Swedes and their envi-

Swedish winters are famous for their longevity, Arctic temperatures and the sun's prolonged absence. But Swedes have learnt how to make the most of it and winter sports are popular with Swedes of all ages. They eagerly await the spring and the return of sunlight with all the excited anticipation of children at Christmas. Like hibernating animals re-emerging after winter, sun-starved Swedes are wont to stand on street corners, at crossings, in traffic lights, and any other spot with a south-facing aspect,

able cradle-to-the-grave welfare system has come under increasing pressure.

Looking to Europe

For years Swedes championed the causes of others, but their own increasingly precarious position has forced them to abandon, albeit unofficially, their policy of neutrality and take closer steps to the Continent. Sweden's entry into the European Union in 1995 was part of an effort to bring Sweden in line with a changing Europe. New social and economic policies are helping the country adapt to a global economy, while the Swedes themselves are learning to adapt to their new role – as Europeans. ❏

LEFT: Swedish fathers are more involved than their European counterparts in caring for their children.
ABOVE: glass-blowing in Småland.

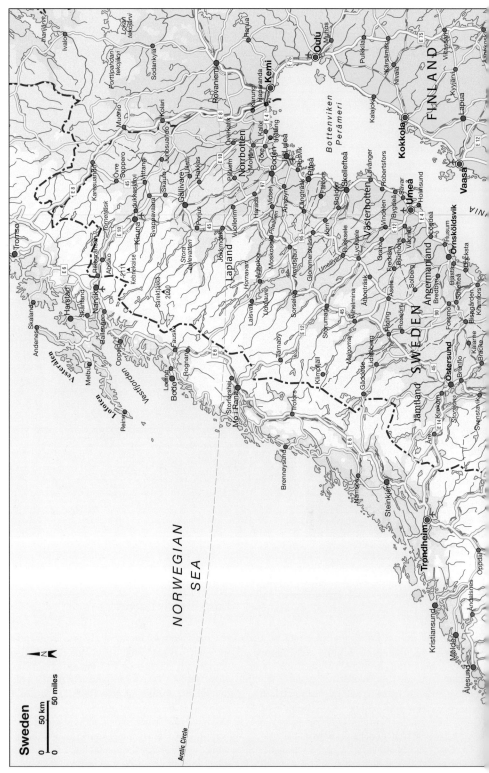

Sweden

0   50 km
0   50 miles

N

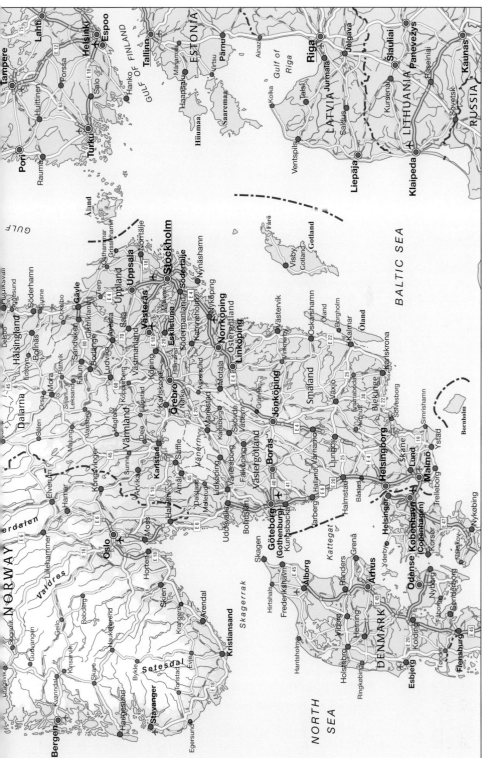

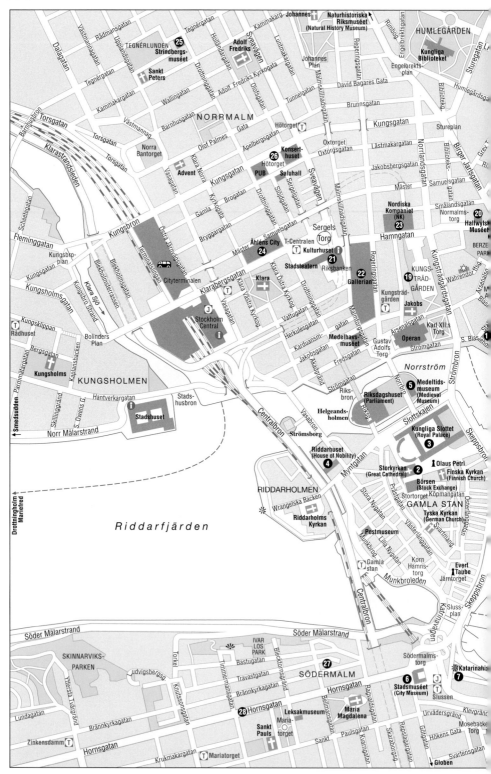

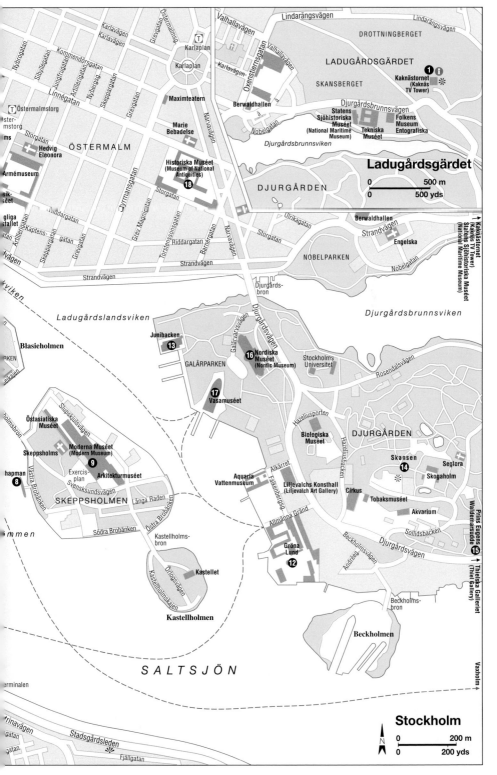

Karlavägen
Östermalms
Valhallavägen
Lindarängsvägen
Lindarängsvägen
Karlavägen
Greygatan
DROTTNINGBERGET
Kommendörsgatan
Nybrogatan
Sibyllegatan
Jungfrugatan
Artillerigatan
Nybergsg.
Skeppargatan
Greygatan
Karlaplan
Karlaplan
Karlavägen
Valhallavägen
Oxenstiernsgatan
LADUGÅRDSGÄRDET
SKANSBERGET
Kaknästornet
(Kaknäs
TV Tower)
1
Linnégatan
Maximteatern
Berwaldhallen
Djurgårdsbrunnsvägen
Östermalmstorg
öster-
mstorg
ms
Marie
Bebadelse
Narvavägen
Statens
Sjöhistoriska
Muséet
(National Maritime
Museum)
Folkens
Museum
Tekniska
Muséet
Entografiska
Storgatan
Nobelgatan
Hedvig
Eleonora
ÖSTERMALM
Djurgårdsbrunnsviken
Armémuseum
Historiska Muséet
(Museum of National
Antiquities)
18
Ladugårdsgärdet
sik-
séet
Jyrmansgatan
Storgatan
DJURGÅRDEN
0   500 m
0   500 yds
gliga
stallet
Riddargatan
atan
Artillerig.
Kaptens-
gatan
Skeppargatan
Greygatan
Grev Magnigatan
Torstensonsgatan
Riddargatan
Barnrégatan
Narvavägen
Ulrikagatan
Storgatan
Berwaldhallen
Strandvägen
Engelska
Kaknästornet
(Kaknäs TV Tower)
Statens Sjöhistoriska Muséet
(National Maritime Museum)
vägen
Strandvägen
Strandvägen
NOBELPARKEN
Nobelgatan
viken
Djurgårds-
bron
Ladugårdslandsviken
Djurgårdsvägen
Galärvarvsvägen
Djurgårdsbrunnsviken
Junibacken
13
Blasieholmen
RKEN
elkalen
GALÄRPARKEN
16 Nordiska
Muséet
(Nordic Museum)
Stockholms
Universitet
Rosendalsvägen
17
Vasamuséet
Östasiatiska
Muséet
Skeppsholms
Slupskjulsvägen
Moderna Muséet
(Modern Museum)
9
Hazeliusporten
Biologiska
Muséet
DJURGÅRDEN
Hazeliusbacken
Skansen
14
Seglora
holmsbron
hapman
8
Exercis-
plan
Arkitekturmuséet
Svensksundsvägen
Västra Brobänken
Aquaria
Vattenmuseum
Alkärret
Falkenbergsg.
Skogaholm
SKEPPSHOLMEN
Långa Raden
Östra Brobänken
Liljevalchs Konsthall
(Liljevalch Art Gallery)
Cirkus
Tobaksmuséet
Akvarium
Pins Eugens
Waldemarsudde
mmen
Södra Brobänken
Kastellholms-
bron
Allmänna Grand
Beckholmsvägen
Andreas
Sollidsbacken
Djurgårdsvägen
15
Thielska Galleriet
(Thiel Gallery)
Kastellet
Gröna
Lund
12
Örlogsvägen
Kastellholmsvägen
Beckholms-
bron
Kastellholmen
Beckholmen
Vaxholm
SALTSJÖN
rminalen
Stockholm
rinavägen
gatan
gatan
Stadsgårdsleden
Fjällgatan
N
0   200 m
0   200 yds

STOCKHOLM

*Sweden's capital is a city of islands where palaces and peaceful
hideaways line the shores, and where cobbled streets lead
to chic shops, cafés and lively cultural attractions*

Map
on pages
230–231

The novelist Selma Lagerlöf called Stockholm "the city that floats on
water". Nowhere do you see this more clearly than from the dizzy observation platform on top of the **Kaknästornet** ❶ (Kaknäs Television
Tower; June–Aug daily 9am–10pm; Sept–May 10am–9pm; entrance charge;
tel: 08 667 21 05), Ladugårdsgärdet, which rises 155 metres (508 ft). Below,
Stockholm spreads out in a panorama of blue water, the red of the old buildings contrasting with the stark white and glass of the new, and swathes of
trees and grass.

Fresh and salt water are separated by the island of Gamla Stan (Old Town)
and the great lock gates of Slussen at the southern end. This island barrier is
where Stockholm originated some time before the 13th century. Today, with
a population of 1.9 million, Stockholm is a modern and sophisticated metropolis, famous for Scandinavian design in furniture, textiles and interiors and
a hotbed for innovation in information technology – Europe's Silicon Valley.
The city features some of the most exciting cuisine in Europe. Stockholm's
nightlife has exploded into an array of young, hip clubs and older, more
sedate nightspots. Infusing the old with the new is a speciality of today's
vibrant Stockholm.

LEFT: Gamla Stan,
the old town of
Stockholm.
BELOW: outdoor
café, Stortorget.

FACT FILE

Situation On a cluster of 14 Baltic coast islands between
the sea and Lake Mälaren.
Population 1.9 million people live in the Stockholm area.
Climate In summer the daytime temperature can reach
20–25°C (68–77°F); in winter -7°C to +2°C (19–36°F).
Transport Comprehensive bus and Tunnelbanan (under-
ground) network; ferry services; sightseeing boats.
Best ferry ride Djurgårdsfärjan (Slussen to Djurgården).
Essential purchase Stockholmskortet (Stockholm Card),
for free admission to museums and free public transport.
Top attractions Drottningholms Slott; Historiska Muséet;
Kungliga Slottet (Royal Palace); Moderna Muséet; Stads-
huset; Vasamuséet; Ekoparken.
For children Skansen; Junibacken; Aquaria; Gröna Lund.
Views Fjällgatan, Södermalm; Katarina Hissen; Slussen.
Annual festivities Walpurgis Night (end Apr); Midsummer
celebrations, Skansen (late June); St Lucia celebrations
(mid-Dec).
Best coffee Vete-Katten, Kungsgatan.
Best smörgåsbord Ulriksdals Slottspark; tel: 08 85 08 15.
Tourist information Stockholm Information Service,
Sweden House, Hamngatan 27; tel: 08 508 285 08;
www.stockholmtown.com.

Stockholm's history starts in **Gamla Stan** (Old Town), which still has the character of a medieval city. Its narrow lanes follow the same curves along which the seamen of former times carried their goods. The best place to start a tour is **Stortorget**, the centre of the original city, from which narrow streets fan out in all directions.

The Vasa capital

In medieval times, Gamla Stan's Stortorget was a crowded, noisy place of trade, where German merchants, stallholders, craftsmen, and young servant girls and boys jostled and shouted. In the cobbled square today, people laze on benches or sit at one of the outdoor cafés, and it is hard to visualise that in 1520 the cobbles ran with blood during the Stockholm Bloodbath. Despite a guarantee of safety, the Danish King Kristian II, known as The Tyrant, murdered 82 people, not only nobles but innocent civilians unlucky enough to have a shop or a business nearby. This gory incident triggered the demise of the Kalmar Union, which had united Sweden with Denmark and Norway. Three years later, Sweden's first heroic king, Gustav Vasa, put an end to the union and made Stockholm his capital.

From the square, it's a short walk to **Storkyrkan ❷** (cathedral; guided tours Thur 11am; free; tel: 08 723 30 16). This awesome Gothic cathedral is the oldest building in Gamla Stan, in part dating to the 12th century. It has high vaulted arches and sturdy pillars stripped back to their original red brick. Its most famous statue is St George and the Dragon, the largest medieval monument in Scandinavia, a wooden sculpture carved by Bernt Notke in 1489, which has retained its original colouring.

BELOW: Stadshuset, the City Hall, on Lake Mälaren.

A CITY AND ITS SYMBOL

From any part of Stockholm that lies south of Lake Mälaren, Stadshuset (City Hall) dominates the skyline. Situated on the lake shore overlooking Riddarfjärden, Stadshuset is the work of architect Ragnar Östberg. A massive square tower rises 105 metres (450 ft) from one corner of the elegant building. Constructed of decorated brickwork with an open-fronted portico facing the lake, the building is topped with spires, domes and minarets. The roofs are clad in copper. Above them gleam the Tre Kronor, the three golden crowns that symbolise the city.

Östberg began work in 1911 and devoted the next 12 years of his life to the City Hall. It was formally opened in 1923 and used 8 million bricks and 19 million gilded mosaic tiles, the latter mostly in the famous Golden Hall. The effect is stunning. The walls are entirely clad in gilded mosaics. The gardens of the southern terrace feature a statue of the 15th-century Swedish patriot, Engelbrekt, who championed the peasants in his native Dalarna. A procession of St George and the Dragon emerges twice a day as the bells play a medieval tune. Guided tours: year-round at 10am and noon, May and Sept also 2pm, June–Aug also 11am, 2pm and 3pm; tower: June–Aug 9am–5pm, Sept 10am–4pm; entrance fee; tel: 08 508 290 58.

Våsterlånggatan is a favourite shopping street for locals and tourists alike. Here and on nearly every other cobbled lane in the Old Town you will find shops, restaurants and cafés to suit every taste. Particularly enjoyable are the cellar restaurants with their musty smell and stone walls. It's easy to imagine the Swedish troubador Evert Taube (1890–1976) raising a beer stein to his compatriots as he composed yet another lyric to the Swedish way of life.

Map
on pages
230–231

The present **Kungliga Slottet ❸** (Royal Palace; June–Aug daily 10am–5pm; last half of May and first half of Sept 10am–4pm; last half of Sept–Dec and Feb–mid-May noon–3pm; entrance charge; tel: 08 402 61 30) was built on the site of the Tre Kronor Palace, which burnt down in 1697, some say not without the help of Nicodemus Tessin the Younger, who had already built a new northern wing and who obviously relished the glory of rebuilding the palace to his Renaissance designs. His father, Nicodemus the Elder, had been architect to the old Tre Kronor palace, and the grandson, Carl Gustaf, was responsible for supervising the completion of the new palace many years later. The palace comprises 608 rooms. Various suites are open to the public and the oldest interiors from the 1660s are in the north wing.

For more of Sweden's aristocratic heritage, head for **Riddarhuset ❹** (House of Nobility; Mon–Fri 11.30am–12.30pm; entrance charge; tel: 08 723 39 90) on the nearby island of **Riddarholmen**, built in 1641 as a meeting place for the nobles. It is arguably the most beautiful building in Gamla Stan, with two pavilions looking out across the water. Inside, the erstwhile power of the nobles is matched by the grandeur of the Main Chamber, where the nobles deliberated, watched from above by a painting of Mother Svea, who symbolises Sweden.

Royal guardsman on duty outside the Royal Palace.

BELOW: ceremonial display at the Royal Palace, Gamla Stan.

Doorman at Stockholm's famous Grand Hotel.

The refurbishment of the Swedish **Riksdaghuset** (Parliament Building) on Helgeandsholmen to the north of Gamla Stan some years ago led to a remarkable archaeological find and a new museum. When the builders started to excavate the Riksdaghuset terrace to form an underground car park, they discovered layer upon layer of the past, including part of the medieval wall and the cellars of an apothecary shop. Stockholm's **Medeltidsmuseum ❺** (Medieval Museum, Strömparterren; currently closed because of nearby building works: due to reopen 2010; tel: 08 508 317 90; www.medeltidsmuseet. stockholm.se), incorporates the old wall and other treasures uncovered during the excavations.

From the southern end of Gamla Stan it is worth making a detour to visit the **Stadsmuseet ❻** (City Museum, Ryssgården; Tues–Sun 11am–5pm, Thur until 8pm; entrance charge; tel: 08 508 316 00), voted Stockholm's best museum in 2007. While Stockholm received virtually no mention until the 13th century, the museum makes it clear that this strategic spot had been inhabited for many centuries. After the museum, it would be a pity not to make a quick trip up **Katarinahissen ❼** (mid-May–Aug 8am–10pm, Sept–mid-May 10am–6pm; entrance charge), a 19th-century lift rebuilt in 1935 that carries you to the heights of Södermalm.

Stockholm's playground

BELOW: gilded tiles decorate the walls of the Golden Hall, Stadshuset.

From Gamla Stan, it is just 10 minutes by boat across the harbour to the island of **Djurgården**. Once a royal deer park, much of Djurgården is still in its natural state, with paths and woods where you may spot small creatures, both everyday and rare, such as hares and the occasional deer. The island is part of

Ekoparken, the world's first city national park *(see page 239)*. A good way to get around is to hire a bike at the bridge which forms the road entrance.

Between Djurgården and Gamla Stan lies **Skeppsholmen**. The sleek schooner moored off the island is the 100-year-old *af Chapman* ❽, now a youth hostel and a café. Also on the island is the spectacular new building of the **Moderna Muséet** ❾ (Modern Museum; Tues 10am–8pm, Wed–Sun until 6pm; entrance charge; tel: 08 519 552 00), designed by the Spanish architect Rafael Moneo, with a collection of 20th-century art that is considered one of the finest in the world, including works by Dali, Picasso and Magritte among others. Its large restaurant-café is worth visiting for a beautiful panorama of the city skyline.

Northwest of Skeppsholmen is the **Blasieholmen** waterfront area where the sumptuous big building is one of Scandinavia's most famous hotels, the **Grand** ❿. Nearby is the **Nationalmuseum** ⓫ (National Museum of Fine Arts, Södra Blasieholmshamnen; Tues and Thur 11am–8pm (June–Aug until 5pm), Wed, Fri–Sun 11am–5pm; entrance charge; tel: 08 519 543 00) featuring Sweden's national collection of art, with most of the great masters from 1500–1900. Rembrandt is particularly well represented. In summer, the National Museum holds concerts in the evening, a lovely setting for music.

As the ferry slides into the Djurgården quay, there is no mistaking that this is an island devoted to enjoyment. On the right is **Gröna Lund** ⓬, an amusement park with its roots in the 18th century (May–mid-Sept: hours vary; tel: 08 587 501 00; www.gronalund.com).

Fans of Astrid Lindgren's children books should not miss **Junibacken** ⓭ (Sept–May Tues–Sun 10am–5pm; June and Aug daily 10am–5pm; July daily

Tunnelbanan, Stockholm's metro system, is described as the "world's longest art gallery". Many stations have paintings, sculptures, mosaics and engravings – and all can be seen for the price of a ticket.

BELOW: winter in the city.

Spinning is one of the many traditional skills still practised at Skansen, the open-air museum.

BELOW: the *Vasa*, a remarkable work of restoration.

9am–6pm; entrance charge; tel: 08 587 230 00), a museum dedicated to her life's work. An electrically operated indoor tram, with narration in English, allows the rider to experience *Astrid's World*, floating over miniature scenes from her books with moving figures, lights and sound, as familiar figures suddenly pop out of corners.

Heading south on Djurgården, where the island rises in steps to a hilltop, is **Skansen ⓮** (Mar–Apr, Oct–Nov daily 10am–4pm; May–mid-June daily until 8pm; mid-June–Aug daily until 10pm; Sept daily until 5pm; Dec–Feb Mon–Fri until 3pm, Sat–Sun until 4pm; entrance charge; tel: 08 442 80 00), the oldest open-air museum in the world. In 1891, Artur Hazelius decided to preserve the fast-disappearing Swedish way of life by collecting traditional buildings. Today there are some 150, including an 18th-century church, still used for services and weddings. Many of the houses and workshops are grouped together to form the town quarter along a steep cobbled street. They include authentic workshops where tradesmen once practised their craft. During the summer, many of the buildings revive their traditional use.

While on Djurgården it's worth visiting the lovely former home overlooking the sea and collection of the "Painter Prince" **Prins Eugens Waldemarsudde ⓯** (Prins Eugens väg 6; Tues–Sun 11am–5pm, Thur until 8pm; entrance charge; tel: 08 545 837 00).

If you choose bus instead of boat and enter the island over Djurgårdsbron from Strandvägen, the first museum you come to is the **Nordiska Muséet ⓰** (Nordic Museum; June–Aug daily 10am–5pm; rest of year Mon–Fri 10am–4pm, Sat–Sun 11am–5pm, to 8pm Wed; entrance charge; tel: 08 519 546 00), which depicts Nordic life from the 16th century. It has peasant costumes, a collection

Map on pages 230–231

of bridal gowns and the traditional silver and gold crowns worn by Swedish brides, exhibits on Lapland culture, folk art, and more.

Marine treasure

To the west of the Nordiska Museet on the waterfront is the huge, oddly shaped **Vasaméet** ⑰ (Vasa Museum, Galärvarvet; June–Aug daily 8.30am–6pm; Sept–May Mon and Thur–Sun 10am–5pm, Wed until 8pm; entrance charge; tel: 08 519 548 00). Inaugurated in 1990, the museum houses the *Vasa* warship, built in the 1620s for the Thirty Years' War, on the orders of Sweden's warrior king, Gustav II Adolf. She was a magnificent ship, decorated with 700 sculptures and carvings, but her oak was too solid. In 1628 she sank in Stockholm harbour on her maiden voyage. In 1956 the Swedish marine archaeologist, Anders Franzén, found her and, in 1961, brought her up from the depths. More than 24,000 objects have been salvaged from the sea bed, including skeletons, sails, cannon, clothing, tools, coins, butter, rum and many everyday utensils.

A short walk across the bridge is the spectacular **Guldrummet** (Gold Room), an underground vault featuring more than 3,000 prehistoric gold and silver artefacts at the **Historiska Museet** ⑱ (Museum of National Antiquities, Narvävägen; May–Sept daily 10am–5pm; Oct–Apr from 11am, Thur until 8pm; entrance charge; tel: 08 519 556 00).

The King's Garden

It's anyone's guess what the Swedish sculptor John Tobias Sergel (1740–1814) might have thought of the huge illuminated obelisk, fountain and square that

BELOW:
Prins Eugens
Waldemarsudde
art gallery and
former home of the
"Painter Prince".

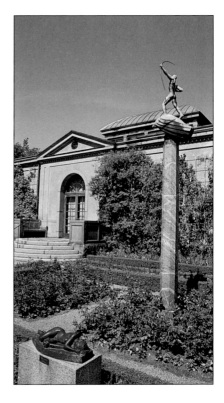

OUTWARD-BOUND IN THE CITY

Ekoparken is the world's first national city park, a huge set of green lungs that stretch out in a 12-km (7-mile) long arch from Ulriksdals Slott (castle) in the north to the Fjäderholmarna archipelago in the south. This green swathe is so large you'll need a full day of serious hiking to explore it, by foot during the warmer months or on skis or long-distance skates in the winter. The inexpensive Brunnsviken Runt (Around Brunnsviken) boat tour is an excellent way of seeing the Ekopark and includes free admission to many attractions.

The Ekopark includes three royal parks, Djurgården, Haga and Ulriksdal, with palaces to tour (Ulriksdals Slott, Gustav III's Paviljong, Rosendals Slott). Visit the tropical Fjärilshuset (Butterfly House) where hundreds of colourful species land lightly upon your shoulder, or the Bergianska (Bergianska Botanical Gardens) and Naturhistoriska Riksmuseet (Museum of Natural History).

For a pleasant retreat on northern Djurgården, you'll find Rosendalsträgård (Rosendals Garden) with orchards, flowers and vegetables, garden shops and a café. For many Stockholmers this has become the ideal retreat after a day on Djurgården. For Ekoparken information, call the Stockholm tourist office (tel: 08 508 285 08).

Prehistoric artefact in the Gold Room, Museum of National Antiquities.

bear his name, and of the modern city around it. The heart of this business and commercial area is not large, but it sits somewhat uneasily with the rest. From **Sergels Torg** it is hard to miss the five towering office blocks on Sveavägen, which cast their shadow over the other buildings. In the 1960s, Stockholm City Council, like so many others, succumbed to the temptation to knock things down and build concrete and glass high-rise buildings.

The destruction of many fine old buildings continued until it threatened **Kungsträdgården ⑲** (King's Garden) with the statue of the warrior king Karl XII on its southern side. At this point the Stockholmers had had enough. Normally placid and biddable, they mustered at the King's Garden, climbed the trees that were in danger of the axe, and swore that if the trees went so did the people. The City Fathers retreated and Kungsträdgården survives to soften the edges of the new buildings and harmonise with the older buildings that are left. This is the place to take a leisurely stroll or sit beside the fountains on a summer day and enjoy a coffee at its outdoor café. In summer it is the venue of many outdoor festivals and rock concerts. In winter, part of Kungsträdgården is flooded with water and becomes a popular ice rink, and the restaurant moves indoors.

A short stroll east is the early 20th-century private palace housing one of Stockholm's most unusual museums, the **Hallwylska Museet ⑳** (Hallwyl Collection, Hamngatan 4; guided tours in English mid-June–mid-Aug daily 1pm; mid-Aug–mid-June Sun only; entrance to the first-floor state rooms year round Tues–Sun 1–4pm; entrance charge; tel: 08 402 30 99). It's the magpie collection of one person, Countess von Hallwyl, from her ornate piano to china, beautiful furniture and personal knick-knacks.

BELOW: Stockholm's underground is an artistic wonder.

Map on pages 230–231

On the southern side of Sergels Torg, the **Kulturhuset ㉑** (Culture House; Tues–Sun 10am–7pm) is a popular meeting place and venue for lectures and entertainment with Stockholm's main tourist information centre on the ground floor (Mon–Fri 9am–7pm, Sat 10am–5pm, Sun 10am–4pm; tel: 08 508 285 08). The centre can advise and book tours and other entertainment, sells the Stockholmskortet (Stockholm Card), and has a well-stocked bookshop. One block east on Hamngatan is **Gallerian ㉒**, a huge covered shopping arcade that stretches to Jakobsgatan.

Sweden's equivalent of Harrods or Bloomingdales is **Nordiska Kompaniet (NK) ㉓**, on Hamngatan (just opposite Sweden House), whose rooftop illuminated sign, constantly turning, is visible from far and wide in the city. NK sells everything from shoes to sporting equipment, men's and women's clothing, glass, pottery and silver, jewellery and perfume; its services range from personal shoppers to post office and travel agency, and multilingual staff are always on hand to assist with changing currency and shipping your purchases back home.

Swedish design is world renowned. Wherever you go in the city you'll never be far from shops selling crystal, china and ceramics, and the fashions of designers like Pia, Wallén, Filippa K and Anna Holtblad.

Find a bargain

Shopping in Sweden is rarely cheap, but it is always good value. For a bargain, the words to look out for are *rea*, which means sale, and *extrapris*, which does not mean extra, but special low price.

Åhléns City ㉔ is on the corner of Sergels Torg and Drottninggatan. It has a similar range and quality to NK, and a visit to its supermarket food department is a sightseeing tour in itself. The third of this trio of stores is **PUB**, on Drottninggatan at Hötorget (*see overleaf*), which is a galleria featuring a variety of Swedish and international-brand shops.

BELOW: cycling through the Old Town.

Contemporary Swedish crystal design.

Drottninggatan (Queen's Street), an old street which leads directly through the Riksdagshuset and over the bridge from the Royal Palace, is one of Stockholm's main pedestrian ways. In summer, it is full of casual crowds strolling or sitting at one of the outdoor cafés. Immigrants sell their wares on the pavement. This area is a haven for pickpockets, so be careful.

Not to be missed is **Strindbergsmuséet ㉕** (Strindberg Museum, Drottninggatan 85; Tues–Sun noon–4pm; Mar–Oct Tues hours extend until 7pm; entrance charge; tel: 08 411 53 54), housed in the top-floor flat of the **Blåtornet** (Blue Tower) where Sweden's greatest playwright spent his last years and wrote his last epic play *The Great Highway* in 1908. Even at the end of his life, Strindberg was astonishingly prolific; he produced some 20 books in his four years in the Blue Tower.

Fruit and finery

Walking south along Drottninggatan to Kungsgatan, on your left you'll come to **Hötorget ㉖**, with its open-air food stalls and indoor market. This is where Swedes shop for food. Here you can find Swedish delicacies such as elk steak and reindeer and the many varieties of Scandinavian cured herring.

In addition to exploring Gamla Stan's antique shops, take the Tunnelbanan (underground railway) south to Slussen station on **Södermalm ㉗**, once the great working-class area of the city; the journey takes just 5–10 minutes. Nowadays, this district is a popular place for local artists to live and work. It has become a trendy place to hang out, and new cafés, restaurants and boutiques seem to open here daily. The steep slope of **Hornsgatan ㉘** has a cluster of galleries.

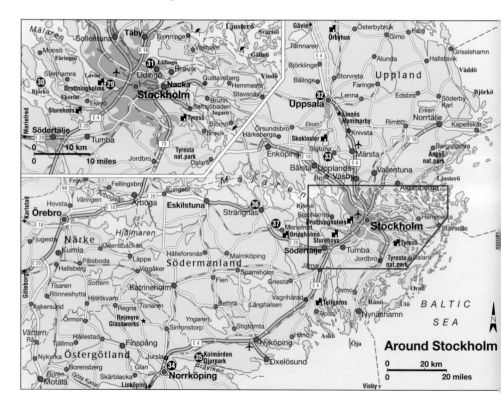

Around Stockholm

Islands by the thousand

It is a rare city that has 24,000 islands on its doorstep and 100 km (60 miles) of lake at its heart, but this is Stockholm's eternal good fortune. Until the building of the Tunnelbanen, boats were the only means of getting around these vast expanses of water, and today boats are still part of Stockholm life. Boat operators Waxholmsbolaget and Strömma Kanalbolaget transport passengers across Lake Mälaren and around the archipelago *(see page 246)* in a variety of craft from old coal-fired steamers to modern ferries.

The most popular place to visit in the archipelago is the royal palace, **Drottningholms Slot** ❷ on Lovön *(see page 245)*, to the west of the city. West of Lovön is **Björkö** ❸, the site of Sweden's oldest city, **Birka**. Between AD 800 and 975, Birka was the trading centre for the 40,000 inhabitants of the rich Mälaren area and the meeting point for traders. This was also where Christianity first came to Sweden, when Ansgar, the Saxon missionary, landed in the 9th century. Almost nothing is left of Birka above ground, but many archaeological digs have revealed the past at sites which include the old town. The **Birka Vikingastaden** (May–Sept 10am–5pm; entrance charge; tel: 08 560 514 45) features the most recent finds.

Although it is now easy to get there by underground train (T–Ropsten), in summer it is worthwhile taking the boat to the island suburb of **Lidingö** ❸, to visit **Millesgården**, the summer home of sculptor Carl Milles and his wife, the Austrian painter Olga Granner (mid-May–Sept 11am–5pm, Oct–mid-May Tues–Sun noon–5pm; entrance charge; tel: 08 446 75 90). Here, Milles patiently reproduced the statues that had made him more famous in his adopted country of the US than in Sweden. His creations seem to defy gravity: they appear to soar and fly, and step lightly over water, emphasised by their position on terraces carved from the cliffs.

Maps:
City 230
Area 242

August is the time for a "kräftskiva" (crayfish party). Under the glow of paper lanterns, Swedes enjoy this beloved shellfish, once plentiful in freshwater lakes, but now imported.

BELOW: Stortorget, the square at the heart of Gamla Stan.

Map on page 242

A Carl Milles sculpture at Millesgården.

BELOW: Uppsala's Gothic cathedral.

North of Stockholm

Less than an hour's drive north of Stockholm on the E4 lies **Uppsala** ❸, Sweden's ancient capital, last bastion of heathenism and seat of one of Europe's greatest universities. This is the birthplace of Ingmar Bergman and the setting for his film *Fanny and Alexander*. The town is also an Episcopal See and has the largest Gothic cathedral to be found in Scandinavia, **Domkyrkan** (May–Aug daily 8am–6pm; Sept–Apr Mon–Fri 8am–4pm, Sat–Sun 8am–6pm). Its vaults, from 1435, house the shrine of Saint Erik, a former king and the patron of Sweden.

Across the town's lush parks rises **Uppsala Slott**, a fortress from the days of the Vasa dynasty (now a conference and exhibition venue; tel: 018 544 811). A few minutes north of the town lies **Gamla Uppsala** (Old Uppsala), the 5th-century bastion of the Yngling dynasty. The three huge grave mounds of kings Aun, Egil and Adils (described in the opening passages of *Beowulf*) dominate the evocative grave fields that lie beyond the **Gamla Uppsala Museum** (May–Aug daily 11am–5pm; Sept–mid-Dec and Jan–Apr Mon, Wed, Sat–Sun noon–3pm; entrance charge; tel: 018 23 93 12), which does a good job of explaining the Viking world outside its windows.

Near Uppsala, where the sea meets the forest, you'll find **Sigtuna** ❸, Sweden's oldest town. In the 11th century this was the commercial centre for the Svea and Vandal tribes. Merchant ships from as far away as Asia dropped anchor here; monasteries and abbeys competed with one another in building glorious churches. Today, Sigtuna is a picturesque town with crooked lanes, quaint wooden houses and a miniature town hall. Tant Brun's café on the main pedestrian lane is a lovely place to stop for a cup of strong Swedish coffee and a freshly baked cinnamon bun.

South to Södermanland

To the south of Stockholm is **Norrköping** ❸, with its tree-lined avenues, outdoor café society, fascinating 19th-century canalscape, trams and elegant architecture. The town's main attraction is **Kolmården Djurpark** ❸. This is Scandinavia's wildlife safari, natural habitat and amusement park supreme (early May–late Aug daily 10am–5pm, June–mid-Aug until 6pm; Sept Sat–Sun 10am–5pm; entrance charge; tel: 011 24 90 00).

Heading north towards Lake Mälaren's bays and inlets you come to **Strängnäs** ❸, a delightful small town dominated by a magnificent Gothic cathedral. Next to the church at **Boglösa**, 20 km (12 miles) north, are hundreds of Bronze Age rock carvings.

On the lake, about 15 km (9 miles) to the east, lies idyllic **Mariefred** ❸ and the impressive **Gripsholms Slott** (castle; mid-May–mid-Sept daily 10am–4pm; entrance charge; tel: 0159 101 94), which contains the royal portrait collections and a marvellous theatre from the late 1700s. Best of all is the architecture of this fortress, begun in the 1370s and continually updated. Around the edge of the moat is a collection of rune stones carved with serpents, ships and magic inscriptions. Mariefred is a lazy, summer lake town, with cafés and restaurants to suit all tastes, and ferry connections to Stockholm. ❏

A ROYAL TREAT: DROTTNINGHOLM PALACE

Often referred to as Sweden's "mini Versailles",
the island palace of Drottningholm with its exquisite
gardens and historic theatre is not to be missed

The most popular place to visit in Stockholm's archipelago is Drottningholms Slott (May–Aug daily 10am–4.30pm; Sept noon–3pm; Oct–Apr Sat–Sun noon–3pm; entrance charge; tel: 08 402 62 80) on Lovön. Now the main home of the Swedish royal family, the 17th-century palace is surrounded by formal Baroque and rococo gardens of fountains, statues, flowerbeds, box hedges and a variety of trees.

The palace was built for Eleonora, the widow of King Karl X, by the Tessin family of architects headed by Nicodemus the Elder (1615–81). Work began in 1662 and was completed by his son, Nicodemus the Younger.

Although the royal family live at Drottningholm, much of the palace is open to the public. Interior highlights include a magnificent Grand Staircase with trompe l'oeil paintings by Johan Sylvius, the Baroque Karl X Gallery, Queen Hedwig Eleonora's State Bedroom with its richly painted ceiling, and the library of Queen Louisa Ulrika who married King Adolf Fredrik in 1744.

In the parkland stands the exotic pagoda roofs and ornamental balconies of the Kina Slott (Chinese Pavilion; May–Aug daily 11am–4.30pm; Sept daily noon–3.30pm; entrance charge; tel: 08 402 62 70), a birthday present to Queen Louisa Ulrika from her husband. In one of four adjoining pavilions the king had his carpentry workshop. In Kanton, a small village built next to Kina Slott, silkworms that had been introduced perished in the freezing winter, thwarting the court's attempt to produce cheap silk.

Top Left: formal gardens at Drottningholm.
Above Left: Chinese Pavilion. **Top Right:** ballet at the Slottsteater. **Right:** palace entrance.

The island's greatest treasure is undoubtedly the 18th-century Drottningholms Slottsteater (Court Theatre; May–Sept guided tours only; entrance charge; tel: 08 759 04 06).

The theatre was designed for Queen Louisa Ulrika by Carl Fredrik Adelcrantz and opened in 1766. The queen's son, Gustav III, was an actor and playwright who became known as "The Theatre King". He invited French troupes of actors to perform at Drottningholm and the theatre soon became an influential centre for performing arts. Gustav went on to found Stockholm's Dramatic Theatre and developed a native theatre and opera.

The building fell into disrepair in the 19th century, then in the early 20th century it underwent extensive restoration. Today it is the oldest theatre in the world still using its original backdrops and stage machinery for productions. Attending a performance of opera or ballet here on a summer evening is like experiencing magic from an earlier age. ❑

STEAMING OUT AMONG THE SKERRIES

When summer comes, the Swedes set off by boat to the thousands of idyllic islands that dot the waterways between Stockholm and the Baltic

Every summer thousands of Swedes in boats navigate carefully through waters loaded with 24,000 islands, rocks and islets in the Stockholm archipelago. The brackish waters start in the centre of Stockholm and extend 80 km (50 miles) out into the open Baltic Sea. Close to the mainland, the islands are larger and more lush, the bays and channels wider. Hidden here are idyllic island communities, farmlands and small forests. But as you travel further out, the scenery becomes more rugged, finally ending in sparse windblown islets formed by the last Ice Age.

ISLAND RETREATS

In the middle of the 19th century affluent Stockholm families began to build their second homes along the shores of the various islands in the archipelago. Over the years, "commoners" had more money and leisure time and soon they, too, sought their way to the archipelago. The combination of wilderness, sea, fresh air and closeness to the city satisfied many leisure needs. Today, Swedes either own their cottages or rent them, and enjoy swimming, fishing, boating, nature walks and socialising with friends.

▷ **YOUNG VOYAGER**
Dressed for the ferry ride and a deck-side view of the steam boats and yachts that ply the waters.

△ **ON THE WATERFRONT**
More than 50,000 chalets offering varying degrees of comfort are spread throughout Stockholm's inner archipelago.

▽ **LAZY DAYS**
The archipelago is such a important factor in Stockholmers' leisure tim that every tenth resident now owns a boat.

▽ HOME FROM HOME
More than 10,000 people live year round on the 150 inhabited islands, working in farming, fishing, boat transport and retailing.

▽ WALK IN THE WILD
Escaping to the islands for summer weekends and holidays, mainly in July, is a perfect antidote to the bustle of city life.

A QUICK GUIDE TO ISLAND HOPPING

The archipelago can be explored on guided tours from Stockholm's city centre. But if you want to travel like the locals, then buy a *Båtluffarkort* (Interskerries card, Skr 340) from the Waxholm boat company (www.waxholmsbolaget.se; tel: 08 679 58 30), which allows you to see as many islands as you can in five days, including:

● Sandön, with its attractive sailing centre village of Sandhamn, sandy beaches and some good restaurants (a 5-hour round trip).

● Fjäderholmarna, featuring a boat museum, aquarium, fish-smoking plant, restaurants and crafts shops (20 minutes by boat from Stockholm).

● Vaxholm, with its famous fortress (1 hour by boat).

● Utö, where a 12th-century iron mine is the

ISLAND HARVEST
rry and mushroom king are popular stimes enjoyed by all es. Swedes also love ture walks, birdwatching d picnicking.

▷ PADDLE POWER
Swedes take time to enjoy the scenery by water. Although sailing is a very popular water sport, canoeing and kayaking come in a close second.

main ttraction, is a great place for bike-riding (3 hours by boat from the city).

SOUTHERN SWEDEN

Across the Öresund bridge from Denmark, southern Sweden is home to the lively city of Malmö. Castles and Stone Age sites abound, while bathers and birdwatchers head for Öland

Map on page 250

Stockholm

Skåne is Sweden's most southerly province, so close to Denmark across the narrow sound that even the accent is faintly Danish. For centuries Swedes and Danes fought over this area, along with the provinces of Halland and Blekinge, until Sweden established its sovereignty in 1658.

Since 2000, however, the two countries have been joined by the Öresund road and rail bridge that links Malmö and Copenhagen. The project has prompted a renaissance for southern Sweden as a centre of the Danish-Swedish Öresund region, with a total of 3 million people and one-fifth of the total combined GNP of Sweden and Denmark.

Skåne is often called Sweden's food store because of its rich farmland, mild climate and good fishing. Along the coast the landscape is undulating and lush and especially spectacular in the southeast corner, Österlen. Inland, there are lakes and three large ridges with lovely walks.

Skåne is renowned for its castles and manor houses. There are said to be 240 in the province, most of which are in private ownership, but it is usually possible to walk round the gardens such as at **Sofiero ❶**, 4 km (2½ miles) north of Helsingborg (daily mid-Apr–Sept 10am–6pm; entrance charge; tel: 042 14 52 59). Built in 1857, Sofiero was used by King Gustav VI Adolf as his summer palace until his death in 1973. He was a keen botanist, as the gardens show.

Malmö: city of the south

Malmö ❷ is Sweden's third city, a lively place with a population of about 280,000. In the 16th century, Malmö competed with Copenhagen to be Scandinavia's leading capital. In those days it was an important port, not far from rich fishing grounds.

Today, the harbour is still busy and many of the old buildings remain. **Malmöhus**, the dominating castle built by King Christian III when Skåne was still part of Denmark, is Scandinavia's oldest remaining Renaissance castle. It houses the **Malmö Museer** (Malmö Museums; June–Aug daily 10am–4pm; Sept–May noon–4pm; entrance charge; tel: 040 34 44 00), which includes the Art Museum, Museum of Natural History, City Museum, Science and Technology/Maritime Museum and the **Kommendants Hus** (Commander's House) in Malmöhusvägen.

From the same period is **Rådhuset** (City Hall), which you will find in **Stortorget**, one of the largest squares in Scandinavia. **Stadshuset** (August Palms Plats; Mon–Fri 8am–4.30pm; tel: 040 34 34 34) was built in 1546 in genuine Dutch Renaissance style. In 1860 it was given a facelift by the architect Helgo Zettervall, with niches, bays, allegorical paintings, and colonnades. Northeast from Stortorget is **St Petri Kyrka**, Göran

LEFT: gathering for the Midsummer Festival.
BELOW: Sweden's Town Hall, Malmö.

Sweden leads the world in glass-making. Many of the famous glassworks, such as Kosta and Boda, are located in the southeast of the country.

Olsgatan 1, built in the Baltic Gothic style and dating from the 13th century, although its towers were built in the 15th century and its copper spires in 1890. This elegant cathedral features a beautiful altar area created by sculptors in 1611.

A particularly idyllic place to sit and relax is **Lilla Torg** (Little Square), with its cobblestones, carefully restored houses and 16th-century charm. Through an arch on the south side of the square is Hemanska Gården. Once a merchant's home and trading yard, it now houses the **Form/Design Center** (Tues–Fri 11am–5pm, Thur until 6pm, Sat–Sun noon–4pm; free; tel: 040 664 51 50), where Swedish industrial design and handicrafts are displayed.

When you get hungry, head for **Saluhallen** (10am–6pm; Sat 10am–4pm), on the northwest corner of Lilla Torg, where you can choose from fish restaurants, cafés, delicatessens and an abudance of fresh food.

Walking east from Lilla Torg, a rewarding visit can be made to the contemporary art gallery **Rooseum** (Gasverksgatan 22; Wed 2–8pm, Thur–Sun noon–6pm; entrance charge; tel: 040 12 17 16), founded in 1988 by the Swedish financier Fredrik Roos. In this fascinating former power station, you'll see changing international exhibitions from artists such as Jean-Michel Basquiat, Julian Schnabel and Susan Rothenberg.

Towards Helsingborg

Heading northeast from Malmö, **Lund ❸** is a university town with a fine cathedral, **Domkyrkan**, built in the 12th century. Don't miss **Kulturen** (Cultural History Museum, Tegnérs platsen; mid-Apr–Sept daily 11am–5pm; Oct–mid-Apr Tues–Sun noon–4pm; entrance charge; tel: 046 35 04 01), an open-air museum with dozens of buildings, silver, textiles, ceramics and art. Along with

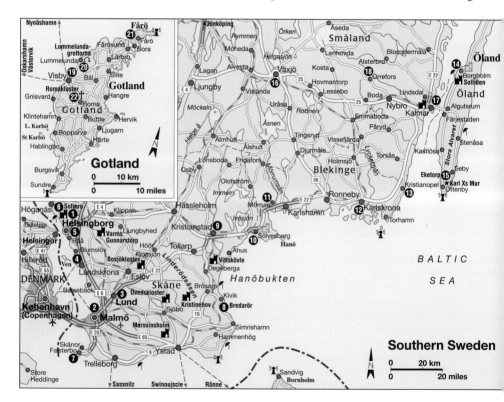

Southern Sweden

the University of Uppsala, Lund is one of the two ancient Swedish universities. About 30 km (19 miles) north along the coast, **Glumslöv** ❹ offers memorable views. From the hill above the church, on a clear day you can see 30 churches and seven towns, including Copenhagen and Helsingør in Denmark.

Helsingborg ❺, 60 km (37 miles) north of Malmö, is an interesting town of cobbled streets, dominated by the ruined castle, **Kärnan**. Frequent ferries to Helsingør in Denmark leave from its bustling harbour. **Höganäs** ❻, 20 km (12 miles) north, is devoted to potters and artists. The large pottery is worth a visit.

Along the south coast

Forty km (25 miles) southwest from Malmö are the summer idylls of **Skanör** and **Falsterbo** ❼. **Skanörs Ljung** is recommended for bird lovers, particularly in September and October, when a large number of migrating birds gather.

Southeast of Kivik is **Bredarör** ❽, site of the Bronze Age **Kiviksgraven** (King's Grave). Scientists still wonder about the mysterious markings on the stones, unearthed in 1748, which are different to any others found in the region.

Kristianstad ❾ is the birthplace of the Swedish film industry, which started around 1910. The original studio is intact and is now a museum where you can watch old films on video (**Filmmuséet**, Östra Storgatan 53; mid-June–mid-Aug Tues–Fri 1–4pm, Sun noon–5pm; Sept–May Sun noon–5pm; free; tel: 044 13 57 29). Nearby, **Kristianstad Vattenriket** (Water Kingdom) is a rich wetland on the Helge River, with a diversity of birds, wildlife and plants.

Blekinge is a tiny province with sandy beaches and Sweden's most southerly archipelago. It is excellent for sea fishing. You can enjoy peaceful angling in some of the lakes, or good sport for salmon in the Mörrum River. Canoeing is popular. Driving to Blekinge from Skåne, you first reach **Sölvesborg** ❿, and the ruins of 13th-century **Sölvesborg Castle** (Slott).

Mörrum ⓫, 30 km (19 miles) north of Sölvesborg, is noted for its salmon fishing: at **Laxens Hus** you can see salmon and trout at different stages of their development (Apr–Sept daily 9am–5pm; Oct daily until 4pm; entrance charge; tel: 0454 501 23).

The biggest town in Blekinge is **Karlskrona** ⓬, a naval centre built in the 17th century, with wide streets and impressive buildings. In the Björkholmen district you'll find quaint 18th-century cottages built by ships' carpenters. The nearby village of **Kristianopel** ⓭ is renowned for its smoked herring.

Öland: an ornithologist's delight

The island of **Öland**, off the east coast, is one of the most visited areas of Sweden and, with its diverse landscape and superb beaches, it is a paradise for birdwatchers, nature lovers and sun worshippers.

Once you've crossed the Öland bridge from Blekinge, you soon see the ruins of **Borgholm Slott** (castle) rising above the main town of **Borgholm** ⓮, a once splendid residence from the 12th century (May–Aug daily 10am–6pm, Sept–Apr until 4pm; entrance charge).

The island has many ancient burial places and there are remains of 16 fortified dwellings from earlier times. The most interesting is **Eketorp** ⓯, in the

TIP

Råå, on the outskirts of Helsingborg, is a picturesque fishing village with an excellent inn.

BELOW: Kalmar Castle, Småland.

Map
on page
250

*Brightly painted
timber buildings
are a feature of
southern Sweden.*

BELOW: glass-
blowing is a highly
valued skill in
southern Sweden.

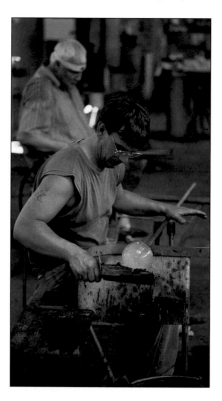

south, which has been partly restored. Sweden's prime birdwatching can be enjoyed at the **Ottenby bird station**, on the island's southerly tip, where more than 350 species have been recorded. Nearby, you can see **Karl Xs Mur** (Karl X's Wall), impressive for its sheer size; it was built in 1650 to distinguish Ottenby's domain and keep out the peasants' animals. **Stora Alvaret**, an expanse of bare limestone soil in central southern Öland, is a starkly beautiful landscape offering rare flowers and flocks of cranes in the autumn.

The emigrants

During the late 19th and early 20th centuries, Sweden's population exploded, and many families could no longer eke out a living on the land. So began the years of migration to North America. A popular place to visit is **Utvandrarnas Hus** (House of the Emigrants; Sept–Apr Tues–Fri 9am–4pm, Sat 11am–4pm; May–Aug Tues–Fri 9am–5pm, Sat 11am–4pm; entrance charge; tel: 0470 201 20) in **Växjö ⑯**, 70 km (43 miles) west of Kalmar, which tells the story of the exodus *(see box page 35)*.

Kalmar ⑰, one of Sweden's oldest cities, was of great importance in the Swedish–Danish wars. Sweden's best-preserved Renaissance castle, **Kalmar Slott** (Apr Sat–Sun and Easter 11am–3.30pm; May–Sept daily 10am–4pm, July until 6pm, Aug until 5pm; Oct Sat–Sun 11am–3.30pm; Nov 1st and 2nd weekend 11am–3.30pm; Dec–Mar 2nd weekend 11am–3.30pm; entrance charge), was begun in the 12th century but was completely renovated during the 16th century by the Vasa kings. The castle's coffered ceilings, panelled halls, fresco paintings and magnificent stonework have inspired the Renaissance Festival, held every July, featuring tournament games, market, music and theatre.

Kingdom of glass

Northwest of Kalmar, about 20 km (12 miles) is **Orrefors ⑱**, part of Sweden's **Glasriket** (Glass Kingdom). The first glass was melted in Sweden in 1556 but it was not established as an industry until 1742, when **Kosta**, the oldest works, was founded to the west of Orrefors. Anders Koskull and Georg Bogislaus Stael von Holstein took the first two syllables of their respective surnames to create "Kosta".

Orrefors started in the glass business by producing windowpanes and bottles. In 1913 the works was taken over by Johan Ekman, an industrialist from Göteborg. Ekman recruited two artists who with their creative flair were to transform Orrefors into one of the world's foremost glassworks: Simon Gate, a portrait and landscape painter, and Edvard Hald, a pupil of Matisse.

Most of the 11 major glassworks are open to visitors for demonstrations and many have shops (Mon–Fri 9am–4pm, Sat 10am–4pm, Sun noon–4pm; Orrefors Glasbruk, tel: 0481 341 95; Kosta Glasbruk, tel: 0478 345 00; Johansfors Glasbruk, tel: 0471 402 70).

Look out for *hyttsill* ("glassworks herring") evenings. In bygone times the glassworks were also a social centre where the locals would gather for a chat and bake herrings and potatoes in the furnace, with music provided by an accordionist or fiddler. Some of the works have revived this tradition for visitors. ❏

GOTLAND: THE SUNSHINE ISLAND

With its medieval towns, sandy beaches and curious rock formations, tranquil Gotland – the largest island in the Baltic – is a favourite holiday spot

Gotland is an island of gaunt rocks, forests, wild flowers, cliffs and sandy beaches, blessed with more hours of sunshine than anywhere else in the country. Swedes naturally flock here for their summer holidays.

Gotland was created over thousands of years as the animals and plants of the ancient Silurian Sea slowly sank into the sediment that was to become the limestone platform of modern Gotland. Million-year-old fossils and the island's monumental sea-stacks *(raukar)*, can still be found on the coast.

In the Viking Age the island was a busy trading post. **Visby** ⑲, the principal centre of population, later became a prosperous Hanseatic town. Great stone houses were erected, churches were founded, and a city wall was built. Today, 3 km (2 miles) of the medieval limestone wall remains virtually intact, interspersed with 44 towers and numerous gates. It is now a UNESCO World Heritage site.

Limestone has created one of the island's major attractions – the impressive subterranean tunnels and stalactite caves of **Lummelundagrottan** ⑳ (May daily 10am–3pm; June and Aug daily 9am–4pm; July daily 9am–6pm; guided tours only; entrance charge; tel: 0498 27 30 50), 13 km (8 miles) to the north of Visby, which should not be missed. Dress warmly, it's 8°C (46°F) inside.

About 50 km (30 miles) north of Visby lies **Fårö** ㉑; the "island of sheep". Take a ferry to the island from Fårösund, and enjoy sites such as Gamlehamn, a medieval harbour, and the ruins of a chapel to St Olof. You can

also see one of Gotland's most bizarrely shaped *raukar*, "The Camel", and visit the beach of Sundersand. After you have been here a little while, you will begin to understand why Fårö was Ingmar Bergman's favourite place.

Sweden's most primitive horse, the Russ, has lived in the forests of the island from time immemorial. The name Russ comes from the Old Norse *hross*, and it is thought that the horse is a descendant of the wild Tarpan. You can see them, only 123–6 cm (46–52 inches) tall, around the island.

Wherever you travel in Gotland you'll come across at least one of its 92 medieval churches. At **Romakloster** ㉒, in the centre of the island, there is a ruined monastery from the 12th century. There are many other relics of the past including runic stones and burial mounds. If you reach Gotland's southernmost tip, you'll see some of the most impressive *raukar* on the island. ❑

TOP LEFT: Gotland beach. ABOVE LEFT: Visby, a Hanseatic town. TOP RIGHT: Visby's medieval town wall. RIGHT: an unusual sea stack *(raukar)*.

SWEDEN'S WEST COAST

From the sandy beaches of Halland to the bustling city
of Göteborg and the rocky shores of Bohuslän, the west coast
has long been a summer playground for Swedes

Map on page 256

The west coast of Sweden, generously dotted with beaches and fishing villages, is 400 km (250 miles) of glorious coastline divided in two by the city of Göteborg (Gothenborg). It has been a favourite holiday spot since the early 20th century. The best beaches are in the southern province of Halland. North of Göteborg, in Bohuslän, is a majestic coast of granite rocks and islands.

The E6 connects all the larger cities, but follow the small coastal roads to discover the gems. Starting along the coast in the northwestern corner of the county of Skåne, a number of small towns offer views into the past. **Gamla Viken ❶**, 15 km (9 miles) north of Helsingborg on Highway 22, is a picturesque fishing village. **Torekov**, at the tip of the next peninsula, has a seaside golf course and boats to the island of **Hallands Väderö** where you can spot seals basking offshore.

Sand and salmon

Halmstad ❷, the largest town in Halland, lies on the River Nissan. **Halmstads Slott** (castle), the provincial governor's residence, was built in the 17th century by the Danish king Kristian IV. In front of the castle is moored the old sail-training vessel *Najaden* (July–Aug Tues and Thur 5–7pm, Sat 11am–3pm), built in 1897. Other sights include **St Nikolai**, a 13th-century church. **Tylösand**, 8 km (5 miles) west of Halmstad, is a popular holiday resort with a predominantly sandy beach and two golf courses. There are good beaches at **Östra Strand**, **Ringenäs** and **Haverdalsstrand**.

Falkenberg ❸, 40 km (25 miles) north of Halmstad, is on the Ätran, a river famous for its salmon. The old part of the town with its 18th-century wooden houses and cobbled streets is centred on the 14th-century **St Laurenti Church**. There is an old toll bridge *(tull-bron)* from 1756 and the oldest pottery in Sweden, **Törngrens Krukmakeri**, which has been run by the Törngren family since 1789 (Mon–Fri; tel: 0346 103 54). Good beaches are found at **Olofsby** (north of the town) and **Skrea Strand** (south of the town).

Continue 30 km (19 miles) north on the E6 to **Varberg ❹**, a bustling place combining spa, resort, port and commercial centre with a ferry service to Grenå in Denmark. **Varbergs Fästning** (Fortress) stands beside the water and houses a youth hostel, restaurant, apartments and a **museum** (mid-June–mid-Aug 10am–6pm, mid-Aug–mid-June Mon–Fri 10am–4pm, Sat–Sun noon–4pm; entrance charge). Pride of place goes to the Bocksten Man, the only preserved figure in the world wearing a complete costume from the Middle Ages. Reminders of Varberg's late 19th-century development as a holiday resort include **Societetshuset** (1883), an elaborate wooden pavilion in the park, and the bathing station (1903), a rectangular wooden structure open to

LEFT: holiday cottage on Klädesholmen.
BELOW: rocky north Bohuslän coast.

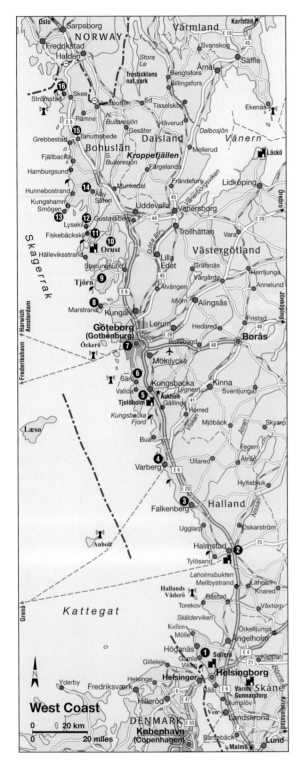

the sea, with changing huts and deck chairs round the sides. After a quick plunge in this sea-water swimming pool, bathers can relax over coffee and waffles.

A taste for Tudor

Heading 30 km (19 miles) north towards **Kungsbacka** you will pass the most out-of-character building along the entire coast. **Tjolöholm Castle ❺** (mid-Mar–mid-June and Sept, Sat–Sun 11am–4pm; mid-June–Aug daily 11am–4pm; Oct–Nov and Jan–mid-Mar Sun noon–2pm; entrance charge; tel: 0300 54 42 00) was built in the early 20th century in an English Tudor style, with a splendid Art Nouveau interior.

Instead of beaches, a dramatic landscape of rocks, inlets and islands takes over at the little seaside resort of **Särö ❻** (immediately north of Kungsbacka). In the early 19th century Särö was a fashionable resort, popular with the Swedish royal family. It remains in a time warp. You can walk along the Strandpromenaden and through **Särö Västerskog**, one of the oldest oak woods on the west coast.

Göteborg

Göteborg ❼ (Gothenburg) is the second-largest city in Sweden (490,000 inhabitants) and home to beautiful parks and a thriving cultural and industrial life. Dutch architects planned the city in the 17th century for King Gustav II Adolf, giving it an architectural character of its own. The shipping industry, particularly trade with the Orient by the Swedish East India Company in the 18th century, shaped the history of the city. Today it is Scandinavia's largest seaport. The harbour area is its soul and a good place to start your sightseeing.

The bold **Göteborgsoperan ❹** (opera house; tel: 031 13 13 00 for bookings, 031 10 80 00 for info), stands on the water just west of the commercial centre. Built in ship-like style in 1994, it is well worth a visit for its architecture alone. Near the Opera is Göteborg's **Maritiman ❽** (maritime centre; Apr, May and Oct daily 10am–4pm; June–Aug until 6pm;

Mar and Nov Fri–Sun 10am–4pm; entrance charge; tel: 031 10 59 50), on Packhuskajen. The world's largest floating ship museum, it features 19 ships, including a submarine, destroyer and lightship.

Maps:
Area 256
City 258

The heart of Göteborg lies along Östra Hamngatan and Kungsportsavenyn. Start at the northern end of Östra Hamngatan; heading south you will pass **Nordstan**, one of northern Europe's largest covered shopping centres. Along the intersecting streets of Norra and Södra Hamngatan are dozens of small and inviting boutiques. Cross Stora Hamnkanalen (Great Harbour Canal) and continue south to **Kungsportsplatsen**, where you can pop into the **Göteborgs Turistbyrå** ● (tourist office; call for opening hours; tel: 031 61 25 00).

Across the street is **Saluhallen** ●, a large indoor marketplace (1886–89) stocked with Swedish specialities such as seafood, cheese and meats. This is a good place to sit and enjoy a cup of coffee, a light snack or a full lunch.

Kungsportsplatsen is also the place to embark on a **Paddan** (Swedish for "toad"), one of the flat-bottomed sightseeing boats that cruise through the old moat, under some 20 bridges, along 17th-century canals, out into the harbour and back again (May–Sept: first departure 10.30am; tel: 031 60 96 70).

From Kungsportsplatsen, cross the moat into Kungsportsavenyn – known as "**Avenyn**" ● (The Avenue). The Avenyn, 40 metres (130 ft) wide and just under a kilometre long, is a boulevard lined with trees, restaurants, pubs and cafés. Halfway along the Avenyn, you are just a block away from the **Röhsska Museet** ● (Vasagatan 37–39; Tues noon–8pm, Wed–Fri noon–5pm, Sat–Sun 11am–5pm; entrance charge; tel: 031 36 83 150), the Swedish museum for design and handicrafts. At the southern end of the Avenyn is Göteborg's cultural centre, **Götaplatsen**, with the Poseidon fountain by the Swedish sculptor Carl Milles.

A Göteborg Pass gives free parking, unlimited travel on city buses and trams, a boat trip and free admission to many museums and to Liseberg.

BELOW: Göteborg's harbourfront and lookout tower.

Götaplatsen is flanked by the **Konstmuseum** ⓖ (Art Museum; Tues and Thur 11am–6pm, Wed until 9pm, Fri–Sun until 5pm; entrance charge; tel: 031 368 35 00), with an extensive collection of Scandinavian art, including work by Munch, Zorn, Rembrandt and Pissarro. Also on the square is the **Konserthuset** ⓗ (Concert Hall), home of the Gothenburg Symphony Orchestra.

Bohuslän is noted for its fine Bronze Age rock carvings. The "Bridal Pair" at Vitlycke, near Tanumshede, is among the best known of the carvings in the area.

Liseberg ⓘ (late Apr–Sept; entrance charge; tel: 031 40 01 00), in the middle of town, is the largest amusement park in northern Europe. Also great for families is **Universeum** ⓙ (10am–6pm; entrance charge; tel: 031 335 64 50), an impressive science and nature centre with shark tunnel and rainforest zone. For a calmer experience, explore the **Botaniska Trädgården** ⓚ (Botanical Gardens) or **Slottsskogen** ⓛ, two of Göteborg's 20 parks.

The rugged coast

The province of **Bohuslän** begins north of Göteborg. To see the coast, head 15 km (9 miles) west from Kungälv on Road 168 past Tjuvkil, where you can catch a ferry to **Marstrand** ⑧. A town without cars, Marstrand is a popular holiday resort and sailing centre. In summer it is also a good place to buy crafts. **Carlstens Fästning** (Fortress) dominates the town and offers the best views of the island. King Oskar II (1872–1907) used to come here every summer to holiday and his statue stands in front of the Societetshuset.

Beyond Marstrand lie the islands of Tjörn and Orust, connected by bridge to the mainland. **Tjörn** ⑨ is beautiful with some barren areas inland and a fascinating coastline. A magnificent curved bridge, which provides good views in either direction, links Tjörn and **Orust** ⑩. This island, the third-largest in Sweden, has its quota of fishing villages, including Mollösund, Ellös and Käringön.

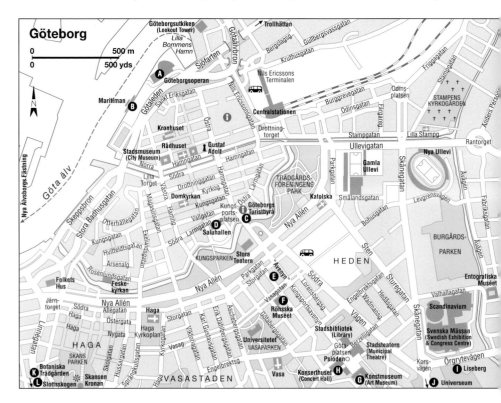

Returning to the mainland, take a ferry across the **Gullmarn**, Sweden's only genuine fjord, from **Fiskebäckskil** ⑪ to **Lysekil** ⑫. Lysekil comes to life in the summer with boat excursions to the islands and sea fishing trips. **Havets Hus** (sea aquarium; mid-June–late-Aug daily 10am–6pm, late-Aug–mid-Nov and mid-Feb–mid-June until 4pm; entrance charge; tel: 0523 66 81 61) includes a tunnel aquarium containing rays, sharks, halibut and cod from Gullmarn and Skagerrak.

North of Lysekil on the Sotenäs peninsula, the small harbour of **Smögen** ⑬ is a favourite stop for boats. The main attraction is the wooden, waterside boardwalk, where you can shop, stroll and lounge. The other attraction is fresh shrimp. Watch a fish auction and then go round the corner to buy some of the catch.

At **Åby Säteri** ⑭, 17 km (11 miles) northeast of Smögen, is **Nordens Ark** (daily Jan–late Apr 10am–4pm; late Apr–late June and Sept 10am–5pm, late June–late Aug until 7pm; entrance charge; tel: 0523 795 90), a nature park featuring endangered species and old breeds of Nordic farm animals.

Towards Norway

Near **Tanumshede** ⑮, a small town about 50 km (30 miles) north on Route 168, is Europe's largest collection of Bronze Age rock carvings and a UNESCO World Heritage site. The petroglyphs include detailed depictions of battles, ships, hunting and fishing scenes, and mating couples.

The last town before the Norwegian frontier is **Strömstad** ⑯, a health resort noted for its long hours of sunshine. Strömstad shrimps are considered by the local inhabitants to be in a class of their own, with a distinctive mild flavour. The district has more than a touch of Norwegian about it, having been part of Norway until 1717. ❑

Maps:
Area 256
City 258

*Thrills for all:
Liseberg amusement
park in Göteborg.*

BELOW: sailing
competition on the
island of Tjörn.

SWEDEN'S GREAT LAKES

Map on page 262

Two of Europe's largest lakes, Vänern and Vättern, lie at the heart of southern Sweden. In this area of farmland and forests, painted churches, grand castles and literary hideaways abound

Two enormous lakes, Vänern and Vättern, dominate the map of Sweden. The larger of the two is Vänern, a vast stretch of water with an area of 5,585 sq km (2,156 sq miles). It is not only the biggest lake in Sweden but also the largest in Western Europe, and its western shore embraces two provinces, Dalsland and Värmland.

Dalsland is a province of neat farms and prosperous small towns and villages, with empty roads running through its forests. The greatest attraction here is nature and, thus, the most interesting activities are outdoors: namely, camping, hiking and canoeing. West of Mellerud is **Kroppefjällen ❶**, an upland area which is a nature reserve. One of the best ways to explore the region is to hike along the 15-km (9-mile) **Karl XIIs Väg** (trail); maps can be obtained from the tourist office in Mellerud (tel: 0530 183 08).

A local feature is the **Dalslands Kanal**, a network of interconnected lakes and rivers. It was designed by Nils Ericsson and built between 1864 and 1868 to provide better transport for the local ironworks and sawmills. Today, it is popular for sailing and canoeing. The aqueduct at **Håverud ❷**, 14 km (9 miles) north of Mellerud, is a dramatic piece of engineering. Made of iron and 33 metres (108 ft) long, it carries the canal over the rapids of the River Upperud.

Along the Klarälven

An old parish register in Western Värmland states: "Between Sweden and Norway lies Värmland." Even today, a certain rugged independence, plus a slight Norwegian accent, persists. The region has strong traditions and has produced a rich crop of writers of both prose and poetry. Spruce and pine forests cover the county and are often referred to as "Värmland's gold".

The province is crisscrossed with narrow lakes and rivers, and the **Klarälven** can claim to be among its most beautiful rivers. It begins turbulently in Norway, where it is called Trysilelva, but gradually becomes broader, winding and sluggish before emptying into Lake Vänern near the province's largest town, **Karlstad ❸**. Highlights in this 400-year-old town include the cathedral (built in 1730), the longest arched stone bridge in Sweden (168 metres/550 ft) and a popular park, **Mariebergsskogen**.

The Klarälven was the last Swedish river used for floating logs. The practice ended in 1991, but in **Dyvelsten ❹**, 17 km (10 miles) north of Karlstad, the **Flottningsmuséet** (Log Rafting Museum; mid-June–mid-Aug daily 11am–5pm; entrance charge; tel: 054 87 12 26) shows how it was done.

At **Ransäter ❺**, 40 km (25 miles) north of Karlstad on the Klarälven, the **Hembygdsgården** (Heritage Village; mid-June–mid-Aug 11am–6pm; entrance

LEFT: fishing on the tranquil waters.
BELOW: watery landscape.

charge; tel: 0552 303 43) includes museums devoted to mining, forestry, agriculture and rural life, which provide a fascinating picture of the Värmland of yesteryear. Ransäter hosts an annual folk music festival in June and the largest accordion festival in Scandinavia in July.

The Klarälven may no longer be used for floating logs, but many Swedes holiday on the river – drifting along on the gentle current on a raft they assemble themselves. Contact the Karlstad tourist office (tel: 054 29 84 00) for more details.

To the south of Lake Vänern, Lidköping's square is said to be the largest in northern Europe. A big market is held here on Wednesday and Saturday mornings.

Nobel prize-winner

West of Ransäter, on the eastern shore of Mellan-Fryken, is **Mårbacka** ⑥ (tours Oct–Apr Sat 2pm, mid-May–early July and late Aug daily 10am–4pm; early July–mid-Aug daily 10am–5pm; entrance charge; tel: 0565 310 27), the manor home of the Swedish writer Selma Lagerlöf, the first woman to receive a Nobel prize for literature, in 1909. Through her books, including *The Wonderful Adventures of Nils* and *The Story of Gösta Berling*, she made famous the

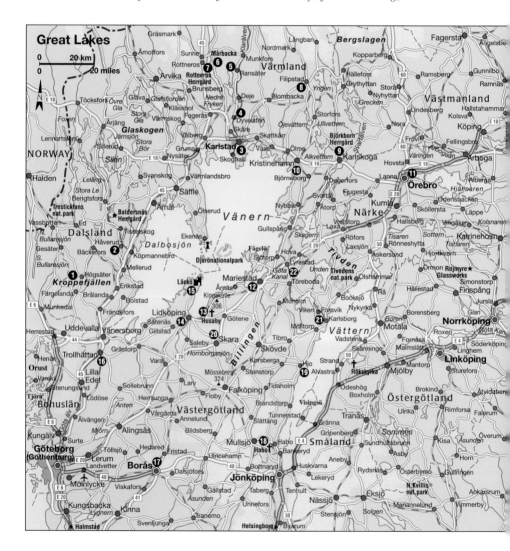

Fryk valley and lakes. On the western side of the lake is **Rottneros Park** ❼ (mid-May–mid-June and mid-Aug–mid-Sept 10am–4pm; mid-June–mid-Aug until 6pm; entrance charge; tel: 0565 602 95), whose elegant manor house appears as Ekeby in Lagerlöf's *The Story of Gösta Berling*. This beautiful park has an arboretum and works by Scandinavian sculptors, including Milles, Eriksson and Vigeland.

Inventive feats

North of Lake Vänern, the bedrock is rich in minerals and this area has long been associated with Sweden's early industrial development. Many Americans make the pilgrimage to **Filipstad** ❽, which has the mausoleum of John Ericsson, the gifted inventor and engineer.

Mariestad Slot, on the eastern shore of Lake Vänern.

Björkborn Herrgård ❾, near Karlskoga, was the home of the Swedish inventor Alfred Nobel. The manor house is now a museum, **Nobelmuséet** (mid-May–mid-Sept daily 10am–5pm; mid-Sept–mid-May Tues–Sun 11am–5pm; entrance charge; tel: 08 534 818 18). At **Kristinehamn** ❿, 24 km (15 miles) west of Karlskoga, a 15-metre (49-ft) high sculpture by Picasso is the most striking feature on Lake Vänern.

To the east, in the province of Närke, is **Örebro** ⓫, with a dramatic 17th-century lakeside **castle** (early June–late Aug, guided tours 1pm; entrance charge; tel: 019 21 21 21), parts of which date back to the late 1200s.

Between the lakes

The region separating Lake Vänern from Lake Vättern offers rich pickings for the visitor. This is the province of Västergötland. In 1746 the indefatigable Swedish botanist Carolus Linnaeus said: "Truly no one could ever imagine such splendour as in Västergötland who had not seen it for himself."

BELOW: ready with a smile.

Heading south along the eastern shore of Vänern, you come to **Mariestad** ⓬, which is dominated by the spire of the 17th-century Renaissance-style cathedral, one of the few churches of this period remaining in Sweden.

Most Swedes learn in school that the king who first united the Svea and Göta tribes, Olof Skötkonung (994–1022), was baptised in 1008 at Husaby Källa (Husaby Spring) at the southern tip of Kinnekulle. Despite disputes, historians would like to establish Husaby as the cradle of the Swedish state. **Husaby Church** ⓭ (Apr–Sept daily; tel: 0511 34 31 41) has an imposing stone tower with three spires.

Nestled into Kinneviken (Kinne Bay), 51 km (32 miles) south of Mariestad, is **Lidköping** ⓮, a town founded in 1446 and renowned for its porcelain. **Rörstrand** (Mon–Fri 10am–6pm, Sat until 4pm, Sun noon–6pm; tel: 0510 823 46), the second-oldest porcelain factory in Europe and maker of the Nobel china, has its own museum featuring royal pieces, and a large shop. For a modest-sized town, Lidköping has several fine cafés. The best is Garströms Konditori, established in 1859, on the main square (daily).

North of Lidköping on the Kållandsö peninsula, stands the restored Baroque-style 17th-century **Läckö Slott** ⓯ (May–Sept, call for opening hours;

Map on page 262

Map on page 262

TIP

On the east of Lake Vättern, historic sites of note include the stone of Rök at Rökeskyrka with its 800 runes (E4 north of Ödeshög) and Alvastra Kloster, Sweden's first Cistercian monastery (Road 50 north of Ödeshög).

BELOW: cycling along the Göta Kanal.

entrance charge; tel: 0510 48 46 60), one of the most impressive castles in Sweden. In summer it holds cultural exhibitions and is a venue for outdoor concerts.

Trollhättan ⑯, at the southern tip of Lake Vänern, is the home town of Saab Automobile and has a rich industrial heritage. The town has long been famous for the magnificent falls of the Göta River. The water level drops by about 32 metres (105 ft), and when the Göta Kanal was built a flight of locks was required to give ships access to Lake Vänern. Today, the river is diverted to generate electricity and the falls are silent. But during the annual Falls Festival in July it is released to follow the old course, providing an impressive spectacle.

The southern part of Västergötland was the heartland of Sweden's textile industry, with the focal point at **Borås ⑰**, where there is a **Textilmuséet** (Textile Museum; Tues and Thur 10am–8pm, Wed and Fri until 4pm, Sat and Sun noon–4pm; entrance charge; tel: 033 35 89 50).

Around Lake Vättern

Lake Vättern, the second-largest lake in Sweden, covers an area of 1,912 sq km (738 sq miles). Near the southern tip of the lake, on the west side, is the 14th-century timber-built **Habo Kyrka ⑱** (church), southwest of Habo village. It features an outstanding painted interior, the work of Johan Christian Peterson and Johan Kinnerus, both of Jönköping, between 1741 and 1743. Their paintings illustrate Luther's catechism and Biblical scenes.

Travelling north along the lake, stop at the small waterside resort of **Hjo ⑲** to enjoy freshly smoked whitefish. Then tour the town in a horse-drawn carriage, or cruise on the lake in the 1892 steamer, *Trafik*. In the summer, Hjo hosts Scandinavia's largest craft festival. **Skara ⑳**, 50 km (31 miles) to the west of Hjo, has Sweden's second-oldest cathedral (after Lund), dating from the 11th century. **Skara Sommarland** (June Sun–Fri 10am–5pm, Sat until 6pm; early July–mid-Aug daily until 7pm; entrance charge; tel: 0511 770 300), 8 km (5 miles) east of Skara on Road 49, is a delight for children with numerous attractions from lunar vehicles to a giant water park.

For more relaxed pursuits, head 10 km (6 miles) southeast of Skara on Road 184 to the lake of **Hornborgasjön**, a wildlife area with more than 100 species of birds. The biggest attraction is the annual mating dance of the crane, best seen in April.

Mighty fortress

Karlsborg ㉑, on the western shore of Lake Vättern, 30 km (19 miles) north of Hjo, is dominated by its huge fortress, **Fästning** (mid-May–Aug daily guided tours; entrance charge; tel: 0505 188 30). In 1809, when Sweden lost Finland to the Russians, the Swedes decided to build two fortresses to house the government and the treasury. The first, at Karlsborg, was started in 1819 and required 250,000 tons of limestone. It was quarried by prison labour on the eastern side of the lake and ferried across by boat.

The castle has walls 2 metres (6 ft) thick with 5 km (3 miles) of ramparts, but by the time the building was finally finished, in 1909, fortresses were out of fashion. The second castle was never built. ❏

CROSSING SWEDEN BY CANAL

One of the most leisurely ways of sampling the country's history is to cruise along the Göta Kanal between Stockholm and Göteborg

The challenge of linking the lakes and rivers through the interior of Sweden, from Stockholm on the east coast to Göteborg on the west coast, had exercised the minds of many industrialists and kings before Baltzar von Platen succeeded at the beginning of the 19th century.

At the time, the country needed this new artery from east to west to transport timber, iron and food, and also to build up industry along its banks. For 22 years, 58,000 men laboured to build the 190-km (118-mile) long **Göta Kanal ㉒**. The canal was designated an "International Historic Civil Engineering Landmark", giving it the same status as the Golden Gate Bridge and the Panama Canal, and in 2007 was officially recognised as Sweden's greatest feat of engineering. Today, there is no commercial traffic on the canal, but many Swedes travel it in their own boats.

For the visitor, the classic way is to take a cruise between Stockholm and Göteborg on one of the vintage vessels operated by the Göta Kanal Rederiaktiebolaget (Göta Kanal Steamship Company). The oldest of the three vessels is *MS Juno*, built in 1874.

The four-day westbound cruise starts from Stockholm, finishing the first day's cruise at the village of Trosa. On the second day the boat passes through Mem – where the canal was officially inaugurated in 1832 – before reaching Berg, where there is time to visit the historic monastery church at nearby Vreta, once the richest religious establishment in Sweden.

The route crosses two picturesque lakes, Asplången and Roxen, where there are ospreys and herons during the breeding season. The canal then takes you through 15 locks in 3 km (2 miles), lifting you 37 metres (120 ft). The next night is spent at Motala, a town founded by Baltzar von Platen.

On the third morning the boat crosses Lake Vättern to Karlsborg, site of a huge fortress built at the same time as the canal, and Forsvik, an old metal-working village and the site of the canal's oldest lock, built in 1813. Here, the boat is often greeted by a local family singing hymns and offering passengers wild flowers. This 100-year-old custom originated as a blessing for passengers as they embarked on what was then regarded as the hazardous crossing of Vättern. In the evening the boat reaches Sjötorp, marking the beginning of Lake Vänern.

At the south side of Lake Vänern, the boat enters the gorge at Trollhättan early the next morning for the last stage of the voyage down the Göta river to Göteborg. ❑

TOP LEFT: safety first. **ABOVE LEFT AND RIGHT:** two of the vintage vessels that cruise the Göta Kanal. **TOP RIGHT:** waiting for a catch.

DALARNA

Map on page 268

Dalarna is Sweden's folklore province, as famous for its scarlet Dala horses as its music and merrymaking at Midsummer. Winter attracts skiers challenged by championship events

Dalarna is often regarded as the heart of Sweden's folklore district, and indeed it represents all that is quintessentially Swedish. With its colourful costumes, centuries-old traditions of music and dance, Midsummer festivals, and evocative rural landscape, its folklore and beauty attract an increasing number of visitors each year.

Dalarna is the third-largest tourist site in Sweden, after Stockholm and Göteborg. The culture that gave us the red-painted Dalahäst (Dala horse) and inspired two of Sweden's most beloved artists, Carl Larsson and Anders Zorn, can best be experienced in the twilight of *fäbodar*, the old pasture cottages nestled in the hills of Dalarna; in the company of some elderly but amazingly energetic fiddlers; or at the magic of Midsummer, when a young woman places nine different flowers under her pillow to dream of the man she will marry.

Music-making

Music is one of the most defining characteristics of Dala culture. Music on Lake Siljan (Musik vid Siljan) is a huge annual festival, held in late June/early July, that attracts visitors from all over Sweden and abroad. Distinctly Dala are the *spelmansstämmor*, folk musicians' rallies, particularly the one held each July in **Bingsjö ❶**, 30 km (19 miles) east of Rättvik, where fiddlers in their eighties turn the classic polka into a musical performance that rivals any blues master.

An exotic setting for listening to music is **Dalhalla** (June–Aug guided tours daily 10am–4pm; entrance charge; tel: 0248 79 79 50), a cavernous outdoor concert arena set in the depths of an abandoned limestone quarry near the town of **Rättvik ❷**. The quarry, abandoned in 1990, was inaugurated with a performance of Wagner's *Der Ring des Nibelungen*. The annual summer festivals feature artists of international standing.

Pastoral scenes

For a change of pace, the gentle quiet of the region's *fäbodar* offer a taste of back-to-the-land living. These pasture cottages and surrounding buildings, dating from the 15th and 16th centuries, are found all over Sweden but are most often associated with Dalarna. They constitute a living museum, where cows are milked, butter is churned, *messmör* (a type of goat's cheese) is made, and the classic *tunnbröd* (thin bread) is baked. Many *fäbodar* are open to the public and sell products or serve food.

One worth visiting is **Ljusbodarnas Fäbod** (June–Aug; tel: 0247 233 45) about 20 km (12 miles) south of Leksand on Route 70 towards Mockfjärd,

LEFT: midsummer celebrations are an annual highlight. **BELOW:** folk art telephone box.

where children are encouraged to pet the cows, calves, hens, sheep and pigs, and you can enjoy a meal of *sill* (herring) on some nights.

If trying your own hand at 15th-century farming appeals, **Prästbodarnas Fäbod** (June–Sept daily, book in advance; tel: 0248 141 59), near Bingsjö, has a variety of native Swedish farm animals, and offers one-day courses in butter churning, milking and cheese-making. The farming life seems a natural accompaniment to the breathtaking scenery of the province.

At the northern extremity of Dalarna is the deceptively gentle start of the mountain range which marches north, gaining height all the time until it culminates in the snow-topped peaks of the Kebnekaise range in Lapland. Dalarna is a transition zone between the softer landscapes of southern Sweden and the more dramatic, but harsher landscapes of the north. It is even divided within itself between the more densely populated area south and east of Lake Siljan (dense by Swedish standards) and the relatively uninhabited zones to the north and west of the lake.

Mora on Lake Siljan is best known as the home of the Swedish artist Anders Zorn (1860–1920). His house and studio, Zorngården, and the Zornmuseet (both open daily) are well worth visiting.

Industrial traditions

Dalarna is not exclusively rural. The Bergslagen district has been mined for a millennium, and the whole area is now a UNESCO World Heritage site. The most impressive industrial site is the 17th-century **Falu Gruva** (Falu Mine; open year-round, phone for times; tel: 023 78 20 30), on the edge of the provincial capital, **Falun ❸**, with machinery, museum and tours into the depths.

Hedemora ❹ claims to be the oldest town in Dalarna, with a charter dated 1459; its privileges as a market town go back even further than that, while parts of the church are 13th-century. The locals have devised **Husbyringen**, a 56-km

BELOW:
local musician.

(35-mile) "museum trail" which you can take by car through the area northeast of the town to see a number of industrial archaeology sites.

Map on page 268

Also worth visiting is **Säter ⑤**, one of the seven best-preserved wooden towns in Sweden. Compared with Hedemora it is quite an upstart, with a town charter dated 1642. The ravines of the Säter Valley were created at the end of the Ice Age and are of interest for their flora.

Traditional handicrafts

In the province that inspired the distinctive Dala horse, it is not surprising that the region is known for its abundance of carvers, potters, silversmiths, weavers, painters and bakers. This is a mecca for *hemslöjd* (crafts), all of which have their ancient roots in the farming culture. At **Sätergläntan ⑥**, 3 km (2 miles) south of Insjön Lake, **Hemslöjdens Gård** (tel: 0247 645 70) offers a wide array of handicrafts as well as week-long courses. At **Nittsjö Keramik** (Mon–Fri 9am–6pm, Sat 9am–2pm; June–Aug Sun noon–4pm; tel: 0248 171 30), 6 km (4 miles) north of Rättvik, clay goods are made following a tradition that goes back over 100 years.

The Dalahäst (Dala Horse), a more readily recognised Swedish symbol than the nation's flag.

Cross-country ski challenge

Dalarna's ski resorts are the principal winter tourist attraction, both for cross-country skiing and downhill. **Romme Alpin ⑦** is Sweden's most-visited ski resort outside the proper mountain areas, with some 200,000 visitors annually. Together, **Sälen ⑧** and Idre, in northwest Dalarna, have almost half of Sweden's ski-lift facilities and Sälen is famous for being the starting point for a 85-km (53-mile) cross-country skiing race to **Mora ⑨**: the Vasaloppet, the most popular sporting event in Sweden. ❑

BELOW: decorating the Maypole.

LARSSON

Carl Larsson (1853–1919) is Sweden's best-loved artist. The greatest source of inspiration for Larsson was the life he shared with his wife Karin, a textile artist, and their children at their home at **Sundborn ⑩** (May–Sept daily 10am–5pm; other times by appointment; entrance charge; tel: 023 600 53).

Carl Larsson was born to a poor family in Stockholm and during his youth he suffered all the deprivations of poverty, a period he later described as "hell on earth". He was determined to leave those hard times behind him and thus it was no coincidence that he became the artist who would best portray the happy, harmonious Swedish family, bathed in light, colour, and joyous celebration of home and hearth. In their wooden farmhouse, where Karin and Carl lived with their eight children, they created the simple interiors that were to influence so much of modern design. Stripped floors strewn with rugs, brightly painted furniture and hand-painted friezes were the key elements.

Larsson's paintings were strongly influenced by the local Dalarna folk-art traditions. In his autobiography, Larsson wrote, "My art: it is just like my home; there is no place there for fine furniture... it is simple, but harmonious. Nothing extravagant... just good, strong work."

CENTRAL SWEDEN

Map on page 272

Brilliant blue lakes, rushing rivers, the mysterious outlines of mountains, and above all the space and silence beckon hikers and anglers to this untouched landscape

Five provinces stretch across central Sweden. In the east are Gästrikland, Hälsingland and Medelpad, which share the long coastline known as Jungfrukusten (Virgin Coast). Further inland come Härjedalen and Jämtland, which stretch west to the Norwegian border, the land of lakes and coniferous or birch forests. Härjedalen marks the beginning of the great northern mountain ranges and the further north you go, the more dramatic the scenery is.

The small province of **Gästrikland** has one major town, **Gävle ❶**, in the southeast corner of the region. Gävle was one of Sweden's great shipping towns, and the most treasured exhibit at the local museum, **Länsmuséet** (Tues–Fri 10am–4pm, Wed until 9pm, Sat–Sun noon–4pm; entrance charge; tel: 026 65 56 00), is the Björke boat, built in AD 100 and among the most notable finds in northern Europe.

Railway enthusiasts should make a point of visiting the **Sveriges Järnvägsmuseum** (Swedish Railway Museum; June–Aug daily 10am–4pm; Sept–May closed Mon; entrance charge; tel: 026 144 615) on the outskirts of Gävle. The collection embraces 29 gleaming locomotives, 30 coaches and wagons and the 1874 coach of King Oscar II.

LEFT: a family day out.
BELOW: lynx, resident of northern Scandinavia.

THE INLAND RAILWAY

A trip on the Inlandsbanan (Inland Railway) is an enjoyable way of seeing some of Sweden's most dramatic scenery. The route stretches through the Central heartlands from Mora in Dalarna to Gällivare in Lapland.

The idea of building such a long railway through a harsh and inaccessible landscape was first promoted in 1894, but it was to take another 40 years of hard labour before it was completed. The 1,100-km (680-mile) line was finally inaugurated in Jokkmokk in Lapland on 6 August 1937, and a monument was erected to commemorate the event.

Today the train stops along the way so passengers can visit local artists and craftspeople or simply admire the views. Sometimes it has to halt to avoid running into herds of reindeer resting on the track. With luck, passengers may also spot elks or bears.

It is possible to make stopovers along the route and stay for a night or two in local towns and villages to do some walking in the mountains, or just enjoy the magnificent landscape. Various packages are available combining rail travel with hotel accommodation, or trekking. For more information contact Inlandsbanan AB, Box 561, SE-831 27 Östersund, Sweden. Tel: +46 63 19 44 00; fax: +46 63 19 44 06; www.inlandsbanan.se.

Relive the life of the charcoal burners of old at Albert Vikstens Kojby (Albert Viksten's Cabin Village) at Lassekrog, 40 km (25 miles) northwest of Ljusdal. Visitors can spend a night in a cabin and bake their own "charcoal bread" over the fire (tel: 0651 850 55).

For children, **Furuviksparken** (June and mid-Aug–Sept 10am–5pm; July–mid-Aug until 7pm; entrance charge; tel: 026 17 73 00), 10 km (6 miles) south of Gävle, combines extensive zoological gardens with a variety of other attractions, including a theatre and a circus.

Grilled herring and potatoes with dill butter is a favourite dish all along the Virgin Coast. At **Bönan**, 10 km (6 miles) northeast of Gävle, visit **Engeltofta** to sample the town's famous golden-brown smoked herring, cured over spruce wood – in summer you can catch the boat over from Gävle.

Gästrikland is at the eastern end of the swathe of land which gave Sweden its early mining and smelting industries. Steam trains ply the 4.5 km (2¾ miles) from **Jädraås ❷**, northwest of Gävle, to **Tallås**. The railway is typical of those used to haul minerals or timber, and the coach used by King Oscar II (ruled 1872–1907) when he went hunting bears in Dalarna is still in service.

The good-time town

Follow the E4 north to **Söderhamn ❸**, the starting point for boat trips around the archipelago. Söderhamn was founded in 1620 as an armoury for the Swedish army, and the museum is situated in part of what was the gun and rifle factory. Although a commercial centre, the town has an impressive town hall, plus a church to match and a pleasant riverside park.

Around 120 years ago, when the timber industry was at its peak, **Hudiksvall ❹** had a reputation for high living. A reminder of the era is the town's theatre, opened in 1882. Hudiksvall also has a group of the best-preserved 19th-century wooden buildings in Sweden, the **Fiskarstan**.

The interior of **Hälsingland** has the best scenery, particularly the valley of the

BELOW: folk dancers prepare for the Hälsingehambo festival at Järvsö.

river Ljusnandalen, which is laced with lakes along its entire length. West of Ljusdal **5**, where the Ljusnan meets the Hennan river, the forests begin.

Map on page 272

Dancing in the valley

About 12 km (7 miles) south of Ljusdal is **Järvsö 6**, a small town in farming and forestry country. Once a year, its peaceful routine is broken by an unforgettable festival: the **Hälsingehambo**, a competitive event involving 3,000 folk dancers. At dawn on a July morning competitors in traditional costumes begin to dance to the tune *Hårgalåten* all the way up the Ljusnan valley, from **Bollnäs 7** and Arbrå, to a grand finale 50 km (31 miles) away in Järvsö, in front of Stengård Manor.

Of the mountains around Järvsö, **Gluggberget**, 515 metres (1,689 ft), has a viewing platform at the summit, while **Öjeberget**, 370 metres (1,214 ft), has the advantage that you can drive to the top.

To absorb this region you need to drive first along the minor road 30 km (18 miles) east from Järvsö to **Delsbo 8**, which attracts large numbers of folk fiddlers for the annual **Delsbostämman**, and then on through Friggesund and Hassela and back to the coast. Surrounded by dark forests, this is **Dellenbygden**, rural Sweden at its best, and includes the Dellen lakes area, with boat and canoe trips, and walking trails.

Anglers' paradise

Together the provinces of **Härjedalen** and **Jämtland** are as big as Denmark, but with a population of only 135,000. To the east and southeast are extensive forests with hills, rivers and lakes. The higher mountains begin in Härjedalen.

Snow scooters are the most practical form of transport in winter.

BELOW: the dense forests are a good hunting ground.

*The E14 from
Östersund to the
Norwegian frontier
is an age-old route
once used by
pilgrims on their trek
to the grave of
St Olav at Trondheim
(see page 209).*

BELOW: Swedes
take to their skis in
the winter months.
RIGHT: "fairy
cottage" at Åre.

This heartland has four main rivers, the Ångermanälven, Indalsälven, Ljungan and Ljusnan, all well stocked with fish, especially trout and grayling. Perch, pike and whitefish are the most common in the forested regions, but many tarns have been stocked with trout. You may need a fishing permit, bought cheaply nearby or at the tourist offices. The vast tracts of near-uninhabited territory are also home to wildlife such as bears, wolverine, lynx and the ubiquitous elk.

When tourism was in its infancy, Härjedalen was one of the first Swedish provinces to attract skiers, who still return to pit their skills against its varied terrain, and come back in the summer for mountain walking. The scenery is impressive and, north of **Funäsdalen**, not far from the Norwegian border, the province has Sweden's highest road over the **Flatruet Plateau**, up to 1,000 metres (3,280 ft) high.

At the crossroads of the north–south route, Highway 45, and east–west, Highway 84, is **Sveg**, a small town but Härjedalen's largest at around 4,000 people. **Vemdalen ❾**, 60 km (37 miles) northwest, has an eight-sided wooden church with a separate onion-domed bell tower. Beyond the village the road climbs between two mountains, **Vemdalsfjällen**, before entering Jämtland.

Jämtland is the biggest province in central Sweden, a huge territory of lakes, rivers and mountains. Its heart is the lake of **Storsjön**, the fifth-largest stretch of inland water in the country, which is reputed to have its own monster, a Swedish version of Scotland's "Nessie". Present-day monster-seekers can take a cruise on the lake in the 1875 steamer *Thomée*. On the banks of Storsjön is Jämtland's largest town, **Östersund ❿**, connected by a bridge to the beautiful island of **Frösön**. The island was home to the noted Swedish composer and critic Wilhelm Peterson-Berger (1867–1942). His most popular work, the opera *Arnljot*, is performed every summer on the island.

In Östersund, **Jamtli** (open late June–late Aug daily 11am–5pm; late Aug–late June Tues–Sun 11am–5pm; entrance charge; tel: 063 15 01 00) is one of biggest open-air museums in the country, comprising 18th- and 19th-century buildings including a *shieling* (summer farm), baker's cottage, smithy, and an old inn. The food in the café is recommended.

North of Storsjön, on the north bank of Lake Alsensjön at **Glösa ⓫**, are a number of *hällristningar*, primitive rock carvings.

Mountains and canyons

In western Jämtland, the peaks rise up to nearly 1,800 metres (6,000 ft). It is a splendid area for trekking in summer and skiing in winter. Centuries ago, melting ice left many strange and unusual formations such as the deep canyon between the Drommen and Falkfångarfjället mountains. The region is also rich in waterfalls, such as **Ristafallet** near Hålland, **Storfallet**, northwest of Höglekardalen and **Tännforsen**, to the west of Åre ⓬.

Åre is a popular winter sports resort with a funicular railway that goes from the town centre part way up the local mountain, Åreskutan, and a cable car that continues almost to the summit. Lakes and mountains on every side make up a superb view. ❏

NORTHERN SWEDEN

Lapland, land of the Midnight Sun and home to the Sami, offers a richly rewarding experience for the traveller. Fishing villages and holiday islands dot the Bothnian Coast

Map on page 278

I n the search for natural landscapes Lapland, which stretches across Northern Sweden and Finland, has become increasingly popular. The uplands, lakes and mountains of the region are among the finest in Europe, and although distances are great there are quality roads and a rail link. Anglers are attracted to the coast of Bottenviken (Gulf of Bothnia), the stretch of water that separates Sweden from Finland. There are excellent opportunities for both river and sea fishing along the coast; holiday-makers and sailors gravitate to its sheltered coves and islands.

The best way to absorb the immensity of Swedish Lapland is to take the inland Highway 45, from south to north. The first town across the border from Ångermanland is **Dorotea ❶**. Its claim to fame is the Dorotea Hotel, which is renowned for its cuisine. **Vilhelmina ❷**, 100 km (60 miles north) on the Ångermanälven river, is of greater interest. It is a well-preserved church village where travellers can find accommodation in its wooden houses.

West of Vilhelmina is the **Kittelfjäll** mountain region and the border with Norway. To the north lies an important road junction at **Storuman ❸** where the 45 is bisected by the E12, known as the Blå Vägen (Blue Highway) because it follows a succession of lakes and the Umeälven river on its route from the east coast. It passes through **Lycksele ❹** where there is a zoo, **Lycksele Djurpark** (daily from 10am; closing times seasonal; entrance charge; tel: 0950 163 63), that has Nordic species including bear, elk, musk-ox, wolf and reindeer. From Storuman the E12 continues west through Tärnaby to Mo i Rana in Norway.

The Silver Road

From Slagnäs, on Highway 45, a secondary road leads through glorious lakeside scenery to **Arjeplog ❺**, one of Swedish Lapland's most interesting towns. The main attraction is the **Silvermuséet** (Silver Museum; June–mid-Aug daily 9am–6pm; mid-Aug–May Mon–Fri 10am–noon, 1–4pm, Sat 10am–2pm; also Jan–Mar Tues 8–10pm, Sat 10am–2pm; entrance charge; tel: 0961 612 90). Housed in an old school, it provides a fascinating insight into the region's history and the Sami people of Lapland. It owes its existence to Einar Wallqvist, "doctor of the Laplanders", who, besides his medical work, collected cultural objects. He established a museum which today has the finest collection of Sami silver in the world. Arjeplog's church is 17th-century and also worth a visit.

Arjeplog is roughly halfway along Highway 95, the Silvervägen (Silver Road) between Skellefteå in the east and Bodø on Norway's west coast. In the 17th century there were silver mines around **Nasafjäll** and the ore was transported, by reindeer and boat, to the

LEFT: on top of the world in Lapland.
BELOW: Sami in traditional garb.

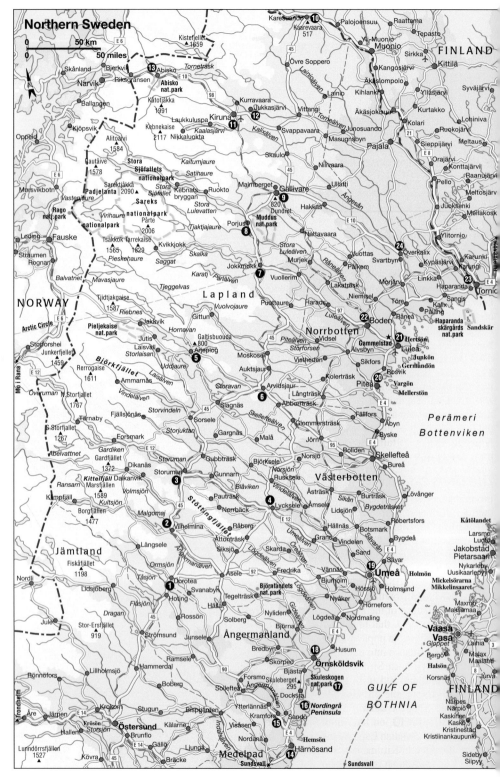

Map on page 278

east coast. Not until 1974 did it become an asphalted highway opening up an area of outstanding beauty. There are magnificent views from Galtisbuouda, 800 metres (2,620 ft) high, just north of Arjeplog.

Arvidsjaur ❻, once a trading post, now a junction of roads and railways, has the atmosphere of a frontier town. The major attraction is **Lappstaden** (daily; July guided tours; tel: 0960 175 00), the oldest surviving example of a Sami village, with *kåtor*, tent-shaped wooden huts, and *härbren*, wooden storehouses. In summer, Arvidsjaur is a tourist centre and in winter, when it is intensely cold, both Arjeplog and Arvidsjaur are taken over by the motor industry to test products in sub-zero temperatures.

Across the Arctic Circle

The **Arctic Circle** is 156 km (97 miles) north of Arvidsjaur and you can buy a certificate to prove you crossed the line at a nearby café. Further north is **Jokkmokk ❼**, the second-largest *kommun* (municipal district) in Sweden covering an area of 19,425 sq km (7,500 sq miles) with a population of 5,500.

Jokkmokk is a centre for the Sami culture and in summer you can see nomadic Sami here. An annual winter market in February attracts thousands of people, although temperatures can drop to –35°C (–31°F). First held in 1605, the market soon became a meeting place for the Sami and merchants from the coastal communities. Today it is as much a social occasion as an opportunity to trade and events such as weddings and baptisms take place. The **Ájtte Fjäll-och Samemuseum** (Swedish Mountain and Sami Museum; mid-June–mid-Aug daily 9am–6pm, call for opening hours rest of year; entrance charge; tel: 0971 170 17) portrays the local culture as well as the mountain world, placing mankind in a natural, cultural and ecological perspective.

Exploring Muddus National Park.

BELOW: the altar at Jukkasjärvi church shows Sami influences.

Highway 45 continues through a sparsely populated area to **Porjus ❽**, a major centre for hydroelectric power. To the east of the town is a wild area, **Muddus National Park** (certain areas are closed during the breeding season, mid-Mar–July; tel: 0971 222 50), home of bear, lynx and wolverine. **Dundret Mountain**, 820 metres (2,690 ft) high, northeast of the park, is a bustling ski centre (tel: 0971 145 60). In summer, the region abounds with activities – riding, walking, windsurfing, fishing, golf and rafting – contact Gällivare tourist office (tel: 0970 166 60) for details.

Gällivare

Gällivare ❾ (pop. 18,900), and its twin town, Malmberget, owe their growth to the discovery of iron ore. Gällivare is the end of the railway line, Inlandsbanan *(see box, page 271)*, that follows Highway 45 north from Östersund. It is a popular tourist route and jumping-off point for treks into the region that include the Padjelanta and Stora Sjöfallet national parks. The town has a museum and an 18th-century Sami church. Beyond Gällivare, the 45 joins the E10 and continues north to **Svappavaara**, a former mining centre, and **Karesuando ❿**, on the Finnish frontier. Many place names in Swedish Lapland owe more to Finnish than to Swedish. In Kiruna, for example, a fifth of the population are Finnish immigrants.

Wolverines thrive in the national parks of Sweden's far north.

The most northerly church in Sweden can be found in Karesuando which also has the lowest average winter temperatures and Sweden's only tundra. From the top of **Kaarevaara Mountain**, 517 metres (1,696 ft) high, you can see three countries: Sweden, Finland and Norway.

Beyond Svappavaara, the E10 swings northwest to **Kiruna** ⓫ (pop. 23,000). Mining began here in 1900 and is still the main industry. The **Kirunavaara Mine** is the world's largest deep mine with 400 km (250 miles) of underground roadways. In summer visitors can tour it by bus; contact the tourist office (tel: 0980 188 80) to book. With the decline in mining, Kiruna has turned to tourism and scientific research: there is a rocket testing station on the banks of the Vittangi river at Esrange. For a glimpse of Sami life and history, visit **Samegård** (mid-June–Sept daily 10am–6pm; Oct–mid-June Mon–Fri 10am–4pm; entrance charge).

Ice Hotel

East of Kiruna, **Jukkasjärvi** ⓬ has acquired fame for its Ice Hotel, which is rebuilt every winter. Activities in the region include dog-sledging in the snow-covered wilderness and white-water rafting in summer.

The E10 (Nordkalottvägen), from Kiruna via the Norwegian frontier to Narvik, penetrates one of Europe's last wilderness areas. The mountains southwest of the highway can only be reached on foot or by pony and it is here that **Kebnekaise**, Sweden's highest peak at 2,117 metres (6,945 ft), reigns supreme. **Abisko** ⓭, 150 km (93 miles) from Kiruna, is a popular base from which to set out along the **Kungsleden** (King's Trail) which enables even inexperienced walkers to see the mountains.

BELOW: ice sculpture at the Ice Hotel.

FISHING IN THE FAR NORTH

There is nothing quite like fishing against the impressive backdrop of Sweden's mountains. Creeping silently along a river bank and trying to tempt a shy trout or grayling to the fly is an unforgettable experience. Fishing is well organised in the north. If you are driving along the Northeast Coast there are plenty of opportunities to fish en route, particularly in the unspoilt Piteälven, Kalixälven and Torneälven rivers; just ask at the nearest tourist office.

Further afield, the Tjuonajokk fishing camp on the Kaitumälven river in northwest Lapland is renowned for its grayling fishing. South from there is the Miekak fishing camp, 100 km (60 miles) northwest of Arjeplog (accessible by helicopter from Tjärnberg at Silvervägen, or by snowmobile in winter from Silvervägen), providing arguably the best char fishing in Lapland. At the northernmost extremity of Sweden the fishing centre on Rostojaure lake is renowned for its char and grayling. It is accessible in summer only by helicopter.

Not surprisingly, transport can be expensive, but the cost of fishing permits is relatively low compared with other countries. Permits can be bought at a number of outlets, including tourist offices and some fuel stations. The best month for fishing is usually August.

The High Coast

The Bottenviken (Gulf of Bothnia) coastline is low-lying and ranges from polished rock to sand and shingle beaches. The major towns along the coast have grown up from trading settlements. Islands form an almost continuous archipelago – a playground for holiday-makers to indulge the Swedish passion for sailing and the sea. Inland, lakes provide tranquil blue oases in the dense forests.

Starting in the south, the main coastal town of Ångermanland is **Härnösand** ⓮, which is modern except for the town hall, the Domkyrkan (cathedral) and some 18th-century wooden houses. Overlooking the harbour at Murberget there is a large open-air historical museum (Tues–Sun 11am–5pm; free).

Travelling north, the Höga Kusten (High Coast) Bridge, modelled partly on San Francisco's Golden Gate Bridge, is an impressive structure, 1.8 km (1.1 miles) long. It has a restaurant and visitor centre. Northwest of Härnösand is **Kramfors** ⓯, a leading centre for accordionists. The 13th-century church, near **Ytterlännäs** on Highway 90, is an antiquarian wonder.

The heart of the High Coast is the **Nordingrå Peninsula** ⓰, where the bedrock is an intense red *rapakivi* granite. Scenic treasures include **Omne Bay**, the villages of **Måviken** and **Norrfällsviken**, and the view from the church over Vagsfjärden. **Bönhamn** is a tiny place among the rocks, where **Arnes Sjöbod** is renowned for fresh fish and mashed potatoes and **Mannaminne**, near Häggvik, provides home-baked delicacies, handicrafts and musical evenings. The **Höga Kusten walk**, at 25 km (16 miles), starts at Fjordbotten with bathing places at Storsand, Norrfällsviken, Hörsång and Noraström.

Between the E4 and the coast lies **Skuleskogen National Park** ⓱ (open all year), which is noted for its rare birds and mammals.

Map on page 278

TIP

The mosquitoes are rapacious in summer in northern Sweden, so don't forget to pack insect repellent.

BELOW: Bönhamn, on the High Coast.

Map on page 278

Örnsköldsvik **⑱**, known as Övik, is an industrial town and one of Sweden's leading winter sports areas. The islands offshore include **Ulvön** with one of the oldest fishermen's chapels in Sweden; **Trysunda**, a favourite with the sailing fraternity; and **Högbonden**, known for its former lighthouse now converted into a cosy clifftop youth hostel accessible by boat from Bönhamn.

Umeå **⑲** is the principal town of Västerbotten; the main attraction here is **Gammlia Friluftsmuseum**, an open-air museum (mid-June–mid-Aug daily 10am–5pm). Within it is the **Västerbotten Museum** (mid-June–mid-Aug daily 10am–5pm; mid-Aug–mid-June Tues–Fri 10am–4pm, Sat noon–4pm, Sun noon–5pm; entrance charge; tel: 090 17 18 00), which explores local history and contains the oldest ski in the world, which was discovered nearby and is over 5,000 years old.

Continuing north, **Piteå ⑳** can come as a culture shock. Some wooden houses remain from the 17th century but today it is an industrial centre with timber, paper and pulp industries and a large holiday resort. Norwegians come in flocks from their calm northern fjords to the nearby resort of Pite Havsbad.

A traditional Sami hut made from wood and reindeer skins.

From Piteå, the road leads northwest through Älvsbyn to Bredsel and **Storforsen**, Europe's longest natural rapids, with a 81-metre (265-ft) drop over 5 km (3 miles). You can get close to the rushing water via wooden walkways and bridges; it is an awe-inspiring sight. The hotel nearby offers magnificent views.

BELOW: catch of the day.
RIGHT: winter scene in the frozen north.

World Heritage site

Luleå ㉑, the most northerly major town in Sweden, was moved 10 km (6 miles) by the king in 1649 and stands now at the mouth of the Luleälven river. The old church town, **Gammelstad**, was left on its original site and is a

fascinating place to visit with its 400 red-painted cottages and a 15th-century church, still used on important religious occasions. The town is a UNESCO World Heritage site. Beside the original harbour there is an open-air museum, **Friluftsmuséet Hägnan** (open all year from 11am; free; tel: 0920 45 38 09), which includes a hay shed typical of Norrbotten. The **Norrbottens Museum** (June–Aug Mon–Fri 10am–4pm, Sat and Sun noon–4pm; Sept–May closed Mon; free; tel: 0920 24 35 02) in Hermelin Park provides a picture of the province and has Sami artefacts.

Boden ㉒, 35 km (22 miles) inland from Luleå on the Luleälven river, is the largest garrison town in Sweden. In the 19th century, it was referred to as "one of the strongest fortresses of Europe – that is to say, in the whole world". The **Garnisonsmuséet** (Garrison Museum; July–mid-Aug Mon–Fri 11am–4pm, Sat–Sun noon–4pm; tel: 0921 683 99) shows 400 years of Sweden's military history.

Sweden's easternmost town, **Haparanda ㉓**, was built opposite Finnish Tornio on the Torneälven river, which forms the border between the two countries. Road 400 goes north along the river on the Swedish side into the Tornedalen valley to the Kukkolaforsen waterfall. West of the falls, on the Kalixälven river, is **Överkalix ㉔** with fine views from the top of Brännaberget. At the end of June, this is the place to see the amazing tradition of netting whitefish and salmon. ❏

FINLAND

The urban scene may have undergone a transformation, but the serenity of Finland's lakes and forests remains timeless

From the moment your plane lands at Helsinki airport you are confronted with a scramble for mobile phones. Reserved and reticent Finns? You'd never guess it from the constant telephone prattle. The stereotype of the hesitant, sullen Finn was always questionable, but now Finns are really starting to open up.

In the late 20th century Finland's capital, Helsinki, underwent rapid expansion, draining the enormous, sparsely populated rural areas and maturing into a distinctive and vibrant metropolis with its own identity. Startling new buildings, such as the weird and wonderful Kiasma (Museum of Contemporary Art) and the gleaming National Opera, transformed the city's silhouette; restaurants multiplied; and pavement cafés now open at the first glimpse of spring sunshine, bringing life and colour to the streets.

By the time they celebrated Helsinki's 450th birthday and its status of European City of Culture in 2000, the city's residents had found their place in the European scheme of things. Technological innovations, from the ubiquitous phones to state-of-the-art medical equipment and progressive Internet services, have begun to catch up with Finland's substantial pulp and paper industry. This is now under threat as Russia intends to increase the cost of the raw timber it supplies.

For a country of just over 5 million people, Finland has produced an astonishing number of architects, artists, sculptors and designers – and it shows. In Helsinki, in particular, almost every corner reveals an intriguing detail: an elegantly carved facade, a statue, a curved window. In cities such as Turku or Porvoo, where the Swedish influence was strongest, some of the oldest buildings remain. Cultural festivals and artistic events are commonplace.

Finland has seemingly endless expanses of untouched landscape, crossed by straight roads running between tall trees. Nobody has managed to count with any degree of certainty how many lakes and islands there are in the country – almost enough, it seems, for every Finnish family to have an island or lake of its own, with plenty of space for visitors, too. No wonder an ideal Finnish summer is based on a waterside wooden cabin and nearby sauna house. With some fishing, swimming, and a small boat, this is Finnish perfection.

As the road heads north, you scarcely realise at first that the rolling farmland of the south has moved into boundless forests and that, gradually, the dark green gives way to the peat and tundra of Lapland. This is the territory of reindeer, bear, wolf, elk and lynx. Along the west coast of the Gulf of Bothnia, the beaches and surprisingly warm waters are ripe for exploration. ❏

PRECEDING PAGES: Sami life as captured by the Sami artist Alariesto; with the onset of winter, artists turn their hand to making ice sculptures; reindeer transport. **LEFT:** lakeside sauna near the town of Jyväskylä.

THE FINNS

*Cool, but not humourless, the innovative Finns have fought hard
to preserve their identity and move with the times*

People tend mistakenly to describe Finns and their Scandinavian neighbours as cold characters when, in fact, their demeanour can be better described as cool and calm. When one spends some time with Finns in either a social situation or doing business, their dry sense of humour starts to emerge – and it doesn't necessarily need the lubrication of alcohol to loosen things up. Though, of course, the Finns are more at ease away from the work place, in the comfort of their weekend retreat in the country or relaxing in a pub or café.

Finland has come of age since it became a member of the European Union in 1995, taking a more visible, if not more vocal stance. Now growing in confidence as a fully fledged European city, Helsinki is justifiably attracting international recognition as a city to visit rather than just a stopover en route to Russia or other Scandinavian destinations. Helsinki has taken on a more colourful demeanour in recent years, attributable in part to Finland's more relaxed policy towards immigration, which has boosted the foreign population to over 5 percent, many of whom are from Russia and Somalia.

Well-travelled Finns have long considered themselves cosmopolitan, but they were in the minority. Many younger Finns, shedding their parents' unease, go on to study, work and travel abroad, as well as welcoming all things foreign to Finland.

City versus country

For a traditionally rural country, Finland is becoming more urbanised. Some 80 percent of Finns live on 2 percent of the land. Domestic emigration is accelerating – Finns are moving from small towns to Greater Helsinki, Tampere, Turku and Oulu, although many Helsinki business types are relocating to other countries with warmer climates and lower taxes. The much publicised *"etätyö"* (distance working via the Internet) has its attractions, but most people still try to escape to the cities.

Nature is sacred

The Finnish state of mind owes a lot to the land itself and the abundance of lakes and forests: more than 400,000 Finns own a plot of forest

LEFT: thick furs protect the Sami against winter cold.
RIGHT: ice hockey, Finland's most popular sport. Champions start training at an early age.

FINLAND: THE ESSENTIALS

Population 5.2 million.
Capital Helsinki (pop. 570,000).
Notable towns Turku, Tampere, Rovaniemi, Oulu.
Climate Northern winters average −13°C (9°F); in the south −5°C (23°F). Summer temperatures average 20°C (68°F).
Top museums Kiasma, Helsinki; Alvar Aalto Museo, Jyväskylä; Suomen Lasimuseo (Finnish Glass), Riihimäki.
Famous homes Hvitträsk (Saarinen); Ainola (Sibelius).
Top events Helsinki Festival; Savonlinna Opera Festival.
Natural wonders Around 190,000 lakes.
Outdoor activities Water sports, hiking, fishing, skiing.
Tourist information www.visitfinland.com

and everyone has the right of access to the land, which is why Finns take to the woods every summer. Nature is sacred and full of mystery as well as a place of renewal and preparation for the cold, dark months to follow. Which causes one to contemplate whether Finns are manic-depressive by nature, as more suicides are committed after the springtime thaw.

Sisu is a word synonymous with the Finnish character. It means guts or fortitude, a description which aptly fits the heroic,

SPORTING PROWESS

As a nation, Finns are great lovers of the outdoors and of sport, and some young Finns, following in the footsteps of the great Finnish runner Paavo Nurmi, live for little else but their athletic activities.

Russian regime more than 100 years ago and being long dominated by Sweden. These days Finns are feeling more self-confident. Although they may not forget, they are willing to forgive: across the eastern border, Finnish trucks carry emergency assistance to the struggling Russians who not so long ago were dictating internal issues within Finland.

The Finns are well used to change; it is so deep-rooted in the Finnish soul that the nation accepts almost any innovation with little resistance, be it the

patriotic and noble warriors of Finland's national epic, the *Kalevala*. Yet, in private, these strong men are shy and uncertain, and have great difficulty in waxing poetic when they set out to woo and win the girl. The women, in contrast, are strongheaded, matriarchal, and family-orientated. Perhaps this is why Finland has had so many women in political power in recent years, including their latest president, Tarja Halonen, who was elected in 2000 and re-elected for a second six-year term in 2006.

No more identity crisis

In the past, Finland struggled to keep its identity, defending its language against the

euro, or the latest advances in mobile phone technology.

Change is most visible in nature. With spring in the air everything grows rapidly, the summer months are light and hot, then winter arrives and for a few weeks around the solstice nature stops, frozen, for a pause. Finns prepare for Christmas and their New Year's resolutions. The big wheel keeps turning, another year means new opportunities for change. "The only constant is change," Finns will tell anyone who asks, but despite this, traditions are never completely forgotten.

Indeed, there are so many paradoxes in the Finnish character that it would be hard to convince the sceptical foreigner that there isn't more than a dash of schizophrenia in the national psyche. For every ranting drunk, there's a raving teetotaller. For every patriotic Finn, there's one who leaves as soon as he can afford the fare, never to return. For every shrinking violet, there's an arrogant, cigar-smoking bombast who's never happier than when showing off his possessions and singing his own praises.

Nordic links

The "typical Finn" is the result of a genetic combination that is 75 percent identical to that whose ancestors merged with the gargantuan Vikings. Most Finns are fair-haired (though, overall, Finns are the "darkest" of the Scandinavians). Some of the most famous Finns are sportsmen and women, taking advantage of their generally strong and healthy physiques.

Finns have entered the 21st century with both style and class. By nature, they are peacemakers. At war, Finns tend to lose, but at peace, Finns certainly seem to be winning. Pinning down their personality is not easy, but if you go to Finland with preconceived stereotypes at the ready, you will no doubt be able to satisfy any or all of them. ❏

of other Scandinavians, but 25 percent is thought to be derived from tribes that migrated to Finland from east of the Ural Mountains. This more Oriental strain accounts for certain physical traits that set Finns apart from their Nordic neighbours – finely pronounced cheekbones and quite small slatey-grey or blue eyes.

Laplanders tend to be smaller in stature and sturdily built. Karelians are stockier and have sallower complexions. They are slightly smaller in stature than people from the west coast,

LEFT: with the first sign of summer, cafés spill out onto Helsinki's streets and squares.
ABOVE: a Finnish fiddler.

ROMANY GYPSIES

One of the oldest groups in Finland who are not ethnic Finns are the Romany gypsies, whose womenfolk are instantly recognisable by their elaborate embroidered lace blouses and voluminous skirts. Although today most speak only Finnish, few have intermarried, so their dark good looks stand out against fairer Finns.

Most gypsies are no longer nomadic and live instead in houses and flats. Some families still tend to wander, especially in autumn, from one market place to another. Little horse-trading is done these days, however, and the gypsies' appearance at these fairs is little more than a vestige of nostalgia.

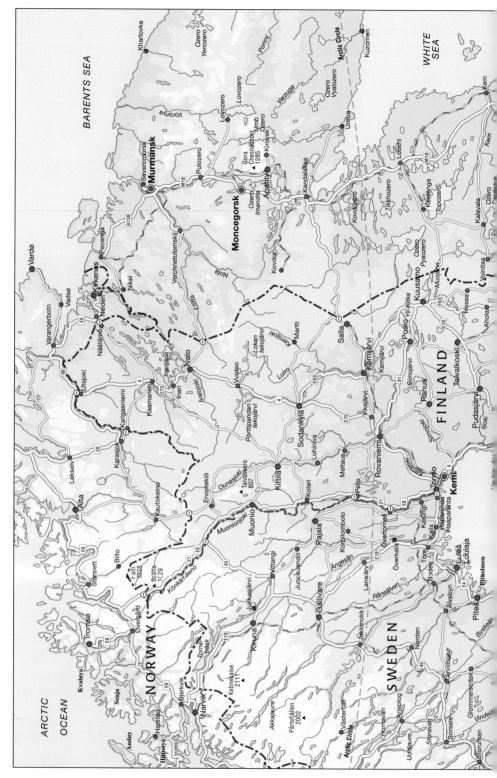

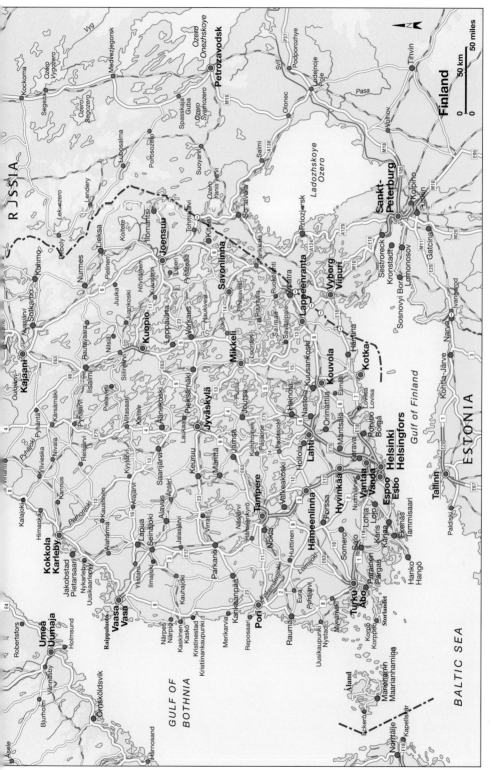

Finland

0   50 km
0   50 miles

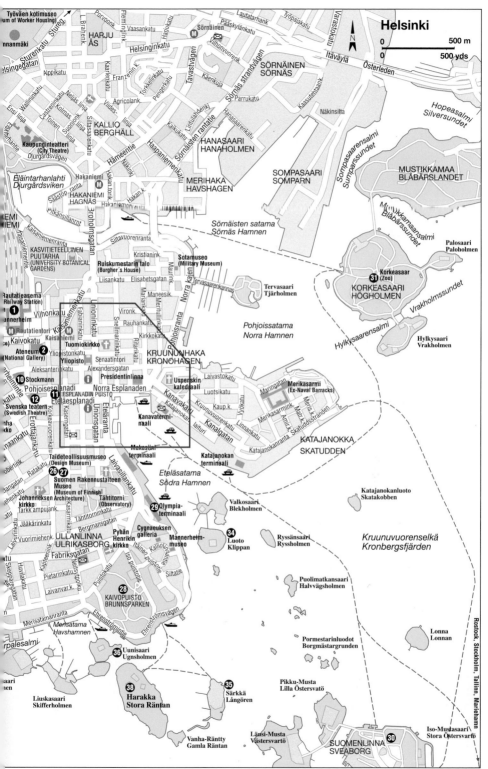

HELSINKI

*An intriguing mix of Swedish and Russian influences combine
with an ultramodern architectural stamp to make
Finland's capital a gem of the northern Baltic*

Map
on pages
298–299

F lying over Helsinki, one sees nothing but lakes and forests. Arriving in the city centre, there are stately granite buildings and people bustling along, purposefully conversing into mobile phones. Although it appears at first glance to be a city in motion, the Finnish capital is surprisingly quiet, except for the buzz of a skateboard, or a tram making its way across town. In recent years, once the spring light and summer sun appear, pavement cafés have become a pleasant addition to city life.

Helsinki

After a complex 450-year history, Helsinki has grown from a picturesque village with a harbour to a modern, confident capital where the quality of life has been ranked as among the highest in Europe. The "Daughter of the Baltic" has gained her own identity.

Building a capital

Before gaining independence in 1917, Finland lived through 500 years of Swedish rule, and more than 100 years under the Russians. These diverse influences from the west and then from the east have contributed to Helsinki's character. Helsinki was founded in 1550 by the Swedish King Gustav Vasa, but the monumental city centre was built in the early 19th century, thanks largely to

LEFT: monument
to Jean Sibelius.
BELOW: young sailor
at the harbour.

FACT FILE

Size 186 sq km (72 sq miles).

Situation Helsinki is the centre of the Greater Helsinki Area, a region with some 1.3 million inhabitants.

Population 570,000.

Climate July is the warmest month, average temperature: 20°C (68°F); January is the coldest: −5.7°C (22°F).

Finest building Finlandia Hall by Alvar Aalto.

Biggest attraction Annual Helsinki Festival which takes place from mid-August to the beginning of September. The festival offers a range of international culture, including classical music, dance, theatre and exhibitions (tel: 0600 900 900; www.helsinginjuhlaviikot.fi).

Newest attraction City Art Museum and Museum of Cultures in Tennispalatsi, the former tennis palace, which also contains a 14-screen cinema complex.

Best excursions City Bus Tour departing from Esplanadi Park and Katajanokan terminal (tel: 2288 1600); and the 50-min round trip by Spårakoff, the pub tram (tel: 20 123 4800).

Best view of the city From the lookout tower/bar of Hotel Torni, one of Helsinki's tallest buildings at 13 storeys.

Meeting place Kappeli café-restaurant, Eteläesplanadi 1.

Tourist information Helsinki City Tourist Office, Pohjoisesplanadi 19 (tel: 09 3101 3300; www.visithelsinki.fi).

the talents of the German-born architect Carl Ludwig Engel. Engel's first commission was a new administrative centre, followed by the cathedral, senate building, university and university library. Engel's neoclassical work can also be seen in St Petersburg and Tallinn. At the same time, Helsinki became the seat of a nationalist movement. Native architects, such as Eliel Saarinen and Alvar Aalto emerged and, after independence in 1917, Finnish Functionalism replaced Art Nouveau as Helsinki's predominant architectural style *(see page 306)*.

Nothing could completely protect the city from the massive Russian air raids of 1944 – nor from fervent, and not always lovely, post-war reconstruction. But Helsinki's position on the sea soon helped it to regain and then increase its stature, not only as a major port, but also as the important site for shipbuilding and international meetings it is today.

Helsinki today

Modern Helsinki is a tranquil but still growing city with some 570,000 occupants. The heart of the city pulses around **Rautatieasema** ❶, the Railway Station, which also contains a metro station and an underground shopping complex. Designed by Eliel Saarinen in 1905 and completed in 1919, it links two of Helsinki's most prevalent styles: National Romanticism and Functionalism.

To the east of the station on the opposite side in another stately building is the **Ateneum** ❷ (Museum of Finnish Art, Kaivokatu 2; Tues and Fri 9am–6pm, Wed and Thur until 8pm, Sat and Sun 11am–5pm; free entrance Wed after 5pm; tel: 173 36401), built in 1887. The museum's collection of Finnish paintings, sculpture and graphic art covers the years 1750 to 1960 and includes works by such notable Finns as Akseli Gallén-Kallela and Albert Edelfelt.

BELOW: the entrance to the Rautatieasema.

Aalto's plan

To get around Helsinki, just remember that all roads lead to **Mannerheimintie**, the city's main thoroughfare and the longest street in Finland. This neighbourhood is evolving based on a plan by Alvar Aalto, which is finally being realised perhaps in ways the great designer would not have anticipated.

From the railway station turn north into Mannerheimintie and on your right you'll see Finland's most-visited museum **Kiasma** ❸ (Tues 10am–5pm, Wed–Sun 10am–8.30pm; entrance charge; tel: 173 36501), a museum of contemporary art, opened in 1998. This remarkable white structure by American architect Steven Holl symbolises the new Helsinki. Outside, the building's proximity to the bronze equestrian statue of Field Marshal Mannerheim makes a striking sight at night.

Behind Kiasma is an eye-catching glass building, **Sanomatalo**, which is headquarters for Helsinki's two daily newspapers. Within this striking complex, which resembles a space station, is a small shopping centre. The main square on the ground floor hosts a variety of free exhibitions.

Joining Kiasma to create a triangle of Functionalist architecture are two other cultural institutions: **Lasipalatsi** (Glass Palace) across Mannerheimintie and the former **Tennispalatsi** ❹ (Tennis Palace) at the other end of the bus station area. Lasipalatsi has been rejuvenated with utmost care to create a media centre which includes an Internet library, television studios, cinema, and fine cafés and restaurants. Tennispalatsi was used during the 1952 Olympic Games and now houses Finland's largest cinema complex (14 screens) and two museums, the **City Art Museum** (Tues–Sun 11am–8.30pm; entrance charge; tel: 3108 7001), and the **Museum of Cultures** (Tues–Thur 11am–8pm, Fri–Sun 11am–6pm; free entrance Tues after 5pm; tel: 4050 9806).

Map on pages 298–299

TIP

See the best of Helsinki with a Helsinki Card, which can be purchased from the Tourist Office, Pohjoisesplanadi 19, hotels and R-kiosks. The card includes free museum admission and free travel on city buses, trams, trains and the metro.

BELOW: Kiasma, the Museum of Contemporary Art.

Traditional Finnish dolls are popular souvenirs.

Opposite Kiasma is the **Eduskuntatalo ❺** (Parliament Building), built between 1925 and 1930 and distinguished by an impressive row of steps and a facade of 14 columns of grey granite. Statues of former Finnish presidents scatter the area between the Parliament Building and the **Kansallismuseo ❻** (National Museum; Tues–Wed 11am–8pm, Thur–Sun until 6pm; entrance charge; tel: 4050 9544) two blocks to the north. The museum's decoration, its collection and the stone bear by the entrance are the work of Emil Wikström. The frescoes on the foyer ceiling, depicting scenes from Finland's national epic, the *Kalevala*, are by Gallén-Kallela. The City Museum branch in the fine **Hakasalmi Villa** (Wed–Sun 11am–5pm; entrance charge; tel: 3107 8519) across Mannerheimintie houses a special exhibition on Helsinki's history.

Finlandiatalo ❼ (Finlandia Hall; tel: 40 241), opposite the National Museum, is undoubtedly the most famous building in Helsinki. Alvar Aalto designed it both inside and out, completing the main section in 1971. Home to the Helsinki Philharmonic Orchestra, it is used regularly for concerts and events.

Around the corner is the **Sibelius Academy** (Pohjoinen Rautatiekatu 9; tel: 020 75390), Helsinki's famous musical conservatory, where concerts are given by top students. Continuing north along Mannerheimintie to where Hesperia Park and Töölö Bay come to an end, the **Suomen Kansallisooppera ❽** (Finnish National Opera House; tel: 4030 2211), which opened in 1993, offers an ambitious season with many international performers.

Nestling, literally, into a small hill west of the Parliament Building behind Mannerheimintie and the winding streets of Töölö, is the ultramodern church, **Temppeliaukion Kirkko ❾** (mid-June–mid-Sept Mon–Tues, Thur–Fri 10am–8pm, Wed and Sat to 6pm, Sun noon–6pm; call for opening hours rest of year;

BELOW: from left, the Parliament Building, Finlandia Hall and the National Museum.

tel: 2340 5920). It is not only an architectural oddity – built as it is directly into the cliffs, with inner walls of stone – but it is also the site of many good concerts. A service for English speakers is held every Sunday at 2pm.

Map
on pages
298–299

Shopping and entertainment

Heading south, back to town on Mannerheimintie, you'll find **Stockmann ⑩**, Finland's largest department store, which has an excellent food hall on the lower level. Behind it, on Keskuskatu, is Scandinavia's largest bookshop, **Akateeminen Kirjakauppa**, a great place to browse or to take a break in the stylish café designed by Alvar Aalto. The bookshop faces another Helsinki landmark, **Esplanadin Puisto ⑪** (Esplanade Park), which was first laid out in 1831 and runs east–west between Mannerheimintie and South Harbour.

The **Svenska Teatern ⑫** (Swedish Theatre), an elegant semi-circular stone building dating from 1866, commands Esplanade Park's western head on Mannerheimintie. In front of the theatre, Bus 20 will take you just five minutes out of town to the **Ruoholahti** area and the Kaapeli Cable Factory complex, where the **Suomen Valokuvataiteen Museo** and **Teatterimuseo ⑬** (Photography and Theatre museums, Tallberginkatu 1; Tues–Sun 11am–6pm) are located.

The **Esplanadi**, an old-fashioned promenade, leads from the theatre across the length of the park, past the central statue of J.L. Runeberg, Finland's national poet, to **Kappeli ⑭** (Eteläesplanadi 1; tel: 010 766 3880) a café-restaurant. The park is a very popular meeting place and is often the scene of free concerts and animated fairs, such as the Christmas Fair in December or Night of the Arts in late August. On May Day Eve it is given over to general lunacy as students wearing white caps revel in the streets alongside workers and members of

Helsinki lies at latitude 60°N, and experiences lengthy summer days as a result. At the summer solstice on 22 June, the sun only drops below the horizon for 1 hr 20 mins.

BELOW: two-wheeled transport, a popular way to get around Helsinki.

ON THE TRAIL OF JUGENDSTIL

Helsinki offers a wealth of interest for lovers of architecture, especially among its flamboyant Art Nouveau buildings

For those who love architecture, Helsinki has lots to offer. After becoming Finland's capital in 1812, the Senate Square, designed by Carl Ludwig Engel (1778–1840), was a bold example of the early period of autonomy after Russian rule. Engel's Graeco-Roman-inspired work is found throughout the city in churches, government buildings and the university.

During the second half of the 19th century, the number of architects and designers grew and building styles became more diverse with references to Classicism and Rationalism.

It was after the turn of the 20th century that a younger generation of architects, inspired by

the Arts and Crafts movement, rose in revolt against Classicism and Eclecticism. These included: Lars Sonck (1870–1956), Bertel Jung (1872–1946), and the trio Herman Gesellius (1874–1916), Armas Lindgren (1874–1929) and Eliel Saarinen (1873–1950), who were committed to creating "a more domestic, freer and more authentic world" with their work.

This Art Nouveau, or Jugendstil, as it is called in Finland, is also known as National Romanticism. It is distinguished by its use of stained glass and murals, timber and bronze accents, interesting windows, heavy ornamentation, grey granite, natural colours, and castle-like features. Some of the most famous tourist attractions in Helsinki are Art Nouveau. Their roots go back to the national epic, the *Kalevala*, which inspired the composer Sibelius and the artist Gallén-Kallela. There are many such buildings to be seen in the Katajanokka area near the harbour and in the stylish Eira quarter – look out for Lars Sonck's hospital, Laivurinkatu 27; Lindahl and Thomé's Lord Hotel, Lönnrottinkatu 29, with a granite facade and romantic turrets, and their Otava publishing house at Uudenmaankatu 10. The Pohjola House, Aleksanterinkatu 44, is by Gesellius, Lindgren and Saarinen, as is the National Theatre. Do not miss spending time at the railway station, which is one of Saarinen's masterpieces, especially the murals in the Eliel restaurant.

Private villas were also prominent in this movement and it is worth making an excursion to Hvitträsk *(see page 318)* at Kirkkonummi, just outside Helsinki, which was designed by the architecture trio as a shared living and studio space for themselves and their families. The best-preserved rooms are essentially a museum to Saarinen, who is buried in the wooded, lakeside environs, along with Gesellius. ❑

TOP LEFT: Eliel Saarinen's railway station.
LEFT: Hvitträsk studio. **TOP RIGHT:** Art Nouveau detail, Korkeavuorenkatu. **ABOVE:** owl motif.

Map
on pages
298–299

political parties. Two boulevards stretch east–west along either side of the park. Nowadays, the fine 19th-century stone buildings along **Pohjoisesplanadi** mostly house design shops including Marimekko, Arabia and Aarikka, known respectively for their colourful clothing, distinctive glassware and wooden jewellery. At number 19, the **Helsinki Information Office** and the **City Tourist Board** ⓯ occupy the ground floor. Both offer extensive selections of maps and brochures.

In 1999 the **Hotel Kämp**, Pohjoiseplenadi 29, a popular rendezvous in Helsinki at the end of the 19th century, reopened its doors as a luxury hotel. The **Kämp Galleria** is an exclusive shopping complex on the lower level.

Market days

Across the road from the Kappeli restaurant is the **Havis Amanda Fountain** ⓰, which created quite a stir when it was first erected in 1908. Surrounded by four sea lions spouting water, the bronze statue represents the city of Helsinki rising from the sea, innocent and naked.

Kauppatori market is the place to look for Sami handicrafts, such as this novel hat.

Opposite the fountain is the bustling **Kauppatori** ⓱ (Central Market Square; Mon–Fri 6.30am–6pm, Sat until 4pm, in summer also Sun 10am–5pm). Shoppers wander from stand to stand looking for the perfect new potato, salmon fillet, bunch of dill or flowers. The small tents serve tasty cinnamon or meat pastries and the ubiquitous coffee which seems to fuel the Finns. Other stands proffer interesting goods and handicrafts, many from Lapland.

To the south of the square at the 100-year-old, yellow-and-red brick **Vanha Kauppahalli** (Old Market Hall), one can buy salmon, reindeer cold-cuts, rounds of Oltermanni cheese, and even Vietnamese *loempia* (egg rolls).

Opposite the market stands the long blue **Kaupungintalo** ⓲ (City Hall) designed by Engel in 1833, and **Presidentinlinna** ⓳ (Presidential Palace), designed in 1818 as a private home and turned into a tsarist palace by Engel in 1843. The Finnish president no longer resides here.

Another major landmark, **Senaatintori** ⓴ (Senate Square), stands one block north of here, on the busy **Aleksanterinkatu** shopping street. Over the centuries the square has remained a very impressive spot. Now, it functions principally as a byway or as the occasional backdrop for an important event. **Tuomiokirkko** ㉑ (Helsinki Cathedral; Mon–Sat 9am–6pm, Sun from noon), at the top of a flight of treacherously steep steps on the north side, is a point of pride for Finns, and the exterior – with its five green cupolas, numerous white Corinthian columns and sprinkling of important figurines posing on its roof – is certainly impressive.

The city's oldest stone building, dating from 1757, is the small blue-grey **Sederholmin Talo** ㉒ (Wed, Fri–Sun 11am–5pm, Thur until 7pm; tel: 310 36529) on the corner of Aleksanterinkatu and Katariinankatu. Across the street is the **Bockin Talo** (Bock House), also 18th-century, which became the meeting place for Helsinki's City Council in 1818.

BELOW: Helsinki's fine cathedral, Tuomiokirkko.

Beyond the centre

After exploring Helsinki's centre, venture into one of the surrounding districts, each of which has its own very particular character. **Katajanokka** lies on a small

The interior of the Uspenski Cathedral.

BELOW: Kappeli, a popular meeting place on Esplanadi.

promontory sticking out into the sea a few blocks east from Senate Square, connected by two short bridges. The spires and onion-shaped domes of the Russian Orthodox **Uspenskin Katedraali** ㉓ (Uspenski Cathedral), built in 1868, tower above a popular restaurant complex across the street. Helsinki's first Russian restaurant, the **Bellevue**, established in 1917, sits at the base of the cathedral, across from Katajanokka Park.

Jugendstil (Art Nouveau) architecture rules in **Luotsikatu** street, just east of the cathedral. Don't miss the charming griffin doorway at No. 5.

On the southern side of Katajanokka the huge Silja and Viking Line ships from Stockholm tie up, and stylish catamarans ply the route to medieval Tallin, the Estonian capital. In recent years, many of the old warehouses have been converted to restaurants, shops and a hotel. The **Tulli-ja Pakkahuone** ㉔ (Customs and Bonded Warehouse, Katajanokan Laituri 5) from 1900 remains the same, with its inventive Jugendstil architecture.

Finding your way back to Esplanadi, head west on **Bulevardi** and the neighbouring streets like Eerikinkatu, Fredrikinkatu and Uudenmaankatu, which in recent years have become filled with fashionable galleries, boutiques, antique bookshops and restaurants. At the end of Bulevardi, past the old opera house, don't miss the flea market, **Hietalahdentori** ㉕ (Mon–Fri 10am–6pm, Sat 8am–4pm, also Sun 10am–4pm in summer).To the south of Bulevardi are the exclusive **Eira** and **Ullanlinna** districts. The **Taideteollisuusmuseo** ㉖ (Design Museum, Korkeavuorenkatu 23; Tues 11am–8pm, Wed–Sun 11am–6pm; in summer daily 11am–6pm; entrance charge; tel: 622 0540) is an essential stop as it is a showcase for Finland's renowned designers, including Alvar Aalto and Lapponia jewellery.

Map on pages 298–299

In the same block is the **Suomen Rakennustaiteen Museo** ㉗ (Museum of Finnish Architecture, Kasarmikatu 24; Tues–Sun 10am–4pm, Wed until 8pm; entrance charge; tel: 8567 5100), which has an excellent archive of architectural drawings and changing exhibitions focusing on Finnish architectural movements.

The southernmost end of the peninsula is lined by parkland, frequented by joggers, skaters and cyclists. In summer, the city sponsors free concerts in **Kaivopuisto** ㉘ (Well Park). In winter, when the sea is frozen, you can actually walk out to some of the closer offshore islands. On the eastern point, embassies fill the chic Ullanlinna district. **Olympiaterminaali** ㉙ (Olympia Quay) is a stopping place for Silja and Viking liners and the start of a popular promenade for walkers who find refreshment at **Café Ursula** or **Carousel**.

Islands abound

Literally hundreds of islands dot the Helsinki coastline. **Suomenlinna** ㉚ (Finland's Castle) is undoubtedly the most important. In reality it consists of five islands, over which the ruins of a naval fortress and its fortifications are spread. Suomenlinna has played an integral part in Helsinki's life since its construction started in 1748. It has been listed by UNESCO as a World Heritage site, and functions today as a thriving local artists' community with the restored bastions being used as studios and showrooms. Water buses ferry visitors here from Market Square every half-hour. They dock on **Iso Mustasaari**, from where a hilly path leads up through **Rantakasarmi** (Jetty Barracks), which house art exhibitions and an interesting restaurant and microbrewery known as **Panimo**.

There are several museums on the island (island open daily; entrance to fortress free; entrance charge to museums; tel: 684 1880). The large **Suomenlinna**

Helsinki has a number of public saunas, but the only wood-heated one is Kotiharjun Sauna in Harjutorinkatu (near Sörnäinen metro station; Tues–Fri 2–8pm, Sat 1–7pm; tel: 735 1535).

BELOW LEFT: taking a break on the harbourside.
BELOW RIGHT: quiet place for a chat.

Map on pages 298–299

Museum is the main historical exhibition of the islands, as well as the main information centre for Suomenlinna. The **Military Museum Manege** exhibits heavy equipment mainly from the 1939–45 period.

Cross the bridge to the rambling remains of the **Kruunulinna Ehrensvärd** (Ehrensvärd Crown Castle) and gardens. The castle courtyard is the best-preserved section of the fortress and contains the 1788 sarcophagus of Count Ehrensvärd himself. His former home is now a museum, with old furniture, arms and lithographs. Try to visit the atmospheric summer restaurant **Walhalla**, where on a clear day it is sometimes possible to see Estonia, some 80 km (50 miles) away. There is also a **Customs Museum** and the **Vesikko Submarine** to explore.

Korkeasaari ㉛ (daily, May–Aug 10am–8pm, Oct–Mar until 4pm, Apr and Sept until 6pm; tel: 3103 7900) is one of those rare zoos in the world set entirely on an island. In summer you can reach it by boat from Market Square. The zoo, perhaps not surprisingly, specialises in "cold climate animals" although there's an interesting enclosure of South American animals. If you want to learn about indigenous Finnish fauna, you'd do just as well at the **Luonnontieteellinen** (Natural History Museum, Pohjoinen Rautatiekatu 13; Tues, Wed and Fri 9am–4pm, Thur until 6pm, Sat–Sun 10am–4pm; entrance charge; tel: 1912 8800). Its excellent exhibitions reopened in 2008 after an extensive refurbishment.

The island of **Seurasaari ㉜** is eminently atmospheric. A pretty, forested place with a national park (open all year), its northeastern side has been made into an **Ulkomuseo** (Open-air Museum; June–Aug daily 11am–5pm; entrance charge; tel: 4050 9660) containing wooden buildings from provinces all over Finland from the 17th to 19th centuries. The island is connected to the Helsinki shore by a wooden footbridge. Take either bus No. 24 from Erottaja (in front of the Swedish Theatre), or cycle along the Meilahti coastal drive which takes you past **Sibeliuksen Puisto ㉝** (Sibelius Park) and the silvery tubular **Sibeliusmonumentti** (Monument) to the bridge.

Off the beaten track

Less well known are the smaller islands that form a string around Helsinki's southern peninsula. Across the "Olympic Harbour" are **Luoto ㉞** and **Valkosaari**, restaurant islands with romantic villas. A long pier outside Kaivopuisto offers a boat service to **Särkkä ㉟**, another island with a popular restaurant.

Uunisaari ㊱ is accessible at the southern end of Neitsytpolku street. It's a popular recreational island with a beach, sauna and restaurant.

Pihlajasaari ㊲ is Helsinki's favourite island for swimming. It actually comprises two islands, with a sandy beach, café and changing cabins on the larger island's western shore. Helsinki's only nudist beach is on the smaller island. Boats to Pihlajasaari depart in summer every 15 to 30 minutes from outside Café Carousel in Eira. The former military island of **Harakka ㊳**, south of Kaivopuisto, is now a wildlife reserve. ❑

BELOW: military might at the castle of Suomenlinna. **RIGHT:** café life, central Helsinki.

THE TRADITIONAL FINNISH SAUNA

An old Finnish proverb says: "First you build the sauna, then you build the house". Even today, there's nothing so uniquely Finnish as a sauna

There are some things along the way which a traveller does not forget – and a real Finnish sauna is one of them. Although its origin is obscure, the sauna came to Finland over 2,000 years ago, and it is a rare Finn who admits to not liking one. Official statistics estimate that there are over 625,000 saunas in Finland, not counting those in private houses or summer cottages that dot the shoreline of the country's lakes. The actual figure could easily be over 1 million in a country of just 5 million people – but then, the sauna is a national institution.

BUSINESS AND PLEASURE

The sauna outgrew its rural roots long ago. Today, be it city or village, you will find public saunas, and it is safe to assume that every new apartment block has a sauna for its tenants. Many companies also have saunas for their employees.

A Finnish sauna is not a meeting place for sex, as it is in some countries; codes of behaviour are strict. Titles and position are, they say, left hanging in the changing room with the clothes. It is not unusual for board meetings and government cabinet meetings to be held in a sauna – perhaps because it's "not done" to swear or raise one's voice. A sauna also leaves you relaxed yet alert.

▽ **FRIENDS AND FOLIAGE**
Tying up birch leaves for the sauna is a social event in summer.

▽ **MORAL CODE**
Despite the nudity, a Finnish sauna is a moral place. Generally, saunas are same-sex only; a mixed sauna is usually a family affair.

▽ **HOT GOSSIP**
There is more to the sauna than just getting clean. It is a happening – a time to meet friends, or to make business deals.

HOW TO TAKE A SAUNA

There is no "right way" to take a sauna – temperature and style vary. The ideal temperature is between 60–80° C (140–175° F) although it can be a cooler 30° C (85° F) on the bottom platform, reserved for children. A common practice is to brush oneself with a wet birch switch, called the *vihta*. This not only gives off a fresh fragrance but increases blood circulation and perspiration.

How long you sit in the sauna is entirely up to you. When you have had enough, you move on to stage two: cooling off. A cold shower is the most common way but, if the sauna is by a lake or the sea, a quick plunge into the cool water is stimulating.

The final stage is to dry off, which should be done naturally, to avoid further perspiration. It is also time for a beer or coffee and a snack to complete the ritual.

△ **STEAM HEAT**
Water thrown over the hot stones creates a dry steam *(löyly)*, which makes the heat tolerable and stimulates perspiration.

◁ **COOLING OFF**
In the winter, brave souls jump through holes in the ice or roll around in the snow – not recommended practice for people with high blood pressure.

SAUNA FASHIONS
he sauna has become uch an integral part of nnish life, that there are ven "designer" outlets pecially geared towards auna accessories.

ANCIENT USES
olden days in rural nland the sauna was not st the place in which to et clean, but also where abies were born and usages smoked.

SOUTHERN FINLAND

Follow the route of the Nordic kings from west to east across Southern Finland through a gentle landscape with painted villages, ancient castles and an island-studded coast

Map on page 316

To follow the south coast of Finland from west to east is to follow a route once travelled by Nordic kings and princes to St Petersburg. Known as The King's Road, the route passes through mainly flat coastal country covered with farmland and dense forest. The area is heavily settled, and it is also heavily Swedish-speaking. From Pargas (Parainen), south of **Turku ❶** *(see page 323)* at the head of the Turunmaa archipelago chain, through Hanko (Hangö), Ekenäs (Tammisaari), Karis (Karjaa) and further east via Porvoo (Borgå) through a cluster of small villages on the approach to Kotka, you will hear a great deal of Swedish being spoken and read it as the first language on signposts. This is all part of the democracy of bilingualism in Finland.

The eastern portion of the coast, past Helsinki, is riddled with fortifications. For the Swedes, then the Russians, and finally the independent Finns, the Russian border has been a crucial dividing line. The Finnish-Soviet borders still have a no-man's-land running between them, and although travel between the two countries has become far easier and more popular since the break-up of the USSR, there is no mistaking the sterner attitude of the Russian customs guards and immediate deterioration of road conditions as soon as one crosses over the border to the east.

LEFT: models of ships traditionally grace the windows of Loviisa's wooden houses. **BELOW:** a summer treat.

Exploring the islands

Richly vegetated but sparsely populated, the archipelago of **Turunmaa ❷** is quieter than the Ålands *(see page 321)* in terms of tourism, and the islands are reached more quickly from the mainland. They are linked by a series of bridges and then ferries. Ferries also service some of the smaller islands that spin off south from the main chain. Local buses connect the larger towns. Many Finnish families have their own islands – the ultimate refuge.

Turunmaa's finest harbour is on the northern spur of **Nagu**. An old wooden house overlooking the marina has been made into a guesthouse-style hotel. Also to be found in Nagu is a small **Hembygdsmuseum** and the 15th-century **St Olof's Church**.

As you approach **Pargas ❸** (Parainen) from west or south you come to **Sattmark**, on the island of Stortervolandet. This tiny log cabin was once a sailor's quarters. It now serves light meals in its prettily furnished rooms and outside on the dock.

Continuing east towards Piikkiö, it is worth making a detour to **Kuusiston Linna ❹** (Kuusisto Castle) on the Kuusisto peninsula. This medieval bishop's castle stood stoutly until Gustav Vasa ordered its demolition in 1528, but enough remains to have encouraged restoration.

Salo ❺, to the east on the mainland in the heart of the apple-growing Salojoki Valley, has a lively market and is set off by a triad of churches – the Lutheran

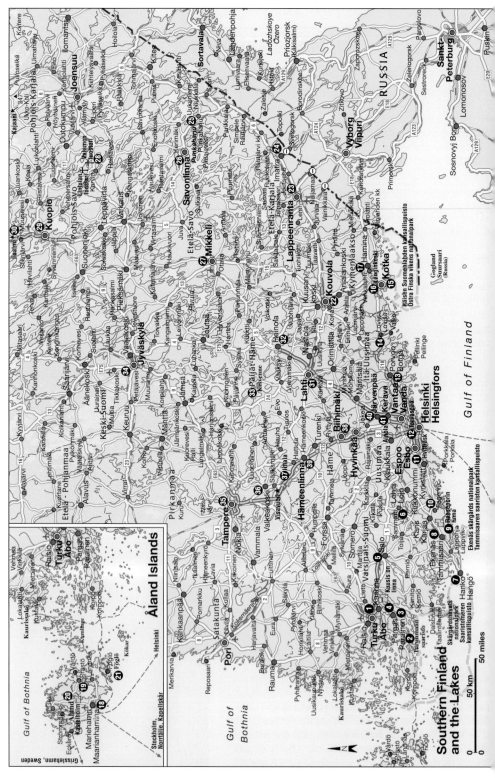

Southern Finland
and the Lakes

Uskela (1832) by C.L. Engel, the Greek Orthodox **Tsasouna** at its foot, and the stunningly modern **Helisnummen** (Helisnummi Church) about 4 km (2 miles) outside the town. At **Sammatti ❻**, 48 km (30 miles) east of Salo, look out for the sign to **Paikkarin Torppa** (Paikkari Cottage), the home of Elias Lönnrot who collected the legends and tales for the *Kalevala (see page 58)*.

Marina life

Due south of Salo is **Hanko ❼** (Hangö), Finland's southernmost town, once a popular spa resort, and now frequented for its annual regatta and its beaches. Hanko is distinguished by an abundance of turreted villas in pastel shades which grace the stretch of beach behind a line of charming white changing huts. These stately homes were built in the late 19th century for the Russian nobility who came for health cures; several offer bed and breakfast accommodation.

Hanko's **Rintamamuseo** (Frontline Museum; June–Aug daily 11.30am–6.30pm), with its wartime bunker, is a reminder of the town's strategic history, such as the destruction of the fortifications during the Crimean War. The Municipal Library and Gallery offers a range of exhibitions and there are several art galleries, notably **Gallery E. Pinomaa**, Korkeavuorenkatu 10, which exhibits contemporary art. **Alan's Cafe**, Raatihuoneentori 4, makes divine pastries and shares a charming garden complex with an antiquarian bookshop and crafts gallery. At the harbourfront, housed in some renovated warehouses, are a couple of restaurants featuring locally caught fish. On 26 August, the annual Night of the Bonfires takes place in the main harbour area and launches the Hanko Days Weekend Festival (note that at the end of August hotels and restaurants virtually shut down).

In summer, seal safaris take off from the eastern harbour Wed and Fri–Sun at 3pm. Book at the tourist office (tel: 019 220 3411). There are also boat excursions to **Bengtskär Lighthouse**, 25 km (15 miles) south of Hanko, which make a memorable day's adventure. Built in 1906, the massive stone structure is Scandinavia's tallest lighthouse at 52 metres (170 ft) high. The climb to the top of the 252 steps is worth it for the view. There is also a café and chapel, and it is possible to lodge here.

Ekenäs ❽ (Tammisaari) is the next main coastal stop along the King's Road. It is a finely laid out old town, with 18th- and 19th-century cobbled streets and charming wooden buildings, and is a great place for a stroll and some delicious Finnish ice cream *(jäätelö)*. Just to the south is the **Tammisaaren Saariston Kansallispuisto**, a national park, resplendent with marshes, forests and water birds.

There is an extremely active boating life in and around Ekenäs, and numerous outdoor concerts in summer. From Ekenäs, take a detour north to the picturesque village of **Fiskars**, a craft, design and art centre and the original home of Fiskars knives and scissors. The area has several galleries and exhibitions. An excellent museum portrays the history of Fiskars company, founded in 1649 (museum May–Sept daily 11am–4pm; Oct–Apr Sat and Sun 1pm–4pm; entrance fee; tel: 019 237 013). The **Knipan** summer restaurant and the steeple of the old granite church (1680) are the town's main landmarks. For an historical background

Setting off for a sail from the marina at Hanko.

BELOW: the flat landscape of southern Finland is ideal for cycling.

Windmills are a feature of the islands and low-lying districts of the south.

on the town, visit **Porvaristalo** (Ekenäs Museum, Wasas gata 11; summer Tues–Sun 11am–5pm; tel: 020-619 3161). There are boat tours from the North Harbour in July and early August. A few kilometres east from Ekenäs is **Snappertuna**, a farming village 15 km (10 miles) from the late-14th-century castle at **Raasepori ❾**. The outdoor theatre in the Raseborg dale stages dramatic and musical evenings and in July you may catch a re-enacted medieval duel. Further east beyond Snappertuna is **Fagervik ❿**, the site of a tremendous old manor overlooking an inlet. This is the place to picnic, horse ride or enjoy good walking paths. The nearby fishing village of **Ingå** (Inkoo) has pretty cafes and craft shops.

Approaching Helsinki from the west it would be a shame to miss Eliel Saarinen's home at **Hvitträsk ⓫** (May–Sept daily 11am–6pm; Oct–Apr Tues–Sun 11am–5pm; entrance charge; tel: 4050 9630). The stone and timber buildings seem to blend with the forest, the great cliffs and the White Lake that give the house its name. This was the studio of three great Finnish architects: Saarinen, Herman Gesellius and Armas Lindgren.

Tarvaspää ⓬ was the home of Finland's national artist Akseli Gallén-Kallela (1865–1931). His Jugendstil-inspired studio has been converted into the **Gallén-Kallela Museum** (mid-May–Aug daily 10am–6pm; Sept–mid-May Tues–Sat 10am–4pm, Sun 10am–5pm; entrance charge; tel: 849 2340) displaying the artist's paintings, stained glass, tools and objects collected on his travels.

BELOW: the former home of Finland's national poet, J.L. Runeberg, Porvoo.

Medieval town

East of Helsinki, **Porvoo ⓭** (Borgå) is one of Finland's most important historical towns. The Swedish king, Magnus Eriksson, gave Porvoo a royal charter in 1346; from this point on it became a busy trading post and, ultimately,

it was the place where the Diet of Porvoo (1809) convened to transfer Finland from Swedish to Russian hands. The striking 15th-century **Porvoo Cathedral** is where this momentous event took place. Sadly, an arson attack in 2006 destroyed the roof: the cathedral is due to open again in 2009.

While its rich history made the town important, Porvoo's writers and artists gave it its real character. The home of Finland's national poet, **J.L. Runeberg** (May–Aug daily 10am–4pm; Sept–Apr Wed–Sun 10am–4pm; entrance charge; tel: 019 581 330) has been restored to its original condition. **Holm House** (May–Aug Mon–Sat 10am–4pm, Sun 11am–4pm; Sept–Apr Wed–Sun noon–4pm; entrance charge; tel: 019 574 7589) is a 1792 merchant's house, formerly the Town Hall, on Rahtihuoneentori (Town Hall Square). It focuses on life as lived by the 19th-century American family who once inhabited it, and includes a fine Art Nouveau furniture collection. The **Albert Edelfelt Atelier** (June–Aug Tues–Sun 10am–4pm) in Haikko, 6 km (4 miles) south of Porvoo, exhibits paintings by Albert Edelfelt – one of Finland's finest 19th-century artists.

For scenery, the medieval atmosphere of **Old Porvoo** has few rivals: its riverbanks are lined with red-ochre warehouses and pastel-coloured wooden houses. On summer weekdays, guided walking tours of the old town start from the town hall square, next to the museum, at 2pm (tel: 019 520 2316). A fine excursion is to take a river cruise to Porvoo from the main harbour in Helsinki.

Towards the border

East of Porvoo, the landscape becomes more rural and less populated. In summer, the grassy hillocks bristle with wildflowers. **Loviisa** ⑭ is a pretty coastal town with an esplanade headed by the New Gothic Church. A town museum tells the local

Map on page 316

Good stopping points on the journey east from Loviisa to Kotka are the excellent sandy beaches of Pyhtää and the holiday island of Kaunissaari with its interesting fishing village.

BELOW: wooden home typical of southern Finland.

Map on page 316

Tsar Alexander III, whose hand-crafted timber fishing lodge at Langinkoski was a gift from the Finnish state.

BELOW: strawberries for sale at a roadside stall.

history, including the role of the Rosen and Ungern bastions, built in the 18th century to protect the trade route between Vyborg and Turku. The Old Town buildings survived the fire of 1855 and tours can be made of the last spirits factory, which today is an artist's atelier. Just 10 km (6 miles) from the centre of town on an island at the mouth of Loviisa Bay is the **Svartholma** sea fortress, built in 1748.

Kotka ⓯ is the next important destination on the King's Road and is considered one of the most beautifully situated cities in Finland. It is around Kotka that the Kymi River breaks up into five branches before rushing off into the sea, making for perfect salmon and trout fishing. The local species of fish can also be found in the **Kotka Maretarium** (Aquarium; Jan–Nov daily 10am–5pm, until 8pm in summer; entrance charge; tel: 040 311 0330).

Tourists fill the modern town of Kotka every July for the largest maritime festival in Finland. The town itself has few attractions, but the nearby islands are worth a visit. The pleasant **Sapokka Harbour** has a nice park, with a high artificial waterfall. Step aboard a water bus for a tour of this beautiful archipelago.

Apart from the Kotka islands, the **Kymenlaakso** (Kymi river valley) extends further inland, where there are forest paths, fishing and white-water rafting. Details are available from the Kotka Tourist Office at Keskuskatu 6, tel: 05 234 4424.

Imperial lodge

The impressive Imperial Fishing Lodge of Tsar Alexander III (1845–94) is at **Langinkoski** ⓰ (June–Aug daily 10am–6pm; May 10am–4pm; Sept–Oct Sat and Sun only; entrance charge; tel: 05 228 1050). The tremendous log building was crafted by the Finns for the Tsar. Several nature paths begin from Langinkoski. You can walk the 5 km (3 miles) to Siikakoski rapids, which are an ideal spot for fishing. On the bank you will find Restaurant Munkkisaari, built on an Orthodox monastery site from 1650–1850. The restaurant sells fishing licences and has boats and cabins for hire (tel: 05 210 7400).

In summer, **Kärkisaari**, just west of Kotka, makes for a lovely excursion. The long swimming dock leads into the island-filled inlet of the Gulf of Finland. On the adjacent peninsula is **Santalahti**; the crescent-shaped beach has grassy knolls at the edge of a sandy bay.

Kotka is only 70 km (45 miles) from the nearest Russian city, Viipuri (Vyborg) and 270 km (170 miles) from St Petersburg; all varieties of Finland–Russia trips can be arranged with the Kotka Tourist Board, but remember to plan overnight trips well in advance so that your visa will be ready.

The circular streets of the 350-year-old town of **Hamina** ⓱ are lined with beautiful wooden buildings with small restaurants, cafes and craft shops. The surrounding area is important in the Finnish military history and has seen numerous battles with foreign powers. The **Military Officer School (RUK) museum** (Kadettikoulunkatu 8; summer Tues–Sun 10am–4pm; tel: 05 181 66498) has local military memorabilia. A major international military music event, Hamina Tattoo, takes place here every second summer (www.haminatattoo.com). Further east lies **Vaalimaa**, a busy border station with huge supermarkets selling goodies to Russians and Finns alike. ❏

ÅLAND ISLANDS: THE ULTIMATE RETREAT

To the west of Finland, the Ålands are a perfect island-hopping destination. Catch a ferry, hire a bike and discover this little-known paradise

The Åland Islands (Ahvenanmaa in Finnish) are a collection of granite skerries comprising some 6,500 islands off the west coast of Finland.

Ålanders have inhabited their islands for thousands of years, and have a strong ethnic culture and a formidable pride in their identity. The population of 27,000 has had its own flag since 1954 and its own postage stamps since 1984. Today, the islands are an autonomous demilitarised zone represented both in the Finnish parliament and the Nordic Council, with Swedish being the official language. Although part of the EU, Åland remains outside the tax union agreement so tax-free shopping is available to travellers.

June to August is the ideal time to visit. Take a Viking or Silja Line ferry from Turku, Helsinki, or Stockholm to **Mariehamn** ⓲, sailing through the maze of skerries en route. There are also Air Åland flights from Helsinki.

Mariehamn is the capital of the main island, Åland, and with 11,000 inhabitants, it is the only town-sized settlement. In the West Harbour, the four-masted museum ship *Pommern*, built in Glasgow in 1904, is worth a visit, as is the nearby Maritime Museum (May, June and Aug daily 9am–5pm; July daily until 7pm; entrance charge). Other museums feature exhibitions on prehistoric and Ice and Bronze Age life, hunting, fishing and even delivering mail.

The islands are a paradise for hiking, fishing, cycling, golfing, swimming and other water sports, and are best explored by bicycle and ferry. Bicycle ferries (June–Aug) link bike routes from island to island, such as **Prästö** ⓳. You can hire bicycles from the Mariehamn harbours and campsites. Most notable in Åland's northeast are the historic Kastelholm and Bomarsund fortresses. **Kastelholm** ⓴ (May–Sept daily from 10am) was once the administrative centre for the islands and dates from the 1300s. The Russians began fortifying it in 1829. Adjacent are the Cultural History Museum and the Jan Karlsgården Open-Air Museum (May–Aug daily; entrance charge).

To the southeast of Åland lies **Föglö** ㉑, once an important vodka smuggling destination. In the eastern part of the island there is a natural bird reserve.

Midsummer celebrations are held in almost every village with the traditional raising of the Midsummer pole and dancing.

Hotels, guest houses, cottages and camping facilities are available. For information, contact Åland's Tourism Board, Storagatan 8; tel: 018 24 000; www.visitaland.com. ❏

TOP LEFT: figurehead, Åland Maritime Museum. **ABOVE LEFT:** Åland flags. **TOP RIGHT:** riding on the islands. **RIGHT:** sauna on the water's edge.

TURKU

Map on page 324

Ancient and modern coexist in Turku, Finland's former historic capital. Colourful restaurant boats line the river; museums, bars and galleries intermingle in the city centre

Surrounded by islands, river and sea, Turku (Åbo in Swedish) is a summer paradise, yet it is also worth a visit during other seasons. The River Aura divides the modern city in two and you can cross its five main bridges or take the little ferry that still carries pedestrians and bicycles free of charge.

Turku is Finland's oldest city and yet many of the buildings go back only to the Great Fire of 1827 which destroyed a town then largely made of wood. In 1300, when it acquired a new cathedral, Turku became the spiritual centre of Finland. Around the same time, the solid lines of a castle began to rise near the mouth of the River Aura as the heart of royal power in Finland, where the Swedish governor lived and visiting dignitaries paid their respects.

After the Great Fire, the market and town moved away from the cathedral to the west bank of the Aura, much of it designed and built to the plan of Carl Ludwig Engel. Turku had the first university in Finland, founded by the 17th-century Governor General of Finland, Count Per Brahe.

Today, **Turun Linna** Ⓐ (Turku Castle; Linnankatu 80; mid-Apr–mid-Sept daily 10am–6pm; mid-Sept–mid-Apr Tues–Sun 10am–3pm; entrance charge; tel: 02 262 0300) looks towards the modern town centre, some 3 km (2 miles) away. Many of its rooms are preserved as the Turku Historical Museum.

LEFT: Turku's 14th-century cathedral.
BELOW: market day in the main square.

Exploring the town

Begin your walking tour at the newly renovated **Turku Art Museum** Ⓑ, the impressive stone building on Puolalanmäki (Tues–Fri 11am–7pm, Sat–Sun 11am–5pm; tel: 02 262 7100). Follow Aurakatu down to the **Ortodoksinen Kirkko** Ⓒ (Orthodox Cathedral), built in 1838 on the orders of Tsar Nicholas I. The church is next to the colourful market square. Be sure to visit the 19th-century **Kauppahalli** Ⓓ (Indoor Markethall), across the street in Eerikinkatu.

Turning down Aurakatu, the Auransilta (bridge) gives the first view of the numerous restaurant boats and the sleek white hull and complicated rigging of the *Suomen Joutsen*, which once plied the ocean between Europe and South America. Nearby is pretty Luostarinmäki, an area that escaped the Great Fire, and the open-air **Käsityöläismuseo** Ⓔ (Handicrafts Museum; mid-Apr–mid-Sept daily 10am–6pm; entrance charge; tel: 02 262 0350) which features traditional crafts people at work.

Tuomiokirkko Ⓕ (Turku Cathedral; daily 9am–7pm) maintains a stately presence. Consecrated in 1300, it is Finland's most important medieval structure. In the Cathedral Park a statue depicts Governor Per Brahe in a classically proud pose. At Vanha Suurtori 3 is the **Turku Cultural Centre** with changing exhibitions, concerts and events. To the north stands

the **Rettig Palace**, built in 1928 for one of Turku's upper-class families. Today it houses the museum complex, **Aboa Vetus and Ars Nova** (Apr–Aug daily 11am–7pm; Sept–Mar Tues–Sun 11am–7pm; entrance charge; tel: 02 250 0552). The main house exhibits 20th-century art and the courtyard (with ruins of a medieval town) provides a glimpse of Turku's history.

Along the riverbank

For a riverbank tour, visit **Qwensel House**, named after a judge, J.W. Qwensel, who bought the plot of land in 1695. This is Turku's oldest wooden building, with a popular courtyard café, and now houses the **Apteekkimuseo** (Pharmacy Museum; Läntinen Rantakatu 13; mid-Apr–mid-Sept daily 10am–6pm; entrance charge; tel: 02 262 0280).

Walk past Myllysilta (Mill Bridge) to the next bridge, Martinsilta, where the *SS Ukkopekka* steamship is moored, and still offers pleasant excursions through the archipelago (early June–late Aug 9.30am). Depending on how far you care to walk, you can continue on this side of the river as far as Turku Castle and the modern harbour areas, with merchant tugs and tankers and the terminals of the Viking and Silja Lines.

On your way to the harbour at Linnankatu 74 is the **Forum Marinum** (Maritime Centre; May–Sept daily 11am–7pm; Oct–Apr Tues–Sun 11am–6pm; entrance charge; tel: 02 282 9511), home of the excellent Maritime Museum and Turku's 12 museum ships, including the handsome three-masted barque *Sigyn*.

Heading back towards the centre you come to the **Wäinö Aaltonen Museum** (Itäinen Rantakatu 38; Tues–Sun 11am–7pm; entrance charge; tel: 02 262 0850). The modern structure contains works by one of Finland's most important

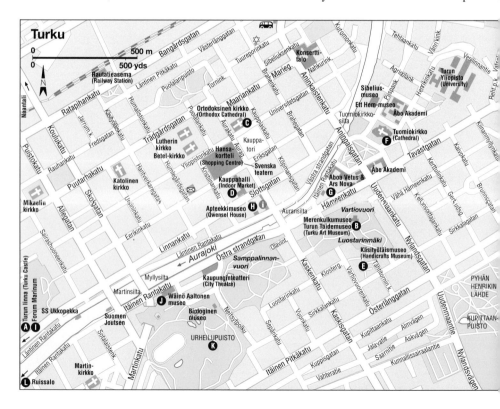

sculptors, Wäinö Aaltonen (1894–1966), plus some interesting temporary exhibitions. In **Urheilupuisto** , the surrounding park, the windmill on Samppalinnanmäki is the last of its kind in Turku. Next to it is the running track where the champion long-distance runner and Olympic gold medallist Paavo Nurmi (1897–1973) trained. His statue stands on Auransilta. The polished granite stone on the slopes of Samppalinnanmäki is Finland's independence memorial, unveiled in 1977 on its 60th anniversary.

Ruissalo Island

Boat services depart several times daily for **Ruissalo Island** ●. An ideal excursion for cyclists, walkers and nature lovers, Ruissalo also has the area's best beaches. The 19th-century **Villa Roma** is typical of the "lace villas" (so-called because of their latticed balconies and windows) built by wealthy merchants. Its owner, the Procultura Foundation, shows summer exhibitions of top-quality Finnish art. In summer, the island is home to Ruisrock, the annual rock festival.

One of the best ways to see the archipelago is with a cruise aboard the *SS Ukkopekka*, which retains something of its steamship past. The bearded skipper, Captain Kangas, is everyone's image of a sea captain. The steamship cruises to different islands and towns, including Captain Kangas's home town of **Naantali**, a charming place north of Turku. Naantali is popular in the summer, when people move into their summer houses and yachts moor in the harbour. Children are attracted by **Moomin World** (mid-June–mid Aug daily 10am–6pm), based on the delightful characters made famous by the Finnish author Tove Jansson. ❏

Turku has become known for its unusual bars in the city centre, housed in buildings that have been converted from a pharmacy, bank, schoolhouse, and even a public toilet.

BELOW: boats moored on the Aura river.

FINLAND'S LAKELAND

A labyrinth of lakes and pine-covered islands extends north from Helsinki. The landscape that was home to Sibelius rewards exploration by lake steamer and canoe

Map on page 316

Helsinki

With some 33,000 islands and peninsulas, the Great Lakes of Saimaa and Päijänne in Central Finland provide a diverse waterscape of lakes, rivers and canals to form Europe's largest inland waterway system. This varied landscape owes its beauty to the Ice Age when glaciers carved out the shape of lakes and ridges. Excellent holiday facilities are offered for most kinds of water sports throughout this region.

The best approach to the lakes is via industrial **Kouvola** ㉒, about 140 km (86 miles) northeast of Helsinki and a junction of road and rail routes into Saimaa. Although not the most interesting town in Finland, Kouvola's Kaunisnurmi quarters house quaint handicraft shops and several museums.

To capture the spirit of Saimaa, ignore the direct routes to Kuopio in the north and head east on Road 6 to **Lappeenranta** ㉓, South Karelia's main town. The fortress next to the harbour was built by the Russians in 1775. Nearby, the suburb of Linnoitus is the most interesting part of the town, where you will find Finland's oldest **Orthodox Church** (1785) and the **Etelä-Karjalan Museo** (South Karelian Museum; June–mid-Aug Mon–Fri 10am–6pm, Sat and Sun 11am–5pm; mid-Aug–May Tues–Sun 11am–5pm; entrance charge; tel: 05 616 2255), with a fascinating section on the old city of Vyborg (just a few miles south in Russia). The **Ratsuväki-museo** (Cavalry Museum; June–mid-Aug Mon–Fri 10am–6pm, Sat and Sun 11am–5pm; entrance charge; tel: 05 616 2257) details the history and distinctive red uniforms of Finland's proud soldiers. Day cruises to Russia operate from Lappeenranta for which Western visitors do not require visas, although they are obligatory for other visits.

A few miles further east is the industrial city of **Imatra** ㉔, once erroneously described as the "Niagara of Finland", but worth a brief visit to see the impressive **Imatrankoski** (rapids).

High on the ridges

About 50 km (30 miles) north of Imatra, Road 6 passes within a few hundred metres of the Russian border. Switching to Road 14, you soon come to **Punkaharju** ㉕, one of Finland's best-loved beauty spots. Punkaharju is one of countless ridges bequeathed to Finland by the last Ice Age. It's around 7 km (4 miles) long and in places is just wide enough to carry the road; elsewhere it widens to accommodate magnificent pine and birch woods.

Lusto, the superb Forestry Museum (May and Sept daily 10am–5pm; June–Aug until 7pm; Oct–Apr Tues–Sun 10am–5pm; entrance charge; tel: 015 345 100) has a comprehensive exhibition on Finland's forests and associated subjects such as design, wilder-

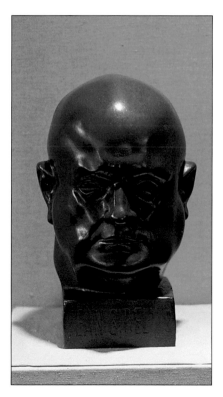

LEFT: peaceful Lakeland waters. **BELOW:** composer Jean Sibelius was born in the town of Hämeenlinna.

ness trekking, forestry industry and research. The **Retretti Arts Centre** (June–Aug daily 10am–5pm; July until 6pm; entrance charge; tel: 015 775 2200), built into the bedrock on the ridge, is well worth a visit. Its annual exhibition, featuring four usually quite different, internationally acclaimed artists, is a major event in Finland. Nearby, in Kerimäki, it is possible to visit the world's largest Christian wooden church built in 1847. In summer, a lake steamer sails between Punkaharju and Savonlinna from Retretti. The two-hour trip is a delightful mini-voyage through the islands.

Operatic odyssey

Savonlinna ㉖ ("the castle of Savo") is the most charming of Finland's main lakeland towns and the best base in Saimaa for making trips. It has the medieval castle of **Olavinlinna** (tours June–mid-Aug daily 10am–5pm; mid-Aug–May daily 10am–3pm; entrance charge), which is the site of the annual International Opera Festival that takes place throughout July. Tickets for, and accommodation during, the festival should be booked well ahead (tel: 015 517 510; www.opera festival.fi). With its massive granite walls, ramparts and shooting galleries topped by three great round towers, Olavinlinna has everything you might expect from a medieval castle.

Near the castle, the museum ship *Salama*, a steam schooner built in 1874, shipwrecked in 1898 and raised from the lake in 1971, is one of three converted old ships that form the inland navigation section of the **Savonlinnan Maakuntamuseo** (Savonlinna Provincial Museum, Riihisaari; Tues–Sun 11am–5pm; July daily 11am–6pm; entrance charge; tel: 015 571 4712).

From Savonlinna to Kuopio by lake steamer is a full day's journey. Road travellers have a choice of continuing west from Savonlinna on Roads 14 and 5 to Mikkeli or staying with Saimaa to its northern limits beyond Kuopio.

Mikkeli ㉗, a pleasant provincial capital, is a historic army town. Near Mikkeli, **Visulahti** amusement park has a vintage car exhibition, plastic dinosaurs and waxworks (park and waxworks open year round; Dinosauria and vintage car exhibition open late-May–early June daily 10am–5pm; early June–mid-Aug daily 10am–7pm; entrance charge; tel: 015 18 281). For the more adventurous, **Xon Action Park** in Anttola offers zorbing (rolling down a hill in a large inflatable ball), bungee jumps, a giant swing and paintball (summer Tues–Fri noon–6pm, Sat 11am–6pm, also Sun noon–4pm in high summer; entrance charge; tel: 015 650 999; www.xonpuisto.com).

Convent culture

The recommended way to Kuopio from Savonlinna is via Varkaus on Road 464, a particularly attractive and watery route. Then take Road 23 heading northeast towards Joensuu in north Karelia, passing by the Orthodox monastery of **Valamon Luostari** ㉘ (daily 8am–9pm; tel: 017 570 111; www.valamo.fi) and the convent of **Lintulan Luostari** (tel: 017 563 106). On all three counts of history, culture and scenery, these merit a visit. *M/S Sergei* cruises along the canal between the two in high summer.

BELOW: the lakes attract windsurfers.

The monastery was formed by monks fleeing from the Lake Lagoda in 1940, after the Finno-Russian Winter War. Valamon Luostari has experienced something of a renaissance in recent years. There is a fine church, completed in 1977, a cafeteria, souvenir shop and a modern hotel. The Lintulan Luostari, a few kilometres away, has a similar but shorter history.

Map on page 316

Music and dance

Kuopio ㉙ has a crowded summer calendar, the highlight of which is the International Dance and Music Festival in June. The town's daily market fills most of the central **Tori** (Market Place) and is one of the most varied outside Helsinki. Sights to see include the **Kuopion Kortellimuseo** (Kirkkokatu 22; mid-May–Aug Tues–Sun 10am–5pm; Sept–mid-May Tues–Fri 10am–3pm, Sat–Sun 10am–4pm; entrance charge; tel: 017 182 625), comprising a number of original dwellings complete with authentic furniture, warehouses, and even gardens dating from the 18th century to the 1930s. The **Kuopion Museo** (Kauppakatu 23; Tues–Fri 10am–5pm, Sat–Sun 11am–5pm; entrance charge; tel: 017 182 603) houses regional collections of a cultural and natural history order in a castle-like building.

Icons – many from the 18th century and some from the 10th century – and sacred objects are on view at the **Ortodoksinen Kirkkomuseo** (Orthodox Church Museum, Karjalankatu 1; May–Aug Tues–Sun 10am–4pm; Sept–Apr Tues–Fri noon–3pm, Sat–Sun until 4pm; entrance charge; tel: 020 6100 266). The treasures were brought here from Valamo and Konevitsa monasteries in Karelia and a few from Petsamo in the far north, all territories ceded to the Soviet Union.

At **Iisalmi** ㉚, 80 km (50 miles) north of Kuopio on Road 5, **Evakkokeskuksen** (Kyllikinkatu 8), a Karelian-Orthodox Cultural Centre, displays valuable

The 19th century recreated in Lappeenranta.

BELOW: Olavinlinna, a dramatic setting for opera.

Street corner kiosks offer everything from culinary delights to fast food.

BELOW: dancers perform at Kuopio's annual festival.

relics recovered from territory now in Russia. You can have a beer on the harbour at **Kuappi**, "the smallest restaurant in the world", or dine at **Olutmestari**, Savonkatu 18, a popular summer restaurant with an attractive terrace.

The western lakes

To the west of the region lies Päijänne, Finland's deepest lake and its longest at 119 km (74 miles). At the southern and northern ends of the lake system are two of Finland's more substantial towns, Lahti and Jyväskylä respectively, which are linked to the west of Päijänne by one of Europe's main highways, E24, and to the east of it by a network of slower more attractive routes.

Lahti ③ lies 103 km (64 miles) north of Helsinki on Road 4 (E75). The **Lahden Urheilukeskus** sports centre is the venue for the annual Finlandia Ski Race and the Ski Games. Lahti is a modern place, one of its few older buildings being the **Kaupungintalo** (Town Hall) designed by Eliel Saarinen in 1912. Three blocks to the north is the market, and two blocks further north, at Kirkkokatu 4, the highly individualistic **Ristinkirkko** (Church of the Cross; daily), built in 1978, and the last church in Finland designed by Alvar Aalto.

The **Lahden Historiallinen Museo** (Lahdenkatu 4; Mon–Fri 10am–5pm, Sat and Sun 11am–5pm; entrance charge; tel: 03 814 4536) in Lahti Manor is an exotic late 19th-century building with very good regional ethnographical and cultural history collections, as well as art and furniture. A few kilometres northwest to Tiirismaa is the tourist centre of **Messilä**, combining an old manor house, downhill skiing in winter and camping.

From Lahti it's only 35 km (21 miles) northeast on Road 4 to the pleasant little town of **Heinola ②**. Taking the summer lake route, it is four hours by steamer.

Map on page 316

The **Jyrängönkoski** (rapids) provide good sport for local canoeists and for fishermen casting for lake and rainbow trout. Rent a rod at the **Siltasaari Fishing Centre** and have your catch smoked to eat on the spot or take it away.

An attractive route to Jyväskylä is along the minor road 314 from Asikkala. This will take you along the **Pulkkilanharju** (ridge), which vies with that of Punkaharju for magnificent views. Continue via Sysmä and Luhanka, through various waterscapes that make up Päijänne's contorted eastern shore. To rejoin Road 9 (E63) at Korpilahti for the final leg to Jyväskylä you can use the enormous bridge across Kärkistensalmi, one of Päijänne's many narrow straits. On the other side, don't miss the Muurame sauna village with 30 saunas from various parts of the country and an exhibition of sauna culture. Book ahead to try a traditional smoke or peat sauna (June–Aug Tues–Sun 10am–6pm; tel: 014 373 2670).

A beauty spot inside the **Päijänteen Kansallispuisto** (Päijänne National Park) is the long, slender island of **Kelvenne** ⓪, 60 km (37 miles) north of Lahti, with its lakes, lagoons and curious geological formations. You can reach it from the Ravintola Laivaranta camping area at Padasjoki.

Alvar Aalto's city

Jyväskylä ㉞ is situated on the northern shore of Lake Päijänne. Alvar Aalto grew up here and there are no fewer than 30 major buildings by him around the area, including the university, theatre and the Museum of Central Finland. Don't miss the **Alvar Aalto Museum** (7 Alvar Aallonkatu; Tues–Sun 11am–6pm; entrance charge; tel: 014 624 809) with its collection of architectural plans, photographs, scale models and Aalto's furniture designs. There are a number of winter and summer sports facilities in Jyväskylä, but the town is best known

BELOW: a boat is an essential part of Lakeland life.

internationally as the venue for the well-attended Neste Rally in August, Finland's premier motor-racing event. The Jyväskylä Arts Festival is a major cultural event held in July, always with a different theme.

Tampere

With over 200 lakes in the area, make sure to take a boat journey from Tampere, either south on the Silverline route, or north on the Poet's Way, or hop on a boat to Viikinsaari to retreat into nature.

Tampere ❸, Finland's industrial capital, lies 150 km (94 miles) southwest of Jyväskylä. It was officially founded in 1779 by King Gustav III of Sweden-Finland and owes its fortunes to the Tammerkoski (rapids), which first brought power and industry to the area. The Tammerkoski have largely lost their working factories, and in their place are hotels, shopping centres and museums.

Significant churches, museums and buildings include the 20th-century **Kirjasto ❹** (City Library) by husband and wife architects, Reima and Raili Pietilä, the design of which is said to be based on the open wings and spread tail feathers of a wood grouse; and **Tampere-talo ❺** (Tampere Hall), a spectacular blue-white structure designed in 1990 by Esa Piiroinen and Sakari Aartelo.

Tuomiokirkko ❻ (Tampere Cathedral, Tuomiokirkonkatu 3), designed by Lars Sonck in National Romantic style and completed in 1907, contains some of the best of Finnish art, including Magnus Enckell's altar fresco of the Resurrection and Hugo Simberg's masterpiece, *The Wounded Angel*.

In a park on the eastern side of town is another Pietilä design, the stark-looking **Kalevan Kirkko** (Kaleva Church; Liisanpuisto 1). Built in 1966, its most striking feature is the organ with 3,000 pipes shaped like a sail.

The Tampella foundry, built in 1850, was transformed in 1996 into an impressive museum centre and renamed **Museokeskus Vapriikki ❼** (Veturiaukio 4; Tues, Thur–Sun 10am–6pm, Wed 11am–8pm; entrance charge; tel: 03 5656 6966).

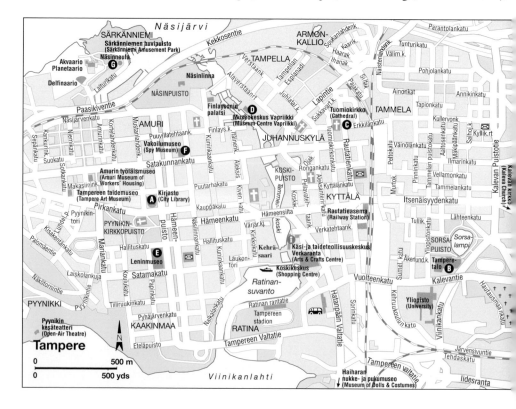

Maps:
Area: 316
City: 332

It features exhibitions on the Tampere region from archaeology to technology. There is a café-restaurant, and museum shop. The **Leninmuseo** ❸ (Lenin Museum; Hämeenpuisto 28; Mon–Fri 9am–6pm, Sat–Sun 11am–4pm; tel: 03 276 8100) introduces the time Lenin spent in Tampere before the Russian revolution in 1905–6. Another fascinating small museum reveals the tricks of spies who often worked from Finland during the Cold War (**Spy Museum** ❺, Satakunnankatu 18B; daily at least 10am–5pm; tel: 03 212 3007).

Across the northern harbour entrance from Näsinpuisto (park) is the highest viewpoint in Finland, the **Näsinneula Observation Tower** ❻ (noon–11.30pm). It stands 120 metres (400 ft) high at the centre of Särkänniemi Park. The park is a favourite place for children with its aquarium, dolphinarium, planetarium, children's zoo and amusement park (for opening hours tel: 02 07 130 200; www.sarkanniemi.fi).

South of Tampere

From Tampere, the 175-km (110-mile) route back to Helsinki passes through the industrial centre of **Valkeakoski** ㊱. In the Middle Ages, Valkeakoski was only a hamlet, later a mining village in the parish of Sääksmäki; but, even then, it had the rapids that meant water power, first to grind corn and then to make paper. In contrast, the 19th-century National Romantic movement brought artists to Sääksmäki and these two ingredients – industry and art – still combine today.

The old **Voipaalan Kartano** (Voipaala Manor) on Rapola Hill was once the home of the sculptor Elias Ilkka who owned the manor and farm where the Valkeakoski Summer Theatre performs. From the car park, a marked path leads you round the faint ruins of Finland's largest hill fort, dating back to the 11th century. Make your way to **Visavuori** (June–Aug 10am–6pm; Sept–May Tues–

Tampere Library houses "Moomin Valley", an exhibition of the characters from Tove Jansson's popular books.

BELOW: Kaleva Church, Tampere.

Map
on page
316

Sun 10am–4pm), the studio home of one of Finland's best-known sculptors, Emil Wikström (1864–1942). Aged 29, he won a competition to design the frieze for Helsinki's House of Estates, and designed this lakeside house, complete with rooftop observatory.

Glass-blowing centre

Of all Finland's glassmakers, **Iittala ③** is the most famous. In the **Iittalan Lasimuseo** (Iittala Museum; June–mid-Aug daily 10am–6pm; entrance charge; tel: 02 0439 6230) beautiful functional glassware and *objets d'art* such as glass birds and fruit shapes are on display, along with designs by Alvar Aalto and Timo Sarpaneva. Visit the Iittala shop where seconds are often indistinguishable to the inexpert eye and less than half the price of perfect work.

It's also worth visiting the **Suomen Lasimuseo** (Finnish Glass Museum; Tues–Sun 10am–6pm; entrance charge; tel: 020 758 4108) in **Riihimäki ③**, just off Road 3, 35 km (26 miles) south of Hämeenlinna. The museum is housed in an authentic glassworks from 1914. Exhibits trace the history of glassmaking from the early days of windowpane production to the era of glass as a fine art in the 20th century.

Häme Castle, Hämeenlinna, built by the Swedes in the 13th century.

BELOW: keeping up the glassmaking tradition at Iittala.

Sibelius country

Continuing south from Iittala, Road 57 leads to the lake of Hattula and **Hattulan Pyhän Ristin Kirkko** (Hattulan Church of the Holy Cross), one of Finland's best-known and oldest churches, built in 1320. Just off the E12, **Aulangon Puisto** (Aulanko Forest Park) is ideal for a break, overlooking Aulankojärvi (lake). Jean Sibelius, who was born in nearby **Hämeenlinna ③**, is said to have commented on Aulanko: "I was thinking of these scenes from my childhood when I composed *Finlandia*."

Hämeenlinna has two claims to fame: first, the early 13th-century **Häme Castle** (June–mid-Aug daily 10am–6pm; mid-Aug–Apr Mon–Fri 10am–4pm, Sat–Sun 11am–4pm; entrance charge; tel: 03 675 6820) and, second, the fact that it was the birthplace of Jean Sibelius. Sibelius was born in December 1865 in the little timberboard house of the town physician, Christian Gustaf Sibelius, now the **Sibeliuksen Syntymä-koti** (Sibelius Home Museum, Hallituskatu 11; May–Aug daily 10am–4pm; Sept–Apr from noon; entrance charge; tel: 03 621 2755). The big dining room is used for recitals, and the house is full of memorabilia.

Heading south through Hyvinkää to **Järvenpää ④**, you are only 45 km (30 miles) from Helsinki. The area's **Tuusulanjärvi** (lake) attracted late 19th-century artists and intellectuals away from their city haunts to build studio-villas on the eastern side, just beyond Järvenpää. Among them was the portrait painter Eero Järnefelt, noted for his rural and folk scenes, and Jean Sibelius and his wife Aino.

Ainola ④ was the Sibelius home for 53 years (May–Sept Tues–Sun 10am–5pm; entrance charge; tel: 09 287 322). Designed by Lars Sonck, the house is still furnished as it was in Sibelius's time and the drawing room holds the composer's piano. Floral tributes adorn the couple's grave in the garden. ❏

CANOEING THE OPEN WATERS

Paddling a canoe on the lakes and rivers of Finland is one of the most pleasurable ways to explore the country. For the energetic there are annual races

One of the more testing annual events on the European canoeing calendar is the Arctic Circle Race which takes place every summer north of the Arctic Circle from Kilpisjärvi to Tornio along 537 km (334 miles) of the border rivers between Finland and Sweden. Another is the six-day 700-km (435-mile) Finlandia Canoe Relay each June, usually through the complex Saimaa system.

With 187,888 lakes (at the last count) and innumerable rivers, it's surprising that canoeing has only become popular in Finland in recent years. There is a growing range of packages whereby you can canoe well-tried routes of varying lengths with the option of hiring equipment, camping or staying in farmhouse accommodation.

A particularly well-tried series of routes forms an overall 350-km (217-mile) circuit beginning and ending at Heinola. This needs 10–15 days, but can also be divided into shorter sections. Another, along 320 km (200 miles) of the Ounasjoki river in Lapland from Enontekiö to Rovaniemi, features sections of true Arctic wilderness; the rapids are mainly Grade I, but it is possible to portage round the most daunting of these. Yet another follows a 285-km (180-mile) lake-and-river route taken by the old tar boats from Kuhmo to Oulu.

If you're attracted to the idea of pioneering across the lakes the possibilities are legion. Any of the 19 road maps which cover the entire country on a scale of of 1:200 000 will be sufficient for general planning, but absolutely essential for more detail are the special inland water charts, for example, for Saimaa on a scale of 1:40 000/1:50 000. It's not until you are in your canoe, however, that navigation problems become clear. From water level one island of rock and pine trees looks like another with few helpful landmarks. You will appreciate those other vital aids to canoeing the Finnish lakes: a compass and a pair of binoculars.

The greatest inconvenience you are likely to encounter is wind. Squalls blow up quickly and across these great expanses, waters are soon whipped up into turbulence. Head for shelter at the first sign.

Seek permission to camp whenever possible, since the right to pitch your tent anywhere has been abused by some foreigners and is no longer permitted. Often, of course, there is no one to ask. It is one of the joys of canoeing in Finland that you may travel for days without sign of humanity, other than a tugboat hauling timber, or a fisherman. ❏

TOP LEFT: canoeists stop for a well-earned rest. **ABOVE:** kayakers in action. **ABOVE RIGHT:** paddle power. **RIGHT:** slalom competitor.

FINLAND'S WEST COAST

*The beautiful Bothnian coastline preserves its rich
maritime heritage and its blend of Finnish-Swedish culture
in the islands and towns along the road to Lapland*

Map
on page
338

Helsinki

The west coast of Finland is a fascinating mixture of past and present: stately churches and old wooden houses, museums and modern industry. With its close proximity to Sweden, Swedish remains the first language for many communities and some towns have both Swedish and Finnish names.

The first main town north of **Turku** *(see page 323)* on Road 8 is **Uusikau-punki ❶** (Nystad). The **Kulttuurihistoriallinen Museo** (Museum of Cultural History; Tues–Fri noon–5pm, in summer Mon–Fri 10am–5pm, Sat and Sun noon–3pm; entrance charge; tel: 02 8451 5399) is in the house of F.W. Wahlberg, a former shipowner and tobacco manufacturer. **Myllymäki Park** is a reminder that many retired sailors became millers and the countryside was once dotted with windmills; four windmills and a tower remain.

Palaces and timber homes

Rauma ❷ is the largest medieval town in Scandinavia, listed as a UNESCO World Heritage site with 600 or so wooden buildings painted in traditional pastel shades. Many of these are still private homes. Although the dwellings and shops are 18th- and 19th-century buildings, the narrow streets date back to the 16th century.

Pori ❸, some 47 km (37 miles) north of Rauma, was founded by Duke Johan of Sweden in 1558. With a population of 76,600, it is one of Finland's chief export harbours and hosts a jazz festival every July. Interesting sights include the **City Hall**, built in the style of a Venetian Palace. More off-beat is the **Jusélius Mausoleum** (May–Aug daily noon–3pm; Sept–Apr Sun only until 2pm; free) at Käppärä Cemetery, built by a Pori businessman in memory of his young daughter.

Satakunta Museum (Tues–Sun 11am–6pm, Wed until 8pm; entrance charge; tel: 02 621 1078), dating from 1888, is the largest Finnish cultural history museum and includes a fine collection of 19th- and 20th-century Finnish art. The **Porin Taidemuseo** (Pori Art Museum, Eteläranta; Tues–Sun 11am–6pm, Wed until 8pm; free entrance on Wed after 6pm; tel: 02 621 1080) features contemporary art.

The peninsula leading from Pori to **Reposaari** has a long sandy beach and is one of Finland's best resorts. **Kristinestad ❹** (Kristiinankaupunki), 95 km (59 miles) to the north was founded by the Swedish governor, Count Per Brahe, in 1649. A master of diplomacy, he gave the town the name of both his wife and Queen Kristina of Sweden-Finland.

Vaasa ❺ (Vasa), established in the 14th century, has been devastated by wars and fire. Today it is a handsome town with wide, attractively laid-out streets and a large market square. Notable buildings include the Orthodox Church, the Court of Appeal (1862),

LEFT: sparkling water in the Gulf of Bothnia.
BELOW: Rauma's Franciscan monastery church.

West Coast

```
0        50 km
0            50 miles
```

and the Town Hall (1883). For the best view of the town, clamber up the 200 steps in the tower behind the police station headquarters.

Vaasa is well-endowed with museums, the most important being the **Pohjanmaan Museo** (Ostrobothnian Museum, Museokatu 3; Tues–Fri 10am–5pm, Wed until 8pm, Sat and Sun noon–5pm; entrance charge; tel: 06 325 3800), which covers local history and art. **Bragen Ulkomuseo** (Open-Air Museum; June–Aug Tues–Sun; entrance charge; tel: 06 312 7166) features 19th-century Ostrobothnian farm life. Offshore islands add to the charms of Vaasa. Ala-Härmä has an amusement park with a karting circuit named after the Formula 1 driver Mika Salo, who also helped to plan it (signposted from the Road 19).

Jakobstad ⑥ (Pietarsaari) gained repute as Finland's shipbuilding centre, producing vessels that opened new trade routes around the world. One of the town's best-known sailing ships *Jakobstads Wapen*, a 1767 galleon, still makes cruises. Some 300 or so restored wooden houses may be seen in the old part of town.

Road of seven bridges

From Jakobstad to **Kokkola ⑦**, take the attractive route called the "road of seven bridges", which runs from island to island across the archipelago. Kokkola's Town Hall was designed by Carl Ludwig Engel, who has left his mark on so many Finnish towns, and there is an English park and boathouse commemorating an episode in the Crimean War with the British fleet. On the 230-km (140-mile) road north between Kokkola and Oulu, the town of **Kalajoki ⑧** is a popular spot for fishing, bathing and sailing.

Oulu ⑨ is the largest city in northern Finland, with a population of 115,500. **Turkansaaren Ulkomuseo ⑩** (Turkansaari Open-Air Museum; June–mid-Aug daily 10am–6pm; mid-Aug–mid-Sept until 4pm; entrance charge; tel: 08 5586 7191) can be found on a small island in the Oulujoki, 14 km (8 miles) east of Oulu. It has an interesting collection of Ostrobothnian buildings, including a church, farm buildings and windmills. In town, the **Tietomaa Science Centre** (daily 10am–4pm, until 6pm in summer; entrance charge; tel: 08 5584 1340) has a wealth of hands-on exhibits. The elegant **Oulun Taidemuseo** (daily 10am–6pm; entrance charge; tel: 044 703 7472) has an exhibition of contemporary art. Visit **Koskikeskus** (Rapids Centre) on the mouth of the Oulujoki, with 12 fountains.

Map on page 338

Snow and the Midnight Sun

From Oulu to **Kemi** ⓫ one begins the approach to Lapland. Kemi lies at the mouth of the Kemijoki River and is known as the seaport of Lapland. In winter, you can take an excursion on the 1961 icebreaker, *Sampo*. A sight not to miss is **Lumilinna** (Snow Castle; daily late-Jan–early-Apr 10am–8pm; entrance charge; tel: 016 259 502) with its dazzling white walls and illuminated towers. The castle, which also has an ice hotel, is rebuilt every year.

On the border a short distance west is **Tornio** ⓬, near the mouth of the Tornionjoki. The **Aineen Taidemuseo** (Aine Art Museum; Tues–Thur 11am–6pm, Fri–Sun until 3pm; entrance charge; tel: 016 432 438) houses a fine collection of Finnish art from 1814 to the present. For a great view, visit the **Vesitorni** water tower (daily mid-June–mid-Aug 11am–7pm).

Lumilinna, the annual snow castle at Kemi, makes an impressive sight.

At the **Green Zone Golf Course** (June–Oct) on the Finnish-Swedish border, you can play nine holes in Sweden and nine in Finland. It is a rare delight to play a night round in summer, thanks to the Midnight Sun.

If you drive 9 miles (15 km) north of Tornio off Road E78, you will come to **Kukkolankoski** ⓭, the longest free-flowing rapids in Finland at 3,500 metres (11,485 ft). Fishermen here still use the traditional long-handled net. ❑

BELOW: tranquil scene on the West coast.

Map
on page
342

KARELIA AND KUUSAMO

*Easterly Karelia with its distinctly Orthodox heritage is the
setting for Finland's epic poem, "Kalevala". Traditions
abound, the air is pure and the landscape untouched*

Helsinki

BELOW: the Karelian
Orthodox Cultural
Centre (Evakkokes-
kuksen); many Kar-
elians belong to the
Orthodox Church.

Karelia is the general name for the area whose westernmost part is still in
Finland and the larger, easternmost part – which was ceded to the Soviet
Union as a result of the Treaty of Paris in 1947 – is in Russia. There are
many holiday options, including renting a cottage or log cabin by the water or
staying in a "working" farmhouse. Depending on the season, one can enjoy a
range of water or winter sports, fishing, hiking, and berry-picking.

Joensuu ❶, the "capital" of North Karelia, is famous for its Festival of Song
every June. The **Carelicum Cultural and Tourism Centre** (Koskikatu 5; Mon–
Fri 9am–5pm, Sat and Sun 10am–3pm; entrance charge; tel: 013 267 5222) has
exhibitions on the history and the folk culture of this part of Karelia. Along the
same street there is the **Taidemuseo** (Art Museum, Kirkkokatu 23; Tues–Sun
10am–4pm, Wed until 8pm; entrance charge; tel: 013 267 5388), containing an
icon collection and Finnish paintings from the 19th and 20th centuries.

Before turning north, go east to **Ilomantsi ❷**. Ilomantsi is the oldest inhabited area of North Karelia and a stronghold of the Orthodox Church. Easter is
the most impressive festival here, and other colourful events are held throughout the summer. Ilomantsi was one of the main battlegrounds in the war of
1939–45 and the **Fighter's House** on Hattuvaara Hill has exhibitions about that

period. Nearby in the village of **Runokylä** at the Singers Lodge on Parppein-vaara Hill, the ancient folk poems of the *Kalevala* are still sung by women in traditional costume (accompanied by the *kantele*, a zither-like instrument). The **Parppeinpirtti** restaurant (tel: 013 881094) on the hill features Karelian cuisine, including tiny fish *(vendace)*, cold smoked whitefish, hearty meat casseroles and pies, *pirakka* pastries, and baked cheese with cloudberry jam.

TIP

Mountain biking is a popular way to explore Karelia. Hire a bike locally, or join a week-long guided trail bike expedition from Lieksa (details from Karelia Expert Tourist Service, tel: 0400 175 323).

Gateway to the wilderness

Heading north from Joensuu, take Route 6 and the eastward fork to Route 73 to **Lieksa ❸**, where the **Ruuankoski** (rapids) must be seen, and possibly experienced, under the supervision of a guide. Lieksa, one of the many forest centres in Finland, is only about 20 years old and has a population of 19,000 in an area larger than London. The **Pielisen Museo** (Pielisen Open-Air Museum, Pappilantie 2; May–Sept daily 10am–4pm; entrance charge; tel: 013 689 4151) has 70 buildings, some dating to the 17th century, which document local settlement.

At **Vuonisjärvi ❹**, 29 km (18 miles) from the centre, is **Paateri** (Mar, June–Aug; daily; entrance charge), the former studio of Eeva Ryynänen (1915–2001), a wood sculptor noted for her spectacular Wilderness Church (adjacent).

Lieksa is the gateway to Finland's wilderness. "Never go hiking on your own" is the warning motto of this region, whose dense forests are inhabited by bears, wolves, elk and reindeer. At **Kaksinkantaja**, 40 km (26 miles) from the centre, there is an exhibition of bear skulls and stuffed animals by Väinö Heikkinen, a renowned bear hunter (June–Aug daily; entrance charge). From Lieksa, Road 73 leads to **Nurmes ❺**. First mentioned in documents in 1556, Nurmes is a beautiful town. The **Bomba House** (Suojärvenkatu 1; tel: 013 687 2501) is a traditional

BELOW: traditional way of life on a Karelian farm.

KARELIA: SOUL AND SAUNA

If Finland has a soul, that soul lives on in Karelia. When Finns have gone to war, it has concerned Karelia. A Karelian theme runs through the music of Sibelius and his *Karelian Suite* reaches sublime heights of patriotism.

The Karelians were one of the earliest of the Finnish communities; they are evident in Bronze and Iron Age discoveries. The *Kalevala*, the great epic saga of ancient life in the far north, is really about Karelians. The poem, which in the 18th and 19th centuries became the cornerstone of the struggle for national culture, recounts everyday events and rituals and finally the heroes' joy as they celebrate in song the salvation of the land of Kalevala from its enemies.

True Karelia exists only as a fragment of its former self. The greater part of the region lies east of the Russian border, lost to Finland after the Winter War (1939–40). As a result 400,000 Karelians had to be resettled in the 1940s. Since then, people of Karelian origin can be found in all parts of Finland. They tend to be lively and talkative, in contrast with the more taciturn nature of other Finns.

It is they who are responsible for the sauna. Early Karelians cleared woodland to grow crops and used steam heat to dry their grain. The therapeutic benefits of this heat were later realised and so the sauna was born in Finland.

wooden Karelian house at Ritoniemi, about 2 km (1¼ miles) from the town, surrounded by a "Karelian village" which provides visitors not only with comfortable accommodation, but also with delicious meals of local specialities.

Nurmes is the place to leave the car and take a scenic ride on Finland's largest inland waterway ferry down Lake Pielinen to **Kolin Kansallispuisto** ❻ (Koli National Park). Here you will see views that inspired some of Finland's greatest painters as well as the composer Sibelius.

Before reaching the Oulu area, if your choice is Road 6 north you could detour to the remote national park, **Tiilikkajärven Kansallispuisto** ❼, near Rautavaara. It was established to conserve the uninhabited area of Lake Tiilikka and the surrounding bogs.

Another national park, **Hiidenportin Kansallispuisto** ❽, is southeast of Sotkamo and also best reached from Road 6. This is a rugged area with the narrow Hiidenporti Gorge, a rift valley with rock sides dropping 20 metres (70 ft) to the floor. There are well-marked trails and camp sites in the park.

Both in and outside the parks you may find reindeer. These animals are the main source of income for many people living in the region and it is very important to take special care on roads when reindeer are around, especially at dusk.

The Finnish frontier

Kuhmo ❾ is a frontier town surrounded by dense forests in the wilderness area of Kainuu. It is known for its annual Kuhmo Chamber Music Festival. A fascinating recreated **Kalevala Village** (June–Aug daily; entrance charge; tel: 08 652 0114) in a wooded park on the outskirts of Kuhmo displays numerous local folk traditions. The aim is to give modern-day visitors an idea of Finnish culture as it was immortalised in Finland's epic poem, *Kalevala*. The **Hotel Kalevala** specialises in regional cuisine (tel: 08 655 4100).

A long straight road through some of Finland's darkest forests leads west out of Kuhmo to Sotkamo and then onwards to **Kajaani** , the area's main town, on the eastern edge of Oulujärvi (lake). Kajaani still has the ruins of the 1604 castle and its town hall was designed by Carl Ludwig Engel, who was responsible for so much of early Helsinki. The road from Kajaani towards **Oulu** hugs the shores of Oulujärvi, plunging first into thickly wooded hill country. Before entering Oulu, the route goes through **Muhos** which has the second-oldest church in Finland, dating from 1634.

Kuusamo

The only other main centre in this scantily populated area is **Kuusamo** ⓫, almost at the Russian border, some 360 km (225 miles) northeast across the breadth of the country along Road 20. The Kuusamo region is marvellous wilderness country, ideal for canoeing and fishing, and the main sound in these parts is a mixture of rushing water and the wind high in the pines. This is also berry country, with several varieties growing in great profusion on the Arctic tundra. The only snag is the number of mosquitoes: take plenty of protection.

The Carelicum Cultural and Tourism Centre at Joensuu traces the region's social history.

Map on page 342

    Karhuntassu Tourist Centre (tel: 0205 64 6804) provides information on activities, accommodation and most other aspects of the region. In winter, the area is excellent for skiing and snowmobiling. There are two national parks: the largest, **Oulangan Kansallispuisto** ⓬, to the north, covers a largely untouched region bordering the Oulanka river. **Karhunkierros**, the most famous walking route in Finland, stretches some 100 km (60 miles) through the Oulanka canyon to the **Rukatunturi Fells** ⓭. A smaller national park, **Riisitunturi**, lies to the southwest of Oulanka. Moving further north approaching Lapland, the landscape and culture change from the traditions of Karelia to the ancient ways of the Sami people. ❑

BELOW: white-water expedition.

FINNISH LAPLAND

*For some travellers, Lapland is the land of the Midnight Sun,
a haven for fell-walkers and anglers. For others, it's the land
of Father Christmas, reindeer racing and dog-sledging*

Map on page 346

Whatever the season, Lapland offers a variety of interesting natural phenomena and cultures, from the mysterious Northern Lights and the dark Kaamos skies to the magical contrast of the Midnight Sun. However you choose to arrive – by air, sea, train, or car, be prepared to experience Lapland and the Arctic Circle on foot, whether reindeer spotting, cross-country skiing, snowmobiling, ice golfing, salmon-fishing, gold-panning, discovering the Sami culture, or simply hiking the rich swampland in search of cloudberries. These activities will only whet your appetite for the delicious Lappish cuisine.

Two main roads bore their way northwards through the province of Lapland (Lappi). Road 4 (E75), sometimes called the Arctic Highway, links Kemi (coming from Oulu) with Rovaniemi before continuing northeastwards into Norway at Utsjoki. The other is Road 21 (E8), which follows the Tornio Valley upstream from Tornio, continuing beside various tributaries that form the border with Sweden, eventually to cross into Norway near Kilpisjärvi.

When exploring this region, the need for proper clothing and equipment cannot be over-stressed: climatic changes are rapid and, for all its magnificence, the Arctic wilderness can be a ruthless place. In summer take plenty of mosquito repellent, preferably purchased from a local *apteekki* (pharmacy), which will be able to recommend the most effective product.

LEFT: snow travel.
BELOW: tending reindeer.

Rovaniemi, Lapland's capital

From Kemi, Road 4 follows the valley of the Kemi-joki. You reach **Rovaniemi ❶** within 115 km (70 miles). This administrative capital of Lapland, on the cusp of the Arctic Circle, is the launching point for most trips into the province.

The town has been completely rebuilt since World War II, and the population now stands at 60,000, including students at the University of Lapland. The reconstruction plan for Rovaniemi was made by Alvar Aalto who also designed the fine **Lappia House** complex on Hallituskatu, containing a theatre, library and congress facilities.

Half underground, the eye-catching **Arktikum** (Pohjoisranta 4; June–Aug daily 9am–7pm; Sept–May Tues–Sun 10am–5pm or 6pm; entrance charge; tel: 016 322 3260) houses the Arctic Centre and the Provincial Museum of Lapland. The Arctic Centre illustrates Arctic history and culture; it is a good introduction to Lapland's nature, Sami traditions and Rovaniemi's history. Get a feeling for bygone days in the 19th-century farm buildings at **Pöykkölä Museum** (June–Aug Tues–Sun noon–6pm; entrance charge; tel: 050 325 2017), by the Kemi river, 3 km (2 miles) to the south. **Rovaniemen Taidemuseo** (Rovaniemi Art Museum, Lapinkävijäntie 4; Tues–Sun noon–5pm; entrance

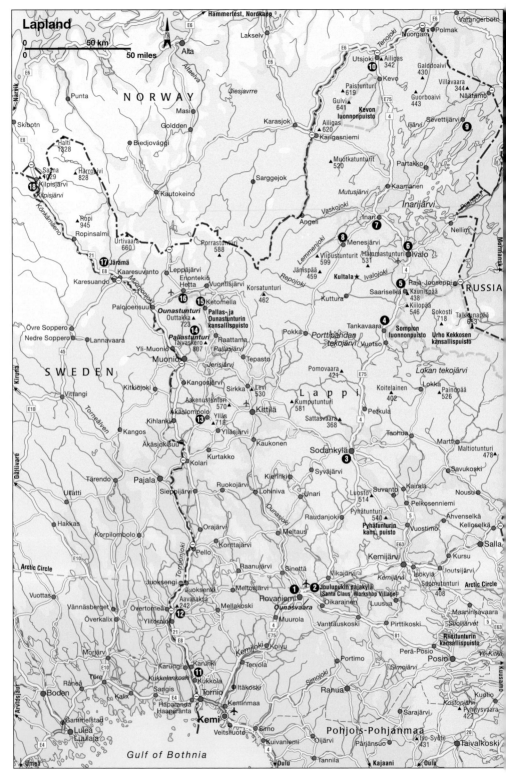

charge; tel: 016 322 2822) has the Wihuri collection of modern Finnish art and various changing exhibitions.

Rising up from the confluence of the Ounasjoki and Kemijoki to the south of Rovaniemi are the wooded slopes of **Ounasvaara**, a well-developed skiing area and the site of annual international winter games. It's also a favourite gathering place on Midsummer Night.

Map on page 346

Land of Santa Claus

About 8 km (5 miles) from the town on Road 4, soon after the turn-off for Rovaniemi airport, **Joulupukin Pajakylä** ❷ (Santa Claus' Workshop Village; June–Aug daily 9am–6pm or 7pm; Sept–May 10am–5pm; free; tel: 016 356 2096) straddles the Arctic Circle. Its post office annually handles thousands of letters from children. There are some good shops, a puppet theatre, art exhibitions, a glass factory, a few reindeer and, of course, Santa Claus.

At Syväsenvaara, 5 km (3 miles) from Rovaniemi, is **Santapark** (for opening hours tel: 016 333 0000; www.santapark.com), an amusement park which has fun rides and attractions for children.

Rovaniemi lies just 8 km (5 miles) south of the Arctic Circle.

You will notice that the landscapes – predominantly forested – are becoming progressively emptier as you travel north. However, there are reindeer aplenty and the occasional elk, so do drive slowly; keep your eyes open and your camera handy – they say white reindeer bring good luck. One of the best fell areas east of Road 4 is centred on **Pyhätunturi**, about 135 km (84 miles) northeast of Rovaniemi. Another, just north of it, is **Luostotunturi**, south of Sodankylä.

Sodankylä ❸, 130 km (80 miles) from Rovaniemi, is the first substantial place along this route. It is the home of the Midnight Sun Film Festival held each June. Next to its 19th-century stone church, its wooden predecessor is Lapland's oldest church, dating from 1689.

BELOW: Santa Claus out for a stroll.

Gold country

Northwards, there's little to detain you for the next 100 km (60 miles) or so until, a few miles beyond Vuotso, you reach **Tankavaara** ❹. Gold panning has been practised in various parts of Lapland for well over a century, and at **Tankavaara Gold Village**, its **Kulta-museo** (Gold Museum) not only chronicles man's historical endeavours to find gold, but for a modest fee gives tuition and allows you to pan for gold. There are cabins where you may lodge and a simple restaurant (tel: 016 626 171; www.tankavaara.fi).

About 40 km (25 miles) further north there is more self-catering accommodation, together with modern hotels and sports facilities, centred on **Laanila** and **Saariselkä** ❺, an immensely popular winter sports centre with good facilities.

Ivalo and Inari

Another 23 km (14 miles) north is the turning for Ivalo airport, Finland's northernmost. **Ivalo** ❻ is the largest community in northern Lapland, though in terms of Sami culture it is much less important than Inari. There is, however, an attractive wooden Orthodox church tucked away in the woods, serving the

Skolt Sami, a branch of the Sami people who formerly lived in territory ceded to the Soviet Union in 1944. They have different costumes, language and traditions from the Finnish Sami, and some now breed sheep as well as reindeer. Ivalo's Lutheran Church stands near the bridge which carries Road 4 over the Ivalojoki; then it's a further 39 km (27 miles) to **Inari ❼**, much of it a delightful route along parts of the shores of Inarijärvi. Inari village is an excellent base for wilderness exploration; you can lodge at the traditional Hotel Inarin Kultahovi (tel: 016 671 221; www.hotelkultahovi.fi).

Though smaller than Ivalo, Inari is the administrative centre for a vast if sparsely populated area, and a traditional meeting place for colourfully costumed Sami people, especially during the church festivals of Lady Day and Easter Day.

Inarijärvi is Finland's third-largest lake, covering 1,300 sq km (500 sq miles) and is dotted with 3,000 islands, some of them considered sacred according to Sami tradition. Boat trips and sightseeing flights are available during the summer to the holy **Ukko Island**.

Inari's excellent **Saamelaismuseo** (Siida Sami Museum; June–Sept daily 9am–8pm; Oct–May Tues–Sun 10am–5pm; entrance charge; tel: 0400 898 212; www.samimuseum.fi) comprises a modern museum building and an open-air section *(skansen)* with old buildings and equipment illustrating the traditionally nomadic way of life. There are also some exhibits on early Skolt Sami culture and modern Sami life. The Siida building also houses the **Ylä-Lapin Luontokeskus** (Northern Lapland Nature Centre), which sells fishing permits and assists in hiking plans for those wishing to explore the wilderness. Be sure to leave time to shop at Inari's many fine handicraft shops that include a silversmith's shop and a knife-making studio.

BELOW: reindeer sledging is a popular activity.

SLEDGING

The easiest way to get across Lapland's vast, icy and largely flat landscape has always been on skis or sledges, the latter less exhausting for longer distances. There are many types of sledging, but the most popular and readily associated with northern Finland is the dog sledge. Four or six husky dogs, hardy beasts naturally acclimatised to snow and ice, are harnessed to the front of the sledge, with passengers standing on the back runners. Unlike horses, the huskies are not readily controllable, so keeping the sledge stationary is done with a hook wedged deep in the snow. Once the hook is withdrawn, the dogs lurch forward.

Reindeer-sledging, as epitomised by images of Santa and his sleigh at Christmas, is another method of getting around, with the advantage that these animals can cover longer and more snowy distances, although they travel more slowly than dogs.

Many centres in Lapland now offer the chance of sledging excursions for tourists – contact tourist offices in main towns for details. It is essential that the right equipment is worn: thermals, waterproofs, hats and goggles are necessary to combat the dampness and brightness of the snow.

Towards Norway

Road 955 from Inari leads 40 km (25 miles) southwest to **Menesjärvi** , a Sami settlement from which one can continue by road then river boat or on foot up the wild and beautiful **Lemmenjoki Valley** ("river of love") to a remote gold prospectors' camp. From Menesjärvi, Road 955 continues across Lapland to join Road 79 at Kittilä. Around Inari and north of it, the road passes a number of attractive holiday centres, mostly of the self-catering variety. After 26 km (16 miles) you come to Kaamanen from which a minor road branches northeast 100 km (60 miles) to **Sevettijärvi** ●, the modern main settlement for the Skolt Sami. An interesting time to be there is during the Easter Orthodox festival. While there, visit the Sami graveyard, with its unusual turf-covered graves.

A couple of kilometres north of Kaamanen take the minor road to **Utsjoki** ●, 94 km (58 miles) away on the border with Norway, passing a series of beautiful lakes close to the eastern fringes of the **Kevon Luonnonpuisto** (Kevo Nature Park). Utsjoki is an important Sami community close to Finland's northernmost point. Its church (built 1860) is one of the few pre-World War II churches still standing in Lapland.

The village and road follow the Utsjoki downstream to join with the Tenojoki, a renowned salmon river. As you approach the Norwegian border at **Kirkenes**, the landscape changes dramatically. You can connect with a variety of routes, eventually returning into western Lapland at Kilpisjärvi or Enontekiö.

Leather goods and "puukko" knives are among the best buys in Lapland.

Western Lapland

Your route through western Lapland is likely to begin at **Tornio** about 80 km (50 miles) south of the Arctic Circle. The earlier stretches of the **Way of the Four Winds** (E8) present a very different face of Lapland from the Arctic Road, for the lower section of the Tornio valley is much more populated, and served by Finland's northernmost railway branch to Kolari.

BELOW: panning for gold, Tankavaara.

In its southern stages the road passes through a string of small communities mainly based, in these marginally milder and more fertile conditions, on agriculture and dairy farming. The Tornionjoki is a good salmon river. Perch, whitefish, grayling, trout and even Arctic char can be found in Lapland's waters. Local travel agencies will organise guided fishing trips complete with gear and permits. At **Kukkola** ⓫ look out for the **Kukkolankoski rapids**; people used to ride the rapids while standing on a log.

About 70 km (43 miles) north of Tornio, beyond Ylitornio, is the 242-metre (794-ft) high **Aavasaksa Hill** ⓬, the most southerly point from which the Midnight Sun can be seen, attracting considerable throngs for Midsummer Eve festivities. A few miles nearer Juoksenki, you cross the Arctic Circle. The scenery becomes wilder as you pass between Pello and Kolari.

Fell country

About 10 km (7 miles) north of Kolari, a detour by Road 940 to the right leads to **Akäslompolo** ⓭. This well-equipped tourist resort and skiing centre, on the shores of a small lake, is set among magnificent

Map on page 346

In northern Lapland the sun stays above the horizon from late May to late July. Autumn is known as "Ruska", when the leaves turn explosive shades of red, yellow and orange.

BELOW: traditional wooden cabin.
RIGHT: Lemmenjoki National Park.

forested hills and bare-topped fells; the highest is **Ylläs**, at 718 metres (2,355 ft), served by chair lifts. A marked trail follows the chain of fells stretching northwards from here, eventually leading in about 150 km (90 miles) to the **Pallastunturi ⓴** fell group. It's a glorious trail with overnight shelter available in untended wilderness huts. Off-road biking is also a possibility with trails for various levels of expertise.

From Akäslompolo you can continue north along minor roads and in 31 km (19 miles) turn left onto Road 79. This is the main road from Rovaniemi, providing an alternative approach to western Lapland. Road 957 to the right is recommended as the best approach to Enontekiö. A further branch left off this route leads from Road 79 to the lonely hotel complex of **Pallastunturi ⓯**, magnificently cradled in the lap of five of the 14 fells which make up the Pallastunturi group. From here the choice of fell walks includes the long-distance 60-km (37-mile) trail north from Yl.lästunturi across the fells to Enontekiö.

Enontekiö ⓰, also known as Hetta, sprawls along the northern shore of Ounasjärvi (lake), looking across to the great rounded shoulders of the Ounastunturi fells. Most of Enontekiö's buildings are modern, including the pretty wooden church which has an altar mosaic depicting Sami people.

Soaring mountains

From **Palojoensuu**, Road 21 continues northwest along the Muonionjoki and Könkämäeno valleys, the scenery becoming even wilder and more barren. A little north of Kaaresuvanto you cross the coniferous tree line and pass the last of the spindly pines.

At **Järämä ⓱**, 10 km (6 miles) further from the tiny settlement of Markkina, German soldiers built fortifications during a standstill in the Lapland War of 1944. Many of these bunkers have been restored and are now open to the public. South and north of **Ropinsalmi**, the mountains reach ever greater heights; the highest, **Halti**, soars up to 1,328 metres (4,357 ft) on the Norwegian border at Finland's northwesternmost point. More accessible and distinctive is Saana, at 1,029 metres (3,376 ft), above the village and the resort of **Kilpisjärvi ⓲**.

Kilpisjärvi is an excellent launching pad for wilderness enthusiasts. There is a lake of the same name whose western shore forms the border with Sweden, and a marked trail which takes about a day and leads to the boundary stone marking the triple junction of Finland, Sweden and Norway.

Motorboats take visitors to the **Mallan Luonnonpuisto**, a nature reserve to the north of the lake (entry permit required: details from Kilpisjärven Retkeilykeskus, tel: 016 537 771). Within the reserve, there is a pleasant 15-km (9-mile) trek.

The rest of these immense, empty, rugged acres are as free to all comers as the elements – and as unpredictable. Never set off without proper equipment and provisions and, unless you are experienced in such landscapes, a guide; always inform someone where you are heading and when you expect to return. Simple advice, but it cannot be said often enough. ❑

INSIGHT GUIDES

TRAVEL TIPS

SCANDINAVIA

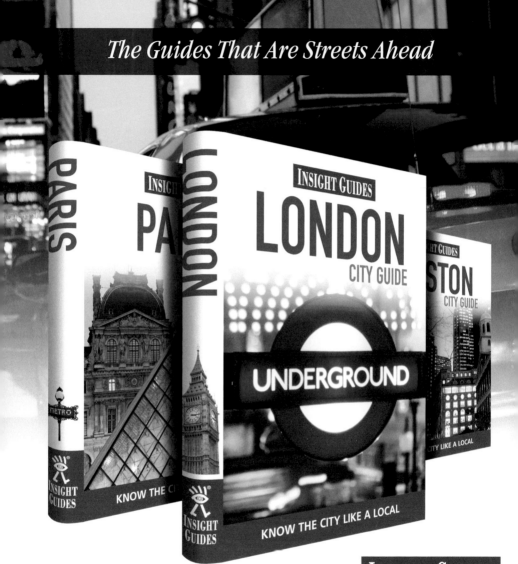

TRAVEL TIPS

DENMARK

A – Z

Activities **356**
Before You Go **356**
Business Hours **356**
Children **357**
Climate **357**
Disabled Travellers **357**
Embassies & Consulates .. **357**
Health **358**
Language **358**
Media **359**
Money **359**
Nightlife **359**
Postal Services **360**
Public Holidays **360**
Shopping **361**
Telecommunications **362**
Tourist Offices **362**
Transport **362**
Visas and Passports **364**
What to Bring/Read **364**

Accommodation

Copenhagen **365**
Zealand **366**
Bornholm **367**
Funen **367**
Jutland **367**
Greenland **368**
Faroe Islands **368**

Eating Out

Copenhagen **369**
Zealand **370**
Bornholm **370**
Funen **370**
Jutland **371**
Greenland **371**
Faroe Islands **371**

NORWAY

A – Z

Activities **372**
Before You Go **373**
Business Hours **373**
Children **373**
Climate **374**
Culture **374**
Disabled Travellers **375**
Embassies in Oslo **375**
Health **375**
Language **376**
Media **377**

Money **377**
Nightlife **377**
Shopping **378**
Telecommunications **378**
Tourist Information **378**
Tour Operators **379**
Transport **380**
Visas and Passports **385**
What to Bring/Read **385**

Accommodation

Oslo **388**
Around Oslo **388**
Stavanger **389**
Bergen **389**
Trondheim **390**
Tromsø **390**

Eating Out

Oslo **392**
Stavanger **392**
Bergen **393**
Trondheim **393**
Tromsø **393**

SWEDEN

A – Z

Activities **394**
Business Hours **395**
Children **395**
Climate **396**
Culture **396**
Disabled Travellers **397**
Embassies & Consulates .. **397**
Health **397**
Language **397**
Media **398**
Money **399**
Nightlife **399**
Postal Services **401**
Public Holidays **401**
Shopping **401**
Telecommunications **402**
Tourist Information **402**
Transport **403**
Visas and Passports **406**
What to Bring/Read **406**

Accommodation

Stockholm **408**
Around Stockholm **409**
Malmö **409**
Göteborg **409**
Southern Sweden **410**
Gotland **410**

The West Coast **410**
The Great Lakes **410**
Göta Kanal **411**
Dalarna **411**
The Central Heartlands **415**
Lapland **415**
The Northeast Coast **415**

Eating Out

Stockholm **412**
Around Stockholm **413**
Southern Sweden **414**
Gotland **414**
The West Coast **414**
The Great Lakes **414**
Göta Kanal **415**
The Central Heartlands **415**
Lapland **415**
The Northeast Coast **415**

FINLAND

A – Z

Activities **416**
Business Hours **417**
Before You Go **417**
Children **417**
Climate **417**
Culture **417**
Disabled Travellers **418**
Health **419**
Language **419**
Media **420**
Nightlife **420**
Postal Services **421**
Public Holidays **421**
Shopping **421**
Telecommunications **422**
Tourist Information **422**
Transport **422**
What to Bring/Read **424**

Accommodation

Helsinki **425**
The South **426**
Lakeland **426**
The West Coast **427**
Karelia **427**
Lapland **427**

Eating Out

Helsinki **428**
The South **429**
Lakeland **429**
The West Coast **430**
Lapland **430**

A – Z

A HANDY SUMMARY OF DENMARK, ARRANGED ALPHABETICALLY

A Activities 356	**G** Gay and Lesbian Travellers 358
B Before You Go 356	**H** Health 358
Business Hours 356	**L** Language 358
C Children 357	**M** Media 359
Climate 357	Money 359
D Disabled Travellers 357	**N** Nightlife 359
E Embassies and Consulates 357	**P** Postal Services 360

S Shopping 361
T Telecommunications 362
Tourist Offices/Operators 362
Transport 362
V Visas and Passports 364
W What to Bring 364
What to Read 364

A ctivities

Outdoor Sports

Angling
Anglers must have fishing permits, which can be obtained at any post office or tourist office, or online at www.fisketegn.dk. Fishing rights in lakes and streams are usually privately owned but permits can often be hired from the local tourist office.

Golf
There are more than 140 golf courses in Denmark. Guests are welcomed at Danish golf clubs on presentation of a valid membership card from their home club. Two worth trying are:
Smørum Golfklub
Skebjergvej 46
Tel: 44 97 01 11
www.smorumgolfklub.dk
Danish Golf Union
Broendby Station 20
Tel: 43 26 27 00. Fax: 43 26 27 01
www.dgu.org

Hiking
There are many beautiful places for hiking in Denmark. Local tourist offices have maps of tested walks and will help you to plan routes. Try walking from Rødvig (just an hour

south of Copenhagen) along the lovely wooded chalk cliffs of Stevns to Bøgeskov harbour (22 km/ 13 miles).

Sailing
Boats and yachts are available for hire on a weekly basis. Visitors should ask to see a certificate from the Shipping Inspection office before hiring a boat. Contact the main tourist office of the region you will be visiting to obtain lists of local boat-hire companies.

Swimming
There are excellent swimming facilities in most Danish towns as well as several funparks with water slides etc. for children. Tourist offices have details. Copenhagen has a superb swimming-pool complex containing six different pools: Vandkulturhuset, DGI-byen, Tietgensgade 65, near the Central Station. Tel: 33 29 80 00.

B efore You Go

● **UK** VisitDenmark, 55 Sloane Street, London SW1X 9SY; tel: 020 7259 5959; fax: 020 7259 5955; e-mail: london@visitdenmark.com; www.visitdenmark.com.
● **US** VisitDenmark, PO Box 4649, Grand Central Station, New York, NY 10163-4649; tel: 212-885 9700; fax: 212-885 9726. e-mail: info@goscandinavia.com; www.visitdenmark.com.
The following websites provide useful information:
● **Denmark Hotel list**
www.dkhotellist.com

Business Hours

Offices: 8/9am–4/5pm.
Shops: Mon–Thur until 5.30pm; Fri until 7pm (8pm in Copenhagen); Sat 9am–noon or 5pm. All are closed on Sunday except for bakeries and kiosks, some of which are open around the clock.
Pharmacies: As shops except Steno Apotek in Copenhagen

(across the street from the train station) which opens all hours.
Supermarkets: until 7/8pm, at least in Copenhagen. The one at the railway station opens all hours.
Banks: Mon–Fri 10am–4pm, some till 6pm Thur.
Post offices: Mon–Fri 9am–5pm, Sat 9am–noon.

● **Wonderful Copenhagen**
Guide to the city:
www.visitcopenhagen.com
● **The Faroe Islands Tourist Board**
www.faroeislands.com
● **Greenland Tourism**
www.greenland-guide.gl or
www.greenland.com

C hildren

Denmark is a peaceful, safe country
with many suitable attractions, such
as amusement parks, playgrounds,
parks and children's theatres. Many
museums have opened children's
sections, and music festivals are
often arranged so kids can take part.
Highlights include:

Copenhagen

Experimentarium (Science Centre)
Tuborg Havnevej 7, Hellerup
Tel: 39 27 33 33
www.experimentarium.dk
A hands-on science museum where
you can try more than 300 experiments with sound, light, water,
currents and more. With short
demonstrations and special exhibits.
Open Mon–Fri 9.30am–5pm (Tues
until 9pm); Sat and Sun 11am–5pm.
Zoologisk Have (Zoo)
Roskildevej 32
Tel: 72 200 200
www.zoo.dk
There is a special children's zoo
here, where children are allowed to
pet the animals, watch chickens
peck their way out of eggs and ride
on ponies. Open daily 9am–4pm or
6pm.
Puppet Theatre
Over the summer there are free
puppet shows for small children in
Kongens Have (the Royal Gardens)
near Rosenborg Palace. At 2pm and
3pm, Tues–Sun.
Tivoli
Vesterbrogade 3
Tel: 33 15 10 01
www.tivoli.dk
The world-famous amusement park,
Tivoli, just across from Central
Station, is a delight, with a huge
variety of rides, parades and summer
pantomimes. Open mid-Apr–mid-Sept
Sun–Thur 11am–11pm, Fri and Sat
11am–midnight.

Outside Copenhagen

Bakken
A traditional amusement park in the
beautiful Dyrehaven area near
Klampenborg. This is also a perfect
place for a walk in the countryside.
Open daily mid-Mar–31 Aug, times
vary. Tel: 39 63 35 44; www.bakken.dk
Benneweis Circus
The largest touring circus in northern

ABOVE: riding high in Tivoli Gardens.

Europe. Check the website for tour
dates; www.benneweis.dk.
Legoland
The original Legoland, built out of 45
million bricks, with rides and a water
playground. Open daily mid-Mar–end
Oct. Tel: 75 33 13 33; www.legoland.dk
Lejre Research Centre
Historical-archaeological centre in
Zealand with a reconstructed Iron
Age village. Children can grind flour,
chop wood, paddle log canoes
and make Viking bread. Open
May–mid-Sept and 3rd week in Oct.
Tel: 46 48 08 78. www.lejre-center.dk

Climate

Denmark's temperate marine climate
keeps the weather mild, with the North
Atlantic Drift, part of the Gulf Stream,
providing a warming influence. Average
rainfall is 660 mm (26 in) a year.
The swimming season starts
(except for true masochists) in mid-
May and ends in September.

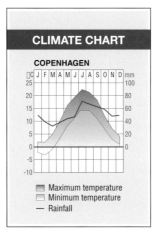

CLIMATE CHART

COPENHAGEN

■ Maximum temperature
□ Minimum temperature
— Rainfall

Be prepared for a variable climate
and remember to dress for cold and
wet weather in the winter and spring.

D isabled Travellers

The Danish tourist board publishes
an excellent disabled travel guide,
although it only covers the West
Jutland region to date (www.disabled
travelguide.com).
For a list of hotels with facilities
for disabled guests, consult the
Danish Accommodation Guide.
Tourist information offices have a
list of restaurants and businesses
with special facilities for disabled
guests. In Denmark as a whole, a lot
of thought and consideration is given
to the comfort and unhindered
access to all parts of society for
citizens and visitors with disabilities.
For further information contact:
Danske Handicaporganisationer,
Kløverprisvej 10b, DK-2650 Hvidovre
Tel: 36 75 17 17. Fax: 36 75 14 03.
www.handicap.dk

E mbassies and Consulates

The following embassies and
consulates are in Copenhagen.
● **Australia**
Dampfaergevej 26
Tel: 70 26 36 76
www.denmark.embassy.gov.au
● **Canada**
Kristen Bernikowsgade 1
Tel: 33 48 32 00
www.canada.dk
● **Germany**
Stockholmsgade 57
Tel: 35 45 99 00
www.kopenhagen.diplo.de
● **UK**
Kastelsvej 40
Tel: 35 44 52 00
www.britishembassy.gov.uk/denmark

DENMARK

NORWAY

SWEDEN

FINLAND

● **US**
Daghammarskjölds Allé 24
Tel: 33 41 71 00
www.denmark.usembassy.gov

ay and Lesbian Travellers

Denmark is one of the most liberal and gay-friendly countries in the world. It has had anti-discrimination laws since 1987, and in 1989 was the first nation to recognise same-sex marriages. The age of consent for homosexuals is 15, the same as for heterosexuals.

Copenhagen is a very welcoming city for gay people and has been for years. Its first gay bar, Centralhjørnet, opened over 80 years ago and is still open today. There are smaller gay scenes in towns such as Århus and Odense.

Tourist offices in Copenhagen will provide a list of the latest venues and events or visit the comprehensive website www.copenhagen-gay-life.dk. The National Association for Gays and Lesbians, **LBL**, is at Teglegårdstræde 13, 1452 Copenhagen, tel: 33 13 19 48; www.lbl.dk.

In August Copenhagen has an annual gay pride parade, **Copenhagen Pride** (www.copenhagen pride.dk), and every October hosts a **Gay and Lesbian Film Festival** (www.cglff.dk).

Some of the most popular gay venues include:
Oscar Bar café
Rådhuspladsen 77, tel: 33 12 09 99; www.oscarbarcafe.dk.
Cosy Bar
Studiestræde 24, tel: 33 12 74 27; www.myspace.com/cosybar
Masken Bar
Studiestræde 33, tel: 33 91 09 37; www.maskenbar.dk
For more information see www.out-and-about.dk.
www.gayguide.dk

ealth

Standards of hygiene in Scandinavia are among the highest in the world. There are no major health hazards and the tap water is safe to drink.

The Danish medical system will assist anyone in an emergency; however you should take out travel insurance before you leave. British nationals should take a European Health Insurance Card (EHIC), which you can apply for online (www.ehic.org.uk), by phone (0845 606 2030), or by post (form available from any post office in the UK). You will be charged for doctors' and dentists' consultations and prescriptions, but not hospital treatment. To get a refund, take the receipts and your EHIC and passport to the local council. Citizens of other countries should ensure that they take out private health insurance before departing for Denmark.

Medical Services

Health care is generally free in Denmark. Acute illnesses or accidents will be treated at the casualty department of the nearest hospital. You can contact a doctor on 70 13 00 41; outside normal business hours, tel: 70 13 00 41 or 38 88 60 41.

Pharmacies

Most operate normal business hours. But there is also a 24-hour pharmacy in every region, the name and address of which is posted on the door of every pharmacy (or look in the *Yellow Pages* telephone directory under *Apotek*).

Dental Services

Dental care is available by appointment only. Check the listings under *Tandlæger* in the *Yellow Pages*. **Tandlægevagten**, Oslo Plads 14, Copenhagen, tel: 35 38 02 51, is open for personal callers on an emergency basis daily 8–9.30pm and weekends and holidays 10am–noon.

anguage

Pronunciation

The old joke says that Danish is not so much a language as a disease of the throat, and so it sometimes seems. Danish has three extra letters – æ, ø, and å – plus unpronounceable sub-glottal stops, and myriad dialects and accents. Here are a few simple rules of thumb for pronouncing vowels:
a = a, as in bar
å = aw, as in paw
æ = e, as in pear
e = e, as in bed
i = ee, as in sleep
ø = u, as in fur

General

yes/no *ja/nej*
big/little *stor(t)/lille*
good/bad *god(t)/dårlig(t)*
possible/impossible *muligt/umuligt*
hot/cold *varm/kold*
much/little *meget/lidt*
many/few *mange/få*
and/or *og/eller*
please/thank you *vær så venlig/tak*
I *jeg*
you *(formal) du (De)*

he/she *han/hun*
it *den/det*
we *vi*
you *(plural, formal) I (De)*
they *de*
foreigner *udlænding*
foreign *fremmed*

Medical

pharmacy *(et) apotek*
hospital *(et) hospital*
casualty *(en) skadestue*
doctor *(en) læge*

Food and Drink

breakfast *morgenmad*
lunch *(break) frokost (pause)*
dinner *middag*
tea *te*
coffee *kaffe*
beer *(bottle/draught) øl/fadøl*

Getting Around

left *venstre*
right *højre*
street *(en) gade/vej*
bicycle (path) *(en) cykel (sti)*
car *(en) bil*
bus/coach *(en) bus*
train *(et) tog*
ferry *(en) færge*
bridge *(en) bro*
traffic light *(et) trafiklys*
square *(et) torv*
north *nord*
south *syd*
east *øst*
west *vest*

Buying a Ticket

ticket *billet*
adult *voksen*
child *barn*
single *enkelt*
return *retur*

Money

How much is it? *Hvad koster det?*
Can I pay with... *Må jeg betale med...*
travellers' cheques *rejsechecks*
money *penge*
notes/coins *sedler/mønter*
Please may I have...? *Må jeg få...?*
the bill *regningen*
May I have a...? *Må jeg få en...?*
receipt *kvittering*
bank *(en) bank*
exchange *veksle*
open *åben*
closed *lukket*
MOMS *value-added tax (VAT)*

Time

good morning *godmorgen*
good day/evening *goddag*
goodnight *godaften/godnat*
today *i dag*
tomorrow *i morgen*
yesterday *i går*

morning *formiddag*
noon *middag*
afternoon *eftermiddag*
evening *aften*
night *nat*
What time is it? *Hvad er klokken?*
It's five o'clock *Den er fem*

Place Names

Copenhagen *København*
Elsinore *Helsingør*
Zealand *Sjælland*
Funen *Fyn*
Jutland *Jylland*

Days of the Week

Monday *mandag*
Tuesday *tirsdag*
Wednesday *onsdag*
Thursday *torsdag*
Friday *fredag*
Saturday *lørdag*
Sunday *søndag*

Numbers

1 *en/et*
2 *to*
3 *tre*
4 *fire*
5 *fem*
6 *seks*
7 *syv*
8 *otte*
9 *ni*
10 *ti*
11 *elleve*
12 *tolv*
13 *tretten*
14 *fjorten*
15 *femten*
16 *seksten*
17 *sytten*
18 *atten*
19 *nitten*
20 *tyve*
21 *enogtyve*
30 *tredive*
40 *fyrre*
50 *halvtreds*
60 *tres*
70 *halvfjerds*
80 *firs*
90 *halvfems*
100 *hundrede*

Media

Newspapers and Magazines

English-language newspapers are widely available at all main train stations, as well as kiosks. You can also read them free at the Central Library, Krystalgade 15 or Café Europa, Amagertorv 1, Copenhagen.

The English-language weekly *The Copenhagen Post* (www.cphpost.dk) has information, Danish news, entertainment and restaurant guides (from tourist offices and newsstands). The very informative booklet *Copenhagen This Week* (www.ctw.dk), actually published monthly, offers the most comprehensive listings information.

Books

Many of the public libraries have a good selection of books in English, and Copenhagen has bookshops that specialise in foreign literature *(see Shopping, page 361).*

Television

There are many satellite/cable channels featuring CNN, BBC and MTV in English. In addition, there are often movies in English without subtitles on the national channels DR1, DR2 and TV2.

Radio

A high percentage of music on Danish radio is in English. For news in English, tune in to Radio Denmark at 1062kHz medium wave Mon–Fri 8.40am, 5.10pm and 10pm.

Internet

To get the latest on what's going on in and about town, consult the following websites:
www.ctw.dk: *Copenhagen This Week*.
www.aok.dk: all about Copenhagen.
www.visitcopenhagen.dk: the Tourist Board site.
www.woco.dk: shopping, eating etc.
www.out-and-about.dk: gay life.

Music Festivals

These are just a few of the music festivals taking place in Denmark every year.
Copenhagen Jazz Festival
For 10 days in July the streets of Copenhagen are filled with the sound of jazz. One of the world's best jazz festivals;
www.jazzfestival.dk.
Skanderborg Festival
"Denmark's most beautiful festival" featuring Danish and international acts is held in August in a beechwood;
www.smukfest.dk.
Roskilde Festival
Late June/early July near Roskilde on Zealand. The largest music festival in Denmark and one of the biggest in Europe, featuring major acts from around the world;
www.roskilde-festival.dk.
Skagen Festival
In July at the northernmost tip of Denmark – beautiful windswept Skagen. One of Denmark's largest folk music festivals;
www.skagenfestival.dk.

Money

Currency

Danish krone (crown); plural kroner; marked kr in shops or DKK internationally; and split into 100 øre. Notes come in 50, 100, 200, 500 and 1,000 denominations. There are 25 and 50 øre coins (both copper coloured), 1 krone, 2 krone, 5 krone (silver-coloured with a hole in the centre), and 10 and 20 krone (solid gold-coloured coins that are similar-looking except the 20 krone piece is a little bigger than the 10 krone).

Changing money

Exchanges are open outside normal business hours at the Copenhagen Central Railway Station, and in the city centre. Forex is open daily 8am–9pm. There are several 24-hour machines near Copenhagen City Hall.

How to pay

Visa and MasterCard are widely accepted in shops. Diner's Club is accepted in many restaurants. American Express cards can sometimes be used in major hotels and shops. All banks and a few shops take travellers' cheques.

Banks and ATMs

Most banks have 24-hour cash machines (ATMs) – look for the word *Kontanten* – and you can draw out up to 2,000DKK, but expect to pay a commission whether you use the machine or cash a cheque at the counter.

Tipping

Service is included in all bills, but a sign of appreciation is often welcomed. In restaurants it is a friendly gesture to pick up the notes but leave the coins. Taxi drivers appreciate it if the fare is rounded up to the nearest 5 or 10DKK.

Nightlife

Information

The best entertainment is found in Copenhagen, Århus and Odense. Check the local newspapers or call tourist information offices for current listings.

BILLETnet is an information network where you can reserve tickets and get details on entertainment events. Tel: 70 15 65 65; www.billetnet.dk.

For details about musical events, contact the **Danish Arts Agency Music Centre**: tel: 33 74 45 00; www.danishmusic.info.0

Copenhagen

Theatre

Most theatre is in Danish even though the piece may have been written in another language.

The London Toast Theatre
Kochsvej 18
Tel: 33 22 86 86
www.londontoast.dk
The only English-language theatre in Copenhagen, showing plays of a high standard. It is most famous for its annual Christmas show, the "Crazy Christmas Cabaret" held in Tivoli Gardens.

Det Kongelige Teater
(The Royal Theatre) Kongens Nytorv
Tel: 33 69 69 69
www.kglteater.dk
Major plays, ballets and symphonies.

The Opera House
Ekvipagemestervej 10
Tel: 33 69 69 69
www.operaen.dk
The impressive new Opera House on the south bank of the river holds major operas.

Wallmans
The Circus Building, Jernbanegade 8
Tel: 33 16 37 00. Fax: 33 16 37 06
www.wallmans.dk
A very popular international dinner show.

Live music

Copenhagen Jazz House
Niels Hemmingsensgade 10
Tel: 33 15 26 00
www.jazzhouse.dk
The place for jazz.

Mojo Blues Bar
Løngangstræde 21C
Tel: 33 11 64 53
www.mojo.dk
Live blues every night.

Pumpehuset
Studiestræde 52

Tel: 33 93 19 60
www.pumpehuset.dk
Big names in modern music.

Rust
Guldbergsgade 8
Tel: 35 24 52 00
www.rust.dk
With three floors, this venue is popular with students and the trendy young.

Vega
Enghavevej 40
Tel: 33 25 70 11
www.vega.dk
Housed in a large 1950s trade union building, this is one of the most popular night life venues in Copenhagen.

Odense

Brandts Klædefabrik
Brandts Passage 37–43
Tel: 66 13 78 97
Music, dance and theatre, with free open-air concerts on summer Saturdays.

Jazzhus Dexter
Vindegade 65
Tel: 63 11 27 28
www.dexter.dk
Live jazz. Denmark's biggest jazz club.

Odense Koncerthus
Claus Berg Gade 9
Tel: 66 12 44 80
www.odensesymfoni.dk
Classical music.

Odense Theatre
Jernbanegade 21
Tel: 66 12 00 52
www.odenseteater.dk
Theatre and opera performances.

Posten
Østre Stationsvej 35
Tel: 66 13 60 20
www.postenlive.dk
Occasional blues/rock/metal gigs.

Public Holidays

● **1 January**	New Year's Day
● **April**	Maundy Thursday, Good Friday, Easter Day and Easter Monday
● **1 May**	Workers' Day
● **May/June**	Whit Monday Ascension Day
● **5 June**	Constitution Day
● **24–6 Dec**	Christmas
● **31 Dec**	New Year's Eve

A floating holiday is **Prayer Day** *(Store Bededag)*, which falls on the fourth Friday after Easter. All shops close on holidays.

Århus

Nightlife is centred around Skolegade.

Fatter Eskil
Skolegade 25
Tel: 86 19 44 11
www.fattereskil.dk
Jazz and blues music, Tuesday to Saturday.

Musikcaféen
Mejlgade 53
Tel: 86 76 03 44
www.musikcafeen.dk
Rock, blues, folk of all kinds.

Musikhuset Århus
Thomas Jensens Allé
Tel: 89 40 40 40
www.musikhusetaarhus.dk
The city's main concert hall, with theatre, dance and music performances.

Train
Toldbodgade 6
Tel: 86 13 47 22
www.train.dk
Concert venue and nightclub, hosting several national/international bands each week.

Cinema

All foreign films are shown with their original soundtrack. Local newspapers have all the details of what's on where.

P ostal Services

Post offices are generally open 9am–5pm on weekdays, and 9am–noon (smaller branches closed) on Saturday. In Copenhagen, the most central **post office**, at the main railway station, opens Mon–Fri 8am–9pm, Sat–Sun 10am–4pm.

Poste restante letters should be collected at the main post office in the region you are in, unless they are specifically addressed to a local post office.

Money orders can be collected or dispatched at all post offices during normal business hours, and

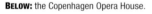

BELOW: the Copenhagen Opera House.

telegrams can be sent by phone –
dial 122 – or from any post office. To
send a fax ask for assistance at a
post office or at your hotel.

R eligious Services

Services are normally on Sunday at
10am, and they are often repeated at
2pm. There are several foreign
congregations in Copenhagen.
St Albans Anglican Church
At Esplanaden near Amaliegade.
English.
Sankt Petri Church
On the corner of Nørregade and Skt
Pedersstræde. In German.
Ohureh of the Reformation
At Gothersgade across the street
from Rosenborg Castle. Shared by a
German and French congregation.
Jewish Synagogue
Krystalgade.
Nusrat Jahan Mosque
Eriksminde Alle 2.
Roman Catholic Church
Skt Ansgars, Bredgade 64.

S hopping

What to Buy

Danish design is famous all over the
world, especially in kitchenware,
furniture and stereo equipment.

Beautiful amber necklaces are to
be found in all jewellery stores, along
with exquisite replicas of ancient
Viking jewellery in silver and gold.

Ceramics and glassware are a
tradition in Denmark and, in addition
to Royal Copenhagen Porcelain, there
are many small ceramic studios
scattered throughout the country.

Danish furs are very popular
among tourists and countless shops
specialise in traditional and modern
knitwear.

Lego bricks originated in Denmark,
but most Danish children's toys are
made of strong, durable wood with
designs and functions that are based
on educational principles.

Feather bedding is a Danish
speciality and many stores sell
down duvets, eiderdowns, quilts and
pillows and can arrange shipment of
bulky items.

Danish pipe makers carve wood
and meerschaum pipes with excellent
craftsmanship.

Tax-free Shopping

Part of the reason for the high prices
is a value-added tax (called MOMS) of
25 percent, added to all sales and
services.

All visitors can avoid making this
contribution to the Danish state by
having their purchases shipped home
directly. Non-EU residents can get a

ABOVE: Illums Bolighus features the best in Danish design.

tax refund by shopping in stores that
offer a tax-free service – minimum
spend is 300DKK. See www.global
refund.com for details. *(See Customs,
page 355 for further details.)*

Shopping in Copenhagen

The main shopping in Copenhagen is
along the "walking street" Strøget,
which is actually four streets that
stretch from the Rådhuspladsen for
about 1 km (¾ mile) to Kongens
Nytorv. Unfortunately, in the last
couple of years or so rising rents
have forced out many of the
characterful small stores and they
have been replaced, mainly, by large
chain stores. But small stores still
remain in the streets parallel and to
the side of Strøget, particularly the
interesting Strædet.

Amber

Copenhagen is the capital of amber,
and in recent years the **House of
Amber** (www.houseofamber.dk) has con-
solidated its position as the leading
retailer in the city and now has five
stores, with the most prominent
being at Kongens Nytorv 2 – which
also includes the Amber Museum,
tel: 33 11 67 00; Nygade 6, tel: 39
55 14 00; Frederiksberggade 34, tel:
33 11 26 44, Langelinie Allé 36, tel:
35 26 36 88 and Vesterbrogade 1B,
tel: 33 11 35 30 – between Tivoli
and the Town Hall Square.

Books

The following shops all have good
selections of foreign-language
literature:
Arnold Busck
Købmagergade 49
Tel: 33 73 35 00.
Atheneum Boghandel
Norregade 6
Tel: 33 12 69 70. Fax: 33 14 69 33.

The Book Trader
Skindergade 23
Tel: 33 12 06 69
www.booktrader.dk
GAD, Central Station
Tel: 33 32 85 58
www.gad.dk
Politikens Boghallen,
Rådhuspladsen 37
Tel: 33 47 25 61. Fax: 33 11 14 10.

Danish Design

DZOO, Designer Zoo
Vesterbrogade 137
Tel/fax: 33 24 94 93
www.dzoo.dk
In this part of now fashionable
Vesterbrogade you will find an
innovative and interesting collection
of clothing, jewellery and
houseware.
Illums Bolighus
Amagertorv 10
Tel: 33 14 19 41
www.royalshopping.dk
Mouthwatering collections of
homeware, from shining teaspoons
to curvy chairs and sofas.
Ofelia
Amagertorv 3
Tel: 33 12 41 98.
Fax: 32 53 38 83
www.ofelia.dk
Found in the heart of Strøget,
this offers the best selection of
goose-down comforters (duvets),
available in international sizes.

Department Stores

Magasin du Nord
Kongens Nytorv 13
Tel: 33 11 44 33
www.magasin.dk
Once the Hotel du Nord and facing
the famous Kongens Nytorv, this
is Denmark's most famous department store and has branches in
other cities in the country.

Fashionwear

Axel Kaufmann
Nygade 2, DK-1164
Tel: 33 13 61 65
This is Europe's largest sweater store. Besides favourites like Dale of Norway it offers a range of stylish Scandinavian products like Sirri (www.sirri.fo), whose products are made out of organic, all-natural, dye-free yarn from the Faroe Islands.

Bruuns Bazaar
Kronprinsensgade 8 & 9
Tel: 33 32 19 99
www.bruunsbazaar.dk
A leading men's and women's fashion design shop, with other branches around Europe and in North America.

Munthe plus Simonsen
Grønnegade 10
Tel: 33 32 03 12
www.muntheplussimonsen.com
A highly fashionable women's store, with a second branch in Århus.

Handicrafts

Danish Crafts, an information centre for Danish handicrafts is situated at Amagertorv 1
Tel: 33 12 61 62
www.danishcrafts.dk

Outdoor Wear

Guns & Gents
Skindergade 31
Tel: 33 91 24 24. Fax: 33 91 24 23
www.gunsandgents.dk
Although primarily a hunting shop, this also has the best collection of waterproof and windproof Barbour jackets – often needed in Copenhagen even in summer.

Helly Hansen
Nøregade 47
Tel: 33 12 20 58
www.hellyhansen.com
This Norwegian based company is famous for its wet- and cold-weather clothing, skiwear, summer wear and children's jumpsuits, particularly popular in Scandinavia.

Porcelain

Royal Copenhagen Porcelain
Amagertorv 6

Copenhagen Card

We recommend that you buy a Copenhagen Card (CPHCARD) at your hotel, the central railway station or the Copenhagen tourist information office. The card gives you free entry to 60 attractions across Copenhagen and north Zealand, free bus/train rides in the same area, and an informative guide. The card is available for periods of 24 and 72 hours.

Tel: 33 13 71 81
www.royalcopenhagen.com
Located in a beautiful building on Strøget, this company celebrated its 230th anniversary in 2005. This flagship store also contains a museum and mini-production line.

Silverwear

Georg Jensen
Amagertorv 4
Tel: 33 11 40 80
www.georgjensen.com
Look no farther than here, on Strøget, for all kinds of beautifully designed silver jewellery.

Stereo Equipment

Bang & Olufsen
Kongens Nytorv 26
Tel: 33 11 14 15
www.bang-olufsen.com
The company's flagship shore, where you can admire their full range of top-quality stereo equipment.

T elecommunications

Phone calls to foreign countries can be made from Statens Teletjeneste offices, above the post office in the Central Railway Station, and next door to the post office in Købmagergade in Copenhagen.

Useful Numbers

● **Police, ambulance, fire** 112
● **Danish directory enquiries** 118
● **International directory enquiries** 113
● **International dialling code** +45

Tourist Offices

There is a tourist office in almost every city, with knowledgeable and friendly staff. They can assist in planning a trip, make reservations, or provide directions and leaflets.
For access to websites and information about all tourist offices in Denmark, visit the central www.visitdenmark.com. Some of the tourist bureaus are:

Copenhagen

Vesterbrogade 4A (across from the Tivoli main entrance)
Tel: 70 22 24 42
www.visitcopenhagen.com

North Zealand

Havnepladsen 3, 3000 Helsingør
Tel: 49 21 13 33. Fax: 49 21 15 77
www.visithelsingor.dk

Southwest Zealand

Stændertorvet 1, 4000 Roskilde
Tel: 46 31 65 65. Fax: 46 31 65 60
www.visitroskilde.com

Bornholm

Ndr. Kystvej 3, 3700 Rønne
Tel: 70 23 20 77. Fax: 56 95 95 68
www.bornholminfo.dk

Funen

Rådhuset, 5000 Odense C
Tel: 66 12 75 20. Fax: 66 12 75 86
www.visitodense.com

East Jutland

Banegårdpladsen 20, 8000 Aarhus C
Tel: 87 31 50 10
www.visitaarhus.com

North Jutland

Østerågade 8, 9000 Aalborg
Tel: 99 31 75 00. Fax: 99 31 75 19
www.visitaalborg.com

West Jutland

Nytorv 9, 8800 Viborg
Tel: 87 87 88 88
Fax: 86 60 02 38
www.viborg.dk

South Jutland

Torvet 3–5, 6760 Ribe
Tel: 75 42 15 00
www.visitribe.dk

Greenland

Greenland Tourism, PO Box 1615, Hans Egedesvej 29, DK-3900 Nuuk, Greenland
Tel: 299 34 28 20
Fax: 299 32 28 77
E-mail: info@greenland.com
www.greenland.com

The Faroe Islands

Vaglið, PO Box 379, FO-110 Tórshavn
Tel: 298 30 24 25. Fax: 298 31 68 31
www.visit-faroeislands.com

Tour Operators

Throughout Denmark

Copenhagen Excursions
Tel: 32 54 06 06. Fax: 32 57 49 05
www.cex.dk

Copenhagen

● To hire an authorised guide to the city, contact: **Meet the Danes**, Ravnsborggade 2, DK-2200 Copenhagen N
Tel: 23 28 43 47
E-mail: info@meetthedanes.dk
www.meetthedanes.dk
● Copenhagen This Week (www.ctw.dk; available free at most hotels and tourist agencies) has a list of tours.

Transport

Getting There

By Air
The two main international airports in Denmark are Copenhagen Kastrup

Airport and Billund Airport in Jutland. Denmark's national carrier is SAS (Scandinavian Airlines System), which is primarily for international traffic. Sterling Airlines flies to other Scandinavian cities, while Cimber Air serves most of the domestic routes. From the UK, British Airways flies daily from London Heathrow to Kastrup Airport. The low-cost operator easyJet flies daily from London Stansted to Copenhagen. Ryanair flies from Stansted to Århus and Billund. Flybmi flies daily from London Heathrow to Copenhagen. SAS, Delta and Continental fly direct from the US to Copenhagen.

From the UK
British Airways Tel: 0844 493 0787
www.ba.com
easyJet Tel: 0871 244 2366
www.easyjet.com
flybmi Tel: 0870 6070 555
www.flybmi.com
Ryanair Tel: 0871 246 000
www.ryanair.com
SAS Tel: 0871 521 2772
www.flysas.com
Sterling Airlines Tel: 0870 787 8038
www.sterling.dk

From the US
Although several airlines fly directly to Copenhagen, an interesting option is to fly **Icelandair** (tel: 800-223 5500; www.icelandair.com), who have direct services from New York, Orlando, Minneapolis and Boston to Reykjavik, Iceland, with connections on to Copenhagen and many other destinations in Europe.
Continental Tel: 1-800 231 0856
www.continental.com
Delta Airlines Tel: 1-800 241 4141
www.delta.com
SAS Tel: 1-800 221 2350
www.flysas.com

By sea
From Germany and Poland
From Germany, ferries connect Puttgarden and Rødby (Lolland). Ferries also run between Rostock and Gedser, and in the summer, Sassnitz and Rønne (Bornholm). Swinoujscie in Poland sends around four ferries per week to Copenhagen.

From Sweden
Sweden operates several lines from Helsingborg to Helsingør (North Zealand) and from Varberg to Grenå (East Jutland); other ferries go from Göteborg to Frederikshavn (North Jutland). From Rønne (Bornholm) there is a ferry to Ystad.

From Norway
Boats go from Oslo to Copenhagen, or to Hirtshals and Frederikshavn in

On Your Bike

The best way to enjoy the Danish landscape is on a bicycle. You would do best to bring your own bike if you want to tour the country, but for getting around the city, a rented one will do. The local tourist information office can tell you where to pick one up.

● For information on routes and practical advice, contact:
Dansk Cyklistforbund (Danish Association of Cyclists)
Rømersgade 7, 1362 Copenhagen K
Tel: 33 32 31 21. Fax: 33 32 76 83
www.dcf.dk
Open Mon–Fri 10am–5.30pm,
Sat 10am–2pm.

● In the centre of Copenhagen you can borrow bikes for free under a scheme operated by City Bikes, from mid-April to November during daylight hours (the bikes have no lights!). You pay 20DKK (inserted into one of the racks scattered

about the inner-city area), which is refunded when you deliver the bike back to one of the stands.
City Bikes
Tel: 36 16 42 33; www.bycyklen.dk

● In addition, there are plenty of places to rent bikes at reasonable prices. Contact:
Cyklebørs
157 Gothersgade
Tel: 33 14 07 17
www.cykleboersen.dk
Københavns Cykler
Reventlowsgade 11
Tel: 33 33 86 13
www.copenhagen-bikes.dk

● Cycle tours of Copenhagen are also available from April to September. Contact:
City Safari Strandgade 27B
Christianshavn
1401 Copenhagen
Tel: 33 23 94 90
www.citysafari.dk

North Jutland; from Bergen and Kristiansand (Norway) there are ferries to Hanstholm and Hirtshals. Ferries from Larvik (Norway) go to Frederikshavn.

From the UK
DFDS Seaways ferries run from Harwich to Esbjerg.

By Rail
Trains arrive daily from Germany, Britain (via Eurostar to Brussels) and Sweden.
● For trains from Britain:
Tel: 08448 484 064
www.raileurope.co.uk
● For train information in Denmark:
Tel: 70 13 14 15
www.rejseplanen.dk

By Coach
Eurolines is the leading operator of scheduled coach services, including nine destinations in Denmark with regular departures from London to Copenhagen, Køge, Ålborg, Århus, Nykøbing Falster and Rødby.
● **Eurolines** Tel: 08717 818181
www.eurolines.co.uk

Getting Around
On Arrival
Almost all international flights arrive and depart from Copenhagen Airport. Trains run six times an hour directly from Terminal 3, the international terminal at Copenhagen Airport, to Central Station and take 13 minutes.

Intercity express trains run from the airport direct to Helsingør and Bornholm.
Trains run between the airport and many major Swedish cities.
The Øresund bridge connects Denmark and Sweden. Starting near Kastrup Airport, you can reach the Swedish city of Malmö in 20–30 minutes, Stockholm in 5 hrs and Gothenburg in 3 hrs 20 minutes.
There is a taxi stand next to Terminal 3.

By Air
If you fly you can be on the other side of Denmark in less than an hour. The main domestic operator, Cimber Airways, has daily flights from Copenhagen to Billund, Bornholm, Karup, Sønderborg and Ålborg.
Cimber Air
Tel: 70 10 12 18
www.cimber.dk

By Metro
Copenhagen's new Metro system (www.m.dk) was extended out to Copenhagen Airport in 2007. Trains run to the city centre every 3–6 minutes from 5am–midnight Sunday to Wednesday, with a less frequent (every 15 minutes) round-the-clock service from Thursday to Saturday.

By Coach (Long-distance Bus)
There is an extensive network of buses throughout Denmark. For details contact Movia Customer

DENMARK

NORWAY

SWEDEN

FINLAND

Service, tel: 36 13 14 15;
www.moviatrafik.dk
Open daily 7am–9.30pm.

By Train
There is a very efficient train service
linking all major cities and some of
the smaller towns.
    There is a boat-train link from
Copenhagen to Rønne, Bornholm.
● For train information, contact the
DSB **Customer Centre**
Tel: 70 13 14 15
www.dsb.dk

By Car
Rules of the Road
Drive on the right, and always give
way at pedestrian crossings and look
out for bicycles when turning right.
Look over your left shoulder every
time you open the doors on the
driver's side – bicycles are everywhere. Overtake on the left only.
    Drivers and passengers must
wear seat belts, and dipped headlights are required. Using a mobile
phone while driving is illegal at all
times. Strict drink-driving laws set
the legal limit for blood-alcohol
content at 0.05 percent – one
drink may put you over.

Speed limits
These are standard speed limits,
which are enforced:
Built-up areas 50 kph (30 mph)
Main roads 80 kph (50 mph)
Motorways 110 kph (70 mph)
For a car with a trailer, the limits are
50 kph (30 mph), 70 kph (40 mph)
and 90 kph (55 mph) respectively.
Roadside assistance

Harbour Tours

One of the best ways of seeing
Copenhagen is on a boat cruising
the main harbour and the canals
around Slotshomen and
Christianshavn.

DFDS Canal Tours
Tel: 32 96 30 00;
www.canaltours.com
DFDS's 60-minute guided tours are
the most popular. Prices are 60DKK
(30DKK for children).They also offer
dinner cruises that last two hours
and cost about 600DKK.

The Netto Boats
Tel: 32 54 41 02
www.nettobaadene.dk
The open-top Netto Boats also
make a 60-minute guided tour of
the harbour and the canals but
cost significantly less at 30DKK
(15DKK for children).

In the event of a breakdown, contact
your car rental company or your own
private insurer.

Car rental
It pays to shop around. Ask travel
agents about special offers, or try
Yellow Pages. **Avis** (tel: 33 26 80
00); **Europcar** (tel: 89 33 11 33);
Budget Rent A Car (tel: 33 91 39
00); **Hertz** (tel: 33 17 90 00);
National Car Rental (tel: 70 25 05
67) and **Sixt Rent A Car** (tel: 32 48
11 00) all have offices all around
the country. You need a valid driving
licence and must be at least 20–25
years old.

By Taxi
Taxis are available at airports, central
train and bus stations and in city
centres. Pick them up at taxi ranks
or flag them down in the street.
● **Århus Taxi**
Tel: 89 48 48 48
● **Copenhagen Taxi**
Tel: 35 35 35 35
● **Odense Mini-Taxi**
Tel: 66 12 27 12

Visas and Passports

A valid passport entitles you to a
stay of up to three months. Visas
are not required for EU citizens, or
those from Canada and the US.
Denmark is a member of the
Schengen Agreement, whereby
citizens of other member states
don't need passports to enter
Denmark. Other nationalities may
need to obtain a visa before arriving.
If in doubt, ask at the nearest
Danish Embassy or Consulate. If
you arrive from another Scandinavian country, you will often find that
passports aren't checked at all. If
you intend to stay longer than three
months you will have to obtain a
resident's permit.

Customs Regulations

Danish customs formalities are
usually painless and baggage is
rarely opened, but it's sensible to
observe the duty-free limits and
other rules.
    Cigarettes, spirits, perfume,
cameras and other luxury items are
relatively expensive in Denmark. The
rules about how much one can bring
into Denmark depend on whether or
not you are coming from an EU
country. Most EU citizens can now
carry almost any amount across EU
borders, so long as it is for "personal
use". If you are coming from outside
the EU, you can bring only 1 litre of
spirits or 2 litres of wine; 200
cigarettes or 50 cigars or 250 g of

tobacco; 500 g of coffee; 100 g of
tea; 50 g of perfume; 250 ml of eau
de toilette; and goods/gifts not
exceeding 1.350DKK in value. It is
wise to check with your local Danish
consul if in doubt. The Danish
customs and tax authority website is:
www.skat.dk.
    Money and cheques may be
brought in freely.

What to Bring

The time of year you are most likely to
encounter good weather is mid-May
to mid-June. Even if you are lucky
enough to travel in a year with a fine
summer, you should still expect some
cold and rainy days. Whatever time of
year you are visiting, it is wise to
bring a sweater and a raincoat.
    Danes dress casually both in their
free time and at work. When going
out for the evening men rarely have
to put on a suit and tie.

What to Read

General

*Complete Hans Christian Andersen
Fairly Tales* (Gramercy Books). The
classic collection of children's tales
by Denmark's master storyteller.
A Conspiracy of Decency by Emmy
Werner (Westview Press). The story
of how Denmark's Jews were saved
from the Nazis, based partly on living
eyewitness accounts.
Culture Shock! Denmark by M.
Strange (Kuperard). A short guide to
Denmark's customs and culture.
Miss Smilla's Feeling for Snow by
Peter Høeg (Flamingo). A worldwide
best-selling novel that spawned a
mediocre film.
The Name of this Book is Dogme 95
by Richard Kelly (Faber). Was
Denmark's most famous cinematic
innovation a genuine breakthrough or
just a clever marketing ploy? Includes
interviews with all the key figures,
including Lars von Trier.
Seven Gothic Tales by Isak Dinesen,
aka Karen Blixen (Penguin Classics).
Dark. dreamy fairytales for adults
from one of Denmark's most
enigmatic 20th-century authors.
The Sixth Floor by Robin Reilly
(Cassell). Dramatic account of the
Danish resistance in World War II
and the tragic consequences of the
British RAF raid on the Gestapo's
Copenhagen headquarters.

Other Insight Guides

Insight Guides which highlight
destinations in this region
are *Smart Guide Copenhagen*,
Step by Step Copenhagen and
Insight Guide Denmark.

A CCOMMODATION

HOTELS, YOUTH HOSTELS, BED AND BREAKFAST

Choosing a Hotel

Danish hotels are not cheap, but have first-class facilities and are very much business-orientated. They are classified by one to five stars by HORESTA (Danish Hotel, Restaurant and Tourist Employers' Association).

Greenland

In Greenland hotels come into the expensive category and there is not a wide selection of alternatives. Make sure of your accommodation before you go.
Greenland Tourism
Tel: 299 34 28 20
www.greenland.com

Faroe Islands

Hotels here were until recently largely designed for visiting sailors. Apart from a few in Torshavn (of which at least two have good facilities), modern hotels are not

plentiful. Private houses and youth hostels provide an alternative.
Faroe Islands Tourist Board
Tel: 298 30 24 25
www.visit-faroeislands.com

Information and reservations

Danish Hotels, www.dkhotellist.com have a very comprehensive list of hotels and other places to stay.
You can book a hotel at the tourist information office opposite Central Station in Copenhagen (open Mon–Fri 9am–4pm, Sat till 2pm; tel: 70 22 24 42).

Family Holidays

Camping/caravanning

You can hire stationary caravans or huts on many campsites (all high standard), or take your own tent. You will need a Camping Card Scandinavia, which you can buy at the first campsite you stay at, or online before travelling. For a list of sites, ask Visit

Denmark or contact:
Camping Rådet (Danish Camping Board)
Tel: 39 27 88 44.
www.campingraadet.dk

Farm Holidays

For details contact:
Landboferie i Danmark
www.bondegaardsferie.dk

Youth Hostels

Denmark has around 100 youth hostels *(vandrerhjem)*. You need to be a member of the Youth Hostel Association in your home country or get in touch with Danhostel www.danhostel.dk for a free catalogue and a list of sites.

Hotel Listings

Hotels are grouped by area, starting with Copenhagen. Within each city or region, they are listed alphabetically.

COPENHAGEN

Hotel d'Angleterre
Kongens Nytorv 34, DK-1050
Tel: 33 12 00 95
www.remmen.dk
Elegant rooms with a rather formal, old-fashioned ambience, plus a palm court, several banquet rooms. **$$$**
Bertram's
Vesterbrogade 107, DK-1620
Tel: 33 25 04 05
www.hotelguldsmeden.dk

Found in trendy Vesterbro, this is a beautiful boutique hotel where all rooms have four-poster beds, balconies and a French colonial decor. Service is superb. 47 rooms. **$$$**
CabInn City
Mitchellsgade 14
Tel: 33 46 16 16
www.cabinn.com
Attractive, functional budget hotel with modern

Danish decor. A good option for families. Only a short walk from the buzzing Tivoli. **$**
Hotel Carlton
Vesterbrogade 66, DK-1620
Tel: 33 12 15 00
www.hotelguldsmeden.dk
Found in a 19th-century building in a popular part of Copenhagen, Bertram's sister hotel has a similar rustic,

French-Colonial feel and equally friendly service. 64 rooms. **$$$**

PRICE CATEGORIES
Price categories are based on the average cost (including tax) of a double room, usually with breakfast: $ = under 1,000DKK $$ = 1,000–1,400DKK $$$ = over 1,400DKK

ABOVE: the grand facade of the Hotel d'Angleterre.

Copenhagen Plaza
Bernstorffsgade 4, DK-1577
Tel: 33 14 92 62
www.profilhotels.se
Commissioned by King Frederik VIII in 1913, this hotel retains its aristocratic style. It has the famous Library Bar, and a location directly between the Central Station and Tivoli Gardens. $$$

First Hotel Sankt Petri
Krystalgade 22, DK-1172
Tel: 33 45 91 00
www.hotelsktpetri.com
This upmarket, modern five-star hotel is located in the ancient centre of the town.

The bathrooms are stunning. There is a good restaurant and a pretty atrium where live jazz is played. You can sit outside in the summer. $$$

First Hotel Vesterbro
Vesterbrogade 23, DK-1620
Tel: 33 78 80 00
www.firsthotels.dk/vesterbro
Centrally placed in Vesterbrogade. All the rooms are a decent size and look down onto an internal airy atrium where you have breakfast. In days of yore it used to be the local porn cinema. $$$

Hilton Copenhagen Airport
Ellehammersvej 20, DK-2770
Tel: 32 50 15 01
www.hilton.com/copenhagen
Featuring Scandinavian furnishings and decor, even the smallest rooms here are the largest in Copenhagen. Although it's right next door to Terminal 3, fantastic soundproofing cuts out all aeroplane noise. $$$

Radisson SAS Royal Hotel
Hammerichsgade 1, DK-1611
Tel: 33 42 65 00
www.royal.copenhagen.radissonsas.com
In a landmark building overlooking Tivoli Gardens, this hotel was designed by the world-renowned architect Arne Jacobsen in 1960. It now has all modern facilities to complement the innovative Scandinavian design. $$$

Radisson SAS Scandinavia Hotel
Amager Boulevard 70, DK-2300
Tel: 33 96 50 00
www.scandinavia.copenhagen.radissonsas.com
Found just outside town, Denmark's largest hotel has rooms in a variety of innovative styles. $$$

The Square
Rådhuspladsen 14, DK-1550
Tel: 33 38 12 00
www.thesquarecopenhagen.com
This exclusive 3-star minimalist-style hotel – the only one of its class with air-conditioning – has a fantastic if noisy location overlooking the Town Hall Square. $$$

Danhostel Copenhagen City
H.C. Andersens Boulevard 50
DK-1553
Tel: 33 11 85 85
www.danhostel.dk/copenhagencity
Europe's largest designer hostel with a great location right in the centre of town and a few minutes' walk from the Central Station. You will need an international YHA card, but the investment is covered by the saving on the cost of a bed. $

Hotel Fy and Bi
Valby Langgade 62, 2500 Valby
Tel: 36 45 44 00
www.hotelfyogbi.dk
A charming 100-year-old hotel and restaurant built around a courtyard and painted in traditional Danish yellow. Close to the zoo. $

ZEALAND

Fredensborg

Hotel Store Kro
Slotsgade 6, DK-3480
Tel: 48 40 01 11
www.storekro.dk
Built as a guest annexe to Fredensborg Castle, this old-fashioned hotel plays up its past. $$

Frederiksværk

Hotel Frederiksværk
Torvet 6, DK-3300
Tel: 47 72 22 88
www.frvhotel.dk
235 years old and located in the centre. $$

Helsingør

Marienlyst Hotel & Casino
N. Strandvej 2, DK-3000
Tel: 49 21 40 00
www.marienlyst.dk
Relaxed hotel complex with

views over the sea and Kronborg Castle. $$$

Køge

Hotel Hvide Hus
Strandvejen 111, DK-4600
Tel: 56 65 36 90
www.hotelhvidehus.dk
Modern hotel with sea views. $$$

Næstved

Hotel Kirstine
Købmagergade 20, DK-4700
Tel: 55 77 47 00
www.hotelkirstine.dk
A charming option, cosy and full of character. $$

Rødby

Hotel E4
Maribo Landevej 4, DK-4970
Tel: 54 60 14 85
www.hotele4.dk

A practical, motel-style option, just 8 km (5 miles) north of the ferry. $

Roskilde

Hotel Prindsen
Algade 13, DK-4000
Tel: 46 30 91 00
www.prindsen.dk
Royal-style building over 300 years old, comfortable and central. $$$

Slagelse

Hotel Frederik d.11
Idagårdsvej 3, DK-4200
Tel: 58 53 03 22
www.fr2.dk
A modern red-brick building near Antvorskou ruins. $$$

Stege

Præstekilde Kro and Hotel
Klintevej 116, Keldby DK-4780

Tel: 55 86 87 88
www.praestekilde.dk
Modern hotel in a pretty area 20 km (12½ miles) from Møn cliffs. $$

Tisvildeleje

Strandhotel
Hovedgaden 75, DK-3220
Tel: 48 70 71 19
www.strand-hotel.dk
Young and arty, near the beach. Popular with both Danes and tourists in summer. $$

Vedbæk

Hotel Marina
Vedbæk Strandvej 391,
DK-2950
Tel: 45 89 17 11
www.choicehotels.dk
Modern hotel, overlooking Vedbæk marina and the beach. $$$

BORNHOLM

Allinge

Hotel Pepita
Langebjergvej 1 Sandvig, DK-3770
Tel: 56 48 04 51
www.pepita.dk
Cosy family-run hotel near beach composed of a traditional 17th-century half-timbered house and modern annexe. $–$$

Hotel Romantik
Strandvejen 68, DK-3770
Tel: 56 48 03 44
www.hotel-romantik.dk
Found right on the shore at Sandvig and very convenient for swimming and fishing. It has newly renovated rooms and flats. Most rooms have views of the Baltic Sea. $$

Svaneke

Hotel Siemsens Gaard
Havnebryggen 9, DK-3740
Tel: 56 49 61 49
www.siemsens.dk
A lovingly restored 17th-century merchant's house found right at Svaneke harbour and with magnificent Baltic Sea views. First

class restaurant. 49 rooms. $$–$$$

Rønne

Det Lille Hotel
Ellekongstæde 2, DK-3700
Tel: 56 90 77 00
www.detlillehotelbornholm.dk
This newly-opened place is a homely choice. $

FUNEN

Odense

Hotel Ansgar
Østre Stationsvej 32, DK-5000
Tel: 66 11 96 93
www.hotel-ansgar.dk
One of the old mission hotels with all facilities. 64 rooms. $$$
City Hotel Odense
Hans Mulesgade 5, DK-5000
Tel: 66 12 12 58
www.city-hotel-odense.dk
Moderately priced three-star with all modern comforts. $$

Det Lille Hotel
Dronningensgade 5, DK-5000
Tel/fax: 66 12 28 21
A friendly and good-value little family hotel on a quiet street near the centre. $
Hotel H.C. Andersen
Radisson SAS
Claus Bergs Gade 7, DK-5000
Tel: 66 14 78 00
www.radisson.com
Good, modern hotel in the old part of town. Conference facilities. $$$
Motel Brasilia/
Blommenslyst Kro

Middelfartvej 420,
DK-5491 Blommenslyst
Tel: 65 96 70 12
www.blommenslyst-kro.dk
Beautiful motel, 8 km (5 miles) west of Odense, added to an old *kro* (inn) with lovely garden. Excellent traditional food. $$
Odense Congress Centre
Ørbækvej 350, DK-5220
Tel: 65 56 01 00
www.occ.dk
Both a congress centre and four-star hotel with 109 rooms. $$$

Ydes Hotel
Hans Tausensgade 11,
DK-5000
Tel: 66 12 11 31
www.ydes.dk
Small hotel. English breakfast. $

Rudkøbing

Rudkøbing Skudehavn
Havnegade 21, DK-5900
Tel: 62 51 46 00
Modern hotel with many facilities. Overlooking the harbour. $$

JUTLAND

Ålborg

Park Hotel
J.F. Kennedys Plads 41, DK-9000
Tel: 98 12 31 33
www.park-hotel-aalborg.dk
Built in 1900, central hotel close to the station. $$

Århus

Hotel Guldsmeden
Aarhus
Guldsmedgade 40, DK-8000
Tel: 86 13 45 50
www.hotelguldsmeden.dk
In a traditional old building that was carefully restored in 1999, this small hotel is one of the most charming in Aarhus. 27 rooms. $$–$$$
Helnan Marselis Hotel
Strandvejen 25,
DK-8000
Tel: 86 14 44 11
www.marselis.dk
Newly renovated, this smart hotel has a swimming pool and all

rooms have impeccable sea views. $$–$$$
Radisson SAS Scandinavia
Margrethepladsen 1, DK-8000
Tel: 86 12 86 65
www.radissonsas.com
Stylish steel and glass building, with large comfortable rooms. $$$
Hotel Royal
Store Torv 4, DK-8000
Tel: 86 12 00 11
www.hotelroyal.dk
Beautiful building, more than 150 years old, but modernised with a fine conservatory restaurant. $$$
Scandic Hotel Plaza Århus
Banegårdspladsen 14, DK-8000
Tel: 87 32 01 00
www.scandichotels.com
Central, with a bar, fitness centre, Jacuzzi and indoor parking. $$$
Villa Provence
Fredens Torv 10, DK-8000
Tel: 86 18 24 00
www.villaprovence.dk
An oasis of charm and

calm in the heart of the city, near the bus station, with all rooms individually designed in the Provençal style. 36 rooms and 3 suites. $$$

Christiansfeld

Den Gamle Grænsekro
Koldingvej 51, DK-6070
Tel: 75 57 32 18
www.graensekroen.dk
Dating back to nearly 1600 this is one of Denmark's royally licensed inns, and only three families have operated in its long and illustrious history. 20 rooms. $

Esbjerg

Hotel Ansgar
Skolegade 36, DK-6700
Tel: 75 12 82 44
www.hotelansgar.dk
This is a 3-star rated hotel, with a very pleasant ambiance, located in the

heart of Esbjerg. 52 rooms. $$–$$$
Hotel Britannia
Torvegade 24, DK-6700
Tel: 75 13 01 11
www.britannia.dk
Found in the centre of town on the Market Square, this modern-style hotel has recently undergone a complete renovation. Its 108 rooms are in sleek, Scandinavian style. $$$

Fanø

Sønderho Kro
Kropladsen 11, DK-6720
Tel: 75 16 40 09
www.sonderhokro.dk

PRICE CATEGORIES

Price categories are based on the average cost (including tax) of a double room, usually with breakfast:
$ = under 1,000DKK
$$ = 1,000–1,400DKK
$$$ = over 1,400DKK

Built in 1722 this is both the town's oldest building and one of Denmark's oldest and best preserved inns. Idyllic both inside and out. 13 rooms. **$$$**

Frederikshavn

Scandic Stena Line Hotel Frederikshavn
Tordenskjoldsgade 14, DK-9900
Tel: 98 43 32 33

www.scandichotels.com
Modern and central. Good facilities. **$$$**

Hirtshals

Hotel Strandlyst
Strandvejen 20, DK-9850
Tel: 98 97 70 76
www.hotel-strandlyst.dk
Cosy 100-year-old hotel, 10 minutes from the beach. **$**

Ribe

Hotel Dagmar
Torvet 1, DK-6760
Tel: 75 42 00 33
www.hoteldagmar.dk
The oldest hotel in Denmark, established in 1581, is packed with character. Located on the main square in the old town, opposite the cathedral. Lovely staff. **$$$**

Vejle

Munkebjerg Hotel
Munkebjergvej 125, DK-7100
Tel: 76 42 85 00
www.munkebjerg.dk
Modern hotel in the middle of forest with marvellous panoramic views. The hotel has 3 restaurants, a gym, sauna and an indoor heated pool. There is a high level of comfort. **$$$**

GREENLAND

Illulisaat

Hotel Arctic
Box 1501,
DK-3952
Tel: 299 94 41 53
www.hotel-arctic.gl
Modern hotel with a superb view over the bay and Disko Island. The best way to reach it is by helicopter from Søndrestrømfjord Airport. Between May and Sept five "igloos" are also available. **$$$**

Kangerlussuaq

Hotel Kangerlussuaq
Box 1006,
DK-3910

Tel: 299 84 11 80
www.airporthotels.gl
On the tip of one of Greenland's longest fjords with 70 rooms, two annnexe hotels for busy periods and numerous amenities. **$$–$$$**

Narsarsuaq

Hotel Narsarsuaq
The Airport,
DK-3923
Tel: 299 66 52 53.
www.airporthotels.gl
The modern and well-equipped airport hotel with 192 rooms, is around 16km (10 miles) from the start of the inland ice. **$$$**

Nuuk

Hotel Hans Egede
Aqqusinersuaq 1–5, Box 289,
DK-3900
Tel: 299 32 42 22
www.hhe.gl
Modern conference hotel. Has 250 beds with private facilities. **$$$**

Qaanaaq

Hotel Qaanaaq
Box 88, DK-3971
Tel: 299 97 12 34
Fax: 299 97 10 64
www.hotelqaanaaq.dk
A small, simple hotel on the remote northwest coast of Greenland. **$**

Sisimiut

Hotel Sisimiut
Box 70,
DK-3911
Tel: 299 86 48 40
www.hotelsisimiut.gl
One of Greenland's best hotels. The hotel's restaurant, Nasaasaaq, has a reputation for fine dining. **$$$**

● For further information contact:
Greenland Tourism
PO Box 1615,
Hans Egedesvej 29, Nuuk,
DK-3900
Tel: 299 34 28 20
www.greenland.com

THE FAROE ISLANDS

Borðoy, Klaksvík

Hotel Klaksvík
Vikarvegur 38,
FO-700 Klaksvík
Tel: 298 45 53 33
www.hotelklaksvik.fo
Handy for the ferry. 61 rooms, some en suite. Restaurant. **$$**

Eysturoy, Eiði

Hotel Eiði
FO-470

Tel: 298 42 34 56
www.hoteleidi.fo
Has 31 beds with private facilities and mini-bars. Some rooms have a view toward the fjord. Good restaurant. **$**

Hotel Runavík
Heiðavegur 6, FO-620
Tel: 298 77 88 77
www.hotel-runavik.fo
Some rooms have private facilities at this pleasant harbourside hotel. **$–$$**

Viðoy, Viðareiði

Hotel Norð
FO-750 Viðareiði
Tel: 298 45 12 44
www.hotelnord.fo
The island's most northerly hotel is looking very spruce after its recent makeover. A paradise for bird lovers. **$$**

Tórshavn

62°N Airport Hotel
Djúpheiðar 2, Sørvágur,
FO-380
Tel: 298 30 90 90
www.62n.fo
Restaurant serves local food; conference facilities. **$$**

Hotel Føroyar
Oggjarvegur, PO Box 3303,
FO-110 Tórshavn
Tel: 298 31 75 00
www.hotelforoyar.com
Modern but built in traditional style, looking across to the island of Nolsoy. All private facilities. **$$$**

Hotel Hafnia
Áarvegur 4-10, FO-110
Tel: 298 31 32 33
www.hafnia.fo
By the harbour, with 56

rooms and 1 suite all with private facilities. Sauna. **$$$**

Hotel Tórshavn
Tórsgøta 4, FO-110 Tórshavn
Tel: 298 35 00 00
www.hotel.fo
A recently-updated hotel (flatscreen TVs, wireless internet) in Tórshavn centre. Smart and comfortable. **$**

● For further information contact:
The Faroe Islands Tourist Board
Tel: 298 30 24 25
E-mail: tourist@tourist.fo
www.visit-faroeislands.com
● For details of youth hostels on the islands contact:
Ferðaráð Føroya
Tel: 298 31 60 55
www.farhostel.fo

E ATING OUT

RECOMMENDED RESTAURANTS AND CAFÉS

What To Eat

Within the past couple of decades the Danish kitchen has gone through a quiet revolution. Not only have the traditional hearty meals of pork and beef seen new low-calorie, high-fibre varieties, but words like pizza, pasta, quiche and kebab have also gone into the everyday vocabulary.

However, the food that is usually associated with Denmark has not suffered from this clash of cultures: open sandwiches (smørrebrød) are still most common for lunch. Smorgåsbord is a lunch buffet of cold dishes, where you can pick and choose from a range of Danish specialities. Beer and aquavit are also traditional.

Take advantage of the varieties of fish from the Baltic and North seas. Fowl and game are common, especially in autumn.

Many restaurants offer "a two-course meal of good, Danish food". This is where one finds roast pork, minced beef, meat or fish balls, and other traditional dishes.

Restaurant Listings

Restaurants are grouped by area, starting with Copenhagen. Within each city or region they are listed in alphabetical order.

RESTAURANT LISTINGS

COPENHAGEN

Michelin Star Restaurants

Era Ora
Overgaden Neden Vandet 33B
Tel: 32 54 06 93

BELOW: dining out in Copenhagen.

www.eraora.dk
Considered to be the best Italian restaurant in Northern Europe, it also has a wine cellar containing over 72,000 bottles and

450 labels that can be visited by those so interested. **$$$**

Formel B
Vesterbrogade 182, DK-1800
Tel: 33 25 10 66
www.formel-b.dk
This has a very stylish and modern dining area, and is famous for its French/Danish cuisine. Its six-course menu is one of the country's finest. **$$$**

Noma
Strandgade 93, DK-1401
Tel: 32 96 32 97
www.noma.dk
Found in an old riverside building in Christianshavn, this has a minimalist style of decor and is renowned for its traditional Danish cuisine and innovative presentation. Received a second star in 2007. **$$$**

The Paul
Vesterbrogade 3, DK-1630

Tel: 33 75 07 75
www.thepaul.dk
Opened in 2003 and located in Tivoli; Paul Cunningham only had to wait one year to be awarded a Michelin star. Spacious open dining areas, and exquisitely prepared and presented cuisine. **$$$**

Other Restaurants

Ida Davidsen
Store Kongensgade 70, DK-1264
Tel: 33 91 36 55
www.idadavidsen.dk

PRICE CATEGORIES

Price categories are based on an average two-course meal (excluding drinks but with tax) per head:
$ = under 100DKK
$$ = 100–200DKK
$$$ = over 200DKK

Open weekends only, this is *the* place to try traditional Danish *smørrebrød* (open sandwiches), with over 250 to choose from.
India Palace
H.C. Andersens Boulevard 13, DK-1553
Tel: 33 91 04 80
www.indiapalace.dk
Found very close to the Town Hall Square; the lunch and evening buffets have been favourites for years. **$–$$**
Krogs Fiskerestaurant
Gammel Strand 38, DK-1202
Tel: 33 15 89 15
www.krogs.dk
Originally opened in 1910, this is undoubtedly the finest fish restaurant in Copenhagen and it has an international reputation. It is also the first restaurant in Denmark to employ a sommelier. **$$$**
Restaurationen
Møntergade 19, DK-1116

Tel: 33 14 94 95
www.restaurationen.com
With its one fixed Danish-style menu of five courses (changed weekly and presented in a frame on an easel), this is a real Copenhagen favourite and has been run by Lisbeth and Bo Jacobsen since 1991. **$$$**
Restaurant Cofoco
7 Abel Cathrines Gade, DK-1654
Tel: 33 13 60 60
www.cofoco.dk
Top quality French/Danish cuisine at an excellent price. Eat at private tables, or turn it into a shared dining experience at the restaurant's sociable long table. **$$**
Restaurant Godt
Gothersgade 38, DK-1123
Tel: 33 15 21 22
www.restaurant-godt.dk
If you're looking for a cosy atmosphere and personal service, this tiny family-run

restaurant (seats 20) serves finely balanced seasonal menus. Reservations are advised. **$$–$$$**
Riz Raz
Store Kannikestræde 19, DK-1169
Tel: 33 32 33 45
Kompagnistræde 20, DK-1208
Tel: 33 15 05 75
www.rizraz.dk
With two locations in Copenhagen, Riz Raz is famed for its ultra-good-value vegetarian buffet, bursting with Mediterranean flavours. Very popular with the locals. **$**
Spiseloppen
Christiania
Tel: 32 57 95 58
www.spiseloppen.dk
Featuring an international menu prepared by chefs from around the globe, Spiseloppen is an ever-surprising restaurant at the heart of Christiania. **$$**

Copenhagen's Cafés

Café Dan Turell
Store Regnegade 3, 1110 K
Tel: 33 14 10 47
www.danturell.dk
Artists frequent this café. **$**
Café Katz
1 Frederiksholms Kanal
Tel: 33 93 33 87
www.cafe-katz.dk
Great waterside location. **$**
Krasnapolsky
Vestergade 10, 1456 K
Tel: 33 32 88 00
Popular with the young. **$**
Park Café
Østerbrogade 79, 2100 Ø
Tel: 35 42 62 48
www.parkcafe.dk
Often has live contemporary music. **$**
Zirup
Læderstræde 32
Tel: 33 13 50 60
www.zirup.dk
Perfect place for people-watching. **$$**

ZEALAND

Kongens Lyngby

Restaurant Brede Spisehus
I.C. Modewegsvej, DK-2800
Tel: 45 85 54 57
www.aok.dk/infosites/7846
Danish/French cuisine. Set in wonderful natural

surroundings in a small village just outside Copenhagen. **$$$**

Hillerød

Slotskroen
Slotsgade 67, 3400
Tel: 48 20 18 00

www.slotskroen.dk
Typical Danish lunch. **$$**

Helsingør

Madam Sprunck
Stengade 48F, DK-3000
Tel: 49 26 48 49
www.madamsprunck.dk

A varied international menu awaits at this atmospheric courtyard restaurant. **$$**
Rådmand Davids Hus
Strandgade 70, DK-3000
Tel: 49 26 10 43
The perfect Danish lunch, served in one of town's quaintest buildings. **$$**

BORNHOLM

Gudhjem

Restaurant Bokulhus
Bokulvej 4
Tel: 56 48 52 97
Modern Danish food using the best local produce. Fish platters with salmon, herring and shrimp. **$$$**

Svaneke

Rogeriet I Svaneke
Fiskergade 12
Tel: 56 49 63 24
The best smokehouse on Bornholm has a selection of fish smoked in the huge ovens – eel, salmon and

trout, and of course Baltic herring on rye bread. **$–$$**

Rønne

Restaurant Fyrtøjet
Store Torvegade 22
Tel: 56 95 30 12
www.fyrtojet.dk

"The Tinderbox" offers a decent choice of fish and meat mains, with lunch and evening buffets. **$$**
Fredensborg
Strandvejen 116, Rønne
Tel: 56 95 44 44. Fax: 56 95 03 14
High gastronomic standard with a sea view. **$$$**

FUNEN

Odense

Den Gamle Kro (The Old Inn)
Overgade 23
Tel: 66 12 14 33
www.den-gamle-kro.dk
International cuisine in a

building dating back to 1683. **$$$**
Olivia Brasserie
Vintappperstræde 37
Tel: 66 17 87 44
www.cafeolivia.dk
This smart, welcoming

brasserie serves epic brunches, light lunches and a "rustic" evening menu. **$$**
Restaurant and Café Vestergade 1
Vestergade 1,

5000 Odense
Tel: 66 12 52 53.
www.vestergade1.dk
A good choice for brunch and excellent Danish home cooking. Great sandwiches. **$$**

JUTLAND

Aabenraa

Krusmølle
Krusmøllevej 10, Feldstedskov
Tel: 74 68 61 72
www.krusmoelle.dk
Linger over coffee and cake or a light lunch at this café, which shares an old mill building with glass and ceramics workshops. $$

Ålborg

Restaurant "Mortens Kro"
Møllåå 4, 9000
Tel: 98 12 48 60
www.mortenskro.com
Super-swish gourmet restaurant, with its own champagne bar. $$$

Arden

Rold Gammel Kro
Hobrovej 11, 9510
Tel: 98 56 17 00
www.roldkro.dk
Traditional Danish dishes. $$

Århus

Emmery's
Guldsmedgade 24

Tel: 86 13 04 00
www.emmerys.dk
Gourmet bakery and tapas. $$

Latin Brasserie & Crêperie
Klostergade 2
Tel: 86 13 78 12
Elegant, romantic French restaurant with chefs of the highest calibre. $$$

L'Estragon
Klostergade 6
Tel: 86 12 40 66
www.lestragon.dk
Top-class classic French food. $$$

Pind's Café
Skolegade 11
Tel: 86 12 20 60
www.pindscafe.dk
An Århus institution serving traditional Danish fare. $$

Svineriet
Mejlgade 35-Bag gården
Tel: 86 12 30 00
www.svineriet.dk
Italian-inspired food in the laid-back Latin quarter. $$$

Christiansfeld

Restaurant Kongens Kælder
Lindegade 25, 6070
Tel: 74 56 17 10. Fax: 74 56 36 40

Top-class restaurant at Brødremenighedens Hotel, specialising in classic Danish cuisine. $$$

Nykøbing Mors

Sallingsund Færgekro
Sallingsundvej 104
7900 Nykøbing Mors
Tel: 97 72 00 88
www.sallingsung-faergekro.dk
High-class menu of traditional and "nouvelle" Danish dishes. $$$

Randers

Restaurant Mad og Vin

BELOW: shellfish are always on the menu.

Storegade 9, 8900
Tel: 87 10 00 98
www.restaurantmadogvin.dk
Stylishly presented Danish/international food. Excellent summer lunch buffet, served in a sunny courtyard. $$$

Skagen

Brøndums Hotel
Anchersvej 3, 9990
Tel: 98 44 15 55
www.broendums-hotel.dk
Established in 1840. Good-quality wine and traditional Danish cuisine. Book ahead. $$

GREENLAND

Nuuk

Restaurant Charoen Porn
Aqqusinersuaq 3, 3900
Tel: 299 32 57 59
Cuisine as far away from the icebergs as it's possible to get – here

you'll find spicy flavours from the Far East at a genuine Thai restaurant. $–$$

Restaurant Gertrud Rask
Hotel Hans Egede, 3900
Tel: 299 32 42 22
On the fifth floor of Hotel

Hans Egede, this is another top-class restaurant serving traditional Greenland dishes. With fine views. $$$

Restaurant Nipisa
Hans Egedesvej 29, 1st Floor, 3900
Tel: 299 32 12 10

An elegant option, serving fascinating fusion food – Greenlandic ingredients such as ptarmigan, reindeer and wild thyme are used to create French-inspired dishes. $$$

THE FAROE ISLANDS

Tórshavn

Glasstovan at Hotel Føroyar
Oyggjarvegur 45, FO-110
Tel: 298 31 75 00
An upmarket choice with fine views over Tórshavn, Glasstovan offers classic dishes such as lobster bisque, rack of lamb or baked salmon – or try the speciality Faroese platter (125DKK). $$$

Restaurant Marco Polo
Sverrisgøta 12, 110
Tel: 298 31 34 30
A well-priced family restaurant, serving pizzas, burgers, steaks and fish mains. $–$$

Restaurant Merlot
Magnus Heinasonargøta 20, FO-100
Tel: 298 31 11 21
Fax: 298 31 11 20
Traditional meat and fish dishes, in the town centre. Good fish menu. $$

Toscana
Nólsoyar Pálsgøta 13, FO-100
Tel: 298 31 11 09
www.toscana.fo
Exceedingly pleasant Italian restaurant, with rich dishes of venison, seafood, meat and pasta. $$$

Eysturoy, Eiði

Hotel Eiði
FO-470
Tel: 298 42 34 56

With a small menu of meaty meals. Good for its Sunday evening buffet (June to August only). $$

PRICE CATEGORIES
Price categories are based on an average two-course meal (excluding drinks but with tax) per head:
$ = under 100DKK
$$ = 100–200DKK
$$$ = over 200DKK

A – Z

A HANDY SUMMARY OF NORWAY, ARRANGED ALPHABETICALLY

A Activities 372	**G** Gay and Lesbian Travellers 375	**T** Telecommunications 378
B Before You Go 373	**H** Health 375	Tourist Information 378
Business Hours 373	**L** Language 376	Tour Operators 379
C Children 373	**M** Media 377	Transport 380
Climate 374	Money 377	**V** Visas and Pasports 385
Culture 374	**N** Nightlife 377	**W** What to Bring 385
E Embassies in Oslo 375	**S** Shopping 378	What to Read 385

Activities

Outdoor Sports

If Norwegians can contrive a sport as an excuse to be outdoors, they'll do it. That's why there are such great facilities here. For a full listing of the range of sports and sports facilities in the Oslo region, see the Outdoor Activities pages of the *Oslo Guide* from tourist offices.

Canoeing

Some of the best canoeing and kayaking lakes and rivers are in the Femund area, Østfold, Aust and Vest Agder, Telemark and suburban Oslo. Contact the local tourist office for details.

Cycling

For details *see Getting Around, page 384.*

Fishing

The fishing is excellent in Norway, whether you're at sea or on a fjord, lake or river. You need a local fishing permit to fish sea char, salmon or sea trout and a national fishing licence for inland fishing in Norway. You can buy a fishing permit at or near your holiday spot. See the tourist board's *Angling in Norway* for full details.

Golf

Norwegian golf courses are by and large difficult and challenging. Most require either a Green Card or a handicap under 20. Green fees are in line with most European golf courses. Some nine-hole courses offer day fees.

In the Oslo region professional competitions are held at Bogstad, Larvik, Borre and Vestfold golf clubs, but by far the most beautifully situated is the Tyrifjord golf links. For information, contact:
Norges Golfforbund
Ullevål Stadion,
N-0840 Oslo
Tel: 21 02 91 50
www.golfforbundet.no

Hiking

The country's extensive mountain ranges and high plains make ideal walking terrain. The most popular areas include the Jotunheim, Rondane and Dovrefjell mountains; the Hardangervidda plateau in the Trollheimen district; and the Finnmarksvidda plain. Mountain cabins are open from the end of June until mid-September, plus over the Easter holiday.

The Norwegian Mountain Touring Association (DNT) runs about 300 guided hikes in summer, and glacier walks in winter. Membership includes hut access. For details:
Den Norske Turistforening
Youngstorget 1, 0181 Oslo
Tel: 40 00 18 68
Fax: 22 42 64 27
www.turistforeningen.no

Glacier Hiking

Glacier hiking is an exhilarating and exciting experience – which should be attempted only with an experienced local guide. Several Norwegian tour companies offer guided glacier walks *(breer)*, particularly in the following areas:

Fjord Norway: Hardangerjøkulen, Folgefonna, Buarbre, Bondhusbre, Smørstabbre, Fannaråkbre and Nigardsbre.
Oppland: Styggebre.
Norland Reiseliv: Svartisen and Engenbreen.
Sognefjord: Jostedalsbreen and Fjæland.
For details, contact **Glacier Information Centres** in western Norway at Oppstryn (tel: 57 87 72 00), Fjærland (tel: 57 69 32 88) and Josterdalen (tel: 57 68 32 50).

Winter Norway

Norway is often dubbed the "Cradle of Skiing". What we today know as a sport is the way Norwegians used to get around, and Norway is said to be responsible for the invention of ski waxing and the laminated ski.

But skiing is just one of Norway's winter attractions. There are snowmobile trips to the North Cape, reindeer safaris and dog-sled races over the plain of Finnmarksvidda.

You can go on horse-drawn sleigh rides, or try your hand at sledding, ice fishing, snow boarding or ice skating. Several companies offer winter train journeys along the spectacular coast.

For details of tour operators who specialise in winter holidays in Norway, see *Specialist Tour Operators* on page 379. Or contact the Norwegian Tourist Board, which has a list of holiday agents offering packages.

Horse Riding
There are riding centres and hotels all over Norway where you can hire a horse for organised trekking or take lessons. For further details contact tourist offices, or:
Norges Rytterforbund
Serviceboks 1 Ullevål Stadion
Tel: 21 02 96 50. Fax: 21 02 96 51
www.rytter.no

Skiing
Along with hiking, this is the primary participant sport in Norway. Even in summer Norwegians take to the slopes (as a rule from June to September), and the sight of people swooping down the slopes in bikinis and trunks is something to behold.

The main ski resorts are at Lillehammer, Trysil, Geilo, Hemsedal, Norefjell (the nearest to Oslo) and Voss, but there are many more; all tourist offices can advise on local ski facilities for cross-country and slalom. Also check the Norwegian ski guide on www.skiinfo.no.

Sailing
Foreign visitors are always welcome in boating circles, and there are sailing and boating clubs and associations throughout Norway. Without your own boat, sailing of any sort can be expensive, and the closest you may get is a small catamaran or even a windsurfer. In Oslo you can hire equipment from:
SrfSnoSk8
Munkedamsvejen 20
Tel: 22 83 78 73. Fax: 93 37 41 37

Norges Seilforbund
Serviceboks 1, Ullevål Stadion,
0840 Oslo.
Tel: 21 02 90 00. Fax: 21 02 97 15

Swimming
Temperatures along the coast and inland reach 25°C (77°F) in summer, and even in the north it can be warm enough to swim. Nude beaches are to be found in Oslo, Moss, Halden, Tønsberg, Larvik, Molde, Ålesund, Bergen, Trondheim and Salten. Most larger hotels have pools and there are numerous leisure centres throughout Norway.

Water Sports
There are several possibilities for waterskiing and windsurfing along the coast, as well as on Norway's numerous lakes.

White-water rafting is available on the following rivers: Sjoaelva in Oppland, Trysilelva in Hedmark and Driva in Sør-Trøndelag.

The Norwegian coast offers very good conditions for diving. There are several diving centres along the west coast, particularly in the counties of Møre and Romsdal, and in north Norway.
Norwegian Diving Federation
Sognsveien 75L, Serviceboks 1
Ullevål Stadion, N-0480 Oslo
Tel: 21 02 97 42
www.ndf.no
Sjoa Raftingsenter
Varphaugen Gård, 2670 Otta
Tel: 47 66 06 80
E-mail: rafting@sjoaraftingsenter.no

B efore You Go
Australia
The embassy deals with tourist information.
17 Hunter Street, Yarralumla,

Canberra ACT 2600
Tel: 02 6273 3444
E-mail: emb.canberra@mfa.no
www.norway.org.au

UK
Innovation Norway
Charles House, 5–11 Lower Regent Street, London SW1Y 4LR
(no walk-in service)
Tel: 020 7389 8800
Fax: 020 7839 6014
E-mail: infouk@invanor.no
www.visitnorway.com

USA/Canada
Innovation Norway
655 Third Avenue, Suite 1810,
New York NY 10017-9111
Tel: 212-885 9700
Fax: 212-885 9710
E-mail: newyork@invanor.no
www.visitnorway.com

Business Hours

● **Offices** 9am–4pm or 8am–4pm; lunch is taken early, 11.30am–12.30pm, or noon–2pm at a restaurant.
● **Shops** Mon–Fri 9am–5pm, Thur until 8pm, Sat from 9am until 1, 2 or even 3pm.
● **Shopping centres** Until 8 or 9pm on weekdays, 6pm on Sat.
● **Banks** 9am–3.30pm weekdays, Thur until 5pm.
● **Pharmacies** Mon–Fri 9am–5pm, Saturday mornings and on a rota basis in larger cities.

C hildren
Norway is a welcoming and safe place for children; this is one reason why you will see them out on their own here at a young age. You can usually get child rates for

BELOW: dog-sledding is one of Norway's winter attractions.

DENMARK

NORWAY

SWEDEN

FINLAND

ABOVE: the spectacular Northern Lights.

travel and accommodation. Family attractions include:

In and around Oslo

International Children's Art Museum (exhibits and workshops), Lille Frøens vei 4, tel: 22 46 85 73 (open all year; entrance fee).
Horse riding, minigolf and Minizoo Ekeberg near Ekeberghallen, tel: 22 68 26 69 (open summer only).
Puppet Theatre Frognerveien 67, tel: 22 34 86 80 (open May–Sept).
Tusenfryd Amusement Park Ås, Østfold. Open June–Aug (May and Sept weekends). Transport by the TusenFryd Bus from Oslo bus station, every ½ hr, tel: 64 97 64 97; www.tusenfryd.no. Attractions include: roller-coaster, water park, flume ride, carousel, magic carpet, climbing wall and so on. Height restrictions apply on some rides.
Youth Information in Oslo provides information on all subjects for young people:
Møllergata 3, Oslo
Tel: 24 14 98 20
www.unginfo.oslo.no
Open Mon–Fri 11am–5pm.

Around Norway

The Troll Family Park
Near Lillehammer

Tel: 61 27 55 30
www.hunderfossen.no
Main attractions are: river rafting, the fairy-tale castle, the world's largest troll, fairy-tale cave, racing-car track, high-wire forest course, raft ride, Wax Museum and Experience Centre for Ice Cream. Open mid-June–late August.
Kongeparken
Near Stavanger
Ttel: 81 52 26 73
www.kongeparken.no
Over 40 attractions, including life-sized model of The Giant Gulliver (85 x 7.5 metres), riding tracks, bob track, farm, car track, Wild West City, birds and fun fair. Open mid-June–late August.
Telemark Sommarland
Bø in Telemark
Tel: 35 06 16 00
www.sommarland.no
Norway's biggest water park with various wet and dry attractions, including many waterslides and Magasuget, a 26-metre (80-ft) - high water chute; Flow Rider, said to be the world's biggest surf wave, and a floating river. Plus live entertainment,
pony rides, Wild West City and children's playground. Open early June–mid-August.

Kristiansand Dyrepark
Tel: 38 04 97 00
www.dyreparken.no
Norway's largest wildlife park and most-visited tourist attraction. The park has a wide range of other attractions: amusement park, water park, show and entertainment park, leisure park and Kardemomme By, a tiny village from a well-known children's book by the Norwegian author Thorbjørn Egner. Open all year, times vary.

Climate

Oslo is one of the warmest places in Norway during winter; in January the average 24-hour high is -2°C (28°F) and the low is -7°C (19°F). Up north it's a different story, with sub-zero temperatures reigning for months and a good number of roads shut over winter due to long-term snow. February and March are the best skiing months. March, April and early May are the wet spring months when roads are buckled due to thaws and

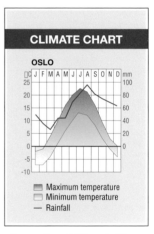

refreezes; through this period the temperature slowly lifts from about 4°C (39°F) to 16°C (61°F).
Come summertime and the season of the midnight sun, Oslo enjoys average temperatures in the low-to mid-20s°C (70s°F), while the sunlight-bathed north has a perfect hiking temperature, around 20°C (68°F). October is the time for autumn rains as temperatures dip below 10°C (50°F), then continue their slide towards zero. The first snow arrives mid-October.

Culture
Music and Opera

In summer the arts take to the outdoors in Norway, and classical music and opera are no exception.

Night Skies

Midnight sun In the north of Norway the sun does not sink below the horizon for several weeks in the summer. The best time to see the "midnight sun" is mid-May to late July. Longyearbyen on Svalbard has the longest period of midnight suns, from about 20 April to 20 August.

Aurora borealis The northern lights, or aurora borealis, are best seen from November to February. You need to go north of the Arctic Circle, which cuts through Norway just south of Bodø on the Nordland coast. There is, unfortunately, no guarantee they will not be obscured by clouds.

For Oslo dates, pick up the *What's On in Oslo* guide. The very active Oslo Philharmonic, founded by Edvard Grieg, is conducted by Jukka-Pekka Saraste, with frequent visits by acclaimed guest conductors and soloists. Den Norske Opera (National Opera) stages big productions such as *La Boheme* and *Don Giovanni* during the year. The opera moved to a brand-new opera house on the waterfront east of Akershus in April 2008.

Akershus Fortress and the Henie Onstad Art Centre (Høvikodden) are two other fine settings for summer concerts, and there are several outdoor rock and pop festivals from June through to August.

Whether the performers are Norwegian or foreign, the season winter or summer, Norway has a rich and varied musical and operatic life (consult area guides for festival schedules; some English and American newspapers give a pan-European list of festivals at the start of each summer). This may be your chance to listen to some of the conductors and performers you'd previously only heard on Deutsche Gramophone CDs, or a first opportunity to see Grieg performed by Norwegian musicians.

Theatre and Dance

Theatre is booming in Norway, with small, contemporary theatres springing up everywhere; but performances are in Norwegian. Some plays are held in English during the Ibsen Theatre Festival, held every other August in Oslo.

Dance has also come into its own. Classical ballet is performed at the Oslo Opera House. Traditional folk dances can be seen in many towns on National Day (17 May), and at Oslo's Konserthus.

Cinema

The Norwegians love films, hence the vast number of cinemas; Oslo has around 40 screens including the impressive wide-screen cinema at Colosseum in Frogner. First-run and repertory films are always shown in the original language, with Norwegian subtitles. Kiosks, newspapers, and local city guides have listings. Booking tickets is recommended for Fridays and Saturdays.

D isabled Travellers

Visitors in need of assistance should contact **Norges handikapforbund**, Schweigaardsgt. 12, 0134 Oslo; tel: 24 10 24 00; e-mail: nhf@nhf.no; www.nhf.no.

Electricity

220 volts AC, 50 cycles. Plugs have two small round pins, so you may need an adapter for appliances you bring with you.

Hotel listings in accommodation guides have symbols designating disabled access and toilets. Under the "Oslo for all" section of the VisitOslo website (www.visitoslo.com), wheelchair users and visitors with hearing or visual impairments can search for accommodation, restaurants and attractions that are tailored to accommodate their needs.

The **Euro Terra Nova AS**, at Prinsensgate 3B, 0152 Oslo, offers brochures on coach tours around Norway especially for wheelchair users. They also provide hotel bookings and hire cars, tel: 22 94 13 50; fax: 22 94 13 61; www.euroterranova.no. Guidebooks for Nordland county (north Norway) can be ordered free of charge from Nordland Reiseliv.

The Society for Accessible Travel and Hospitality (SATH) provides information and advice for travellers with disabilities. Their website is: www.sath.org.

E mbassies in Oslo

Canada
Wergelandsveien 7
Tel: 22 99 53 00
www.canada.no
UK
Thomas Heftyesgate 8
Tel: 23 13 27 00
www.britain.no
United States
Henriklbsens gate 48
Tel: 22 44 85 50
www.usa.no

G ay and Lesbian Travellers

In common with the rest of Scandinavia, Norway has a very relaxed attitude to homosexuality. There is very little open hostility to gays and lesbians in general society and, partly as a result, the commercial gay scene is relatively small. Tourist offices *(see page 379)* carry details of the main places and events, including the Gay Pride.

H ealth

The are no major health hazards in Norway. No vaccinations are necessary to enter Norway and the

tap water is (generally) good. A degree of common sense is required when travelling in remote areas, especially during the winter. When hiking/skiing in the mountains always let someone know of your travel intentions, and use guides wherever possible.

Treatment

Norway has reciprocal treatment agreements with the UK and many other European countries; your own National Insurance should cover you to receive free treatment at public hospitals. EU citizens should obtain the relevant documentation to entitle them to this (for British citizens an EHIC, European Health Insurance Card, is available from post offices or online at www.ehic.org.uk). People from countries without such agreements, and those without an EHIC card, will have to pay a small fee. If you are concerned whether you need extra cover, check in your own country before you go. The EHIC card only covers the basics and does not include the cost of medicine, so it is advisable to take out additional medical insurance. You will need to take out extra cover if you are going skiing or considering any other possibly dangerous sports.

Pharmacies

For minor problems, head for a pharmacy, or *Apotek (for opening hours, see page 373)*. Most larger cities have all-night pharmacies *(see below)*. In other cities enquire at your hotel, or try the emergency number in the phone book under *Legevakt* (doctor on duty).

BELOW: a night out at the theatre.

Where there is a rota of 24-hour pharmacies in a city, a list will usually be posted on the door of each one.

Oslo
Jernbanetorvets Apotek, across from Central Station, Jernbanetorget 4B. Tel: 23 35 81 00. Open 24 hours.
Bergen
Apotek Nordstjernen, Strømgata 8. Tel: 55 21 83 84. Open Mon–Sat 8am–11pm, Sun 10am–11pm.
Stavanger
Loeveapoteket, Olav V's gt 11. Tel: 51 91 08 80. Open daily until 11pm, Christmas, New Year, Easter and Whitsun 9am–8pm.
Trondheim
St Olav Vakt-apotek, Beddingen 4. Tel: 73 88 37 37. Open Mon–Sat 8.30am–midnight, Sun 10am–midnight.

Dentists

Emergency dental treatment in Oslo, outside regular dentists' office hours, is available from:
Oslo Kommune Tannlegevakt, Schweigaards gate 6, 3rd floor, (near the central railway station) Tel: 22 67 30 00.
Open Mon–Sat 7–10pm, Sat–Sun and public holidays 11am–2pm.

Internet Cafés

Free internet access is available at most public libraries in Norway. Screen time is limited and you may need to reserve your slot in advance. The Oslo Tourist Information Service publishes a list of internet cafés in the capital. These include:
Arctic Internet, Oslo Central Station. Open daily 9am–11pm. Tel: 22 17 19 40.
Galleriet Internettkafé, Schweigaardsgate 6, Oslo (Oslo Central Bus Terminal). Open Mon–Sat 11am–9pm. Tel: 22 17 19 00.
Qba, Olaf Ryes Plass 4. Open weekdays 8am–1am, Sat–Sun 11am–1am. Tel: 22 35 24 60.

Language

Introduction

Germanic in origin, Norwegian is one of the three Scandinavian languages, and is closely related to Danish and Swedish. There are two official forms of Norwegian, *bokmål* and *nynorsk*. The former reflects Norway's 400 years of Danish domination, while *nynorsk* is built on native Norwegian dialects. The Sami population (Lapps) in north Norway speak Lappish. English is widely understood.

Useful Words and Phrases

Yes *Ja*
No *Nei*
Good morning *God morgen*
Good afternoon *God eftermiddag*
Good evening *God kveld*
Today *I dag*
Tomorrow *I morgen*
Yesterday *I går*
Hello *Hei*
How do you do? *Står det til?*
Goodbye *Adjø/Ha det bra/Hadet*
Thank you *Takk*
How much is this? *Hvor mye koster det?*
It costs *Det koster...*
How do I get to...? *Hvordan kommer jeg til...?*
Where is...? *Hvor er...?*
Right *Høyre*
To the right *Til høyre*
Left *Venstre*
To the left *Til venstre*
Straight on *Rett frem*
Phrase book *Parlør*
Dictionary *Ordbok*
Money *Penger*
Can I order please? *Kan jeg få bestille?*
Could I have the bill please? *Kan jeg få regningen?*
What time is it? *Hvor mye er klokken?*
It is (the time is...) *Den er (Klokken er...)*
When? *Når*
Where? *Hvor?*
Could I have your name please? *Hva er navnet?*
My name is *Mitt navn er...*
Do you have English newspapers? *Har du engelske aviser?*
Do you speak English? *Snakker du engelsk?*
I only speak English *Jeg snakker bare engelsk*
May I help you? *Kan jeg hjelpe deg?*
I do not understand *Jeg forstår ikke*
I do not know *Jeg vet ikke*
It has disappeared *Den har forsvunnet*
Chemist *Apotek*
Hospital *Sykehus*
Doctor *Lege*
Police station *Politistasjion*
Parking *Parkering*
Department store *Hus/Stormagasin*
Toilet *Toalett/WC*
Gentlemen *Herrer*
Ladies *Damer*
Vacant *Ledig*
Engaged *Opptatt*
Entrance *Inngang*
Exit *Utgang*
No entry *Ingen adgang*
Open *Åpent*
Closed *Stengt*
Push *Skyv*
Pull *Trekk*
No smoking *Røyking forbudt*

Numbers

1	*en*
2	*to*
3	*tre*
4	*fire*
5	*fem*
6	*seks*
7	*syv or sju*
8	*åtte*
9	*ni*
10	*ti*
11	*elleve*
12	*tolv*
13	*tretten*
14	*fjorten*
15	*femten*
16	*seksten*
17	*sytten*
18	*atten*
19	*nitten*
20	*tjue*
21	*tjue-en*
22	*tjue-to*
30	*tretti*
40	*førti*
50	*femti*
60	*seksti*
70	*sytti*
80	*åtti*
90	*nitti*
100	*hundre*
200	*to hundre*
1,000	*tusen*

Breakfast *Frokost*
Lunch *Lunsj*
Dinner *Middag*
Eat *Spise*
Drink *Drikke*
Cheers! *Skål!*
Hot *Varm*
Cold *Kald*
Aircraft *Flymaskin*
Car *Bil*
Train *Tog*
Ticket *Billet*
Single/return *En vei/tur-retur*
To rent *Leie*
Free *Ledig*
Room to rent *Rom til leie*
Chalet *Hytte*
Can we camp here? *Kan vi campe her?*
No camping *Camping forbudt*
Grocery store (in countryside) *Landhandel*
Shop *Butikk*
Food *Mat/kost*
To buy *Kjøpe*
Sauna *Badstue*
Off licence/liquor store *Vinmonopol*
Clothes *Klær*
Overcoat *Frakk*
Jacket *Jakke*
Suit *Dress*
Shoes *Sko*
Skirt *Skjørt*

Blouse *Bluse*
Jersey *Genser*

Days and Months

Sunday *søndag*
Monday *mondag*
Tuesday *tirsdag*
Wednesday *onsdag*
Thursday *torsdag*
Friday *fredag*
Saturday *lørdag*

January *januar*
February *februar*
March *mars*
April *april*
May *mai*
June *juni*
July *juli*
August *august*
September *september*
October *oktober*
November *november*
December *desember*

Media

Newspapers

Most larger kiosks (like the *Narvesen* chain) and some bookshops sell English-language newspapers. Norwegian news in English is found on the website of Norway's main newspaper *Aftenposten*: www.aftenposten.no.

Deichmanske Bibliotek, the main public library, is at Arne Garborgs plass 4 in Oslo; you'll find a selection of international papers and periodicals in its reading rooms, as well as free internet access. Open Mon–Fri 10am–7pm, Sat 10am–4pm.

Bookshops

There are several bookshops in Oslo with English-language sections, including; **Erik Qvist** at Drammensveien 16, tel: 22 54 26 00; **Litteraturhuset** at Wergelandsveien 29, tel: 22 95 55 30; and **Norli** at Universitetsgaten 20–24, 0162 Oslo, tel: 22 00 43 00.

Radio

English broadcasts on short wave can be picked up if atmospheric conditions are favourable. Best results can usually be heard on short-wave frequency 9410.

During the winter months **BBC radios 1**, **2**, **3** and **4** can sometimes be received on AM but reception is often distorted. **Radio 5** can be picked up on 909 and 693 medium wave (best reception in the evening). For local frequencies of the **BBC World Service** enquire at the nearest tourist office.

Television

Norway has five main television stations: **NRK1**, **NRK2**, **NRK3** (Norsk Rikskringkasting), **TV2** and **TV Norge** (TVN). Cable TV is common here and allows you to pick up a variety of channels, including **BBC Prime**, **BBC World**, **CNN**, **Swedish TV1** and **TV2**, **Discovery**, **MTV**, **French TV5**, **Eurosport**, **TV3** and so on, depending on the distributor. Most hotels have pay channels in addition to the above. English films on Norwegian television are subtitled, not dubbed.

Money

The Norwegian krone (NOK) is divided into 100 øre. Notes come in denominations of NOK 50, 100, 200, 500 and 1,000 and coins are 50 øre and NOK 1, 5, 10 and 20.

You can change currency at post offices, the Oslo S train station, international airports, some hotels and commercial banks. The relatively new FOREX offices have good rates and no fees. It is always useful to carry a certain amount of cash with you in case of emergency.

Credit Cards/ Travellers' Cheques

Use of credit cards is widespread in Norway, with Eurocard, Visa, MasterCard, American Express and Diner's Club the most common. Check with your own credit card company about acceptability and other services.

Travellers' cheques are not very widely used now, but they are

BELOW: National Independence Day.

accepted in the bigger hotels and should be purchased before travelling to Norway. In most banks you can generally get cash on a debit card or a Visa or MasterCard.

Tipping

Tipping is quite straight forward in Norway. Hotels include a service charge and tipping is generally not expected. Restaurants usually have the service charge included, in which case it's your choice to add anything (5–10 percent is customary). The same applies to taxis. Table service in bars (particularly outdoor tables) requires tipping. With hairdressers a tip isn't quite as customary, but again 5–10 percent would be appropriate – and appreciated. Cloakrooms usually have a fixed fee of about NOK 5–10; if not, leave a few krone for the attendant.

Nightlife

Oslo, once considered a big yawn at night, is now vying with Stockholm and Copenhagen to be Scandinavia's nightlife capital. Loads of new bars, pubs and clubs have come on to the scene, but many can't recoup their investments quickly enough and go out of business. So check locally for up-to-date venue listings, see the official *Oslo Guide* provided free by Oslo Promotion, or check the website www.visitoslo.com. All the major cities have both official and unofficial nightlife guides.

In Bergen, Stavanger, Trondheim and Tromsø nightlife exists to a much lesser extent. But you can guarantee that most large hotels have nightclubs and bars. In small towns, you may be out of luck altogether.

International rock, folk, and jazz musicians often include Oslo on European tours.

There are only two things you need to be warned about before a night out: the high cost of drinking, and age restrictions: some clubs have minimum ages as high as 26 (although 21 and 23 are more common).

Public Holidays

1 January	New Year's Day
March/April	Easter: Thursday to Monday inclusive
1 May	Labour Day
17 May	National Independence Day
May	Ascension Day
May/June	Whit Monday
25 December	Christmas Day
26 December	2nd Christmas Day

P ostal Services

Post offices in Oslo open Mon–Fri 9am–5pm and Sat 9am–3pm.

Letters and postcards cost the same price to send to the UK and continental Europe, slightly more to send outside Europe. Post takes 2–3 days to Europe and 7–10 days to North America.

R eligious Services

The Lutheran church is Norway's state church, with around 83 percent of the population registered as Lutherans. Oslo has many Lutheran places of worship, including one American Lutheran church (Fritzners g. 15; tel: 22 44 35 84; fax: 22 44 30 15; www.alcoslo.org).

Services are held in English at the **American Lutheran church** and the **Anglican/Episcopalian church** (St Edmund's, Møllergate 30; tel: 22 69 22 14; www.osloanglicans.net).

Minority religious groups are Pentecostalists, Baptists, Seventh Day Adventists, Evangelical Lutherans, Methodists, Catholics, Jews (the **synagogue** is at Bergstein 13, near St Hanshaugen; tel: 22 69 65 70) and Muslims. The **Oslo Cathedral** (Protestant), Domkirke at Storgate, tel: 23 31 46 00, was closed for renovations at the time of writing, but check with the tourist office for interesting concerts, previously held there on Wednesdays. For up-to-date information, consult the daily press, the tourist office or www.visitoslo.com.

S hopping

What to Buy

Popular souvenirs from Norway include knitted jumpers, cardigans, gloves and mittens, pewter, silver jewellery and cutlery, hand-painted wooden objects (like bowls with rose designs), trolls and fjord horses carved out of wood, goat and reindeer skin, enamel jewellery, woven wall designs, furs, handicrafts, glassware and pottery – to name just a few (see *Tax-free Shopping, below,* on how to reclaim tax).

Department Stores

The major department stores are *Glasmagasinet* and *Steen & Strøm*, both of which have a good selection of most of these items. *House of Oslo* at Ruseløkkveien 26 is a new department store specialising solely in design. Karl Johansgate, Grensen, and Bogstadveien are all major shopping streets. With the exception of Oslo, most Norwegian towns are

ABOVE: colourful glassware for sale.

so compact that your best bet is to window shop and go into the places that look most appealing.

Buying Art

Anyone interested in buying Norwegian art will have ample prospects – from south to north, Norway abounds in galleries. Get a local recommendation.

Food

If you are food shopping, fruit and vegetable prices vary considerably throughout the year. Look out for *lavpris* (low-price) shops offering discounts. The first Saturday of each month is "Super Saturday" when shops in Oslo open longer and offer special discounts. Bear in mind that most bottles (whether plastic or glass) have a returnable deposit of NOK 1.

Tax-free Shopping

If you are a resident of a country other than Norway, Sweden, Denmark or Finland, you are entitled to tax-free shopping on purchases in excess of NOK 315 at any of the 3,000 stores connected to the scheme.

The store issues you with a tax-free voucher for the amount of VAT paid. When you leave Norway, a refund of 12–19 percent (depending on the sale price) will be refunded on presentation of the goods, the tax-free voucher and your passport, on condition that the item has not been used while in Norway.

Global Refund has its own representatives at a total of 100 refund places, including airports, international ferry terminals and at the main border crossings. Check

opening times, as they are not open 24 hours, and make sure there is a refund desk if you are using a small border crossing. Customs officials cannot refund VAT. For details, contact Global Refund Norge, Grini Næringspark 15, PO Box 48 N-1332 Østerås; tel: 67 15 60 10; fax: 67 15 60 29.

T elecommunications

International dialling code: +47 When calling from Norway to foreign countries always dial 00 first. Cheapest calling times are outside business hours: 5pm–8am. Extra-cheap international calling cards, such as Eurocity, can be purchased from a variety of kiosks (corner shops) in most major towns.

Calls abroad can be made from hotels – with a hefty surcharge – or from phone booths or the main telegraph office at Kongensgate 21 (entrance Prinsensgate), Oslo. You can also send faxes from this office.

Norwegian payphones take 1, 5, 10 and 20 kroner pieces. Phone-cards, which can be used in the green phone booths, can be bought in *Narvesen* kiosks and at post offices. Credit cards are accepted in card phones.

Telephone directories have a page of instructions in English in the index. When looking up names, remember the vowels æ, ø, and å come at the end of the alphabet, in that order.

Some US phone companies have their own international access numbers, to allow US citizens cheaper calls, as follows:
Sprint 800-19 877
AT&T 800-19 011
WorldPhone 800-19 912

Tourist Information

There are around 350 local tourist offices around Norway, as well as 18 regional tourist offices. For general information, contact:
The Tourist Information Centre Fridtjof Nansens Plass 5, Oslo

Emergency Numbers

Fire 110
Police 112
Ambulance 113
Medical problems For emergency medical treatment in Oslo *(legevakt)* ring 22 11 80 80.
Internal directory enquiries 1881/1880
International directory enquiries 1882

Tel: 24 14 77 00
Fax: 22 42 92 22
E-mail: info@visitoslo.com
www.visitoslo.com

Regional Information

Regional tourist offices are experts in the county they cover. They are not usually open to personal callers, with the exception of the VisitOslo offices, but will supply advice and information in writing or over the phone.

Oslo/Oslofjord

The Tourist Information Centre
(details as above)
Akershus Tourist Board
Kultur- og næringspark N-2060
Gardermoen
Tel: 64 82 22 99
Fax: 64 82 22 98
E-mail: info@akershus.com
www.akershus.com

East Norway

Fjell og Fjord Ferie
Gamlevegen 6
N-3550 Gol
Tel: 32 02 99 26

Specialist Tour Operators in the UK

Activity Holidays

Inntravel
Whitewell Grange,
Nr Castle Howard, York YO60 7JU
Tel: 01653 617 949
www.filoxenia.co.uk
Scantours
73 Mornington St,
London NW1 7QE
Tel: 020 7554 3530
www.scantours.co.uk

Arctic Voyages/Dog-sledging/Whale Watching

Arctic Experience and Discover the World
8 Bolters Lane, Banstead,
Surrey SM7 2AR
Tel: 01737 218800
www.arctic-experience.co.uk
Arcturus Expeditions
PO Box 41, Hereford HR1 9DP
Tel: 01432 850886
www.arcturusexpeditions.co.uk

Christmas Holidays

Page and Moy
Compass House, Rockingham
Road, Market Harborough,
Leicester LE16 7QD
Tel: 0870 833 4012
www.pageandmoy.com

Norway specialists

Norsc Holidays
The Court, The Street,
Charmouth DT6 6PE

Fax: 32 02 99 28
E-mail: info@eventyrveien.no
www.eventyrveien.no
Hedmark Reiseliv BA
Grønnegate 11
N-2317 Hamar
Tel: 62 55 33 20
Fax: 62 55 33 21
E-mail: hedmark@villmarksriket.com
www.hedmark.com

South Norway

Arendal Turist Kontor
PO Box 324, Sam Eydes plass
N-4803 Arendal
Tel: 37 00 55 44
Fax: 37 00 55 40
www.arendal.com
Destinasjon Sørlandet
Vestre Strandgate 32
N-4612 Kristiansand
Tel: 38 12 13 14
Fax: 38 02 52 55
E-mail: info@visitsorlandet.com
www.visitsorlandet.com
Telemarkreiser
Nedre Hjellegate 18
N-3724 Skien
Tel: 35 90 00 30

Tel: 01297 560033
www.norsc.co.uk
Taber Holidays
PO Box 176, Tofts House,
Tofts Road, Cleckheaton,
West Yorkshire BD19 3WX
Tel: 01274 875 199
www.taberhols.co.uk

Skiing/Walking

Crystal Holidays
King's Place, Wood Street,
Kingston, Surrey KT1 1JY
Tel: 0870 166 4971
www.crystalholidays.co.uk
Exodus Travel
Grange Mills, Weir Road,
London SW12 0NE
Tel: 0845 863 9600
www.exodus.co.uk

Tours

Explore Worldwide
55 Victoria Road, Farnborough,
Hampshire GU14 7PA
Tel: 0845 013 1537
www.explore.co.uk
ScanMeridian
73 Mornington Street,
London NW1 7QE
Tel: 020 7554 3530
www.scantours.co.uk
Great Rail Journeys
Saviour House, 9 St Saviourgate,
York YO1 8NL
Tel: 01904 521936
www.greatrail.com

Time Zone

Central European Time, 1 hour ahead of Greenwich Mean Time, 6 hours ahead of Eastern Standard Time. The clock is set forward an hour to summer time at the end of March, and back an hour at the end of September.

Fax: 35 90 00 21
E-mail: info@telemarkreiser.no
www.visittelemark.com

Fjord Norway

Bergen
Slottsgaten 3, 3rd floor
N-5835 Bergen
Tel: 55 55 20 00
Fax: 55 55 20 01
E-mail: info@visitbergen.com
www.visitbergen.com
Fjord Norge AS
Lodin Leppsgt 2B, N-5003 Bergen
Tel: 55 30 26 40
Fax: 55 30 26 50
E-mail: info@fjordnorway.no
www.fjordnorway.com
Hordaland Reiseliv
PO Box 416 Marken
N-5828 Bergen
Tel: 55 31 66 00
Fax: 55 31 52 08
E-mail: info@hordalandreiseliv.no
www.visithordaland.no
Møre og Romsdal Reiselivsråd
Fylkeshuset, N-6404 Molde
Tel: 71 24 50 80
Fax: 71 24 50 81
E-mail: mr-reiselivsrad@eunet.no
www.visitmr.com
Rogaland Reiseliv
PO Box 130
N-4001 Stavanger
Tel: 51 51 67 88
E-mail: gen@rogfk.no
www.rogfk.no
Sogn and Fjordane Tourist Board
PO Box 370
N-6782 Stryn
Tel: 57 87 40 40
E-mail: mail@nordfjord.no
www.sfr.no

Central Norway

Trøndelag Reiseliv AS
PO Box 65
N-7004 Trondheim
Tel: 73 84 24 50
E-mail: touristinfo@trondelag.no
www.trondelag.com

North Norway

Finnmark Tourist Board
NO-9509 Alta
Tel: 78 44 90 60
Fax: 78 44 90 79
E-mail: post@finnmark.no
www.visitnorthcape.com

Fjord Tours

Whether you are planning a short break or a long holiday, many companies offer tours of the fjord, coastal and mountain scenery. Two of the main ones are:
Fjord Tours
Strømgt 4
5015 Bergen
Tel: 47 81 56 82 22
www.fjord-tours.com
Fjord Travel Norway
Østre Nesttunvei 4–6
5221 Nesttun, Bergen
Tel: 47 55 13 13 10
www.fjordtravel.no

Nordland Reiseliv AS
PO Box 434
N-8001 Bodø
Tel: 75 54 52 00
Fax: 75 54 52 10
E-mail: nordland@nordlandreiseliv.no
www.visitnordland.no
Svalbard Reiseliv
PO Box 323
N-9171 Longyearbyen
Tel: 79 02 55 50
Fax: 79 02 55 51
E-mail: info@svalbard.net
www.svalbard.net
Troms Reiseliv
PO Box 326
N-9305 Finnsnes
Tel: 77 85 07 30
Fax: 77 85 07 31
E-mail: post@visittroms.no
www.visittroms.no

Transport

Getting There

Scandinavia's flagship carrier, **SAS** (Scandinavian Airline System; www.scandinavian.net), runs a wide range of flights between Oslo Gardermoen Airport and other world capitals (usually involving a feeder service to and from one of the main European hubs – usually London, Copenhagen or Frankfurt), with some direct services to and from Bergen, Oslo, Stavanger, Tromsø and Trondheim.

SAS is joined by other major international airlines – including **British Airways, Lufthansa, Air France**, and **KLM** – in connecting Oslo and other cities with daily flights to Europe.

Approximate flying times to Oslo are: London, 2 hours, Frankfurt, 1 hour 50 minutes, Paris, 2 hours, Budapest, 3 hours 35 minutes, and Warsaw, 3 hours 25 minutes.

SAS offers several daily flights from Heathrow to Oslo and two to Stavanger, plus direct flights to

ABOVE: farmhouses look out onto Geirangerfjord.

Bergen and Ålesund; there are also flights in and out of Manchester. **BA** (www.ba.com) operates from Heathrow to Oslo. **Ryanair** offers low-cost flights from London Stansted and Glasgow Prestwick to Oslo Torp, near Sandefjord (in fact 130 km/80 miles south of the capital) and from London Stansted to Haugesund.

Wideroe (www.wideroe.no) flies to 33 destinations within Norway and has flights from Aberdeen, Edinburgh, Newcastle, Copenhagen and Gothenburg. It is based at Oslo Torp airport in Sandefjord, 130 km (80 miles) south of Oslo. **Norwegian Air Shuttle** (www.norwegian.no) is a low-cost airline operating from 10 airports in Norway; flights go to Oslo and Stavanger from London Gatwick and Edinburgh, and from London Stansted to Oslo, Bergen, Tromsø and Trondheim. All airports are serviced by buses and taxis. Oslo's Gardermoen Airport has a number of train services (see page 381).

By Sea

DFDS Seaways cancelled its services from the UK to Norway in September 2008.
Smyril Line
Head office:
J. Broncksgøta 37, PO Box 370,
Tórshavn, Faroe Islands
Tel: +298 345 900
UK agent:
Scantours UK Ltd,
73 Mornington Street,
London NW1 7QE
Tel: 020 7554 3530
www.smyril-line.com
Operates a weekly sailing from Torshavn in the Faroe Islands to Bergen via Scrabster in Scotland.

Color Line
PO Box 1422, Vika N-0115 Oslo
Tel: 47 81 00 08 11
www.colorline.com
The main ferry service linking Oslo to the continent, with big new cruise-ferries sailing to Kiel in Germany.

By Rail

Numerous rail services link Norway with the rest of Scandinavia and Europe. From the continent, express trains operate to Copenhagen, where inter-Scandinavian trains connect to Oslo. There are train connections in Oslo to other cities in Norway. First- and second-class coaches are available on these express trains, plus sleeper coaches on all of the overnight expresses.

Seat reservations are required on all night and long-distance day trains, as well as on express and high speed services.

The Norwegian State Railways (NSB) is part of the InterRail, EuroDomino, Eurailpass and Eurail Youthpass system, which offers various discount tickets (including to students). InterRail: www.interrail net.com, Eurail: www.eurail.com.

There are frequent connections from Copenhagen, Stockholm and Gothenburg to Oslo.

You can also get to northern Norway from Stockholm, with Trondheim and Narvik the principal destinations, again usually twice daily (the line in Norway terminates at Bodø).

International arrivals and departures are located at Sentralstasjon (Oslo-S). Gardermobanen, the high-speed rail link to/from Oslo Gardermoen Airport has a terminal at Oslo S, and trains also run to/from

Asker via Nationalteatret station. NSB provides train information and also operates as a travel bureau across Norway:

Norwegian State Railways
NSB Reisesenter
Prinsensgate 7–9, N-0048 Oslo
Tel: 81 50 08 88
www.nsb.no

By Road
Most major shipping lines to Norway allow passengers to bring cars. But coming by car increases sea travel costs, and petrol is expensive in Norway.

Norges Automobil Forbund
(NAF or Norwegian Automobile Association)
Østensjøveien 14, 0609 Oslo
In Norway tel: 08 505
From abroad tel: +47 926 08505
www.naf.no

Kongelig Norsk Automobilklub
(KNA or Royal Norwegian Automobile Club)
Cort Adelersgt. 16, 0201 Oslo
Tel: 21 60 49 00
Emergency tel: 800 31 660
(members only).

Getting Around

Public Transport
There is an excellent network of domestic transport services – a necessity in a country so large and often impassable by land. You may have to use more than one means (for example, train and bus or plane and bus) but if you're travelling beyond Oslo you'll find these services indispensable.

Although covering great distances can be expensive, Norway offers transport bargains through special tourist cards like the Fjord Pass, the Bonus Pass (which covers the whole of Scandinavia), plus some of the pan-

European programmes like InterRail and Eurail. Within larger cities, tourist passes cover urban transport and give free entry to many museums.

From the Airport
Gardermoen Airport is 50 km (30 miles) north of Oslo. It is served by the Airport Express Train/Flytoget to Oslo S (the Central Station) every 10–20 minutes and takes 22 minutes. Details at www.flytoget.no. For about half the price, regional and local trains also connect Oslo and the airport and take about 37 minutes; there is normally a train at least every hour. Note that rail passes are not valid on the Airport Express. See also www.nsb.no.

The airport bus departs six times an hour to and from the Radisson SAS Scandinavia Hotel via Oslo Busterminal, Helsfyr and Furuset. It takes 45 minutes.

The regular bus No. 344 from the Radisson SAS Scandinavia Hotel via Oslo S departs three times an hour and takes 50 minutes. Buses 332 and 355 also make the journey. Tel: 177 or 22 80 49 71; www.flybussen.no.

Nor-Way Busekspress. No. 114 stops in Oslo and the Oslo fjord area en route to Gardermoen. There are four departures per hour from the Oslo suburbs. Tel: 81 54 44 44; www.nor-way.no.

If you arrive from London Stansted at **Torp Airport** at Sandefjord on the southwest side of the fjord, buses and trains will take up to 2½ hours to reach the capital, depending on traffic conditions.

Bergen Airport is at Flesland, 19 km (12 miles) south of the city. The airport bus goes to the Radisson SAS Royal Hotel at Bryggen, via Radisson SAS Hotel Norge and the

Tickets and Info

For tickets, routes, times and all other queries about public transport, **Trafikanten** in Oslo offers an information and booking service. Its office is at Jernbanetorvet 1, by Oslo Sentralstasjon (at the bottom of the glass tower at the front of the station). Office open Mon–Fri 7am–8pm, Sat–Sun 8am–6pm. Tel: 81 50 01 76 (lines open Mon–Fri 7am–11pm, Sat–Sun 8am–11pm). Info line: 177.

bus station. There are around 3 buses per hour, taking from 30 to 45 minutes depending on traffic. For details, tel: 177.

All other major city airports are serviced by buses and taxis.

By Air
Considering its size, Norway is exceptionally well served by domestic airlines, with about 50 airports and airfields throughout the country.

The main domestic airlines are SAS, Widerøe and Norwegian Air Shuttle. Each offers discount travel passes.

SAS Scandinavian Airlines
At Oslo and Bergen airports
Bookings tel: 915 05 400
Main office tel: 67 59 70 00
Widerøe's Flyveselskap ASA
Vollsvien. 6, PO Box 131, N-1324 Lysaker, and Bergen Airport
Tel: 75 11 11 11
Bookings tel: 81 00 12 00
Norwegian Air Shuttle
PO Box 115, N-1330 Fornebu
In Norway tel: 81 52 18 15
Outside Norway tel: +47 2149 0015
In the UK tel: 020 8099 7254

By Rail
Rail services are far more comprehensive in the south than in the north, and tend to fan out from Oslo, so you will have to supplement your trip with ferries and buses, unless you are travelling strictly in the south or to the major towns.
Oslo S (Oslo Sentralstasjon) is Norway's busiest railway station, located in central Oslo at the eastern end of Karl Johansgate on Jernbanetorget. Long-distance, express and local suburban trains arrive and depart here. It is also the terminal for the Oslo Gardermoen Airport high-speed rail link (some trains continue under the city to Asker via Nationalteatret station). The end of the line in Norway is at Bodø, but the most northerly railway station is at

Norway in a Nutshell

One of the most pleasurable ways of seeing western Norway is to take a **Norway in a Nutshell** journey *(see page 197)*. The trip uses various forms of public transport and takes you from Myrdal to Flåm, Gudvangen and Voss through some of the country's most beautiful scenery. A selection of packages is on offer. Tel: 81 56 82 22. www.norwaynutshell.com.

The railway line from Myrdal to Flåm is a masterpiece of engineering. When you have made the 850-metre (2,800-ft) descent you are at the head of one of the longest fjords

in the world, Sognefjorden, and on the brink of another scenic high.

The trips can be made in either direction and from any of the stations between Oslo and Bergen.
Norway in a Nutshell round trip: train from Oslo to Myrdal/Flåm, boat to Gudvangen, bus to Voss, train to Oslo.
Norway in a Nutshell one way: train from Oslo to Myrdal/Flåm, boat to Gudvangen, bus to Voss, train to Bergen.

Tickets are sold at the railway stations in Oslo and Bergen or from travel agencies. See www.norway nutshell.com for more details.

Narvik, which is reached through Sweden by train or by bus from Fauske. Most of Norwegian State Railways (NSB's) lines run through tourist country, presenting continuous panoramas of unspoiled scenic beauty. The Oslo–Bergen line is hailed as one of the world's most spectacular for its scenery.

Most trains are modern and efficient, but the older rolling stock has a touch of nostalgic luxury. New inter-city express (ICE) trains offer one class only. There is a wide range of special offers that can make your holiday better value for money.

Rail passes make travelling in Norway cheaper. If you live in Europe, the InterRail Norway Pass gives 3, 4, 6 or 8 days' unlimited 1st- or 2nd-class travel within a one-month period. It also offers discounts on some ferry services. See www.interrailnet.com for details.

If you live outside Europe, the Eurail Scandinavia Pass entitles you to unlimited second-class travel across Scandinavia, for 4, 5, 6, 8 or 10 days within a two-month period. Buy the pass before you travel from www.scandinavianrail.com.

If you plan to take special fast trains, you must book ahead. Ticket sales are from the main hall of the train station (tickets for ordinary trains may also be bought on board).

For information about timetables, ticket prices and bookings contact Trafikanten, Jernbanetorvet 1, by

Travel Passes

The Oslo Pass, issued for 24, 48 or 72 hours, with half price for children, is your ticket to unlimited public transport (including city ferries) and free entry to many museums. If you want a card for travel only, there are all kinds of passes including a Dagskortet (valid for 24 hours) and Flexikort (eight rides at a discount), plus passes appropriate for longer stays.

The Oslo Pass may be purchased at the Central Railway Station (Oslo S), Trafikanten, as well as all Narvesen kiosks and hotels, camp sites and tourist offices.

Other cities offer similar tourist travel cards: for example, the Bergen Card, a 24-hour or 48-hour pass available from tourist information offices, the railway station, hotels, camp sites and the Hurtigruten terminal.

Oslo S, tel: 81 50 01 76 or 177; www.nsb.no

By Bus
Where the rail network stops, the bus goes further: you can get to practically anywhere you want by bus on an ever-growing number of bus lines. Time Express is a popular one (see www.nettbuss.no). Usually it is not necessary to book in advance; just pay the driver on boarding. NOR-WAY Bussekspress (bus pass) guarantees a seat for all passengers. Children up to the age of 4 travel free, 4 to 16 years pay 75 percent of the adult price.

NOR-WAY Bussekspress AS, Karl Johans gt. 2, N-0154 Oslo; tel: 81 54 44 44; www.nor-way.no.

Water Transport
Ferries
You are never very far from the sea in Norway. Ferries are an invaluable means of transport that allow short cuts across fjords to eliminate long road journeys; in built-up areas they are crucial to commuters, like the Horten-Moss ferry across Oslofjord between Vestfold and Østfold. Ferries to the fjord islands around Oslo leave from the Vippetangen quay near Akershus Castle.

Almost all town marinas have places for guest boats. A mooring fee is required.

The following company operates the ferries which run between the centre of Oslo and the Bygdøy Peninsula, where many of the main museums are located.
Bygdøfærgene Skibs
Rådhusbrygge 3, Oslo
Tel: 23 35 68 90
www.boatsightseeing.com

Long-distance Ships
Hurtigruten, the Norwegian Coastal Express service, is a vital means of water transport for Norwegians, but also a superb way for visitors to see Norway's dramatic coast. In summer, boats leave daily, travelling between Bergen and Kirkenes in 11 days and putting in at 34 ports.

Children (between 4 and 15 years old) pay a child's fare. The steamers take cars, and should be booked well in advance. Either contact your local travel agent or:
Hurtigruten
Tel: 81 03 00 00
www.hurtigruten.com
Kystopplevelser (Coastal Experiences)
Tel: 75 54 17 10
www.kystopplevelser.no
Two days in Geiranger fjord. Fly to Ålesund, sail to Geiranger, stay overnight and then return to Oslo. Prices from NOK 2,900.

Buses and Trams
Oslo's bus and tram system is comprehensive and punctual; there are detailed timetables at every stop. Trafikanten can suggest bus or tram routes to get you where you wish to go. There are night buses on some routes and very early morning buses (starting at 4am) so that public transport is available virtually around the clock. Bergen and Trondheim also have tram systems.

Underground
Oslo's underground is called the T-bane (see map on inside back cover) and is simple to use. There are five lines that converge under the centre of Oslo. A circle line linking the station of Storo with Carl Berners

BELOW: going by boat is the only way to travel.

ABOVE: the Lærdal tunnel, the longest in the world, links Oslo with Bergen.

plass was completed in 2006. You can catch any train to any of the far-flung suburbs from any of the stations between Tøyen and Majorstuen. Station entrances are marked with a "T". Trafikanten has route maps. The most scenic route is T-bane 1 up to Frognerseteren. From there enjoy panoramic views back down to Oslo.

Taxis

Taxis are widely available, even in many suburban and rural areas, so you need never risk drink driving (for which penalties are severe).

No matter where you are in Oslo, telephone 023 23 and your call will be transferred to the nearest taxi rank. Mini-buses and taxis (for up to 16 people) can also be booked on 22 38 80 70. Otherwise, you can take a taxi from one of the many taxi ranks scattered around the city.

In Oslo, taxis are more expensive at night or if ordered by phone. At night there are two things to watch out for: when everyone leaves the bars and restaurants late, long queues build up at taxi ranks. This can be extremely uncomfortable in the winter if you are not dressed appropriately. The problem has given rise to a second difficulty: "pirate" taxis. These either cruise up out of the blue or a "dummy" comes and asks you if you want a taxi without queuing. Pirate taxis are a risk, but if you do use one, make sure you agree a price beforehand. They tend to gather at Stortorget, opposite GlassMagasin.

Private Transport
By Car

Norway's roads are extremely good, particularly in view of the treacherous weather conditions encountered in winter. Be prepared for tunnels, though, as some routes have long lengths of road underground.

EU driving licences are valid in

Norway, but drivers from other countries must carry an international driving licence. Drive on the right.

Traffic regulations are strictly enforced *(see Rules of the Road, below)*.

Winter Driving

With Norway's winters, you should never assume all roads are passable. Small roads in the north are often closed so the authorities can put all manpower into keeping main roads safe, and even the E6 highway from Oslo to Trondheim has been known to close. If you intend to travel on minor roads, seek a local's advice or phone the 24-hour Road-User Information Centre (tel: 175 in Norway; tel: 08 15 48 991 from abroad) and go prepared for anything. Your car must be equipped with winter tyres.

Snow-tyre Hire

If you're driving in Norway in winter you can hire the appropriate tyres and snow chains by the week. Ask in any petrol station. In the UK contact:
Snowchains Europroducts
Tel: 01732 884408
Fax: 01732 884564
www.snowchains.co.uk

Breakdown and Accidents

The AA and RAC are affiliated to the AIT (Alliance Internationale de Tourisme), so members receive free assistance (with journey planning as well as backup in case of breakdown or accident) from Norway's NAF (Norges Automobilforbund). More comprehensive repairs can be carried out at NAF-contracted garages (for which you will have to pay). NAF also patrol Norway's main roads and mountain passes from mid-June to mid-August. They have emergency phones along the mountain passes.

NAF
Østensjøveien 14, 0609 Oslo

Tel: 08 505
24-hour emergency service (for members of AIT clubs), tel: 22 34 16 00/81 00 05 05.

If you are involved in an accident where there are no injuries, telephone **Falck Rescue Service** on 02222/810 30 333 or **Viking Redningstjeneste AS** on 06000. Their offices provide a 24-hour service for all Norway.

In an emergency you can contact **Alarmsentralen** (Air Ambulance), tel: 67 92 74 00.

It is not necessary to call the police for minor accidents, but drivers must exchange names and addresses; leaving the scene without doing so is a crime.

Only call the **police** (on **112**) or an **ambulance** (on **113**) if it's a real emergency.

Rules of the Road

It is essential for visitors to Norway to be aware of Norwegian driving regulations, some of which vary significantly from those in the UK and on the continent. Here are a few tips to help you drive safely, but for further guidance it's worth getting a copy of *Velkommen på norske veier* (Welcome to Norwegian Roads), which includes an English section and is available at tourist offices.

Speed Limits The maximum speed limit is usually 80 kph (50 mph), though 100 kph (62 mph) is permitted on some roads (mainly motorways). The limit is reduced to 40 kph (24 mph) in built-up areas, and even 30 kph (18 mph) on certain residential roads. On-the-spot fines are given for drivers found speeding (this may be as much as NOK 3,500). Speed cameras and radar traps are both used.

Giving Way This can be very confusing to the visitor. Roads marked at intervals by yellow diamond signs indicate that you have priority. On all other roads you are

DENMARK

NORWAY

SWEDEN

FINLAND

required to give way to traffic entering from the right. This is further confused by the fact that some roads have a series of white triangles painted across them at junctions, which mean stop and give way, though as you can imagine these easily become obliterated by snow and ice in the winter.

On roundabouts, priority is from the left. Always give way to trams, buses and taxis. Many roads have a right-hand lane exclusively for buses and taxis.

Drinking and driving You are strongly advised not to drink at all if you anticipate driving within at least eight hours. The current permissible limit is 0.02 per ml, and penalties are severe (imprisonment, a high fine and loss of licence are automatic).

Documentation and equipment You must always have the following with you in your car: driving licence, car registration documents, European accident statement form, insurance policy and a reflective warning triangle. A snow shovel and tow rope are also useful in winter. For regularly updated information in the UK, the AA runs a very good fact line for just a small charge on tel: 0870 600 0371; www.theaa.com

Lights It is obligatory to drive with dipped headlights on during the daytime, even on the brightest summer day. This rule applies to all vehicles, including motorcycles and mopeds. We recommend you carry spare bulbs. Do not forget that right-hand drive cars require black adhesive triangles (often supplied by ferry companies), or clip-on beam deflectors, so you don't dazzle oncoming drivers.

Seat belts must be worn, both front and back (again, there are on-the-spot fines for failing to comply). Motorcycle and moped drivers and their passengers must wear helmets.

Tyres It is obligatory to use winter tyres from October to April. These are either tyres with studs (*piggdekk*) or specially designed tyres for use in ice and snow. Studded tyres are preferred but these may soon be prohibited in urban areas for environmental reasons.

Car Hire

Hiring a car in Norway can be expensive, but may be worthwhile if shared between several people. Otherwise, watch for special weekend and summer prices.

Avis Bilutleie-Liva Bil AS
PO Box 154, N-1376 Billingstad

(near Oslo)
Tel: 66 77 11 11
Fax: 66 77 11 30
Booking tel: 81 53 30 44
www.avis.no
Europcar
Grini Næringspark 10, PO Box 173, 1332 Østerås
Tel: 67 16 58 00
Booking tel: 67 16 58 20
www.europcar.no
Hertz Bilutleie
PO Box 331, N-1324 Lysaker/Oslo
Tel: 67 16 80 80
Booking tel: 67 16 80 00
www.hertz.no

Cycling

Cycling in Norway is safe, as there is so little traffic on many minor roads. But you must ride with caution as, though there are a few cycle routes, it is not an integrated system. Cyclists are not allowed to go through the larger tunnels, for example (because of car fumes). Out in the countryside you'll find surfaced cycle paths. Cycling is a good way of exploring outside Oslo: bicycles are allowed on most trains and buses for a small charge.

Special cycle trains are laid on during the summer. Tourist offices have details of mountain cycle tours.

The **Syklistens Landsforening** (Cycling Association) can help plan tours and cycling holidays: Storg. 23D, Pb. 8883 Youngstorget, 0028 Oslo; tel: 22 47 30 30; fax: 22 47 30 31; e-mail: post@syklistene.no.

Sykkelturisme i Norge (Institute for Cycle Tourism) was set up in conjunction with the Norwegian Tourist Board to help promote cycling in Norway: C. Sundtsgate 10, N-5004 Bergen; fax: 55 23 04 42;

e-mail: post@bike-norway.com; www.bike-norway.com.

To organise cycle routes and transport for bicycles, contact Skiforeningen, Kongeveien 5, 0787 Oslo; tel: 22 92 32 00; fax: 22 92 32 50; e-mail: ski@skiforeningen.no

Cycle Rental

In Oslo and Bergen, bikes can be hired from hotels, campsites, local tourist offices or sports shops, as well as small cycle-hire shops.
A/S Skiservice, dept. bike, Voksenkollen Stasjon, Tryvannsveien 2, 0394 Oslo
Tel: 22 13 95 00
Vestbanen Bike Rental
Brynjulf Bulls plass 2, 0250 Oslo
Tel: 22 83 52 08

On Foot

There is almost nowhere in Norway you can't go happily on foot; it is a nation of devout walkers, and walking is one of the most popular outdoor activities at weekends.

The law of access to the natural environment, known as "everyman's right", allows you to walk wherever you want in the wilderness such as seashore, forests, mountains and in other non-cultivated regions. This should be done with consideration. Use paths and roads when walking in agricultural and populated areas.

It is preferable to make use of campsites if you are staying overnight outdoors. If you pitch a tent in the wilderness, it should be situated at least 150 metres/yards from the nearest house or hut. Open fires are prohibited from 15 April to 15 September.

Detailed maps are available from the Norwegian Trekking Association

BELOW: cycling is a good way to see the fantastic views.

(DNT). Membership gives you rights to use the association's huts. The map and guidebook selection is excellent; survey maps of Norway are sold; sketch maps are free.

The Norwegian Tourist Board publishes a handbook, *Mountain Hiking in Norway*, which gives suggested itineraries for mountain walks and details of chalets and where to stay. Contact Scandinavia Connection, 26 Woodsford Square, London W14 8DP; tel: 020 7602 0657; www.scandinavia-connection.co.uk.

Den Norske Turistforening, (Norwegian Trekking Association) Storgata 7, PO Box 7 Sentrum, 0101 Oslo; tel: 40 00 18 68; www.turistforening.no.

Visas and Passports

A valid passport is all that is necessary for citizens of most countries to enter Norway. Visas are not required. Norway is a member of the Schengen agreement, allowing citizens of other Schengen countries to enter without passports. If you enter from another Nordic country (Denmark, Finland, Iceland, or Sweden), you won't get an entry stamp. Tourists are generally limited to a three-month visit; it is possible to stay longer, but you must apply for a visa after the initial three months (Scandinavian passport holders are exempt from this requirement) or if you plan to work in Norway.

Customs Regulations
The following can be brought into Norway by visitors:
Money Notes and coins (Norwegian and foreign) up to NOK 25,000 or equivalent. If you intend to import more, you must fill in a form (available at all entry and exit points) for the Customs Office.
Alcohol Permitted imports for people aged 20 and over include 1 litre of spirits (up to 60 percent vol.) plus 1 litre of fortified wine (up to 22 percent vol.) or 3 litres of wine (if no spirits) and 2 litres of beer, or 5 litres of beer.
Tobacco European residents over the age of 18 may bring 200 cigarettes or 250 g of other tobacco goods.
Sweets 1 kg (2.2 pounds) duty-free chocolate and sweets.
Meat and dairy products Meat, meat products, cheese and foodstuffs except dog and cat food, totalling 10 kg (22 pounds) altogether from EEA (European Economic Area) countries. From countries outside the EEA, it is prohibited to bring meat, meat products, milk and milk products with you in your luggage.

Sundries Other goods (excluding articles for personal use) may be brought in duty-free up to a value of NOK 6,000.
Prohibited goods Narcotics, medicines (except for personal use), poisons, firearms, ammunition and explosives. Note: the mild narcotic leaf khat is illegal in Norway.
Agricultural produce This comes under strict surveillance. If it concerns you, get specific details beforehand.

Animals
Dogs, cats and ferrets from all EU countries except Sweden must have pet passports, ID marking, a valid rabies vaccination, and valid blood-test documentation (this does not apply to ferrets). Dogs and cats must also be given approved tapeworm treatment during the week before and the week after they have been brought into the country.

What to Bring
You're in for a pleasant surprise if travelling to Norway in summer. As it is influenced by the Gulf Stream it can get even warmer than some of its southern neighbours. In the south, temperatures above 25°C (77°F) are not unusual. The average temperature for the country as a whole in July, including the far north, is about 16°C (60°F), 22°C (71°F) in Oslo. Bring swimming gear, as the water in most fjords, except northern Norway, is 20°C (68°F) in midsummer.

A first-aid kit is recommended for those who plan to make any trips to remoter parts. And be sure to include medicines for preventing and treating mosquito bites, as from midsummer into early autumn biting insects are rife, especially in Finnmark.

What to Read
Snorri Sturlson
The Prose Edda, Penguin Classics, 2005.
Heimskringla, History of the Kings of Norway, University of Texas Press, 1991.
King Harald's Saga (an excerpt from the *Heimskringla*), Penguin Classics, 1976.

Miscellaneous
Garrison Keillor's Lake Wobegone Series.
A Happy Boy, Bjørnson Bjørnstjerne.
Constance Ring, Amalie Skram, Northwest University Press, 2002.
Shyness and Dignity, Dag Solstad, 2006.

Weights and Measures
Metric. Distances are given in kilometres (km) but Norwegians often refer to a *mil* which is 10 km (thus 10 mil = 100 km). When talking about land area you will often hear the word *mål*. This old measure of 984.34 sq. metres has been rounded up to 1,000 sq. metres (or 1 decare).

Kristin Lavransdatter, Sigrid Undset, Penguin, 2005.
Writing on the Wall, Gunnar Staalesen, Arcadia, 2002.
Punishment, Anne Holt, Time Warner, 2006.

Henrik Ibsen
A Doll's House
Peer Gynt, Oxford Classics.

Edvard Munch
Edvard Munch: Behind the Scream, Yale University Press, 2005.

Arctic Explorers
Scott and Amundsen: Last Place on Earth, Roland Huntford, Abacus 2000.
The South Pole: An Account of the Norwegian Antarctic Exploration in the Fram, 1910–12, Roald Amundsen, Cooper Square Press, 2001.
Kon Tiki: Across the Pacific by Raft, Thor Heyerdahl, Simon and Schuster Press, 1995.
Kon Tiki Expedition, Flamingo 1996.
In the Footsteps of Adam, Heyerdahl's autobiography, Abacus, 2001.
No Horizon is So Far, Ann Bancroft, Da Capo, 2003. About Liv Arnesen's journey.

Knut Hamsun
Hunger, Canongate Books, 2006.
Mysteries, Souvenir Press, 1992.
The Growth of the Soil, Souvenir Press, 1989.
Wanderer, Souvenir Press, 2001.
In Wonderland, IG Publishing, 2004.
Wayfarers, Souvenir Press, 1994.
Women at the Pump, Souvenir Press, 1978.

Jostein Gaarder
Orange Girl, Phoenix, 2005.
Sophie's World: A Novel about the History of Philosophy, Phoenix, 1996.
Ringmaster's Daughter, Orion, 2003.

Other Insight Guides
Insight Guide titles in the region include *Insight Pocket Guides Oslo & Bergen*, *Insight Guide Norway* and *Insight Fleximaps Norway*.

A CCOMMODATION

HOTELS, YOUTH HOSTELS, BED AND BREAKFAST

Norwegian hotels can be expensive, but, in common with the rest of Scandinavia, they reduce their rates during the outdoor summer holiday period when business decreases. This makes May to September attractive when compared with standard rates. Weekends are also usually cheaper. Normal weekday rates outside summer are geared towards business occupants, but are generally in line with, sometimes even lower than, hotels elsewhere in Europe or the US.

When it comes to places to stay, Norway has something to suit every requirement. The range covers hotels from the luxurious to the simple, to more modest guesthouses, camp sites, cosy self-catering cottages, and youth and family hostels.

The British-style bed and breakfast is developing in Norway, and country or farm holidays offer an opportunity to experience day-to-day farm life at close quarters.

Full-board terms are available to guests staying at the same establishment for at least three to five days. Children often go for free, providing the child stays in the parents' room. Guesthouses *(pensjonat)* offer lower rates and may have shared baths (the bathroom may be down the hall).

The state-run visitors' site, www.visitnorway.com, can be a good starting point for tracking down accommodation.

An online hotel-booking service is available at www.hotels-in-norway.com.

Hotel Chains

Some of the major hotel chains are well-represented in Norway's major cities, but many are not, or they operate through a local brand.

Several local chains, meanwhile, offer passes and discount schemes to help reduce the cost of accommodation. These passes, available for sale at participating hotels, usually involve a modest one-time fee (around NOK 100) and then entitle the holder to discounted rates, mostly in the summer and on weekends. Some passes also offer a free night of accommodation after the pass holder has logged several nights on the programme.

Among the hotel chains in Norway:
Best Western Hotels Norway
Kronprinsens gt 1
0251 Oslo
Tel: 22 94 40 60
Toll-free: 800 11 624
www.bestwestern.no
Choice Hotels AS
Frederik Stangs gate 22–24,
PO Box 2454 Solli
0201 Oslo
Tel: 22 40 13 00
www.choicehotels.no
Fjord Tours AS
Norway Fjord Pass
Strømgate 4
5015 Bergen
Tel: 815 68 222, ext 2
www.fjordpass.no
Norlandia Hotels
Norlandia Guest Card
Tel: 815 44 144
www.norlandia.no
Radisson SAS Hotels
Tel: 800 160 91
Toll-free from UK: 0800 374411
www.radisson.com
Rica Hotels
Rica Hotels Loyalty Card
Slependveien 108
1375 Billingstad
Tel: 66 85 45 60
www.rica.no
Scandic Hotels
Sjølyst pl 5
Tel: 23 15 50 00
www.scandichotels.com
Thon Hotels
Stenersgate 2

BELOW: fishermen's cabins *(rorbuer)* in the Lofoten Islands.

Norway's Historic Hotels

Tradition runs strong in Norway, and Norwegians are known for preserving their heritage. Massive investment in historic properties has made it possible for visitors to stay in a wide range of them, while enjoying every modern convenience and gourmet meals as well.

A few hotel organisations have been formed during the past decade to keep Norway's historic hotels alive and up-to-date, while maintaining their character and charm. Some of these fairy-tale-like structures are in towns and cities, but many are in the mountains,

along fjords and frankly in relatively obscure but often beautiful locations, making them a destination in themselves. All of the properties are unique, and most include dinner and breakfast as part of the room rate. Overnight accommodation for two including dinner and breakfast generally runs to around NOK 2,000, plus drinks. A couple worth trying:

De historiske
PO Box 196 Sentrum
5804 Bergen
Tel: 55 31 67 60
www.dehistoriske.no
This is a group of around 30 historic

hotels, manor houses or timbered lodges and 14 selected restaurants around Norway, catering to visitors keen on style and good food.
The Great Life Company
Karenslyst allé 11, PO Box 54
Skøyen, 0212 Oslo
Tel: 24 12 62 10
www.thegreatlifecompany.com
Controlled by a shipowning Oslo family that's made a business out of restoring gracious old lodging establishments. The group consists of around 20 mostly historic inns and restaurants, with a few modern surprises.

Thon Guest Card
Tel: 23 08 02 00
www.thonhotels.no

Hotels

The hotels are listed geographically, and given a price category. There is a separate box above with information on booking rooms at some of Norway's historic hotels, many of which are a destination in themselves.

Breakfast Included

Norwegian hotels almost always offer a breakfast buffet that's included in the room rate. All hotel taxes are also included in the quoted rates, so there are rarely any nasty surprises upon checkout (unless you have used the phone in your room to make external calls).

Booking in Oslo

In Oslo, the Tourist Information centres at Fridtjof Nansens Plass 5 (Mon–Sat 9am–5pm), and at the Central Station (daily 8am–8pm; will book accommodation in the capital for those requesting it in person. This service covers private rooms, pensions and hotels.

City Packages

The Oslo Package offers great value for money. It is available at weekends and during the holiday seasons (Easter, summer holidays and Christmas time). The price includes accommodation with breakfast (there are 40 hotels to choose from in Oslo) plus the Oslo card which includes free entrance to many museums and attractions, free inner city transport and numerous discounts. The packages can be booked through

tourist information offices in Oslo or through a travel agency, but not directly with the hotel.

Chalets *(Hytter)*

There are abundant holiday *hytter* (cabins or chalets) available for rent. These usually house four to six people. If you want to spend just one night in a chalet and then move on, you can stay in one on a campsite without booking ahead. See accommodation guides at www.visitnorway.com, or try the Cultural Heritage Association's website at www.olavsrosa.no/en.

Fishermen's Cabins (Rorbuer)

In the Lofoten Islands in northern Norway, and at numerous places elsewhere along the coast, you can rent a traditional former fisherman's cabin, called a *rorbu*. The fishermen used to come to Lofoten from other parts of the coast for the winter cod-fishing season from January to April, and would make these cabins their temporary homes. Most of them have been modernised, and some have their own shower and toilet.
Lofoten Tourist Office
Tel: 76 06 98 00. Fax: 76 07 30 01

Camping

Norway has more than 1,000 campsites, classified by 1–5 stars, depending on the standard and facilities available. The fixed charge per plot is usually NOK 80–160, with additional charges per person.

With the Norwegian camping card *(Norsk Campingkort)* you receive a faster checking-in service along with special discount deals. The card is available from participating campsites. Many campsites have cabins that may be booked in advance.

Some are small and basic, but others are large and well equipped. Both close to Oslo, Ekeberg Camping (tel: 22 19 85 68) and Bogstad Camping – the largest campsite in Norway – also have cabins (tel: 22 51 08 00).

For further information, write to: Norwegian Camping Guide, Essendropsgt. 3, PO Box 5465 Majorstuen, N-0305 Oslo or log onto www.camping.no

Bed and Breakfasts

British-style bed and breakfasts are catching on in Norway, and they are all of a high standard. You can book at local tourist offices or at Oslo's central railway station. Or look out for signs for *Rom* or *Husrom* houses as you drive. A guidebook, *The Norway Bed and Breakfast Book*, with listings throughout the country, is available from tourist offices and book shops in Norway or from:
Scandinavia Connection
26 Woodsford Square,
London W14 8DP
Tel: 020 7602 0657
www.scandinavia-connection.co.uk

Youth and Family Hostels

There are approximately 100 youth hostels in Norway, all of a relatively high standard.

A night's accommodation costs from NOK 200, breakfast NOK 60–75 for members of the YHA. Further information can be obtained by contacting *Hostelling International Norway*, or your local YHA office.

Reserving space during the high season is essential, as hostel accommodation is the cheapest way to travel and everyone knows it.
Norske Vandrerhjem
(Hostelling International Norway),
P.B. 53 Grefsen, 0409 Oslo
Tel: 23 12 45 10; www.vandrerhjem.no

DENMARK

NORWAY

SWEDEN

FINLAND

OSLO

Hotel Bristol
Kristian IV's Gate 7
Tel: 22 82 60 00
www.bristol.no
Now part of the Thon Hotels chain, the Bristol remains a classy place to stay in the heart of downtown. Known for its "Bibliotek (Library) Bar" in the lobby and its Bristol Grill restaurant, the hotel is a popular meeting place for journalists, politicians and local celebrities. **$$$**

Cochs Pensjonat
Parkveien 25
Tel: 23 33 24 00
www.cochspensjonat.no
A friendly relatively low-price alternative with a loyal following, just at the foot of one of Oslo's most popular shopping streets (Hegdehaugsveien-Bogstadveien) and a block from the park around the Royal Palace. Not all rooms have private baths. **$**

Comfort Hotel Boersparken
Tollbugaten 4
Tel: 22 47 17 17
www.choicehotels.no
Another member of the reliable Choice Hotels family, Boersparken is comfortable, friendly and handy for the station. Rooms overlooking the harbour, with superb views of Oslo's brand-new Opera House, are the best. **$$–$$$**

Hotel Continental
Stortingsgate 24–26
Tel: 22 82 40 00
www.hotel-continental.no
This five-star family-run hotel often ranks among the best in northern Europe, and is famed for its classic Theater Café, a Viennese-style café that's the place to see and be seen in Oslo. **$$$**

First Hotel Grims Grenka
Kongens Gate 5
Tel: 23 10 72 00
www.firsthotels.com
Billed as Oslo's first "design hotel without the attitude". 42 rooms and 24 suites, rooftop lounge. Opened in Sept 2007. **$$**

First Hotel Millennium
Tollbugaten 25
Tel: 21 02 28 00
www.firsthotels.com
Suite-style family rooms available in a downtown location, also popular with business travellers. **$$**

Gabelshus Hotel
Gabels Gate 16
Tel: 23 27 65 00
www.choicehotels.no
This ivy-clad hotel in a quiet residential neighbourhood near downtown is now part of the Clarion Collection of hotels. It opened in 1912. **$$**

Grand Hotel
Karl Johans Gate 31
Tel: 23 21 20 00
www.grand.no

This is where the Nobel Peace Prize winner stays every year, and where the Nobel Banquet is held. Located just across from the Norwegian Parliament, its venerable Grand Café also was a favourite haunt of playwright Henrik Ibsen. **$$$**

Holmenkollen Park Hotel
Kongeveien 26
Tel: 22 92 20 00
www.holmenkollenparkhotel.no
This magnificent wooden hotel is perched high above Oslo in the hills adjacent to the famed Holmenkollen Ski Jump. There are outstanding views over the city and fjord, with hiking and skiing trails out the front door. Rooms are located in a modern annexe. **$$**

Karl Johan Hotel
Karl Johans Gate 33
Tel: 23 16 17 00
www.norlandia.no/karljohan
Now part of the mid-price Norlandia chain, this stately old hotel is a cut above most of its sister properties and the location can't be beaten, right next door to the Grand and in the heart of Oslo's downtown. **$$**

Perminalen Hotel
Øvre Slottsgate 2
Tel: 23 09 30 81
www.perminalen.no
A recently renovated hotel near the Parliament that appeals to young people on

a tight budget. Simple rooms, where it's possible to pay just for a bed in a four-bunk room. All rooms have private baths. **$**

Radisson SAS Scandinavia Hotel
Holbergs Gate 30

Radisson SAS Plaza Hotel
Sonja Henies Plass 3
Toll-free tel (UK): 0800 374411
www.radisson.com
Classic high-rise business-orientated hotels, with favourable rates in the summer. **$$**

Hotel Savoy
Universitets Gate 11
Tel: 23 35 42 00
www.choicehotels.no
A landmark hotel that recently re-emerged in ultra-modern style, sporting one of Oslo's best restaurants (Restaurant Eik). Part of the Clarion Collection of hotels. **$$**

Thon Hotel Vika Atrium
Munkedamsveien 45
Tel: 22 83 33 00
www.thonhotels.no/vikaatrium
Mid-range hotel in a great location near the City Hall plaza and Aker Brygge. **$$**

Thon Opera
Christian Frederiks Plass 5
Tel: 24 10 30 00
www.thonhotels.no/opera
Also a good central choice, Thon Opera is a harbourside business hotel with decent if rather impersonal rooms. **$$**

AROUND OSLO

Oscarsborg Festning
1443 Oscarsborg
Tel: 815 51 900
www.nasjonalefestningsverk.no/oscarsborg
Here you can stay in an historic fortress on an island off Drøbak in the Oslo Fjord. It's good value for money and open all year, although arguably most appealing in the summer months. The ferry service is from Drøbak, a picturesque coastal town in itself. **$**

Radisson SAS Airport Hotel
Oslo Airport Gardermoen
Tel: 63 93 30 00
www.radisson.com
If you need to be near Oslo's main airport, then you can't beat this for convenience. You can walk from baggage claim to this elegant and comfortable hotel in a matter of minutes. **$$**

Hotell Refsnesgods
Godset 5, 1518 Moss
Tel: 69 27 83 00
www.refsnesgods.no
Located right on the Oslo

Fjord on the island of Jeløy, about an hour south of Oslo, this is an elegant getaway spot known for its wine cellar and art collection. Several rooms face the beach. **$$$**

Scandic Asker
Askerveien 61
Tel: 23 15 54 00
www.scandichotels.com
Suburban hotel, completely renovated in 2008, near the train station and the main motorway into Oslo. **$**

Thon Hotel Oslofjord
Sandviksveien 184
1337 Sandvika
Tel: 67 55 66 00
www.thonhotels.no/oslofjord
This hotel on the busy E18 motorway in the western suburb of Sandvika has been part of several chains and is now in the Thon group. It's close to downtown Sandvika, Bærum Kulturhus and Ikea at Slependen. Also close to the fjord. **$**

STAVANGER

Radisson SAS Atlantic Hotel
Olav V's Gate 3
Tel: 51 76 10 00
www.radisson.com
High-rise business hotel in the heart of town, overlooking Lake Breiavatnet. Five-minute walk to the harbour and all its restaurants and bars, with deeply discounted room rates in the summer. **$$**

Radisson SAS Royal Hotel
Løkkeveien 26
Tel: 51 76 60 00
www.radisson.com
Located behind its sister property Atlantic, this is a mid-rise luxury hotel most memorable for its themed floors. Swimming pool, sauna and jacuzzi. **$$–$$$**

Sola Strand Hotel
Axel Lundsveien 27
4050 Sola
Tel: 51 94 30 00
www.sola-strandhotel.no
"Strand" means "beach" in Norwegian, and this hotel is located on one of the many windswept beaches along the North Sea, about a 20-minute drive from downtown Stavanger. A classic, traditional hotel with plenty of space to unwind. **$$**

Thon Hotel Maritim
Kongsgaten 32
Tel: 51 85 05 00
www.thonhotels.no/maritim
Tucked into a side-street across from Stavanger's downtown lake, this mid-range hotel offers discounted rates on weekends and in the summer. **$**

Utstein Kloster Hotel
Mosterøyveien 661
4156 Mosterøy
Tel: 51 72 01 00
www.utsteinklosterhotell.no
Another waterfront hotel, this one is located on an island north of Stavanger near the historic Utstein Cloister. It's connected to the mainland, though, by an underwater tunnel. Excellent area for cycling and seeing historic sites. **$$**

Victoria Hotel
Skansegate 1
Tel: 51 86 70 00
www.victoria-hotel.no
Historic, first-class, family-run hotel on the harbour, in the heart of the bar and restaurant district yet somehow quietly removed. **$$**

BERGEN

Clarion Admiral
C. Sundtsgate 9–13, 5004
Tel: 55 23 64 00
Fax: 55 23 64 64
www.choicehotels.no
Part of the Choice chain and one of Bergen's finest hotels. There are 210 rooms in varying categories, many of which have superb views over the harbour to Bryggen, while the restaurant has excellent cuisine. **$$**

Comfort Hotel Holberg
Strandgaten 190
Tel: 55 30 42 00
www.choicehotels.no
This place represents perfect value for money. Although rooms are small, they're clean, comfortable, and were all newly renovated (with flatscreen TVs) in 2007. There's free wifi access, tea and coffee, and a brand-new Chili Bar and Restaurant. **$$**

Hotel Park Pension
Harald Hårfagresgt 35, 5035
Tel: 55 54 44 00
Fax: 55 54 44 44
E-mail: booking@parkhotel.no
www.parkhotel.no

This family-operated hotel with 40 rooms has its own unique flavour and character due to the owner's taste for original antiques. It is located in the university quarter. **$**

Radisson SAS Hotel Norge
Nedre Ole Bulls Plass, 5807
Tel: 55 57 30 00
Fax: 55 57 30 01
www.radissonsas.com
One of Bergen's best-loved hotels and meeting places, right in the centre, with 345 rooms and suites of the highest standard. Three restaurants including gourmet Ole Bull. Winter garden, swimming pool, nightclub. **$$$**

Radisson SAS Royal Hotel
Bryggen, 5835
Tel: 55 54 30 00
Fax: 55 32 48 08
www.radissonsas.com
The classic Norwegian architectural style makes this an unusually handsome hotel as it is actually several old warehouses. Upmarket facilities. **$$$**

Hotel Rosenkrantz
Rosenkrantzgate 7, 5035
Tel: 55 30 14 00
Fax: 55 31 14 76
www.thonhotel.no/rosenkrantz
Comfortable, early 20th-century hotel located in the street behind Bryggen (the wharf) in the heart of the old town; well modernised in light, airy colours. The best rooms have a view of the harbour but get booked up, so plan ahead. There's a restaurant and piano bar. Hotel nightclub entrance is next door. **$$**

Scandic Hotel Bergen
Håkonsgaten 2, 5015
Tel: 55 30 90 80
Fax: 55 30 90 91
E-mail: bergencity@scandichotels.com
www.scandichotels.com
Newly extended and now the biggest Scandic hotel in Norway. Wireless internet access available. Near the city centre. **$$**

Strand Hotel
Strandkaien 2B, 5013
Tel: 55 59 33 00
Fax: 55 59 33 33
E-mail: post@strandhotel.no
www.strandhotel.no
Superb harbour views make for a pleasant stay. Family-run hotel with a cosy breakfast room, bar (rated among the five best in Norway) and dinner served in the Lido restaurant. **$$**

PRICE CATEGORIES

Price categories are based on the average cost of a double room for two, with breakfast in high season.
$ = Less than NOK 1,100
$$ = NOK 1,100–1,700
$$$ = More than NOK 1,700

DENMARK

NORWAY

SWEDEN

FINLAND

TRONDHEIM

Britannia Hotel
Dronningensgate 5
Tel: 73 800 800
www.britannia.no
A brand-new spa opened
here in 2008. Otherwise
the Britannia is an old-
fashioned, independently-
owned place, with
comfortable rooms and
four restaurants. $$$
Clarion Collection Bakeriet
Brattorgata 2
Tel: 73 99 10 00
www.choicehotels.no
Based in an old bakery, this
pleasant hotel keeps up
traditions by offering guests
freshly baked afternoon
waffles. Unusually for
Scandinavia, many of the
rooms have bath tubs. $$
Elgeseter Hotel
Tormodsgate 3

Tel: 73 82 03 30
Fax: 73 82 03 31
E-mail: elgeseter.hotell@munken.no
www.elgeseter-hotell.no
Conveniently located just
10 minutes' walk from the
centre. $
Grand Olav Clarion Hotel
Kjøpmannsgaten 48
Tel: 73 80 80 80
Fax: 73 80 80 81
E-mail: cc.grand.olav@choice.no
www.choicehotels.no
Top-class hotel situated in
the heart of Trondheim,
close to shops, bars and
restaurants. Renovated in
2007. Runs an airport bus.
$$$
Prinsen Scandic
Kongensgate 30
Tel: 73 80 70 00
Fax: 73 80 70 10
E-mail: prinsen@scandichotels.com

www.scandichotels.com
A wealth of facilities here
including 81 rooms, the
fine Pinocchio restaurant, a
bistro, bar, grill room, wine
tavern and beer garden. $$
Quality Hotel Augustin
Kongensgate 26
Tel: 73 54 70 00
Fax: 73 54 70 01
E-mail: hotel-augustin@hotel-
augustin.no
www.hotel-augustin.no
Close to the main city
square, this huge old brick
hotel has 139 comfortable
rooms, bar, fitness room,
internet access and
covered parking. $$
**Radisson SAS Royal
Garden Hotel**
Kjøpmannsgt 73
Tel: 73 80 30 00
Fax: 73 80 30 50

www.radisson.com
Has 298 well-appointed
rooms plus solarium, indoor
pool, gymnasium, sauna
and several good
restaurants. Runs an airport
bus every 15 minutes. $$
Thon Hotel Gildevangen
Søndre gate 22B
Tel: 73 87 01 30
Fax: 73 52 38 98
E-mail: gildevangen@thonhotels.no
www.thonhotels.no/gildevangen
In a grand building in the
centre of town, near the
bus and train stations, and
with a stop for the airport
shuttle right outside. All the
rooms are a good size and
decorated to a high
standard. The restaurant,
on the second floor, only
serves breakfast; bar,
internet access. $$

TROMSØ

Ami Hotel
Skolegata 24
Tel: 77 62 10 00
www.amihotel.no
More B&B than hotel, this is
a great-value option for
those on a budget. All rooms
have fridges, and there's a
guest kitchen so you can
self-cater. Some rooms have
private facilities. $

Grand Nordic
Storgt 44
Tel: 77 75 37 77
Fax: 77 75 37 78
E-mail: Resepsjon.gnt@nordic.no
www.nordic.no
Close to the centre, 4 km
(2½ miles) from the airport.
Full conference facilities
and well-appointed rooms.
$$

Quality Hotel Saga
Richard Withs plass 2
Tel: 77 60 70 00
Fax: 77 60 70 10
www.choicehotels.no
Small conference hotel
with relaxing atmosphere.
$$
Rica Ishavshotel
Fr. Langesgt. 2
Tel: 77 66 64 00
Fax: 77 66 64 44
E-mail: rica.ishavshotel@rica.no

First-rate luxury hotel close
to the centre, specialising
in conferences and
comfort. $$$
Scandic Tromsø
Heiloveien 23
Tel: 77 75 50 00
Fax: 77 75 50 11
E-mail: tromso@scandichotels.com
www.scandichotels.no/tromso
Modest conference hotel
located in Tromsø suburb
close to the airport. Free
bicycle hire for guests. $$
Hotel With
Sjøgata 35–37, N-9257
Tel: 77 68 42 00
Fax: 77 68 96 16
www.clarionhotel.com
A first-class hotel with a
difference. Situated by the
waterfront in Tromsø's
dock district, it offers a
beautiful view to the
Tromsø bridge and the
famous Arctic Cathedral,
and has a maritime
atmosphere. $$

BELOW: the Rica Ishavshotel at Tromsø.

PRICE CATEGORIES
Price categories are based on the average cost of a double room for two, with breakfast in high season. $ = Less than NOK 1,100 $$ = NOK 1,100–1,700 $$$ = More than NOK 1,700

E ATING OUT

RECOMMENDED RESTAURANTS AND CAFÉS

What to Eat

Norwegians eat hearty breakfasts, but light lunches; the size of the evening meal *(middag)* depends on the day of the week and the occasion.

With the abundant supply of seafood and what can be gleaned from forest and field, the Norwegian diet has traditionally been healthy and appetising. For example, white bread is rarely purchased as most Norwegians prefer brown bread or dry crackers for breakfast. However, the younger generation has a tendency to eat frozen pizzas and easily prepared meals.

The hunting season (early autumn) offers some irresistible temptations: pheasant, grouse, elk and reindeer steaks served with peppercorns and rich mushroom sauces. It is also a good time of year to make the most of seafood (with cod considered best in months with an R in them).

Outside main meals there are many coffee breaks, often served with pastries, including *bolle* (raisin buns) and *wienerbrød* (lighter pastries laced with fruit or nuts).

Frokost (breakfast) is more or less a variation of the lunch *Kaldtbord*, a spread including breads (try *grovbrød* and *knekkebrød*), sausage, cheese (try the piquant *Gudbrandsost*, a delicious burnt goats' milk cheese with a dark golden colour), eggs, herrings, *gravlax* (marinated salmon), and coffee and tea.

The lunch version has hot dishes, such as sliced roast meats, meatballs or fish. *Øllebrød* (beef marinated in beer and served inside pitta bread with salad) makes a hearty, inexpensive lunch; an open-faced shrimp or ham sandwich is another staple.

Dinner in a city restaurant can be

Drinking Notes

No one talks about a trip to Norway without complaining of the high cost of alcohol. For those who can afford the prices, serving hours are long; in Oslo you can drink spirits until midnight and wine or beer until 3am. Outside Oslo, times are less predictable; a conservative Lutheran culture holds sway in many west-coast areas, rendering some counties virtually dry. But there are exceptions to this: in Oslo, for example, there are some no-alcohol hotel/restaurants and in the "dry" counties it is always possible to find a hotel/restaurant

anything you wish. In someone's home you might eat mutton stew or a fish ragout. Boiled potatoes with dill or parsley usually accompany a hot main course. When dining in more remote places, the menus will invariably be limited by availability. *Smørbrød* is a snack (called *aftens* when eaten late at night), usually of bread or crackers with butter, cheese and salami or ham.

For dessert, ice cream is a favourite, as is apple pie. In summer there are all kinds of puddings based on the fresh berries that grow profusely in the Norwegian woods.

Where to Eat

There has been a significant increase in what's on offer when you choose to eat out in Norway. Pizza is very popular and the cynic may even describe it as the Norwegian national dish. Asian food has also become a local favourite, although Indian restaurants tend to tone down the spices to suit the

that serves some form of alcohol.

The *Vinmonopolet* (state off-licences/liquor stores) in cities are open Mon–Fri 10am–6pm and Sat 9am–2pm; they are closed on election days, holidays and the preceding day of a holiday.

Most Norwegians drink beer and/or wine. Traditional *Akevitt*, similar in taste to Schnapps, is derived from potato and caraway seeds, and is also a favourite. It can be sipped neat in small glasses at room temperature, or served cold with beer to accompany salty, spicy or pungent dishes.

more delicate Norwegian palate, so you may wish to tell the waiter to beef it up a bit. Continental European dishes have always played a role in Norwegian cuisine (such as Viennese- and French-style dishes), but pride in native foods and an interest in "new Scandinavian" cuisine is prevalent.

At lunch time many restaurants offer special fixed-price menus. More casual meals can be had from informal establishments, which come under a range of names such as *stovas, kros, bistros, kafés, kafeterias,* and *gjæstgiveris* and may sell alcohol as well as coffee and soft drinks. For an even more casual meal buy a hot dog *(pølse)*, kebab or a waffle from a kiosk; these stay open late to catch pubcrawlers. And yes, there is McDonald's.

Restaurant Listings

Restaurants are grouped by area starting with Oslo. They are listed alphabetically.

RESTAURANT LISTINGS

OSLO

Norwegian Classics

De Fem Stuer
Holmenkollen Park Hotel
Tel: 22 92 20 00
Elegant dining inside the historic timbered salons of this fairy-tale-like hotel overlooking the city and fjord. Five separate dining areas as the name suggests. Booking recommended. **$$$**

Det Gamle Raadhus
Nedre Slotts Gate 1
Tel: 22 42 01 07
Housed in the capital's old city hall from the 1600s, now best known for its *lutefisk* in the months leading up to Christmas. **$$**

DS Louise
Stranden 3
Tel: 22 83 00 60
This was one of the first restaurants to open at the waterfront complex Aker Brygge, and it's still going strong. Nostalgic maritime decor and a wide range of traditional dishes. **$$**

Ekeberg Restaurant
Kongsveien 15
Tel: 23 24 23 00
Take the No. 18–19 tram to Sjømannsskolen and walk up the hill to this recently restored gem. Knockout view over the city and fjord, with a large outdoor terrace complementing the restaurant inside. **$$**

Grand Café
Karl Johans Gate 31
Tel: 23 21 20 00
Henrik Ibsen's former haunt, known for its murals and stylish surroundings just across from the Parliament. **$$**

Kaffistova
Rosenkrantz Gate 8
Tel: 23 21 41 00
Cafeteria-style place dishing up authentic rural Norwegian food. Fast and filling. **$**

Maud's
Tollbugate 24
Tel: 22 83 72 28
Old-fashioned Norwegian-style restaurant, named after Norway's first modern queen, the former Princess Maud of England. **$$**

Solsiden
Sondre Akershus Kai 34
Tel: 22 33 36 30
One of the best seafood restaurants in Oslo, situated right on the harbour under the historic Akershus Fortress. Try the shellfish platter or catch of the day. Summer only. **$$**

Sult
Th. Meyers Gate 26
Tel: 22 87 04 67
Named after Knut Hamsun's novel *Hunger*, this was one of the first restaurants to pop up in the newly revitalised Grünerløkka district. Simple, fresh food dubbed "neo-Norsk." **$$**

Theatercafeen
Stortings Gate 24–26
Tel: 22 82 40 50
Famed Vienna-style café; classic dishes served with flair, live violin music. The place to see and be seen in Oslo. **$$**

Continental/International

Alex Sushi
Cort Adelers Gate 2
Tel: 22 43 99 99
The *New York Times* lavished praise on this neighbourhood sushi place. Book well in advance. **$$**

Bagatelle
Bygdøy allé 3
Tel: 22 12 14 40
Simply the best, with the Michelin stars and prices to prove it. Fabulous seafood. All dishes use market-fresh ingredients. **$$$**

Bambus
Kirkeveien 57
Tel: 22 85 07 00
Blend of Thai, Vietnamese and Japanese food in a stylish setting in Oslo's trendy Majorstuen district. **$**

Brasserie France
Øvre Slottsgate 16
Tel: 23 10 01 65
You'll think you're eating in Paris, but the quality of the shellfish is definitely Norwegian. The children's menu is highly recommended. **$$**

Dinner
Stortingsgate 22
Tel: 23 10 04 66
Spicy Szechuan cuisine, hailed by Chinese aficionados. **$$**

La Rosa Magra
Arbins Gate 1
Tel: 22 56 14 00
Excellent Italian food, from small pizzas to full-course meals, located just under the flat where Henrik Ibsen lived after returning from years in Italy. Splendid view across to the Royal Palace. **$–$$$**

Oro Restaurant and Bar
Tordenskiolds Gate 6A
Tel: 23 01 02 40
Elegant dining in the main gourmet restaurant, tapas in the adjacent bar/café. Excellent fixed-price menu. **$–$$$**

Restaurant Eik
Universitetsgata 11
Tel: 22 36 07 10
Arguably the best of Oslo's "menu-based" restaurants, where you select how many courses you want from a carefully planned multi-course meal. Next to Oslo's National Gallery. **$$**

Statholdergaarden
Rådhus Gate 11
Tel: 22 41 88 00
Danish chef Bent Stiansen is host in the elegant restaurant upstairs and the bar downstairs, in an urban home from the 1700s. **$$$**

STAVANGER

Charlottenlund
Kongsgaten 45
Tel: 51 91 76 00
Graceful, Norwegian- and French-inspired cuisine served in a former private mansion on the lake in the heart of town. **$$**

Craigs Kjøkken
Breitorget
N-4006
Tel: 51 93 95 90
This transplanted North American cook has a lot of fans, and with good reason. The menu may be limited but the quality of the food is top-notch. There is a well-stocked wine cellar. **$$**

Hall Toll
Skansengaten 2
Tel: 51 51 72 32
Housed in a former customs hall on the waterfront, this relatively new restaurant is cavernous with an innovative international-style menu and chic clientele. **$$**

N.B. Sørensens Dampskibsexpedition
Skagen 26
Tel: 51 84 38 20
One of the most traditional restaurants in Stavanger, located at the Vågen promenade and marina. An international menu using fresh Norwegian ingredients. **$$**

PRICE CATEGORIES

The symbols give an indication of prices, based on a three-course evening meal per head, excluding wine.
$ = Less than NOK 150
$$ = NOK 150–400
$$$ = More than NOK 400

BERGEN

Bryggen Tracteursted
Bryggen 6
Tel: 55 33 69 99
Traditional Norwegian fare and great fish dishes. **$$**

Dickens
Kong Olav V's Plass
Tel: 55 36 31 30
This informal setting is popular and relaxed, serving good meals, light snacks and just drinks. **$$**

Fiskekrogen Fisk and Vilt Restaurant
Fish Market
Tel: 55 55 96 40
The very best of Norwegian cuisine. Superb fish dishes served by friendly and knowledgeable waiters. **$$$**

Fløien Folkerestaurant
Top of Fløien funicular
Tel: 55 33 69 99
Good, reasonably priced food with intoxicating view. Work up an appetite by walking there. **$$**

Holbergstuen
Torgallmenningen 6
Tel: 55 55 20 55
In the heart of the town. Good traditional dishes. **$$**

Louisiana Creole Restaurant
Vågsallmenningen 6
Tel: 55 54 66 60
An intimate restaurant offering first-class Creole and Cajun food, located in the centre next to the tourist information office. **$$**

Mongolian Barbecue Restaurant
Olav Kyrresgt. 39
Tel: 55 32 39 15
Diners can combine lamb, pork, beef, chicken, vegetables and sauces to suit their own tastes at this Mongolian barbecue buffet. Best for confirmed meat-eaters. Fully licensed. **$$**

Pygmalion Økocafe
Nedre Korskirkeallmenning 4
Tel: 55 32 33 60
An eco-friendly café that serves up healthy organic food, although service can be a little erratic – drop in for coffee or a light lunch. **$**

Stragiotti Bar & Ristorante
Vestre Torggate 3
Tel: 55 90 31 00
This family restaurant

makes a change from Norwegian staples; it's located in pleasant surroundings and offers authentic Italian food with good service. **$$**

To Kokker (Two chefs)
Bryggen, Bergen
Tel: 55 30 69 55
On the Bryggen in Bergen, this well-known restaurant serves Norwegian and French dishes. Specialities include game, fish and seafood. **$$$**

Wesselstuen
Ole Bulls plass 6
Tel: 55 55 49 49
Traditional Norwegian fish and stews are served to a loyal local crowd. Good atmosphere. **$$**

TRONDHEIM

Bari Café and Bar
Munkegata 25
Tel: 73 60 60 24
Bari has an Italian-influenced menu with dishes ranging from lunchtime burgers to more sophisticated fish and meat evening mains. **$$**

Big Horn Steakhouse
Munkegt. 14, Ravnkloa
Tel: 73 50 94 90
Specialises in tasty spare ribs and juicy steaks. **$$**

Credo Restaurant and Bar
Ørjaveita 4A
Tel: 73 53 03 88
International-style restaurant known for its original food and no fixed menu. The wine cellar is one of Norway's best. **$$**

Grenaderen
Kongsgårdsgt. 1e
Tel: 73 51 66 80
In a 16th-century forge with a large terrace. Offers a traditional menu including

fish and reindeer. **$$**

Havfruen
Kjøpmannsgt. 7
Tel: 73 87 40 70
Some of the finest Norwegian fish and seafood, plus meat. Trendy bar. **$$**

Palmehaven Restaurant
Dronningensgate 5
Tel: 73 80 08 00
Palmehaven, an old favourite, has been going since 1918, and creates a

frisson with its Moorish garden and live classical music on Fridays and Saturdays. **$$**

To Rom og Kjøkken
Carl Johansgate 5
Tel: 73 56 89 00
One for special occasions, this excellent restaurant uses the freshest Norwegian ingredients and gives them a Mediterranean twist. Try the bouillabaisse, made with the day's catch. **$$$**

TROMSØ

Compagniet
Sjøgata 12
Tel: 77 66 42 22
Gourmet fare. **$$$**

BELOW: there is always an abundance of fresh ingredients.

Emmas Drømmekjøkken
Kirkegata 8
Tel: 77 63 77 30
Emma's Dream Kitchen

delivers high-quality Norwegian fish, seafood, duck and lamb dishes, pepped with ginger, enriched by truffle sauces, and generally turned into culinary triumphs. Recommended. **$$$**

Lasperanza
Rederveien 66
Tel: 77 65 43 00
Friendly Italian restaurant, with an outdoor eating area in summer. **$–$$**

Peppermøllen Mat-og Vinhus
Storgata 42
Tel: 77 68 62 60
Menu features about 160 dishes using mainly

Norwegian ingredients, with fish being a clear favourite. **$$**

Store Norske Fiskekompani
Storgata 73
Tel: 77 68 76 00
Just fish served here, to the highest quality and taken straight from the harbour. The seafood is cooked in a variety of styles, from traditional to "New Scandinavian". Meat-eaters need not attend. **$$$**

Vertshuset Skarven
Strandtorget 1
Tel: 77 60 07 20
This popular restaurant serves several varieties of steak. **$$**

A – Z

A HANDY SUMMARY OF PRACTICAL INFORMATION, ARRANGED ALPHABETICALLY

A Activities 394

B Business Hours 395

C Children 395

Climate 396

Culture 396

D Disabled Travellers 397

E Embassies and Consulates 397

G Gay and Lesbian Travellers 397

H Health 397

L Language 397

M Media 398

Money 399

N Nightlife 399

S Shopping 401

T Telecommunications 402

Tourist Information 402

Tour Operators 403

Transport 403

V Visas and Passports 406

W What to Bring 406

What to Read 406

Activities

Spectator Sports

Göteborg is probably the most sport-focused town in Sweden, and its Scandinavium is the venue for many major events, including tennis, ice hockey and table tennis. The city's other main arena is Ullevi Stadium, where international tournaments in football, athletics and speedway are staged regularly.

Tennis must come top of the list of spectator sports, with Swedish players still doing well on the international circuit. The main tournaments are the Swedish Open at Båstad, on the southwest coast, in mid-July and the Stockholm Open in early November.

Athletics Meetings are usually held in early July. In addition, Stockholm stages one of the world's biggest marathons each year – usually in early June with some 16,000 competitors from about 30 nations.

Horse-racing and trotting are popular in Sweden, with the best-known courses at Stockholm (Täby), Göteborg (Åby) and Malmö (Jägersro). The Swedish Derby is held in July at Jägersro, which is also the venue for a major horse show in August. Another important annual international horse show is held at the Göteborg Scandinavium in April.

Participant Sports

Sweden is a health-conscious nation, offering copious sports facilities nationwide.

Tennis

The country's tennis facilities are excellent. There is a wide range of both indoor and outdoor courts for public use throughout Sweden, and tennis is not at all considered an exclusive sport.

Horse-riding

Almost every town has riding stables or a riding school, and more experienced riders can enjoy a pony-trekking safari in the Kebnekaise mountain range.

Golf

Another very popular sport, golf is played at more than 300 courses. The best are located in the south, but you can even play a round in the light of the midnight sun inside the Arctic Circle at Boden. The more popular golf courses can be extremely busy in the summer so booking is advisable.

Watersports

With almost 100,000 lakes and thousands of kilometres of waterways, Sweden has a lot to offer to watersports devotees, including water skiing, windsurfing, canoeing and whitewater rafting. Dalsland and Värmland are good areas for canoe safaris.

Fishing

You can fish in the sea with rod and line free of charge around the Swedish coastline. Fishing is also free from the shores of the five largest lakes: Vänern, Vättern, Mälaren, Hjälmaren and Storsjön. In other lakes, rivers and streams the fishing rights are privately owned and a permit is required. Special conditions may apply, covering permitted equipment, close seasons, minimum size and catch limits. Close seasons may also apply to salmon and sea trout fishing along the coast. Trolling and similar fishing which requires the use of a boat is free only on public waters. Permits are available through local tourist information offices. Poaching is severely punished.

Skiing

Swedes learn to ski when they are toddlers so there are plenty of facilities for both downhill and cross-country enthusiasts. The best-known resorts are Åre, which was a close contender for the 1994 Winter

Olympics, and Sälen in the province of Dalarna. Summer skiing can be enjoyed at Riksgränsen in the far north of the country.

Hiking
In the countryside, serious walkers will find plenty of long-distance paths, including the *Kungsleden* (King's Trail), which traverses the high peaks of Lapland. The Swedish Tourist Federation *(Svenska Turistföreningen)* maintains a network of cabins for overnight accommodation and also operates Sweden's youth hostels.

For more details contact:
Svenska Turistföreningen
Box 25, 101 20 Stockholm
Tel: 08-463 21 00
E-mail: info@stfturist.se
www.stfturist.se

Information
Contact the following organisations for details on participant sports:
Swedish Walking Association
Kvibergs Idrottscenter,
415 82 Göteborg
Tel: 031-726 61 10
E-mail: svenskagang@vsif.o.se
www.gangsport.se
Swedish Angling Federation
Svartviksslingan 28, 16739 Bromma
Tel: 08-704 44 80
E-mail: info@sportfiskarna.se
www.sportfiskarna.se
Svenska Cykelförbundet (Cycling)
Idrottens Hus, Fiskartorpsvägen 15A,
114 73 Stockholm
Tel: 08-699 60 00
Fax: 08-699 63 70
www.scf.se
Svenska Ridsportförbundet (Riding)
Ridsportenshus, 734 94 Strömsholm
Tel: 0220-456 00
www.ridsport.se

Business Hours

● **Shops** on the whole open 9.30am–6pm on weekdays and until between 1 and 4pm on Saturdays. In larger cities many shops are open on Sundays as well, usually noon–4pm. Shops generally close early the day before a public holiday.
● **Department stores** may remain open until 8pm or 9pm and possibly also on Sundays.
● **Banks** Monday–Friday 9.30am–3pm (6pm in some larger cities), but closed on Saturdays. The bank at Stockholm Arlanda Airport's arrival hall is open daily 8am–10.30pm and at the departure hall Monday–Friday 6.30am–9pm, Saturday–Sunday 6.30am–8pm.

ABOVE: having fun at Asrid Lindgren's World in Småland.

Svenska Skidförbundet (Skiing)
Riks Skidstadion,
791 19 Falun
Tel: 023-874 40
Fax: 023-874 41
E-mail: info@skidor.com
www.skidor.com
Svenska Seglarförbundet (Sailing)
Af Pontinsvägen 6,
115 21 Stockholm
Tel: 08-459 09 90
Fax: 08-459 09 99
E-mail: ssf@ssf.se
www.svensksegling.se
Sweden's National Parks
Valhallavägen 195,
106 48 Stockholm
Tel: 08-698 10 00
Fax: 08-20 29 25
www.naturvardsverket.se
Svenska Kanotförbundet (Canoeing)
Rosvalla, Idrottsvägen
611 61 Nyköping
Tel: 0155-20 90 80
Fax: 0155-20 90 81
www.kanot.com
Svenska Tennisförbundet (Tennis)
Lidingövägen 75,
115 41 Stockholm
Tel: 08-450 43 10
E-mail: info@tennis.se
www.tennis.se
Svenska Golfförbundet (Golf)
Kevingestrand 20,
182 11 Danderyd
Tel: 08-622 15 00
Fax: 08-755 84 39
E-mail: info@sgf.golf.se
www.golf.se

Active Holidays
If you want to centre your holiday around sport:
● Request the brochure *Active Holidays in Sweden* from www.visitsweden.com.
● *See pages 403* for a list of tour operators that offer activity and sporting holidays.

Children

The Swedes are good at devising excellent attractions for the whole family, like amusement parks such as **Liseberg** (www.liseberg.se) in Göteborg and **Gröna Lund Tivoli** (www.gronalund.com) in Stockholm.

Astrid Lindgren fantasies
The famous author Astrid Lindgren is a master at creating fantasy characters that appeal to children. Pippi Longstocking, Emil and Karlsson on the Roof are just some of the attractions at Junibacken, a wonderful fairy-tale house in Stockholm, where characters from many favourite children's books come to life and kids can play, discover and learn. All activities are indoors, and there's also a restaurant and a bookshop with Sweden's largest selection of children's books.
Junibacken, Galärvarvsvägen, close to Gröna Lund Tivoli, Stockholm
Tel: 08-587 230 00
Fax: 08-587 230 99
E-mail: info@junibacken.se
www.junibacken.se
In Vimmerby in the province of Småland you can also visit Astrid Lindgren's World, another fairy-tale land with living characters from her books. It is open from mid-May until the end of August.
Astrid Lindgren's World
Tel: 0492-798 00
E-mail: info@alv.se
www.alv.se

Sommarland Centres
There are several Sommarland developments in Sweden (www.sommarland.se), the largest of which is at Skara, northeast of Göteborg. It has 50 attractions,

CLIMATE CHART

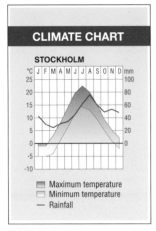

STOCKHOLM

- ▨ Maximum temperature
- ▢ Minimum temperature
- — Rainfall

including a water-slide, a grand prix race track, a railway and three boating lakes. Tel: 0511-77 03 00.

Zoos

The best-known zoo/safari park is at Kolmården (tel: 011-24 90 00; www.kolmarden.com) near Norrköping. It has lions, giraffes and so on, as well as Sweden's only dolphinarium. Other zoos of note are in Borås, Furuvik, Molstaberg and Skansen in Stockholm. In a park in Grönklitt (tel: 0250-462 00; www.orsa-gronklitt.se) near Orsa in Dalarna, bears live in their natural forest habitat.

Santaworld

Not far from Orsa is Tomteland (Santaworld; tel: 0250-287 70; www.santaworld.se), where children can explore Santa's house, workshop and animals and the Snow Queen's Palace, and place orders for Christmas.

Vintage Railways

Sweden has a number of vintage railways, some of which still operate steam locomotives. The longest preserved railway is the 32-km (20-mile) narrow-gauge line from Uppsala to Lenna, which operates during summer weekends.

Cowboy Capers

An unusual visitor attraction in Småland is **High Chaparral** (tel: 370-82785; www.highchaparral.se), a mock Wild West town.

Climate

In summer Sweden's weather is similar to that in Britain – and just as unpredictable – although in a good year some remarkably high temperatures can be recorded in the Arctic

regions. The area round Piteå on the Gulf of Bothnia is known as the Northern Riviera because of its warmth. But in the north, autumn and winter arrive early and spring comes in late May.

Winter can be cold; even in Stockholm, maximum temperatures in the day are likely to remain below freezing in January and February.

Culture

Music

The musical scene in Sweden is busiest in the autumn, winter and spring, but there is still a lot going on in summer. In Dalarna, for example, several communities organise music festivals.

Stockholm

The main concert hall is the Konserthuset, the home of the Stockholm Philharmonic Orchestra, whose season runs from September to May or June.

The Berwald Concert Hall is the base for Swedish National Radio's musical activities, with regular performances by the Radio Symphony Orchestra.

Stockholm's famous Royal Opera House hosts top international performances from mid-August to June.

Göteborg

The Concert Hall hosts the Göteborg Symphony Orchestra, which is known worldwide and performs every week, often with guest artists, from August to June. The final concert in June is given outdoors. Göteborg's modern Opera House offers a varied programme (including opera, ballet and musicals) from August to June.

Malmö

The 1,300-seat concert hall is the permanent home of the Symphony Orchestra.

Theatre

Sweden has a lively theatrical scene in the major cities, but many theatres close during the peak summer months. Performances are usually in Swedish.

Stockholm

The most prestigious theatre is the Royal Dramatic Theatre on Nybroplan, with four auditoriums. The most unusual one is the Drottningholm Court at Drottningholms Palace, founded by King Gustav III in 1766. More than 30 sets from then are still in use today, and in the summer there are ballet and opera performances.

Current performances are listed in the *Stockholm What's On* booklet. There is a booth on Norrmalmstorg Square, Biljett Direkt, where you can buy last-minute theatre seats.

Göteborg

The two main theatres are Stadsteatern and Folkteatern, both open from late August to early June. The Göteborg Card gives you a discount in May and June. Even though the major stages are closed in summer, Göteborg has a lot to offer. The amusement park hosts many famous artists, and during the midsummer Göteborg Party music is performed in several venues.

Malmö

The Stadsteater is a modern building with three stages. Plays are in Swedish, but you can often catch an opera or musical performance.

BELOW: Göteborg Opera House.

Mystery plays

If you're in the right place during the summer, you may be able to see one of the traditional mystery plays. In Leksand there are performances in mid-July of *Himlaspelet (The Road to Heaven)*. In Visby, on the island of Gotland, there are open-air performances in the ruins of St Nicolaus Church during the Gotland Chamber Music Festival, around the end of July.

Cinema

Virtually all foreign films are shown with their original sound-tracks and Swedish subtitles (rather than being dubbed). Local newspapers have full details of programmes and times. In Stockholm, cinemas showing first-run international films include Filmstaden Sergel, Filmstaden Söder, Rigoletto and Filmstaden Kista.

The film company SF has a website where you can book your ticket for any cinema around the country; www.sf.se

D isabled Travellers

Access

In line with its enlightened social attitudes, Sweden has long been a pioneer in accommodating travellers with disabilities. Many hotel rooms and facilities are adapted for the needs both of people with mobility problems and those suffering from allergies. New public buildings are all accessible to people with disabilities, and toilets with the handicap symbol can be found almost everywhere.

In Stockholm, most buses are designed for easy access for people with wheelchairs and pushchairs. Mainline and underground trains have elevators or ramps.

For general information on travel for those with disabilities, and to request a guide to Swedish restaurants with disabled access contact:
DHR De Handikappades Riksförbund
Box 47305, SE-100 74 Stockholm
Tel: 08-685 80 00
E-mail: info@dhr.se
www.dhr.se

Hotel Guide

The "Hotels in Sweden" directory (order from www.visitsweden.com) lists hotels with wheelchair access.

Wheelchair rental

Contact Hjälpmedelsinstitutet
Tel: 08-620 17 00
E-mail: registrator@dhr.se
www.hi.se

Cinemas, museums, theatre

A guide to accessible cinemas, museums, theatres and libraries can be ordered from Kultur- och Idrottsförvaltningen in Stockholm. Tel: 08-508 26 000

Stockholm cultural walking tours for the disabled

"Kulturpromenader för personer med funktionshinder" by Elena Siré och Sten Leijonhufvud is a guide to Stockholm written in Swedish and English.
Order from Elena Siré
Tel: 08-790 85 24

E mbassies and Consulates

UK

Skarpögatan 6-8
Tel: 08-671 30 00
Fax: 08-662 99 89
www.britishembassy.se

US

Dag Hammarskjölds Väg 31
Tel: 08-783 53 00
Fax: 08-661 19 64
www.usemb.se

Canada

Tegelbacken 4, 7th floor
Tel: 08-453 30 00
Fax: 08-453 30 16
www.canadaemb.se

Australia

Sergels Torg 12, 11th floor
Tel: 08-613 29 00
Fax: 08-613 29 82
E-mail: reception@austemb.se
www.sweden.embassy.gov.au

G ay and Lesbian Travellers

Sweden is renowned for its liberal attitudes to sex, and its age of consent is 15 for heterosexuals and gays. But there is nevertheless little open affection between gay couples and the gay scene is less apparent in Stockholm than in other capitals, with few places for gays only.

QX is a gay/lesbian magazine that offers information about clubs, restaurants, bars and shops mainly in Stockholm, Gothenburg, Malmö and Copenhagen. www.qx.se.

H ealth

Precautions

Standards of hygiene in Sweden are among the highest in the world. No inoculations are needed, and tap water is safe to drink. Food poisoning or related problems are unlikely. However, in the far north of Sweden in high summer, precautions need to be taken against the vicious mosquitoes. Even the strongest

ABOVE: lunch is served.

insect repellents are not entirely successful.

Medical Treatment

Sweden has reciprocal agreements with the UK and other countries, under which visitors are entitled to the same medical treatment as Swedes. To qualify, EU nationals must obtain an European Health Insurance Card (EHIC; available in the UK through post offices and online at www.ehic.org.uk), which allows visitors to pay the same fees as Swedes. Without this card you might have to foot the bill for the actual cost of the treatment.

Visitors from outside the EU pay higher consultation fees, although these are modest compared with those charged in North America.

For hospital visits you will also have to pay for treatment; it is important to take out adequate medical insurance coverage before your visit so that you can reclaim the money on your return.

If you are interested in planned medical treatment or a medical check-up while you are in Sweden, you can contact Stockholm Care (tel: 08-672 24 00), but its fees are higher than those of a normal doctor.

L anguage

The Alphabet

The Swedish alphabet has 29 letters; the additional three are å, ä and ö and come after the letter Z. To find Mr Åkerblad in the phone book, therefore, look at the end of the listings.

Useful Words and Phrases

Yes *Ja*
No *Nej*
Hello *Hej*

Goodbye *Hejdå*
Thank you *Tack*
Please *Tack/Var så god*
Do you speak English?
talar du engelska?
I only speak English
jag talar bara engelska
Good morning *God morgon*
Good afternoon *God eftermiddag*
Good evening *God kväll*
Today *Idag*
Tomorrow *I morgon*
Yesterday *I går*
How do you do *Goddag*
What time is it? *Hur mycket är klockan?*
It is (the time is) *Den är (klockan är)*
Could I have your name please?
Hur var namnet?
My name is *Jag heter*
Can I help you? *Kan jag hjälpa till?*
I do not understand *Jag förstår inte*
I do not know *Jag vet inte*

Eating and Drinking
breakfast *Frukost*
lunch *Lunch*
dinner *Middag*
eat *Äta*
drink *Dricka*
cheers *Skål!*
off-licence *Systembolaget*
Can I order please? *Får jag beställa?*
Could I have the bill please?
Kan jag få notan?
Accommodation
to rent *Att hyra*
room to rent *Rum att hyra*
chalet *Stuga*
sauna *Bastu*
launderette *Tvättomat*
dry cleaning *Kemtvätt*
dirty *Smutsigt*
clean *Ren*

Getting Around
aircraft *Flygplan*
bus/coach *Buss*
car *Bil*
parking *Parkering, Garage*
train *Tåg*
How do I get to? *Hur kommer jag till?*
Where is ...? *Var finns...?*
Right *Höger*
To the right *Till höger*
Left *Vänster*
To the left *Till vänster*
Straight on *Rakt fram*

Shopping
to buy *Att köpa*
department store *Varuhus*
food *Mat*
free *Ledigt*
grocery store (in countryside)
Lanthandel
handicraft *Hemslöjd*
money *pengar*

shop *Affär*
clothes *Kläder*
overcoat *Kappa, Överrock*
jacket *Jacka*
suit *Kostym*
shoes *Skor*
skirt *Kjol*
jersey *Tröja, jumper*
How much is this? *Vad kostar det?*
It costs *Det kostar*
Do you have English newspapers?
Har du engelska tidningar?

Health and Security
chemist *Apotek*
Accident and emergency clinic
Akutmottagning/Vårdcentral
hospital *Sjukhus*
doctor *Doktor*
police station *Polisstation*

Miscellaneous
toilet *Toalett*
gentlemen *Herrar*
ladies *Damer*
vacant *Ledig*
engaged *Upptagen*
no smoking *Rökning förbjuden*
entrance *Ingång*
exit *Utgång*
no entry *Ingen ingång*
open *Öppen/öppet*
closed *Stängt*

Days of the Week
Monday *måndag*
Tuesday *tisdag*
Wednesday *onsdag*
Thursday *torsdag*
Friday *fredag*
Saturday *lördag*
Sunday *söndag*

Numbers
1 *en/et*
2 *två*
3 *tre*
4 *fyra*
5 *fem*
6 *sex*
7 *sju*
8 *åtta*
9 *nio*
10 *tio*
11 *elva*
12 *tolv*
13 *tretton*
14 *fjorton*
15 *femton*
16 *sexton*
17 *sjutton*
18 *aderton*
19 *nitton*
20 *tjugo*
21 *tjugoen*
22 *tjugotvå*
30 *trettio*
40 *fyrtio*
50 *femtio*
60 *sextio*

70 *sjuttio*
80 *åttio*
90 *nittio*
100 *hundra*
200 *tvåhundra*
1,000 *tusen*

Media

Newspapers and Magazines

English-language newspapers are widely available at kiosks in larger cities, usually on the day of publication. Kulturhuset (the cultural centre) in Stockholm at Sergels Torg has a good selection of English newspapers and magazines that can be read for free, as does the City Library in Göteborg on the main square, Götaplatsen. For a wide selection of English-language magazines try a Press Stop Store (in Stockholm there's one in the Gallerian, across from NK on Hamngatan).

Books

English-language books are widely available. In Stockholm, excellent bookshops include:
Akademibokhandeln, Mäster Samuelsgaten 32, on the corner of Regeringsgatan,
www.akademibokhandeln.se
Hedengrens Bokhandel, Stureplan 4,
www.hedengrens.se
New York Stories, Odengatan 100,
www.newyorkstories.se
Sweden Bookshop, Slottsbacken 10,
www.swedenbookshop.com

For maps and guides, try
Kartbutiken, Kungsgatan 74,
www.kartbutiken.se
Kartcentrum, Vasagatan 16,
www.kartcentrum.se

Television

Sweden's state-run STV1, STV2 and Kanal 4 show a film most evenings. The commercial STV3 and Kanal 5 run American chat shows, sport, movies and soap operas. Plus there are many satellite/cable channels, featuring CNN, BBC and MTV, broadcast in English with subtitles.

Radio

Radio Sweden has programmes in English with news and information about Sweden on medium wave 1179 KHz (254m), and also in the Stockholm area on FM 89.6 MHz. A variety of BBC and NPR programmes is also available on channel 89.6 FM. Broadcast schedules are available at most hotels in Stockholm or can be requested from:
Radio Sweden, tel: 08-784 50 00,
www.sr.se/international

Money

There is no limit on the import of either Swedish or foreign currency.

Travellers' cheques can be exchanged without difficulty at banks all over Sweden. A foreign exchange service is also provided by post offices with the "PK Exchange" sign. Forex and Wexex, bureaux de change with branches in most major towns, usually have better exchange rates than the banks and post offices and don't charge any commission.

All the leading credit cards are accepted by most hotels, restaurants and shops throughout the country, and you can also take out cash on these cards at foreign exchange offices and banks.

Currency

Swedish krona (plural kronor), marked ":-" or "kr" or "Skr" in shops, or SEK internationally, and split into 100 öre. Coins are 50 öre, 1 krona, 5 and 10 kronor. Notes are 20, 50, 100, 500 and 1,000 kronor.

Tipping

● In hotels and restaurants a service charge is included in the bill and a further tip is not expected, although it's usual to round up the bill to the nearest 10 or 20 SEK.
● Taxi drivers usually get an extra 10 SEK, but this is optional.
● Cloakrooms at restaurants and clubs charge about 15–20 SEK.
● Tipping for special services provided by hotel staff is fine but not expected.

Nightlife

Where to Go

As in other countries, there is an active nightlife in the larger cities but nothing particularly hectic in the smaller communities. Many of the hotels listed have bars, nightclubs and sometimes even live dance music. The university cities like Uppsala, Lund, Linköping and Umeå have quite a busy nightlife, at least for the students.

Skiing resorts like Åre and Sälen are also good for nightlife (mainly for younger people) during the season, from December to April. Après-ski is often very lively with bands playing covers of well-known tunes to packed crowds.

Out in the countryside and in smaller towns *dansband* music is very popular – Swedish-style country music to which people dance foxtrot and a kind of jive. If you like dancing this could be a fun thing to try and a chance to meet the locals. Dancing

may not begin until midnight.

Given the high cost of drinking in Sweden, a night out on the town can be expensive. The best value is probably at one of the jazz clubs favoured by the young or at one of the piano bars, which offer a quieter and more relaxing environment for a late-night drink.

Nightclubs and Discos

Opening Hours

Nightclubs and discos usually close around 3am, but in Stockholm some places have extended this to 5am. Unfortunately, numerous nightclubs have long queues outside after 9 or 10pm, even if it's not full inside. This is an irritating way of showing that the club is popular. One way to avoid the queue is to get there early or to book a table and have dinner there so that you don't have to pay the entrance fee to the nightclub.

Stockholm

Absolut Ice Bar
Vasaplan 4
Tel: 08-505 631 24
www.nordicseahotel.se
The world's first permanent ice bar. The -5°C interior is entirely sculpted from ice – including the glasses. Reservations normally required. See website for details.

Akkurat
Hornsgatan 18
Tel: 08-644 00 15
Popular Söder hangout for those who enjoy listening to good blues, rock and soul, played here on Sunday nights. Also has a wide selection of whiskies and beers.

Bern's
Berzelli Park 6
Tel: 08-566 325 15
www.berns.se

This entertainment palace at Berzelli Park has been in existence since 1863 but it has never been in better form since Sir Terence Conran redesigned it a few years ago. It now has several stylish bars, including the Berns bar under crystal chandeliers, the cocktail bar in a sober glass veranda and a cellar bar that attract the trendy crowd. Wherever you order them, the drinks are truly delicious.

Café Opera
Operahuset
Tel: 08-676 58 07
www.cafeopera.se
Expensive but ever-popular bar, restaurant and club (which starts around midnight) with a mix of young people and older regulars. There is an impressive classical architectural interior.

Café Tivoli
Mariatorget 1A
Tel: 08-644 54 18
www.cafetivoli.se
Local bar, restaurant and nightclub in Södermalm.

Mälarsalen
Torkel Knutssonsgatan 2
(closed June–August)
Tel: 08-658 00 20
www.malarsalen.se
This club always features live music. On Fridays younger people dance *bugg* (a kind of jive) and on Saturdays a slightly older crowd dance to *dansband* music. There is also a separate dance floor dedicated to salsa music (although this is not live).

Mosebacke Etablissement
Mosebacke Torg 3
Tel: 08-556 098 90
www.mosebacke.se
At this classic restaurant, nightclub and bar in Söder you can eat typical Swedish dishes and enjoy one of the

BELOW: keep your cool in the Absolut Ice Bar.

best views in the city, dance to popular music on the outdoor dance floor, or listen to jazz, rock or blues in the club.

Nada
Åsögatan 140
Tel: 08-644 70 20
Pleasant, cosy bar with DJs spinning indie-pop tunes.

Patricia
Stadsgårdskajen 152
Tel: 08-743 05 70
www.patricia.st
The steamship M/S Patricia is now a party boat, with three floors of bars and dancing. Gay club night on Sundays.

Spy Bar
Birger Jarlsgatan 20
Tel: 08-545 076 55
Ever-popular dance club.

Sturecompagniet
Sturegatan 4
Tel: 08-545 076 01
www.sturecompagniet.se
Restaurant, bar and nightclub on three floors in the centre of the city.

Göteborg
Blissresto
Magasinsgatan 3
Tel: 031-13 85 55
www.blissresto.com
Awarded Best Musik Bar Sweden 2006. Perfect cocktails.

Excet
Vasagatan 52
Tel: 031-711 99 11
Three-storey nightclub which attracts a mixed crowd.

Glow
Avenyn 8
Tel: 031-10 58 20
www.glownightclub.se
Top DJs and great club nights. Attracts an older crowd.

Jazzhuset
Erik Dahlbergsgatan 3
Tel: 031-13 35 44
There's always live music here. It has a club during the week for younger people, while at weekends rock, blues and sometimes jazz attract a slightly older crowd.

Lounge(s)
Kungsportsavenyen 5
Tel: 031-711 15 41
www.lounges.se
Stylish club with themed lounges, resident DJs and a very sleek casino.

Nefertiti
Hvidfeldtsplatsen 6
Tel: 031-711 40 76
Popular jazz club.

Park Lane
Kungsportsavenyn 36–38
Tel: 031-20 60 58
An upmarket nightclub with an international atmosphere. There are three bars, a restaurant, a casino and live performances.

ABOVE: taking part in Midsummer festivities.

Malmö
Crown Nightclub
Amiralsgatan 23
Tel: 040-611 80 88
In this popular club there are different themes for different days of the week, from 1960s music to soul and R&B, or 1980s music/disco.

Etage
Stortorget 6
Tel: 040-23 20 60
Popular place with young people.

Kulturbolaget
Bergsgatan 18
Tel: 040-30 20 11
A popular haunt among rock lovers, but also features pop music and sometimes disco.

Panora
S:t Gertrudesgatan 4
Tel: 040-611 27 07
www.panora.nu
Live music and club nights.

Slagthuset
Jörgen Kocksgatan 7A
Tel: 040-10 99 31
Three dance floors with different music, including oldies, house and disco.

Swing Inn
Stadt Hamburgsgatan 2C
Tel: 040-12 22 21.
Popular among 30-somethings, the music is soft disco; jacket and tie required. Minimum age limit 28.

Bars and Live Music

Stockholm
Debaser
Karl Johans Torget 1
Tel: 08-462 98 60
www.debaser.nu
Hip live rock and pop.

Fasching
Kungsgatan 63
Tel: 08-543 829 60
www.fasching.se
This is Stockholm's largest and most popular jazz club.

Glenn Miller Café
Brunnsgatan 21A
Tel: 08-10 03 22
Small bar and restaurant where bands often play jazz music.

Nalen
Regeringsgatan 74
Tel: 08-505 292 00
Classic ballroom that is currently enjoying a revival as a restaurant and music venue – concerts encompass jazz, folk and pop.

Pelikan
Blekingegatan 40
Tel: 08-556 090 90
Unpretentious bar and beer hall. The bar to the left is very lively and popular among the locals and the beer hall to the right serves simple Swedish *husmanskost*.

Riche
Birger Jarlsgatan 4
Tel: 08-545 035 60
The cosy Lille Bar, to the side of the main Riche bistro, has DJs Tuesdays to Saturdays, and a live band weekly.

Stampen
Stora Nygatan 5
Tel: 08-20 57 93
Lively well-known jazz pub in the Old Town.

Sturehof/Obaren
Stureplan 2
Tel: 08-440 57 30
www.sturehof.com
One flight up from Sturehof's tiled bar and traditional dining room sits the very busy, funky Obaren bar – especially popular among Stockholm's trendy media and advertising sets.

Tranan
Karlbergsvägen 14
Tel: 08-527 281 00
Trendy and lively local restaurant and basement bar which sometimes offers live music performances.

Göteborg
Brasserie Lipp
Kungsportsavenyn 8

Public Holidays

Sweden has several official holidays:
- **1 January** New Year's Day
- **6 January** Epiphany
- **March/April** Good Friday and Easter Monday
- **1 May** Labour Day
- **May** Ascension (usually second part of the month); Pentecost (10 days after Ascension)
- **6 June** National Day
- **June** Midsummer's Day (around the 24th)
- **November** All Saints' Day (usually at start of the month)
- **25 and 26 December** Christmas

Tel: 031-10 58 30
Classic French bistro/bar catering to a slightly older crowd, with DJs on summer weekends.
Dancin' Dingo
Kristinelundsgatan 16
Tel: 031-81 18 12
Australian bar offering live music performances.
Klara
Viktoriagatan 1
Tel: 031-13 38 51
Vaguely bohemian bar with music provided by a DJ.
Nivå
Kungsportsavenyn 9
Tel: 031-701 80 90
Popular bar and restaurant with dance music covering five floors.
Palace
Södra Hamngatan 2
Tel: 031-80 75 50
www.palace.se
Classic bar, especially popular among business people after work on Friday.
Jazzhuset
Erik Dahlbergsgatan 3
Tel: 031-13 35 44
www.jazzhuset.se
Live music is guaranteed here, with a club for the young set during the week and at weekends rock, blues and sometimes jazz for a slightly older crowd.
Trädgår'n
Nya Allén
Tel: 031-10 20 80
Restaurant with live performances and club arrangements.
Smaka
Vasaplatsen 3
Tel: 031-13 22 47
Classic Swedish bar and restaurant popular with students.

Malmö
Brogatan
Brogatan 12
Tel: 040-30 77 18
The place to be seen, this is a

popular bar among Malmö's celebrities.
Harry's
Södergatan 14
Tel: 040-12 34 90
Bar and disco with a friendly and relaxed atmosphere.
Hipp
Kalendegatan 12
Tel: 040-97 40 30
Beautiful, late 19th-century-style restaurant and bar with club arrangements, such as salsa evenings.
Tempo Bar & Kök
Södra Skolgatan 30
Tel: 040-12 60 21
A popular bar and restaurant.

New in Malmö
There is an area in Malmö called Lilla Torg (Small Square) near the market hall where new bars are opening up all the time. It's always worth trying some of these out.

Bars on the Web
For the most happening clubs and bars check out www.stockholmtown.com and www.goteborg.com. For gay clubs and bars throughout Sweden see www.qx.se.

Age Limits
If you're in your early 20s or younger, you may not be able to get into some clubs. Some have remarkably high minimum age limits, so it's advisable for younger visitors to check first. It is even possible to find some of the more upmarket night-clubs imposing a minimum age of 26 for men and 24 for women.

Dance Boats
A popular outing – among young and old as well as conference parties – is to take the boat from Stockholm to Finland for a day's visit to Helsinki or Åbo. This takes about 40 hours and includes two nights on the boat and one day in Helsinki or Åbo. The boats have several dance floors, bars and a restaurant to entertain the captive audience. Contact Silja Line (tel: 08-22 21 40) or Viking Line (tel: 08-452 40 00) for information.

P ostal Services

Post offices have been phased out and their services taken over by supermarkets, grocery stores and petrol stations. Stamps (frimärken) are also on sale at Pressbyrån newsstands, bookstalls and stationers' shops. Mailboxes are blue for local letters and yellow for all other destinations.

R eligious Services
The Swedish State Church is in the Lutheran tradition and has churches throughout the country.
Stockholm has the widest range of places of worship, including a Greek Orthodox church, several synagogues and three Islamic mosques.
Protestant services in English are usually held once a week in major cities. Inquire at your hotel for more information.

S hopping
Where to Shop
Sweden is famous the world over for its elegant design, and you will find plenty of good buys in glassware, stainless steel, silver, pottery, ceramics, textiles and leather goods. Department stores such as NK and Åhléns are noted for their high-quality, inexpensive kitchenware.
Glass The best bargains are found in "Glass Country" – Småland, in the southeast – where there are over 15 glassworks. Major glassworks like Orrefors, Kosta-Boda, Älghult and Skruf have shops adjoining their factories where you can buy seconds very cheaply. For flawless glass products, shop at department stores like NK, Crystal Art Centre or Nordiska Kristall in Stockholm.
Porcelain Sweden is also renowned for its high-quality porcelain, and bargains can be found at the Gustavsberg factory outside Stockholm and at the Rörstrand factory in Lidköping.
Fashion For cheap clothing, try Hennes & Mauritz (H&M), Lindex, JC and KappAhl. The best shopping area is probably Borås, near Göteborg, and the centre of the Tygriket (Weavers' Country). Knallebygden is a large shopping centre in Borås where you can get bargains from the leading direct-mail companies.
The centre of the fur business is Tranås in the province of Småland, where you can usually find bargains.

Markets
These are found in all the major cities: Stockholm has markets at Hötorget and Östermalmstorg, which are worth a visit, while Göteborg has its "Fish Church", a thriving fish market built in the ecclesiastical style.
Göteborg also has a fascinating market hall (Saluhallen) selling mainly food. Malmö has a similar, more upmarket Saluhallen in Lilla Torg, with restaurants, cafés and delis.
Stockholm has what is claimed to be northern Europe's largest flea market at Skärholmen, 20 minutes on the underground from the city

centre. It's open daily, but Saturday and Sunday are the best days to go.

Factory Outlets

Below are factory outlets selling Swedish and international brand names:
Stockholm Quality Outlet
Majorsvägen 2–4, Järfälla (outside Stockholm, 40 brand name shops)
Tel: 08-564 720 31
www.qualityoutlet.com
Abecita
Borås (ladies' underwear, swimsuits, dressing gowns)
Tel: 033-23 76 00
Ge-Kås
Ullared (clothes, kitchenware, food)
Tel: 0346-375 00
www.gekas.se
Miss Mary of Sweden
Borås (ladies' underwear)
Tel: 033-22 22 50
Visko
Skene
Tel: 0320-322 90
Shoes and more near Göteborg.

Local Crafts

All over Sweden you can see craftspeople at work and buy their work at low prices. In the countryside, look out for *Hemslöjd* handicraft centres, where you can buy locally produced items. Women's and children's clothes are especially good buys, as well as furs and needlework.

Below is a selection of outlets in Stockholm and Göteborg. The *Yellow Pages* website (www.gulasidorna.se; in Swedish) lists shops in Sweden: search for *hantverk*.
Gamla Stans Hantverk AB
Västerlånggatan 27, Stockholm
Tel: 08-411 01 49
Svensk Hemslöjd
Sveavägen 44, Stockholm
Tel: 08-23 21 15
www.svenskhemslojd.com
Bohusslöjd

BELOW: glassware is a popular gift.

Kungsportsavenyn 25, Göteborg
Tel: 031-16 00 72
Kronhusbodarna
Central Göteborg
Tel: 031-61 25 00
Handicraft centre with glass, ceramic, chocolate and jewellery workshops.

Design

For contemporary Swedish (and international) design, several shops in Stockholm are worth visiting:
DesignTorget
Kulturhuset, Sergelgången 29, tel: 08-21 91 50 and Götgatan 31, tel: 08-644 16 78
www.designtorget.se
G.A.D.
Birger Jarlsgatan 34
Tel: 08-545 480 08
www.gad.se
Norrgavel
Birger Jarlsgatan 27
Tel: 08-545 220 50
www.norrgavel.se
Nordiska Galleriet
Nybrogatan 11
Tel: 08-442 83 60
www.nordiskagalleriet.se
R.O.O.M.
Alströmergatan 20
Tel: 08-692 50 00
www.room.se
Svenskt Tenn
Strandvägen 5
Tel: 08-670 16 00
www.svenskttenn.se
Carl Malmsten
Strandvägen 5B
Tel: 08-23 33 80
www.malmsten.se
Design House Stockholm
Smålandsgatan 11
Tel: 08-509 081 13
www.designhousestockholm.com
Bruka Design
Humlegårdsgatan 1
Tel: 08-660 14 80 and

Regeringsgatan 44
Tel: 08-22 39 30
www.brukadesign.se

Ikea
Ikea stores are usually on the outskirts of towns, and they have an export service.

T elecommunications

Telephones

There are plenty of payphones, credit card phones (signposted CCC) and special telegraph offices (marked Tele or Telebutik). Most of the payphones operate only with a telephone card *(telia telefonkort)*, so to be sure that you can use all public telephones it's a good idea to buy a card. They are available in Pressbyrån, kiosks, bookstalls and stationers' shops.

As elsewhere, it is expensive to phone from hotel rooms; use payphones instead where you can. The telephone directory enquiry service *(see Useful Numbers, below)* is also expensive.

To call abroad, dial 00 followed by the country code (44 for the UK, 1 for the US and Canada, 353 for Ireland, 61 for Australia and 64 for New Zealand), then dial the number, omitting any initial 0.

To call from your mobile phone you dial the area code (e.g. 08 for Stockholm) followed by the number. To ring another British visitor's mobile phone in Sweden you have to dial 00 followed by your country code and then the area code (omitting the 0), plus the number.

Useful Numbers

- **Police, fire, ambulance**
  112 (calls are free)
- **Swedish directory enquiries**
  118 118
- **International directory enquiries**
  118 119
- **International dialling code:** +46

Internet

Most hotels offer Wi-Fi Internet access; cybercafés are easy to find in towns and cities.

Tourist Information

A good starting point for national tourist information is:
VisitSweden
Stortorget 2-4, 831 30 Östersund
E-mail: info@visitsweden.com
www.visitsweden.com

Local offices

Sweden has a country-wide network of tourist information offices, or

Turistbyrå, in more than 350 cities and towns, which can be identified by the international "I" sign. They usually have a hotel booking service, *rumsförmedling* or *hotellcentral*, and supply information about local sightseeing and sporting activities. Some are open during the summer only. A complete list can be obtained from VisitSweden *(see above)*. The main offices are as follows:

Stockholm
Sverigehuset, Hamngatan 27, (enter on Kungsträdgården)
Tel: 08-508 285 08
E-mail: info@svb.stockholm.se
www.stockholmtown.com
This is the country's busiest tourist office. Run by the Stockholm Visitors Board, it can book tickets, tours and accommodation for you. It also publishes a monthly *What's On* magazine.

Göteborg
Kungsportsplatsen 2,
SE-411 10 Göteborg
Tel: 031-61 25 00
Fax: 031-368 42 18
www.goteborg.com

Gotland
Skeppsbron 4–6, Visby
Tel: 0498-20 17 00
Fax: 0498-20 17 17
E-mail: info@gotland.info
www.gotland.info

Lapland
Lars Janssonsgatan 17, Box 113,
SE-981 22 Kiruna
Tel: 0980-188 80
Fax: 0980-182 86
www.lappland.se

Skåne
Kyrkogatan II 25, SE–222 21 Lund
Tel: 046-35 50 40
Fax: 046-12 59 63
E-mail: turistbyran@lund.se
www.skaneturist.nu

Småland
Resecentrum, Järnvägsstationen,
55189 Jönköping
Tel: 036-10 50 50
Fax: 036-10 77 68
E-mail: turist@jonkoping.se
www.visit-smaland.com

Tour Operators

A brochure on Sweden containing a complete guide to tour operators offering holidays in Sweden is available from VisitSweden. Catalogues can also be downloaded from the VisitSweden website.
A selection of tour operators with interests in Sweden includes:

UK
Arctic Experience
Arctic House, 8 Bolters Lane,
Banstead, Surrey SM7 2AR
Tel: 01737-21 88 00
Fax: 01737-36 23 41
E-mail: sales@discover-the-world.co.uk
www.arctic-experience.co.uk
Specialist in guided tours, plus hiking and winter holidays.
DFDS Seaways
Scandinavia House, Parkeston,
Harwich, Essex CO12 4QG
Tel: 0871-522 99 55
Fax: 0191-293 62 45
www.dfds.co.uk
For ferries, motoring, cruises, lake and mountain breaks, self-catering and country cottages.
Scantours
73 Mornington Street,
London NW1 7QE
Tel: 020-755 435 30
Fax: 020-738 744 96
E-mail: info@scantours.com
www.scantours.co.uk
Offers holidays and tours, including city breaks, lake and mountain holidays, fly-drive, motoring, self-catering, coach and rail tours, golf, angling, activity and winter holidays.
Simply Sweden
5 Hill Road, Springthorpe,
Lincolnshire, DN21 5QB
Tel: 0845-890 03 00
Fax: 0845-890 07 62
E-mail: info@simplysweden.co.uk
www.simplysweden.co.uk
Offers tailor-made Swedish holidays including Ice Hotel, city breaks, log cabins, rafting etc.

Ireland
Go Hop
Tel: 01-241 23 89
E-mail: info@gohop.com
www.gohop.com
Internet travel company offering city breaks, fly-drive, motoring, lake and mountain breaks and farm holidays.

US and Canada
There are numerous tour operators in the US, a complete list of which can be obtained from the Scandinavian Tourist Board in New York *(see opposite)*. The following is just a selection:
Nelson's Scandinavia
Tel: 1-800-542 16 89
Fax: 312-236 51 35
www.nelsonsscandinavia.com
Nordic Saga Tours
Tel: 1-800-848 64 49
Fax: 425-488 09 79
www.nordicsaga.com
Scantours Inc
Tel: 1-800-223 72 26
Fax: 310-390 04 93
www.scantours.com

Australia
Contact American Express or Thomas Cook.

Unique Holidays
Ichi Ban Events
Tel: 08-715 86 00
www.ichiban.se
A network of swan yachts for private hire April–October.
Vildmark I Värmland
Tel: 05601-40 40
www.vildmark.se
One, four and seven day cruises on the Klarälven river. Not just any cruise though, they assist you in building a log raft and provide camping equipment for your journey.
Wildlife Worldwide
UK tel: 0845 130 69 82
www.wildlifeworldwide.com
Offer various wildlife holidays, including bird-watching and reindeer trekking in Lapland.

Transport
Getting There
By Air
From the UK and Ireland
Scandinavian Airlines (SAS) and British Airways operate direct daily flights from London Heathrow to Stockholm Arlanda. SAS also flies direct to Stockholm from Manchester. Ryanair also operates flights from London Stansted to Stockholm's Vasterås and Skavsta airports, both about an hour and twenty minutes drive from the capital (to the northwest and southwest respectively).
From London, SAS and British Airways fly daily to Göteborg (Gothenburg); and Ryanair flies to Göteborg. From Glasgow Prestwick, Ryanair flies daily to Skavsta (Stockholm) and Göteborg. From Birmingham and Liverpool, Ryanair flies several times per week to Skavsta. From Dublin, Ryanair has regular flights to Skavsta and Göteborg. City Airline flies around four times per week from Manchester to Göteborg. Travelling time from the UK is around 2½ hours.
From the US
Services between Stockholm and North America are operated by SAS, Finnair, Iceland Air, and by the US airlines Delta and American.

Airline offices in the UK and Ireland
SAS, tel: 0871-521 2772;
www.flysas.com
Finnair, tel: 0870-241 44 11;
www.finnair.com
British Airways, tel: 0844-493 0787 50; www.ba.com
Ryanair, UK, tel: 0871-246 00 00;
www.ryanair.com
Dublin, tel: 0818-30 30 30
City Airline, tel: 0870-220 68 35;
www.cityairline.com

Airline offices in the US
SAS, tel: 1-800-221 23 50;
www.flysas.com
Finnair, tel: 1-800-950 50 00;
www.finnair.com
Icelandair, tel: 1-800-223 55 00;
www.icelandair.com

By Sea
There are no longer any ferries from
the UK to Sweden. To get there by
boat, you will have to take the ferry
from Harwich to Esbjerg in Denmark
(which runs three or four times a
week) and then drive up to Grenå or
Frederikshavn and catch another
ferry from there to Sweden. There
are many ferry links between
Denmark and Germany to Sweden,
as well as from Sweden to Finland.

By Train
The fastest rail route from the UK to
Sweden is via the Eurostar service,
through the Channel Tunnel from
London St Pancras to Brussels, with
onward trains to Copenhagen and
then connecting services to Sweden.
    For further information call:
Eurostar, tel: 08705-18 61 86;
www.eurostar.com
European Rail, tel: 020-761 910 83;
www.europeanrail.co.uk

By Car
With the 16-km (10-mile) Öresund
bridge connecting Copenhagen with
Malmö, you can drive all the way to
Sweden from Denmark. The drive
from Copenhagen Airport to Malmö
takes about 45 minutes.

Getting Around
On Arrival
All three of Sweden's major
international airports – Stockholm
(Arlanda), Göteborg (Landvetter) and
Malmö (Sturup) – have excellent
links to their respective city centres.
From Arlanda, passengers can use
the Arlanda Express high-speed train
which operates four times an hour
to Stockholm Central Station in only
20 minutes. There are also frequent
bus services from Arlanda's
international and domestic
terminals to the city Terminal at
Klarabergsgatan above Central
Station. In Göteborg and Malmö,
coaches operate from the airport to
the city's Central Station.
    A connecting bus meets all
Ryanair flights at Vasterås and
Skavsta airports and goes directly to
the Cityterminalen bus terminal in
central Stockholm, taking around 1
hour and 20 minutes from both.
    Taxis are always available but
make sure that you get a price for
your destination before getting into

ABOVE: travelling by rail is fast and efficient.

the taxi. At Arlanda airport, beware of
catching Taxi Stockholm, Taxi Kurir
and a handful of other companies
which have fixed fares for rides into
the city centre, as these will cost you
at least double the price that other
firms will charge.

By Air
Air travel is part of everyday life in a
country as large as Sweden, and all
major cities and towns are linked by
an efficient network of services
operated mainly by SAS. Stockholm
alone has flights to more than 40
places within Sweden.
    Cheap flights are available on
selected domestic services all year,
as well as standby flights for under
25s and special fares for senior
citizens. But many of the best deals
are during the summer peak season
in July when few business executives
are travelling.
    Air Passes, sold in conjunction
with an international fare, allow up to
six flights within Scandinavia at
affordable prices. For more
information call:
SAS, www.flysas.com
Malmö Aviation, www.malmoaviation.se
Skyways, www.skyways.se

By Train
Swedish State Railways, or SJ (tel:
0771-75 75 75; www.sj.se) operate an
efficient electrified network covering
the entire country. The route from
Trelleborg in the south to
Riksgränsen in the far north is
reckoned to be the longest
continuous stretch of electrified rail
line in the world.
    Swedish trains run at a high
frequency, particularly on the main
trunk route linking Stockholm with
Göteborg, on which there is an hourly
service. The high-speed train X2000
travels at up to 200 kph (125 mph)
and is a good choice if you want to

travel long distances; the journey
from Göteborg to Stockholm, for
example, takes only three hours.

Rail Passes
Swedish state railways offer a wide
range of fares for both business and
leisure travellers. Conditions and
prices may depend on whether you
buy your ticket in Sweden or abroad.
A number of discount fares are
available, including the following,
which must be purchased outside
Sweden:
● **The Interail Scandinavian Passes**
offer travellers who live outside
Sweden unlimited rail travel within
Sweden. Check www.interailnet.com, or
European Rail, www.europeanrail.co.uk,
for details.
● *Resplus* If you want to combine
rail, bus and boat in one ticket, the
best way is probably to buy a *Resplus*
ticket that enables you to reach over
3,000 destinations within Sweden.
For more information, prices and
bookings call: 08-762 4400,
www.resplus.se.
    To get a *förköpsbiljett* (reduced
rate ticket) in Sweden, you must
book 7 days in advance. For more
information, prices and bookings call:
0771-75 75 75.
    For rail travel in Lapland, call
Connex, tel: 0771-26 00 00.
Scenic Train Route
One very beautiful journey to take by
train is the *Inlandsbanan* (Inland
Railway), which runs for more than
1,300 km (800 miles) down the
spine of Sweden from Gällivare,
north of the Arctic Circle, to Mora in
the south. The ticket is valid for 10
days and you may stop and continue
wherever you please within the time
limit.
    More information is available from
Inlandsbanan AB, PO Box 561, S-831
27 Östersund. Tel: 0771-53 53 53,
www.inlandsbanan.se.

By Underground

Stockholm is justifiably proud of its underground railway, known as T-banan (the "T" stands for "tunnel" – all stations are identified by the "T" sign). The T-banan is spotless, with almost 100 stations covering more than 95 km (60 miles).

The commuter trains *(pendeltåg)* take you very quickly to the suburbs of Stockholm as well as down to Nynäshamn, where you can board the ferry to the island of Gotland.

By Bus

Travelling by bus is usually cheap compared to rail but travelling time is longer. There are weekend-only services on a number of key routes.

An efficient network of express bus services links all major towns and cities, operated mainly by:
Svenska Buss, tel: 0771-67 67 67.
Swebus Express, tel: 0771 21 82 18.

Stockholm

The local bus network in Stockholm is claimed to be the world's largest and is run by the Stockholm Transit Authority (www.sl.se), which also operates the underground and local mainline rail services.

Instead of paying cash on the bus, it is cheaper to buy a *Förköpsremsa,* which is a set of 16 vouchers which you use according to how many of the three travel zones you pass through on your journey. The driver stamps your ticket when you start your journey and you are allowed to travel freely within one zone on the bus, train and underground for an hour on the same ticket. One-, three- and seven-day travel cards are available; or if you buy the worthwhile *Stockholmskortet* tourist card, this gives free public transport in the Greater Stockholm area for a period of 24 or 72 hours.

Göteborg

Göteborg has a superior tram system, as well as a good network of bus routes.

By Boat or Ferry

For a country that boasts about its 96,000 lakes and countless rivers and canals, water transport plays a surprisingly small part in Sweden's public transport system. The main ferry links the Baltic island of Gotland and has services from Nynäshamn and Oskarshamn. For more information check with the local tourist office or call Destination Gotland, tel: 0498-20 18 00; www.destinationgotland.se.

There are also innumerable commuter services in the Stockholm archipelago operated by the famous white boats of the Waxholm Steamship Company. In the summer, visitors can buy a range of discounted tickets which give unlimited travel on the Waxholm boats. For information call: 08-679 58 30, www.waxholmsbolaget.se.

Strömma Kanalbolaget's website also has information on sightseeing and excursions in Stockholm: www.stromma.se.

By Taxi

Swedish taxis are usually efficient, but rely more on the telephone than being flagged down. In larger cities, a computer system gives instructions to drivers to indicate where the next person is to be picked up.

Fares are steep. There is a minimum charge, and the meter goes on as soon as the taxi arrives at your address. If you are late, the meter starts at the time you ordered the taxi – even a five-minute delay can be costly. The bigger firms accept credit cards.

In Stockholm, some companies have a maximum fare for rides within the centre. This is good value if you want to travel, for example, from the north to the south of town or if there is a traffic jam.

By Bicycle

Many of Sweden's towns are ideal for exploring by bike, with good cycle lanes. Cycling holidays are also popular in Sweden; a favourite among cyclists is the Sweden Trail *(Sverigeleden)*, which links a large number of tourist centres and ports.

Bikes can be hired in most places; just enquire at the local tourist office. Costs are per day or per week.

Cykelfrämjandet, tel: 08-545 910 30, www.cykelframjandet.se, publish a cycling holidays guide in English.

On Foot
Sightseeing

All three of Sweden's largest cities, Stockholm, Malmö and Göteborg, are compact enough to sightsee on foot. They are pedestrian-friendly to the extent that they have traffic lights that motorists actually observe; conversely, Swedish pedestrians are disciplined, and respect red lights even when there is not a car in sight.

Hitchhiking

This is officially discouraged, and in any case finding a lift can be difficult in the holiday season, when every Swedish car seems to be packed with children, baggage and camping gear.

Driving
Main Routes

Sweden's roads are uncrowded, with toll-free motorways covering more than 1,100 km (700 miles), trunk roads some 80,500 km (50,000 miles) and then there are thousands of kilometres of often picturesque byroads.

Rules of the Road

• Traffic gives way to approaching traffic from the right, unless signs indicate otherwise, and gives way to traffic already on a roundabout.
• Everyone must wear seat belts.
• Headlights are obligatory both day and night.
• Drivers are not required to call the police after accidents but must exchange names and addresses. If you do not stop at all you may be liable to a fine or imprisonment.
• In the event of a breakdown,

BELOW: the Øresund bridge links Denmark and Sweden.

contact the police or Larmtjänst, an organisation run by the Swedish insurance companies with a 24-hour service (tel: 020-91 00 40). The emergency number 112 should be used only for accidents or injury.

● Sweden's drink-drive laws are strictly enforced, with spot checks and heavy fines imposed. You can be prosecuted for drinking even the equivalent of a can of beer.

● Drivers must stop at pedestrian crossings when a person is crossing or indicates an intention to cross.

● Swedes often forget to indicate when changing lanes, so be careful.

Speed Limits
Motorways 110 kph (70 mph)
Dual carriageways 90 kph (55 mph)
Unsigned roads 70 kph (43 mph)
Built-up areas 50 kph (31 mph), or 30 kph (19 mph) around school areas.

Car Hire
All the major companies have desks at the airports.

Stockholm
Avis, Vasagatan 10B and Arlanda airport; tel: 0770-82 00 82; www.avis.se
Budget, Klarabergsviadukten 92 and Arlanda airport; tel: 0770-11 00 12; www.budget.se
Europcar, Hotel Sheraton, Tegelbacken 6 and Arlanda airport; tel: 0770-77 00 50; www.europcar.se
Hertz, Östermalmstorg 4 and Arlanda airport; tel: 0771-21 12 12; www.hertz.se

V isas and Passports

A valid passport entitles you to stay for up to three months, and visas are not normally required. Immigration rarely causes problems in Sweden. If you arrive from another Scandinavian country, passports aren't usually checked at all. If you intend to stay longer than three months you will need to obtain a resident's permit, which you can do once you are in Sweden.

Customs Regulations

There are no restrictions on importing/exporting goods for people travelling between Sweden and other EU countries, as long as the goods are for personal use and not resale; guide levels are 3,200 cigarettes, 400 cigarillos, 200 cigars, 1kg tobacco, 10 litres of spirits, 20 litres of fortified wine, 90 litres of wine and 110 litres of beer. Visitors travelling to/from non-EU countries can import duty-free 200 cigarettes/100 cigarillos/50 cigars or 250g tobacco, 1 litre of spirits or 2 litres of dessert

wine (maximum 22 percent alcohol by volume), 2 litres of wine plus 16 litres of beer.

Gifts

Presents up to a value of 1,700 SEK may be taken into the country; the value of any food you are bringing is included in this limit.

W hat to Bring

Sweden's weather is unpredictable, so plan for any eventuality. In summer, even in the Arctic North, you could have hot sunny days that call for shorts and T-shirts, or it could be one of those summers when the sun never appears and sweaters and rainwear are needed. Winters can be very cold, but this is "dry" cold, which is not uncomfortable. Still, you should take a heavy coat and warm headgear as well as sturdy footwear for the slushy streets.

What to Read

Good books on Sweden are few and far between, but the best source of information on publications in English is the Swedish Institute, which itself publishes a good range of guides. Its website has a good list and has an ordering service.
Svenska Institutet
Slottsbacken 10, Box 7434, SE-103 91 Stockholm.
Tel: 08 453 78 00.
Fax: 08 20 72 48.
www.si.se (also search under Sweden bookshop; www.swedenbookshop.com)

History

Sweden: A Traveller's History by Eric Elstob (Boydell Press). Swedish history from its beginnings.
Swedish History in Outline by Jörgen Welbull (Swedish Institute).

BELOW: be prepared for all weathers.

The Vikings, Lords of the Seas by Yves Cohat (Thames & Hudson). History of the Vikings, with excellent colour photography.

Architecture

A Home by Lena Rydin (Carl Larsson Gården/Dalaförlaget). Artist Carl Larsson's farm in Sundborn in the Dalarna region in photographs and paintings.
Great Royal Palaces of Sweden by Göran Alm (M.T. Train/Scala Books). A dozen castles, palaces and pavilions belonging to Swedish royalty over the past 500 years.

Art and Design

Carl and Karin Larsson: Creators of the Swedish Style by Michael Snodin and Elisabet Stavenow-Hidemark (eds.). A profile of two of Sweden's most influential designers.
A History of Swedish Art by Mereth Lindgren, Louise Lyberg, Birgitta Sandström and Anna Greta Wahlberg (Bokförlaget Signum). A bird's-eye view of Swedish painting, sculpture and architecture.
The Swedish Room by Lars Sjöberg and Ursula Sjöberg (Frances Lincoln Limited). Some of Sweden's most classic interiors.

Food

The Swedish Kitchen: A Culinary Journey by Lennart Hagerfors (Norstedts). A cookbook by one of the best-known chefs in Sweden, with 198 modern Swedish recipes.
Smörgasbord: A Swedish Classic by Kerstin Torngre (Swedish Institute). A short guide to Sweden's traditional buffet spread.

Fiction

The Wonderful Adventures of Nils and *The Further Adventures of Nils* by Selma Lagerlöv. Captivating stories about a boy who flies around Sweden on a goose, have made Lagerlöv one of the nation's most popular children's authors.

Guides

Live and Work in Scandinavia by Andre de Vries et al (Vacation Work Publications). Jobs and how to obtain them.
National Parks in Sweden: Europe's Last Wilderness edited by Clæs Grundsten (The National Environment Protection Board, available through the Swedish Institute).

Other Insight Guides

Insight Guide titles in the region include *Insight Pocket Guide Stockholm* and *Insight Guide Sweden*.

A CCOMMODATION

HOTELS, YOUTH HOSTELS, BED AND BREAKFAST

Choosing a Hotel

Swedish hotels are of a uniformly high standard, and can be expensive. However, hotel rates do come down in high summer when the expense-account business travellers are on holiday. Scandic and Sweden Hotels are the country's leading multiples. Away from the big cities, there are plenty of privately owned hotels with the individuality lacking in chains. Visit www.hotelsinsweden.net for details on hotels in most towns and cities.

The Hotel Online accommodation booking service is based at the main tourist information office in Stockholm. Their services are free if you book by telephone or through their website; if you book in person, there's a charge of 75Skr for a hotel room and 25Skr for a room at a Youth Hostel.

Hotel Online, Hamngatan 27 (Entrance Kungsträdgården), Stockholm. Tel: 08 508 285 08; www.stockholmtown.com.

Discounts

All the hotel groups run discount schemes during summer. Stockholm, Göteborg and Malmö also offer special discount packages at weekends year-round and daily in summer. These often include free public transport and free admission to visitor attractions.

Nationwide Chains

The big international hotel chains like Hilton or Sheraton have made little impact. Accommodation is dominated by Scandinavian chains such as Scandic or Sweden Hotels.
Best Western Hotels
Skytteholmsvägen 2, Box 28
SE-171 11 Solna.

Tel: 08 566 293 70
www.bestwestern.se
Choice Hotels
Master Samuelsgaten 42, Box 7620
SE-103 94 Stockholm
Tel: 08 691 35 00
www.choicehotels.no
First Hotels
Linnégatan 89A
SE-104 51 Stockholm
Tel: 020 41 11 11
www.firsthotels.com
Scandic Hotels
Hälsingegatan 40, Box 6197
SE-102 33 Stockholm
Tel: 08 51 73 50 50
www.scandichotels.com
Sweden Hotels
Tel: 0771-777 800
E-mail: info@gastklubben.se
www.swedenhotels.se

Bed and Breakfasts

The bed and breakfast system is becoming more popular. Look for the *Rum* sign (it means "room" and does not include breakfast). Ask at local tourist offices if any *rum* accommodation is available. Prices are very reasonable.

Youth Hostels

Sweden has over 300 youth hostels *(vandrarhem)*, from mansion houses and castles to renovated ships like the 100-year-old *af Chapman* in Stockholm harbour, and modern purpose-built hostels. These are mailny in southern and central Sweden. There are also plenty of youth hostels in the Stockholm archipelago. This is an excellent facility for an inexpensive holiday. Most have two- and four-bedded rooms or family rooms. Hostels have self-catering facilities, but meals or snacks are provided in some. There is often use of a washing machine. Most hostels will charge extra for bed linen, so bring your own sheets and towels. Always book ahead in the summer.

For details:
Svenska Turistföreningen (STF).
Tel: 08 463 21 00.
www.stfturist.se.

Camping

There are about 750 officially approved sites, many in pretty locations and are generally of a high standard. Most open from early June to the end of August. Rates are claimed to be among the cheapest in Europe.

You can also rent camping chalets and cottages, cabins and mountain huts, caravans and motor homes. For fast check-in and check-out plus insurance while at the site, you should get the Camping Card Scandinavia. This costs around 125Skr, and you can apply for it before you leave for Sweden. The card is available (allow one month for delivery) from:
Sveriges Camping – och Stugföretagares Riksorganisation, Mässens Gata 10, PO Box 5079, SE-402 22 Göteborg. Or visit the very useful www.camping.se

Hotel Listings

Hotels are grouped by area, starting with Stockholm. Within each city or region, they are listed alphabetically.

DENMARK
NORWAY
SWEDEN
FINALND

STOCKHOLM

Adlon Hotell
Vasagatan 42, 111 20 Stockholm
Tel: 84 02 65 00
www.adlon.se
Rooms are on the small side, but this is great value for a central location. **$–$$**

Af Chapman & Skeppsholmen
Flaggmansvägen 8, SE-111 49
Tel: 08 463 22 66
www.stfchapman.com
A Youth Hostel situated in a landmark 1888 ship with spectacular views of the Gamla Stan. Af Chapman has 136 beds plus a 152-bed building facing the ship's gangway. Café has a terrific view. **$**

Hotel Bentleys
Drottninggatan 77, SE-111 60
Tel: 08 14 13 95
www.bentleys.se
Found at the top, and quieter, end of this famous shopping street, this is a mid-size charming hotel where all the rooms are individually designed. **$$**

Berns Hotel
Näckströmsgatan 8, SE-103 27
Tel: 08 566 322 00
www.berns.se
Historic but ultra-modernised hotel and "salons" in the heart of town close to shopping and nightlife. **$$$**

Birger Jarl Hotel
Tulegatan 8, SE-104 32
Tel: 08 674 18 00
www.birgerjarl.se
This is the first hotel in Stockholm to have rooms with uniquely Swedish design, and also just a short walk from the centre of town. **$$$**

City Backpackers
Upplandsgatan 2A, SE-111 23
Tel: 08 20 69 20
www.citybackpackers.se
A busy central hostel with excellent facilities, including free bike hire. Ideal location, although can get noisy at weekends. **$**

Columbus Hotel
Tjärhovsgatan 11, SE116 21
Tel: 08 503 112 00
www.columbus.se
This former hostel is now a three-star hotel in Södermalm, an area popular among younger people, artists and writers. The renovated hotel is close to pubs, galleries and designer shops. **$$–$$$**

Crystal Plaza
Birger Jarlsgatan 35, SE-111 45
Tel: 08 406 88 00
www.crystalplazahotel.se
Centrally located. Different room rates on offer. **$–$$**

Hotell Diplomat
Strandvägen 7C, SE 104 40
Tel: 08 459 68 00
www.diplomathotel.com
Beautiful waterside location on the city's most exclusive street. **$$$**

First Hotel Amaranten
Kungsholmsgatan 31, SE-104 20
Tel: 08 692 52 00
www.firsthotels.se

BELOW: the comfortable rooms at Hotel J.

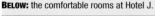

This is a large, modern hotel with much style that also features a spa. Found in a neat area just a short walk from the Town Hall and Central Station. **$$$**

First Hotel Reisen
Skeppsbron 9, SE-111 30
Tel: 08 22 32 60
www.firsthotels.se
With origins from the 18th century, this has a classical ambiance, a waterfront location and sauna and cold pool in the vaulted cellar. **$$$**

Grand Hôtel Stockholm
S. Blasieholmshamnen 8, SE-103 27
Tel: 08 679 35 00
www.grandhotel.se
This five-star hotel, the only one of its class in Sweden, has an unparalleled view of the waterfront and Royal Palace. Its new "Restaurant Mathias Dahigren" received its first Michelin star in 2008. **$$$**

Gustav Vasa Hotel
Västmannagatan 61, SE-113 25
Tel: 08 34 38 01
www.gustavvasahotel.se
In popular residential area near restaurants and shops. Three underground stops from centre. **$$**

Hotel Hellsten
Luntmakargatan 68, SE-113 51
Tel: 08 661 86 00
www.hellsten.se
Situated in what is fast becoming a trendy area, only a few minutes from the town centre. The building dates from 1898 and it has large rooms with much style at a very reasonable cost. **$$–$$$**

Hilton Stockholm Slussen
Guldgränd 8, SE-104 65
Tel: 08 517 353 00
www.hilton.com
A very impressive modern hotel with spectacular views over the water to Gamla Stan and the Town Hall. **$$$**

Hotel J
Ellensviksvägen 1
131 28 Nacka Strand
Tel: 08 601 30 00
www.hotelj.com

Decorated in contemporary marine style, reminiscent of the boathouses in New England. The city centre is 15 minutes away by boat or car. Restaurant J is highly recommended. **$$–$$$**

Lord Nelson Hotel
Västerlånggatan 22, SE-111 29
Tel: 08 506 401 20
www.lordnelsonhotel.se
Located in a popular location in Gamla Stan, this is part of a small chain featuring a Nelsonian theme. **$$**

Mälardrottningen
Riddarholmen, SE-111 28
Tel: 08 545 187 80
www.malardrottningen.se
This is your one and only chance to sleep on a 1920s' luxury yacht that was once owned by the American millionaire Barbara Hutton, and now moored against Riddarholmen. **$$**

Radisson SAS Strand Hotel
Nybrokajen 9, SE-103 27
Tel: 08 5066 4000
www.radissonsas.com
Featuring a modern interior within a classical-style building, with views across the water to the impressive Strandvägen street. **$$$**

Rex Hotel
Luntmakargatan 73, SE-113 51
Tel: 08 16 00 40
www.rexhotel.se
In a building dating from 1866, this is just across from its sister-hotel the Hellsten and shares much of its character and charm. **$$**

Sheraton Stockholm Hotel and Towers
Tegelbacken 6, SE-101 23
Tel: 08 412 34 00
www.sheraton.com/stockholm
Found between Central Station and Gamla Stan, this has the largest rooms in town and fabulous views of Lake Mälaren, the Town Hall and the Old Town. **$$$**

Tre Små Rum Hotel
Högbergsgatan 81, SE-118 54
Tel: 08 641 23 71

www.tresmarum.se
Simple but very good-value B&B in the trendy suburb of Södermalm. **$**
Victory Hotel
Lilla Nygatan 5, SE-111 28

Tel: 08 506 400 00
www.victoryhotel.se
In the heart of Gamla Stan, this has a maritime ambiance reflecting the war vessel it is named after

and has a great deal of character. **$$$**
Villa Källhagen
Djurgårdsbrunnsvägen 10, SE-115 27
Tel: 08 665 03 00

www.kallhagen.se
Modern, charming hotel with an excellent restaurant run by an award-winning chef. Close to parks. **$$**

AROUND STOCKHOLM

Grythyttan

Grythyttans Gästgivaregård
Prästgatan 2, SE-712 81
Tel: 0591 633 00
www.grythyttan.com
Sweden's best-known inn in a lovely setting. Expensive but exquisite restaurant and wine list. **$$–$$$**

Mariefred

Gripsholms Värdshus and Hotel
Kyrkogatan 1, SE-647 23
Tel: 0159 347 50

www.gripsholms-vardshus.se
A 400-year old inn west of Stockholm and across the road from Gripsholms Castle. Its rooms are full of antiques. **$$–$$$**

Norrköping

Elite Grand Hotel
Tyska Torget 2, SE-600 41
Tel: 011 36 41 00
www.elite.se
First-class early 20th-century hotel by the Motala river, by the town hall, in the centre of town. **$$–$$$**

Sigtuna

Sigtuna Stadshotell
Stora Nygatan 3, SE-193 30
Tel: 08 592 501 00
www.sigtunastadshotell.se
A renovated, early 20th-century hotel in the heart of this historic town. **$$–$$$**

Skokloster

Skokloster Wärdshus & Hotel
SE-746 96 Skokloster
Tel: 018 38 61 00
www.skokloster.se

Newly renovated hotel built in what used to be the nearby castle's stables. Many rooms offer views of the castle and lake. **$–$$**

Uppsala

First Hotel Linné
Skolgatan 45, SE-750 02
Tel: 018 10 20 00
www.firsthotels.com
Modern hotel with a view over Linnaeus Garden. Situated in a quiet area, five minutes walk from the centre. **$$**

MALMÖ

Hotell Baltzar
Södergatan 20, SE-211 34
Tel: 040 66 55 700
www.baltzarhotel.se
Turn of the 20th century building, centrally located. **$$**
Elite Hotel Savoy
Norra Vallgatan 62, SE-201 80
Tel: 040 664 48 00
www.elite.se
Opposite the train station.

Has a restaurant, a French-style brasserie, and a pub, The Bishop's Arms with a large selection of beers. **$$**
First Hotel Garden
Baltzarsgatan 20, SE-211 36
Tel: 040 66 56 200
www.firsthotels.com
This has a charming roof garden making the hotel an oasis in the centre of town. **$$**

Hilton Malmö City
Triangeln 2, SE-200 10
Tel: 040 693 47 00
www.hilton.com
Modern high-rise glass building. Top floor rooms and fitness centre have nice views of Malmö. **$$$**
Hotel Noble House
Gustav Adolfstorg 47, SE-211 39
Tel: 040 664 30 00
www.hkchotels.se

Right in the centre, close to shops and restaurants. **$$**
Hotell Royal
Norra Vallgatan 94, SE-211 22
Tel: 040 664 25 00
www.hotellroyal.com
Small hotel, recently acquired by Best Western, in an old building close to shops, station and ferries. In summer, breakfast is served in the garden. **$**

GÖTEBORG

Hotel Eggers
Drottningtorget, SE-404 24
Tel: 031 333 44 40
www.hoteleggers.se
Historic 19th-century railway hotel with individually furnished rooms. By the station and near the city centre. **$$**
Elite Plaza Hotel
Västra Hamngatan 3, SE-404 22
Tel: 031 720 40 00
www.elite.se
New luxury hotel in the centre. **$$$**
First Hotel G
Nlls Ericonsplatsen 4, SE-411 03
Tel: 031 63 72 00
www.firsthotels.com

Functional design combined with modern technology and a pleasing ambiance. **$$**
Hotel Lorensberg
Berzeliigatan 15, SE-412 53
Tel: 031 81 06 00
www.hotel-lorensberg.se
Hotel with beautiful mural paintings, close to Götaplatsen, main street, Avenyn, and Liseberg amusement park. **$$**
Novotel Göteborg
Klippan 1, SE-414 51
Tel: 031 720 22 00
www.novotel.se
Overlooking the harbour and near good public transport. **$$**

Scandic Crown
Polhemsplatsen 3, 411 11
Tel: 031 75 15 100
www.scandichotels.com
Handy for the train station, the Crown has light, tasteful rooms, great views from the upper balconies, and one of the best breakfast spreads in town. **$$**
St Jörgens Hotell & Pensionat
Gamla Lillhagsvägen 127B, SE-422 49
Tel: 031 55 39 81
www.st-jorgen.nu
Charming and small in rural setting within easy reach of the centre. **$**

Vanilj Hotell
Kyrkogatan 38, 411 15
Tel: 031 71 16 220
www.hotelvanilj.se
A pleasant little hotel, on a quiet street yet handy for the city centre. Close to the cathedral. **$–$$**

PRICE CATEGORIES

Price categories are based on the average cost (including tax) of a double room for two, usually with breakfast:
$ = under 1,000Skr
$$ = 1,000–1,800Skr
$$$ = over 1,800Skr

SOUTHERN SWEDEN: SMÅLAND AND ÖLAND

Helsingborg

Hotel Mollberg
Stortorget 18, SE-251 14
Tel: 042 37 37 00
www.elite.se
Dating back to the 14th century, this beautiful hotel is the oldest in Sweden. **$$**

Kalmar

First Hotel Witt
Södra Långgatan 42,
SE-392 31
Tel: 0480 15250

www.firsthotels.com
This, Kalmar's oldest hotel, has hosted many famous personalities and is where the popular dish "Biff à la Lindstöm" originated. **$$**
Slottshotellet
Slottsvagen 7, SE-392 33
Tel: 0480 882 60
www.slottshotellet.se
A romantic and old-fashioned atmosphere in Kalmar's old town. Opposite the park and castle. **$$**

Öland

Guntorps Herrgård
Guntorpsgatan, SE-387 36
Borgholm
Tel: 0485 130 00
www.guntorpsherrgard.se
Beautiful manor house just outside Borgholm, with lovely restaurant, pool and charming rooms. **$$**

Ystad

Ystads Saltsjöbad
Saltsjöbadsvägen 15,

SE-271 39
Tel: 0411 13 630
www.ystadssaltsjobad.se
Spa hotel with panoramic Baltic view. Relaxing accommodation. **$$**

Växjö

Elite Stadshotellet
Kungsgatan 6, 351 04
Tel: 04 70 134 00
www.elite.se
One of the best options in Växjö. The airport bus stops right outside. **$$**

GOTLAND

Visby

Clairon Hotel Wisby
Strandgatan 6, SE-621 56
Tel: 0498 25 88 00
www.wisbyhotell.se
An old brewery turned into a stylish hotel, located in the town centre, just a 15-minute walk from the port. Steam room, sauna and

indoor pool located in the medieval cellar. Relax in the Winter Garden bar. **$$**
Hotel Stenugnen
Korsgatan 4-6, 621 57
Tel: 0498-210 211
www.stenugnen.nu
Pleasing, bright rooms with a nautical theme, spruced up each year to keep them fresh. **$–$$**

Tofta Strandpensionat
Solbacksvägen 19
Tel: 0498 29 70 60
www.toftastrand.se
Basic but pleasant boarding house plus self catering-chalets. Excellent location right on the beach 20 km (12 miles) from Visby. Bikes for hire, tennis and badminton. **$$**

Fårösund

Fårösunds Fästning
Bungenäs, 62035
Tel: 0498-22 12 40
www.pontusfrithiof.com
To experience Danish minimalism at its best, look no further than this sleek design hotel, just yards from the beach. **$$$**

THE WEST COAST

Halmstad

First Hotel Mårtenson
Storgatan 52, SE-302 43
Tel: 035 17 75 75
www.firsthotels.com
A very pleasant hotel in the centre of town beside the River Nissan and near the

park. **$–$$**
Hotel Tylösand
Tylöhusvägen, SE-301 16
Tel: 035 305 00
www.tylosand.se
A first-class hotel overlooking the beach that includes a great spa, and has golf courses nearby. **$$**

Marstrand

Grand Hotel Marstrand
Rådhusgatan 2, SE-440 30
Tel: 0303 603 22
www.grandmarstrand.se
Attractive late 19th-century hotel. Located by the water. **$$**

Villa Maritime Marstrand
Hamnen SE-440 30 Marstrand
Tel: 0303 610 25
www.villa-maritime.se
First class hotel with apartments located right on the harbour and close to golf courses, sailing and other activities. **$$**

THE GREAT LAKES

Borås

First Hotel Grand
Hallbergsplatsen 2, SE-503 05
Tel: 033 799 00 00
www.firsthotelgrand.se
First-class and modern, bar and nightclub. A range of entertainment including dance bands and DJs. **$$**

Karlstad

Clarion Hotel Plaza
Västra Torggatan 2, SE-652 25
Tel: 054 10 02 00

www.radissonsas.com
Modern hotel in the centre with great views of the city. Close to the railway station. Piano bar and wine cellar. **$–$$**
Elite Stadshotellet Karlstad
Kungsgatan 22, SE-651 08
Karlstad
Tel: 054 29 30 00
www.elite.se
Late 19th-century hotel with a good restaurant and English pub, on the banks of the Klara river. **$$**

Lidköping

Hotel Ekoxen
Klostergatan 68, SE-582 23
Tel: 013 25 26 00
www.ekoxen.se
First-class hotel with spa and golf packages, in the centre of town. **$$**
Stadt Lidköping
Gamla Stadens Torg 1,
SE-531 32
Tel: 0510 220 85
www.stadtlidkoping.se
Very distinguished hotel with a fine waterfront

location. Close to Läckö Castle and Röstrand porcelain factory. **$$**

Örebro

Elite Stora Hotellet
Drottninggatan 1
Tel: 019 15 69 00
www.elite.se
An historic hotel, built in 1858, centrally located near Örebro castle, the art gallery and concert hall. Stylish comfortable rooms. Popular restaurant. **$$**

GÖTA KANAL

Karlsborg

Kanalhotellet
Storgatan 94, SE-546 32
Tel: 0505 121 30
www.kanalhotellet.se
Late 19th-century hotel
with views of the canal. **$**

Motala

Hotel M
Kungsgatan 1, SE-591 30 Motala
Tel: 0141-21 66 60
www.hotelm.se
Marine-style hotel, newly
renovated. **$$**

Söderköping

Hotel Söderköpings Brunn
Skönbergsgatan 35, SE-614 21
Tel: 0121 109§ 00
www.soderkopingsbrunn.se
Charming spa hotel
situated in a park. **$$$**

Villa Linnéa
Nybrogata 1, 61430
Tel: 0121-218 10
www.villalinnea.se
A peaceful, B&B which
practically dips its toes
into the Göta Kanal. You
can't get much closer. **$**

DALARNA

Falun

First Hotel Grand
Trotzgatan 9–11, SE-791 71
Tel: 023 79 48 80
www.firsthotels.se
Dalarna's biggest hotel
located in the town centre.
Close to golf courses. **$$**

Mora

Mora Hotell
Strandgatan 12, SE-792 30
Tel: 0250 59 26 50
www.morahotell.se
Modern hotel in the centre
close to Lake Siljan, the
Zorn museum, and the

finishing line of the famous
cross-country ski race,
Vasaloppet. Several
restaurants are nearby. **$$**

Tällberg

Hotell Klockargården
Siljansvägen 6, SE-793 70

Tel: 0247 502 60
www.klockargarden.com
Traditional timber houses
built around a peaceful
courtyard, with an Arts and
Crafts yard nearby. Lovely
surrounding gardens and
superb views of Lake
Siljan. **$–$$**

THE CENTRAL HEARTLANDS

Åre

Åregården
SE-830 13
Tel: 0647 178 00
www.diplomathotel.com
First-class hotel with an
indoor pool. Skiing

facilities, shops and
nightclubs nearby. **$$–$$$**
Åre Ski Lodge
Trondheimsleden 44, SE-830 13
Tel: 0647 510 29
www.areskilodge.se
This hostel is a cheap
option with comfortable

rooms and good facilities
including sauna and
kitchen. **$**

Sundsvall

First Hotel Strand
Strandgatan 10, SE-851 06

Tel: 060 64 19 50
www.firsthotels.se
This, the largest hotel in
town, the Neptune wing
has a marine theme, the
Bacchus wing is more
classical in style. Popular
restaurant and bar. **$$**

LAPLAND

Arvidsjaur

Laponia Hotel
Storgatan 45, SE-933 33
Tel: 0960 555 00
www.hotell-laponia.se
Modern hotel offering
various winter sports
facilities such as dog
sledging and scooter rides
as well as winter golf. **$$**

Kiruna

Hotel Rallaren
Bangårdsvägen 4, 98134
Tel: 0980-611 26
www.hotelrallaren.se
Choose between Rallar-
en's standard hotel
rooms or one of their
traditional Sami dwellings
in the garden. Outdoor

hot tub and sauna.
$$–$$$
Hotell Vinterpalatset
Järnvägsgatan 18, SE-981 21
Tel: 0980 677 70
www.vinterpalatset.se
Small privately owned
hotel built in 1904 and
renovated into a modern
hotel with all facilities.
$–$$

Riksgränsen

Riksgränsen
Riksgränsvägen 15,
SE-981 94
Tel: 0980 400 80
www.riksgransen.nu
Rooms and self-catering,
with skiing facilities and
opportunities for hiking
nearby. **$$**

THE NORTHEAST COAST

Haparanda

Haparanda Stadshotell
Torget 7, SE-953 31
Tel: 0922 614 90
www.haparandastadshotell.se
Early 20th-century hotel
in the town centre. The
restaurant's specialities
include reindeer, elk
and grouse. **$$**

Piteå

Piteå Stadshotell
Olof Palmes Gata 1,
SE-941 21
Tel: 0911 23 40 00
www.piteastadshotell.com
Restored late 19th-
century hotel located
in the centre of town.
$$

Umeå

Hotell Dragonen
Västra Norrlandsgatan 5,
SE-903 27
Tel: 090 12 58 00
www.hotelldragonen.se
Hotel with restaurant,
bar and Umeå's biggest
nightclub. Live music
Friday and Saturday **$$**

PRICE CATEGORIES

Price categories are based
on the average cost
(including tax) of a double
room for two, usually with
breakfast:
$ = under 1,000Skr
$$ = 1,000–1,800Skr
$$$ = over 1,800Skr

DENMARK

NORWAY

SWEDEN

FINLAND

E ATING OUT

RECOMMENDED RESTAURANTS AND CAFÉS

Choosing a Restaurant

Sweden, once known as the land of *husmanskost* (homely fare), is currently enjoying a culinary renaissance, thanks to a new generation of chefs who know how to give a sophisticated twist to classic Swedish dishes such as reindeer, elk, lingonberries, salmon or herring.

Eating out has become increasingly popular, but can seem expensive if you drink a lot of wine or beer. Stockholm has more than 700 restaurants covering at least 30 national cuisines. Göteborg is particularly good for seafood, and Malmö claims to have more restaurants per head than any other Swedish city.

For travellers on a tight budget there is no shortage of inexpensive places to eat. Look for the *dagens rätt* (dish of the day), a lunch that usually includes bread, a simple salad and soft drink for around 65–75Skr. Traditional Swedish food like meatballs, *pytt i panna* (fried potatoes, onions, meat and sausage served with beetroot), and pea soup

is widely available. The famous *sill* (pickled herring) is served mostly around midsummer with new potatoes. You can find all kinds of pickled herring; with onions, mustard, barbecue sauce, garlic or herbs, or *matjessill* (with sour cream and chives).

Salmon has less of a luxury connotation than in other countries. *Gravad lax* (marinated salmon) and *rökt lax* (smoked salmon) can be found on the *smörgåsbord* and on most Swedish menus.

Fast food outlets are everywhere. The ubiquitous *korvkiosk* sells grilled chicken, sausages, hamburgers and *tunnbrödsrulle* (a parcel of mashed potato, sausage and ketchup or mustard wrapped in soft bread). Some serve *strömming* (fried herring) and mashed potato.

The Swedes generally eat early. Restaurants start serving lunch at about 11am and some small hotels, particularly in country areas, serve evening meals around 6pm. In the cities you can eat much later. Many of the top restaurants in Stockholm close in July for staff holidays.

Traditional Dishes

Ärtsoppa Hearty yellow pea and pork soup, served with pancakes *(plättar)* and traditionally eaten on Thursday.
Janssons frestelse Jansson's Temptation, a creamy baked dish of shredded potatoes layered with herring and onion.
Kåldomar Meat stuffed cabbage leaves.
Köttbullar Beef or pork meatballs served with a tangy lingonberry sauce.
Potatissallad Potato salad richly spiced with dill, a traditional accompaniment to pickled herrings.
Sjömansbiff Beef casserole with a sliced potato and onion topping.

Restaurant Listings

Below is a selection of restaurants around the country. Restaurants are grouped by area with Stockholm first, and are listed alphabetically.

RESTAURANT LISTINGS

STOCKHOLM

The Bull and Bear Inn
Birger Jarlsgatan 16
Tel: 08 611 10 00
Stockholm's most authentic English pub, with typical pub food combined with a huge selection of draught and bottled beers and over 200 types of malt whisky. **$–$$**

Den Gyldene Freden
Österlånggatan 51
Tel: 08 24 97 60
www.gyldenefreden.se
Dating from 1722, and with an atmosphere almost unchanged since then, this is the classical restaurant in Stockholm where you'll combine excellent cuisine

with a historical environment. **$$$**
Eriks Bakficka
Fredrikshovsgatan 4
Tel: 08 66 01 599
www.eriks.se
A longstanding and reliable restaurant, Bakficka serves traditional Swedish dishes. **$$**

Fredgatan 12
Fredgatan 12
Tel: 08 24 80 52
www.f12.se
A very fashionable bar-club-restaurant serving excellent food. **$$$**
Gondolen
Stadsgården 6
Tel: 08 641 70 90

www.eriks.se
Highly recommended.
Eating here is a real
Stockholm experience.
Offers excellent traditional
Swedish cuisine with a
great view over the city.
$$$
GQ restaurang
Kommendörsgatan 23
Tel: 08 545 67 430
www.gqrestaurang.se
Opened in August 2005 this
is one of the city's newest
restaurants; the name
signifies Gastronomic
Intelligence and represents
a new, comprehensive,
total concept of a dining
experience. **$$$**
Indian Curry House
Scheelegatan 6
Tel: 08 650 20 24
Small, basic restaurant
with good Indian food at
reasonable prices. **$**
Järnet Matsal and Bar
Österlänggatan 34–36
Tel: 08 10 71 37
www.jarnet.nu
With a delightful corner
location and outside tables
in summer, this
combination of bar and
restaurant has much charm
and good, reasonably
priced dishes. **$$**
Mathias Dahlgren
Grand Hotel, Södra
Blasieholmshamnen 6
Tel: 08 679 35 84
www.mathiasdahlgren.com
The Michelin-star-winning
chef uses the best Swedish
ingredients to create
elegant, unusual, melt-in-
the-mouth dishes. Superb.
$$$
Operakällaren
Operan (Royal Opera House)

Tel: 08 676 58 00
www.operakallaren.se
Arguably Stockholm's
best-known restaurant and
is worth visiting for the
fantastic decor alone. **$$$**
Pontus by the Sea
Tullhus 2,
Skeppsbron
Tel: 08 20 20 95
www.pontusfrithiof.com
Found in the old Gamla
Stan Bryggeri, and on
the quayside of Skepps-
bron, this has a more
lighthearted Mediter-
ranean flavour and
ambiance than its more
established sister
restaurant. **$$**
Restaurant Pontus
Brunnsgatan 1
Tel: 08 545 273 00
www.pontusfrithiof.com
One of Stockholm's
great restaurants, with
superbly presented
cuisine served in a an
ambiance resembling what
you might expect in your
own dining room. **$$$**
Sturehof
Stureplan 2
Tel: 08 440 57 30
Stylish Swedish food.
Has a popular bar and
live music. **$$**

Cafés

Café Blå Porten
Djurgårdsvägen 64
Tel: 08-663 87 59
Unpretentious café with
good cakes and a light
food menu.
Café String
Nytorgsgatan 38
Tel: 08-714 85 14
Café with hip 1950s

and '60s decor that is
all for sale.
Chokladkoppen
Stortorget 20
Tel: 08 20 31 70
A small and cosy café,
with outdoor seating in
one of the best people-
watching spots in
Stockholm.
Fåfängan
Klockestapelsbacken 3
Tel: 08-642 99 00
A visit here is essential in
the summer if you can
manage the long, steep
walk up – the view over
Stockholm is fantastic.
Konditori Sturekatten
Riddargatan 4
Tel: 08-611 16 12
Classic, cosy café, worth a

visit for the old-fashioned
decor alone. Home-baked
bread and pastries are on
offer.
Rosendals Trädgård
Rosendalsterrassen 12
Tel: 08-545 812 70
This café within the
garden by Rosendal
Palace, on Djurgården,
attracts hordes of visitors
in fine weather.
Taxinge Slottscafé
Nykvarn
Tel: 0159-701 14
Located a 45-minute
drive south of Stockholm
approximately, this
beautiful castle's café
features a buffet of
40–50 different cakes
and buns.

BELOW: delicious dishes at Mathias Dahlgren.

AROUND STOCKHOLM

Grythyttan

Grythyttans Gästgivaregård
Prästgatan 2
Tel: 0591 633 00
www.grythyttan.com
Well-known romantic inn
serving excellent modern
Swedish food. **$$–$$$**

Södertälje

Oaxen Skärgårdskrog
Oaxen (30km/19 miles

from Södertälje)
Tel: 08 551 531 05
www.oaxenkrog.se
Beautiful location in the
Stockholm archipelago.
Excellent Swedish cooking.
$–$$

Mariefred

**Gripsholms Värdhus &
Hotel**
Kyrkoplan 1
Tel: 0159 347 50

www.gripsholms-vardshus.se
Sweden's oldest inn
has a first class restaurant
that specialises in local
produce, international
cooking as well as fine
wines. **$$–$$$**

Norrköping

Restaurang Knäppingen
Våstgötegatan 19
Tel: 011 10 74 45
www.knappingen.gastrogate.com

Fabulous modern Swedish
food in a medieval vaulted
cellar. Homemade bread
and soups. **$$–$$$**

PRICE CATEGORIES

Price categories are based
on an average three-course
meal (excluding drinks but
with tax) per head:
$ = under 200Skr
$$ = 200–400Skr
$$$ = over 400Skr

SOUTHERN SWEDEN AND SMÅLAND

Malmö

Brogatan
Brogatan 12
Tel: 040 30 77 17
Popular among the famous.
Organic Swedish food and
live music. **$–$$**
Restaurang Johan P
Lilla Torg, Landbygatan 3
Tel: 040 97 18 18
www.johanp.nu
Excellent and beautifully
presented fish dishes. **$$**
Restaurang Möllan
Bergsgatan 37C

Tel: 040 12 10 15
A good choice for filling,
good-value traditional
Swedish home cooking. **$$**
Skeppsbron 2
Börshuset
Tel: 040 36 62 02
www.skeppsbron2.com
Modern and inventive
cuisine in a building
overlooking the sea. **$$**
● There is an area worth
visiting in Malmö called Lilla
Torg (Little Square), where
the market hall is located
and new restaurants are

opening all the time offering
various cuisines.

Helsingborg

Pålsjö Krog
Drottninggatan 151
Tel: 042-149 730
www.palsjokrog.com
For beautifully presented
Swedish fish and meat
mains. **$$**

Kalmar

Calmar Hamnkrog

Skeppsbrogatan 30
Tel: 0480 41 10 20
www.calmarhamnkrog.se
Gourmet restaurant with a
sea view. Classic and
international food. **$$**

Simrishamn

Karlaby Kro
In the village of Tommarp,
7km/4 miles from Simrishamm
Tel: 0414 20 300
www.karlabykro.se
Cosy restaurant serving
fresh local produce. **$$–$$$**

GOTLAND

Visby

Bakfickan
Stora Torget 1
Tel: 0498 27 18 07
www.bakfickan-visby.nu
Gotland's only seafood
restaurant. Warm, cosy

atmosphere serving
excellent dishes. **$–$$**
Clematis
Strandgatan 20
Tel: 0498 21 0288
www.clematis.se
Medieval dishes served in a
13th-century house,

accompanied by jesters,
musicians and fire-eaters. **$$**
Donners Brunn
Donners Plats
Tel: 0498 27 10 90
www.donnersbrunn.nu
Friendly gourmet restaurant
with the "Best Lamb Chef"

in Sweden. **$$**
Isola Bella
Södra Kyrkogatan 20
Tel: 0498 21 87 87
www.isolabella.se
An airy Italian restaurant
with a long pizza menu.
Friendly service. **$$**

THE WEST COAST

Göteborg

Bliss Resto
Magasinsgatan 3
Tel: 031 13 85 55
www.blissresto.com
Swedish and Oriental
dishes. **$$**
Fiskekrogen
Lilla Torget 1
Tel: 031 10 10 05
www.fiskekrogen.com
Best fish restaurant in
town; exciting wines at
good prices. **$$$**
Heaven 23
Hotel Gothia Towers, Mässansgata

Tel: 031-75 08 805
www.heaven23.se
Excellent food, with city
views to match. The King
Size shrimp sandwich is
their best-seller. **$$–$$$**
Hemma Hos
Haga Nygata 12
Tel: 031 13 40 90
Cosy local restaurant
serving great fish dishes
and tasty desserts. **$$**
Junggrens Café
Kungsportsavenyn 37
Tel: 031 16 17 51
A classic café that is
popular with young people.

Trädgår'n
Nya Allén
Tel: 031 10 20 80
www.tradgarn.se
Exotic award-winning
international restaurant.
Also has live music
performances. **$$$**

Halmstad

Pio & Company
Storgatan 37
Tel: 035 21 06 69
www.pio.se
Traditional Swedish food,
planked steak a classic. **$$**

Hamburgsund

Skäret
Strandvägen 10
Tel: 0525 345 80
Charcoal-grilled fish. **$$**

Tanumshede

Tanums Gestgifveri
Apoteksv 7, 30km (19 miles) from
Strömstad
Tel: 0525 290 10
www.tanumsgestgifveri.com
Traditional Swedish food.
Fish and oysters feature
high on the menu. **$$**

THE GREAT LAKES

Jönköping

Mäster Gudmunds Källare
Kapellgatan 2
Tel: 036-10 06 40
www.mastergudmund.se
Atmospheric medieval
cellar-restaurant, with a
Swedish/International
menu focusing on simple
home cooking. **$$**

Karlstad

Café Artist
Norra Strandgatan 9–11
Tel: 054 77 64 700
Swedish and French cuisine
located in the Scandic Winn
hotel. **$$–$$$**
Legends Bar and Grill
Drottninggatan 4
Tel: 054 770 5500

A trendy meeting place
located in the Scandic
Karlstad City Hotel, serving
steaks and cocktails.
$$–$$$
Tiffanys
Västra Torggatan 19
Tel: 054 15 33 83
Stylish restaurant
specialising in local fish
and game. **$$–$$$**

PRICE CATEGORIES

Price categories are based
on an average three-course
meal (excluding drinks but
with tax) per head:
$ = under 200Skr
$$ = 200–400Skr
$$$ = over 400Skr

GÖTA KANAL

Dalarna

Värdshuset Dala Floda
Badvägen 6, Dala Floda
(40km/25 miles from Borlänge)
Tel: 0241 220 50
Excellent well-known inn/
restaurant. International
menu. $-$$

Falun

Dössbergets Värdshus
Bjursås (20km/12 miles from
Falun)

Tel: 023 507 37
www.dossbergets.se
Beautifully located
restaurant with fabulous
views. Traditional Swedish
and gourmet food. $$

Leksand

Åkerblads Hotell &
Gästgiveri
Sjögattu 2, Tällberg (13 km/8 miles
from Leksand)
Tel: 0247 508 00
www.akerblads.se

Traditional Swedish fare.
Buffet lunch and
smörgåsbord at weekend.
Children's menu. $$

Söderköping

Romantik Hotel
Söderköpings Brunn
Skönbergsgatan 35
Tel: 0121 109 00
www.soderkopingsbrunn.se
Fine Swedish and
international cooking; some
vegetarian dishes. $$

Vadstena

Starby Kungsgård
Ödeshögsvägen
Tel: 0143 751 00
www.starbykungsgard.se
Excellent. Traditional
Swedish and gourmet
international cuisine. $$
Vadstena Valven
Storgatan 18
Tel: 0143 123 40
www.valven.se
Excellent food, using local
produce. $$

THE CENTRAL HEARTLANDS

Åre

Villa Tottebo
Parkvägen 1
Tel: 0647 506 20
www.villatottebo.se
Pleasant restaurant serving
mostly local products. $$

Östersund

Brunkullans Krog
Postgränd 5
Tel: 063 10 14 54
A beguiling little bar-

restaurant with some good
traditional dishes. $$
Innefickan Restaurant and
Bar
Postgränd 11
Tel: 063 12 90 99
Former warehouse, now
turned into a successful
bar and restaurant serving
Italian food. $$-$$$
Mikado
Grytan, Brunflo (10km/6 miles from
Östersund)
Tel: 063 209 08
www.mikadosweden.com

Beautifully presented
Japanese food created by
chef Tsukasa Takeuchi.
$$-$$$

Sundsvall

7 Kryddor
Trädgårdsgatan 25
Tel: 060-61 50 80
www.7kryddor.com
For a touch of spice, head
to this Turkish restaurant.
The barbecued meat dishes
are recommended. $$

Restaurang Grankotten
Norra Stadsberget
Tel: 060 61 42 22
www.grankotten.com
A fine place for summer
dining, with great views
over Sundsvall and outdoor
tables. $$
Saffran
Nybrogatan 25
Tel: 060 17 11 07
Small cosy Spanish
restaurant with tapas bar.
Very reasonable with a
varied menu. $-$$

LAPLAND

Jukkasjärvi

Jukkasjärvi Wärdshus
Marknadsvägen 63
Tel: 0980 668 00
www.icehotel.com
Excellent restaurant based
at the famous Ice Hotel,
specialising in local products

such as reindeer, grouse,
char and cloudberries. $$

Kiruna

Restaurang Rallaren
Bangårdsvägen 4
Tel: 0980 611 26
www.hotelrallaren.se

Tärnaby

Sånninggården Restaurang
& Pensionat

For traditional Sami bread
(*gahkku*), and game dishes
complimented by traditional
Lapp ingredients. $-$$

Klippen, Hemavan (25km/
15 miles from Tärnaby)
Tel: 0954 330 00
www.sanninggarden.com
Beautifully located
restaurant; specialising in
local game and poultry. Try
the cheese crepes with
Arctic char roe. $-$$

THE NORTHEAST COAST

Luleå

Cafe Tallkotten
Luleå Stadshotel, Storgatan 15
Tel: 0920 27 40 20
Busy hotel restaurant with
an international menu. $$
Margaretas Värdshus
Lulevägen 2, Gammelstad
(10km/6 miles from Luleå)
Tel: 0920 25 42 90
www.margaretasvardshus.se
Picturesque inn, close to

the church, with a
restaurant, serving local
specialities. $-$$

Umeå

Restaurant Sävargården
Gammlia
Tel: 090-77 02 22
www.savargarden.nu
Patronised by royalty,
Sävargården is one of the
region's finest haute-

cuisine restaurants. $$$
Rex Bar & Grill
Rådhustorget
Tel: 090 12 60 50
Trendy, stylish bar and
restaurant that mixes local
produce with inspiration
from the Med. Located
inside the town hall. $-$$
Sjöbris
Kajen 10
Tel: 090 77 71 23
Enjoy the *sjöbris* (sea

breeze) on board this
fishing-boat restaurant,
and some delicious
seafood. $-$$
Great Eastern
Magasinsgatan 17
www.greateastern.se
Tel: 090 13 88 38
The dishes are cooked
on the open grill in a
variety of styles such as
Cantonese, Mongolian,
Thai and Indian. $

DENMARK

NORWAY

SWEDEN

FINLAND

A – Z

A HANDY SUMMARY OF PRACTICAL INFORMATION, ARRANGED ALPHABETICALLY

A Activities 416
B Before You Go 417
Business Hours 417
C Children 417
Climate 417
Culture 417
D Disabled Travellers 418

E Embassies and Consulates 419
G Gay and Lesbian Travellers 419
H Health 419
L Language 419
M Media 420
Money 420
N Nightlife 421

S Shopping 421
T Telecommunications 422
Tourist Information 422
Tourist Offices 422
Transport 422
W What to Bring 424
What to Read 424

A ctivities

Participant Sports

Finland is known as a sporting nation, and has won more Olympic medals per head than any other country. Devotion to training is constant; it is not unusual on a hot summer's day to see squadrons of muscular youths out on roller-skis to make sure they do not lose their touch for the coming winter.

Cycling
Bicycling is big in Finland. The countryside is ideal for cyclists, dead flat on the west coast leading to gently rolling hill areas. Contact **Mountain Bike Club Finland**, Paavo Nurmen Kuja 1, 00250 Helsinki; tel: 09-454 6466. 13 excellent cycling maps cover the country, see www.karttakeskus.fi.

Sailing
Boating exists in all forms, and most harbours have guest marinas where one can dock for reasonable overnight fees. Canoeing is also popular in the Lakelands region.

Other Sports
For information on any sport in Finland, please contact **Suomen Urheilu ja Liikunta (Finnish Sports Federation)**, Radiokatu 20, 00240 Helsinki (Ilmala); tel: 09-348 121; fax: 09-348 12602; www.slu.fi.

Spectator Sports

There is a near endless list of spectator sports in Finland, but a shortlist of the most popular must include ski-jumping, regatta sailing and ice-hockey.

Summer
One of the biggest sailing events of the year is the Hanko Regatta, which takes place in early July off Finland's south coast. Kotka also sponsors a yearly Tall Ships event.
The biggest inland sailing regatta is on Lake Päijänne, also in July. Details are available from the **Finnish Sailing Federation**, Westendinkatu 7, 02160 Espoo; tel: 0207 96 4200; www.yachting.fi.
Before mid-June is the **Finlandia Canoeing Relay**, held in the large Lakeland region – the venue changes annually. It lasts six days and covers over 545 km (350 miles), with day and night action. See www.suomimeloo.fi for details.

Winter
Lahti, about 105 km (65 miles) north of Helsinki, is the best place to watch ski-jumping.

For winter spectator sports, the **Finlandia Ski Race** in mid-February is one of the top events. This 60-km (37-mile) event attracts the best Finnish skiers and has ample spectator opportunities.
For information, contact:
Finlandia Ski Race Office
Urheilukeskus, 15110 Lahti
Tel: 03-816 813
Fax: 03-751 2079
www.finlandiahiihto.fi
As is the case with participant sports, all general sport queries can

BELOW: welcome to Moomin World.

Business Hours

Shops In larger cities generally 9am–5pm, with late-night opening on Thursday. In Helsinki, many open until 9pm on weekdays and 6pm on Saturday. Larger food stores usually open 9am–8pm weekdays and 9am–4pm on Saturday. The only really late shops are in the tunnel under the Helsinki railway station: open weekdays 10am–10pm and weekends noon–10pm.
Banks Mon–Fri 9.15am–4.15pm, *bureaux de change* open a bit later. The one at the airport opens daily 6am–10pm.

be directed to the Suomen Urheilu ja Liikunta (Finnish Sports Federation).

Skiing in Finland

Finns are particularly famous as cross-country runners and skiers, as well as ski-jumpers. You'll find facilities for any of these sports excellent; in most major urban areas there are maps of the non-auto paths set aside for such pastimes. Ask for the *Ulkoilukartta* (outdoor map) from tourist boards.

One can ski cross-country anywhere in Finland, but Lapland is a favourite spot for this very Nordic sport, as well as for downhill skiing (try to avoid school holiday weeks). Unlike Norway and even Sweden, Finland has very little in the way of mountains, except in the far north, where the Lappish hills, the highest over 1,400 metres (4,000 ft), are called *tunturi*.

There are many participant cross-country ski events as well; information is available from **Suomen Latu (Finnish Ski Trek Association)**, Fabianinkatu 7, 00130 Helsinki; tel: 09-4159 1100; fax: 09-663 376.

B efore You Go

● **UK**
Finnish Tourist Board
PO Box 33213, London W6 8JX
Tel: 020 8600 5680 (UK) or
01 407 3362 (Ireland)
Fax: 020 8600 5681
www.visitfinland.com/uk
● **US/Canada**
Finnish Tourist Board
PO Box 4649, Grand Central Station, New York NY 10163-4649
Tel: 212 885 9700 or
800-FIN-INFO (North America)
www.visitfinland.com/us
● **Australia**
The Embassy supplies tourist information.

12 Darwin Avenue, Yarralumla, ACT 2600
Tel: 02 6273 3800
Fax: 02 6273 3603
www.finland.org.au
● **Websites**
Finland: http://virtual.finland.fi
www.visitfinland.com
Helsinki: www.hel.fi/english

C hildren

In Helsinki, the Tourist Board can provide a list of babysitters.

Attractions

Heureka, the Finnish Science Centre (in Tikkurila 15 minutes by train from downtown Helsinki), has exhibitions, a planetarium/cinema and hands-on experiments, and opens daily year round. Tel: 09 85799; www.heureka.fi
Moomin World, theme park based on the popular Moomin characters created by Tove Jansson. Situated 16km from Turku; open daily year round. Tel: 02 511 1111; www.muumimaailma.fi.

There are several good spots in the Lakeland region:
The Snow Centre, Messilä, in Hollola near Lahti, features many supervised activities, including pony riding and (in winter) skiing. Tel: 03 860 11; www.messila.fi.
The Musta and Valkea Ratsu Dollshouse and Puppet Theatre is north from Hollola, towards Hartola, on Road 52 (signposted), 19230 Onkiniemi. Tel: 03 718 6959.
Santa Claus's Village, Rovaniemi, near the Arctic Circle. Rumour has it Santa stops off here when travelling from his secret hideaway. Open daily year round. Tel: 016 356 2096; www.santaclausvillage.info.
Åland Islands Check out the amusement park by the west harbour, Pommern ship museum at the west harbour, and Lilla Holmen bird park on the east harbour.

Climate

Finland has cold winters and fairly warm summers. In July, the south has similar temperatures to southern England, with less rain and more sunshine. The hottest months are July–Aug, when temperatures average 18°C (65°F); the coldest are Jan–Feb, averaging -4°C (25°F). In south and central Finland snow settles at the start of Dec and melts mid–late Apr (or May in the forests). In the north snow comes about five weeks earlier and ends about three weeks later.

Culture

Museums

Finland is a country of small museums. The grandest in scale is the Ateneum in Helsinki, which could fit neatly into London's National Gallery at least three times. Art dominates the museum scene, with the greatest variety of venues in Helsinki. In total, there is probably more contemporary art to be seen than older art.

Museum opening hours are almost always reduced in winter. Most museums close on Monday. Be prepared that many museums also close for public holidays.

Classical Music and Opera

Most larger cities have a steady itinerary of concerts throughout the year, but music festivals abound in Finland in summer, and many of these are held in stunning settings. The most famous of these are held in July: the Savonlinna Opera Festival at Olavinlinna Castle in eastern Finland, the Kuhmo Chamber Music Festival, also in eastern Finland and the Kaustinen Folk Festival in western Finland. The festivals feature Finnish and international performers.

Finnish opera has a great following, and much of it features Finnish composers and performers.

Helsinki Events

In late summer are the Helsinki *Juhlaviikot* (festival weeks) featuring broad-ranging programmes with artists from Finland and abroad, set at different venues around the city. Information from:
Helsinki Festival Office
Lasipalatsi, Mannerheimintie 22–24, FI-00100 Helsinki
Tel: 09-6126 5100

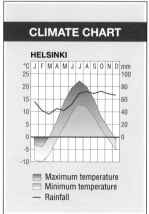

CLIMATE CHART

HELSINKI

Maximum temperature
Minimum temperature
— Rainfall

Also, try the weekday evening series of concerts at the unique Temppeliaukio (Church in the Rock) in Töölö, Helsinki.

During the rest of the year, main events are at Finlandia Concert Hall, many by the Radio Symphony Orchestra and the Helsinki Philharmonic Orchestra. The National Opera House (and ballet) in Helsinki opened in 1993.

Turku Events
Turku is a lively musical city, with concerts given by the Turku City Orchestra, a series of concerts in the Sibelius Museum, and others in the cathedral and the castle. The Turku Musical Festival is one of the oldest in Finland and ranges from medieval music to first performances. Held in mid-August, it attracts international composers and musicians.

Further information is available from the **Foundation for the Turku Music Festivals**, Aninkaistenkatu 9, 20100 Turku; tel: 02-262 0814; www.tmj.fi.

Tampere Events
Tampere has always had its share of music. Since 1975 the city has held an international choir festival each year and the Tampere Biennale, started in 1986, is a festival of new Finnish music, arranged in co-operation with the Association of Finnish Composers. For information contact:
Tampere
Tullikamarinaukio 2
33100 Tampere
Tel: 03-5656 6172
Since the opening of the Tampere Hall, interest has soared. The auditorium is one of the great concert halls of the world and the

acoustics are acknowledged to be far better than those of Helsinki's Finlandia Hall. The small auditorium is used for chamber music, and the Hall is also a conference venue. Tampere holds numerous concerts in its cathedral, churches and halls.

Jazz and Rock
The most famous of Finland's jazz festivals is PoriJazz. Big open-air concerts are held in the concert park by the Kokemäki river and evening venues vary between intimate clubs and large concert halls. For more information contact the **Pori Jazz Office**, Pohjoisranta 11 D, 28100 Pori; tel: 02-6262 200; www.porijazz.fi.

In Tampere there is an annual jazz festival called Jazz Happening. For information on dates and concerts, contact **Tampere Jazz Happening**, Tullikamarinaukio 2, 33100 Tampere; tel: 5656 6172.

There is also Ruisrock on the island of Ruissalo in Turku, Finland's oldest and highly popular rock festival (see page 325).

Theatre
Helsinki
The Finnish National Theatre and Svenska Teatern in Helsinki both enjoy long traditions of performance in, respectively, Finnish and Swedish. Unfortunately, there is no foreign-language theatre to speak of, but you may be interested in touring the theatre buildings themselves, or even going to a play you know well enough to overcome the language barrier.

Turku
Plays performed are of a high standard but rarely in languages other than Finnish or Swedish. In

winter, there is the Turku City Theatre on the bank of the River Aura and Swedish Theatre on the corner of the Marketplace – the oldest theatre in Finland still in use.

Tampere
Tampere rivals Helsinki for year-round theatrical events but, again, the difficulty is language. One exception is the Pyynikki Outdoor Summer Theatre where you can see plays from mid-June to mid-August, with synopses in English. This is particularly worthwhile if you want to enjoy the setting at the edge of the Lake Pyhäjärvi. Booking is necessary; tel: 03-216 0300; www.pyynikinkesateatteri.com.

The Tampere Theatre Festival in August includes many international companies who produce plays in their own languages.

Further information is available from **Tampere International Theatre Festival**, Tullikamarinaukio 2, 33100, Tampere; tel: 03-222 8536; www.teatterikesa.fi.

Cinema
Finns do not dub foreign films, and you can enjoy as good a selection of movies here as in any other European city of moderate size. The **Kansallinen Audiovisuaalinenarkisto** at the Orion Film Archive (Pursimiehenkatu 29–31A; tel: 09-615 40 201; www.sea.fi) has endless stocks of older films, both Finnish and foreign. Helsinki has two big cinema complexes, **Kinopalatsi** in Kaisaniemenkatu 2 and **Tennispalatsi** at Salomonkatu 15. Smaller cinemas are dotted around the town, often showing a wider range of titles.

Film showings are usually at 6pm and 8.30pm. The kiosk outside the east entrance to Helsinki railway station has comprehensive listings, as do the newspapers; listings are also available at the Tourist Board. Seats are reserved at the time you buy the tickets, and box offices usually open 30–45 minutes before show time but at some cinemas may be purchased even earlier.

Tampere has a cinema centre, **Finnkino Plevna**, in the Finlayson area (Itäinen katu 4). In Turku most cinemas are found in the Hansa Shopping Centre (see page 207).

D isabled Travellers

For disabled people, travelling should not pose tremendous problems in Finland. Most newer buildings have access for disabled people, in terms of ramps and lifts.

BELOW: the Pori Jazz Festival at Tampere.

Check the Finland Hotel guide which indicates by symbols which hotels have access and facilities for disabled people. With careful planning, transport should also go smoothly; when ordering a taxi, specify your needs (wheelchair is "*pyörätuoli*"). Helsinki metro is accessible for wheelchair users but other forms of public transport may be a bit more problematic, although some city buses "kneel", making it easier to board. If you have queries related to disabled travel in Finland, contact:
Rullaten ry
Kauppamiehentie 6, 02100 Espoo
Tel. 09-805 7393
www.rullaten.fi

E mbassies and Consulates

UK
Itäinen Puistotie 17, Helsinki
Tel: 09 228 65100
US
Itäinen Puistotie 14B, Helsinki
Tel: 09 161 250
Canada
Pohjoisesplanadi 25B, Helsinki
Tel: 09 228 530
South Africa
Rahapajankatu 1 A 5, Helsinki
Tel: 09 6860 3100

G ay and Lesbian

Finns have a tolerant attitude to gay and lesbian travellers. Helsinki's scene is less lively than other Scandinavian capitals – for listings, pick up the *Gay Guide* from the main tourist office. For general information, contact **SETA**, Mannerheimintie 170, 00300 Helsinki; tel: 09-681 2580; www.seta.fi.

H ealth

You'll have little to worry about healthwise in Finland. However, you may have an uncomfortable time with the mosquitoes in northern and central parts in July and August. Ask your GP about appropriate mosquito treatment before you go and enquire at chemists in Finland about the most effective repellent.

Finland's medical facilities have an excellent reputation worldwide. The country has reciprocal health arrangements with other EU members, so visitors are entitled to the same treatment as Finns. British nationals should take a European Health Insurance Card (EHIC), which you can apply for online (www.ehic.org.uk), by phone (0845 606 2030), or by post (form available from any post office in the UK).

ABOVE: there is usually a pharmacy open late in larger towns.

Hospitals

If you need medical treatment, almost any *Terveysasema* (health clinic) or *Sairaala* (hospital) will treat you for a nominal fee or will bill your insurance firm. All doctors speak English. Casualty is generally called *Ensiapu*. Visitors needing hospital care in Helsinki should contact the following:
For surgery and medicine:
Meilahti Hospital, Haartmaninkatu 4, Helsinki. Tel: 09 4711, or the 24-medical advice hotline *(see Emergency Numbers, page 422).*
For serious accidents:
Helsinki University Hospitals' Töölö Hospital, Topeliuksenkatu 5, Helsinki. Tel: 09 4711.
For 24-hour private medical care:
Mehiläinen, 3rd floor, Runebergin-katu 47a, Helsinki. Tel: 010 414 0444.

Pharmacies

A pharmacy is called *apteekki.* There is at least one open late at night in larger towns. In Helsinki, the Yliopiston Apteekki at Mannerheimintie 96 is open 24 hours a day.

Dentists

Emergencies in working hours: Dentarium, 6th Floor, 7A Mikonkatu, Helsinki. Tel: 09 622 1533. Out-of-hours emergencies: Oral, 2nd Floor, 5A Erottajankatu, Helsinki. Tel: 010 400 3000

L anguage

Getting By

Good morning *Hyvää huomenta*
Good day *Hyvää päivää*
Good evening *Hyvää iltaa*
Today *Tänään*
Tomorrow *Huomenna*
Yesterday *Eilen*
Hello *Terve or hei*
How do you do? *Kuinka voit*
Goodbye *Näkemiin or hei hei*
Yes *Kyllä or joo*
No *Ei*
Thank you *Kiitos*

How much does this cost? *Paljonko tämä maksaa?*
It costs... *Se maksaa...*
How do I get to..? *Miten pääsen..?*
Where is...? *Missä on...?*
Right *Oikealla*
To the right *Oikealle*
Left *Vasemmalla*
To the left *Vasemmalle*
Straight on *Suoraan*
What time is it? *Paljonko kello on?*
It is (the time is) *Kello on*
Could I have your name? *Saisinko nimesi?*
My name is... *Nimeni on...*
Do you speak English? *Puhutko englantia?*
I only speak English *Puhun vain englantia*
Can I help you? *Voinko auttaa sinua?*
I do not understand *En ymmärrä*
I do not know *En tiedä*

Eating Out

Breakfast *Aamiainen*
Lunch *Lounas*
Dinner *Illallinen*
To eat *Syödä*
To drink *Juoda*
I would like to order... *Haluaisin tilata*
Could I have the bill? *Saisko laskun?*
Could I have the key? *Saisko avaimen?*
Toilet *Vessa*
Gentlemen *Miehet (Swedish: Herrar)*
Ladies *Naiset (Swedish: Damer)*
Vacant *Vapaa*
Engaged *Varattu*
Entrance *Sisäänkäynti*
Exit *Uloskäynti*
No entry *Pääsy kielletty*
Open *Avoinna, Auki*
Closed *Suljettu, Kiinni*
Push *Työnnä*
Pull *Vedä*

Shopping

Clothes *Vaatteet*
Overcoat *Päällystakki*
Jacket *Takki*
Suit *Puku*

Shoes *Kengät*
Skirt *Hame*
Blouse *Pusero*
Jersey *Neulepusero or villapusero*
Grocers *Ruokakauppa*
Shop *Kauppa*
Food *Ruoka*
To buy *Ostaa*
Off licence *Alko*
Money *Raha*

Days of the Week

Monday *Maanantai*
Tuesday *Tiistai*
Wednesday *Keskiviikko*
Thursday *Torstai*
Friday *Perjantai*
Saturday *Launantai*
Sunday *Sunnuntai*

Numbers

1 *yksi*
2 *kaksi*
3 *kolme*
4 *neljä*
5 *viisi*
6 *kuusi*
7 *seitsemän*
8 *kahdeksan*
9 *yhdeksän*
10 *kymmenen*
11 *yksitoista*
12 *kaksitoista*
13 *kolmetoista*
14 *neljätoista*
15 *viisitoista*
16 *kuusitoista*
17 *seitsemäntoista*
18 *kahdeksantoista*
19 *yhdeksäntoista*
20 *kaksikymmentä*
30 *kolmekymmentä*
40 *neljäkymmentä*
50 *viisikymmentä*
60 *kuusikymmentä*
70 *seitsemänkymmentä*
80 *kahdeksankymmentä*
90 *yhdeksänkymmentä*
100 *sata*
200 *kaksisataa*
1,000 *tuhat*

Useful Words

Chemist *Apteekki*
Hospital *Sairaala*
Doctor *Lääkäri*
Police station *Poliisilaitos*
Parking *Paikoitus*
Phrase book *Turistien sanakirja*
Dictionary *Sanakirja*
Car *Auto*
Bus, Coach *Bussi, Linja-auto*
Train *Juna*
Aircraft *Lentokone*
Cheers *Kippis (Swedish: skål)*
To rent *Vuokrata*
For sale *Myytävänä*
Free, no charge *Ilmainen*
Room to rent *Vuokrattavana
huone*

Media

Newspapers and Books

With the exception of the *International Herald Tribune*, which arrives on the afternoon of its publication date, you'll have to wait a day and a half for English-language newspapers to get to Helsinki. Foreign papers are sold at **Helsinki railway station** and **Akateeminen Kirjakauppa** (Academic Bookstore) at Keskuskatu 1 (tel: 09 121 41; www.akateeminen.com), where you can also get books in English, and at the **larger hotels** in other cities, as well as at **main airports**.

The *Helsinki Times* is an English-language newspaper published on Fridays, giving news about Finland. It is also available at newsstands, stations, hotels and airports.

Tourist publications

Helsinki This Week, free from the tourist office at Vantaa Airport and most hotels, is an English-language guide to cultural and tourist events in the capital, also online www.helsinkiexpert.fi.

City, a weekly newspaper, has separate Finnish editions for the major Finnish cities and a quarterly English edition with a calendar of events and restaurant listings. It is available free in shopping centres, bars and hotels.

SixDegrees is a free monthly magazine in English with events, trends and current affairs, also online www.6d.fi.

Radio and Television

For news in English, you can tune in to the Finnish national broadcasters' YLE Capital FM (97.5 FM) in most of Southern Finland. This broadcasts hours of programmes in Spanish,

BELOW: the Hartwall Arena in Helsinki.

French and Russian, but mainly English, using American, Canadian, Australian and South African stations as well as the BBC and Ireland's RTE. The news in English is broadcast daily on YLE Radio 1 (87.9 FM in the Helsinki region) daily at 3.55pm. For up-to-date schedules, contact YLE on 09-14801. YLE 1 also broadcasts news in English on weekdays at 7.30am, and the BBC's World Service and other English-language channels are usually available in hotels.

Money

Finland's unit of currency is the euro (€). Notes are available in 500, 200, 100, 50, 20, 10 and 5 euros and coins in 2 and 1 euros, 50, 20, 10, 5, 2, and 1 cents. Shops do not have to accept 2 and 1 cent coins.

How to pay

Credit cards MasterCard, Visa, Diner's Club and American Express are accepted in most establishments in main cities.
Travellers' cheques and common currencies can easily be exchanged in banks.
ATMs Automatic Teller Machines marked OTTO give local currency if you have a card with an international PIN number (Visa, Cirrus, PLUS, MasterCard and so on).

Nightlife

Pubs, Bars and Clubs

Pub crawling remains popular and there are several clubs that attract the best pop bands. Increasing numbers of international stars make a stop at the **Hartwall Arena** (www.hartwall-arena.com) in Helsinki on their world tours.

The minimum age for drinking

alcohol is 18 but some clubs have an age limit of 21. Entrance fees vary.

Nightclubs and discos have become more popular in recent years. The popular **Helsinki Club** and **Tenth Floor** dance bar at the Hotel Vaakuna in Helsinki are good examples. For good nightlife try:

Helsinki
Highlight
Frederikinkatu 42; tel: 010 766 3780; www.ravintolahighlight.com
A nightclub for young people built in an old church.
Corona Bar
Eerikinkatu 11; tel: 09 7517 5611; www.corona.fi
Attracts a young hip crowd who come to talk, drink beer, eat toasted sandwiches and play pool.
Lost and Found
Annankatu 6; tel: 09 680 1010; www.lostandfound.fi
Several Finnish rock stars use the café upstairs as their living room. Downstairs has a popular gay club
Storyville
Museokatu 8; tel: 09 408 007; www.storyville.fi
A cosy jazz club to have a late drink. There is a cover charge.
Studio 51
Fredrikinkatu 51–53; tel: 020 775 9330; www.studio51.fi
A popular retro club modeled after the studio 54 in New York. Age limit 24.
Tavastia
Urho Kekkosenkatu 4; Tel: 09 7746 74 20; www.tavastia.fi
This University-owned club attracts some of Helsinki's best live music.
Torni
Yrjönkatu 26; Tel: 09 4336 6340; www.ravintolaopas.net/ateljeebar
The expensive Ateljee bar on the 13th floor is famous for its great views over Helsinki.
Zetor
Mannerheimintie 3–5, Kaivopiha; tel: 010 766 4450; www.ravintolazetor.fi
This "tractor-style" rock 'n' roll bar has to be seen to be believed. Experience the surrealism of the Finnish countryside.

Tampere
Nightlife is very evident on the main street, **Hämeenkatu**. Bar hopping is easy, although more "traditional" pubs are elsewhere, such as **Salhojankadun Pub** on Salhojankatu, and **Ohranjyvä** at Näsilinnankatu 15. Locally brewed beer is available at **Plevna** (Itäinenkatu 8) and **Wanha Posti** (Hämeenkatu 13A).

Turku
Panimoravintola Koulu
Eerikinkatu 18; tel: 02 274 5757;

www.panimoravintolakoulu.fi
This former school has a brewery and the classrooms are now pubs or restaurants.
Old Bank
Aurakatu 3; tel: 02 274 5700; www.oldbank.fi
Once a very fine bank, this pub serves more varieties of beer than any other in town.
Uusi Apteekki
Kaskenkatu 1; tel: 02 250 2595; www.uusiapteekki.fi
Literally "new pharmacy", this pub is set in an old chemist.

P ostal Services
Post offices are open 9am–5pm weekdays. Services include stamps, registered mail and *poste restante*. The *poste restante* address is Elielinaukio, 00100 Helsinki. It's on the railway square side of the main post office (Mannerheiminaukio 1) and is open Mon–Fri 9am–6pm.

R eligious Services
The Lutheran Church is the state church of Finland, with 82 percent of Finns counted as Lutherans. There is a small Greek Orthodox population, and just two Catholic churches in Finland.

In Helsinki, services in English are held at the Temppeliaukio church, the Church in the Rock on Lutherinkatu; there are both Lutheran and ecumenical services here. There is also one synagogue and one mosque in Helsinki, for those of Jewish or Muslim faith.

S hopping
What to Buy
Finnish Design
Choose from jewellery, woodwork, clothing, glass or kitchenware.
Lapponia Aarikka and **Kalevala Koru** jewellery are particularly Finnish, the first being a mainly contemporary

collection and the second a collection based on designs from the Finnish epic poem *Kalevala*, rendered in silver, gold, and brass. Aarikka also supplies some fine woodwork products, including chopping boards, Christmas decorations, toys and wooden jewellery.

The most impressive ceramic work is commissioned by **Arabia**, one of the older Finnish firms. Its factory (about 20 minutes' tram ride from Helsinki centre) has a small museum upstairs, and pristine goods as well as seconds on sale downstairs. **Pentik** is known for its ceramics as well as beautifully crafted leather clothing.

Iittala makes beautiful glassware at its factory. **Marimekko** is the quintessential Finnish clothing designer, with its typical brightly coloured fabrics for men, women and children, as well as more elegant clothing for women and textiles for home use. These companies can be found both in their own stores and department stores in most Finnish towns of any size, including three shops on the Pohjoisesplanadi in Helsinki.

A good place for an overview of contemporary Finnish design is at the **Design Forum** in Helsinki (Erottajankatu 7; tel: 09 622 0810; www.designforum.fi).

Shopping Areas
Helsinki
Apart from mainstream department stores, shopping centres (**Kampii**, **Aleksi 13**, **Forum** and **Kämp Galleria**) and boutique shopping in Helsinki, there are several market squares that sell both fresh food and a range of other consumer goods of greatly varying quality, from second-hand clothes and records to designer jewellery, Sami mittens and fur hats.

Kauppatori is the main market, followed by **Hietalahdentori** and **Hakaniementori**, all near the centre. Markets have extended hours in summer and are open until about 8pm, but close briefly from about 2pm. Otherwise, **the Esplanadi** is the hub of shopping delights in Helsinki.

Turku
Turku has its own **Stockmann** store at Yliopistonkatu 22. Also on Yliopistonkatu are **Pentik** (No. 25), famous for ceramics, and **Aarikka** (No. 27), for handmade wooden crafts and decorations. For crafts, look into **Sylvi Salonen**, specialising in linens and decorative crafts at Yliopistonkatu 26. Markets are generally open daily except Sunday. Turku's **open-air market** features

flowers, fish, fruit, vegetables and some crafts. The **indoor market hall** offers all that and more, including bread, cheese, coffee, tea, spices, snacks and many handicrafts.

Tampere
Tampere has most of the medium-sized department stores found in Helsinki and Turku, as well as a host of smaller boutiques. A good collection is at **Kehräsaari Boutique Centre**, Laukontori 1, Keräsaari, in a converted textile mill. Visit the **Verkaranta Arts and Crafts Centre** at Verkatehtaankatu 2 for a good selection of handicrafts and toys. The main **Tampere Market Hall**, at Hämeenkatu 19, is open Mon–Fri 8am–6pm, Sat 8am–3pm.

Department Stores
The king of department stores in Finland is Stockmann's; it is the place Finns go to when they want to hunt down some elusive item, or some exotic gift. To the outsider it will probably seem merely a large, pleasant place to shop, but it is something of an institution; branches are also in Tampere, Turku and Tapiola (Espoo). Stockmann's also owns the Akateeminen Kirjakauppa, Finland's best-known bookstore. Another good department store to look out for throughout Finland is Sokos, with its fine food hall.

T elecommunications

International dialling code: 358
Finland is a world leader in telecommunications, with a highly sophisticated, deregulated phone system. Public call boxes take either coins or phonecards (on sale at most kiosks and tourist offices). The best way to call overseas cheaply is at certain internet cafes in main cities. Hotels usually add a surcharge for calls made from your room. In Helsinki, there are internet call centres at Vuorikatu 8 (Mon–Fri 10am–9pm, Sat 11am–9pm, Sun noon–9pm) and Hämeentie 23 (Mon, Thur, Sat 11am–6pm, Tue, Wed and Fri until 9pm).
    Callers from outside Finland should dial the international code, then the country code (358) followed by the area code, omitting the initial zero (0).

Mobile phones
Finland is the home of Nokia and has the world's highest ownership of mobile (cell) phones – around 70 percent of Finns own one. There are several operators; two major ones are Radiolinja and Sonera.

Emergency Numbers
● **Ambulance, rescue services, fire department and police** 112
● **Police** 10022
● **24-hour medical advice hotline** (Helsinki only) 10023

Tourist Information

Finland has over 50 main tourist information offices, marked with an "i", as well as many summer tourist offices. The following are the main tourist offices, but a full list can be obtained at most offices:
Finnish Tourist Board
PO Box 625, Töölönkatu 11, 00101 Helsinki; tel: 010 605 8000; e-mail: mek@mek.fi; www.visitfinland.com
Helsinki City Tourist Office
Pohjoisesplanadi 19, 00100 Helsinki; tel: 09 3101 3300; e-mail: tourist.info@hel.fi
Rovaniemi Tourist Information
Sampo Shopping Centre, Maakuntakatu 29–31, 96200 Rovaniemi; tel: 016 346 270; fax: 016 342 4650; e-mail: travel.info@rovaniemi.fi
Tampere City Tourist Office
Railway station, Rautatienkatu 25A, 33100 Tampere; tel: 03 56 56 6800; e-mail: gotampere@gotampere.fi

Tourist Publications
Useful publications in Helsinki include *City*, a weekly newspaper featuring a calendar of cultural events and restaurant listings; *Helsinki This Week* and brochures put out by the Tourist Board.
    The Tourist Board also has a useful internet travel guide (www.visitfinland.com) which allows you to search for accommodation by region and by type among other things.

Transport
Getting There
By Air
Finnair is the national carrier of Finland and operates international and national routes. Both Finnair (www.finnair.com) and British Airways (www.ba.com) connect London and Helsinki with daily flights. Finnair (and many other airlines, including Lufthansa and Scandinavian Airlines) fly direct between Helsinki and most European capitals. Finnair also links with several North American cities including New York. You may be able to find value-for-money package fares and charter flights from New York or London, but they are rare; watch newspaper advertisements for offers.
    From Helsinki, Finnair and Blue 1 (www.blue1.com) fly numerous domestic routes to more than 20 cities,

Tourist Offices

Finnish Tourist Board
www.visitfinland.com
Eteläesplanadi 4, 00130 Helsinki, tel: 09-4176 9300, fax: 09-4176 9301; postal address: PO Box 625, 00101 Helsinki.
Helsinki City Tourist Office
Pohjoisesplanadi 19, PO Box 1, 00099 Helsinki, tel: 09-169 3757, fax: 09-169 3839.
Rovaniemi Tourist Information
Rovakatu 21, 96200 Rovaniemi, tel: 016-346 270, fax: 016-3424 650.
Tampere City Tourist Office
Verkatehtaankatu 2, FIN-33101 Tampere, tel: 020-7166 800, fax: 020-7166 463.
Turku City Tourist Office
Aurakatu 4, 20100 Turku, tel: 02-262 7444, fax: 02-262 7673.

including several to North Finland airports, and have cross-country flights between some of them. Budget airline Ryanair (www.ryanair.com) flies between Tampere and London, Riga, Frankfurt and Dublin.

By Sea
You can travel to Finland by boat from Sweden, Estonia and Germany. **Silja Line** and **Viking Line** have daily routes between Stockholm and Helsinki. These ferries are luxurious with restaurants, saunas, swimming pools, tax-free shops and children's playrooms. There is no direct link from Germany to Finland but Silja Line's refurbished Finnjet boat sails between Rostock–Tallinn–St Petersburg from the end of April to mid-September – a route that you can conveniently join in Tallinn.
    There are plenty of services to choose from for a trip between Helsinki and Tallinn. For a fast trip Silja Line's SuperSeaCat and Linda Line's hydrofoil take the trip in 1½ hours during the ice-free period. These fast boats are dependent on weather conditions, whereas Viking and Eckerö Lines' bigger boats manage also in rough weather.
    It's less expensive to travel by ferry from Stockholm to Turku or Naantali in western Finland and then overland to Helsinki rather than by direct ship to Helsinki. Viking provides very cheap bus tickets for the overland trip; the ferry ticket is also cheaper as the voyage is shorter. One can also travel to Finland's Åland islands by boat from Stockholm or Turku – Viking has a daily service to Mariehamn. Also, RG Line operates a cargo boat between

Vaasa and Umeå.
Eckeröline
Tel: 09-2288 544
Linda Line
Tel: 0600 066 8970
www.lindaliini.ee
RG Line
Tel: 0207 716 810 (Finland) or
090-185 200 (Sweden)
Silja Line
Tel: 02 335 6500 (Finland) or
08 666 3333 (Sweden)
Viking Line
Tel: 09-12351 (Finland) or
08 452 4000 (Sweden)

By Rail
It's a long haul to Finland from just
about anywhere by rail, because you
inevitably finish the long rail trip
north with a 15-hour journey by boat
and train from Stockholm to Helsinki.
From Britain, the handiest route is
Sealink from Harwich to the Hook of
Holland, overland to Copenhagen,
then the connecting train to
Stockholm and boat/boat and train
to Helsinki. Total travel time is about
45 hours. This is cheaper than an
Apex flight only if you get a special
fare rail ticket; residents of Nordic
countries now qualify for Interrail
tickets regardless of age.

Getting Around
On Arrival
Finland's main international airport,
Helsinki-Vantaa, is connected by
Finnair bus and local bus to
Helsinki; fares are usually a little
more on the Finnair bus. There is
also a "shared" taxi stand at the
airport, with a reasonable fare
available to any destination in the
centre of the city.

Public Transport
By Air
Finnair and Blue 1 both operate
domestic flight services. Fares are
relatively inexpensive; in July, fares
are very cheap. It is a good idea to
fly if, for example, you want to get to
Lapland from the south without
spending days on the road.
Discounts are available for groups,
families and senior citizens.

By Rail
The Finnish rail network is limited,
but service is adequate in most
cases and very good between major
points like Turku and Helsinki. Rail
travel to north Finland requires
completion by bus as Finnish rail
lines only run as far as Rovaniemi
and Kemijärvi (in winter to Kolari).
Finnrail passes are available for 3-
day, 5-day, and 10-day periods; first-
class passes are also available.

From June to August, a special
Lomapassi (Holiday Pass) costs
about €139 for adults and entitles
you to 3 travel days in a month. More
information on family tickets, group
tickets and other types of discounts
is available on-line at www.vr.fi/heo/eng
or contact:
VR Ltd, Finnish Railways
VR Passenger Services, Eteläinen
asemakatu 2A, 11130 Riihimäki
Tel: 0600 41902

Water Transport
Ferries and passenger boats in
Finland play a strong role where
international destinations are
concerned but there are some
lakeland ferry routes worth pursuing.
There are the **Silverline and Poet's
Way**, which begin in Tampere and
cover much of the western lakelands,
tours in the **Päijänne** region and over
Finland's largest lake, **Saimaa**, in
eastern Finland. Many other operators
run trips on the lakes; for more information, contact the central or regional
tourist boards (*see page 422*).
   Helsinki's only real commuter
island is Suomenlinna, with ferries
travelling back and forth roughly
every half-hour (schedule depends on
season). Most of these ferries are
part of the public transport network
of Helsinki. Other Helsinki islands
closer to the coast are connected by
road.
Silverline and Poet's Way
Tel: 010 422 5600
Lake Päijänne Cruises
Tel: 010 421 7800
Roll Risteilyt
Tel: 017-266 2466

Bus and Coach
Finland is greatly dependent on
buses for transporting the bulk of its
passenger traffic. There are coach
services on 90 percent of Finland's
public roads (40,000 long-distance
departures a day) which also cover
the areas that trains don't,
particularly in the north and in
smaller places throughout the
country. The head office for long-
distance bus traffic is **Matkahuolto**,
Lauttasaarentie 8, 00200 Helsinki,
tel: 09-682701, fax: 692 2082.
Timetable enquiries can be made at
the **National Timetable Service**, tel:
0200 4000 (€1.50 per minute plus
local telephone charges) or on-line at
www.matkahuolto.info.
   There is no penalty for buying a
ticket on the coach but you cannot
get group discounts (for three adults
or more on trips over 80 km/50
miles) from the coach ticketseller.
Senior citizens and full-time students
(university and lower) are also eligible

for discounts, but must purchase, for
€5, a coach card entitling them to
this discount – at least 30 percent.
Bring a photo, ID and international
ISIC student card. Accompanied
children under four travel free.
   Visitors can reserve long-distance
coach seats (for a small fee) by
calling Matkahuolto or visiting the
main bus station, situated at the
corner of Mannerheimintie and
Simonkatu in Helsinki.

Driving
Finland's roads are not too plagued
by traffic although they do get very
busy between the capital and the
countryside on Fridays and Sundays
during the summer. There are few
multi-lane motorways. Most are two-
lane only.
   Pay attention to road signs
showing elk and reindeer zones.
Collisions with these animals are
usually serious. Use caution at all
hours, but especially at dusk when
elk are most active. For winter
driving, studded tyres should ideally
be used from November to March
and are strongly recommended
throughout December at all times.

Rules of the Road
Drive on the right, overtake on the
left. All cars must use their lights
outside built-up areas. Elsewhere,
lights must be used at dusk or at
night or in bad weather (UK cars
must sweep their lights right).
Wearing of seat-belts is also
compulsory.
   Traffic coming from the right has
right of way. Exceptions are on roads
marked by a triangle sign; if this is
facing you, you must give right of way;
similarly if you are on a very major
thoroughfare it is likely that the feed-
in streets will have triangles, giving
you the right of way. On roundabouts
(*rotaries*), the first vehicle to reach
the roundabout has right of way.
   Speed limits are signposted, and
range from 30 kmph (18 mph) in
school zones to 100 kmph (62 mph)
on motorways.

Taxis
Finnish taxis run throughout the
country, with fares starting at around
€4.50. Helsinki city centre and the
centres of other large cities, as well
as most major airports, bus and
railway stations, have taxi stands.
Otherwise local telephone books list
the number of the nearest dispatcher
(under *Taksi* in the White Pages).
Finding the closest one is worthwhile,
especially in Helsinki, as taxis charge
from embarkation point (plus an
order fee). You can also hail a cab on

the street, but this is a rarer way of getting a taxi in Finland than those mentioned above.

Bicycles

Finland is a good cycling country with its well-engineered cycle paths and gently rolling landscape. In Helsinki in summer, there's a free city bike scheme. For better-quality bicycles, try Greenbike rental shop (Fredrikinkatu 31, tel: 50 550 1020). You can rent bikes from the harbours of Mariehamn in the Åland islands (a popular summer cycling destination).

The **Finnish Youth Hostel Association** also offers planned route tours at good-value prices (which can also include accommodation). Also ask the Finnish Tourist Board *(see page 422)* about other firms that run planned cycling tours in the country.
Finnish Youth Hostel Association
Yrjönkatu 38B, 00100 Helsinki
Tel: 09-565 7150
Fax: 09-565 71510
www.srmnet.org

Hitchhiking

Thumbing is still a time-honoured way to get a cheap ride in Finland, but you may have to wait a long time to get picked up, particularly at weekends and in the furthest reaches of Lapland where traffic can be pretty thin. Hitchhiking is prohibited on Finland's motorways; the smaller secondary routes are a better bet. As with any country in the world however, safety can never be guaranteed on the road, and this mode of transport is not recommended.

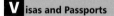isas and Passports

Citizens of most Western countries do not need visas to travel to Finland; a valid passport will suffice. EU citizens may enter with a valid ID card.

Customs Regulations

The following items may be brought into Finland.

Cigarettes/tobacco

Visitors from non-EU countries or travelling from the new eastern European member states over 17 years of age may bring in 200 cigarettes, 50 cigars or 250 g (1–2 lb) tobacco products duty free.

Alcohol

Visitors from non-EU countries aged 20 or over can bring in 16 litres of beer, 2 litres of other mild alcohol (drinks containing not more than 22 percent by volume of alcohol) and

ABOVE: Finland is perfect cycling country.

1 litre of strong alcohol (spirits). For visitors of 18 years of age, the quantity limit is the same, but must not include strong alcohol.

W hat to Bring

The best advice on packing for Finland is to bring layers of clothes, no matter what the season. While it is famous for frigid winters – when gloves, long underwear, hats, woollen tights and socks, and several layers of cotton topped by wool and something waterproof are recommended – Finland is less known for its very sunny temperate summers. As a result, sun block and a sun hat are as essential at these times as warm clothes are in the winter.

What to Read

General Interest

Facts about Finland (Otava). The most comprehensive coverage of Finland's history and culture, by a range of Finnish authors.
A Brief History of Finland (Otava, 1999) and *Finland in Europe* (Otava, 2003) by Matti Klinge offer a concise account of nation's history and role in the European Union. Manuel Castells' and Pekka Himanen's excellent and thought-provoking *The Information Society and the Welfare State: The Finnish Model* (WSOY, 2003) discusses the development of Nokia and the reasons behind the success of Finnish innovation.
Skating on the Sea: Poetry from Finland by (Bloodaxe Books, 1997) and *The Kalevala* (Oxford University Press – The World's Classics, 1989), translated by Keith Bosley, provide an introduction to Finnish literary culture. *The Maiden Who Rose from the Sea* by Helena Henderson (Hisarlik Press). An entertaining collection of Finnish folk tales.

Scandinavia

Scandinavia by Tony Griffiths. Two hundred years' worth of Scandinavian history, culture and art in this highly readable volume.
In Forkbeard's Wake: Coasting Around Scandinavia by Ben Nimmo. A very lively and up-to-date account of sailing around the region. With an array of colourful and amusing characters.
The Cambridge History of Scandinavia Vol. 1 by Knut Helle et al. An academic look at the early years of Scandinavian history to 1520 with further volumes to come. *Scandinavian Design* by Charlotte Fiel. A survey *c*.1900 to the present day that illustrates virtually all areas of design: furniture, ceramics, textiles, lighting, industrial and product design.

Other Insight Guides

Insight Guide titles in the region include *Insight Guide Finland*, and *Insight Pocket Guide Helsinki*.

Send Us Your Thoughts

We do our best to ensure the information in our books is as accurate and up-to-date as possible. However, some mistakes and omissions are inevitable and we are ultimately reliant on our readers to put us in the picture.

We welcome your feedback, especially your experience of using the book on the road and will acknowledge all contributions. We'll offer an Insight Guide to the best letters received.

Please write to us at:
Insight Guides
PO Box 7910
London SE1 1WE
Or email us at:
insight@apaguide.co.uk

ACCOMMODATION

HOTELS, YOUTH HOSTELS, BED AND BREAKFAST

Choosing a Hotel

Hotels throughout Finland are clean and well equipped, though expensive. A good breakfast buffet is usually included and one can find bargains at the chain hotels (generally up to 60 percent of standard prices) at weekends, and in summer when they lose their business and conference trade.

Budget accommodation includes youth and family hostels, farmhouses, guesthouses, family villages, camping and various forms of self-catering. During the summer holidays, some student residences become Summer Hotels, opening on 1 June. Details of youth hostels are available from:
The Finnish Youth Hostel Association, Yriönkatu 38B 15, 00100 Helsinki. Tel: 09 565 7150. Fax: 09 565 71510.
E-mail: info@srm.fi; www.srmnet.org
Local tourist offices and booking centres will provide up-to-date prices, including details of weekend and summer discounts. General information on accommodation is available from the Finnish Tourist Board in your home country, or from the head office in Helsinki *(see Tourist Information, page 422)*. Or Helsinki has its own booking centre at the railway station:
Hotel Booking Centre
Central Railway Station, 00100 Helsinki
Tel: 09 2288 1400.
Fax: 09 2288 1499.
E-mail: hotel@helsinkiexpert.fi
www.helsinkiexpert.fi

Hotel Chains

Finland has many large hotel chains of its own, as well as foreign ones. Scandic, Sokos and Cumulus offer fairly comfortable standard services in most big towns; Radisson SAS and others have even more comfortable facilities. Some of the best known are:
Best Western Finland
Nuijamiestentie 10, 00320 Helsinki
Tel: 09 622 622 649 00
www.bestwestern.fi
Cumulus
Restel Hotel Group
Tel: 09 733 5421
www.cumulus.fi
Scandic
Tel: 08000 6969
www.scandichotels.com
Sokos Hotels
Tel: 020 1234 600
www.sokoshotels.fi

Discounts

A systematic way to get discounts is to enrol in the Finncheque scheme, in which some 250 hotels participate. By spending around €39 on Finncheque vouchers, you get a night's free accommodation in these hotels. Vouchers are refundable at place of purchase.

Hotel Listings

Hotels are grouped by area, starting with Helsinki. Within each city or region, they are listed alphabetically.

ACCOMMODATION LISTINGS

HELSINKI

Academica
Hietaniemenkatu 14, 00100
Tel: 09 1311 4334
www.hostelacademica.fi
Basic summer hostel providing small, modern rooms with their own kitchen. Family rooms available. €
Crowne Plaza
Mannerheimintie 50, 00260
Tel: 09 2521 0000
www.crowneplaza-helsinki.fi
A newly refurbished upmarket hotel with a gym and spa. €€€
Eurohostel
Linnankatu 9, 00160
Tel: 09 622 0470
www.eurohostel.fi
Located on Katajanokka Island by the ferry terminals, this no-frills hostel has shared facilities including kitchen, laundry, sauna and café. €
Hotel Kämp
Pohjoisesplanadi 29, 00100
Tel: 09 576 111
www.hotelkamp.fi
The top hotel in town, popular with state guests, actors and rock stars. €€€
Klaus K
Bulevardi 2–4, 00120
Tel: 020 770 4700
www.klauskhotel.com
A brand new designer hotel

PRICE CATEGORIES

Price categories are based on the average cost (including tax) of a double room with breakfast:
€ = under €145
€€ = €145–215
€€€ = over €215

in a beautiful national romantic era building. €€€

Hotel Linna
Lönnrotinkatu 29, 00180
Tel: 09 5840 9711

BELOW: the sheer luxury of Klaus K.

www.palace.fi
A Finnish Jugend-style castle in one of the most fashionable areas of Helsinki. €€

Radisson SAS Plaza
Mikonkatu 23, 00100
Tel: 020 123 4700
www.radisson.com
All modern amenities. €€

Scandic Hotel Simonkenttä
Simonkatu 9
Tel: 09 68380
www.scandichotels.com
Recently opened hotel in the city centre. Comfortably furnished; some rooms have their own terrace with magnificent views. €€€

Hotel Seurahuone Helsinki
Kaivokatu 12, 00100
Tel: 09 69 141
www.hotelliseurahuone.fi
An older, characterful hotel refurbished in 2007, this is a great choice for centrality (opposite the train station) and service (choose your pillow from the "pillow menu"!). €€

Sokos Hotel Torni
Yrjönkatu 26, 00100
Tel: 020 123 4604
www.sokoshotels.fi
Gracious 13-storey hotel with an older Art Deco-style section. €€

THE SOUTH

Hanko

Pensionat Garbo
Esplanaadi 84, 10900
Tel/fax: 019 248 7897
www.pensionat-garbo.com
Like a Hollywood museum – each themed room features a star from the silver screen. €

Villa Maija
Appelgrenintie 7, 10900 Hanko
Tel: 050 505 2013
www.villamaija.fi
This fine 19th-century villa is one of many on this attractive street. €

Kotka

Sokos Hotel Seurahuone
Keskuskatu 21, 48100
Tel: 020 123 4666
www.sokoshotels.fi

This very central hotel has superb rooms and a fine restaurant. €€

Naantali

Naantali Spa & Congress Hotel
21100 Naantali
Tel: 02 445 5100
www.naantalispa.fi
In a charming seaside town near Turku, this unique hostelry offers luxury in a yacht next to the spa. €€

Turku

Best Western Hotel Seaport
Matkustajasatama (Passenger Harbour), 20100
Tel: 02 283 3000
www.hotelseaport.fi

By the castle, a 19th-century warehouse with red-brick facade in original neo-Gothic style with beautiful wooden beams. €

Marina Palace Radisson SAS
Linnankatu 32, 20100
Tel: 020 123 4700
www.radisson.com
Reopened in 2006 after extensive renovation, rooms are modern and some have river views. €€€

Omenahotelli
Humalistonkatu 7, 20100
Tel: 0600 18018
www.omena.com
A budget hotel in a building designed by Alvar Aalto. €

Park Hotel
Rauhankatu 1, 20100
Tel: 02 273 2555
www.parkhotelturku.fi

This elegant Jugendstil building (1902) was once a private mansion. Each of the well-furnished rooms is different, some with a park view. €

Scandic Hotel Plaza Turku
Yliopistonkatu 29
Tel: 02 33200
www.scandichotels.com
Designed in 1929 by Erik Bryggman, a friend of Alvar Aalto, this hotel has 107 comfortable and simply styled rooms. Good restaurant and popular bar. €€

Turku Hostel
Linnankatu 39
Tel: 02 262 7680
www.turku.fi/hostelturku
A reasonably priced alternative within walking distance of sights. €

LAKELAND

Imatra

Rantasipi Imatran Valtionhotelli
Torkkelinkatu 2, 55100
Tel: 05 625 2000
www.rantasipi.fi

Art Nouveau castle, next to the Imatra rapids. €

Jyväskylä

Hotelli Yöpuu
Yliopistonkatu 23, 40100

Tel: 014 333 900
www.hotelliyopuu.fi
Centrally located right in the heart of the city. Idyllic hotel in a historic building with a fine restaurant serving excellent lunches. €€

Sokos Hotel Alexandra
Hannikaisenkatu 35, 40100
Tel: 020 123 4642
www.sokoshotels.fi
Centrally located modern hotel, within easy walk of the lake. €

Kuopio

Scandic Hotel Kuopio
Satamakatu 1
Tel: 017 195 111
www.scandichotels.com
This large hotel on the waterfront is one of the finest in town. €€

Sokos Hotel Puijonsarvi
Minna Canthinkatu 16, 70100
Tel: 017 192 2000
www.sokoshotels.fi
Modern, pleasant ambience. €€

Spa Hotel Rauhalahti
Katiskaniementie 8, 70700
Tel: 030 60830
www.rauhalahti.com
This fine spa hotel also includes a wing with budget apartments. €–€€

Lappeenranta

Scandic Hotel Patria
Kauppakatu 21, 53100
Tel: 05 677 511
www.scandichotels.com
Modern hotel situated close to the harbour and fortress area; 130 rooms, restaurants and saunas. Some rooms have balconies and views over Lake Saimaa. €

Punkaharju

Fontana Punkaharjun Valtionhotelli
58450 Punkaharju 2
Tel: 020 752 9800
www.lomaliitto.fi
Wooden Russian-style villa with lots of atmosphere and 24 rooms. €

Savonlinna

Fontana Spa Hotel Casino
Kylpylaitoksentie 5, 57130
Tel: 015 739 5430
www.lomoliitto.fi
Large complex, on an island. Cheap hostel beds in summer. €€

Perhehotelli Hospitz
Linnankatu 20, 57130
Tel: 015 515 661
www.hospitz.com
Cosy, family-run hotel. Very popular and often fully booked in summer. €

Tampere

Cumulus Koskikatu
Koskikatu 5, 33100
Tel: 03 242 4111
www.cumulus.fi
Modern with good bar and

food. Their restaurant offers a good menu. €

Scandic Tampere City
Hämeenkatu 1, 33100
Tel: 03 244 6111
www.scandichotels.com
A new centrally located hotel with a gym and a sauna. €

Sokos Hotel Tammer
Satakunnankatu 13, 33100
Tel: 020 123 4632
www.sokoshotels.fi
Dramatic hotel, and a tribute to Finnish Art Deco. Set in a green, hilly district. €€

Hotel Victoria
Itsenäisyydenkatu 1, 33100
Tel: 03 242 5111
www.hotellivictoria.fi
Simple hostel with a lively bar and restaurant (group discounts). €

WEST COAST

Oulu

Holiday Club Oulun Eden
Holstinsalmentie 29, 90500
Tel: 0201 234 905
www.holidayclub.fi
Indoor pools, water slides, luxury spa and steam rooms in a beach area. Good restaurant. €€

Rauma

Hotel Cumulus Rauma
Aittakarinkatu 9, 26100 Rauma
Tel: 02 837 821
www.cumulus.fi
A simple canalside hotel, with small swimming pool and two saunas. €

Hotel Vanha Rauma
Vanhankirkonkatu 26
Tel: 02 837 86150
www.hotelvanharauma.fi
A small hotel situated right in the centre of old Rauma, in a renovated Art Deco warehouse. Well-equipped comfortable rooms. and a restaurant. €€

Kemi

Kemi SnowHotel
Tel: 016 259 502
www.snowcastle.net
The magical SnowHotel opens from January to mid-April. Snug arctic sleeping bags hold the cold at bay. Book well in advance. €€€

KARELIA

Joensuu

Finnhostel Joensuu Hostel
Kalevankatu 8
Tel: 013 267 5076
www.islo.fi
Located right in the city centre. Suites are self-contained single, double and triple rooms. The

Sportti restaurant serves inexpensive meals. €

Sokos Hotel Vaakuna
Torikatu 20, 80100
Tel: 020 123 4661
www.sokoshotels.fi
A newly refurbished modern hotel with a sauna and jacuzzi. Located by the market place. €

Nurmes

Bomba Holiday Resort
Suojärvenkatu 1
Tel: 013 687 200
www.bomba.fi
On the shore of Lake pielinen, this is a good destination for families. Sample Karelian cooking. €€

Kuusamo

Sokos Hotel Kuusamo
Kirkkotie 23, 93600 Kuusamo
Tel: 020 1234 693
www.sokoshotels.fi
Pleasant rooms, close to the ski slopes and wilderness. Saunas and swimming pool. €

LAPLAND

<table>
<tr><td>

PRICE CATEGORIES

Price categories are based on the average cost (including tax) of a double room with breakfast:
€ = under €145
€€ = €145–215
€€€ = over €215

</td></tr>
</table>

Rovaniemi

Guesthouse Borealis
Asemieskatu 1
Tel: 016 34 20 130
www.guesthouseborealis.com
Friendly B&B accom-modation run by a local family very close

to the train station. There are single, double and triple rooms as well as an apartment accommodating seven people in two bedrooms. Own bathroom and cooking facilities. €

Rantasipi Pohjanhovi
Pohjanpuistikko 2, 96200

Tel: 016 33 711
www.restel.fi
E-mail: pohjanhovi.rantasipi@restel.fi
Legendary luxury riverside hotel with swimming pool, nightclub and casino. Located on the banks of the Kemijoki waterfront with lovely river views. €€

E ATING OUT

RECOMMENDED RESTAURANTS AND CAFÉS

What to Eat

Finnish cuisine has broadened and improved enormously in recent years. The wild game dishes (reindeer, elk and bear) are a real treat and are usually served with exquisite mushroom and berry sauces. In summer, you are strongly recommended to try *ravut* (crayfish). Crayfish feasts are often held in hotel restaurants and include lots of *schnapps* and songs.

Finns tend to eat a large hot lunch, then a smaller cold meal in the evening. Dining out has become more popular, with Italian, Chinese and French restaurants in almost all major towns. The best Russian cuisine outside of Russia is found in Helsinki.

Where to Eat

In the past, it was difficult to get a really cheap meal in Finland, but you can find places where you will definitely get value for money. Fixed-price lunches are often very good deals and are usually advertised on boards outside restaurants. The Sokos and Stockmann department stores have excellent food halls; otherwise, for snacks there are more and more cafés sprouting up that supply sandwiches, quiche, soups and salads at reasonable prices.

Many hotels (particularly Sokos and Scandic) in Helsinki, Turku, Tampere and elsewhere have good places to eat, ranging from gourmet restaurants to wine bars and cafés.

Restaurant Listings

Restaurants are listed in alphabetical order by region, with the most expensive first.

Drinking Notes

Alcohol is expensive in Finland due to high taxes.

Beer The Finnish *tuoppi* is slightly smaller than the British pint. If you do not specify, you will usually be served a *keski-olut*, (3.5 percent alcohol. The strongest beer is number 4 (*nelosolut*, 4.5 percent) and the weakest number 1 (*ykkösolut*, just over 1 percent).

Wine in Finland is imported and very costly. There is more choice in Alko outlets (the state alcohol monopoly).

RESTAURANT LISTINGS

HELSINKI

Aino
Pohjoisesplanadi 21
Tel: 09 624 327
www.marcante.fi
A Finnish restaurant using traditional seasonal ingredients. Try 'Aino's snaps', the restaurants

PRICE CATEGORIES

Price categories are based on an average cost per head of a three-course meal (excluding drinks but with tax):
€ = under €15
€€ = €15–35
€€€ = over €35

own version of schnapps, which is served in hand-made stoneware cups. €€€
Bar Tapasta
Uudenmaankatu 13
Tel: 09 640 724
www.marcante.fi
Where the young and hip come for tapas, pasta and good wine. Great atmosphere. €
Bellevue
Rahapajankatu 3
Tel: 09 179 560
www.restaurantbellevue.com
Superb cuisine in Helsinki's oldest and most refined Russian restaurant, located in the shadow of the

Uspenski Orthodox Cathedral. Try the blinis with herring caviar or the pot-roast bear steak. €€€
Café Bar No 9
Uudenmaankatu 9
Tel: 09 621 4059
www.bar9.net
A few minutes walk away from the Swedish Theatre, this little restaurant/bar has become a popular hot-spot. The single page menu offers a surprisingly wide variety of sandwiches, salads, soups, and stir-fried dishes at very economical prices. €
Chez Dominique
Rikhardinkatu 4

Tel: 09 612 7393
www.chezdominique.fi
A Scandinavian cuisine restaurant with two Michelin stars, owned by Hans Välimäki, probably Finland's most famous chef. Chez Dominique is renowned for inventive cuisine such as seared fois gras with a white port and golden raisin sauce. Menu changes weekly. €€€
G. W. Sundmans
Eteläranta 16
Tel: 09 6128 5400
www.royalravintolat.com
This esteemed restaurant is next to Market Square in

a 19th-century Empire-style building designed by Engel. Although the building and decor are traditional, the cuisine is not. Expect light, seasonal dishes. The extensive wine list includes some surprisingly inexpensive wines. €€€

KarlJohan
Yrjönkatu 21
Tel: 09 612 1121
www.ravintolakarljohan.fi
Traditional Finnish dishes at fair prices. Homely atmosphere. €€

Kynsilaukka Garlic Restaurant
Fredrikinkatu 22.
Tel: 09 651 939
www.kynsilaukka.com
The chef brings fresh market produce to the garlic-centred dishes served here. €€

Lappi
Annankatu 22
Tel: 09 645 550
www.lappires.com
An authentic Lapland experience is a bonus when sampling anything made of reindeer, tasty fish, salted fungi and exotic berries. Try the Lappish plate to savour a full range of northern specialities. €€

Maxill
Korkeavuorenkatu 4
Tel: 09 638 873
www.maxill.fi
Has a loyal clientele who come for the consistently good menu. €€

Restaurant Klippan
Luoto
Tel: 09 633 408
www.palacekamp.fi
The red roof of this distin-guished wooden villa is

easily recogned on the island of Luoto, in the South Harbour. Reached by ferry it is a summer restaurant only open from May to September. One of the specialities is the local crab. €€

Romanov
Yrjänkatu 15
Tel: 09 642 394
www.romanov.fi
This is the latest addition to Helsinki's array of Russian restaurants. The interesting menu is in two parts – one featuring classic dishes, the other offering new Russian cuisine, and two set menus are available. The grilled steak Romanov is recommended. €€

Sandeep
Lönnrotinkatu 22
Tel: 09 685 6206

www.sandeep.fi
Top-quality Indian dishes including tandoori specialities. €€

Saslik
Neitsytpolku 12
Tel: 09 7425 5500
www.saslik.fi
Excellent Russian restaurant for bear meat dishes and a good place to experience the autumn bear festival. €€€

Walhalla
Suomenlinna
Tel: 09 668 552
www.restaurantwalhalla.com
Open in summer, this restaurant is set in the archways of the old fortress on historic Suomenlinna island. Seafood and game are specialities. €€€

THE SOUTH

Turku

Summer in Turku is not complete without a session in one of the dozen boat restaurants on the River Aurajoki.

Bossa
Kauppiaskatu 12
Tel: 02 2515 880
www.restaurantebossa.fi
For something different, try this authentic Brazilian

restaurant, with exotic dishes and live music on Tuesday evenings. €€

Enkeliravintola
Kauppiaskatu 16
Tel: 02 231 8088
www.enkeliravintola.fi
Fine restaurant serving delicious food. Desserts are excellent. €€

Panimoravintola Herman
Läntinen Rantakatu 37
Tel: 02 230 3333

www.ravintolaherman.com
This brewery-restaurant serves a popular inexpensive lunch buffet on its ground level, while upstairs more gourmet food is offered. €–€€

Pizzeria Dennis
Linnankatu 17
Tel: 02 469 1191
www.dennispizza.fi
Tasty and authentic

pizzas, good toppings. €

Ravintola Linnankatu 3
Linnankatu 3
Tel: 02 233 9279
www.linnankatu3.fi
A gourmet restaurant continuing a tradition from 1682. €€€

Viking Restaurant Harald
Aurakatu 3
Tel: 02 276 5050
www.ravintolaharald.com
A theme restaurant with

LAKELAND

BELOW: a platter of mixed fish.

Kuopio

The small *muikku* (whitefish) is a speciality in Kuopio, although more famous is the *kalakukko* (loaf of rye bread crust filled with fish and pork) that can be found at the market.

Musta Lammas
Satamakatu 4
Tel: 017 5810 458
www.ravintolamestarit.net/mustalammas
A pleasant restaurant, considered Kuopio's best. €€

Vapaasatama Sampo
Kauppakatu 13
Tel: 017 261 4677
Informal atmosphere, serving excellent fish. €€

Wanha Satama
Matkustaja-Satama
Tel: 017 197 304
www.wanhasatama.net
Rustic and lively; located by the passenger harbour. Serves tasty *muikku* fish with garlic and mashed potatoes. €

Savonlinna

The market is busy and popular. Prices are steep during the opera festival, but the market is also at its liveliest here.

Hilpeä Munkki (Cheerful Monk)
Riihisaari
Tel: 015 515 330

www.jarvisydan.com/munkki
A popular medieval restaurant, open only in summer. €€
Majakka
Satamakatu 11
Tel: 015 206 2825
www.ravintolamajakka.fi
A popular place near the market serving fish. €€
Sillansuu
Verkkosaarenkatu 1
Tel: 015 531 451
www.sillansuu.net
Popular pub near Market Bridge. €€

Tampere

Astor
Aleksis Kivenkatu 26
Tel: 03 260 5700
www.ravintola-astor.fi
Live piano music every night. Try the fillets of Baltic herring in mustard sauce. €€
Eetvartti
Sumeliuksenkatu 16
Tel: 020 123 4630
www.eetvartti.fi
Run by the Pirkanmaa Hotel and Restaurant School.

High-quality food cooked by the students. €
Hella & Huone
Salhojankatu 48
Tel: 03 253 2440
www.huone.info
Genuine French gourmet restaurant. Ever-changing menu. €€€
Näsinneula
Särkänniemi
Tel: 03 248 8234
www.sarkanniemi.fi
Revolving restaurant high in the Näsinneula Observation Tower where you dine 168

metres (635 ft) above the scenic landscape of Tampere. €€€
Plevna
Itäinenkatu 8
Tel: 03 260 1200
www.plevna.fi
Lively pub/café specialising in steaks, sausages. Beers are brewed on the premises. €
Salud
Tuomiokirkonkatu 19
Tel: 03 233 4400
www.salud.fi
Popular tapas restaurant. €

WEST COAST

Vaasa

Gustav Wasa
Raastuvankatu 24
Tel: 050 466 3208
www.gustavwasa.com
Cellar restaurant serving excellent meat portions and some fish. The rustic dining hall used to be a coal-storing cellar. €€€
Strampen
Rantakatu 6
Tel: 041 451 4512

www.strampen.com
A summer-only pavilion restaurant, with a fine terrace for people-watching. Good selection of evening dishes and lighter lunches. €€–€€€

Oulu

Pannu
Kauppurienkatu 12
Tel: 0207 928 200
www.ravintolapannu.com
Popular grill restaurant in

the basement of Stockmann department store. Large pizza selection, also serving standard Finnish dishes such as wild boar and fresh fish. €
Ravintola Matala
Rantakatu 6
Tel: 08 333 013
www.matala.fi
Oulu's finest restaurant, with dishes such as spiced dove's breast with truffle butter. Separate vegetarian

choice, and a four-course "surprise" menu. €€–€€€

Pori

Raatihuoneen Kellari
Hallituskatu 9
Tel: 02 633 4804
www.raatihuoneenkellari.fi
First class establishment serving Finnish-style meat and fish dishes. Located in the basement of ther old town hall. €€–€€€

LAPLAND

Rovaniemi

Fransmanni
Sokos Vaakuna Hotel, Koskikatu 4

Tel: 020 123 4695
www.fransmanni.fi
Rather pricey, but excellent food. A good

BELOW: smoked fish is a Baltic delicacy.

place to try Lappish specialities, such as reindeer and cloudberry liquer. Quite an expensive menu, but well worth the experience. €€€
Restaurant Nili
Valtakatu 20
Tel: 0400 369 669
www.nili.fi
Nili is a snug place, decorated with Lappish wood carvings and furs. It offers traditional Lapp food – Arctic char, fresh salmon and reindeer, served with seasonal accompaniments. €€€
Restaurant Sky Ounasvaara
Ounasvaara
Tel: 016 323 4333
For startling beautiful views, head for this panoramic restaurant 3km (2 miles) outside town in the Hotel Sky Ounasvaara. There's a selection of classy international

dishes, or try local treats from the Lapp menu. €€€

Saariselkä

Ravintola Pirkon Pirtti
Honkapolku 2, 99830
Tel: 016 668 050
www.pirkonpirtti.fi
Popular restaurant serving reindeer and game dishes, and pizzas for the less adventurous. Also on the menu is marinated fillet of elk, and crispy fried char. Round off the meal with Arctic cloudberry sorbet. Closes summer. €€€

PRICE CATEGORIES

Price categories are based on an average cost per head of a three-course meal (excluding drinks but with tax):
€ = under €15
€€ = €15–35
€€€ = over €35

ART & PHOTO CREDITS

DENMARK

Numbers in italics refer to photographs

A

Absalon of Roskilde, Bishop 31, 98
Æbelø 126
Ærø 126
Ærøskøbing 126
agriculture 44
Åkirkeby 120
Åkirke (church) 120
Ålborg 134
Jomfru Ane Gade 134
Stenhus (Stone House) 134
Almindingen forest 119
Als Island 131
amber 133
Ancher, Anna and Michael 52–3, 134
The Girl in the Kitchen (Anna Ancher) *50*
Andersen, Hans Christian 36, 51, 100, 104, 116, 117, 123, *127*
Hans Christian Andersen Museum (Odense) *122,* 124
Shadow Picture of a Journey to the Harz Mountains and Saxony 127
The Emperor's New Clothes 51
The Improvisatore 127
The Little Match Girl 117
The Little Mermaid 51
The Nightingale 127
The Princess and the Pea 51, 127
The Tinder Box 117, 127
The Ugly Duckling 51, 116
Århus 129
Århus Kunstmuseum (Museum of Art) 129
Den Gamle By (Old Town) 129
Domkirken (Cathedral of St Clement) 129
Rådhus (City Hall) 129
art and crafts 51–3
in Bornholm 119
CoBrA movement 53, 131, 132
Danish Design 54, 99, *110–11*
Danish Design Centre (Copenhagen) 99, 110
in Funen 123
Royal Academy of Fine Arts (Copenhagen) 102
Scandinavian design 54
Skagen painters 52–3, 107, 134
arts and entertainment
Danish Film Institute (Copenhagen) 102
Det Kongelige Teater (Royal Theatre) (Copenhagen) 51, 102, 103
Faroese Cultural Evening 143
Nordisk Film Kompagni 52
Royal Danish Ballet 51
Royal Danish Opera 51
Royal Danish Orchestra 51
Royal Theatre Orchestra 127

Sjællands Symphony Orchestra 99
Aurora Borealis see **Northern Lights**
Avernakø 126

B

Bagenkop 126
Bagger, Erik 111
Balka 121
Bang, Jens 134
beaches 65–6
Bagenkop (Langeland) 126
Balka 121
Dueodde 121
Hennes Strand *135*
Hvide Sande 133
Køge 116
Liseleje 115
Marielyst (Falster) 117
Risting (Langeland) 126
Tisvilde 115
in Western Jutland 133
Billund 131
Legoland 131
Blåvands Huk (lighthouse) 133
Blixen, Karen 51, *115,* 126
Out of Africa 51, 115
Bogense 126
Gyldensteen castle 126
Bohr, Niels 99
Borðoy Island 143
Bornholm 118–21
see also individual place names
Bournonville, August 51–2
Brahe, Tycho 102

C

Caroline Matilde 35
castles and fortresses
Aalholm Slot (Nysted) 117
Absalon's Old Fortress (Copenhagen) 97, 107
Egeskov Slot (Funen) 125, *126*
Gamleborg (Almindingen Skov, Bornholm) 118–9
Gamleborg (Paradisbakkerne, Bornholm) 118–9
Gavnø Slot 116
Gissfeld Slot 116
Gyldensteen (Bogense) 126
Hammershus (Bornholm) 119
Kalø Slot (Jutland) 129
Kronborg Castle (Helsingør) 35, 115, 116
Liselund Slot 117
Nyborg Slot (Nyborg) 123
Rosenborg Slot (Copenhagen) 97, 107
Ruins of Absalon's Old Fortress (Christiansborg, Copenhagen) 107

Shackenborg Slot (Møgeltønder) 132
Sønderborg Slot (Sønderborg) 131
Valdemars Slot (Tåsinge) 126
Vikingeborgen Trelleborg (Viking fortress) 116
Christian IV 161
churches and cathedrals
Åkirke (Åkirkeby) 120
Alexander Nevski Russian Orthodox Church (Copenhagen) 103
Chapel (Frederiksborg, Hillerød) *113*
Den Tilsandede Kirke (Sand-Covered Church) *134*
Domkirke (Cathedral) (Roskilde) 115
Domkirken (Cathedral of St Clement) (Århus) 129
Frederikskirken (Marble Church) (Copenhagen) 103–4, *104*
Københavns Domkirke (Cathedral) (Copenhagen) 101
Østerlars Kirke (St Laurentius) (Gudhjem) 120
Palace Chapel (Christiansborg, Copenhagen) 107
Ribe Domkirke (Cathedral) (Ribe) 132
"round churches" of Bornholm 120–21
round church (Olsker) *118,* 120
Sankt Petri Kirke (St Peter's) (Copenhagen) 100
Skt Knuds Domkirke (Odense) 124
Skt Mariæ Kirke (Helsingør) 115
Skt Nikolai Kirke (Køge) 116
Skt Nikolai Kirke (Rønne) 120
Vor Frelsers Kirke (Church of Our Saviour) (Copenhagen) 97, 108
Christiansen, Ole Kirk 131
Christiansfeld 131
climate 89, 97
of the Faroe Islands 141
of Greenland 139
Copenhagen 77, 97–108, 113
Absalon's Old Fortress, ruins 97, 107
Alexander Nevski Russian Orthodox Church 103
Amagertorv *86,* 100
Amaliehaven 104
Amalienborg Museum 104
Amalienborg Slot (Palace) 104, *104*
Børsen (Stock Exchange) 98, 108
Botanisk Have (Botanical Gardens) 107, *108*
canal boat trips 97, *107*
Carlsberg Brewery and stables 102, *108*
Charlottenborg 102
Christiania *106,* 108

Christiansborg *98,* 107–8
Folketinget (House of Parliament)
   107
Kongelige Stalde & Kareter
   (Museum of the Royal Stables
   and Coaches) 108
Palace Chapel 107
Ridebanen 107
Royal Reception Chambers 107
Teatermuseet 108
Thorvaldsens Museum 107
Christianshavn 108
Christianskirke 108
Churchillparken 105
Danish Design Centre 99, 110
Danish Film Institute 102
Dansk Arkitektur Center (Danish
   Architecture Centre) 108
Den Hirschsprungske Samling
   (Hirschsprung Collection) 105,
   107
Den Lille Havfrue (Little Mermaid)
   104, *105*
Det Kongelige Bibliotek (Royal
   Library) *105,* 108
Det Kongelige Teater (Royal
   Theatre) 51, 102, 103
Fiolstræde 101
Frederikskirke (Marble Church)
   103–4, *104*
Frederiksstaden 103
Frihavnen (Free Harbour) 105
Frihedsmuseet (Danish
   Resistance Museum) 40, 105
Gammeltorv (Old Square) 100
Gefionspringvandet fountain 104
Georg Jensen 101
Gråbrødretorv (Greyfriars Square)
   101
"Guided Walking Tour of
   Copenhagen" 103
Hotel d'Angleterre 102, 103
Hotel Kong Frederik 98
Hovedbanegården (Central
   Railway Station) 99
Illums Bolighus 101, 110
Istedgade 100
Kastellet (The Citadel) 105
Københavns Domkirke
   (Cathedral) 101
Købmagergade 100
Kompagnistræde 100
Konditori La Glace 100
Kongens Have 107
Kongens Nytorv (King's New
   Square) 102
Kunstindustrimuseet (Danish
   Museum of Decorative Art)
   103, 110
Krystalgade 101
Latin Quarter 101
Little Mermaid *see* Den Lille
   Havfrue
Museum Erotica 102
Nationalmuseet (National
   Museum) *22,* 97, 100
Nyboder 105
Ny Carlsberg Glyptotek 97, 99,
   100
Nyhavn *102,* 103

Palace Hotel 98
Paustians Hus 105
Rådhuset 97, 98
Jens Olsen's World Clock 98
Rådhuspladsen (City Hall Square)
   98, *99*
Ripleys Believe It or Not! Museum
   98
Royal Academy of Fine Arts
   102
Rundetårn (Round Tower) 97,
   101–2, *103*
Rosenborg Slot (Castle) 97, 107
Royal Copenhagen Porcelain 101,
   103
Sankt Petri Kirke (St Peter's
   Church) 100
shopping 97, 100–101
Slagteren ved Kultorvet (Coal
   Square) 101
Slotsholmen (Castle Island) 107
Sømod's Bolcher 101
Statens Museum for Kunst
   (National Museum for Fine
   Arts) 97, 105
Strandgade 108
Strøget 100
Tivoli Gardens *96,* 97, 98
Tobaksmuseet (Tobacco
   Museum) *101*
tourist information 97, 100
transport 97
University of Copenhagen 101
Vesterbro 99–100
Vestergade 100
Vor Frelsers Kirke (Church of Our
   Saviour) 97, 108
culture and traditions
   of the Faroe Islands 143
   Greenland traditional costume
   138

D

"Daisy Routes" 126
Dinesen, Isak *see* **Blixen, Karen**
Dreyer, Carl Th. 52
Dueodde 121
Dybbøl 131–2
   Dybbøl Mill and museum 132

E

Ebeltoft 129
Eckersberg, C.W. 52
economy 43–4
Egeskov Slot 125
   maze 125
   Veteranmuseum (Veteran Motor
   Museum) 125
Eiríksson, Leifur 26
Eiríksson, Thorvaldur 26
Elmelund 117
Enniberg 142
Eriksen, Edvard 104
Ertholmene Islands 120
   Christiansø 120
   Frederiksø 120
Esbjerg 133
Esturoy 143

F

Fåborg 125
   Fåborg Museum for Fynsk Kunst
      125
   Klokketårnet 125
Falster 117
   see also individual place names
Fanefjord 117
Fanø 133
Faroe Islands 77, *140,* 141–3
   see also individual place names
Fensmark 116
   Holmegård Danish Glassvæk
      (glassworks) and museum 116
festivals and events
   Århus festival week 129
   Bornholm Classical Music
      Festival 120
   Folk Music Festival (Tórshavn,
      Faroe Islands) 143
   Horsens Middle Ages Festival 131
   Midsummer's Eve celebrations
      117
   Summartonar Music Festival
      (Faroe Islands) 143
   Tórshavnar Jazz, Folk and Blues
      Festival (Faroe Islands) 143
   Viking life re-enactments 132
food and drink 62–3
   alcohol restrictions in Faroe
      Islands 143
   aquavit/schnapps 62, 134, 143
   Bornholm specialities 121
   Greenland specialities 139
   smørrebrød 61–2
   Sønderborg sausages 131
Fredensborg (palace) 115
Freydis 26
Funen 28, 123–7
   see also individual place names
   cycling tours 123
Fyrkat 28, *29,* 132

G

Gammel Skagen (Old Skagen) 134
Geocenter Møns Klont 117
Gilleleje 115
   Hos Karen og Marie restaurant
      115
Greenland 40, 77, 137–9
   see also individual place names
   climate 137
   tourism 137
Grenen 134
Gudhjem 120
   Bornholms Model Jernbane
      (model train) Museum 120
   Østerlars Kirke (St Laurentius)
      120

H

Hærvejen cycle and walking trail 69
Harald Bluetooth 26, 132
Haslev 116
Hastings 25–6
Helsingør 115
   Carmelite Kloster (Convent) 115

Kronborg Castle 35, 115, 116
Skt Mariæ Kirke 115
Henne 133
Henne Kirkeby Kro 133
Henningsen, Poul 110
Hillerød 115
Frederiksborg 115
Chapel *113*
Natural History Museum 115
Himmelbjerget (Sky Mountain) 131
Hobro 132
Hobro Museum 132
Holberg, Ludvig 51
Høm, Poul 121
Horsens 131
Høst, Oluf 120
Hovu 131
Hoyvik 143
Fornminnisavn (National Museum) 143
Humlebæk 115
Louisiana Museum for Moderne Kunst (Louisiana Museum of Modern Art) 52, 115
Hvide Sande 133

I

industry
film 52
fishing 61, 141
oil 44
Ishoj 116
Arken Museet for Moderne Kunst *116*
Ittoqqortoormiit 137
Ivar the Boneless 26

J

Jacobsen, Arne 54, 110, 111, 129
Jelling 28, 132
Jellingstenene (Jelling Stones) *132*
Johansen, Viggo 134
Jorn, Asger 53, 131
Jutland 28, 53, 129–34
see also individual place names

K

Kangerlussuaq 137
Keldby 117
Kerteminde 123, 124
Johannes Larsen Museum 124
Kierkegaard, Søren 36, 51, 100
Kirkjubøur 142, 143
Smoke Room 143
Klaksvík 143
Nordoya Fornminnisavn (North Islands Museum) 143
Klampenborg 113
Klampenborg Dyrhavn (deer park) 113
Bakken fun fair 113
Ordrupgaard 113
Peter Lieps' restaurant 113
Køge 116
Hugo's Vinkælder inn 116
Skt Nikolai Kirke 116

Knud of Denmark and England 207, 209
Knud II 124
Knuthenborg safari park 117
Kolding 131
Koldinghus Slot 131
Kunstmuseet Traphold (Trapholt Museum of Art) 131
Kristian II *31*, 33, 34, 234
Kristian IV 34, 98
Kristian VII 34
Krøyer, P.S. 52–3, 134

L

Ladby 123
Viking Burial Ship Museum 28, 123
Langeland 126
language 21–2, 91, 143, 366
Lassen, Anders 40
Lego *131*
Lind, Jenny 127
Lindholm Høje 28, *29,* 132
Liseleje 115
literature 51
see also individual writers' names
Anglo-Saxon Chronicle 23, 26
Beowulf 22
Hamlet 115, 116
Lolland 117
see also individual place names
Lønstrup 134
Lunkebugten Bay (Tåsinge) 126
Lyø 126

M

Margrethe II *42*
Marielyst 117
Marstal 126
Melsted 120
Landbrugsmuseet Melstedgård (agricultural museum) 120
Middlefart 126
Midnight Sun 138
Moesgård 129
Forhistorisk Museum (Museum of Prehistory) 129
Møgeltønder 132
Shackenborg Slot 132
Mols Bjerge 129
Møn 116–7
see also individual place names
Grønjægers Høj barrow grave 117
monarchy 42
Møns Klint *112*
Munch-Petersen, Ursula 110
museums and galleries
AROS Århus Kunstmuseum (Museum of Art) (Århus) 129
Arken Museet for Moderne Kunst (Ishoj) *116*
Bornholms Model Jernbane (model train) Museum (Gudhjem) 120
Bornholms Museum (Rønne) 120
Carl Nielsen Museet (Odense) 124–5
Danmarks Grafiske Museum

(Danish Museum for Printing) (Odense) 125
Danmarks Mediemuseum (Danish Media Museum) 125
Dansk Arkitektur Center (Danish Architecture Centre) (Copenhagen) 108
Den Fynske Landsby (Funen Village) (Odense) 125
Den Gamle By (Old Town) open-air museum (Århus) 129
Den Hirschsprungske Samling (Hirschsprung Collection) (Copenhagen) 105, 107
Dybbøl Mill and museum (Dybbøl) 132
Fåborg Museum for Fynsk Kunst (Fåborg) 125
Fornminnisavn (National Museum) (Hoyvik) 143
Forsvarsmuseet (military museum) (Rønne) 120
Frihedsmuseet (Danish Resistance Museum) (Copenhagen) 40, 105
Glass Museum (Fensmark) 116
Hans Christian Andersen Museum (Odense) *122,* 124
Hobro Museum (Hobro) 132
Johannes Larsen Museum (Kerteminde) 124
Kongelige Stalde & Kareter (Museum of the Royal Stables and Coaches) (Christiansborg, Copenhagen) 107–8
Kunsthallen (art gallery) (Odense) 125
Kunstindustrimuseet (Danish Museum of Decorative Art) (Copenhagen) 103, 110
Kunstmuseet Traphold (Trapholt Museum of Art) (Kolding) 131
Landbrugsmuseet Melstedgård (agricultural museum) (Melsted) 120
Lindholm Høje museum 28, *29,* 132
Louisiana Museum for Moderne Kunst (Louisiana Museum of Modern Art) (Humlebæk) 52, 115
Moesgård Museum (Museum of Prehistory) (Moesgård) 129
Museet for Fotokunst (Museum of Photographic Art) (Odense) 125
Museet Louis Tussaud's (Copenhagen) 98–9
Museum Erotica (Copenhagen) 102
Nationalmuseet (National Museum) (Copenhagen) *22,* 97, 100
Natural History Museum (Frederiksborg, Hillerød) 115
Nordoya Fornminnisavn (North Islands Museum) (Klaksvík) 143
Silkeborg Museum (Museum of Art) (Silkeborg) 131

Skagens Museum (Skagen) 134
Statens Museum for Kunst
  (National Museum for Fine
  Arts) (Copenhagen) 97,
  105
Teatermuseet (Christiansborg,
  Copenhagen) 108
Thorvaldsens Museum
  (Christiansborg, Copenhagen)
  107
Tidens Samling (Time Collection)
  (Odense) 125
Tobaksmuseet (Tobacco
  Museum) (Copenhagen) 101
Tønder Museum (Tønder) 132
Veteranmuseum (Veteran Motor
  Museum) (Egeskov Slot) 125
Viking Burial Ship Museum
  (Ladby) 28, 123
Vikingeskibsmuseet (Viking Ship
  Museum) (Roskilde) 115–6
Mykines Island 142

N

Næstved 116
Narsarsuaq 139
national parks and nature reserves
  Rebild Bakker 68
  Svanninge Bakker 68, 125
nature and outdoor life 65–69,
  71–2
Nielsen, Anne Marie 125
Nielsen, Carl 124–5, 127
  Carl Nielsen Museet (Odense)
  124–5
  My Childhood 127
Nordby 131
  Samsø Labyrinten (maze) 131
Northern Lights 138
Nuuk (Godthåb) 137
Nyborg 123
  Nyborg Slot 123
Nyker 120
Nykøbing 117
  Czarens Hus (Tsar's House) 117
Nylars 120
Nysted 117
  Aalholm Slot 117

O

Odense 123–5
  Brandt's Klædefabrik 125
  Carl Nielsen Museet 124–5
  Danmarks Grafiske Museum
  (Danish Museum for Printing)
  125
  Den Fynske Landsby (Funen
  Village) 125
  Hans Christian Andersen
  Museum 122, 124
  Kunsthallen (art gallery) 125
  Munkemøllestræde 124
  Museet for Fotokunst (Museum
  of Photographic Art) 125
  Nørre Lyndelse 125
  Skt Knuds Domkirke 124
  Tidens Samling (Time Collection)
  125

Oehlenschläger, Adam 51
Olsker 120
  round church 118, 120
Oresund bridge 44, 45, 77, 249
Ørsted, H.C. 126

P–Q

Paradisbakkerne (Hills of Paradise)
  118, 119
people
  Danes 89–91
  Faroe Islanders 141
  Inuit of Greenland 137
Petersen, Carl-Henning 132
plant life 119
population
  of Copenhagen 97
  of Denmark 89
Poskjær Stenhus barrow 132
Qeqertarsuaq (Disko Island) 137

R

Råbjerg Mile 134
religion 26
Ribe 132
  Ribe Domkirke (Cathedral) 132
Ringkøbing Fjord 133
Risting 126
Rolf ("Rolo") the Ganger 26
Rønne 119–20
  Bornholms Museum 120
  Kastellet (Citadel) 120
  Forsvarsmuseet (military
  museum) 120
  Skt Nikolai Kirke 120
Roskilde 115–6
  Domkirke (Cathedral) 115
  Vikingeskibshallen (Viking Ship
  Museum) 115–6
Rudkøbing 126
Rungsted
  Rungstedlund 113, 115

S

Samsø 129, 131
Silkeborg 131
  Silkeborg Kunstmuseum
  (Museum of Art) 131
Sisimiut 137
Skagen 134
  see also Gammel Skagen
  Anchers Hus (Ancher's House)
  134
  Skagens Museum 134
Sønderborg 131
  Café Druen 131
  Sønderborg Slot 131
Sønderho 133
Spodsbjerg 117
sport
  angling and ice fishing 70, 138,
  142
  boating and sailing 14, 65–6, 97,
  138
  football 71
  hiking and walking 66–7, 69,
  138, 141

  ice skating 99
  pony trekking 138
Stege 117
Stevns Klint 116
Struensee, Johann Friederich
  34–5
Svaneke 120
Svendborg 125

T

Tårs 117
Tasiilaq 137
Tåsinge island 126
Thorvaldsen, Bertel 107
Thyborøn 133–4
  shell-covered house 133, 134
Tisvilde 115
Tønder 132
  Tønder Museum 132
Tórshavn 141
tourist information 89
transport
  bicycles 68–9, 98, 120, 121
  boat trips and cruises 131,
  137–8, 141
  dog-sled trips in Greenland 137,
  138
  helicopter tours in Greenland 138
  IC3 Train 111
Trelleborg 28
Troense 126
  Troense Inn 126
Tybrind Vig 126

U–V

Uppsala 26
Valdemar I 31
Valdemar II 31
Valdemar IV 32
Vestmanna 142
Vestmannabjørgini 142

W–Z

Wegner, Hans J. 54, 110
wildlife 138, 141
  Arctic Fox 138
  Puffin 142
windmills 68
Zealand 113–7
  see also individual place names

FINLAND

Numbers in italics refer to photographs

A

Aalto, Alvar 57, 331
Aaltosen, Wäinö 324–5
Aavasaksa Hill 349
  Midsummer Eve festivities
    (Aavasaksa Hill) 349
accommodation
  camping 68, 335
  wilderness huts 68
Akäslompolo 349
  Ylläs fell 349
Åland Islands 321
  see also individual place names
Alexander III 320
architecture 57, 291, 302, 306
  Jugendstil (Art Nouveau) 306,
    308
  Suomen Rakennustaiteen Museo
    (Museum of Finnish
    Architecture) (Helsinki) 308–9
  traditional wooden buildings 337,
    338
Arctic Circle 345, 347, 349
art and craft 57–8
  Finnish Design 57
  Scandinavian design 54
  tradtional Finnish dolls 304
arts and entertainment
  Finlandiatalo (Finlandia Hall)
    (Helsinki) 57, 301, 304
  Helsinki Philharmonic Orchestra
    (Helsinki) 304
  Suomen Kansallisooppera
    (Finnish National Opera House)
    (Helsinki) 291, 304
  Sibelius Academy (Helsinki) 58,
    304
  Svenska Teatern (Swedish
    Theatre) (Helsinki) 305
  Teatterimuseo (Theatre Museum)
    (Helsinki) 305
  Valkeakoski Summer Theatre
    (Valkeakoski) 333
Aulangon Puisto (Aulanko Forest
  Park) 334
Aurora Borealis see Northern
  Lights

B

beaches 65, 291
  Hanko (Hangö) 317
  nudist beach 310
  Pihlajasaari 310
  Pyhtää 319
  Reposaari 337
  of Ruissalo Island 325
  Santalahti 320
Bobrikov, Nikolai Ivanovich 39

C

churches and cathedrals
  Hattulan Pyhän Ristin Kirkko

  (Hattulan Church of the Holy
    Cross) 334
  Helisnummen (Salo) 317
  Kaleva Kirkko (Tampere) 332
  Orthodox (Lappeenranta) 327
  Ortodoksinen Kirkko (Orthodox
    Cathedral) (Turku) 323
  Porvoo Cathedral 319
  Ristinkirkko (Church of the Cross)
    (Lahti) 330
  St Olof's (Nagu) 315
  Temppelinaukion Kirkko (Helsinki)
    304–5
  Tsasouna (Salo) 317
  Tuomiokirkko (Cathedral)
    (Helsinki) 307
  Tuomiokirkko (Cathedral)
    (Tampere) 332
  Tuomiokirkko (Cathedral) (Turku)
    323
  Uskela (Salo) 317
  Uspenskin Katedraali (Cathedral)
    (Helsinki) 308
climate 293, 301
culture and traditions 57

E

economy 43
Edelfelt, Albert 57, 319
Ekenäs (Tammisaari) 317–8
  boat tours 317–8
  Porvaristalo (Ekenäs Museum)
    317
Engel, Carl Ludwig 57, 302, 306,
  323, 338
Enontekiö 350

F

Fagervik 318
festivals and events
  Christmas Fair (Helsinki) 305
  Easter Orthodox festival
    (Sevettijärvi) 349
  Festival of Song (Joensuu) 340
  Hanko Days Weekend Festival
    (Hanko) 317
  Helsinki Festival 301
  International Dance and Music
    Festival (Kuopio) 329
  International Opera Festival
    (Savonlinna) 58, 328
  jazz festival (Pori) 58, 337
  Jyväskylä Arts Festival (Jyväskylä)
    332
  Kuhmo Chamber Music Festival
    (Kuhmo) 342
  May Day Eve (Helsinki) 305
  Midnight Sun Film Festival
    (Sodankylä) 347
  midsummer celebrations in the
    Åland Islands 321
  Night of the Bonfires (Hanko)
    317

  Ruisrock (Ruissalo Island) 325
Föglö 321
  bird reserve 321
food and drink 62–3
  aquavit 62
  cloudberry 348
  Panimo microbrewery
    (Suomenlinna) 309
  smörgåsbord 62

G–H

Gallén-Kallel, Akseli 57–8, 318,
  337
Gesellius, Herman 57, 306, 318
Gulf of Bothnia 291
Halti mountain 350
Hämeenlinna 334
  Häme Castle *334*
  Sibeliuksen Syntymäkoti Museo
    (Sibelius Home Museum) 334
Hamina 320
  Military Officer School (RUK)
  Museum 320
Hanko (Hangö) 317
  Alan's Café 317
  boat trips to Bengtskår
    Lighthouse *317*
  Hanko Days Weekend Festival 317
  Linnoitusmuseo (Frontline
    Museum) 317
  Loft Gallery E. Pinomaa 317
  Night of the Arts (Helsinki) 305
  Night of the Bonfires 317
  regatta 317
Harakka wildlife reserve 310
health 405
  mosquitoes 343, 345
Heinola 330
Helsinki 77, 291, 301–10
  see also Harakka, Lauttasaari,
    Luoto, Pihlajasaari, Särkkä,
    Seurasaari, Suomenlinna,
    Uunisaari, Valkosaari
  Akateeminen Kirjakauppa
    bookshop 305
  Aleksanterinkatu 307
  Ateneum (Museum of Finnish Art)
    302
  Bellevue Russian restaurant 308
  Bockin Talo (Bock House) 307
  Bulevardi 308
  Café Ursula 309
  Carousel café 309
  Christmas Fair 305
  City Art Museum 301, 303–4
  Design Forum 303
  Eduskuntatalo (Parliament
    Building) *304*
  Eira 308
  Esplanadi 305
  Esplanadin Puisto (Esplanade
    Park) 305
  Finlandiatalo (Finlandia Hall) 57,
    301, *304*

Hakasalmi Villa 304
Havis Amanda Fountain 307
Helsinki Festival 301
Hietalahdentori (flea market)
  308
Hotel Kamp 307
Kamp Galleria 307
Hotel Torni 301
Kaivopuisto park 309
Kansallismuseo (National
  Museum) *304*
Kappeli café-restaurant 301,
  305, *308*
Katajanokka 307–8
Kauppatori (Central Market
  Square) 307
Kaupungintalo (City Hall) 307
Kiasma (Museum of
  Contemporary Art) 291, *303*
Lasipalatsi (Glass Palace) 303
Luotsikatu 308
Mannerheimintie 303
May Day Eve 305
Museum of Cultures 301, 304
Night of the Arts 305
Olympiaterminaali (Olympia Quay)
  309
Pohjoisesplanadi 307
Presidentinlinna (Presidential
  Palace) 307
Pulp restaurant 303
Rautatieasema (Railway Station)
  302, 306
Ruohalahti 305
Sanomatalo 303
Sederholmin Talo 307
Senaatintori (Senate Square) 307
shopping 305, 307
Sibelius Academy 58, 304
Sibelius Monument 310
Sibeliuksen Puisto (Sibelius Park)
  310
Stockmann 305
Suomen Kansallisooppera
  (Finnish National Opera House)
  291, 304
Suomen Rakennustaiteen Museo
  (Museum of Finnish
  Architecture) 308–9
Suomen Valokuvataiteen Museo
  (Photography Museum) 305
Svenska Teatern (Swedish
  Theatre) 305
Taideteollisuusmuseo (Museum
  of Art and Design) 308
Teatterimuseo (Theatre Museum)
  305
Temppelinaukion Kirkko 304–5
Tennispalatsi (Tennis Palace) 303
tourist information 301, 307
Tulli-ja Pakkahuone (Customs and
  Bonded Warehouse)
  308
Tuomiokirkko (Helsinki Cathedral)
  307
Ullanlinna 308
Uspenskin Katedraali (Uspenski
  Cathedral) 308
Vanha Kauppahalli (Old Market
  Hall) 307

Hildén, Sara 333
Hvitträsk 318

I

Iisalmi 329
  Evakkokeskus Cultural Centre
  329
  Kuappi restaurant 329
  Olutmestari beer hall 329
Iittala 334
  glass museum 334
Ilkka, Elias 333
Ilomantsi 340–41
  Fighter's House 341
Imatra 327
  Imatrankoski (rapids) 327
Inari 348
  Saamelaismuseo (Siida Sami
  Museum) 348
  Ylä-Lapin Luontokeskus
  (Northern Lapland Visitor
  Centre) 348
Inarijärvi Lake 348
  boat trips 348
  Ukko Island 348
industry
  fishing 61
  pulp and paper 291
Ivalo 347–8

J

Jakobstad (Pietarsaari) 338
  historic sailing ship trips 338
Jansson, Tove 58, 325, 333
Järämä 350
  World War II bunkers 350
Järnefelt, Eero 334
Järvenpää 334
  Ainola 334
  Tuusulanjärvi (lake) 334
Joensuu 340
  Festival of Song 340
  Pohjois-Karjalan Museo (North
  Karelia Museum) 340
  Taidemuseo (Art Museum) 340
**Joulupukin Pajakylä (Santa Claus
  Workshop Village)** 347
Jung, Bertel 306
Jyrängönkoski 330–31
  Siltasaari Fishing Centre 330–31
Jyväskylä 331–2
  1,000 Lakes Rally 332
  Alvar Aalto Museo *57*, 331
  Jyväskylä Arts Festival 332

K

Kajaani 343
Kaksinkantaja 341
Kalajoki 338
Karelia 77, 340–43
  see also individual place names
Karelian Circle Trek 68
Karhunkierros walking route 343
Karhuntassu Tourist Centre 343
Kärkisaari 320
Kastelholm fortress 321
  Cultural History Museum 321

  Karlsgården Open-Air Museum
  321
Kaunissaari Island 319
Keisarin Kosket Lodge 320
Kelvenne Island 331
Kemi 339
  icebreaker excursions 339
  Lumilinna (Snow Castle) 339
Ketomella 350
Kilipsjärvi 335, 350
Kirkenes 349
Kivi, Aleksis 58
  Leah 58
  Seven Brothers 58
Kokkola 338
Kotka 320
  boat trips 320
  Kotka Maretarium 320
  Sapokka Harbour 320
Kouvola 327
Kristinestad (Kristiinankaupunki)
  337
  Merimuseo 337
Kuhmo 342
  Hotel Kalevala 342
  Kalevala Village 342
  Kuhmo Chamber Music Festival
  342
Kukkola 349
Kukkolankoski rapids 339, 349
Kuopio 329
  International Dance and Music
  Festival 329
  Kuopion Kortellimuseo 329
  Kuopion Museo 329
  Ortodoksinen Kirkkomuseo
  (Orthodox Church Museum)
  329
  Tori (Market Place) 329
Kuusamo 343
  see also individual place names
Kuusistan Linna 315
Kymenlaakso (Kymi river valley) 320

L

Laanila 347
Lahti 330
  Kaupungintalo (Town Hall) 330
  Lahden Historiallinen Museo 330
  Lahden Urheilukeskus sports
  centre 330
  Ristinkirkko (Church of the Cross)
  330
lakes 66, 327–35, 343
Langinkoski 320
  Tsar Alexander III's fishing lodge
  320
language 21–2, 36, 294, 315, 321,
  337
Lapland 70, 77, 291, 339, 345–50
  see also individual place names
Lappeenranta 327, *329*
  day cruises to Russia 327
  Etelä-Karjalan Museo (South
  Karelian Museum) 327
  Orthodox Church 327
  Ratsuväkimuseo (Cavalry
  Museum) 327
Lemmenjoki Valley 348

Lieksa 341
  Pielisen Museo (Pielinen Open-Air
    Museum) 341
  Ruuankoski (rapids) 341
Lindfors, Stefan 54
Lindgren, Armas 57, 306, 318
Lindroos, Peter 58
Lintulan Luostari 328–9
literature
  see also individual writers'
    names
  Anglo-Saxon Chronicle 23, 26
  Beowulf 22, 244
Lönnrot, Elias 34, 58
  Kalevala 34, 58, 294, 317, 340,
    341, 342
Loviisa 319–20
Luostotunturi 347
Luoto 310

M

Mäkinen, Tommi 71
Mannerheim, Marshal 41
Mariehamn 321
  Maritime Museum 321
  Pommern museum ship 321
Marti Ahtissari 19
Mattila, Karita 58
media 303
Menesjärvi 348
Messilä 330
Midnight Sun 77, 339, 345, 349,
  350
Mikkeli 328
  Visulahti Family Leisure Centre
    328
Mikkola, Hannu 71
Muhos 343
museums and galleries
  Aboa Vetus and Ars Nova (Turku)
    324
  Aineen Taidemuseo (Aine Art
    Museum) (Tornio) 339
  Alvar Aalto Museo (Jyväskylä) 57,
    331
  Apteekkimuseo (Pharmacy
    Museum) (Turku) 324
  Arctic Centre (Rovaniemi) 345
  Ateneum (Museum of Finnish Art)
    (Helsinki) 302
  Borstö Folk Museum (Nagu)
    315
  Bragen Ulkomuseo (Brage Open-
    Air Museum) (Vaasa) 338
  City Art Museum (Helsinki)
    303–4
  Cultural History Museum
    (Kastelholm fortress) 321
  Design Forum (Helsinki) 303
  Etelä-Karjalan Museo (South
    Karelian Museum)
    (Lappeenranta) 327
  Evakkokeskus Cultural Centre
    (Iisalmi) 329
  Forum Marinum (Maritime Centre)
    (Turku) 324
  Gallén-Kallela Museum
    (Tarvaspää) 318
  glass museum (Iittala) 334

Helsinki Art Museum (Helsinki)
  301
Kalevala Village (Kuhmo) 342
Kansallismuseo (National
  Museum) (Helsinki) 304
Karlsgården Open-Air Museum
  (Kastelholm fortress) 321
Käsityöläismuseo (Handicrafts
  Museum) (Turku) 323
Kiasma (Museum of
  Contemporary Art) (Helsinki)
  291, 303
Kultamuseo (Gold Museum)
  (Tankavaara) 347
Kulttuuruhistoriallinen Museo
  (Museum of Cultural History)
  (Uusikaupunki) 337
Kuopion Kortellimuseo (Kuopio)
  329
Kuopion Museo (Kuopio) 329
Lahden Historiallinen Museo
  (Lahti) 330
Linnoitusmuseo (Frontline
  Museum) (Hanko) 317
Luonnontieteellinen (Natural
  History Museum)
  (Suomenlinna) 310
Lusto (Finnish Forest Museum)
  (Punkaharju) 327
Maritime Museum (Mariehamn)
  321
Merenkulku-Museo (Turku Art
  Museum) (Turku) 323
Military Museum Manege
  (Suomenlinna) 310
Military Officer School (RUK)
  Museum (Hamina) 320
Museum of Cultures (Helsinki)
  301, 304
Muurame Sauna Village 331
Ortodoksinen Kirkkomuseo
  (Orthodox Church Museum)
  (Kuopio) 329
Oulun Taidemuseo (Art Museum)
  (Oulu) 339
Pielisen Museo (Pielinen Open-Air
  Museum) (Lieksa) 341
Pohjanmaan Museo
  (Ostrobothnian Museum)
  (Vaasa) 338
Pohjois-Karjalan Museo (North
  Karelia Museum) (Joensuu)
  340
Pommern museum ship
  (Mariehamn) 321
Porin Taidemuseo (Art Museum)
  (Pori) 337
Porvaristalo (Ekenäs) 317
Pöykkölä Museum (Rovaniemi)
  345
Provincial Museum of Lapland
  (Rovaniemi) 345
Ratsuväkimuseo (Cavalry
  Museum) (Lappeenranta)
  327
Retretti Arts Centre (Punkaharju)
  328
Rettig Palace (Turku) see Aboa
  Vetus and Ars Nova
Saamelaismuseo (Siida Sami

Museum) (Inari) 348
Sara Hildénin Taidmuseo (Sara
  Hildén Art Museum) (Tampere)
  333
Satakunta Museo (Pori) 337
Savonlinna Maakuntamuseo
  (Provincial Museum)
  (Savonlinna) 328
Sibeliuksen Syntymäkoti Museo
  (Sibelius Home Museum)
  (Hämeenlinna) 334
Suomen Lasimuseo (Finnish
  Glass Museum) (Riihimäki)
  334
Suomenlinna Museum
  (Suomenlinna) 309–10
Suomen Rakennustaiteen Museo
  (Museum of Finnish
  Architecture) (Helsinki)
  308–9
Suomen Valokuvataiteen Museo
  (Photography Museum)
  (Helsinki) 305
Taideteollisuusmuseo (Design
  Museum) (Helsinki) 308
Teatterimuseo (Theatre Museum)
  (Helsinki) 305
Tehdasmuseo Vapriikki museum
  (Tampere) 332–3
Tietomaa Science Centre (Oulu)
  339
Turkansaaren Ulkomuseo
  (Turkansaari Open-air
  Museum) (Oulu) 338–9
Ulkomuseo (Open-air Museum)
  (Seurasaari) 310
Voipaalan Kartano (Voipaala
  Manor) (Valkeakoski) 333
Wäinö Aaltosen Museo (Turku)
  324–5
Ylä-Lapin Luontokeskus
  (Northern Lapland Visitor
  Centre) (Inari) 348
Rovaniemi Art Museum 345, 347

N

Naantali 325
  Moomin World 325
Nagu 315
  Borstö Folk Museum 315
  St Olof's Church 315
national parks and nature reserves
  68
  Hiidenporttin Kansallispuisto 68,
    342
  Kevon Luonnonpuisto 349
  Koli Kansallispuisto 342
  Mallan Luonnenpuisto nature
    reserve 350
  Oulangan Kansallispuisto 343
  Päijänteen Kansallispuisto
    331
  Ramsholmen Nature Reserve
    68
  Riisitunturi 343
  Seurasaari 310
  Tammisaaren Saariston
    Kansallispuisto 317
  Tiilikkajärven Kansallispuisto 342

nature and outdoor life 65–69,
71–2
Noras, Arto 58
Northern Lights 345
Nuovo, Frank 54
Nurmes 341–2
    Bomba House 342
    scenic boat trips 342
Nurmi, Paavo 43, 71, 294, 325

O

Oulu 338–9, 343
    Koskikeskus (Rapids Centre) 339
    Oulun Taidemuseo (Art Museum)
    339
    Tietomaa Science Centre 339
    Turkansaaren Ulkomuseo
    (Turkansaari Open-air Museum)
    338–9
Oulujärvi lake 343

P

Pallastunturi fells 349–50
Pallastunturi Hotel complex 349
Palojoensuu 350
Pargas (Parainen) 315
people 293–5
    Karelians 341
    Romany Gypsies 295
    Sami 21, 37, 55, 70, 292, 343,
    347–8, 349
Pihlajasaari 310
Pori 337
    City Hall 337
    jazz festival 58, 337
    Jusélius Mausoleum 337
    Porin Taidemuseo (Art Museum)
    337
    Satakunta Museo 337
Porvoo (Borgå) 318–9
    Albert Edelfelt Atelier 319
    Edelfelt-Vallgren Art Museum 319
    J.L. Runeberg home 319
    Old Porvoo 319
    Porvoo Cathedral 319
    river cruises 319
Prästö 321
Pulkkilanharju (ridge) 331
Punkaharju 327–8
    lake steamer trip to Savonlinna
    328
    Lusto (Forestry Museum) 327
    Kesämaa (Summerland) Leisure
    Centre 328
    Retretti Arts Centre 328
Pyhätunturi 347
Pyhtää 319

R

Raasepori 318
    castle ruins 318
Rauma 337
Rautio, Erkki 58
Reposaari 337
Riihimäki 334
    Suomen Lasimuseo (Finnish
    Glass Museum) 334

rivers
    Aura 323
    Kemijoki 339
    Kymi 320
    Kymijoki 320
    Oulujoki 339
    Tornionjoki 349
    "road of seven bridges" 338
Ropinsalmi 350
Rovaniemi 345
    Arktikum 345
    Arctic Centre 345
    Provincial Museum of Lapland
    345
    Lappia House 345
    Pöykkölä Museum 345
    Rovaniemi Art Museum 345, 347
Ruissalo Island 325
    Ruisrock festival 325
    steamship cruises 325
    Villa Roma 325
Rukatunturi Fells 343
Runokylä 341
    Parppei Pirtti restaurant 341
    Singers Lodge 341
Ryynänen, Eeva 341

S

Saana mountain 350
Saarinen, Eliel 57, 306, 318
Saariselkä 347
Salo 315, 317
    Helisnummen (Helisnummi
    Church) 317
    Tsasouna Church 317
    Uskela Church 317
Salonen, Esa-Pekka 58
Sammatti 317
    Paikkarin Torppa (Paikkari
    Cottage) 317
Santa Claus 347
Santa Claus Workshop Village see
    Joulupukin Pajakylä
Santapark 347
Santalahti 320
Särkkä 310
Sattmark café 315
saunas 290, 309, 312–3, 341
    Finnish Sauna Society
    (Lauttasaari) 310
Savonlinna 328
    International Opera Festival 58,
    328
    lake steamer trips 328
    Olavinlinna castle 328
    Savonlinna Maakuntamuseo
    (Provincial Museum) 328
Schauman, Eugen 39
Seurasaari 310
    Seurasaari National Park 310
    Ulkomuseo (Open-air Museum)
    310
Sevettijärvi 349
    Easter Orthodox festival 349
shopping
    tax-free shopping 321
Sibelius, Jean 58, 334, 341
    Finlandia 58, 334
    Karelian Suite 341

Kullervo 58
    monument 300
Sillanpää, F.E. 58
Snappertuna 318
Sodankylä 347
    Midnight Sun Film Festival 347
Sonck, Lars 306
sports and pastimes 294
    1,000 Lakes Rally (Jyväskylä)
    332
    Arctic Circle Race 335
    canoeing 335
    dog-sledging and reindeer
    sledging 70, 348
    Finlandia Canoe Relay 335
    Finlandia Ski Race and Ski
    Games 330
    fishing and ice fishing 70, 320,
    321, 330–31
    football 71
    gold-panning 345, 347
    golf 321
    golf under the Midnight Sun 70,
    71, 339
    hiking 66, 68, 321, 341, 343,
    345, 349–50
    Ice Hockey 72, 293
    Kesämaa (Summerland) Leisure
    Centre (Punkaharju) 328
    Koskikeskus (Rapids Centre)
    (Oulu) 339
    Lahden Urheilukeskus sports
    centre (Lahti) 330
    motor racing 71, 332
    mountain biking 341
    regatta (Hanko) 319
    skiing and other winter sports
    72, 330, 345, 347, 349
    snowshoe trekking 70
    Visulahti Family Leisure Centre
    (Mikkeli) 328
    water sports 321
Stahlberg, Kaarlo Juho 40
Suomenlinna (Finland's Castle)
    309, 310
    Iso Mustasaari 309
    Korkeasaaren Eläitarha zoo
    310
    Kruunulinna Ehrensvärd
    (Ehrensvärd Crown Castle)
    310
    Luonnontieteellinen (Natural
    History Museum) 310
    Military Museum Manege 310
    Panimo microbrewery 309
    Rannikotykisto Museo (Coast
    Artillery Museum) 310
    Rantakasarmi (Jetty Barracks)
    309
    Suomenlinna Museum 309–10
    Vesikko Submarine 310
    Walhalla restaurant 310
Svartholma sea fortress 320

T

Tampere 332–3
    boat trips 332
    Kaleva Kirkko (church) 332
    Kirjasto (City Library) 332

Näsinneula Observation Tower 333
Sara Hildénin Taidmuseo (Sara Hildén Art Museum) 333
Särkänniemi Park 333
Tammerkoski (rapids) 332
Tampere-talo (Tampere Hall) 332
Tehdasmuseo Vapriiki museum 332–3
Tuomiokirkko (Tampere Cathedral) 332
Tankavaara 347
Kultamuseo (Gold Museum) 347
Tankavaara Gold Village 347
Tarvaspää 318
Gallén-Kallela Museum 318
Tornio 335, 339, 349
Aineen Taidemuseo (Aine Art Museum) 339
Vesitorni water tower 339
transport
cycling in the Åland Islands 321
Turku 315, 323–5, 337
Aboa Vetus and Ars Nova museums 324
Angel Restaurant 324
Apteekkimuseo (Pharmacy Museum) 324
Forum Marinum (Maritime Centre) 324
horse cabs 324
Käsityöläismuseo (Handicrafts Museum) 323
Kauppahalli (Indoor Market Hall) 323

Merenkulku-Museo (Turku Art Museum) 323
Ortodoksinen Kirkko (Orthodox Cathedral) 323
Rettig Palace see Aboa Vetus and Ars Nova
steamship excursions 324
Tuomiokirkko (Turku Cathedral) 323
Turku Cultural Centre 323
Turun Linna (Turku Castle) 323
Urheilupuisto park 325
Wäinö Aaltosen Museo 324–5
Turunmaa archipelago 315
see also individual place names

U

Utsjoki 349
Uunisaari 310
Uusikaupunki (Nystad) 337
Kulttuuruhistoriallinen Museo (Museum of Cultural History) 337
Myllymäki Park 337

V

Vaalimaa 320
Vaasa (Vasa) 337–8
Bragen Ulkomuseo (Brage Open-Air Museum) 338
Pohjanmaan Museo (Ostrobothnian Museum) 338
Wasalandia 338

Valamon Luostari (monastery) 328–9
Valkeakoski 333–4
Valkeakoski Summer Theatre 333
Visavuori 333–4
Voipaalan Kartano (Voipaala Manor) 333
Valkosaari 310
Vatanan, Ari 71
Vuonisjärvi 341
Paateri 341

W

Way of the Four Winds 349
wildlife 341
reindeer 70, 341, 342, 347
Wikström, Emil 333–4
windmills *318*

X

Xon Park 328

NORWAY

Numbers in italics refer to photographs

A

accommodation
hytta 65, 196
Ålesund *190,* 199
Alta 213
Alta Museum 213
Amundsen, Roald 166, 170
Archer, Colin 170
architecture
Art Nouveau at Ålesund 199
stave churches 56, 153, *170,* 176–7, 189, 197
Arctic Circle 208
Polarsirkelsenteret (Arctic Circle Centre) 208
Arendal 173, 176
Arendal Bymuseum (Town Museum) 173, 176
Rådhus (Town Hall) 176
art and crafts 55–6
prehistoric pictographs 168, 213
rose painting 56, 193
Scandinavian design 54
wood carving 193

arts and entertainment
Grieghallen (concert hall) (Bergen) 186
Hardanger fiddle 181, 182
Harmonien orchestra 186
Nationaltheatret (National Theatre) (Oslo) 164
traditional music and dance 182, 193
Åsgårdstrand 170
Munch's Lille Hus (Munch's Little House) 169–70
Askøy 182
Atlanterhavsveien (Atlantic Road) 200
Aurora Borealis see **Northern Lights**
Aursunden lake 193
Averøya 200

B

balestrand 197
Barents, Willem 214
Bergen 77, 178, 182, 185–9
Bergen Akvariet (Aquarium)

187–8
Bergen Billedgalleri (Municipal Art Gallery) 188–9
Bergen International Music Festival 56, 186
Bryggen *184,* 187
Bryggens Museum 187
Domkirke (Cathedral) 187
Fisketorget (Fish Market) *185,* 187
Fløibanen (funicular) 188
Fløyen mountain 188
Gamle Bergen 153
Grieghallen (concert hall) 186
Håkonshallen 188
Hanseatiske Museum 187
Korskirken 187
Mariakirken (St Mary's Church) 187
Raftohuset – Menneskerettighetenes Hus (Rafto Human Rights House) 189
Rasmus Meyers Samlinger (Rasmus Meyer Collection) 189
shopping 187

Stenersens Samling 189
Torgalmenningen 187
Bodø *207*, 208
Borre Nasjonalpark 169
Brønnøysund 208
Brundtland, Gro Harlem 153
Bud 200
Buekorps 186
Bull, Ole 56, 181, 189
statue in Bergen *187*

C

churches and cathedrals
Domkirke (Cathedral) (Bergen)
187
Domkirken (Cathedral)
(Stavanger) 181
Drøbak Kirke (Drøbak) 168
Fantoft Stave Church (Paradis)
189
Ishavskatedralen (Arctic Ocean
Cathedral) (Tromsø) *203*, 212
Korskirken (Bergen) 187
Mariakirken (St Mary's) (Bergen)
187
Nidarosdom (Nidaros Cathedral)
(Trondheim) 153, *205*, 206,
209
stave church (Borgund) 56, 153
stave church (Heddal) 56, 153,
176–7, *182*
Urnes Stavkirke (stave church)
(Luster) 56, 197
Utstein Kloster (Mosterøy Island)
178
climate 153, 161
arctic 212, 214
culture and traditions 55–6
trolls *191*

D–E

Dombås 193–4
Drøbak 168, *169*
Drøbak Kirke (church) 168
Follo Museum (Heritage Museum)
168
Oscarsborg Festning (Fort)
168
Du Chaillu, Paul Belloni 194
Land of the Midnight Sun 194
Duun, Olav 154
economy 43–4
Eid 198
Eidsvoll 167
Eidsvollbyningen (Memorial
Building) 167–8
Elverum 193
Erik of Pomerania 33, 115

F

Fåberg 192
Norsk Vegmuseum (Road
Transport Museum) 192
Fedje 182
festivals and events
Battle of Stiklestad re-enactment
(Stiklestad) 209

Bergen International Music
Festival (Bergen) 56, 186
blues festival (Hell) 153, 207
Emigration Festival (Stavanger)
179
Haugesund International Film
Festival 155
Hollmenkollen Ski Festival (Oslo)
161, 165
Ibsen Festival (Oslo) 164
International Trad Jazz Festival
(Haugesund) 179
Jazz Festival (Oslo) 161
Lofotfiske (Kabelvåg) 211
Molde International Jazz Festival
(Molde) 200
National Day *189*
Norwegian Film Festival
(Haugesund) 179
Olsok (St Olav's day) 169
Olsokspelet (St Olav's Play)
(Stiklestad) 207–8
St Olav Festival (Trondheim)
208
Finse 67, 195
Fjærland 197
Norsk Bremuseum (Norwegian
Glacier Museum) 197
fjords 66, *76, 153*, 177, 181–2,
187, 191, 196–200
cruises 187, *202–3*
Flam 197
scenic railway *197*
Flekkefjord 173
Florø 198
Sogn og Fjordane Kystmuseet
(Coastal Museum) 198
food and drink 62–3
alcohol restriction 41
aquavit 62
Arctic Ale 212
distilleries 191–2
geitost (goat's cheese) 193
Løten Brænderi distillery (Løten)
191–2
Mack brewery (Tromsø) 212
Førde 197
Førdefjord 197
Sunnfjord Museum 197
Fosse, Jon 154
Foyn, Svend 170
Frederikstad 168
Oldtidsveien (Highway of the
Ancients) 168
Frederiksten 34

G

Gaup, Nils 213
Pathfinder 213
Geirangerfjorden 198–9
Gjende lake 195
glaciers 67
Briksdalsbreen 198
Jostedalsbreen 67, 196, 197,
198, *201*
Norsk Bremuseum (Norwegian
Glacier Museum) (Fjærland)
197
Grieg, Edvard 36, 56, 181, 182,

185–6, 195
Peer Gynt 195
Grimstad 173
Grimstad Bymuseum (Town
Museum) 173
Gudbrandsdalen 191, 193–4

H

Haav, Anne 193
Hafjell 192
Håkon Håkonson 170, 206
Håkon VII 39, 43
Halden 168
Frederiksten Festning (Fort)
museums 168–9
Haldenkanal (canal) 169
see also **Ørje**
Hamar 191
Hedemarksmuseet og
Domkirkeodden (Hedemark
Museum and Cathedral Point)
191
Jernbanemuseet (National
Museum of Railway Transport)
191
Hamsun, Knut 167
Sult (Hunger) 167
Harald Fairhair 25
Harald I Hårfagre 181
Harald V 42
Harald Hardrade 26, 161
Hardangerfjorden 181
Haugesund 179
International Trad Jazz Festival
179
Norwegian Film Festival 179
Heddal 176–7
Heddal Bygdetun (Rural Museum)
177
stave church 56, 153, 176–7,
182
Helberg, Claus 180
Hell 153, 207
blues festival 153, 207
Hella 197
Heyerdahl, Thor 166, 170
Hidra Island 173
Hjemmeluft 213
Honningsvag 214
Nordkappmuséet (North Cape
Museum) 214
Hordaland 173, 181–2, *183*
see also individual place names
Horten 169
Marinemuseet (Naval Museum)
169
Hovig, Jan Inge 212
Husaby, Hallvard *see* **St Hallvard**

I–J

Ibsen, Henrik 36, 56, 164, 173, 176
immigration issue 154–5, 162
industry
fishing and fish farming 61, 182,
199, 211
metal foundries 208
oil 44, 151, 153, 179, 181,
182

Jan Mayen 40
Jonsson, Tor 154

K

Kabelvåg 211
  Lofotfiske 211
Karasjok 213
Karmøy Island 177
Kautokeino 213
Kierulf, Halfdan 56
Kinsarvik 181–2
Kragerø 171, 176, 178
Kristiansand 173
  Christiansholm Festning
    (fortress) 173
  Kristiansand Dyrepark 173
Kristiansund 200
Kvaløya 212
Kvinesdal 173
Kvinnfoss (Lady's Waterfall) 197

L

Laksestudioet 178
  Kolbeinstveit Museum (Rural
    Museum) 178
language 21–2, 36, 154, 213
Lapland 70, 77
Larvik 170
  Farriskilde (Farris Spring) 170
Lillehammer 192
  Maihaugen open-air museum 192
  Winter Olympic facilities 192
Lillesand 173
Lindesnes Fyr (lighthouse) 173
literature
  see also individual writers'
    names
  Anglo-Saxon Chronicle 23, 26
  Beowulf 22, 244
Lofoten Islands 153, 203, 211
  see also individual place names
Longyearbyen 214
Longyear, John 214
Løten 191–2
  Løiten Lys candle factory 192
  Løten Brænderi distillery 191–2
Luster 197
  Urnes Stavkirke (stave church)
    56, 197
Lysøen (Island of Light) 189

M

Maelstrom 211
Magnus 31
Mandal 176
Margarethe 32–3
Mellemverftet 200
Memurubu 196
Midnight Sun 203, 212
Mjøsa lake 191
Mo i Rana 208
Molde 200
  Molde International Jazz Festival
    200
Morgedal 176
Mosjøen 208
Moskenesøya 211

Moskenstraumen 211
Mosterøy Island 178
  Utstein Kloster (church) 178
mountains
  Besseggen ridge 195
  Dovrefjell (Dovre Mountains)
    193–5
  Galdhøpiggen 67
  Glitterind 67
  Gråkallen (Old Man) 205
  Gvepseborg 177
  Hardangervidda 181, 195
  Jotunheimen Mountains 67, 195,
    196
  Rondane range 196
  Snøhetta 194
Munch, Edvard 36, 56, 163
  Shrik (Scream) 56, 163
museums and galleries
  Alta Museum (Alta) 213
  Arendal Bymuseum (Arendal)
    173, 176
  Bergen Billedgalleri (Municipal Art
    Gallery) (Bergen) 188–9
  Borgarsyssel Museum
    (Sarpsborg) 169
  Bryggen Museum (Bergen)
    187
  Det Internasjonale
    Barnekunstmuseet
    (International Museum of
    Children's Art) (Oslo) 161,
    163, 164
  Emanuel Vigeland Museum (Oslo)
    164
  Follo Museum (Heritage Museum)
    (Drøbak) 168
  Frammuseet (Fram Museum)
    (Oslo) 166
  Frederiksten Festning museums
    (Halden) 168–9
  Grimstad Ibsen-museet (Town
    Museum) (Grimstad) 173
  Hardanger Folkemuseum (Utne)
    181
  Hanseatiske Museum (Bergen)
    187
  Heddal Bygdetun (Rural Museum)
    (Heddal) 177
  Hedemarksmuseet og
    Domkirkeodden (Hedemark
    Museum and Cathedral Point)
    (Hamar) 191
  Hermetikkmuséet (Canning
    Museum) (Stavanger) 181
  Ibsen-museet (Ibsen Museum)
    (Oslo) 164
  Jernbanemuseet (National
    Museum of Railway Transport)
    (Hamar) 191
  Kanalmuseum (Ørje) 169
  Kolbeinstveit Museum (Rural
    Museum) (Laksestudioet) 178
  Kon-Tiki Museum (Oslo) 166
  Maihaugen open-air museum
    (Lillehammer) 192
  Marinemuseet (Naval Museum)
    (Horten) 169
  Munch-museet (Munch Museum)
    (Oslo) 163

Nasjonalgalleriet (National
  Gallery) (Oslo) 56, 153,
  163
Nordkappmuséet (North Cape
  Museum) (Honningsvag) 214
Nordnorsk Kunstmuseum (North
  Norway Art Museum) (Tromsø)
  212
Norges Hjemmefrontmuseum
  (Norway's Resistance
  Museum) (Oslo) 40, 164–5
Norsk Bremuseum (Norwegian
  Glacier Museum) (Fjærland)
  197
Norsk Folkemuseum (Oslo) 161
Norsk Industriarbeidermuseum
  (Norwegian Industrial Workers
  Museum) (Rjukan) 177
Norsk Oljemuseum (Norwegian
  Petroleum Museum)
  (Stavanger) 181
Norsk Sjøfartsmuseum
  (Norwegian Maritime Museum)
  (Oslo) 166
Norsk Vegmuseum (Road
  Transport Museum) (Fåberg)
  192
Norwegian Crown Jewels
  (Trondheim) 206
Polarsirkelsenteret (Arctic Circle
  Centre) 208
Rasmus Meyers Samlinger
  (Rasmus Meyer Collection)
  (Bergen) 189
Skimuseet (Ski Museum) (Oslo)
  161, 165
Sogn og Fjordane Kystmuseet
  (Coastal Museum) (Florø)
  198
Sunnfjord Museum (Førdefjord)
  198
Telemark Museum (Skien) 176
Tromsø Museum (Tromsø) 212
Vikingskipshuset (Viking Ship
  Museum) (Oslo) 28, 153, 161,
  166
Myrdal 197
  scenic railway 197

N

Nansen, Fridtjof 166
National Parks 68
  Jostedalsbreen 196
nature and outdoor life 65–69,
  71–2
Nordfjorden 198
Nordhordland 182
Nordkapp (North Cape) 153,
  213–4
  Children of the World Monument
    214
  Nordkapphallen (North Cape Hall)
    214
Norheim, Sondre 72, 176
Northern Lights 203, 212, 214
Notodden 176
Nøtterøy 170
Ny Ålesund 214
  Svalbard Rocket Range 214

O

Olav Haraldsson (St Olav) 154, 205, 206, 207, 209
Olav V 177, 206
Olav Tryggvason 26, 209
  statue (Trondheim) 206
Oluf 32–3
Opsvik, Peter 54
Oseberghaugen Viking site 170
Oslo 77, 161–70
  Aker Brygge (Aker Quay) 161, *167*
  Akershus Slott og Festning (Castle) 161, 164–5
  Norges Hjemmefrontmuseum (Norway's Resistance Museum) 40, 164–5
  Bygdøy peninsula 166
  Det Internasjonale Barnekunstmuseet (International Museum of Children's Art) 161, *163,* 164
  Det Kongelige Slott (Royal Palace) 162–3
  Det Norske Utvandrersenteret (Emigration Centre) (Stavanger) 179
  Emanuel Vigeland Museum 164
  Frammuseet (Fram Museum) 166
  Frogner Park 161, 163, *168*
  Holmenkollbakken (Hollmenkollen Ski Jump) *165*
  Hollmenkollen Ski Festival 161, 165
  Ibsen Festival 164
  Ibsen-museet (Ibsen Museum) 164
  Jazz Festival 161
  Kon-Tiki Museum 166
  Munch-museet (Munch Museum) 163
  Nasjonalgalleriet (National Gallery) 56, 153, 163
  Nationaltheatret (National Theatre) 164
  Norsk Folkemuseum 161
  Norsk Sjøfartsmuseum (Norwegian Maritime Museum) 166
  Oslo Opera House 163
  Oslomarka (Oslo's fields) 165–6
  Oslo Sentralstasjon (Oslo Central Station) 163
  Rådhuset (City Hall) 163
  Skimuseet (Ski Museum) 161, 165
  Stortinget (Parliament) 162
  tourist information 161
  transport 161, 166–7
  Tryvannstårnet (Tryvann Tower) 161
  Vigelandsparken (Vigeland Park) *160, 162,* 163
  Vikingskipshuset (Viking Ship Museum) *28,* 153, 161, 166
Oslomarka 161
Østerdalen 191, 193
Osterøy 182

P–Q

Paradis 189
  Fantoft Stave Church 189
Peer Gyntveien (Peer Gynt Way) *196*
people 151, 153–5, 170, 179, 181
  Sami 21, *37,* 55, *70,* 213, *214*
plant life 214
Polarsirkel see **Arctic Circle**
polar winter 214
politics 153, 167–8
population 153
Preikestolen (Pulpit Rock) 153, *172, 177*
Quisling, Vidkun 43

R

Rafto Prize for Human Rights 189
Rafto, Thoralf 189
Reine 211
rivers
  Glomma 193
  Jølstra 1978
  Lågen 193
  Nidelva 205–6, 209
  Suldalslågen 178
Rjukan 40, 177, 180
  Norsk Industriarbeidermuseum (Norwegian Industrial Workers Museum) 177
Rogaland 173, 177–8
  see also individual place names
Røros 153, *192,* 193
Runde 199–200

S

St Hallvard 166
Sandefjord 170
  Badeparken 170
  Gokstadhaugen Viking burial site 170
  Preståsen 170
Sandvig, Anders 192
Sarpsborg 169
  Borgarsyssel Museum 169
Skien 176
  Telemark Museum 176
Skipper, Essau and John 196
  Three in Norway by Two of Them 196
Skykkjedalsfossen waterfall 182
Sogndal 197
Sognefjorden 196–7
Sogn og Fjordane 196, *197*
  see also individual place names
Sørlandet 173
  see also individual place names
Sotra 182
Sparre, Victor 212
Spitsbergen see **Svalbard**
sports and pastimes 71
  Birkebeiner race 192
  cycling and mountain-biking 170
  dog-sledging and reindeer sleigh rides 70
  fishing and ice fishing 69, 70, 71, 178, 182
  football 71
  golf under the Midnight Sun 70, 71
  hang gliding and paragliding 182
  hiking and walking 67, 165–6, 170, 182, 194, 195–6, 205
  Holmenkollbakken (Hollmenkollen Ski Jump) (Oslo) *165*
  Hollmenkollen Ski Festival (Oslo) 161, 165
  sailing and boating *14,* 165, 170, 177, 178
  skiing and other winter sports 72, 165, 166, 178, 182, 192, 195–6, 199, 205
  Skimuseet (Ski Museum) (Oslo) 161, 165
  snowshoe trekking 70
  Styrkeprøven (Trial of Strength) bicycle race (Trondheim) 207
  Telemark skiing 72, 176
  watersports 165, 182
  Winter Olympics facilities (Lillehammer) 192
Stavanger *179,* 181
  Alexander Kielland Minnesmerke (monument) 181
  Breiavatnet 181
  Det Norske Utvandrersenteret (Emigration Centre) 179
  Domkirken (Cathedral) 181
  Emigration Festival 179
  Gamle Stavanger (Old Stavanger) 181
  Hermetikkmuséet (Canning Museum) 181
  Kvernevik 181
  Norsk Oljemuseum (Norwegian Petroleum Museum) 181
  Sverd i fjell monument 181
Steinkjer 208
Stiklestad 207, 209
  Battle of Stiklestad re-enactment 209
  Olsokspelet (St Olav's Play) 207–8
Stryn 199
Svalbard (Spitsbergen) archipelago 40, 214
Svalbard Satellite Station 214
Svendsen, Johan 56
Svolvær 211

T

Telemark 176–7
  see also individual place names
"Telemark, Heroes of" 40, 177, *180*
Telemarkskanal 1 76
Tjøme 170
Todalfjorden 200
  Svinvik Arboret (Arboretum) 200
Tønsberg 170
  island tours 170
  Nordbyen 170
  Slottsfjellet fortress 170
  Storgata 170
transport
  boat services and sightseeing trips 169, 178–9, 191, 194–5, 200, 202–3, 208

mountain railway *197*
Troldhaugen 186
Trollfjorden *203*
Trollheimen 200
Tromsø 203, 211–2
Fjellheisen cable car *212*
Ishavskatedralen (Arctic Ocean Cathedral) *203*, 212
Mack brewery 212
nightlife 211
Nordnorsk Kunstmuseum (North Norway Art Museum) 212
Tromsø Museum 212
Tromsø Satellite Station 212
Trondheim *204*, 205–7
cycling in the city 206–7
Erkebispegården (Archbishop's Manor) 206
Nidarosdomen (Nidaros Cathedral) 153, *205*, 206, 209
Norwegian Crown Jewels 206
St Olav Festival 208
Styrkeprøven (Trial of Strength) bicycle race 207
Trampe bicycle lift 207
TusenFryd amusement park 168

U

Ulefoss 176
Ullensvang 182
Ulsteinvik 200
Uppdal, Kristofer 154
Utne 181
Hardanger Folkemuseum 181
Utne Hotel 181

V–W

Vardø 213
Verdens Ende (World's End) 170
Vesaas, Halldis Moren 154
Vesterøy peninsula 170
Vigeland, Emanuel 164
Vigeland, Gustav 163
Voss 182
wildlife
bird-watching 178, 199, 203
polar bears *214*
reindeer 70, 195, *214*
Salmon leaping 178

SWEDEN

Numbers in italics refer to photographs

A

Abisko 281
Kungsleden (King's Trail) 67, 281
Åby Säteri 259
Nordens Ark nature park 259
accommodation
Ice Hotel (Jukkasjärvi) 70, 223, 280
Miekak fishing camp 280
mountain stations 67
Tjuonajokk fishing camp 280
Albrecht 32–3
Alvastra Kloster (Cistercian monastery) 264
architecture
fäbodar 267
of Southern Sweden 252
Arctic Circle 279
Åre winter sports resort 72, *274*
Arjeplog 277
Silvermuséet (Silver Museum) 277
art and crafts 53–5
Dalahäst (Dala horse) 267, *269*
Dalarna folk art 269
Nittsjö Keramik (pottery) (Rättvik) 269
Scandinavian design 54
Swedish design 223, 233, 241
Törngrens Krukmakeri pottery (Falkenberg) 255
traditional crafts 238, 269
arts and entertainment
Dalhalla outdoor concert arena (Rättvik) 267
Drottningholms Slottsteater (Stockholm) 53, *245*
folk music 267, 281
Götaplatsen cultural centre (Göteborg) 258
Göteborgsoperan (Opera House) (Göteborg) 256
Göteborg Symphony Orchestra (Göteborg) 223, 258
Konserthuset (Concert Hall) (Göteborg) 258
Kulturhuset (Culture House) (Stockholm) 240
Arvidsjaur 279
Lappstaden Sami village 279

B

beaches 65
Blekinge 251
of Gotland 253
Haverdalsstrand 255
Öland Island 251
Olofsby 255
Östra Strand 255
Ringenäs 255
Skrea Strand 255
West Coast 255
Bellman, Carl 53
Berg 265
Bergman, Ingmar 55, 244, 253
Fanny and Alexander 244
Bergman, Ingrid 55, 59
Bernadotte, Count Folke 43
Bernadotte, Jean-Baptiste 35–6, 42
Bingsjö 267
spelmansstämmor (folk musicians' rallies) 267
Birka 28, 29
Björg, Björn 71
Björkborn Herrgård 263
Nobelmuséet 263
Björkliden 72
Blå Vägen (Blue Highway) 277
Blekinge 251
Boden 282
Garnisonsmuséet (Garrison Museum) 282
Boglösa 244
Bohuslän archipelago 65, 258
Bollnäs 273
Bönan 272
Engeltofta 272
Bönhamn *281*
Arne's Sjöbod restaurant 281
Borås 264
Textilmuséet (Textile Museum) 264
Borgholm 251
Borgholm Slott (Castle) 251
Bredarör 251
King's Grave (Kiviksgraven) 251

C

Carl Gustaf 42
Carl XVI Gustaf 72
castles
Borgholm Slott 251
Carlstens Fästning (Fortress) (Marstrand) 258
Drottningholms Slott (Stockholm) *34*, 233, 243, *245*
Gripsholms Slott (Mariefred) 244
Halmstad Slott 255
Kalmar Slott *251*, 252
Karlsborg 264, 265
Kärnan (Helsingborg) 251
Läckö Slott 263–4
Malmöhus (Malmö) 249
Mariestad Slott 263
Örebro 263
Sölvesborg Slott 251
Tjolöholm 256
Uppsala 244
Varbergs 255
Visborg 33
churches
Domkyrkan (Cathedral) (Lund) 250
Domkyrkan (Cathedral) (Uppsala) *244*

Habo Kyrka (Habo) 264
Husaby Church (Husaby) 263
monastery church (Vreta) 265
St Laurenti (Falkenberg) 255
St Nikolai (Halmstad) 255
St Petri Kyrka (Cathedral)
(Malmö) 249
Sami church (Gällivare) 279
Storkyrkan (Cathedral)
(Stockholm) 234
climate 225, 234, 385
customs and folklore 223, 267
see also etiquette, festivals and
events
Lake Storsjön monster 274

D

Dalarna 77, 267–9
see also individual place names
Dalsland province 261
see also individual place names
Dalslands Kanal 261
Dellenbygden 273
Delsbo 273
Delsbostämman folk fiddlers'
festival 273
Dorotea 277
Dyvelsten 261
Flottningsmuséet (Log Rafting
Museum) 261

E

economy 43–4, 227
Eketorp ancient burial site 251
Ericsson, John 263
Erik I 31, 32, 244
etiquette 226

F

Falkenberg 255
St Laurenti Church 255
Törngrens Krukmakeri pottery
255
Falkoping 33
Falsterbo 251
Falu Gruva (Falu Mine) 268
Falun 268
Bergslagen 268
Fårö 253
festivals and events
Delsbostämman folk fiddlers'
festival (Delsbo) 273
Equestrian Week (Malmö) 249
Falls Festival (Trollhättan) 264
Falu Folk Music Festival 267
folk music festival (Ransäter)
262
Hälsingehambo folk dance
festival (Järvsö) 272, 273
handicraft festival (Hjo) 264
hyttsill ("glassworks herring")
evenings (Orrefors) 252
Midsummer celebrations 233,
266
Music on Lake Siljan 267
Renaissance Festival (Kalmar)
252

St Lucia celebrations (Stockholm)
233
spelmansstämmor (folk
musicians' rallies) (Bingsjö)
267
summer festivals (Rättvik) 267
Walpurgis Night (Stockholm) 233
Filipstad 263
Fiskebäckskil 259
Flatruet Plateau 274
food and drink 62–3, 226
alcohol restrictions 41, 226
aquavit 62
confectionary 273
crayfish 243
schnapps 227
smörgåsbord 62
Strömstad shrimps 259
Swedish specialities 272
Forsvik 265
Frösön 274
Funäsdalen 274
Furuviksparken 271–2

G

Gällivare 279
mining museum 279
Sami church 279
Gamla Viken 255
Gammelstad 282
Friluftsmuséet Hägnan open-air
museum 282
Garbo, Greta 55
Gästrikland 271–2
see also individual place names
Gävle 271
Länsmuséet 271
Sveriges Järnvägsmuseum
(Railway Museum) 271
Glasriket (Glass Kingdom) 252
Glösa 274
prehistoric rock carvings 274
Glumslöv 251
Göta Kanal 77, 223, 264, 265
cruises 265
cycle trails 69
Göteborg (Gothenburg) 223,
256–8, 265
"Aveyn" (The Avenue) 257
Botaniska Trädgården (Botanical
Gardens) 258
Götaplatsen cultural centre 257
Göteborgsoperan (Opera House)
256
Göteborgs Turistbyrå (Tourist
Office) 257
harbourfront 257
Konserthuset (Concert Hall) 258
Kungsportsplatsen 257
Konstmuséet (Art Museum) 258
Lisebergs Nöjespark amusement
park 258, 259
Maritima Centrum (Maritime
Centre) 256–7
Nordstan shopping centre 257
Padden sightseeing boats 257
Röhsska Muséet 257–8
Saluhallen market 257
Slottskogen park 258

transport 257
Gotland 33, 253
see also individual place names
Granner, Olga 243
Gullmarn fjord 259
Gustavus II Adolphus 34
Gustav III 52, 53
Gustav VI Adolf 249
Gustav Vasa 18, 30, 234, 301

H

Habo 264
Habo Kyrka (church) 264
Hallands Väderö 255
Hälsingland 272–3
see also individual place names
Halmstad 255
Halmstad Slott (Castle) 255
St Nikolai Church 255
Haparanda 282
Härjedalen province 273–4
see also individual place names
Härnösand 281
open-air museum 281
Håverud 261
health
mosquitoes 281
Hedemora 268–9
Husbyringen museum trail 268–9
Helsingborg 249, 251
Kärnan (Castle) 251
Sofiero Palace gardens 249
Hemavan 67
Hjo 264
handicraft festival 264
lake cruises 264
Höga Kusten Bridge 281
Höga Kusten walk 282
Höganäs 251
Hudiksvall 272
Fiskarstan 272
Husaby 263
Husaby Church 263
Hydman-Vallien, Ulrika 54

I

immigration issues 227
industry
engineering 265
fishing 61
glass 252
mining 277, 279, 280
motor 44, 264
shipping 256
iron and steel 268, 272
Swedish film industry 251
textiles 264
timber, paper and pulp 282

J

Jädraås 272
steam trains to Tallås 272
Jämtland province 273, 274
see also individual place names
Järvsö 273
Hälsingehambo folk dance
festival 272, 273

Johnson, Eyvind 55
Jokkmokk 279
 Ájtte Svenskt Fjäll-och
  Samemuseum (Swedish
  Mountain and Sami Museum)
  279
Jukkasjärvi 280
 Ice Hotel 280
Jungfrukusten (Virgin Coast) 271

K

Kalmar 33, 252
 Kalmar Slott (Castle) *251*, 252
 Renaissance Festival 252
Karesuando 280
Karl XII 34
Karl XIIs Väg (Trail) 261
Karlfeldt, Erik Axel 55
Karlsborg 264, 265
 Fästning (Fortress) 264, 265
Karlskrona 251
Karlstad 261
 Mariebergsskogen park 261
Kiruna 280
 Kirunavaara Mine 280
 Samegård 280
Klädesholmen *254*
Konghelle 31
Kramfors 281
Kristianopel 251
Kristianstad 251
 Filmmuséet (film museum) 251
Kristinehamm 263
Kungsbacka 256

L

Lagerkvist, Pär 55
Lagerlöf, Selma 53, 55, 262
 Gösta Berlings Saga 53, 262, 263
 The Wonderful Adventures of Nils
  55, 262
lakes
 Asplången 265
 Hornborgasjön 264
 Mälaren 69, 243, 244
 Rostojaure 280
 Roxen 265
 Siljan 268
 Storsjön 274
 Vänern 77, 261–4, 265
 Vättern 77, 261, 264, 265
language 21–2, 402
Lapland 70, 77, *276*, 277–82
Larsson, Carl and Karin 54, 55,
 223, 267, 269
Lassekrog 272
 Albert Vikstens Kijby (Cabin
  Village) 272
Lidköping 262, 263
 market 262
 Rörstrand porcelain factory 263
Lindgren, Astrid 55, 237
 Emil in Lönneberga 55
 Pippi Longstocking 55
Linnaeus, Carl 36
literature
 see also individual writers'
  names

Anglo-Saxon Chronicle 23, 26
Beowulf 22, 244
Ljusbodarnas Fäbodar 267–8
Ljusdal 272
Luleå 282
Lummelundagrottorna caves 253
Lund 250–51
 Domkyrkan (Cathedral) 250
 Kulturhistoriska Muséet (Cultural
  History Museum) 250
Lycksele 277
 Lycksele Djurpark (zoo) 277
Lysekil 259
 boat trips 259
 Havets Hus (Sea Aquarium) 259

M

Malmö 249–50
 Equestrian Week *249*
 Form Design Centre 250
 Lilla Torg (Little Square) 250
 Malmöhus (castle) 249
 Kommendants Hus
  (Commander's House) 249
 Malmömuseer 249
 Rådhuset (City Hall) 249
 Rooseum 250
 St Petri Kyrka (Cathedral) 250
 Saluhallen 250
 Stadshuset 249–50
 Stortorget 249
Mårbacka 262
Mariefred 244
 Gripsholms Slott (Castle) 244
Mariestad 263
 Mariestad Slott (Castle) 263
Marstrand 258
 Carlstens Fästning (Fortress) 258
Martinson, Harry 55
Måviken 281
Mem 265
Midnight Sun 279, *282*
Milles, Carl 243–4
Moberg, Vilhelm 55
 Kristina from Duvemåla 55
 The Emigrants 55
monarchy 42
Mora *268*, 269
 Zorngården *268*
 Zornmuséet 268
Mörrum 251
 Laxens Hus 251
Motala 265
mountains 274
 Dundret 279
 Galtisbuouda 279
 Gluggberget 273
 Kaarevaara 280
 Kebnekaise 280
 Kittelfjäll 277
 Öjeberget 273
 Vemdalsfjällen 274
museums and galleries
 Ajtte Svenskt Fjäll-och
  Samemuseum (Swedish
  Mountain and Sami Museum)
  (Jokkmokk) 279
 Birka Vikingastaden (Stockholm)
  243

Bruksmuséet (ironworks
 museum) (Iggesund) 272
Carl and Karin Larsson museum
 (Sundborn) 54
Filmmuséet (film museum)
 (Kristianstad) 251
Flottningsmuséet (Log Rafting
 Museum) (Dyvelsten) 261
Friluftsmuséet Hägnan open-air
 museum (Gammelstad) 282
Gammlia Friluftsmuseum open-air
 museum (Umeå) 282
Garnisonsmuséet (Garrison
 Museum) (Boden) 282
Guldrummet (Gold Room)
 (Stockholm) 239
Hallsylska Muséet (Hallwyl
 Collection) (Stockholm) 240
Hembygdsgården heritage village
 (Ransäter) 261–2
Historiska Muséet (Museum of
 National Antiquities)
 (Stockholm) 233, 239
Husbyringen museum trail
 (Hedemora) 268–9
Jamtli open-air museum
 (Östersund) 274
Källers Karamellmuseum (Hållbo)
 273
Konstmuseum (Art Museum)
 (Göteborg) 258
Kulturen (Cultural History
 Museum) (Lund) 250
Länsmuséet (Gävle) 271
Malmömuseer (Malmö) 249
Maritiman (Maritime Centre)
 (Göteborg) 256
Medeltidsmuseum (Medieval
 Museum) (Stockholm) 236
mining museum (Gällivare) 279
Moderna Muséet (Stockholm) 55,
 233, 236–7
Nationalmuseum (National
 Museum of Fine Arts)
 (Stockholm) 237
Naturhistoriska Riksmuséet
 (Museum of Natural History)
 (Stockholm) 239
Nobelmuséet (Björkborn
 Herrgård) 263
Nordiska Muséet (Nordic
 Museum) (Stockholm) 238
open-air museum (Härnösand)
 281
Röhsska Muséet (Göteborg)
 257–8
Silvermuséet (Silver Museum)
 (Arjeplog) 277
Skansen open-air museum
 (Stockholm) 233, 237, *238*
Stadsmuséet (City Museum)
 (Stockholm) 236
Strindbergsmuséet (Strindberg
 Museum) (Stockholm) 242
Sveriges Järnvägsmuseum
 (Railway Museum) (Gävle) 271
Textilmuséet (Textile Museum)
 (Borås) 264
Utvandrarnas Hus (House of the
 Emigrants) (Växjö) 252

Vasamuséet (Vasa Museum)
(Stockholm) 233, *238*,
239
Zornmuséet (Mora) 268

N

Nasafjäll 277
national parks and nature reserves
68
Dalby Söderskog 68
Kristianstad Vattenriket (Water
Kingdom) 251
Kroppefjällen nature reserve 261
Muddus *279*
Nordens Ark nature park (Åby
Säteri) 259
Padjelanta 70, *279*
Skuleskogen 282
Stora Sjöfallet 279
Store Moss 68
nature and outdoor life 65–69, 71–2
Nobel, Alfred *36*, 263
Nobel Prizes
literature 55, 58, 167, 262
peace 154
Nordingrå Peninsula 281
Norra Ulvön 282
Norrfällsviken 281
Norrköping 244
Kolmården Djurpark 244

O–P

Öland Island 251
see also individual place names
Olof Skötkonung 263
Omne bay 281
Örebro 263
castle 263
Öresund bridge 44, *45*, 77, 249
Örnsköldsvik 282
Orrefors 252
glass factory visits 252
hyttsill ("glassworks herring")
evenings 252
Orust 258–9
Östberg, Ragnar 234
Östersund 274
Jamtli open-air museum 274
Ottenby bird station 251–2
Karl Xs Mur (Karl X's Wall) 252
Överkalix 282
Övik *see* Örnsköldsvik
Palme, Olof 44
people 225–7
Sami 21, *37*, 55, 70, 223, *277*,
279, *282*
Peterson-Berger, Wilhelm 274
Arnljot 274
Piteå 282
Porjus 279
Prästbodarna Fäbodar 268

R

Ransäter 261
folk music festival 262
Hembygdsgården heritage village
261–2

Rättvik 267
Dalhalla outdoor concert arena
267
Nittsjö Keramik (pottery) 269
summer festivals 267
rivers
Ångermanälven 274
Åtran 255
Göta 264, 265
Indalsälven 274
Kaitumälven 280
Kalixälven 280, 282
Klarälven 261–2
Ljungan 274
Ljusnan 274
Ljusnandalen 272
Mörrum 69, 251
Nissan 255
Piteälven 280
Torneälven 280, 282
Upperud 261
Rökeskyrka 264
stone of Rök 264
Romakloster 253
Romme Alpin ski resort 269
Rottneros Park 263

S

St Erik 244
Sälen winter sports resort 72, 269
Särö 256
Särö Västerskog 256
Säter 269
Sätergläntan 269
Hemslöjdens Gård 269
Sergel, John Tobias 239
Sidén, Ann-Sofi 55
Sigtuna 244
Silvervägen (Silver Road) 277
Sjötorp 265
Skåne 249–52
see also individual place names
Skanör 251
Skanörs Ljung 251
Skara 264
Skara Sommarland 264
Smögen 259
Söderhamn 272
boat trips 272
Södra Ulvön 282
Sölvesborg 251
Sölvesborg Slott (Castle) 251
Sörmlandsleden (Sörmland Route)
67
sports and pastimes
dog-sledging and reindeer sleigh
rides 70, 280
fishing and ice fishing 69, 70,
251, 274, 277, 279, 280
football 71
gold-panning 279
golf 255, 279
golf under the Midnight Sun 70,
71
hiking and walking 66, 67, 261,
273, 274, 279
sailing and boating *14*, 251,
261, 273
skiing and other winter sports

71–2, 269, 274, 282
snowshoe trekking 70
Vasaloppet cross-country ski race
72, 269
white-water rafting 279, 280
Stenmark, Ingemar 71
Stockholm 77, 233–44
Åhléns City 241–2
Aquaria 233
Björkö 243
Birkamuséet 243
Blasieholmen 237
Blåtornet (Blue Tower) 242
boat trips 243, 265
Djurgården *see* Ekoparken
Drottninggatan (Queen's Street)
242
Drottningholms Slott *34*, 233,
243, *245*
Drottningholms Slottsteater
(theatre) 53, *245*
Ekoparken 233, 236, 239
Bergianska Botanical Gardens
239
Fjärilshuset (Butterfly House) 239
Naturhistoriska Riksmuséet
(Museum of Natural History)
239
Rosendalsträgård (Rosendals
Garden) 239
Gallerian shopping arcade
240–41
Gamla Stan (Old Town) *232*,
233–4
Grand Hotel 237
Gröna Lund amusement park
233, 237
Guldrummet (Gold Room) 239
Haga park 239
Hallsylska Muséet (Hallwyl
Collection) 240
Historiska Muséet (Museum of
National Antiquities) 233, 239
Hornsgatan 243
Hötorget 242
Junibacken 233, 237
Kaknästornet (Kaknäs Television
Tower) 233
Katarinahissen 236
Kulturhuset (Culture House) 240
Kungliga Slottet (Royal Palace)
222, 233, *235*
Kungsträdgården (King's Garden)
239–40
Lidingö 243–4
Millesgården 243–4
Medeltidsmuseum (Medieval
Museum) 236
Midsummer celebrations 233
Moderna Muséet 55, 233, 236–7
Nationalmuseum (National
Museum of Fine Arts) 237
nightlife 233
Nordiska Kompaniet (NK) 241
Nordiska Muséet (Nordic
Museum) 238
Prins Eugens Waldemarsudde
238, *239*
PUB 242
Riddarholmen island 235

Riddarhuset (House of Nobility)
235
Riksdaghuset (Parliament
building) 235–6
St Lucia celebrations 233
Sergels Torg 239
shopping 234–5, 240–42
Skansen open-air museum 233,
237, *238*
Skeppsholmen 236
Södermalm 242–3
Stadshuset (City Hall) 233, *234*,
236
Stadsmuséet (City Museum) 236
Stockholm card 233, 234
Stockholms Auktionsverket
(Stockholm Auction House)
241
Storkyrkan (Cathedral) 234
Stortorget *233*, 234, *243*
Strindbergsmuséet (Strindberg
Museum) 242
Strömmen channel 69
Sverigeleden (Sweden Bicycle
Route) 69
tourist information 233
transport 233, 237, *240*
Ulriksdal *see* Ekoparken
Vasamuséet (Vasa Museum)
233, *238*, 239
Våsterlånggatan 234–5
Walpurgis Night 233
Stockholm archipelago 65
Stora Alvaret 252
Storuman 277
Strängnäs 244
Strindberg, (Johan) August 53, 55,
242
The Great Highway 242
The Red Room 53
Strömstad 259
Sundborn 54, 55, 269

Carl and Karin Larsson museum
54
Svappavaara 279–80
Sveg 274

T

Tallås 272
Tanumshede 258, 259
Bronze Age rock carvings 258,
259
Taube, Evert 235
Tjörn 258
Torekov 255
transport
cycle routes 69
Inlandsbanan (Inland Railway)
271, 279
snow scooters *273*
Trollhättan 264, 265
Falls Festival 264
Trysunda 282
Tylösand 255

U–V

Umeå 282
Gammlia Friluftsmuseum open-air
museum 282
Uppsala 26, 244
Domkyrkan (Cathedral) *244*
Gamla Uppsala 244
Gamla Uppsalakyrkan (parish
church) 244
Linnaeus house and botanical
garden 36
Uppsala Slott 244
Varberg 255–6
Societetshuset 255
Varbergs Fästning (Fortress)
255
Värmland 261

Vasa, Gustav 33–4
Västerbotten Museum 282
Västergötland 263–4
see also individual place names
Växjö 252
Utvandrarnas Hus (House of the
Emigrants) 252
Vemdalen 274
Vilhelmina 277
Visby 32, *253*
von Hausswolff, Carl Michael 55
von Heidenstan, Verner 55
von Linné, Carl *see* **Linnaeus**
Vreta 265
monastery church 265

W–Z

Wallenberg, Raoul 43
Wallqvist, Einar 277
waterfalls
Kukkolaforsen 282
Ristafallet 274
Stora Sjöfallet 279
Storfallet 274
Storforsen 282
Tännforsen 274
Wiberg, Pernilla 71–2
Wikström, Elin 55
wildlife 68, 274
bird watching 251, 252,
264
lynx *271*
reindeer 70, 271
Russ horses of Gotland 253
of the wetlands 251
wolverine *280*
Ytterlännäs 271
Zorn, Anders 267, 268

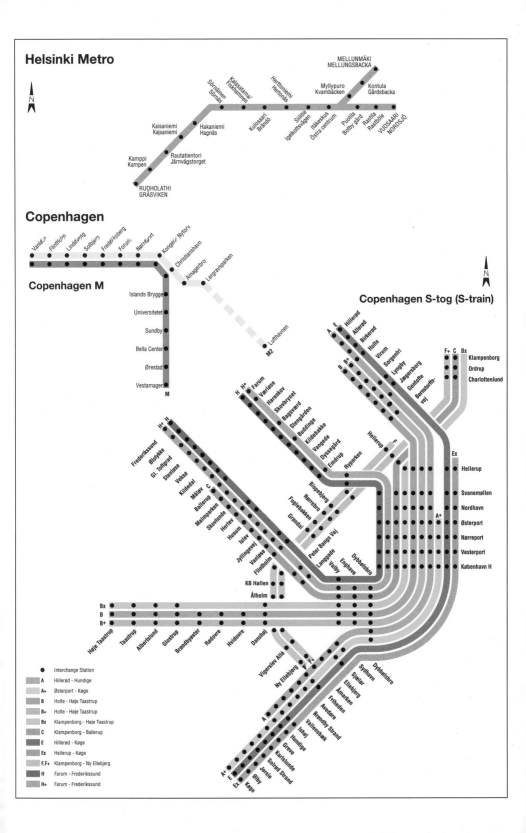

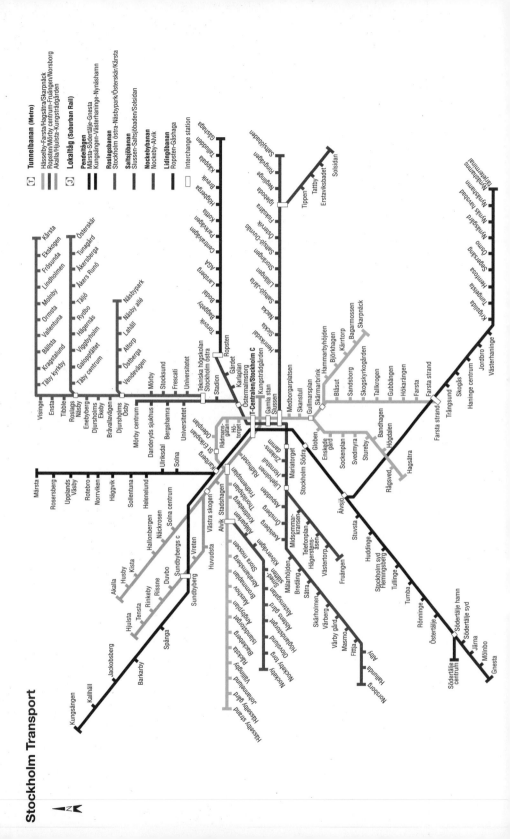